Soundscapes

SECOND EDITION

Map of the World

SECOND EDITION

Soundscapes

EXPLORING MUSIC
IN A CHANGING WORLD

Kay Kaufman Shelemay

W·W·NORTON & COMPANY

NEW YORK · LONDON

W. W. Norton & Company has been independent since its founding in 1923, when William Warder Norton and Mary D. Herter Norton first published lectures delivered at the People's Institute, the adult education division of New York City's Cooper Union. The Nortons soon expanded their program beyond the Institute, publishing books by celebrated academics from America and abroad. By mid-century, the two major pillars of Norton's publishing program—trade books and college texts—were firmly established. In the 1950s, the Norton family transferred control of the company to its employees, and today—with a staff of four hundred and a comparable number of trade, college, and professional titles published each year—W. W. Norton & Company stands as the largest and oldest publishing house owned wholly by its employees.

Copyright © 2006, 2001 by W. W. Norton & Company, Inc.

Editor: Peter Lesser
Assistant Editor: Birgit Larsson
Managing Editor—College: Marian Johnson
Senior Production Manager—College: JoAnn Simony
Project Editor: Kim Yi
Copy Editor: Richard Wingell

Composition by TSI Graphics
Manufacturing by Quebecor World, Versailles
Book design by Chris Welch

Library of Congress Cataloging-in-Publication Data

Shelemay, Kay Kaufman.
    Soundscapes : exploring music in a changing world / Kay Kaufman Shelemay.—2nd ed.
        p. cm.
    Includes bibliographical references and indexes.
    ISBN-13: 978-0-393-92567-8 (pbk.)
    ISBN-10: 0-393-92567-6 (pbk.)
    1. Music appreciation. 2. World music—Analysis, appreciation.
        3. Ethnomusicology—Cross-cultural studies. I. Title.

MT90.S53 2006
    780.9—dc22   2006040017

W. W. Norton & Company, Inc., 500 Fifth Avenue, New York, NY 10110
                                    wwnorton.com
W. W. Norton & Company Ltd., Castle House, 75/76 Wells Street, London W1T 3QT

2 3 4 5 6 7 8 9 0

FOR MY STUDENTS, FROM WHOM I HAVE LEARNED SO MUCH.

Brief Contents

Contents

Part I
Listening to Music

Part II
Transmitting Music

Chapter 6   **Music, Mobility, and the Global Marketplace**   256

Part III
Understanding Music

Chapter 7   **Music and Dance**   300

Listening Guides

Preface

Music is on the move, traveling across international boundaries to reach new and broader audiences. Most places today support a range of musics of different styles and histories. Music can be a medium of expression through which we pray and protest and remember and relax. At the same time, it provides a lens through which we can understand the most deeply felt aspects of human experience. This book offers a fresh approach to this complex world of musical action and interaction, introducing and interpreting a cross section of musical domains called *soundscapes*.

The term *soundscape* plays a special role in this book, providing an inclusive and flexible framework for approaching any music tradition. My use of the term began after I read a 1991 article by the anthropologist Arjun Appadurai, who coined *ethnoscapes* to capture the shifting and nonlocalized quality of group identities in the late twentieth century. I transposed Appadurai's term to a musical context and reimagined *soundscape* in a more defined setting than his parent term *ethnoscape* might have allowed. Another source, which does not use the word *soundscape*, influenced me indirectly: Mark Slobin's extended 1992 essay "Micromusics of the West: A Comparative Approach," revised and reissued in 1993 as *Subcultural Sounds: Micromusics of the West* (Hanover, NH: Wesleyan University Press). There Slobin briefly explores Appadurai's concept of ethnoscapes in relation to present-day musical life. Other appearances of the word *soundscapes* have emerged over the years. The most generative use in the musical arena has been that of the Canadian composer R. Murray Schafer, who in the late 1960s employed *soundscape* as a cover term for his inclusive definition of music. The word can be found in other contexts as well—such as in the music historian Reinhard Strohm's writings about the broader sonic environment of late medieval Bruges—if only fleetingly and usually as a musical corollary to a panoramic landscape. Thus, although I did not invent the term *soundscape* and I do acknowledge a wide array of precedents, I use it in a new and expanded way.

The soundscape concept helps us bring together musics that exist side by side in the lives and imaginations of so many people. A soundscape accommodates the musical dynamism of the twenty-first century: music may be anchored for periods of time in single places, but even when situated locally, it is always changing, subtly or dramatically. Many soundscapes incorporate global connections and influences. As we study the music of many peoples and places, we will find that music-making is a creative practice as well as the ongoing process of selected sounds, shifting settings, and changing significances interacting.

Centuries of human migration have resulted in increasingly heterogeneous populations and a broad range of soundscapes in many places. For this reason, each chapter in *Soundscapes* includes a major case study drawn from a music tradition that has migrated at some point in its history. Also included are two or more shorter case studies that complement and contrast with the primary case study and illustrate the same theme in music traditions with very different geographical roots. While *Soundscapes* is global in its content, all of the music traditions within these pages are also transmitted "at home" in North America. From the rousing presence of bagpipe bands to the calming strains of lullabies, global soundscapes shape the settings in which they are performed.

The ten chapters of *Soundscapes* are grouped into three large sections. Following an Introduction to the soundscapes concept, the chapters in Part I establish a three-part framework for "Listening to Music." Chapter 1 (new for the Second Edition) approaches music as organized sound, providing a guide to the listening experience; Chapter 2 explores musical creativity and performance within contrasting settings; and the manner in which music conveys different meanings is the subject of Chapter 3.

The three chapters in Part II, "Transmitting Music," chart music's transmission through human migration (Chapter 4), trace music's survival in individual and collective memory (Chapter 5), and map music's movement through channels ranging from tourism to the global marketplace (Chapter 6).

Part III, "Understanding Music," contains four chapters that map music's close connection with a particular realm of human experience. Chapter 7 surveys music and dance; Chapter 8 explores the relationships between music and ritual; Chapter 9 traces music's important role in political life and action; and Chapter 10 situates music practices within individual and social identity.

A brief Epilogue brings our musical journey to a close, arriving at a soundscape that incorporates both multiple soundscapes and musical processes charted throughout the book. Indeed, all of the chapters have porous boundaries and are linked by common themes and materials. For instance, changing technologies shape the sounds, settings, and significances of most soundscapes, and dance reappears in many discussions.

Each chapter also contains at least four "capsules" that expand on the chapter narratives through time lines, charts, or focused discussions. Capsules explore the different voices and instruments encountered ("Sound Sources"); supply valuable historical information ("Looking Back"); trace the biographies and contributions of important musicians ("Individual Portraits"); and offer guidelines for further musical exploration ("Studying Music").

For decades, most ethnomusicologists have taken a geographical approach to the study of music, surveying a selected music tradition primarily within the context of its historical homeland. This foreign-cultures perspective has provided significant insights, but it has also distanced and exoticized musical practices that today are more often found closer to home. Beyond providing an introduction to a wide variety of music traditions from around the world, *Soundscapes* invites instructors and students to draw on their personal expertise, their individual backgrounds and interests, and the resources of their local communities.

In addition to its broad focus on music's movement over time and geographical space, *Soundscapes* offers three other innovations. First, it dissolves the long-standing practice in musical pedagogy of separating the study of so-called Western and non-Western musics. Second, it couples the study of varied music traditions with consideration of their transmission and performance in many places internationally, including at home in North America. Finally, *Soundscapes* shifts the emphasis from musical styles to the cultural processes through which people engage in music. *Soundscapes* explores a cross section of international musics while keeping local styles in clear view, making music the anchor for understanding diverse human settings. Through constant dialogue between the present and the past, *Soundscapes* maps music traditions at home and abroad, bringing together many musical styles within an inclusive, interactive context.

Acknowledgments

In many ways, the seeds for *Soundscapes* were sown at the very beginning of my academic career, when I traveled to Ethiopia to do fieldwork on music traditions found only there. Not long after my arrival back home several years later, I noticed that the Ethiopian musical world had begun to migrate and was settling in all around me in New York City. The realization that so many musics once found only in distant places had through the vagaries of migration, tourism, and sound recordings come to be located next door slowly transformed my own research and teaching agendas. *Soundscapes* emerged over a long period of time and draws on almost everything I have read or heard.

The first acknowledgment here should by any measure be extended to the students, both undergraduates and graduates, whom I have taught over the years at Columbia, New York University, Wesleyan, and Harvard. It is to them that this book is dedicated. They have challenged me through their curiosity, introduced me to new worlds of sound, shared unforgettable moments in the field, and dazzled me with their own ambitious research agendas. A number of them have contributed in important ways to *Soundscapes,* whether through research collaboration and assistance, through our work together in the classroom, by offering insightful comments, or by giving me access to materials otherwise unavailable.

Once I began writing the First Edition of *Soundscapes* in 1995, I gained a clearer understanding of why most textbooks have several authors. Although a single-author text permits one to conceptualize and shape the materials in new ways as well as to fairly easily establish continuities of theme and style, no single individual could possibly carry out all the primary research necessary to address a sufficiently wide range of musical materials. As a result, I have intellectual debts to many and have taken particular care to document the sources I consulted. Footnotes throughout the text identify the sources of quotations or important ideas that helped me organize particular sections in significant ways. The bibliographies for each chapter, which contain a detailed listing of all the sources I or my research assistants consulted, are preceded by brief summaries of the research process and acknowledgments to those on whose work I have drawn. Here I will provide an overview of the individuals who have offered advice, lent materials, or extended important critical feedback.

I could not have completed either the First or the Second Edition of *Soundscapes* without abundant assistance from many individuals and organizations. I would like to express special thanks to the Bogliasco Foundation and the Liguria Study Center for the Arts and Humanities for an unforgettable residency, during which several chapters of the First Edition of this book were drafted; to Civitella Ranieri Study Center, where I had the time to think through changes that would become part of this Second Edition; Samantha Chaifetz and Mike Bortnick for tango lessons and insights into ballroom dance culture; Jody Cormack and David Nelson for help in obtaining a recording of *raga nilambari* and photographs; my thanks to those for helping to transcribe and translate song texts—a specific list is included at the end; Caprice Corona and Norma Cantú for discussions of the *quinceañera*; Virginia Danielson, Andrew Wilson, Robert Dennis, Constance Mayer, and Kerry Masteller for advice and guidance in the Eda Kuhn Loeb Music Library at Harvard University; Beverley Diamond for assistance with Native American materials; Anthony DiBartolo and Margaret Keyes of the Harvard University Media Production Center for mastering the Second Edition CDs; Stuart Feder for an introduction to the accordion; Mickey Hart and the Society for Gyuto Sacred Arts for Tibetan Buddhist materials; the Harvard-Radcliffe Office for the Arts for help in obtaining illustrations; Hailegebriot Shewangizou and Danny Mekonnen for information about Ethiopian music in the United States; Robert Hogan and Gregory Morrow for materials on bagpipes; Theodore Levin and David Hykes for information on *khoomii* and an update on the Harmonic Choir; Ezra Mtshotshi, Counsellor, and Juan A. Henriquez, Information Officer, of the South African Embassy, Washington, D.C., for assistance; Pham Duy for exceptional generosity in supplying recordings, videotapes, and scores; Ankica Petrovics and Saint Mary's Ethiopian Tewahedo Church for providing videotapes of Ethiopian Christian rituals in Los Angeles; Ronald Radano for information on the spiritual; Anne Rasmussen for sharing the wonderful Bunai photograph she uncovered and for help with recordings of Middle Eastern music in North America; Adelaida Reyes, Deborah Wong, Terry Miller, and Andrew Talle for supplying recordings, materials, and advice related to Vietnamese music and texts; Gil Rose, the Boston Modern Orchestra Project, and especially to Reza Vali for help with Mr. Vali's Flute Concerto; Judith Vander for sharing materials and an unforgettable field trip to the Shoshone Wind River Reservation; María Teresa Vélez for advice and information on *Santería*; Lee Warren of Harvard University's Bok Center for cogent suggestions on pedagogical concerns; Yo-Yo Ma, Laura Freid, and Isabelle Hunter for materials and advice about the Silk Road Project; Su Zheng for materials on and recordings of Sheung Chi Ng; Evan Ziporyn, Philip Yampolsky, I. Nyoman Catra, and Christine

Southworth for assistance with *gamelan* recordings and analysis; Emmanuel Akyeampong, Gage Averill, Jean–Jacques Nattiez, J. H. Kwabena Nketia, Helen Rees, Daniel Sheehy, Sarah Weiss, Philip Yampolsky, and many other colleagues too numerous to name for advice, materials, or corrections; and Reece Michaelson, Galen Malicoat, Keith Hampton, and Mary Gerbi during their tenures at the Harvard Music Department for a full measure of support in all aspects of my work during the years this project has been in process.

Many staff members at W. W. Norton have offered excellent support and advice. Michael Ochs first approached me to write this book and then faithfully guided the First Edition over the course of six years; dozens of his insightful suggestions are retained in the following pages. Similarly, Neil Ryder Hoos helped with images that bring life and color to these pages. For revisions to the Second Edition, I am deeply grateful to Maribeth Payne and Peter Lesser for sage advice. As this edition assumed its present shape, Pete Lesser took over as editor and provided additional detailed feedback and editorial suggestions. Copy editing by Richard Wingell greatly enhanced the text, as does a lively new design by Chris Welch. Roby Harrington continued to offer wise counsel, and Steve Hoge helped solve technological problems. And throughout, Allison Benter and especially Birgit Larsson, Kim Yi, JoAnn Simony, and Marian Johnson kept this complex project on track and on schedule.

A series of superb research assistants provided help without which this project would never have been completed. David Lyczkowski once again worked on every aspect of the book, compiling many listening guides as well as editing and formatting chapter drafts. Joseph Fishman researched sources for updating the case studies and cross-checked footnotes and the bibliography. Sarah Morelli once again provided indispensable help with the dance chapter (Chapter 7) and South Asian case studies as well as located many wonderful illustrations. Neeraj "Richie" Banerji provided updated ethnographic observations of Mumbai's musical life. Roe-Min Kok, Charles Starrett, and Andrew Talle researched and drafted the segments about musical instruments and helped supply texts. Patricia Tang graciously supplied materials and checked analysis of several examples. The (then) graduate students who helped teach *Soundscapes* during its various iterations at Harvard offered many cogent suggestions: they included head teaching fellows Patricia Tang, Charles Starrett, and Judah Cohen, as well as Suzanne Fatta, David Kaminsky, Roe-Min Kok, Zoe Lang, Sarah Morelli, Julie Rohwein, and Julie Searles. Students who used *Soundscapes* also made excellent observations and suggestions; here I give special thanks to Navlyn Wang and Michael Kozuch.

Many colleagues have contributed greatly by offering advice and materials. Richard Wolf deserves special thanks for his collaboration and guidance on the South Indian lullaby case study carried out with Jeyalakshmi (Sujata) Sundar in

Chapter 3; Amy Bard provided invaluable guidance for the Mumbai case study in Chapter 2. I am very grateful to Sandra Graham for her detailed comments on several chapters. Sarah Weiss, who has prepared the Instructor's Guide for the Second Edition, has made many cogent suggestions. Emmanuel Akyeampong, Daniel Avorgbedor, David Locke, and Herman Kwei provided support for my fieldwork in Accra as well as expert advice and feedback on materials related to that case study. To the anonymous readers of Second Edition proposals and draft manuscripts for Norton, I am exceedingly grateful for your useful feedback on the book's strengths and shortcomings. Many colleagues and students (too many to name) who have taught and studied *Soundscapes* have made suggestions for the Second Edition. I, however, take full responsibility for all interpretations and conclusions, especially those that differ from the original sources.

I could not have completed this large-scale project without special help and support from family and friends. Jack Shelemay was once again my supportive companion in the field and at home, and, as always, Raymond and Lillian Kaufman encouraged this work. A special group of friends and colleagues aided and buoyed me in many ways throughout this project. Adrienne Fried Block, the late Stuart Feder, Tomie Hahn, Steven Kaplan, Ingrid Monson, Patricia Tang, Adelaida Reyes, Nancy Risser, and Su Zheng have given important feedback and support. For their intellectual companionship and friendship, I am indebted to the venerable "Gang": Jane Bernstein, Ellen Harris, Jessie Ann Owens, and Judith Tick. They have all made important suggestions for this edition; Judith and Jessie provided especially useful feedback from their own classroom experiences with the First Edition.

In closing, but foremost in importance, I would like to acknowledge the dozens of musicians whose creativity gives life and meaning to these pages. I hope that this book conveys my concern for the important issues at stake in their music's conception, transmission, and performance, as well as the complex questions raised by its study.

Translators

Lenëën (Senegalese *mbalax*), Patricia Tang and Papa Abdou Diop; *Atumpan*, Daniel Agyei Dwarko and Emmanuel Akyeampong; *Jay Ganesh* ("Praise Ganesh"), Sarah Morelli; *Mum-bhai*, Neeraj "Richie" Banerji; *Fado Lisboeta*, Nicola Trowbridge Cooney; *Hagerei*, Meley Mulugetta; *Araro Ariraro*, Jeyalakshmi Sundar and Richard Wolf; *Amba Nilambari*, T. Viswanathan and Richard Wolf; *Tema para Quinceañera*, David Lyczkowski; *Ng Bak Loi Gimsaan*, translation: Su Zheng, transliteration: Meredith Schweig and Andres Su; *Wakef 'ala shat baher*, John Eisele, Ali Jihad Racy, and Ahmed Jebari; *A Thousand Miles from Home*, Phong T. Nguyen, Terry Miller, and Andrew

Talle; *Come to Hue, Come*, Pham Duy; *Who Is Walking on the Endless Road*, Pham Duy; *Gregorio Cortez*, Américo Paredes; *You God, Are Mighty*, James Robinson; *The Works of God*, Joshua Levisohn; *The Wheat Song*, Nabil Salim Azzam; *Let My Whole Being Testify*, Louis Massry; *Come Let's Dance*, translation by Usha Verma and Rajwinder Singh; *La Cumparsita* (tango song), David Lyczkowski; *Changó*, David Lyczkowski and Marìa Teresa Vélez; *There Is Joy Today*, Getatchew Haile; Shoshone Flag Song, Judith Vander; *He Descended from Heaven*, Thomas Kane and Monica Devens; *Ringo Oiwake*, Takashi Koto and Kazuko Mockett; *Allons à Lafayette*, David Lyczkowski; *Zydeco Sont Pas Sale*, David Lyczkowski; *C'est Moi*, David Lyczkowski.

A Note on the Spelling of Foreign-Language Texts and Terms

Texts and terms from more than twenty-five different languages are found in *Soundscapes*. Terms are spelled consistent with common usage, accompanied when necessary by pronunciation tips in parentheses. In many cases, the most straightforward alternative of several possibilities has been selected. Song texts follow their presentation in the original sources credited; in general, however, diacritical markings used to indicate tonal levels or otherwise mark sounds distinctive to indigenous scripts are not reproduced.

Soundscapes

SECOND EDITION

What Is a Soundscape?

A scene from a 2002 celebration of the Chinese lunar new year, the Year of the Black Horse. This celebration is similar to parades that have been held annually in San Francisco's Chinatown since 1953. These festivities blend aspects of the traditional Chinese Lantern Festival with American parade customs of having floats and marching bands.

Overview

Main Points

- Soundscapes arise from the distinctive setting, sound, and significance of music.

- Music travels geographically, linking soundscapes within and across isolated locales and large urban centers.

- Soundscapes are never static and are always changing.

Introduction

From coast to coast in the United States, a flurry of media activity surrounded a concert tour in the spring of 2003. Feature articles appeared in newspapers several days in advance of each performance, announcing special events at local schools and universities. On their arrival in a city, the musicians were interviewed on local radio stations. The sold-out concerts were covered by area television stations and reviewed enthusiastically in the press. The activities surrounding this concert tour would not be surprising if the musicians were a

The members of the Tuvan ensemble Huun-Huur-Tu pose with traditional string and percussion instruments. The musicians include Anatoli Kuular (top left), Sayan Bapa (top right), Kaigal-ool Khovalyg (bottom left), and Alexei Saryglar (bottom right).

world-famous rock group or a well-known string quartet. What is remarkable and what reflects our changing musical environment is that the tour comprised a series of concerts by a group of singers known as Huun-Huur-Tu, from the Inner Asian Republic of Tuva. After multiple tours of the United States beginning in the 1990s, along with concert and festival performances in nearly every country of Europe, Huun-Huur-Tu has emerged as the foremost international representative of Tuva's remarkable musical culture.

CASE STUDY: The Throat Singers of Tuva

If you had attended one of these concerts, you would have heard some song lyrics telling of life among nomadic peoples in the arid plains and rugged mountains of Inner Asia, while others speak of events in the modern cities of that area. The musical instruments used to accompany the singers included stringed instruments such as a small, graceful fiddle, called an *igil* ("ee-geel"), decorated on top with a carved horse's head.

Some songs are sung without instrumental accompaniment and have no words at all. Most listeners are intrigued by wordless songs that feature the Tuvans' novel vocal style, called *khoomii* ("WHO-mee") singing, heard in Listening Guide 1.

Like many concertgoers, you probably find this music unfamiliar. But other than piqued curiosity, what would you take from this brief encounter with Tuvan music in an international concert setting? What could you learn from this exposure that would broaden your understanding of the world in which you live and the musical traditions that help give it shape and meaning?

Kaigal-ool Khovalyg, a co-founder of Huun-Huur-Tu, sings *khoomii* and plays the *igil,* a two-stringed bowed instrument with a carving of a horse's head on top. As a child, Khovalyg worked as a herder before studying traditional and classical Tuvan music and performing with the Tuvan State Ensemble.

First, let's consider this: Musics from around the globe surround most of us wherever we live and are accessible, if only for an evening in concert or through the media. If we want to hear a particular music, we can often find an opportunity nearby. To expand your musical horizons, keep an eye open for flyers advertising concerts, call up a community arts organization or nearby campus for information, scan the local newspaper for listings, flip on a TV or radio program sponsored by a particular ethnic community, ask an interest group for an events calendar, or search for a music or performing group on the Internet. If live performances are not readily available, the World Music section of your local record shop stocks virtually any music one might wish to hear.

Artii-Sayir ("The Far Side of a Dry Riverbed," *kargyraa khoomii*)

CD 1
Track 1

Date of recording: 1990
Performer: Vasili Chazir

WHAT TO LISTEN FOR:

- The distinctive sound of the *kargyraa khoomii* vocal technique, with a harmonic melody heard above the low fundamental
- A single melody, repeated several times

	STRUCTURE	DESCRIPTION
0:00	Melody presented	The singer begins singing the low fundamental and almost immediately produces the audible upper harmonic. Note how his vowel changes. The lowest harmonic is produced when the singer sings a closed vowel like "oo," the middle harmonics are produced with an "oh" vowel, and the higher harmonics correspond to a more open vowel like "ah." These five harmonics comprise the tune.
0:19	Melody repeated	
0:39	Melody repeated	
1:01		Track ends.

Many musicians provide sound clips on their Web sites that you can listen to at no charge.

Even when we do not actively seek out these new musical experiences, they come to us anyway, clamoring for our attention. They intrude uninvited into our most private spaces through the various media. They enter casually into our perception through recordings played in restaurants and stores, and as background music for television commercials. They catch our eye and ear with the color and vibrancy of their performances as we stroll through local fairs and arts festivals or watch newly released films. They insistently demand our attention and spare change as we walk down the street on an errand or

Two musicians play violin and cello at Pike Place Market, Seattle, Washington.

descend into the subway on our way to work. Performers entice us to attend their concerts and often to lend support to the causes for which they perform.

The burgeoning presence of multiple musics in familiar places is a reality of life around the globe in the twenty-first century. Their inescapable presence reminds us that we all make choices in the sights and sounds with which we surround ourselves, adopting some and rejecting others. Just as we decorate our living spaces, choose clothes for the image we wish to convey, and prepare food according to habit and taste, so we shape much of our sound environment to please, stimulate, inspire, and console us. We cannot help but choose and incorporate several contrasting musical styles in constructing our own sonic space at home, in social interaction, during worship, and in the course of everyday life.

But much more is at stake than simply enjoying a kaleidoscope of sound. If music is an integral part of so much of life, it has unsuspected power as well. Familiar music can inspire us, cheer us, and link us to a network of family, friends, and community. Unfamiliar music can also provide unexpected opportunities. When we encounter the

An unprecedented level of mobility blurs boundaries between soundscapes at home and abroad while providing a constant flow of new subjects for ethnomusicological study. Here we see students from Moscow playing music in front of a church on a crowded New York City street.

STUDYING *Music*

Ethnomusicology—A Definition

Ethnomusicology is a field that joins the study of music with the concerns and methods of anthropology. The research process in ethnomusicology usually depends on observation of and participation in musical events, although most ethnomusicologists also use recorded music and consult a range of documentary sources to expand on information they have gathered from living musicians. Some ethnomusicologists also draw on recordings made in the past or descriptions of older musical practices to carry out historical studies.

Working in an academic field founded in the late nineteenth century (see **"Looking Back: Important Moments in Ethnomusicology"** on the next page), most twentieth-century ethnomusicologists studied music outside the boundaries of the Western classical traditions and focused on styles transmitted by oral tradition. Many, especially those trained in Western Europe and the United States, worked in locations abroad, in contrast to Eastern European and South Asian scholars, who often focused on music of their own countries. Today, ethnomusicologists around the world are involved with any and all musical phenomena in a variety of places.

By the last two decades of the twentieth century, increasing numbers of ethnomusicologists began carrying out research not just abroad, but in their home environments as well, in order to understand better the music around them. Increasing migration and accessible technology contributed to the spread of music traditions across geographical and national boundaries, leading to multi-sited and transnational studies. Today, ethnomusicologists can be found studying any music tradition, and their work includes activity across the boundaries of many disciplines, from cultural studies to neuroscience. Many ethnomusicologists also engage in full- or part-time work outside the confines of the university, called "applied" or "public sector" ethnomusicology, applying the knowledge they gather about a music tradition to enhance the welfare of a community, library, museum, or other local, state, or national arts organization. In part due to the expansion of the field and to concerns that the prefix "ethno" implies an older, elitist approach to music traditions outside the historical West, some have suggested renaming ethnomusicology, offering alternatives such as sociomusicology or simply musicology.

LOOKING *Back*

Important Moments in Ethnomusicology

Ethnomusicology had its roots in Europe, begun as an armchair enterprise called "comparative musicology" by scholars who compared music from early sound recordings and collected musical instruments:

1885	Founding of comparative musicology in Europe and early activity underway by first generation comparative musicologists across Asia, Middle East, Africa, North and South America[1]
1914	In Berlin, Erich von Hornbostel and Curt Sachs publish classification system for musical instruments that facilitates cross-cultural comparisons
Late 1930s	European music scholars begin fleeing Europe during World War II, increasing the ranks of comparative musicologists in North America and elsewhere

Comparative musicology embraced early recording technologies, permanently wedding the use of new technologies to the study of music worldwide:

1890	Walter Fewkes makes first cylinder field recording with Passamaquoddy Indians in Maine
1899–1901	Founding of first sound archives in Vienna and in Berlin
1928	American Folksong Archive begun at US Library of Congress
1939	Moses Asch starts record company that later becomes Folkways Records, a leading publisher of music from around the world

Fieldwork, the study of living music traditions, becomes an important focus of comparative musicology in the early twentieth century:

1904	Hungarian composer Béla Bartók begins fieldwork in Eastern European folk music
1907	Frances Densmore studies the medicine ceremony at White Earth Chippewa Reservation
1916–18	Cecil Sharp and Maud Karpeles discover English ballads (termed the

variety of musics that surround us, we are given a chance to move into different worlds of experience, to travel beyond the musical surface to explore the complex of meanings hidden there. This type of inquiry is undertaken by ethnomusicologists, scholars who seek to document and interpret music as an integral part of life experience (see **"Studying Music: Ethnomusicology—A Definition"** and

"Child ballads") still being transmitted in the rural eastern United States, following up on the famous five-volume study of English and Scottish ballads published between 1883 and 1898 by Frances James Child

1931–1934 John Avery Lomax and his son Alan make field trip to southern US, recording blues singer Leadbelly (Huddie Ledbetter)

The third quarter of the twentieth century marked changes in the name and focus of comparative musicology:

1950 Dutch scholar Jaap Kunst suggests renaming the field "ethnomusicology"

1952 Society for Ethnomusicology founded in the United States

1960 Mantle Hood proposes that all ethnomusicologists should be able to perform in two different music traditions, becoming bimusical

1964 Publication of *The Anthropology of Music* by Alan Merriam marks ascendance of anthropological approaches to music research

The late twentieth century marked major shifts in modes of presentation, preservation, and publication of cross-cultural music traditions by ethnomusicologists:

1978 World Music Institute, presenters of world music concerts, established in New York City

1987 Folkways Records becomes Smithsonian Folkways at the Smithsonian Institution

1998 First volume of the *The Garland Encyclopedia of World Music* published

2004 Alan Lomax's historic collection of international field recordings, film, videotapes, and other research materials deposited in the American Folklife Center's Archive of Folk Culture at the Library of Congress

"Looking Back: Important Moments in Ethnomusicology"). We can begin our **ethnomusicology** studies by paying attention to and delving into the moment of a musical performance in whatever form we encounter it. In this way, we can begin to uncover the soundscape of which any single musical event is a small but telling part.

ethnomusicology A field of study that joins the concerns and methods of anthropology with the study of music.

What Is a Soundscape?

Many musicians and scholars use the term "soundscape" to refer to different aspects of the musical environment, ranging from a single music tradition to all the sounds heard in a particular place. In 1971, the Canadian composer R. Murray Schafer began his World Soundscapes Project to comparatively study all sounds that constitute "the soundscape," his general term for the global "sonic environment."[2] Schafer's project studied both human and animal sounds, incorporating everything audible in the natural environment world-wide. In contrast, this book uses "soundscape" to refer specifically to human music making and to provide a flexible framework for studying the many ways in which human musical creativity and performance shape our daily lives.

While Schafer compared his soundscapes to specific landscapes, likening them to the geographic terrains that typify a place or region, here we will more often compare a soundscape to a seascape, which provides a more flexible analogy to music's ability both to stay in place and to move in the world today, to absorb changes in its content and performance styles, and to continue to ac-crue new layers of meanings.

We can chart our location in a seascape by longitude and latitude and an-chor ourselves in one spot for as long as we wish. Similarly, music traditions can be anchored in a single place for a long period of time, closely associated with a particular setting, whether an individual, family, neighborhood, com-munity, city, state, region, nation, or continent. Consider the strong associa-tion of specific soundscapes to their places and communities of origin, such as jazz with African American musicians in the city of New Orleans, or of the in-strument made of a hollowed-out tree limb known as the *didjeridu* with the aboriginal communities in Australia who created it.

To extend our seascape analogy further, musicians may also decide to set sail, attracted by possibilities beyond the horizon, taking their music traditions along with them. They can also be blown off course by an unexpected storm— that is, forced to move by natural disasters or political circumstances. For more than a century, music has sometimes traveled without the people who created and performed it, moving through recordings or virtual channels simi-lar to the proverbial message in a bottle, cast into the water in one place and washed up on a faraway shore.

The notion of a seascape suggests that we need to take a flexible approach to thinking about not just a soundscape's settings, but also about aspects of its sound and performance. Consider that while we are anchored in a particular place, the movement of the waves may remain calm for long periods of time, or they may shift rapidly all around us. In the same way, the content of a soundscape may remain stable or change more quickly over time, even in the same setting. A variety of local factors may initiate changes—perhaps the entry of a talented musician into the scene, or a shift in generational tastes. Many formerly local soundscapes develop global connections as people travel, migrate, and resettle. Wherever their settings, whether in large metropolitan areas or in small towns, most soundscapes come into contact with other soundscapes, sometimes through geographical proximity, at other times through sharing musicians or other participants. Thus the content of a soundscape is, like the tides, almost always changing.

Wherever they are found, too, soundscapes may convey a wide range of meanings to their performers and listeners. As each of us gazes at a seascape, we perceive different shapes and colors in the patterns of waves and sky. Because of differences in individual experience and predilections, some may perceive the sea as a comforting presence, while others may be frightened by its potential power. Like human behavior in general, many of our interpretations about the significance of music are both shaped by and contribute to those shared patterns of knowledge and experience we call "culture." Each soundscape partakes of and interacts with cultural knowledge, sometimes providing windows on music cultures shared by large groups of people, and at other times connecting to knowledge sustained just by a few. An individual may also be part of more than one culture (and music culture) at the same time.

Locating a Soundscape

We can locate a soundscape most easily through an encounter with a specific musical performance. The music may be part of a larger encompassing scene, such as a parade, festival, or religious ritual. Wherever it occurs, a soundscape signals its presence through a live or a recorded musical performance.

A brief encounter with a single musical event rarely yields more than a preliminary entry into a soundscape. To better understand a soundscape, we need to attend repeated events and to gather a range of additional information about their *sound*, *setting*, and *significance*. Although soundscapes engage several of the senses, they generally imprint themselves first and most definitively on the ear. For this reason, we begin with the sound.

The choir of Mount Pilgrim Church of Christ, Scranton, North Carolina, sings to the accompaniment of a piano.

Sound

Let us take the music heard in Listening Guide 1 as a point of departure for an exploration of sound. This striking singing style, termed *khoomii* ("WHO-mee"), is usually translated as "throat singing" since the name derives from an Inner Asian word for "throat." While most people are accustomed to thinking of the voice as able to produce only a single sound at one time, *khoomii* produces two sounds at the same time, a low, steady tone with a higher tone above. *Khoomii* singing not only provides entry into one very rich soundscape; it also gives us an opportunity to better understand the basics of musical sound.

acoustics The science that deals with *sound*.

Individual voices and instruments are distinguished by differences that arise from their sound properties, studied through the field of **acoustics**, which explores the many factors shaping the production and conveying of sound. Every musical sound is produced by the vibration of some substance—for example, a string (violin, guitar), a column of air (clarinet, organ), a membrane (drum), or a piece of metal (vibraphone, triangle). In the case of the human voice, the vocal cords are set vibrating by air. The number of vibrations per second (termed the frequency) determines what we perceive as the pitch of a tone; faster vibrations produce a higher pitch, and slower vibrations a lower one.

fundamental tone The lowest tone in a *harmonic series*, also referred to as the "first harmonic" or "first partial," which determines the perceived pitch of a sound.

harmonic series See *harmonics*.

harmonics The series of simple vibrations that combine to create a complex pitched sound, also called the *harmonic series*.

However, each voice or instrument produces not a single sound but a blend of a **fundamental tone**—the tone our ear perceives as the frequency or basic pitch of the sound—with a series of tones ascending above the fundamental, an acoustical phenomenon known as the **harmonic series**. These tones are known as harmonics or partials. **Harmonics** (of which the fundamental is in fact the first and lowest partial) are a subtle part of every sound produced by a musical instrument or a voice.

A string, for example, vibrates along its entire length when plucked, producing what is perceived as the fundamental tone. At the same time, the string also vibrates independently at various subdivisions—at half the length of the string, one-third the length, one-fourth the length, and so on—each at a different, higher pitch and a different volume. By gently placing a finger in the middle of the string, on a guitar for example, we can stop the fundamental from vibrating and hear the second partial clearly. The particular combination of partials creates the characteristic tone colors of different instruments. Although in most cases it is difficult to separate the upper partials from the fundamental tone by ear (throat singing being a striking exception), the presence and relative strength of particular partials give an instrument or voice its special tone quality or "timbre." Listening Guide 2 demonstrates how the distinctive sounds of a human singing voice, a Western clarinet, and a Chinese *erhu* are shaped by their particular blend of partials; it also shows how similar the voice and two instruments sound when all the partials except the fundamental are filtered out.

LISTENING GUIDE 2

Demonstration: The role of harmonics in determining sound quality

Created by: Julie Rohwein and Kay Shelemay

Date of recording: 2004

Performers and sound sources: Petra Gelbart, *voice;* Michael Cuthbert, *clarinet;* Julie Rohwein, *erhu* (Chinese bowed string instrument); Kay Shelemay, *narration*

WHAT TO LISTEN FOR:

- The difference in sound quality between sound sources with all partials present and when selected partials have been filtered out. Without a full complement of harmonics, voices and instruments lose their distinctive tone colors and sound alike.

	INSTRUMENT	DESCRIPTION
0:00	Narration	Fundamental pitch A440 sounded by all three sound
0:10	Voice	sources without filtering. (A440 is the standard
0:17	Clarinet	international measurement of cycles per second [cps]
0:22	*Erhu*	or hertz [Hz] to which instruments of the orchestra are tuned.)
0:30	Narration	Fundamental pitch A440 sounded with partials 2, 3,
0:39	Voice	and 4 filtered out.
0:46	Clarinet	
0:51	*Erhu*	
0:59	Narration	All partials filtered out except for the first partial and
1:09	Voice	the fundamental.
1:14	Clarinet	
1:19	*Erhu*	
1:27	Narration	Fundamental pitch A440 sounded by all three sound
1:32	Voice	sources without filtering
1:37	Clarinet	
1:43	*Erhu*	
1:48		Recording ends.

How does the *khoomii* singer produce two tones at the same time? By manipulating the mouth cavity and the position of the tongue, the singer causes one additional partial at a time to be heard quite distinctly above the fundamental, giving the impression that two separate tones are being sung at once. Some singers can sound a third partial at the same time. The higher of the two tones heard in the throat-singing example in Listening Guide 1 is one of the upper partials, sometimes referred to as an "overtone" because it is above the fundamental. Translating this example into Western music writing (musical notation) displays both the fundamental and the precise upper partials sounded in Listening Guide 1.

This example, termed a *transcription*, represents in Western staff notation the fundamental pitch and harmonics heard in Listening Guide 1.

This notation shows a fundamental pitch along with its harmonics. The note heads in red are the five harmonics actually sounded by the singer as the tune above the fundamental heard in Listening Guide 1.

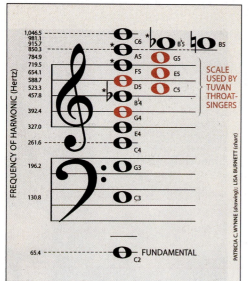

Even if you can't read Western notation, you can follow the numbers of partials above the individual noteheads. There are also other musical traditions besides *khoomii* in which upper partials are rendered audible. Common examples are the Jew's (or jaw's) harp, a small metal instrument found in Inner Asia and North America as well as other places, held in the mouth and plucked by hand on its protruding end. A more subtle but still audible upper harmonic is produced by the musical bow, an instrument widespread in sub-Saharan Africa that we will discuss in Chapter 1 (Listening Guide 7).

You will notice that the *khoomii* singer in Listening Guide 1 does not use all possible harmonics in his singing, but rather sustains the fundamental and repeatedly emphasizes five particular harmonics above it, as shown in the adjacent figure. These specific harmonics become, through repeated use, a familiar set of five tones that are the basis of the melodies the singer performs.

While Tuvan singers refer to this singing style in general as *khoomii*, there are many styles with contrasting sound characteristics in different regions of the country. Some of the most important *khoomii* styles are named within the Tuvan tradition. *Kargyraa* ("car-gee-RAH"), the type of *khoomii* we heard in Listening Guide 1, has a fundamental sung in a low register with a husky vocal quality; sometimes *kargyraa* can have a text. *Kargyraa* is an onomatopoeic word for wheezing or speaking in a hoarse or husky voice.[3]

Another common style is *sygyt* ("SUH-gut"), which has a higher-pitched fundamental than *kargyraa* and produces clear harmonics that sound like whistling. Listening Guide 3 (on pages lvi–lvii) presents a style similar to *sygyt*. Many accomplished singers develop their own personal *khoomii* styles, which are subsequently known by the singer's name and vary according to the pitch of the fundamental, the loudness or softness of the sound, the position of the mouth, and the emphasis on specific harmonics. The manner in which a singer produces the sound, anchored in his nose or chest, has given rise to styles known as "nose" and "chest" *khoomii*.

Beyond its identity as *kargyraa*, the *khoomii* example in Listening Guide 1 also has distinctive properties of pace and rhythm. It has a regular beat that you can tap along with as you listen to the recording, divided into a series of four-beat units that can be counted beginning from the first appearance of harmonic 12, following a two-beat lead-in on harmonics 9–10. Each subsequent group of four beats is marked off in the notation by vertical lines (see previous page).

Our brief discussion of the sound of *khoomii* has introduced some of its distinctive sound characteristics. The contexts within which it is performed play important roles in both shaping and conveying these sounds. This leads us to our next consideration, setting.

setting The context of a musical performance, such as the structure of the performing space or behavior of those present.

Setting

Musical sound is not conceived, taught, or performed in a vacuum. The **setting** of a soundscape includes everything from the *venue* (place of performance) to the behavior of those present.

The setting in which one encounters a soundscape, such as a concert hall, street corner, or even one's room, reveals much about a musical event. For instance, concert halls are generally constructed to contain musical sound, although such spaces vary dramatically in their size, layout, and acoustical properties.

Patrons await the start of a performance at the Kravis Center for the Performing Arts, West Palm Beach, Florida.

A band performs before a large crowd on a summer evening at the Chicago Blues Festival in Grant Park.

In contrast, music performed on a street corner or in a park transforms an otherwise nonmusical venue, effectively redefining that space sonically.

Comparing a musical performance within a concert hall or on a street corner to that on a sound recording illuminates other issues, such as the creative processes and technologies that produce the recorded sound. There is also the paradox that a recording or broadcast that simultaneously reaches millions can, at the same time, constitute an intensely private experience for a single listener.

While the Western concert hall tends to separate performers from audience, the relationship between musicmakers and listeners varies considerably among music cultures. Whereas some ensembles, such as Western symphony orchestras, expect to perform before an attentive and silent audience, other musics are highly participatory, blurring the boundary between performer and audience through clapping, dancing, and verbal responses. In some traditions, including the African American gospel tradition and music of the Arab Middle East, listeners play a vital role by encouraging the performers, responding verbally to the music with feedback, and reinforcing exciting moments in the performance.

Therefore, the setting determines to a great extent what we hear and see. In addition, every musical event is influenced by others that have come before it, whether the performers are part of an established tradition or are trying out a new style and setting for the first time. All such factors force musicmakers to be creative in adapting their traditions to the situation.

Many factors can influence a musical performance, some of which cannot be predicted. The number of musicians may vary, or the absence of an important singer or instrumentalist may require adjustments that change the nature of the sound. The performance space may be unusually large, and performers who are not accustomed to using microphones may have to adapt quickly. Musicians may also somehow alter their sound or other aspects of their performance to communicate better with a particular audience, and so on.

The setting of each performance conveys meanings for both performers and listeners. For instance, traditional venues and those faced by musicians performing abroad can be dramatically different. At the very least, musicians must try to translate for their listeners by changing aspects of their performance and by explaining in some way what they have changed.

When Tuvan singers perform in a concert hall, whether in Seattle, Washington, or present-day urban Tuva, the issues are complex. In the past, throat singing was a largely solitary pursuit, practiced outdoors by individuals during herding or in communion with the natural environment. Particular settings shaped the musical sound. A notable example is *ezengileer* ("eh-ZEN-guh-leer," from the Tuvan word for "stirrup"), a type of *khoomii* that has a galloping rhythm said to reflect the fact that it was sung on horseback.

In the last quarter of the twentieth century, increasing urbanization and the opening of conservatories in Inner Asian cities have created new opportunities for teaching and transmitting Tuvan music. In the 1990s, following the breakup of the Soviet Union and the dissolution of state-sponsored musical

The concert hall used for performances of Japanese Kabuki theater traditionally has a long ramp, called the *hanamichi*, extending from the back of the theater to the right of the stage. In this theater, a second ramp has been added on stage left. The *hanamichi* is used by actors to enter and exit.

ensembles, new musical groups were founded by the musicians themselves.[4] Throat singing, once a part of everyday life, began to appear in formal concerts both at home and abroad. Tuvan musicians have appeared in a wide variety of new settings; the throat-singing ensemble Yat-Kha has traveled around the world to provide live music during screenings of V. I. Pudovkin's 1928 restored Russian silent film *Storm Over Asia: The Heir of Genghis Khan*. Ethnomusicologists also introduced and cultivated throat-singing techniques around the world through research and recordings, leading to new developments based on *khoomii* in other places. Clearly, the relationship of music to its performance setting is not always simple or straightforward.

Musicians adapt to a new performance setting in many ways. Sometimes they adjust the length of the music they perform, substantially shortening traditional musical forms. New performance settings lead some musicians to alter the construction of their instruments, perhaps by replacing traditional gut strings with strings made of more resonant, machine-made steel to produce a louder sound. In the case of Tuvan musicians, their presentations abroad feature groups of musicians who alternate solo *khoomii* singing with instrumental selections performed on instruments such as jaw's harp or fiddle. Clearly, a single *khoomii* singer could not physically sustain a lengthy concert on his own, nor would he likely hold the audience's attention for such a long period of time. The international interest in *khoomii* singing has also encouraged innovations by individual performers who have both combined existing styles and invented new styles altogether.[5]

Musicians performing in settings outside their home environments are often expected to provide oral commentary during concerts as well as supply explanations in the form of program notes. In these situations, they may struggle to distill complex knowledge into a simplified form for an audience that is hearing their music for the first time. Another challenge may be the need to explain aspects of the music tradition historically left unspoken. These demands on musicians can vary greatly depending on whether the setting is a concert hall, a street fair, or a religious ceremony.

Just as performers must adjust to different settings, so must their listeners transform their perceptions in some ways. First-time listeners usually interpret what they see and hear in terms of music they already know and understand. It is common for a listener to frame an unfamiliar musical event within the context of her or his past experience. In a first encounter with a music tradition, the listener is dependent in part on the sensitivity with which that tradition is presented.

fieldwork Research, including observation and participation, of living traditions, also called musical ethnography.

Yet if we are careful in our observations and descriptions—if we employ *critical listening*—we can narrow the distance between a music event and its performance setting. **"Studying Music: Observing and Participating,"** provides guidelines for doing this.

STUDYING *Music*

Observing and Participating

During the first decade of the twentieth century, Alice Fletcher (1838–1923) studied and wrote about music of the Omaha and other Native American communities under the sponsorship of the Bureau of American Ethnology at the Smithsonian Institution.

Most ethnomusicologists study a music tradition through a research process called **fieldwork**, which entails studying music in the settings in which it is created, taught, and performed. As noted earlier in "**Studying Music: Ethnomusicology—A Definition,**" the research site—the "field"—may be located anywhere. One may carry out fieldwork with music and musicians at home or abroad, in urban or rural locales, or in virtual settings such as radio or cyberspace. Most professional ethnomusicologists carry out long-term fieldwork that lasts for months or even years, but it is also possible to carry out brief fieldwork projects. Whatever the location or duration of fieldwork, one needs to develop skill in observation and participation.

First and foremost, an ethnomusicologist needs to develop the ability to observe attentively what is going on within a musical setting. A rule of thumb is that things that are at first new to the eye and ear of the observer will, on repeated encounters, quickly become familiar. Unless observers take the time to make notes about what they observe (called *fieldnotes*) during or shortly after each encounter or musical performance, they will forget important details, noticing some things while ignoring others. Being aware of detail as well as one's changing perceptions by making focused observations and keeping careful records is an important part of the fieldwork process.

Ethnomusicologists doing long-term research often participate actively in the tradition they are studying. Many music traditions are open to participation even by casual observers, permitting a researcher to sing along, clap rhythms, or in some other way contribute to the musical process. Sharing the experience of making music is one of the best ways to learn, in part because it is often the only way to share an insider's experience. Of course, in many circumstances it is not possible for the observer to participate because of lack of musical expertise or because of strict cultural constraints limiting the sex or age of participants. In these circumstances, careful observation may have to suffice. A common mode of nonmusical participation is to discuss the musical event with the musicians or other listeners, both through informal conversations and formal interviews.

Keeping a journal while doing fieldwork is vital, should the observer later want to recall various events and describe and interpret what he or she has heard and seen. The process of doing participant-observation of music is termed *musical ethnography*. "Ethnography" is also used to refer to the outcome of the research process, a description and interpretation of a music culture through writing, film, or other medium.

Focusing our observations while considering the available information about past traditions can help us appreciate both the current setting of a musical event and what the music means.

Significance

Music means or signifies different things to performers and listeners from different backgrounds. Sometimes musicians can convey musical meanings clearly through commentary or action during a performance. Over time, certain musical events can come to symbolize meaningful moments, evoking emotions ranging from celebration to sadness. In other cases, music carries meanings that are hidden, or at least hard to describe. Music can even convey coded information that cannot be transmitted more directly because of political pressure or active repression, as we will see in Chapter 9.

Khoomii provides an example of a tradition with multiple meanings for performers and listeners alike. For many Tuvan musicians in particular, *khoomii* embodies and conveys a deep attachment to their homeland.

By imitating or depicting the sounds of nature, *khoomii* singers reinforce their link to the physical environment of Tuva. This attachment is anchored in part by traditional Tuvan spiritual practices, in which music was used to communicate with spirits believed to inhabit local places ranging from mountaintops to flowing streams. In addition to the belief that *khoomii* is closely linked to the natural environment, some Tuvans trace the origins of *khoomii* to lullabies.[6] *Khoomii* may therefore signify deep-seated associations with a homeland as well as ties to home and family.

The sound of a bugle—here, a trumpet—playing *Taps*, marks the lowering of the US flag at sunset. The use of the bugle at flag lowerings and at military funerals has led to a strong association between these settings and the sound of *Taps*.

The Huun-Huur-Tu musician Kaigal-ool Khovalyg is shown singing and playing outdoors at home in Tuva, while a man sitting nearby taps his stomach to the rhythm of the music. The Tuvan grasslands, visible in the background, provided the inspiration for the name Huun-Huur-Tu. Translated as "sun propeller," the name refers to the refraction of the sun's rays that occurs at dawn and dusk on the Tuvan landscape, a phenomenon said to be similar to the separating or refracting of sound achieved in throat singing.

Sound was also used by Tuvan herders to calm their livestock and to communicate with each other across short distances.[7] Inspired by the wind on the Tuvan steppes and the rushing water of the streams and rivers where they watered their cattle and horses, Tuvans transformed the natural sounds of wind, water, and animals into musical representations. Some styles of *khoomii* mimic the sound of bubbling brooks and blowing winds.

The physical appearance of the Tuvan landscape also influenced musical sound, especially the rugged vistas of the mountains in the southwest of the country and the undulating expanses of the steppes. Tuvan herders shape the melodies of "steppe" and "mountain" *khoomii* to reflect these distinctive features of the topography; the steppe *khoomii* have long flowing lines replicating the undulating contours of the land.[8] Tuvans map the physical landscape in their song texts as well. Thus Tuvan music, unlike much of Western instrumental music, is not considered by its musicians to be abstract, but to be "radically representational."[9]

Outsiders who first encounter *khoomii* music in concert may be so surprised by hearing harmonics made audible that they do not consider the sound's significance. Repeated exposure and consideration of Tuvan points of view, which have been changing because of new settings both at home and abroad, can help outsiders become more sensitive to a range of insider meanings.

The Ever-Changing Nature of Soundscapes

Familiarity with the route a music tradition has traveled can provide insight into both the manner in which it has changed and the way it maintains connections with different places, including its historical homeland. Such knowledge can deepen and broaden our understanding of a particular soundscape's sound, setting, and significance. In some cases, musicians move from one place to another because of economic or political forces. In other instances, an entire community in motion may transplant and eventually transform its music. Some new soundscapes have resulted from serendipitous encounters within settings that bring together multiple streams of music traditions. The latter situation describes the genesis of harmonic chant.

CASE STUDY: David Hykes and the Harmonic Chant

There is no doubt that the world of *khoomii* singers has changed at home in Tuva. However, even before these changes, and before Tuvan musicians began to perform abroad in the 1990s, attracting a global audience, the sound of *khoomii* had begun to travel internationally.

In the early 1970s, a young American musician from New Mexico named David Hykes had a chance encounter with a recording of *khoomii* from Mongolia, a country directly south of Tuva that has its own styles of *khoomii*. Hearing the recording inspired Hykes to try to sing *khoomii*, which he eventually learned to do after six months of experimentation. Hykes also encountered through recordings the vocal techniques used by certain orders of Tibetan monks to produce multiple, subtle harmonics, discussed and heard in Listening Guide 66. In notes distributed to his audiences at concerts, Hykes explained his attraction to these singing styles:

> I found myself listening in a new way. . . . I felt called by a special quality of these musics. I knew it wasn't just technique, but there was plenty to learn about that, too. I set to work.[10]

In 1975, Hykes founded the Harmonic Choir, a small ensemble of men and women who performed Hykes's compositions. Hykes's early works, such as *Hearing Solar Winds,* were wordless songs for a chorus of five to seven voices and soloist. The choir generally began by singing the same fundamental tone, then slowly produced a subtle, shimmering spectrum of upper harmonics similar to those heard in Tibetan chant. Hykes's voice would enter next, performing a *khoomii* solo over the slowly shifting choral sound. Hykes's compositions were partially improvised and were usually performed within large, resonant spaces that amplified the harmonics. The Cathedral of St. John the Divine in New York City was a favorite performance setting, a huge, neo-Gothic structure where Hykes and his Harmonic Choir were in residence from 1979 to 1987. This setting was used to enhance the sound and also to lend added significance; indeed, most of Hykes's performances over the years have been held in resonant church naves lit by candlelight.

The unusual sound of the Harmonic Choir immediately attracted attention in avant-garde musical circles. However, Hykes believed that musical sound should move beyond entertainment to provide a meaningful spiritual experience for both singers and listeners. Drawing freely on a range of Central Asian and Sufi philosophies, particularly the writings of G. Gurdjieff (1872–1949),[11] Hykes conveyed universalist ideas shared by many New Age musicians. Hykes also echoed Inner Asian thinking, suggesting that music that rendered harmonics audible provided a close connection with nature.

Beyond performing in cathedrals and other spaces that allowed for reflection and meditation, Hykes presented concerts on days of universal significance, such as the equinox and summer solstice. Early on, Hykes explained why he drew on unfamiliar sounds for his compositions and why he felt that music based on *khoomii* and Tibetan vocal styles had the potential to provide transcendence:

> Singing combines the science of acoustics and an ancient musical practice which in traditional teachings has helped to "harmonize" the individual and provide glimpses of the music at the heart of the Creation. . . . The Harmonic Choir is searching for a global music at once illuminated by the high standards of tradition and responsive to the present; a music that signals to us through pure sounds, "upstream" from language, independent of culture. Our aim is to bring to life a listening environment where the search for such a music can be shared.[12]

Hykes's comments demonstrate the ways in which musical innovations, even when conceived as "independent of culture," are in fact shaped by their settings. These traditions also come to embody meanings in circulation at the

This 1981 poster advertised a performance of the Harmonic Choir, then in residence at The Cathedral of St. John the Divine in New York City.

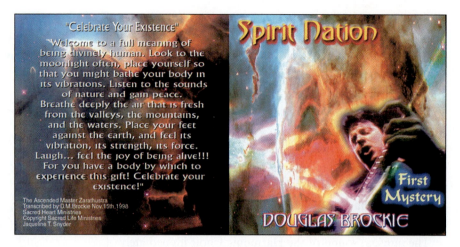

The text accompanying this CD presents traditional musical instruments and concepts within the framework of New Age ideas, describing music as a powerful source for relaxation, meditation, and healing. It also conveys a sense of universalism, suggesting that music is a natural phenomenon that can successfully cross all cultural boundaries.

David Hykes performs "harmonic chant" at a November 1998 concert in Brussels, Belgium.

time they are created, adapted and blended from different sources. Hykes sought to move beyond musical sound to create, perform, and transmit what he terms "a new, global sacred music" through his experiments with the acoustic universals of the harmonic series. Rather than create music independent of culture, however, Hykes began to construct a new soundscape with its own distinctive combination of sounds, settings, and significances.

After a decade in New York City, Hykes moved to France in 1987. There he worked both with his choir and, increasingly, as a soloist. After studying classical Azerbaijani and Armenian music as well as North Indian *raga*, in the late 1980s Hykes began to incorporate aspects of these styles into his solo *khoomii*-based compositions. He added new rhythmic elaborations, adding a Persian goblet-shaped drum, the *zarb*, to his solo compositions, as heard in Listening Guide 3 (on pages l–li). Hykes and accompanying instrumentalists have also brought Middle Eastern visual touches to their performances, sitting on Turkish pillows and dressing like nomads.

Of the soundscape he has created, Hykes has written:

It's a way to create a world of music. We are working with the very elements of sounds, the pure waveforms which in their infinite variety of composition give rise to all the musical sounds we hear. Of course, electronic and computer composers deal with these elements all the time. But I feel the living voice can always make sounds come to life more vividly.[13]

David Hykes's music draws on improvisation during live performance, thereby creating music anew during each performance. Hykes conceives of musicmaking as a search for spiritual enlightenment and believes that each performance reenacts a moment of creation. By performing in sacred spaces, maintaining a devout and solemn atmosphere, and creating music patterned after traditional styles used for worship in different cultures, he purposefully cultivates a spiritual atmosphere in his attempt to formulate a "new traditional or sacred art."

David Hykes and his innovative harmonic chant bring our introduction full circle. Hykes's music draws on Inner Asian throat singing and other historical chant traditions, but at the same time constitutes a new beginning—an example of the distinctive combinations and recombinations you will encounter in the musical world around you.

We will explore many other soundscapes in the following pages, using the framework of sound, setting, and significance to understand music's content and meaning in different global settings. We begin in Chapter 1 with an introduction to sound.

A number of outsiders have learned to perform the *khoomii* singing style. The award-winning documentary *Genghis Blues* traces the experience of Paul Pena, a blind American blues singer of Cape Verdean extraction, who taught himself throat singing and then traveled to Tuva.

IMPORTANT TERMS

acoustics	musical ethnography	sound
critical listening	overtones/harmonics	soundscape
cross-cultural	participant observation	throat singing/*khoomii*
ethnomusicology	pitch	*ezengileer*
fieldwork	register	*igil*
fundamental	setting	*kargyraa*
harmonic chant	significance	*sygyt*

Windhorse Riders (harmonic chant)

Date composed: Late 1980s
Composer: David Hykes
Date performed: 1989
Performers: David Hykes, *voice*
Djamchid Chemirani, *zarb*

WHAT TO LISTEN FOR:

- The influence of *khoomii* vocal technique in a new setting
- The changing vowels on the fundamental that result in different harmonics. The highest harmonics are produced with an "ee" vowel, which changes to "oh" for middle harmonics, and "oo" for the lowest harmonic.
- The *zarb*, a Persian drum
- Subtle changes in the length of each of the eight phrases (sections separated by breaths) sung by the voice. Most contain thirty-two beats each (eight groupings of four beats), except for phrase 4, which is shorter, and phrase 6, which is longer.

	STRUCTURE	DESCRIPTION
0:00	Phrase 1	The lower, sustained pitch—the fundamental—is heard, joined by an upper harmonic seconds later. The high harmonic melody begins on harmonic 12, descends, and

then ascends, ending on harmonic 8. The lowest harmonic in this phrase is harmonic 5. The first phrase is in a free rhythm, perhaps influenced by Middle Eastern customs of having a rhythmically free introduction. There is a pause for breath before phrase 2.

0:32	Phrase 2	Similar to phrase 1, but with the addition of the *zarb*. The *zarb* establishes a regular rhythm with eight groupings of four beats each.
0:48	Phrase 3	
1:03	Phrase 4	This vocal phrase is much shorter than the others, containing only five groupings of four beats each.
1:13	Phrase 5	This phrase, unlike the others, ends on harmonic 7.
1:33	Phrase 6	While this phrase begins (like the others) on harmonic 12, it rises to harmonics 13 and 14 at 1:47 and 1:49, respectively. This phrase is also longer, lasting twelve groupings of four beats each.
1:56	Phrase 7	This phrase again rises as high as harmonic 14.
2:11	Phrase 8	
2:28		The recording fades out and ends.

PART I
Listening to Music

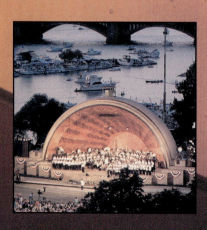

listening to music is one of life's great pleasures. Wherever one lives and whatever music traditions one comes into contact with, hearing music unites sensations of the ear, mind, and body to entertain, inform, inspire, or otherwise transform daily experience. Much of what all of us know about music we absorb through watching, feeling, and listening. Sometimes we listen to music alone through recordings or the radio during private or reflective moments. At the same time, many of our most memorable musical experiences are those shared with others, whether our families, our friends, or a broader community.

Part I of *Soundscapes* introduces you to the listening experience. It links hearing music to thinking and talking about music and provides a framework for listening that is flexible and can be used to explore the diverse music cultures that constitute different soundscapes.

In Chapter 1, we will explore the fundamentals of music and acquire skills for focused listening. We will define important musical concepts illustrated through an international array of music traditions. An important goal of Chapter 1 is to build a vocabulary that will enable you to talk about what you hear.

The setting in which music is performed, our subject in Chapter 2, provides a vital grounding for the listening experience. We will compare settings of musicmaking in three major cities on three different continents—Accra, Mumbai, and Boston. Chapter 2 anchors our discussion of musical sound in specific localities, exploring both the manner in which different settings shape diverse musical sounds and the ways in which these music cultures help construct a sense of place.

Music's significance is the topic of Chapter 3, which provides guidance for understanding music's meanings. In this chapter we will explore ways in which musical sound acquires and conveys significance. We will also consider how musical meanings can change over time and why music is able to accommodate multiple meanings at once.

Chapter 1

Sound: The Materials of Music

Music has always occupied a central role in human life. This wall painting from the tomb of Nebamun, a nobleman who lived in Thebes, Egypt during the eighteenth Dynasty, portrays female musicians listening, clapping, and (in a part of the painting not reproduced, to the right) dancing to the music of the double reed pipe at a banquet. Although musical activity is represented in Egyptian paintings and reliefs from as early as 2500 BCE, this painting dates from around 1350. The musicians are wearing perfumed cones of scented fat on their heads.

Overview

Main Points

- Music is sound organized in ways meaningful to people in a specific time and place.

- Each music culture organizes the four main characteristics of sound—quality, intensity, pitch, and duration—in distinctive ways.

- Musicians may reproduce, reshape, or discard familiar sounds each time they conceive and perform music.

Introduction

How do we talk about musical sound? Different cultures have different ways of thinking and talking about music. Commonly used terms within sound-scapes emerge from a consensus about what constitutes music and its important characteristics.

What Is Music?

As we learned in the Introduction, vibrations give rise to sound waves, which in turn affect the eardrums and set into motion a multi-stage process of auditory perception. So ubiquitous is sound in our lives that we have a term for its absence—**silence**—which is a relative concept. In fact, we rarely experience absolute silence, since the basic processes of our bodies and nervous systems provide a constant sonic backdrop to our existence.

While a wide variety of sources can produce sound, such as the pounding of a hammer or the scream of a tea kettle, music is purposefully constructed from particular types of sounds that have over time come to convey meaning within a given cultural setting. **Music**, therefore, can be defined as organized sound that is meaningful to people within a specific time and place. Beyond this very general definition, we must look to individual soundscapes to understand what sounds people select and how they define music.

Music can be defined quite differently by people in different cultures or sub-cultures. For instance, although in many traditions people define music as or-

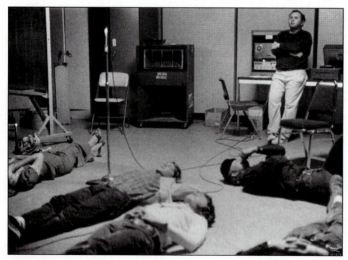

Listening is a part of our daily experience, often involuntary, at times all-encompassing. Here, a group of students at the University of California, San Diego raptly listen to music in 1975.

ganized sound that has a tune or melody, among some of the Venda people of South Africa music "is believed to be founded not on melody, but on a rhythmical stirring of the whole body, of which singing is but one extension." As a result, although some Venda children's songs do not have tunes, their regular rhythms lead Venda people to define these sounds as music, not speech.[1]

Even closely related music cultures sometimes categorize the same sounds differently. An example is a type of singing performed by Inuit, Chukchi, and Ainu peoples living in widely separated polar

Katajjaq on the syllable *"hamma"* (Inuit vocal game)

CD 1
Track 4

Date of recording: 1970s
Performers: Inuit singers, Baffin Land, Canada
Function: Performed by Inuit women as a vocal game for entertainment

WHAT TO LISTEN FOR:
• The combination of four types of vocal sounds which, when repeated, produce a series of short patterns

regions of the Canadian Central Arctic, Siberia, and Japan. All three peoples use a similar and distinctive singing style, almost certainly derived from a common source, characterized by the fast inhalation and exhalation of breath.[2]

In Listening Guide 4, we hear one type of Inuit *katajjaq* ("cat-ta-ZHAHK"), translated as "vocal game." The *katajjaq* (pl. *katajjait)* is generally sung in a playful manner by two Inuit women who stand or sit face to face, sometimes holding each other's shoulders, competing to see who can keep singing longer. Eventually, one woman runs out of breath and both begin to laugh.

The rapid breathing in and out enables the singers to produce two additional sounds called "voiced" and "voiceless" sounds. The vocal cords produce voiced sounds when they vibrate while being pressed together, and produce voiceless sounds when held apart. The result is a complex sound that is very distinctive, as heard in Listening Guide 4.

Among the Inuit today the *katajjait* are considered vocal games, not music. However, the Chukchi and Ainu peoples perform similar songs as part of ritual dances and consider them to be a type of musical expression.[3] Therefore definitions of music may be shaped not only by preferences for different sounds in different settings, but also by disagreements in closely related cultures as to whether particular sounds constitute music or not. It is worth noting that the main entry under "music" in the leading English-language music dictionary cautions us that it is impossible to provide "a universally acceptable definition" of the word "music" because of the many different ideas about what constitutes music in different places at different times.[4]

Alacie Tullaugaq and Lucy Amarualik, female Inuit artists from Puvirnituk, Nunavik (Northern Quebec), are pictured on the cover of their album *Katutjatut Throat Singing*, which was chosen "Best Traditional Album—Historical" at the Canadian Aboriginal Music Awards. Tullaugaq and Amarualik, who learned singing from their mothers and grandmothers, have performed internationally.

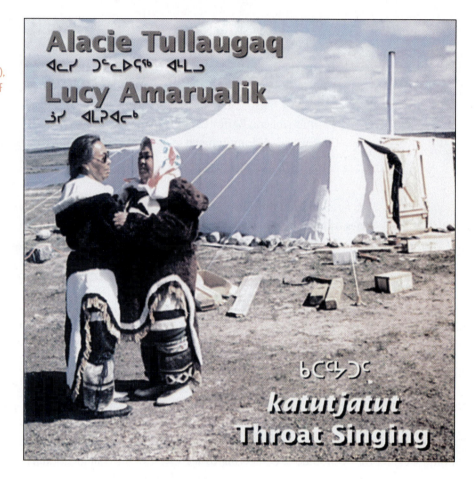

Characteristics of Sound

If music is the purposeful organization of sound that enters our consciousness through the sense of hearing, we need to subdivide the listening process into manageable parts. We can break down sound into four acoustical characteristics that are useful in all cultures: *quality, pitch, duration,* and *intensity.*

At the same time, we will take into consideration which aspects of musical sound are considered important within a given tradition, and what other special concepts might be applicable. We will pay attention to insider words, concepts, and expressions that are used to represent and explain musical sound within a specific soundscape.

Our exploration of the characteristics of sound is made possible by the availability of sound recordings that give us access to music traditions that little more than a century ago could be studied only through live performance in widely scattered locales (see **"Looking Back: The History of Changing Sound Technologies"**). These recordings enable us to compare and contrast the characteristics of musical sound across geographical and cultural boundaries.

The History of Changing Sound Technologies

To study a range of cross-cultural music traditions, we are dependent on sound recordings, a technology invented in the late nineteenth century:

1877–1878	Thomas Edison invents and patents cylinder phonograph
1888	First commercial phonograph. Introduction of six-inch wax cylinder, able to record and play back music

Phonographs no longer record sound, shifting industry focus to marketing prerecorded sound:

1895	Emile Berliner introduces prerecorded 78-rpm twelve-inch discs
1902	First recording of the tenor Enrico Caruso
1910–1912	Pathé and Columbia stop manufacturing wax cylinders, leaving only prerecorded cylinders and discs on market

Recording technology fed the development of other sound-related industries:

1920	First regular radio broadcast in the United States
1924	Microphone and electrical amplifier first used in sound recording
Late 1920s	Custom-built portable disc recording equipment created

By the mid-twentieth century, new technologies enhanced the quality of recorded sound and new methods of sound recording emerged:

1945	45-rpm seven-inch vinyl disc first appears
1948	33⅓-rpm vinyl long-playing disc (the LP) appears
1948	First commercial magnetic tape recorders are manufactured
1955	Stereophonic recording. First stereo LPs and stereo tape recorders

The late twentieth century saw the democratization of sound recording through a series of new technologies permitting easy recording as well as portability:

1963	Cassette tape created
1969	Dutch physicists begin development of the Compact Disc (CD)
1979	Portable cassette player is introduced
1982–1983	CD players first sold
1986	Digital Audio Tape (DAT) introduced
1992	MiniDisc comes on market
1995	Enhanced CDs appear
1998– present	MP3 system compresses audio files into digital formats that take less computer memory than previous technologies
2001– present	Introduction of small, portable, battery-driven digital music (MP3) players that can store and play back thousands of tunes

Quality

quality The color of a *sound,* arising from acoustical properties of the *harmonic* series. Also called *timbre.*

tone color See *quality.*

timbre The distinctiveness of a particular voice or instrument, arising from acoustical properties of the *harmonic* series. Also called *quality.*

sound sources The voices and instruments that produce musical *sound* and whose vibrations give rise to our perceptions of *quality.*

The distinctive sound of a particular voice or instrument is termed its **quality**; sometimes musicians use the expression **tone color** or borrow the French word **timbre** to refer to this characteristic of sound. Quality is the first among the four characteristics because without it, we would not perceive much in the way of difference between musical sounds. We already learned in the Introduction that each musical sound is constituted of a spectrum of harmonics ascending above a fundamental tone, produced by the vibration from either a musical instrument or the human vocal cords. Our discussion of quality, therefore, must take account of **sound sources**, the voices and instruments that produce musical sound and whose vibrations give rise to our perceptions of quality.

We have learned that each sound source generates certain harmonics that render its sound distinctive and enable the listener to distinguish between a piano and a guitar, or to differentiate between the voices of two singers. Factors such as details of the construction of an instrument, including the materials from which it is made or subtle aspects of craftsmanship, also contribute to the quality of a sound. For instance, an instrument made of metal generally has a more resonant quality than one made of wood.

There are also other aspects of sound production that shape quality. These include the ability of a voice or instrument to begin, sustain, and end a sound. The onset of a sound is called its *attack;* the way in which a sound dies out is termed its *decay.* Wind instruments generally have an abrupt attack because of the need to force air into the instrument and the quick action of their keys. Keyboard instruments such as the piano use special pedals to help sustain tones that would otherwise decay rapidly. Some sound sources, such as the voice and string instrument heard in Listening Guide 5, are able to begin a sound gradually and to sustain it as long as the breath holds out, or to prolong a sound by pulling the bow slowly over the strings.

The pioneer ethnomusicologist Frances Densmore (1867–1957) used a wax-cylinder phonograph to record the language and music of Blackfoot Mountain Chief in 1916. Many of her recordings are preserved in the American Folklife Center's Archive of Folk Culture at the Library of Congress.

Sound Sources: The Voice

The voice has always been a source of considerable mystery, in part because, in contrast to many other instruments, its sound-producing mechanism, the vocal cords, are hidden from view. Most of us recognize different vocal qualities, since many coexist within the same geographical or cultural arena. The wide array of vocal sounds all around us is probably the most persuasive evidence that no single vocal quality can be considered to be a "natural" singing

LISTENING GUIDE 5

My Beautiful Hangai Land (Mongolian long song)

Date of recording: 1977
Performers: Sumya (voice), accompanied by Orchirbat on a bowed stringed
    instrument
Function: Used for entertainment and celebrations as well as for personal pleasure

WHAT TO LISTEN FOR:
- The different qualities of the female voice and the bowed string instrument,
  which can be distinguished from each other even as they perform virtually the
  same lines

voice. Rather, as we have already heard with examples of *khoomii* singing, *katajjaq,* and the long song, the voice is an enormously flexible instrument that can produce a variety of sounds, some quite unexpected.

There are many ways in which the voice can produce a distinctive sound. The ability to render an upper harmonic audible as practiced by *khoomii* singers, or to produce the range of vocal articulations as women do in performing a *katajjaq,* is relatively uncommon, and for this reason has attracted the attention of outsiders. Yet there are common vocal articulations that produce qualities encountered in many soundscapes that are easily recognized. These include a purposeful vibration of the tone, referred to in Western music by the Italian term **vibrato;** excellent examples of vibrato can be heard in the voice singing the long song in Listening Guide 5. String instruments can also be played with vibrato introduced through a regular shaking of the hand on the strings, commonly heard in performances on the Western violin. However, the bowed instrument that accompanies the singer in Listening Guide 5 uses very little vibrato, producing a sound described as a **straight tone.**

Terminology describing vocal quality is often subjective—for example, the term **raspy** is sometimes used to describe a singing voice that is rough or gruff in quality. Sometimes words describing vocal quality connect a musical sound to other aspects of the culture, revealing qualities important to insiders within the tradition. For instance, food-related terms are quite commonly used to describe vocal quality, such as the description of a "sweet" vocal sound. Adjectives relating to temperature, such as "warm" or "cold," are also frequently

vibrato A regular fluctuation of a sound, produced by varying the *pitch* of the sound.

straight tone A sound that lacks any *vibrato.*

raspy A singing voice that is rough or gruff in *quality.*

LISTENING GUIDE 6

Wreck of the Old 97 (traditional American folk song)

CD 1 Track 6

Date of recording: 1962
Performer: Dorsey Dixon
Function: Sung to recall an historical event—a catastrophic train wreck—and to entertain

WHAT TO LISTEN FOR:
• The *nasal quality* of singer Dorsey Dixon's voice

chest voice Sound resonated from within the chest, with a low, powerful, throaty vocal *quality*.

head voice A light, bright, high tone resonated in the head.

falsetto The process of singing by men in a high *register* above the normal male singing *range*.

nasal A buzzing vocal *quality* produced by using the sinuses and mask of the face as sound resonators.

applied to vocal quality, as are attributes of "bright" and "dark" tones borrowed from the visual domain. Instruments are frequently described by the materials from which they are made; we speak of "reedy" or "brassy" sounds.

A singer can alter the quality of her voice by generating the sound from within the chest, head, or nose. Generally, the **chest voice** produces a low, powerful, throaty vocal quality often heard in rock music. A good example of a chest voice is heard in the recording of the long song in Listening Guide 5: compare the chest voice used for most of this excerpt with the **head voice** heard at 0:40 on that same track. In European music, the male head voice is known by the Italian term **falsetto**. The contrast between the quality of chest and head voice of a male singer is usually more marked than in the female voice, as can be heard in the South African song *Wimoweh* in Listening Guide 29 (CD 1, TRACK 29). A buzzing vocal quality produced by using the sinuses and mask of the face as sound resonators is sometimes termed a **nasal** quality, and is heard in many music cultures, ranging from those of the Mediterranean area to Chinese opera and American country music. In Listening Guide 6, we hear a strong nasal quality in the voice of American folksinger Dorsey Dixon.

Sound Sources: Instruments

Musical instruments are almost as ubiquitous as the voice, and they tend to be made of materials native to their place of origin. For instance, on islands from the Pacific to the Caribbean, conch shells have long been blown as trumpets; similarly, many instruments from coastal Africa and Southeast Asia were commonly decorated with small cowrie shells that washed ashore. Musical bows were widespread in the rain forest areas of Central and Southern Africa, likely adapted

Mbuti musical bow

CD 1
Track 7

Date of recording: 1957–1958
Performer: Unidentified *Mbuti* musical bow player
Function: For entertainment

WHAT TO LISTEN FOR:

• The rich sound emanating from the single string, producing both a fundamental and harmonics

from hunting bows by peoples for whom hunting was a part of daily life. In Listening Guide 7, we hear the sound of the hunting bow, which is rich in overtones.

Beyond the close connection of musical instruments to the local ecology and economy, musical instruments reflect and embody the technologies of their time and place. Examples are numerous. Bronze metallurgy is known to have entered mainland areas of Southeast Asia by late in the second millennium before the Common Era; Vietnam was the site of the first bronze instruments (drums).[5] Indonesia later developed large instrumental ensembles called *gamelans,* dominated by xylophones and gongs made of bronze (Listening Guide 28, in Chapter 2).

In nineteenth-century Europe, the Industrial Revolution introduced new materials and techniques of mass production that transformed the construction of many musical instruments, incorporating steel wires and iron frames within the piano and fashioning new types of valves for wind instruments such as French horns. In early twentieth-century Trinidad, instruments were made from everyday items such as soap boxes, biscuit tins, and bottles. During the 1930s, discarded fifty-five-gallon steel drums from the oil industry were modified into musical instruments that came to be known as "pans" or "steel drums." Steel drums, which could be played alone or in groups, as heard in Listening Guide 8, subsequently spread throughout the Caribbean. While early in their history steel drums varied in their

A musical bow player from the Ituri Forest in northeast Congo (formerly Zaire) anchors the bow with his right foot, and grasps the other end in his right hand. He strikes the string of the bow with a stick held in his left hand, and rests the top against his lips, allowing his mouth to serve as resonator for the musical sound. Sometimes, a gourd is attached to one end of the musical bow and rests against the chest of the player to act as an external resonator.

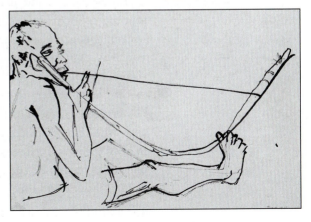

LISTENING GUIDE 8

designs, in recent decades they have been manufactured in standardized forms, making it possible for a player to move from band to band without difficulty.[6]

Musical instruments are an important part of most societies' material culture, a term anthropologists use to refer to objects used in everyday life. Instruments can carry powerful associations to the contexts within which they are played. For instance, the large gong that anchors the music of the Indonesian *gamelan* in ritual contexts has long been considered to have supernatural power (see page 102 for a sketch of a *gamelan*). Instruments can also change functions and gain new associations over the course of time, as can be seen in the case of the Japanese bamboo flute, the *shakuhachi,* over the course of the last 1,000 years. A millennium ago, musicians within the Japanese court first played the *shakuhachi*; later the instrument became a form of Japanese Buddhist musical expression.

The sound of some instrumental ensembles can over time come to represent the political entities by which they were organized and supported; these instruments can also be used in new contexts. For example, military bands, which were first established worldwide following the entry of European colonial powers into the Middle East, Asia, and Africa, are today ubiquitous in ceremonies, parades, and other events whenever national or military power is celebrated. During the period when African nations won independence from European colonial powers in the years following World War II, many African countries established national folklore ensembles consisting of dancers accompanied by indigenous instruments. These groups perform at state occasions and tour internationally, representing their countries at home and abroad.

In many societies, particular instruments are closely identified with either men or women. Horns and drums are often associated with men, particularly those of high rank and royal status. In African courts such as those of the Asante kings in Ghana, musicians playing trumpets and drums perform an important role within state ceremonies. The frame drum is used widely throughout the Middle East to accompany wedding music and remains closely associated with the female musicians who play it. In some places, women are formally or informally prohibited from playing certain instruments; women in Mongolian pastoral communities were historically prohibited from playing all instruments except for the jaw's harp.[7]

Over time, instruments that are markers of ethnic and national identity can attain even deeper associations as people move beyond the boundaries of their historical homelands. One notable example is the Armenian *duduk*, a wind instrument played in the Armenian countryside, heard in Listening Guide 9 (see page 14). The *duduk*'s sound has come to symbolize that country wherever individuals of Armenian descent live.

The *shakuhachi* was played beginning in the Edo period (1603–1868) by *komuso*, wandering mendicant priests who wore wicker baskets over their heads to disguise their identities while working as spies for the government. While their organization was abolished in the Meiji Restoration, the twentieth century still saw wandering *komuso* on the streets of Tokyo.

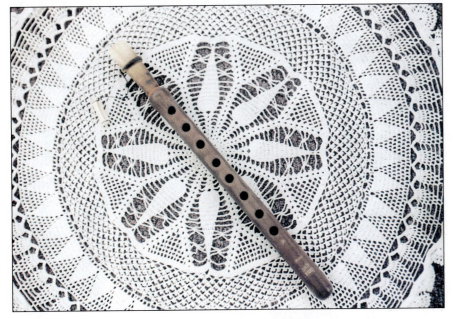

An eight-holed, double-reed Armenian *duduk*. The wood binding attached by a string on the left of the instrument is placed over the mouthpiece to keep its reeds together.

Anush Garun ("Sweet Spring," Armenian *duduk*)

Date of recording: 2002
Performers: Gevorg Dabaghyan and Grigor Takushian
Function: For entertainment at parties and weddings

WHAT TO LISTEN FOR:

- The distinctive nasal quality of the two *duduk*s, one of which plays a high melody while the second produces a continuous, lower line called a *drone*. Listen to the continuous sound of the drone, produced through a special playing technique used for some wind instruments called *circular breathing*. The player breathes in through the nose while simultaneously blowing into the instrument through the mouth.

This harp, made of ivory and okapi hide, was commissioned in the early colonial period by the Mangbetu Chief Okondo. The human figures on the neck of the instrument and the ivory pegs have elongated, wrapped heads that exemplify Mangbetu aesthetic ideals of the late nineteenth and the early twentieth centuries. The figure on the instrument's neck is that of a man, while the five pegs are topped with heads of women, identifiable by their fanlike coiffures.

Instruments often carry prestige or status related to their historical roles in society. Those long associated with social elites, such as keyboard instruments in Europe, commanded respect and often were perceived to raise the status of those outside the elite who acquired and played them. In some places, a high-status instrument has a less prestigious equivalent within the same society, with corresponding differences in sound quality. Such a pairing is found in highland Ethiopia, where aristocrats of the Ethiopian court played the large, ten-stringed lyre (*baganna*), which they associated with King David, to accompany singing of psalms and hymns. Within the same region, professional musicians with low social status played a smaller and less elaborate six-stringed Ethiopian lyre (*krar*). The *krar* was known as "the devil's instrument" because of the myth that it arose from the devil's attempt to mimic the larger *baganna*. Instead of inspiring religious devotion, the sound of the *krar* is said to arouse emotions associated with carnal love or obscenity.[8]

Musical instruments can also have substantial economic value. In many societies, instruments are richly decorated and used for purposes of display. Among the most beautiful instruments are those produced by the Mangbetu people of Zaire (now called the Congo), who carve their instruments from ivory and cover them with rare animal skins.

The Study and Classification of Musical Instruments

So striking are the sounds and shapes of musical instruments that they have long been avidly collected by travelers. This practice led, by the late nineteenth century, to an international marketplace for musical instruments and also spurred the development of a new field called **organology**, the study of musical instruments. As European museums expanded their collections to include musical instruments from different places, the need arose for categorizing and

This modern Ethiopian painting presents an Ethiopian emperor as King David playing the *baganna*, a popular image in Ethiopian art, derived from descriptions in the Book of Psalms. The instrument has a typical lyre structure with its two upright arms connected by a crossbar to which the ten strings are attached.

Voices and Instruments

Although the Sachs-Hornbostel classification system is used all over the world in museums and by scholars, many societies have their own systems of categorization. In ancient China, for example, instruments were classified according to the materials from which instruments were made, including earth, stone, metal, skin, silk, wood, gourd, and bamboo. In European music, instruments were divided into three categories—strings, wind, and percussion—a system derived in part from the ancient Greeks. A scheme used by the sixth century in India anticipates the categories of Sachs-Hornbostel, incorporating "stretched" strings, "covered" drums, "hollow" winds and "solid" idiophones.[9]

Over the course of the twentieth century, some scholars have criticized the Sachs-Hornbostel system for its internal inconsistencies and inflexible hierarchy, and have proposed alternatives. One such suggestion applies the Linnaean system from biology to instruments, grouping them by genus, family, order, class, and phylum.[10]

There is no cross-cultural system used to classify voice types, although an early Indian treatise included the singing voice along with hand-clapping within the five categories of instruments. One ethnomusicologist proposed that the term "corpophones" be used for instruments that are part of the human body.[11] Voices are sometimes named by their sound, as in the common Western designation of soprano, alto, tenor, and bass, or by the musical style they usually sing, such as opera singer, blues singer, or rapper.

Although instruments cover a wider range and variety of sounds than voices, there are frequently similarities between vocal and instrumental quality and style within a given soundscape. Particularly interesting are those traditions in which voices imitate instrumental sounds, as in the "mouth music" with which Scottish singers duplicate the sound of bagpipes, heard in Listening Guide 38 (in Chapter 3).

---

organology The study of musical instruments.

Sachs-Hornbostel system A classification of musical instruments, named after the scholars who developed the system.

comparing instruments. In 1914, Curt Sachs and Erich M. von Hornbostel published a four-part classification system based on the means by which instruments produce sound. What came to be known as the **Sachs-Hornbostel system,** later expanded to include instruments that generate sound electrically, today comprises five categories that accommodate most musical instruments in existence (see the Appendix).

Idiophones

The first of the five categories includes instruments that are self-sounding, that is, the material of which they are made, whether wood, metal, or another substance, is somehow set into vibration. These self-sounding instruments are called **idiophones;** they include gongs, bells, and your two hands and feet, which become idiophones when they are clapped together or stamped on the ground. Idiophones are divided into subcategories according to the manner in which the material is set into motion, such as by striking, shaking, scraping, or stamping. Steel drums are examples of struck idiophones (Listening Guide 8), while rattles are shaken idiophones (Listening Guide 19, in Chapter 2).

Chordophones

String instruments, or **chordophones,** have one or more vibrating strings as the sound source. Chordophones are subdivided into four categories differentiated by shape. Those with a neck and body to which strings are parallel are termed **lutes.** The strings are attached to one end of the neck (usually by pegs) and are anchored on the body; the body of the lute is usually hollow and lends additional resonance. The Tuvan *igil* seen on page xxviii of the Introduction is an excellent example of a long-necked lute; a similar Mongolian lute is heard acompanying the long song in Listening Guide 5.

All lutes can be plucked with the fingers or a pick (*plectrum*), while others are played primarily with a **bow**. A well-known plucked lute is the North Indian *sitar,* heard in Listening Guide 10 (see page 18).

idiophones Instruments that produce sound by being vibrated. One of the five main classes of instruments in the *Sachs-Hornbostel system*, idiophones are further classified by the way they are caused to vibrate: *concussion, struck, stamped, shaken, scraped, plucked,* or *rubbed*.

chordophones Instruments with strings that can be plucked or bowed, one of the five main classes of instruments in the *Sachs-Hornbostel system*, which subdivides them into *zithers, lutes, lyres,* and *harps.*

lute *Chordophone* whose strings are stretched along a neck and body, such as the *'ud, ukulele,* and *guitar.*

bow An implement resembling an archer's bow used to sound string instruments; in some places, the bow itself is plucked to produce sound.

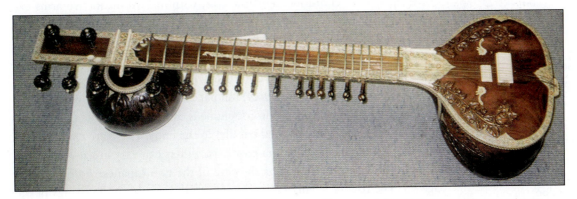

The *sitar's* face is made of carved wood attached to a large gourd. In some styles of playing, another gourd is attached to the top of the instrument's neck (pictured here). The number of strings varies according to style of *sitar,* and they have three basic purposes. The five main strings on the fingerboard of the instrument are used for the melody and can be pulled along the frets (small ridges of wood or metal) to produce large slides and subtle ornaments. Two thinner strings called *chikari* are used for rhythmic punctuation, and the majority of the instrument's strings (attached to smaller tuning pegs running along the side of the instrument) are "sympathetic strings," vibrating with the main melody. These sympathetic strings, along with the instrument's special flat bridge, which raises the strings above the face of the instrument, give the *sitar* its uniquely metallic, resonant sound.

Rag Des (North Indian *sitar*)

**CD 1
Track 10**

Date of recording: 1967
Performer: Ustad Vilayat Khan
Function: Demonstration recording

WHAT TO LISTEN FOR:

- The resonance of the strings as they are plucked with a wire plectrum called a *mizrab,* setting into motion the sympathetic strings that resonate in the background

harp *Chordophone whose strings run at an angle away from the soundboard, subcategorized by shape, playing position, and tunings.*

lyre *Chordophone whose strings are stretched over a soundboard and attached to a crossbar that spans the top of a yoke.*

zither *A chordophone without a neck or yoke whose strings are stretched parallel to the soundboard.*

The second type of string instrument has a sound board to which strings are attached at an angle. Termed **harps,** those with curved necks are sometimes called arched harps or even lute harps, since their construction can be seen as a hybrid with the lute. The musical bow (see page 11) is a good example of a type of single-stringed harp; the Mangbetu harp pictured on page 14 is an arched harp.

A third type of chordophone is the **lyre,** with its two distinctive arms extending up from the body of the instrument and a crossbar running between them to which the strings are attached. Lyres were common in the ancient Mediterranean, especially in Egypt and Greece, but today survive in only a few places, including East Africa and the African Horn, as we have seen in the case of the large Ethiopian lyre (*baganna*) (on page 15). Lyres are always plucked.

The fourth and final type of chordophone is called a **zither.** The zither has a flat body; the strings are attached parallel to the body. There are many zithers with rectangular-shaped bodies in East Asia; zithers can vary in size and have a different number of strings, as is the case of the two Japanese *koto*s seen on page 93. The row of small, white objects protruding above the strings of the *koto* on the left are wooden or plastic supports called bridges. The bridges hold the strings of the *koto* away from the body of the instrument, enabling the performer to pluck the strings with a finger or plectrum.

Zithers with trapezoidal-shaped bodies are also found throughout the Middle East, including the Egyptian *qanun* (see Chapter 4, "**Sound Sources: The 'Ud and the Qanun**"), which has dozens of strings. A common zither encountered in North American folk music is the *dulcimer.*

Aerophones

Aerophones are instruments in which an enclosed column of air vibrates to produce sound, such as flutes, trumpets, and horns. The size and shape of the inside of the instrument, termed its *bore,* determines the range of harmonics produced, and in part shapes each instrument's distinctive quality. Aerophones have an opening, or *mouthpiece,* through which the player blows air. The distinctive aerophone from Australia, the *didjeridu,* is blown through a hole at the end (*endblown*), in contrast to many flutes, which are blown through a mouthpiece on the side (*transverse*). The *didjeridu* produces a drone consisting of a fundamental and one or more harmonics. The instrument is used primarily to accompany songs, and is almost always accompanied by wooden *clapsticks,* as heard in Listening Guide 11 (see page 20).

In contrast to the open end of the hollowed-out log that constitutes the mouthpiece of the *didjeridu,* aerophones such as the European clarinet and the Armenian *duduk* have mouthpieces holding reeds that give each instrument its distinctive sound quality. The reed, which may be made of natural cane or of a synthetic material, is a small rectangular piece held between the lips; it vibrates as it channels the player's breath into the instrument.

Instruments are termed single- or double-reed aerophones, depending on the number of reeds used; the clarinet is a single-reed instrument, while the *duduk* has two reeds. The single reed vibrates against the mouthpiece of the instrument while double reeds vibrate against each other.

Instruments which have enclosed reeds through which air is pushed, such as those within the bagpipe, are classified as *free reed* aerophones (see Chapter 3, "**Sound Sources: The Scottish Highland Bagpipe**"). Finally, there are a few aerophones that act directly on surrounding air without enclosing it, called *free aerophones.* An example is the Australian *bull roarer,* a thin board attached to a string which produces a roaring sound when whirled above the player's head.

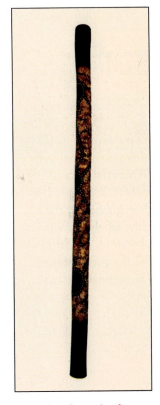

The *didjeridu,* made of a hollowed-out log, may be large enough to require the help of a second musician to support the instrument.

The saxophone is a single-reed instrument whose reed is fixed to the bottom of the mouthpiece with an adjustable metal casing (upper left).

Bushfire (*didjeridu* from Northern Australia)

CD 1
Track 11

Date of recording: 1998
Performers: *Didjeridu* and clapsticks accompanying Alan Maralung (voice)
Function: *Wangga* song performed for rituals and for entertainment

WHAT TO LISTEN FOR:
- The ways in which the player enhances the *didjeridu*'s distinctive tone quality by vibrating his lips and resonating the sound in his mouth. The player sustains an unbroken tone by using circular breathing.

membranophones
Instruments whose sound is produced by a membrane stretched over an opening. One of the five main classes of instruments in the *Sachs-Hornbostel system*, membranophones are distinguished by their material, shape, number of skins (or heads), how the skins are fastened, playing position, and manner of playing.

Membranophones

Membranophones, popularly known as drums, constitute the fourth category of musical instruments. Membranophones are characterized by a membrane (*drumhead*) stretched across one or both ends of the instrument. Membranophones are classified according to their shapes, which may be *cylindrical, bowl (kettle), hourglass,* or *goblet*; according to the ways in which the heads are attached to the body of the instrument (*glued, tacked, laced,* etc.); and according to the ways in which the drumheads are made to sound (by

During the Senegalese *tanibeer*, a convivial celebration of Wolof people in a neighborhood in Senegal's capital city, Dakar, *sabar* drummers accompany dancing for the enjoyment of all.

Lenëën Bàkk (Wolof *sabar* drum rhythm)

CD 1
Track 12

Date of recording: 2003

Performer: Lamine Touré

Function: Named rhythmic pattern (*bàkk*) played on the *sabar* drums in contexts ranging from life cycle rituals to nightclubs

WHAT TO LISTEN FOR:

- The rhythm, named *Lenëën bàkk,* first "spoken" by the drummer (transcribed below) and then "drummed." Each of the syllables represents a different stroke. Three basic hand strokes are represented by "*gin,*" "*pin,*" and "*pax,*" while the other syllables specify different strokes by the stick, some in combination with the hand. "*Ja,*" for example, means that the stick hits the skin and bounces off freely.[12] This rhythm is associated with the Mbaye family of Kaolack and Dakar, Senegal.

TEXT

Te tan pax gin, te tan pax gin chaw ra jan pax, gin jan pax, ja pa ja gin gin jan jan pax gin,/ te tan pax, gi gin, te tan pax gin . . . raw raw ran gin gin

hands or sticks). The *sabar* drum, played by professional musicians in Senegal, is a single-headed drum that uses a combination of hand and stick strokes to produce a variety of sounds. The stick is usually held in the right hand, while the left hand hits the drumhead directly. Listening Guide 12 demonstrates the variety of sounds played on the *sabar.*

Electrophones

The fifth and final category of musical instruments, **electrophones,** was added in the mid-twentieth century in order to include instruments whose sound is produced or modified electronically, such as the *synthesizer* or the *electric guitar.* Instruments such as the electric guitar overlap the chordophone and electrophone categories.

The Sachs-Hornbostel system of classification is provided in detail in the Appendix. The system is useful when discussing instruments from a comparative perspective, enabling one to identify structural similarities in instruments with different names from different places; it also helps one distinguish between instruments that have similar names but are constructed differently

electrophones Instruments that produce sound using electricity, one of the five main classes of instruments in the *Sachs-Hornbostel system,* subdivided into *electromechanical instruments, radioelectric instruments,* and *digital electronic instruments.*

and hence produce different sounds. The human voice is not included within the Sachs-Hornbostel classification system, although it can be said to conform most closely to the aerophone category, with an enclosed column of air setting the vocal cords into vibration.

Intensity

intensity The perceived loudness or softness of a sound.

Closely related to the quality of instruments and voices is **intensity**—the loudness or softness of a sound. Intensity, often referred to as *volume* or *dynamics,* is a vital part of the listening experience. Certain musical instruments, such as many types of bagpipes, were originally constructed for outdoor performance; their construction ensures a high level of intensity and the instruments can be heard over considerable distances, but they are unable to vary the intensity level. Some vocal styles, such as Swiss yodeling, are also *outdoor styles,* as was harmonic singing in the lives of Tuvans and Mongolians. When a large number of instrumentalists or singers perform together, great contrasts in volume are possible. The intensity of a sound is also deeply linked to its cultural setting and function: a woman singing a lullaby while rocking her baby to sleep obviously sings at a lower volume level than when leading her church choir in the performance of a hymn.

Although the loudness or softness of music can be measured precisely by a *decibel meter,* the human ear cannot quantify intensity in the same way. However, the ear and body are quick to sense changes in intensity and to perceive relative levels of loud and soft sounds. Many music traditions have terms to describe different levels of intensity, and some incorporate more contrasts of soft and loud sounds than do others. Clear examples of changing intensity levels can be heard within the Balinese instrumental (*gamelan*) tradition, which employs a wide range of terms drawn from the Indonesian and Balinese languages to describe different dynamics. A strong, loud sound is *keras,* while its opposite is *manis* (sweet, soft); a neutral intensity level in between these two poles is termed *sedeng* (average). *Gamelan* musicians also refer to increases (*nguncab*) and decreases (*ngisep*) in intensity.[13] Contrasting and changing intensity levels can be heard in the Balinese *gamelan* music in Listening Guide 28.

One finds similar attention to dynamics in Western classical music, which uses the Italian words *forte* and *piano* to refer to loud and soft sounds, respectively. Each of these terms can be further modified—*mezzo forte* (moderately loud), *fortissimo* (very loud)—to differentiate further levels of dynamic contrast. Musicians also use the terms *crescendo* and *decrescendo* to refer to an increase or decrease in volume. The term *sforzando* indicates a sudden loud sound.

The relative volume level, or changes in volume, can reflect deeply held emotional or affective values within a music tradition. For instance, Balinese musicians associate dynamics with *rasa* (feeling, expression) in their music, believing that changing dynamics enhance the structure of the music and convey feelings such as strength, sweetness, or softness, as noted earlier.[14]

The widespread use of amplification has reshaped perceptions of intensity within many music traditions. Performers (or sound technicians) often adjust the volume level during live performances as well as during recording sessions. Even the casual listener can reshape intensity by manipulating the volume control on his radio or MP3 player. It is therefore important to consider the potential impact of amplification during any listening experience.

Pitch

The fundamental of the harmonic series vibrates at a specific *frequency,* a faster vibration producing a higher sound and a slower vibration producing a lower sound. The relative highness or lowness of the sound is known as **pitch.**

When the *frequency* of the fundamental is doubled, the ear perceives the sound as the same pitch class, but at a higher level, called an *octave.* When the frequency is halved, the pitch is perceived to drop an octave. Put differently, when a low voice and a high voice sing the same tune, they sing the same pitch classes, but an octave or two apart. This set of equivalent pitches at the distance of an octave is an acoustical phenomenon recognized in many, but not all, music traditions, although it is called by different names. The Western classical tradition uses syllables known as *solfège* to name pitch classes, as illustrated in the figure below.

pitch The highness or lowness of a *sound.*

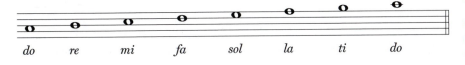

do   re   mi   fa   sol   la   ti   do

This figure presents the syllables used to represent pitch classes in Western music traditions. The fundamental is represented by *do,* which recurs an octave higher.

Hearing and Comparing Pitch Systems and Scales

Each voice and instrument can produce only a certain number of pitches, some more comfortably than others. The overall compass of pitches from the highest to the lowest that an instrument or voice can produce is termed its **range.** Apart from the physical capability of a sound source to produce sounds throughout its range and its greater comfort in certain areas (*registers*) within that range, music traditions inevitably select particular sets of pitches for regular use.

Many music traditions are sung and played at a pitch level comfortable for the singers or instrumentalists, just as we start a tune on any pitch that is convenient. More important are the distances between pitches, which are called **intervals.** The size and arrangement of these intervals, and the resulting relationships among pitches, vary greatly among music systems. Listeners accustomed to one music system often perceive a different set of intervals in an unfamiliar music tradition as sounding "out of tune."

range The distance between the highest and lowest *pitches* that can be sung or played by a voice or instrument.

interval The distance between two *pitches.*

Many music systems have their own special terms for describing and prescribing the set of pitches they use, and by extension, the relationship between any two adjacent pitches. The classical music of North India, for example, organizes its music according to *ragas*, groupings of certain pitches and intervals that move in characteristic patterns. If we return to Listening Guide 10, a *sitar* performing *Rag Des* (pronounced "Rog Desh"), we can hear that the music uses a distinctive set of intervals. While North Indian *ragas* are also much more than just distinctive assortments of pitches (each *raga* is named and has characteristic melodic movements as well as other associations, as we will see in Chapter 3), here we will discuss only the pitch content.

In order to summarize the set of pitches that constitute a particular *raga* (or another music system), musicians commonly arrange all the pitches in order of ascent and descent, called a **scale**. The scale is a concept taken from Western classical music that has been adopted and adapted by many other music traditions in the course of the last century or two. This is true of India, where the pitch content of a *raga* is often represented by syllables widely used for teaching, singing, and writing down melodies, termed *sargam*. This system of representing pitch, similar to Western *solfège,* provides names for the seven most important tones in the Indian scale, moving from the lowest to the highest.

Listen closely to the pitch content of *Rag Des*, which varies as the melody ascends and descends. The most important pitch, or *tonic* note, *Sa*, is easy to hear, since it is reinforced by a drone. The pitch *Ni* is inflected differently in this *raga*, depending on whether the melody is ascending or descending. The musician plays *Ni* slightly higher and repeats it three times as the melody first ascends to the upper *Sa*, but plays it lower as the scale descends.[15]

Mode is a flexible term that can refer, depending on the context, to the general pitch organization of a music tradition or to a particular scale of pitches. Scholars have also sometimes categorized the pitch resources of a given music culture by the number of pitches used. For example, *pentatonic scales*, with five pitches, are quite common in many cultures, although the intervals between the pitches may vary between traditions.

In many traditions, such as the Western and Indian classical traditions, some pitches are perceived as more important than others and serve as points of departure or arrival, especially at the beginning and end of melodies. We should be aware, however, that in some music traditions the individual pitches

The Indian system of *solfège,* called *sargam,* is named after its first four notes, "sa re ga ma." It is presented here in both its English transliteration and in Devanagari, the script in which Sanskrit, Hindi, and several regional languages are written.

The pitches of the Western music system can most easily be understood by looking at a piano keyboard, on which each octave is divided into twelve pitches an equal distance apart. Each pitch is sounded by pressing a white or black key. The seven white keys have letter names and are arranged in the order C–D–E–F–G–A–B. A black key can be called by the letter name of either adjacent white key, along with the sign of a sharp (#) or a flat (♭): the black key between C and D can be named C-sharp or D-flat, depending on the musical context. Each of the twelve keys in the octave can serve as the lowest tone of seven pitches that is a scale. These scales are the basis for the musical language of Western music. Because it is cumbersome to use the names for pitches based on any single music system, ethnomusicologists have developed a system called "cents" to quantify the measurement of intervals and facilitate comparison. The cents system assigns the octave the total value of 1,200 cents and then divides it into twelve equidistant intervals following those of the modern Western scale, each equaling 100 cents. One can through this method measure the frequency of pitches used in different pitch systems and convert the distance between them into cents, quantifying the size of the interval in both absolute and relative terms, comparing the interval to those in the Western music system.

used are not conceived as separate entities, nor are they named; we will encounter one such example in our study of Ethiopian sacred music in Chapter 8. Other traditions have no special vocabulary for describing pitch, or so far, study of the music system has not documented this information.

Melody and Processes of Ornamentation

Most music traditions organize pitches into meaningful units, termed *melody*. A **melody** orders pitches in distinctive patterns that are perceived to have a beginning, middle, and end. Some traditions use relatively few pitches and tend to have melodies with a *narrow range,* such as the Australian *wangga* song heard in Listening Guide 11. Return to that example now and listen closely to

melody A sequence of *pitches,* also called a "tune," heard in the foreground of music.

conjunct motion Step-
wise melodic movement
using small intervals, as
opposed to *disjunct
motion*.

disjunct motion Melodic
motion by leaps of large
intervals, as opposed to
conjunct motion.

ornaments Melodic,
rhythmic, and timbral
elaborations or decora-
tions such as *gracings*,
rekrek, and *grace notes*.

the voice part, which sings the melody. The short melody begins with a number of repeated pitches and then *descends* to end at a lower pitch. The motion
of this melody can be termed **conjunct**—that is, it moves in close and regular
intervals in a stepwise pattern.

Other music systems use a large number of pitches, resulting in melodies
with *wider ranges*. A melody can encompass different numbers of pitches and
often does not use all pitches available within a single vocal or instrumental
part. As an example, return to Listening Guide 5, and listen again to the vocal
melody of the Mongolian long song. In contrast to the Australian *wangga* song,
the melody of the long song has a very wide range; it both *ascends* and descends. The long song melody moves mainly in larger intervals, which is termed
disjunct motion; notice especially the leap of more than an octave at 0:39.

Melodies can be decorated or **ornamented** in a variety of ways. A good example is found in the Mongolian long song (Listening Guide 5), where the
singer uses *trills,* a fast movement between two
adjacent pitches, heard at 0:15, 0:20, and intermittently throughout the excerpt.

Filigree decoration on
jewelry provides a parallel to
ornamentation of a melody

There are names for different kinds of ornaments within most music traditions. For example, North Indian music uses a wide variety of
ornaments, most of which are named. In *Rag Des*
(Listening Guide 10) the most important ornament is the *mind* (pronounced "meend"), a slow
slide from one tone to another.[16] The *mind*
is crucial to establishing *Rag Des*'s identity, particularly when it occurs on the ascent from *Re* to
Ma and on the descent from *Ga* to *Re*. The slide
from *Ga* to *Re* is heard near the beginning of the *sitar* melody, and again in
three different octaves at 1:00 (upper), 1:10 (middle), and 1:12 (lower). Near
the end of the melody, the two *minds* (*Re* to *Ma* and *Ga* to *Re*) are joined
together and emphasized from 1:27 to 1:34. A *mind* is the final sound heard
at 1:43.

Melodies are made up of **phrases**. Here musical terminology borrows from
language: musical phrases, like phrases in speech, carry an idea or thought but
do not constitute a full sentence.

When melodies are sung, they can extend to the very boundaries of the
breath and challenge a singer's endurance; listen to the phrase in the long song
beginning at 0:24, which is so extended that the singer must grab a quick
breath before the sudden ascent at 0:37 in order to sustain the phrase to its end
at 0:47. Conversely, phrases can be short, as heard in Listening Guide 8, where
the steel drums play a melody over and over with some slight variations. The

phrase A brief section of
music, analogous to a
phrase of spoken language,
that sounds somewhat
complete in itself, while
not self-sufficient. One
phrase may be separated
from the next by a brief
pause to allow the singer
or player a moment to
breathe.

steel drum melody subdivides into two phrases of equal length, the second phrase mimicking the first at a slightly lower pitch.

Musical phrases are not always symmetrical. For instance, listen again to the Senegalese *sabar bàkk* presented in Listening Guide 12, in which the drummer speaks the *bàkk* against a background of twelve tapped beats and then plays the *bàkk* on the *sabar* drum. The *bàkk* divides into two main parts of unequal length, marked in the drum syllables by a slash. The *sabar* example also leads us beyond the boundaries of pitch organization to consider the manner in which time is organized.

Duration

Just as music organizes pitch, it also shapes time. When we listen to music, we enter a time continuum different from that of nonmusical experience. We talk about duration by using the terms **pulse** (a regular beat, such as the heartbeat), which produces *rhythms* (patterns arising from different combinations of beats). We can also use the term **rhythm** in a broader sense to refer to the general temporal organization of music.

Music's rate of speed or *pace*, called **tempo** in Western music, is specified (like dynamics) by a variety of terms in different music cultures. Western classical music uses Italian terms, ranging from *adagio* (slow), to *andante* (moderate), and *allegro* (fast). The music of the Balinese *gamelan gong kebyar,* heard in Listening Guide 28, emphasizes changes in pace and has its own terminology.

Hearing and Comparing Durational Systems

The durational aspects of sound can be regular, irregular, or free.

Regular rhythms are quite common in many music traditions; note the strong pulse maintained in the Inuit *katajjaq* heard in Listening Guide 4. Similarly, in the Australian *wangga* song in Listening Guide 11, the clapsticks enter at 0:19 with three sharp strokes and then establish a regular beat.

Much of Western classical and popular music has a regular pulse, organized within a hierarchical durational system called **meter**. Meter subdivides music into groupings of two, three, and four beats, each grouping called a **measure**. We name these **simple meters** according to the number of beats in each measure, terming them duple, triple, or quadruple meters, respectively.

Simple meters are used in many types of music, ranging from symphonies to pop tunes, and are familiar to you from casual listening. For instance, duple meter is commonly heard in marches; each footstep corresponds to one beat, the right foot emphasizing the first beat of each two-beat measure. Emphasis or stress on a beat is termed an **accent**, which often reinforces the first beat of every measure.

pulse The short, regular element of time that underlies *beat* and *rhythm*.

rhythm The temporal relationships within *music*.

tempo *Music*'s rate of speed or pace.

meter A term describing the regular *pulse* of much of *Western classical music* and its divisions into regular groupings of two, three, four, or six *beats*.

measure The unit of time in *Western music* and musical *notation* in which one cycle of the *meter* takes place.

simple meter Groupings of two, three, or four beats per *measure*.

accent Emphasis on a *pitch* by any of several means, such as increased *intensity*, altered *range*, or lengthened *duration*.

The waltz, a well-known ballroom dance, is always set in a triple meter. Most music for social dancing has regular rhythmic patterns that help partners or groups synchronize their movements, as we will see in a study of the polka and tango in Chapter 7.

The American folk song *Wreck of the Old 97*, heard in Listening Guide 6, is an example of quadruple meter; each verse of the song lasts eight measures for a total of thirty-two beats. The otherwise regular quadruple meter is lent more variety by the voice beginning on the last beat of the instrumental introduction, which results in word and verse divisions overlapping the measure boundaries, as seen in the following.

It was **on** one cold No-**vem**ber morning,
The **clouds** were hanging **low**.
Ninety-**seven** pulled out from **Wash**-ington Station,
Like an **ar**-row shot from a **bow**.

compound meter
Groupings of six, nine, or twelve beats per *measure*.

Duple, triple, and quadruple meters can be multiplied by three to produce **compound meters** of six, nine, or twelve beats per measure. Groupings of five, seven, and nine beats are found in many music cultures.

We will begin to explore the ways in which music traditions organize rhythm later in this chapter when we discuss time organization within a Middle Eastern instrumental piece in Listening Guide 18 (see page 41). Here it is important to emphasize that while the term *meter* is of European origin, many music traditions have their own ways of using and naming regular groupings of beats. The length of these regular rhythmic patterns can vary. For instance, the steel band music in Listening Guide 8 has a melody that is eight beats long, subdivided into two four-beat phrases.

It is also possible to have a regular beat reinforced by different rhythms in different voices or instruments. Listen to *Time* (Listening Guide 13), a song describing Judgment Day, performed by men who used to work together on boats gathering sponges off the shore of the Bahamas. Insiders call *Time* a *rhyming spiritual* because of the close coordination between the lead singer, who performs fast couplets, with the chorus, which accompanies him with a repeated verse. The song has a strong quadruple meter with an accent on the first beat of each measure.

Contrast the regular meter of *Time* with the metric asymmetry of the French-American folk song heard in Listening Guide 14 (see page 31). In this humorous song, titled *Old Lady Robert,* we find that the regular meter, divided into eight six-beat (sextuple) measures per verse, is subtly disrupted by the addition of an extra three beats to two of the eight measures. Within the

Time (song from Andros Island, Bahamas)

Date of recording: 1935
Performer: Men from Andros Island, led by David "Pappie" Pryor
Function: Performed by men working in the Bahamian sponging industry and at wakes

WHAT TO LISTEN FOR:

• The four-beat (*quadruple*) rhythmic patterns strongly outlined, with an accent on the first beat, in the low (*bass*) and high (*tenor*) male parts by the chorus (called *bassers*) singing the word "time." All support a rotating lead singer (called the *rhymer*), who performs a text above the chorus at approximately double the rate of speed. Listen to how the fast solo part overlaps and falls between the four beats of the chorus parts.

TEXT

Sinner man, then you need not dwell,
Sinner man, in the region of hell,
Sinner man, you can't dwell there then,
When you reach to God up on high.

O you countin' your finger,
O Lord, till you reach up to your thumb,
. . . can't drink no rum now,
Sinner man, no hidin' place, time.

O way over yonder,
. . .? [text unclear]
Thank God I'm gonna dwell in the . . .
. . . no hidin' place, time.

O one of these mornin',
O Lord, bright and soon,
I'm gonna put on my wing, I'm gonna
    fly God air then,
Sinner man, no hidin' place, time.

Quebecois tradition from which this song originated, asymmetrical tunes such as this one are called *crooked songs* (*air crôche* or *air tordu*). The interruption of a regular rhythmic pattern as heard in *Old Lady Robert* is termed **syncopation**. Syncopation can occur by adding or subtracting beats from an ongoing regular meter, thereby changing the number of beats in a measure, as in this example, or by accenting an unexpected beat within a regular meter without changing the number of beats in a measure.

Many music traditions use **irregular** or asymmetrical meters. Listen again to the *Mbuti* musical bow in Listening Guide 7, which repeats similar phrases that contract and expand, each phrase incorporating a different number of beats.

syncopation A *rhythmic* effect that provides an unexpected accent, often by temporarily unsettling the *meter* through a change in the established pattern of stressed and unstressed *beats*.

irregular meter Asymmetrical groupings with different numbers of beats per *measure*.

The traditional occupation of sponge fishing, practiced by the singers from Andros Island heard in Listening Guide 13, was captured in an 1885 watercolor, *Sponge Fishing—The Bahamas,* by Winslow Homer (1836–1910).

free rhythm *Rhythm* that is not organized around a regular *pulse.*

Some music is so flexible in its rhythmic organization that it may be said to have **free rhythm.** Listen again to Listening Guide 10, *Rag Des,* which has a flexible rhythmic framework without a steady pulse. The *sitar* player lingers over the melody, prolonging some pitches, shortening others, and pausing in between phrases. Both the long song in Listening Guide 5 and the *duduk* music in Listening Guide 9 also exhibit free rhythm.

Listening for Musical Texture and Form

Throughout the previous pages, we have discussed the characteristics of sound as separate elements. But as we have returned repeatedly to the same musical examples for illustrations of different sound characteristics, it has no doubt become clear that all the aspects of sound interact. Indeed, it is only when

La Bonne Femme Robert ("Old Lady Robert," Quebecois song)

CD 1 Track 14

Date of recording: 1999
Performers: Bernie, Normand, Marc, and Michael Ouimet, voices, and clapper?
Function: Entertainment for family events and, more recently, public performances at festivals and clubs

WHAT TO LISTEN FOR:

- The manner in which the regular (and very fast) six-beat measures (sextuple meter) are disrupted by an extra three beats added at the end of measures 4 and 7 in the eight-measure phrase. The extra three beats unsettle the regular rhythm and provide an example of displaced accents called *syncopation*. The six-beat pulse is so fast that you may find it easier to count each measure as containing two beats (marked underneath the beats with X's), adding an extra third beat in the fourth and seventh measures. The text of one verse (beginning at 0:20) is provided below, with each measure numbered above, and broken down below into the number of beats per syllable. The extra beats in measures 4 and 7 are underlined.

0:20 **SOLO**

Measure:	1)	2)	3)
Text:	Mon pere n'a ja -/mais por- te	/de casse car - re /	
Beat:	1 - 2 3 4 - 5 6 /1 - 2 3 4 - 5 - 6	/1 - 2 3 4 - 5 6 /	
Large beat:	X X X	X X X	

Measure:	*4)	5)	6)
Text:	sur sa te - te	/Mon pere n'a ja /mais chan-te	
Beat:	1 - 2 3 4 - 5 6 <u>7 8 9</u>	/1 - 2 3 4 - 5 6 /1 - 2 3 4 5 6 /	
Large beat:	X X X	X X X X	

Measure:	*7)	8)	
Text:	ni - de mes - ses	/ni de ve - pres/	
Beat:	1 2 3 4 - 5 6 <u>7 8 9</u>	/1 2 3 4 5 6 /	
Large beat:	X X X	X X	

Each verse ends with a chorus called a *refrain,* a four-measure verse with a regular rhythm that recurs with the same text and melody sung by the entire group.
Refrain:
Ouich to gais si j'a / vais ma fron-de/ Sap-re gai j'te l'a / rais fron-dec
Recording ends at 0:55.

quality, intensity, pitch, and rhythm combine that we are really experiencing music. How can we think about and talk about the different ways in which the characteristics of sound are organized on a larger scale? We can first consider the vertical structure of music, called texture, and then move on to form, the overall organization of music shaped as the characteristics of sound interact.

Hearing and Comparing Textures

texture The perceived relationship of simultaneous musical sounds.

Musical **texture** results from the ways in which instruments and/or voices combine with each other.

There are five major categories of musical texture, the names of which are based on the root "phone," derived from a Greek word meaning "voice" or "sound." These textures, which include monophony, biphony, homophony, polyphony, and heterophony, are summarized by line drawings in the following figure.

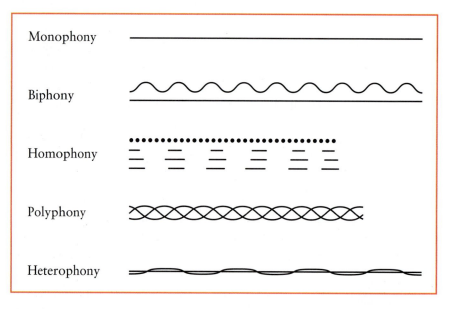

monophony Literally a "single sound," the simplest musical *texture*.

biphonic singing A singing technique of Inner Asian origin in which two tones, the *fundamental* and an *overtone*, are made audible simultaneously by a single singer; also known as harmonic singing.

The simplest musical texture is **monophony**, literally a "single sound." A texture is *monophonic* when an individual voice or melody instrument performs alone (*solo*), or when more than one voice or instrument sing or play the same melody together, sounding the same pitch in the same rhythm at the same time. Listening Guide 15 presents an excerpt from a Roman Catholic Mass, in which one hears first an individual voice and then a small choir singing in monophony.

A **biphonic** texture has two distinct lines, the lower sustaining a continuous pitch (*drone*) while the other performs a more elaborate melody above it. We heard two Armenian *duduk*s playing in a biphonic texture in Listening

Kyrie (Roman Catholic Mass)

CD 1
Track 15

Date of recording: August 12, 2004
Performers: Indiana University School of Music
Function: Roman Catholic worship and historical performances

WHAT TO LISTEN FOR:
- The manner in which a solo male voice sings Kyrie and is joined by a male choir, their voices producing a single (*unison*) sound constituting a monophonic texture

	STRUCTURE AND TEXT	TRANSLATION	DESCRIPTION
0:00	Kyrie Eleison	Lord have mercy	The text is sung three times, with the second rendition by another choir. The third performance of the text is by the soloist and original choir, ending at 0:39.

Guide 9; in Listening Guide 10, the *sitar* and an accompanying drone produce a biphonic texture.

Sometimes a single voice or instrument can produce a biphonic texture by itself, as we have seen in the case of *khoomii* singing in Listening Guide 4. In Chapter 3 we will explore the sound of the bagpipe, which on its own sounds a biphonic texture consisting of drones and a melody.

Homophony, a "same sounding" texture, occurs when a melody is supported by other vocal or instrumental parts, all of which move along in roughly the same rhythm as the melody, but on different pitches. Barbershop quartets and church choirs usually sing in homophony, often referred to as "four-part harmony." This texture, common in Euro-American traditions, usually has one voice part, often the highest of the four parts, singing the melody while the other parts sing the same words in the same rhythm, but on different pitches that combine with the melody to form *chords*, the individual units of Western harmony.

The American folk song *Wreck of the Old 97* (Listening Guide 6) provides another example of homophony; the singer performs the words and melody and the guitar provides supporting harmony as accompaniment. Homophony occurs frequently in European and American folk musics.

homophony A musical *texture*, as in the Western *hymn*, where the parts perform different *pitches* but move in the same *rhythm*.

Thinking about "Western Music"

We have noted throughout Chapter 1 the influence of Western ideas and values on musical terminology. Any discussion of music traditions must also take into account the impact of Euro-American musical sounds, repertory, ensembles, and concepts—often lumped together under the term "Western music"—on so many aspects of music worldwide. Ironically, while "Western" is most commonly used to describe European and American art music of the eighteenth to twentieth centuries, Western music actually consists of many different styles of musical expression from many parts of Europe, and later from North, Central, and South America. We will frequently encounter traces of Euro-American musical sounds and concepts in the soundscapes we study.

Western musics of the eighteenth and nineteenth centuries share a music system termed *tonal music,* in which a single pitch or tone serves as the point of departure and return in any piece of music. As explained in the figure on page 25, the Western tonal system divides the octave into twelve pitches, each of which can serve as the first and last pitch—the center of gravity—for groupings of pitches into scales.

Initially, Western music traveled to different locales along with European missionaries and colonists. In the United States, this imported music tradition quickly established deep roots, supported by an elite dominated until the late nineteenth century by people of European descent. The international impact of the United States in twentieth-century economic and political life, along with the growth and international spread of the US recording industry, also served to disperse Western musical sounds worldwide.

European repertories such as the symphony and opera were transplanted and taken in innovative directions in the New World; at the same time, new American musical idioms interacted with elements of the Western musical system. The extraordinary array of African American musics that emerged in the late nineteenth and early twentieth centuries, including ragtime, blues, and jazz, drew on some aspects of the Western music system, transforming them to create new genres.

Throughout the world in the twentieth century, many primary and secondary schools taught Western music. These shared musical experiences in schools and the pervasive presence of Western popular music on the radio are the reasons many around the globe have at least a passing familiarity with Western tonal music.

Combinations of more than one voice or instrument can create textures called **polyphony**, literally "many sounds." There are many different types of polyphonic textures, some examples of which we've already encountered. The *katajjaq* in Listening Guide 4 is a good example of two-part polyphony, in which two separate but very similar vocal lines interweave and interact with each other.

The song *Lenëën* in Listening Guide 16 (see page 36) provides an example of multi-part polyphony, with different instruments and voices constantly interweaving different melodies and rhythms. In Senegal since the 1970s, the *sabar* drum, heard earlier in Listening Guide 12, has been an increasingly important member of popular music ensembles such as the *mbalax* dance music in Listening Guide 16, a style named after a well-known *sabar* drum rhythm.

The polyphonic texture of *Lenëën* is enhanced by many contrasting rhythms, called **polyrhythms**. The two *sabar* drums establish a fast-changing rhythmic dialogue; as one drummer plays a bass beat and intermittently performs traditional *sabar* rhythms (*bàkks*), the other moves between several drums of different sizes and shapes to give a wider range of rhythms and tone qualities. Both drums play against the quadruple meter established by the synthesizer and bass, following an introduction with a free rhythmic structure. Throughout the song, the voice, saxophone, and trumpets enter and exit, adding their own distinctive rhythms to the texture. Within this multi-layered, polyphonic music, Senegalese audiences recognize familiar *bàkks*, such as *bàkk Lenëën*, which are played during instrumental interludes or between verses by a solo *sabar* drum.[17]

The *mbalax* band Nder and the Setsima Group, featuring vocalist Alioune Mbaye Nder, is pictured here performing at the Parc de la Villette, Paris, in August 1998. Instruments include synthesizer, bass guitar, and drums. On the right side of the photo, percussionist Lamine Touré is playing the drums: the *sabar*, which is prominently displayed, and the *djembe* drum, half hidden behind the *sabar*.

Lenëën (Senegalese *mbalax*)

CD 1
Track 16

Date of recording: 2000

Performers: Nder & le Setsima Group; Alioune Mbaye Nder, *lead vocal;*
Saliou Ba, *bass;* Malick Diaw, *guitar;* Bassirou Mbaye and Mokhtar Samba,
drums; Talla Seck and Lamine Touré, *percussion;* Ibou Tall, Elou Fall, and
Jean-Phillipe Rykiel, *keyboards;* Ibou Konaté, trumpet; Mor Sarr, *saxophone;*
Aïcha Konte and Mbene Seck, *backup vocals*

Composer: Alioune Mbaye Nder

Tempo: Moderate tempo, quadruple meter

Function: Nightclub entertainment and dance accompaniment

WHAT TO LISTEN FOR:

- Five separate but interacting melodic/rhythmic parts played by (1) the saxophone,
  (2) synthesizer and bass accompaniment, (3) *sabar* drums, (4) trumpets, and
  (5) voice
- Repeating harmonic pattern in the synthesized vibraphone, which alternates every
  measure between only two chords
- Entry of *Lenëën bàkk* at 2:16

	STRUCTURE AND TEXT	TRANSLATION	DESCRIPTION
0:00	**Introduction**		A synthesizer carries the melody initially, with a synthesized vibraphone providing harmonic support. Two *sabar* drums interweave intermittently throughout the song, punctuated by recurring calls in the trumpet.
0:14			Electric bass and trumpets join in.
0:30	**Verse** Ndawsi, bul joy Bi ma la seene aeroport Nga laxasu sa borom kër Sa rangantuuru, ci laa xamne Mbëgel metti na	Dear, don't cry When I saw you in the airport Hugging your husband With tears rolling down your face, then I knew Love is painful	The lead vocalist begins the first verse, supported by synthesizer and bass, and often accompanied by a backup singer singing parallel harmonies. The short phrases feature syncopation, rarely beginning on a strong beat.

0:49	Bala nga koy xam
	Nga giss ku yagg loole
	
	xamni mbëgala neex.
	So ame nit ko bëgg ba mu
	   jeex loole,
	so ko gissul weet.
		Before you know it
		If you see a couple that has
		  been together for a long
		  time
		Then you know love is
		  beautiful.
		If you love someone deeply,
		When you don't see him, you
		  feel lonely
			The backup singer adds a
			brief response. Trumpets or
			synthesized horn are used
			occasionally at the ends of
			phrases.

1:07	Weetay bi gënn bonn moy, weetayu guddi ya, so guddi gi xaaje Ba ginaar yi sabbandoo, Nga lambatu lal bi ci wet gune Mu weeta weet Guddi gi yagg lool, mu metti lool, So gëmm di joy, Doo ko tey, mbëgel leneen la.	The worst of loneliness Is that which happens at night Deep in the night Until the cock crows, You feel the bed around you It's so lonely Nighttime is so long So painful So you close your eyes and can't help but cry Love is something else	The singer introduces a new melody, also featuring short, syncopated phrases. Tension builds as the singer climbs into a higher vocal register.
1:33	**Chorus** Ma bëgg jigéén ñi, Mbaye Nder, ma fonk jigéén ñi Ni bilaay, ma yërëm jigéén ñi, Mbaye Nder, ma fonk jigéén ñi	I love women Mbaye Nder, I respect women I swear, I feel sorry for women Mbaye Nder, I respect women	A short phrase is repeated four times. It is high in the singer's range, and features the backup singer harmonizing in parallel fashion.

1:49	Setlul bu baax, jigeen yalla ko
	  teral,
	yalla leen sutural,
	
	Da ngay am sa waay,
	nga bëgg ko lool,
	mu tukki fu sori lool,
	Su guddi jotté,
	ngay joy di joy, di joya joy,
	  (x2)
	Soy gëm di joy do ko tey,
	
	mbëgel leneen la.
		Look carefully, God honored
		  women
		God has respect for women's
		  privacy
		You have your man
		You love him so much
		He travels so far away
		When nighttime falls
		You cry and cry, you cry and
		  cry (x2)
		Close your eyes and can't
		  help but cry
		Love is something else.
			Chorus continues with
			different melody.

2:16	**Bàkk**		A solo *sabar* enters playing the *Lenëën bàkk,* heard in Listening Guide 12; the saxophone plays a melody
2:35			Fade-out

Transcription and translation by Patricia Tang and Papa Abdou Diop

While polyphony generally occurs when several voices or instruments perform different melodies or different rhythms together, some instruments, such as the piano, the accordion, and some zithers, have the capability to produce multiple musical lines on their own.

In musical traditions of the Middle East and parts of Asia, one frequently encounters a distinctive texture called **heterophony**, produced by several voices or instruments that perform similar but slightly different melodies and rhythms at the same time. *Heterophonic* textures can be heard in the Mongolian long song (Listening Guide 5), in which the female voice and fiddle perform in near unison, with slight differences in melody and rhythm.

A large instrumental ensemble of the Naxi people in China's southwestern Yunnan Province performs in heterophony in Listening Guide 17. This instrumental ensemble, which plays at rituals celebrating festivals of various religious deities, includes several aerophones, three different kinds of plucked lutes, bowed two-stringed instruments, and various membranophones and idiophones. When these instruments perform together, all play the same melody with slightly different ornaments.

One type of texture may be maintained throughout a song or instrumental piece, but texture can also vary. Indeed, music would become tedious if it remained the same in all characteristics of sound throughout. Most music therefore changes as it moves through time, varying the relationship between the sound sources, melodies, rhythms, and intensity, shaping textural changes in ways that are familiar within a given music tradition.

Hearing and Comparing Forms

When we speak of the shape or structure of music, we are referring to **form.** When a text is present, one can often identify the form by looking at the relationship of melody to text. For instance, returning to Listening Guide 6, the folk song *Wreck of the Old 97,* one hears a musical structure that follows clearly delineated verses or strophes of text; each subsequent strophe is set to the same music. This form is called **strophic** structure. Strophic structures are very common across historical epochs and geographical and cultural boundaries. Many folk and popular songs have strophic structures in which the verses alternate with a recurring chorus, called a **refrain,** that repeats both the same music and the same text. *The M.T.A. Song* heard in Listening Guide 30 (in Chapter 2) is a strophic folk song with a catchy refrain.

Many forms are named, such as the strophic vocal form that tells a story, known as the *ballad,* which we will study in Listening Guides 31 and 32 (in Chapter 2). Forms of instrumental music tend to vary between music traditions. In the absence of text, one has to listen closely to the characteristics of

---

heterophony A musical *texture* in which two or more *parts* sound almost the same melody at almost the same time; often with the *parts ornamented* differently.

form The structure of a musical piece as established by its *qualities, pitches, durations,* and *intensities,* typically consisting of distinct sections that are either repeated or are used to provide contrast with other sections.

strophic form A form in which all *verses* of text are set to the same melody. Strophic form can include a *refrain* that is sung between *verses.*

refrain A fixed stanza of text and music that recurs between *verses* of a *strophic* song.

Wannian hua ("Eternal Flowers," Lijiang, China)

CD 1
Track 17

Date of recording: 1995

Performers: The Dayan Ancient Music Association

Function: Before 1949, performed at rituals and festivals for deities, as well as by amateur groups for entertainment; since 1949, primarily played for entertainment

WHAT TO LISTEN FOR:

- The heterophonic texture is led off by the flute (*dizi*), almost immediately joined by a high-pitched bowed lute. Next the other bowed lutes, plucked lutes, one plucked zither (*zheng*) and a double-reed pipe enter, the latter quite hard to hear as it pulsates from time to time on long notes. As the other instruments enter, listen closely to how the different playing techniques (whether blowing, plucking, or bowing) result in subtle differences in shaping the basic melody. Important, too, is the range, which can help an instrument shape an upward or downward interpretation of the melody depending on what is possible or more comfortable. The melody played by the higher-pitched bowed lutes is quite ornate, with elaborate ornaments, while the *bobo,* a double-reed pipe, has a more restricted range than the flute and plays the melody more simply.
- A low, plucked chordophone (*pipa*) enters at 0:13, reinforcing important pitches of the melody and emphasizing subdivisions of the pulse beginning at 0:15. One musician plays the *yinqing,* an inverted clapperless bell on a stick, struck with a metal beater that provides a tinkling sound that reinforces the beat throughout the piece.
- Note the subtle differences between instrumental parts by following continuously one distinctive instrumental timbre (whether flute, double-reed pipe, plucked or bowed lute) as it continues throughout the example.
- The heterophony clearly evident at the highest points in the melody (0:14, 0:32, 0:38, etc.), where several of the instruments seem to strain to reach the pitch.

sound to follow the form of an instrumental composition. Many forms become conventional through frequent use over time and are identified by name, such as the *sama'i,* a lively Middle Eastern instrumental piece.

The word *sama'i* means "heard," and refers to being audible.[18] The *sama'i* in modern Middle Eastern music is an instrumental overture with four parts. Each of the four parts is called a *khanah* (pl. *khanat),* and is separated from

"This one goes verse, verse, chorus, train; verse, verse, chorus, train."

the other *khanat* by a refrain, a section of music (and, in vocal music, text) that recurs. The *sama'i* is usually played by a Middle Eastern ensemble which may vary in size, but generally includes one or more violins, plucked lutes (*'ud*), a zither (*qanun*), a goblet-shaped drum (*darabukkah* or *tablah*), a frame drum (*riqq*), and a flute (*nay*); it can also be played by a soloist. Below we explore *Sama'i Bayyati*; the word *bayyati* in the work's title indicates that it is performed in the Middle Eastern musical category or mode (*maqam*) of that name. *Maqam bayyati*; is based on a seven-pitch scale in which the second and sixth pitches are inflected distinctively. The *sama'i* has a standard rhythmic profile: it uses the same rhythmic organization for the first three *khanat* and a different rhythm for the fourth *khanah*. The first three *khanat* are in a slow rhythm known as *sama'i thaqil* ("heavy") which divides into ten-beat patterns; the fourth and final *khanah* is performed in faster, six-beat units that can be heard (as we encountered before in Listening Guide 14) as a strong two-beat pattern.

Throughout the book, we will encounter many other examples that will help us listen for and recognize a wide array of musical forms. Here we will explore the creative processes that create form.

Sama'i Bayyati (Middle Eastern [Egyptian] instrumental piece)

CD 1
Track 18

Date of recording: 1995

Performers: University of California, Santa Barbara, Middle Eastern Ensemble, Scott Marcus, director

Form: *Sama'i,* an instrumental composition with four parts (four *khanah,* pl. *khanat*) separated by refrains

Composer: Ibrahim al-'Aryan (1898–1953)

Function: Performed before a suite or for pedagogical purposes

---

WHAT TO LISTEN FOR:

- The form of the *sama'i,* which is outlined below. The beginning of *Khanat* 2, 3, and 4 are signaled by a change in texture and the sounding of the *tablah* drum.

	STRUCTURE	DESCRIPTION
0:00	*Khanah* 1	This *Khanah* introduces the *sama'i,* setting forth the content of *maqam bayyati.*
0:28	Refrain	The refrain, itself repeated, repeats a descending phrase several times, before ascending to a high point and then descending to the central pitch.
1:22	*Khanah* 2	*Khanah* 2 focuses on a higher register of the *maqam* than the previous *Khanah* or the refrain.
1:48	Refrain	
2:41	*Khanah* 3	*Khanah* 3 remains in the higher register of the *maqam* and moves in conjunct motion up and down the scale of *maqam bayyati,* touching briefly on another *maqam, ajam,* from 2:52 to 3:00.
3:07	Refrain	The *qanun* can be heard playing an ascending scale at 3:32 just before the refrain is repeated.
4:00	*Khanah* 4	Note change in rhythmic pattern and faster tempo for *Khanah* 4, which also includes marked changes in texture, with repeated "calls" and "responses" between different instruments.
4:49		The pace slows markedly, leading back to the refrain.
4:53	Refrain	The instruments slow down at the end and the flute plays a descending scale to bring the piece to a close at 5:51.

Processes of Musical Creativity: Composition, Performance, Improvisation

composition The process of creating *music.*

improvisation The process of composing music as it is performed, drawing on conventions of preexisting patterns and styles. Examples include *cadenzas, jazz riffs,* and *layali.*

The distinctive sounds, textures, and forms of a particular music tradition arise from several interconnected processes of human creativity. **Composition** is a term for the process of creating music; an individual who creates music is known as a composer. In many traditions, however, a composition assumes its shape only during the course of performance. This process is sometimes referred to as **improvisation**, which can be defined as the spontaneous creation of music during performance. Although composition and improvisation have been separated in Western musical thought and approached as mutually exclusive processes, this is a misleading dichotomy. All musical performances incorporate at least some degree of creativity. Similarly, improvisation does not emerge from a void, but is based in large part on the musician's prior musical knowledge and experience. Even in those music traditions that separate composition from performance and have detailed systems of music writing, the performer still retains at least some creative latitude. In sum, we can say that improvisation is the spontaneous composition of music in time.

Some twentieth-century composers have practiced spontaneous composition; we see an example in the music of Pauline Oliveros (see **"Individual Portraits: Pauline Oliveros's 'Deep Listening'"** on pages 44–45).

Many compositional processes exist in many cultures. For instance, Australian *wangga* songs (Listening Guide 11) are owned by individuals who

Lead sheets supply all the information necessary to perform popular and jazz tunes. The melody (usually written on the treble clef) is either sung or played by a melody instrument such as a saxophone. Information about the bass or root movement is supplied by the chord symbols, which also indicate the harmonic possibilities to the keyboard or guitar players.

compose songs in several different ways. Most songs are received by a *songman* from spirits during dreams or other altered states, but it is also possible for a singer to conceive a song without the inspiration of a spirit. Songs may also be inherited from someone else, usually the songman's father.[19]

It may be helpful to think about musical performance as requiring a continuum of choices, some made prior to performance, others made in the moment. Before the performance, musicians decide what instruments or voices to use and how closely to follow musical notation. During the performance, more choices

Pauline Oliveros's "Deep Listening"

Few people devote more time to thinking about how to listen than composers. Composer Pauline Oliveros has devoted her life to exploring the listening process. Throughout her career, Oliveros has united the processes of composition and performance. Oliveros says that "composition gives you time to change your mind, while improvisation provides an edge where what you do is it. I do both. I like collaboration and enjoy opportunities to work with different people from diverse communities." Oliveros further composes and improvises in the context of performance: "I have always loved performance. I wanted to be in contact with sound and moving sound in real time."[20]

Composer/Performer Pauline Oliveros with her accordion.

Pauline Oliveros grew up in rural Texas, where she was influenced by the sounds of the natural environment. She also spent hours listening to the radio, remembering that she "loved the static and tuning whistles to be found in between the stations." Oliveros learned to play the piano from her mother and grandmother, and was fascinated when her mother brought home an accordion in 1942. Oliveros was always interested "in what I could hear and the sensual nature of sound."

After moving from Texas to the San Francisco area in the mid-1950s, Oliveros began to experiment, recording her surroundings by placing a microphone on a window ledge. She discovered that the microphone picked up sounds that she had not heard. Realizing that her own perceptions were selective, filtering some sounds out, she resolved to listen more carefully. Oliveros also continued to play the accordion, composing new works for the instrument over the years, including a 1982 composition, *The Wanderer,* for twenty-three accordions.

Seeking a more organic approach to composition and rejecting conventional musical notation, Oliveros formed the group Sonics with two other composers. Early on, she began to improvise with new resources for electronic and tape music. "It never interested me to cut and splice tape or to wait for numbers to crunch in a computer," she recalls. "I wanted immediate results. . . . It was really thrilling to hear the sounds that I got and to shape them in real time like a performance, even if it were in a studio." Eventually, Oliveros developed the Expanded Instrument System (EIS), which provided control during performance of aspects of pitch and timbre that could usually be shaped only in a studio. EIS (pronounced "ice") is a "continually developing electronic sound-processing environment designed to provide improvising musicians control over various parameters of sound transformation." Foot pedals and switches control various digital delays, reverberation units, mixers, and processors, with output distributed to speakers around the performance space.

In 1988, Oliveros formed the Deep Listening Band, which has performed worldwide and made recordings. The band has used a variety of sound sources, including trombone, *didjeridu*, conch shells, voices, pieces of metal, and, of course, the accordion. The band performs in highly resonant spaces and much of its music features a drone, which Oliveros sees "as connecting it to other musics."

Deep listening has become a central pursuit for Oliveros, who explains the concept as follows:

> The key to multi-level existence is deep listening. Deep listening includes language and its syntax, the nature of sound, atmosphere and environmental context. This is essential to the process of unlocking layer after layer of imagination, meaning, and memory down to the cellular level of human experience. Listening is the key to performance. Responses, whatever the discipline, that originate from deep listening are connected in resonance with being and inform the artist, art, and audience in an effortless harmony. . . . Deep listening is a lifetime practice.

Teach Yourself to Fly (dedicated to Amelia Earhart) is the first of Pauline Oliveros's many *Sonic Meditations*, a series of compositions conceived in the early 1970s that have been performed ever since in many different contexts, always with different outcomes. Here are the Pauline Oliveros's instructions for performing *Teach Yourself to Fly*:

> Any number of persons sit in a circle facing the center. Illuminate the space with a dim blue light. Begin by simply observing your own breathing. Always be an observer. Gradually allow your breathing to become audible. Then gradually introduce your voice. Allow your vocal cords to vibrate in any mode which occurs naturally. Allow the intensity of the vibrations to increase very slowly. Continue as long as possible, naturally, and until all others are quiet, always observing your own breath cycle. Variation: translate voice to an instrument.

are made. These might range from subtle decisions about aspects of musical pace to choices about altering a melody or rhythm through ornaments or syncopation. In addition, the performers might need to substitute a different voice or instrument because of unexpected acoustical factors or a broken string.

We will explore choices made before and during musical performance throughout the book. We will find that the length of a musical performance can be flexible, determined by the constraints of the occasion on which the music is played. We will explore settings of musical performance more closely in Chapter 2, but we've already encountered examples such as the *Mbuti* musical bow tune (Listening Guide 7), and the steel band music (Listening Guide 8), which can be sustained as long as the performers choose and the audience is willing to listen. Contrast these examples to *Sama'i Bayyati* (Listening Guide 18, on page 41), which, while a relatively fixed form, retains some flexibility. The musicians can ornament their melodies differently in each performance, and sections within the *khanat* can be repeated.

Conclusion

Repeated listening to music, primarily through the medium of sound recordings, enables us to develop listening skills, a process discussed in "**Studying Music: Tips on How to Listen.**"

Although recorded sound has helped us launch our exploration and has allowed us to study and appreciate a vast range of musical creativity, we must now turn to the settings in which musical sound is transmitted and performed. In this way, we can expand our understanding of the importance of place to many music traditions and the contributions that musical creativity makes to the settings of which musicmaking is a vital part.

IMPORTANT TERMS

silence
music
quality (tone color, timbre, falsetto, head voice, chest voice, nasal, raspy, straight tone, vibrato)
pitch (conjunct, disjunct, intervals, melody, range, scale)

duration (pulse, irregular rhythm, free rhythm, measure, meter, tempo, accent, syncopation)
intensity
sound sources (idiophone, chordophone, aerophone,

membranophone, electrophone)
organology
texture (monophony, biphony, homophony, polyphony, heterophony)
form (strophic, refrain)

STUDYING *Music*

Tips on How to Listen

Using your knowledge of the characteristics of sound can help you make sense of any music tradition you encounter. Now that you are familiar with the categories of quality, intensity, pitch and rhythm, try to incorporate consistently each characteristic and its associated terminology into your own listening process.

One such process is summarized in the following figure, a mental checklist that can guide you when you are confronted with unfamiliar music. It is usually most efficient to begin with quality—first identifying the sound source(s) performing— but it is best for you to decide in what order you will proceed through the characteristics of sound. It is helpful for an inexperienced listener to settle on a particular sequence of characteristics in order to systematically develop your listening skills and to have an analytical framework to fall back on if you are perplexed by what you hear. Depending on one's musical background and listening experience, one person may find it easier to focus first (after quality) on rhythmic aspects, while another may feel more at home focusing on pitch organization.

As you become a more experienced listener, you will find that identifying a sound source and one other prominent factor related to pitch, rhythm, texture, or form, will provide a strong indication of what you are hearing. For instance, if you encounter an *'ud* (Middle Eastern lute) playing in a heterophonic texture, you should suspect that you are hearing music with its roots in Middle Eastern traditions. At this point, focusing on a third characteristic, such as pitch or rhythmic content, can either confirm your analysis or raise further questions. As you proceed through this book and gain experience listening to music from many different soundscapes, you will also develop your own memories of sounds ranging from the Indonesian *gamelan* to West African drumming, which will build your personal sound archive against which new sounds can be compared.

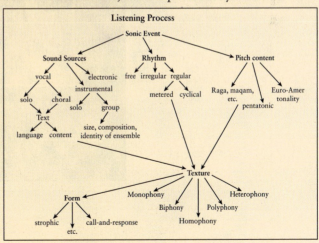

Guide to the listening process.

Chapter 2

Setting: The Study of Local Musics

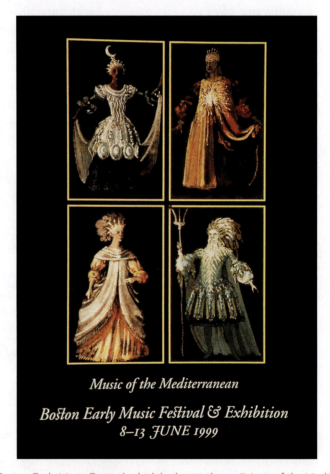

Music of the Mediterranean

Boston Early Music Festival & Exhibition
8–13 JUNE 1999

The 1999 Boston Early Music Festival, which had as its theme "Music of the Mediterranean," included groups such as Ensemble Sarband, which performs music drawing on European, Islamic, and Jewish traditions. The festival program cover featured costume designs by Robin Linklater for *Ercole Amante* ("Hercules in Love"), a seventeenth-century opera composed by Francesco Cavalli.

Overview

Main Points

- Every city, town, and village has its own distinctive musical profile.

- We can map the city's soundscapes by asking what makes up musical life, where is music performed, when is music heard, who makes music, and why.

- Soundscapes existing side by side often interact.

- Soundscapes in different locales may share sounds, settings, and significances.

Introduction: Setting the Stage

"Setting" in its broadest sense encompasses the multiple contexts—a city, a concert hall, a park, a home—in which music is conceived, created, transmitted, performed, and remembered. Since music is more than just sound, we take into account the broad sweep of history and the events of everyday social life.

In this chapter, we will discuss the soundscapes within several urban settings. Our focus here is music in the city rather than in rural settings for two main reasons. First, according to a report of the United Nations Population Fund, by the year 2000, 47 percent of the world's population lived in urban areas; this number is expected to reach 60 percent by 2030. Around 75 percent of the population of Europe, North America, South America, the Caribbean, and Oceania lived in cities in the year 2000; by 2030 both Asia and Africa will have higher numbers of urban dwellers than other continents. Thus, cities—and increasing numbers of "megacities" with populations greater than ten million—will predominate more and more as settings for musical activity worldwide as well as sites for musical research.

Second, wherever their location and whatever their size, most communities today are complex environments that include both distinctive local elements and music traditions from elsewhere. Even a small college campus in a rural location sustains multiple music cultures because of its diverse student population. Small towns also sustain surprisingly varied soundscapes, requiring us to apply many of the same methods to study them as we do to study larger urban areas. Although any environment can provide a stimulating laboratory for studying music, a central goal of *Soundscapes* is to awaken your interest in the musical world immediately around you.

Surprisingly, only in the last quarter of the twentieth century did scholars begin to explore the richness of urban musical life. These studies have focused on the music traditions of ethnic communities, or on musical events accessible in a wide variety of urban public places (see "**Studying Music: Mapping the City**"). In this chapter, we will include music performed in local ethnic communities, as well as styles that have attained worldwide popularity through various media. We will focus on the widest possible variety of music traditions to discover the distinctive musical profile of a given locale. We will, in effect, map the city's soundscapes.

Ethnomusicologists have been reluctant to study multiple music traditions in a single city, partly out of concern that the task may overwhelm an individual fieldworker. One solution to this challenge is to undertake collaborative or team projects, a particularly congenial approach when one is working at home.

STUDYING *Music*

Mapping the City

Ethnomusicologists were slow to discover the rich musical life of cities; only in the last quarter of the twentieth century did they recognize the potential for ethnographic research and carry out fieldwork there. In developing the new subfield of urban ethnomusicology, scholars began by focusing on individual ethnic communities and their music. By the mid-1980s, ethnomusicologists were giving increasing attention to various musics such as rock, rap, and country that are found in urban and rural areas in the United States and abroad.

There are only a few models to guide us in mapping multiple music traditions in a single locale. The most detailed and large-scale study of the music of a single city is Ruth Finnegan's book *The Hidden Musicians,* a study of amateur music-making in the author's hometown of Milton Keynes, England.[1] Finnegan took a close look at what she called the "musical worlds" of her community, which are very similar to the music cultures that constitute our soundscapes. Finnegan's musical worlds however, are almost exclusively European or American, including classical music, brass band music, folk music, musical theater, jazz, country and western music, and rock and pop. Finnegan focused not on professional musicians, but on amateur musical life, observing that amateurs' musical activities are often hidden from both the community at large and musicians who are not involved in them.

We will cast our net wider to investigate international music traditions represented within a single locale, as well as musical activity by both professionals and amateurs, but we can learn a great deal from Finnegan's work. Particularly useful is Finnegan's concept of "pathways," a term she uses to refer to familiar and regular activities, such as work, worship, or recreation, that an individual undertakes in the course of everyday life. Musicmaking is a pathway too often overlooked, constituting for many a regular, part-time group activity that carries substantial meaning for its participants. Finnegan emphasizes that musical pathways are always changing, and people form new pathways to follow, as they maintain and transform longtime ensembles or establish new singing groups or bands. Musical pathways, suggests Finnegan, provide "an invisible structure" through which people choose to conduct their lives.

The failure to look broadly at urban musical life has reduced our appreciation of the many music cultures that exist side by side in most cities and towns, often sharing performance spaces as well as music, musicians, and audiences. By looking at the big picture in several urban centers, we can understand the ways in which a locale can attain its own distinctive profile while partaking of—and contributing to—the musical world beyond. In order to capture the many interactions in urban musical life, our discussions here will incorporate musics—including those labeled "popular" and "classical"—that have rarely been surveyed by musical ethnographers until recently. Many different music cultures are present in most places—for instance, Indian music and African American rap may be performed at the same festival on the same day—and it is important to study the relationship between these contrasting traditions.

Here we will explore the soundscapes of three cities in order to attain a comparative perspective, looking briefly at musical life in an African and an Indian urban area before exploring a North American city in more depth. Our three cities have been chosen because, although they are of different sizes and locations, they share aspects of economic and political history and they sustain multicultural populations. Located on different continents, all three are coastal towns whose character has been shaped by their role as ports. At different moments in their histories, all have been under British colonial domination. This trio therefore presents both similarities and differences; each sustains distinctive local traditions while borrowing from other places around the globe and in turn influencing the content of soundscapes worldwide. All three have been over the course of time central to the music history of their respective countries and regions, and continue to play vital roles today. Our three cities are Accra, Mumbai, and Boston.

CASE STUDY: Accra, Ghana

The surf rolls in under the half moon, stars shining dimly in the hazy sky. It's Friday evening and Next Door, a festive club on the outskirts of Accra, is filled with people listening and dancing to the sounds of the Silver Wings band playing "highlife." This musical style was given its name around 1920 when local melodies were first arranged for urban Ghanaian ballroom orchestras who entertained upper-class audiences. It became popular worldwide through concerts and sound recordings.[2] At the same time, highlife achieved a unique place within Ghanaian consciousness. To quote one Ghanaian listener at Next Door: "Highlife—it's our national music."

Much of the history of Accra echoes through the strains of highlife, which unites several streams of the Ghanaian musical past. In highlife one can hear traces of sea chanteys and folk songs carried by sailors of many nationalities to the coast of West Africa; the instruments and sounds of military bands introduced by European military and colonial forces over the centuries in the area known as the Gold Coast; and piano music and church hymns widely dispersed among the educated elite by the late nineteenth century. Highlife fell somewhat out of fashion in the last decades of the twentieth century as competition from other West African popular musics increased, but it has continued to transform itself, to be widely distributed through recordings, and to be performed in Accra for engagements, weddings, and christenings, at nightclubs, and on the radio. Highlife is so central to Ghanaian life that Silver Wings is just one of several groups recruited and supported by the Ghanaian military to play at official functions and public concerts. With trumpets, guitar, bass, keyboard, two drummers, and several singers, Silver Wings performs highlife classics, most with texts in Twi, the indigenous language of the Akan peoples who constitute about half the population of Ghana.

Multicultural Accra

The location of Accra and its role as a port have over the centuries made it a magnet for cultural exchange, bringing together a wide array of people and their musical traditions. The forced flow of musical influences between the Gold Coast, Europe, and the New World during the centuries of the slave trade was followed by the region's incorporation into the British empire in the late nineteenth century. Global connections were further insured by the early introduction of English, which remains Ghana's official language, since no single indigenous language is spoken in all areas. In 1877 Accra became the capital of the Gold Coast, a British colony, and it remained the capital when the Gold Coast became the independent country of Ghana in 1957. Accra in the

early twenty-first century is a sprawling city of nearly three million people, its streets a chaotic mix of carts, cars, taxis, buses, and ramshackle minibuses known as *tro-tros,* all producing a symphony of honking horns blended with the ubiquitous sounds of Ghanaian radio stations.

Modern Accra was settled by the Ga people in the fifteenth century. The Portuguese arrived shortly thereafter, launched the gold trade, and introduced Christianity. The arrival of Dutch, Danish, and English forces followed, and many of the trading posts and forts they constructed to protect the gold trade were refitted for the slave trade. Migration from inland Ga communities further swelled the population along the coast.[3]

Koo Nimo (Daniel Amponsah) is one of Ghana's most revered musicians, shown here (on right holding guitar) with his *Adadam Agofomma* (Roots Ensemble) from Kumasi, Ghana. Koo Nimo plays a form of acoustic guitar highlife known as palmwine music, named after a drink made from fermented palm tree sap. The musician on the far left plays an idiophone called the *prempresiwa,* or *rumba box.*

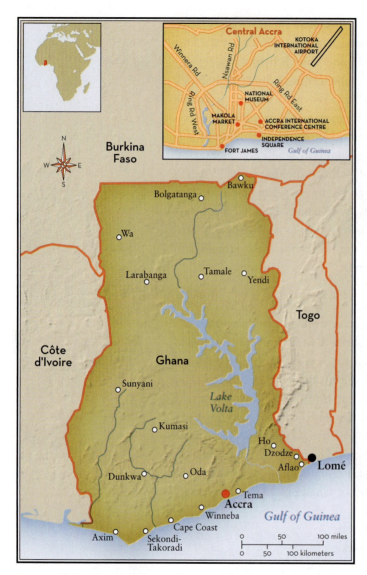

Central Accra

KOTOKA
INTERNATIONAL
AIRPORT

Winnera Rd

Nsawan Rd

Ring Rd East

Ring Rd West

NATIONAL
MUSEUM

MAKOLA
MARKET

ACCRA INTERNATIONAL
CONFERENCE CENTRE

INDEPENDENCE
SQUARE

FORT JAMES

Gulf of Guinea

Burkina
Faso

N
W E
S

Bawku

Bolgatanga

Wa

Larabanga   Tamale

Yendi

Togo

Côte
d'Ivoire

Ghana

Lake
Volta

Sunyani

Kumasi

Ho
Dzodze
Aflao   Lomé

Dunkwa   Oda

Tema

Accra

Winneba   Gulf of Guinea

Cape Coast

Axim   Sekondi-
Takoradi

0   50   100 miles

0   50   100 kilometers

Accra at the beginning of the twenty-first century extended over approximately 200 square kilometers along the central Ghanaian coast.

The establishment of Accra as capital of the Gold Coast in the late nineteenth century intensified the city's political and economic importance and attracted further waves of immigrants, as did Accra's subsequent role as the capital of independent Ghana.

The presence of the Ga ethnic community has long lent Accra much of its distinctive cuisine, including the long strips of fried plantains sold by street vendors, and much of its traditional music. The Ga people celebrate the *Homowo* Festival annually, an occasion for performance of well-known Ga dances, accompanied by drumming. *Homowo* ("Mocking Hunger") marks the Ga community's triumph over famine with a successful harvest, commemorating the period during which the Ga people migrated to the area from regions farther east in what is present-day Nigeria. The seven-day *Homowo* festival, celebrated in August or September throughout Ga neighborhoods in Accra, culminates in the *Great Durbar*, a lively musical celebration attended by all chiefs, sub-chiefs, and a broad cross-section of the community.

Various ethnic festivals dot the Ghanaian calendar and are celebrated publicly; elaborate funerals are also celebrated by most ethnic communities in Accra. Driving through the neighborhoods of the city, one frequently passes crowds observing wakes outdoors; women and men sit in chairs on opposite sides of the road, listening to live or recorded music while eating and drinking. Individuals come together not only to commemorate the dead, but also to celebrate the community of which the deceased was a member. An elaborate funeral, with the full display of music and food not only marks an individual's passing, but also provides evidence of his or her contribution during life.

Mounting a funeral can tax the resources of many families, especially those of struggling immigrants. For this reason, the Ewe people, who until the early decades of the twentieth century lived mainly to the east of Accra in the rural

Volta region and who migrated to the capital for economic reasons, have banded together with others from their hometowns in funeral associations. One such group, *Milo Mianoewo* ("Love Your Neighbor"), was founded in 1972 by Ewe people who came to Accra from Dzodze, a large town near the Togo border. Several hundred members of the association pay dues and meet once a month to socialize and make music. When a member of the

Ga chiefs, strewing corn and accompanied by horn blowers, process through the streets of Jamestown, Accra, on the final day of the *Homowo* festival.

association dies, the society buys the coffin and covers all expenses for the burial, supplying food, drink, and music for the wake. Should a member die in Accra, the association transports the body to the hometown and observes the funeral, a three-day affair. At the monthly meetings of the association, drinks and snacks are served and individuals join in performing traditional Ewe songs and dances.

In Listening Guide 19 (see page 57), we hear the members of the funeral association perform *agbadza* ("ahg-bahd-ZHA"), a dance performed at Ewe social gatherings and at funerals. Said to have derived from a dance performed by fighters returned from war, over the years *agbadza* became a popular social dance, today performed by both men and women.[4] The lyrics of *agbadza* songs change frequently; new texts often allude to migration or current political and social issues.[5] In addition to the alternation of a solo singer and chorus in call-and-response format, *agbadza* involves a number of instruments, including idiophones and membranophones. The *agbadza* rhythms are for many listeners the most familiar aspects of the music and are frequently borrowed for use with new texts in contexts ranging from hymns to popular songs.

Just as *agbadza* rhythms are widely associated with the Ewe people, different drums and their music are linked to other Ghanaian ethnic groups. Perhaps best known is the *atumpan*, ("ah-toom-PAHN") a drum associated with the Akan people, which includes a number of subgroups, including the Asante, Fante, and Akyem. *Atumpan* are the main instruments used for ceremonies by Asante chiefs and for state occasions by the Asante king. These large, goblet-shaped drums have a single drumhead attached by wire to a flexible round frame made of bamboo and secured to the body of the drum by laces tied to protruding tuning pegs. *Atumpan* are produced in pairs of "male" and "female"

Members of the funeral association Milo Mianoewo wear traditional garments made of java cloth to their monthly meeting. (top left) Master drummer Patience Dogba, who performs along with her brothers Lucas and Kofitsey Tagborlo, is seen playing *atsimevu*, holding a stick in her right hand and muting the drumhead with the left hand; a second drummer is beating rhythms with two sticks on the body of the master drum. (top right) Men shake the *axatse*, calabash rattles covered with mesh net threaded with beads. Two seated men play the *sogo* (rear) and *kidi* (foreground) drums. (bottom left) Women sing, dance, and clap the *agbadza*.

drums, but are played by a single drummer, a practice said to reflect the interdependence of men and women in Akan society, which is matrilineal in descent and inheritance customs. The *atumpan* are played as part of the Asante king's orchestra, called the *Fontomfrom,* as well as part of the *Adowa* orchestra performing dances for Asante funeral celebrations.

James Acheampong constructs Akan drums of cordia (tweneboa) wood, leather, cowrie shells, cow hide, brass, and other local materials in his workshop at the Centre for National Culture in Kumasi, Ghana. A pair of recently completed *atumpan* drums are in the foreground, with two *donno*, double-headed drums with laces connecting the two drumheads, resting on the table behind them. Several of James Acheampong's drums are on permanent display in the lobby of the National Theatre in Accra.

Agbadza (Ewe song and dance)

Date of recording: January 11, 2004
Performers: Members of the Dzodzemidodzi Association, Milo Mianoewo
Form: Excerpt from a polyphonic and polyrhythmic form
Function: Used for social events and funerals

WHAT TO LISTEN FOR:

- Rattles (*axatse*) supplying a 2+2+2+3+3 pattern, or timeline, operating as a central rhythmic referent for the drummers, singers, and dancers; clapping follows rattles
- High-pitched stick drums (*sogo* and *kidi*), which fill out the timeline and respond to the master drummers
- Two lower-pitched hand-and-stick master drums (*atsimevu*), whose part is much more varied and tends to converse both with the higher stick drums and with individual dancers
- Call-and-response between lead singers and chorus

DESCRIPTION

0:00	Four distinct parts—rattles (*axatse*), stick drums (*sogo* and *kidi*), hand-and-stick drums (*atsimevu*), and vocal call-and-response—combine throughout. Near the beginning of this recording, the lead male singer calls in an improvisatory manner and tends to overlap the choral responses. The distance of the microphone from the singers and the dense polyphonic texture made it impossible to transcribe the text.
0:16	Lead male singer is heard most clearly here.
0:54	Male lead singer is joined by female lead singer, and the vocal part becomes more fixed.
1:10	The two high-pitched stick drums can be heard especially well here, as the microphone moves closer to the drums.
1:34	Fade-out

In addition to their prominence in Akan social and ceremonial life, the *atumpan* are also "talking drums" that were used in the past for communication. The *atumpan* can produce tones on several different pitch levels, enabling the drum to replicate the patterns of the tonal Akan language, Twi. Listening Guide 20 (see page 58) demonstrates the ability of the *atumpan* to speak, presenting a short narrative about the history of the Denkyira state, a powerful kingdom which ruled over many Akan peoples until its defeat by the Asante at

Atumpan (talking drum from Denkyira state in southwestern Ghana)

CD 1
Track 20

Date of recording: 1992–1993
Performers: Elizabeth Kumi, *appellant;* Joseph Manu, *drummer*
Form: Appellation (naming) text in Twi language
Function: To glorify performer and his/her lineage; to demonstrate drum language

WHAT TO LISTEN FOR:

- Ability of the drum to talk, performing both new text and historical drum language
- Manner in which the tonal contours of the spoken text are replicated by the subsequent drum phrase

	STRUCTURE AND TEXT	TRANSLATION	DESCRIPTION
0:00	Me ma mo atena ase, Nana ne me mpaninfoo	Greetings to those present. I welcome you, Nana, and his elders,	
	Owura dwamtenani, Enanom ne agyanom, ne anuanom a yeahyia ha, yegye me asona.	Mr. Chairman, mothers, fathers, and brethren here gathered. The response to my greeting is *asona.*	
	Saa twenekasa yi fa Odeefuo Boa Amponsem, Denkyira hene no. Odomankoma kyerema, ma no nko!	This drum language is about Odeefuo Boa Amponsem, King of Denkyira. Creator's drummer, let it go!	
0:27	Adawu, Adawu, Denkyira mene sono. Adawu, Adawu, Denkyira pentenprem, Omene sono, ma wo ho ne so.	Adawu, Adawu, Denkyira is the devourer of the elephant. Adawu, Adawu, Denkyira the quicksand, Devourer of the elephant, come forth in thy light, show your glory!	Drum language, glorifying King of Denkyira
	Pentenprem, ma wo ho ne so, Ma wo ho ne so. Kronkron, kronkron, kronkron, Amponsem Koyirifa, ma wo ho ne so. Ako nana ma wo ho ne so.	Quicksand, show your glory, Show your glory. Your holiness, holiness, holiness, Amponsem Koyrifa, show your glory. Grandson of the Parrot, show your glory.	
0:55	Fade-out at 0:57		

A variety of membranophones and idiophones are used by music clubs in Accra to bring together young people to learn a pan-ethnic array of musical styles. The African Star-Dance Group, founded in 1994 for young people in the Darkuman neighborhood, is seen here performing *kuku*, a dance popular in northern Ghana. The dancers are accompanied by several drums (seen at rear behind the dancers), including the *kpanlongo*, *donno*, and *djembe*, the latter a drum from Mali widely distributed today across West Africa.

the end of the seventeenth century. The text in Listening Guide 20 resembles the form used for a traditional ritual, first explaining its purpose and then naming powerful beings, both traditional deities and historical figures.

Music in Ghanaian Christian Life

A substantial amount of musicmaking in Accra occurs within the context of religious rituals. Although many traditional belief systems are still practiced, especially in the rural locales, using indigenous music in their devotional and healing activities, the entry of Christianity into coastal Ghana left a marked Christian influence in rural and urban areas. Throughout Accra, belief is prominently displayed in signs and billboards advertising the numerous churches that dot the city. Many shops carry Christian or Biblical names, such as the By His Grace Chop Shop, the Jesus Dressmaking and Hair Dressing Center, and Faith Art Services.

Churches are located on virtually every block, and most support substantial musical activity. For instance, the large Evangelical Presbyterian Bethel Church in the New Town section of Accra mounts two full services each Sunday morning. The first is trilingual, in Twi, Ewe, and English. The service incorporates a corresponding diversity of musical styles, featuring songs performed in Western harmony by the Church's youth choir accompanied by traditional drumming, hymns accompanied by an organ, and lively worship songs performed with the support of amplified bass guitar, synthesizer, and drum set. The music unites Western musical influences with Ewe rhythmic

The Youth Choir of the Evangelical Presbyterian Bethel Church in Accra marches into the sanctuary for the Sunday morning early service, singing as they process.

Banners mounted throughout Accra advertise the January 2004 performances by African American ragga/rap star Shaggy (Richard Oriville Burrel) at the Accra Sports Stadium. Ghanaian hiplife musicians, who perform a blend of highlife combined with hip-hop, participated in the concerts, which drew record crowds.

complexity. The repertory ranges from new worship songs to traditional Methodist hymns sung in either the Twi or Ewe languages. Once a month, when everyone in the congregation marches forth from their pews to deposit a cash donation in one of seven boxes corresponding to the day of the week on which the individual was born, that month's birthdays are announced and the congregation sings *Happy Birthday* in unison.

Many churches in Accra hold healing rituals that seek to cure illnesses through prayer and participation in musicmaking. Many of these rituals incorporate traditional indigenous healing practices.

One such group, The Kwabenya Prayer Camp of the Bethel Prayer Ministry International Church, holds daily rituals as well as "Breaking Sessions" to cure diseases; their newsletter invites everyone to "Bring the sick, barren, demon-possessed and people with all kinds of problems for healing and deliverance."[6] Songs accompanied by instruments including synthesizer, guitar, and a drum set are the main venue through which healing is accomplished, and members of the congregation join their ministers in ecstatic speaking in tongues, followed by singing and dancing in the aisles. The Bethel Prayer Ministry, which has a congregation of more than 1,000, is also an international organization, with congregations located elsewhere in Africa, Europe, and the United States. Their activities bring us full circle, demonstrating once again the striking international reach of seemingly local traditions in Accra.

Accra's Global Connections

In Accra, the complex blend of local and international traditions emerges in all aspects of musical life and gives the city's music a distinctive, cosmopolitan flavor. An example is the range of musics heard on Ghanaian radio: Listeners can tune into Radio Globe 91.5, which features foreign offerings; switch to Joy FM 99.7, which mixes local and foreign styles; or listen to popular Peace Radio 104.3, which often plays highlife recordings. Among the explicitly local broadcasts is a music show in Ewe every Sunday to help the Ewe in Accra keep current on "what's happening back home."

Like much of Africa, Accra continues to listen to cassettes, which have been displaced by new digital technologies in the United States, Canada, and most of Europe. Small kiosks at sites ranging from traditional marketplaces to modern supermarkets sell new and used cassettes. A few shops in downtown Accra display recent CDs and DVDs, arranging recordings under a mix of familiar and novel rubrics. One finds bins for

Reggae, Jazz/Country, and R&B/Hip Hop alongside a space for Locals/Gospel, an important Christian musical genre in Accra. One shelf, marked "Cools," contains selections considered to be Cool Music, including various blues recordings and CDs by superstars such as Michael Jackson, Lionel Ritchie, and Elton John.

Accra's role as Ghana's capital extends into musical life; a number of musical ensembles reinforce national identity, helping to unite the many historically independent ethnic groups brought together as a nation less than fifty years ago and representing Ghana to the world. In addition to the National Symphony Orchestra, the Pan-African Orchestra under the direction of Nana Danso Abiam issues recordings and mounts tours abroad. The National Theatre houses both Abibigroma, the National Drama Company of Ghana, and the National Dance Company. Founded in 1962 by musicians from the University of Ghana, the National Dance Company merges traditional Ghanaian dances with contemporary dance styles; it performs both at home and abroad. In its mission to export Ghanaian culture, the National Dance Company of Ghana is, like the musical profile of the city it represents, at once local and global, achieving "a dramatic fusion of African and Contemporary Dance."

Nowhere is the ongoing relationship between traditional Ghanaian music cultures and international musical styles made more clear than in works by Ghanaian composers. Listening Guide 21 (see page 64) contains an excerpt from a composition by Ghanaian composer J. H. Kwabena Nketia that fuses the sounds and styles of traditional Akan music with a European musical idiom. This composition, titled *Cow Lane Sextet,* emerges from the composer's blending of his local roots with cosmopolitan experience, a process discussed in detail in "**Individual Portraits: J. H. Kwabena Nketia, Composer, Educator, Ethnomusicologist**" (see page 62). Composed for a combination of Western melody instruments and Ghanaian membranophones, the *Cow Lane Sextet* is performed on synthesizer for reasons explained by the composer himself: "This piece was not composed for synthesized instruments. The computer came in solely for illustrative and educational purposes when I did not have competent performers on hand."[7] The *Cow Lane Sextet* seeks to convey the soundscape of a particular Ghanaian place—the street called Cow Lane in the center of Accra—through an intentionally hybrid musical style. It then conveys these distinctive sounds through modern technology.

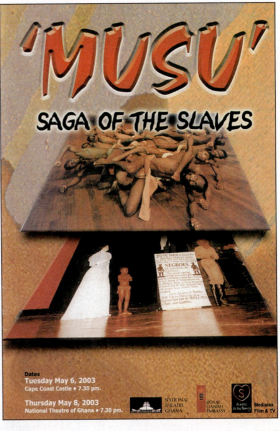

'MUSU'

SAGA OF THE SLAVES

Dates
Tuesday May 6, 2003
Cape Coast Castle • 7.30 pm.

Thursday May 8, 2003
National Theatre of Ghana • 7.30 pm.

NATIONAL THEATRE GHANA

ROYAL DANISH EMBASSY

Medialex Film & TV

Since 1998, secondary school students have participated in the Noyam (Ga for "Moving On") African Dance Institute, a program of the National Dance Company of Ghana. The troupe has undertaken international and national tours to perform *Musu* ("Abomination"), a synthesis of poetry, dance, and music recounting the story of the Danish involvement in the Gold Coast slave trade starting in the late seventeenth century. The program for this event describes *Musu* as "an attempt to stimulate mankind to reflect on the whole issue of slavery worldwide."

J. H. Kwabena Nketia, Composer, Educator, and Ethnomusicologist

Joseph Hanson Kwabena Nketia has long represented the study of African music to the outside world. That he is also revered within his native Ghana is clear from his official designation by the government as a national "Living Treasure" in 2003. Born in 1921 and educated in Ghana, with graduate training in the United Kingdom, Nketia served as Professor of Music at the University of Ghana, where he founded the Ghana Dance ensemble, and also taught at UCLA and the University of Pittsburgh. Since 1993, Nketia has been at home in Accra as Professor Emeritus and Director of the Centre for African Music and Dance. His work as an educator and founder of institutions is well-known to ethnomusicologists, but provides only a partial picture of his life as a musician, for J. H. Kwabena Nketia is also a composer.

J. H. Kwabena Nketia in 2004 at the Archive of African Music and Dance that he founded at the University of Ghana.

Nketia was born to an Akan family in Mampong, a town less than an hour's drive north of Accra. A small town in a hilly, forested region, Mampong was among the first parts of the Ghanaian interior to be settled by Europeans and was an early locus for missionary activity. Mampong was also the site of the first cocoa farm in Ghana in the late nineteenth century, a crop that revolutionized the Ghanaian economy. Nketia was educated at the Presbyterian Training College in nearby Akropong, and later taught there.

During his school years in England in the 1940s, Nketia became interested in musical composition. He followed in the footsteps of other distinguished Ghanaian composers, such as Ephraim Amu (1899–1995), who was also educated in England and was known for his choral compositions.[8] Nketia learned Western composition and realized that he needed to figure out how to create distinctive African compositions: "I studied harmony and counterpoint," Nketia recalls. "I did all the exercises and knew which ones I could not apply."[9] Nketia decided that in Africa a composer must use not just countermelodies, but also counterrhythms.

From the beginning, Nketia wanted to combine indigenous tradition and colonial influence, the dual heritage that shapes so many aspects of Ghanaian musical life. Nketia believes in a pan-ethnic Ghanaian music and sees musical creativity intersecting with and relating to social life and cultural policy. One sustains tradition, he suggests, "by embracing multiple streams of history and multiple ethnicities. As a result, new things constantly emerge."

Nketia has compiled a four-volume CD and cassette collection of his compositions, which are written for instruments and voices. The works are performed on synthesizer and his scores are being made available online. Most of Nketia's music draws its inspiration and aspects of its musical style from specific Ghanaian soundscapes. His Akan background figures heavily in his compositions, and he draws on a variety of traditional repertories as the basis for his compositions. One of his compositions, *The King Walks Majestically,* is based on a praise song for the *Asantehene,* the King of the Asante. This slow and stately composition is written for piano, flute, and oboe, with prominent parts for the Asante talking drum (*atumpan*), bell, and rattle.

Nketia has spent much of his adult life in Accra, and the cacophony of that urban area has had an impact on his compositions. One composition, conceived in 1959 while he was a visiting professor at Northwestern University in Evanston, Illinois, is a work for six instruments titled *Cow Lane Sextet.* Cow Lane is a crowded road in the central part of Accra, adjacent to a lively market area. Nketia considers the sextet "a very avant-garde piece." He adds: "This is about as far as I can go; I always have to have the local audience in mind. I always have local connections."

The *Cow Lane Sextet,* composed for piccolo/flute, clarinet, trumpet, xylophone, timpani standing in for *atumpan,* and snare drum standing in for the traditional *brekete*, is intended to capture the bustle and confusion of Cow Lane. That Nketia composed this piece while residing in quiet, suburban Evanston, Illinois, is a fitting testimony to the multifaceted world of the modern African composer. It also demonstrates the manner in which Nketia is interested in "transferring and transforming" sound. In listening to *Cow Lane Sextet,* we can understand, with Nketia, that "music always transforms tradition, and listening to it is transformative."

Cow Lane Sextet

CD 1
Track 21

Date of recording: October 2003

Composer: J. H. Kwabena Nketia

Performer: Transcribed, programmed, and performed on computer by Andrews K. Agyemfra-Tettey

Tempo: Moderate tempo, mainly in sextuple (6/8) meter

WHAT TO LISTEN FOR:

- Incorporation of substitutes for traditional Ghanaian instruments and Ghanaian musical elements into a contemporary composition
- Melodic aspect of the xylophone and tympani (*atumpan*) parts
- Syncopation and frequently shifting accent patterns that obscure the underlying sextuple meter and provide a sense of polyrhythm

	STRUCTURE	DESCRIPTION
0:00	**Section A**	Xylophone enters, followed two beats later by tympani, which substitutes for the a*tumpan*.
0:02		Clarinet enters, followed by snare drum substituting for the *brekete;* clarinet introduces main theme, which has a descending contour and syncopated rhythm.
0:06		Trumpet enters, with ascending melody.
0:13		Flute enters.
0:19		Cadence in trumpet part.
0:20	**Section B**	Xylophone plays regular, six-beat pattern accompanying syncopated flute melody.
0:29		Percussion drops out briefly.
0:32		Regular xylophone beat resumes.
0:37		Snare drum roll.
0:39		Shift to duple meter.
0:41		Flute trill; tempo accelerates, followed by intense polyphony and implied polyrhythm.
1:04		Return to sextuple meter.
1:08		Flute trill.

Fade-out and track ends at 1:11.

CASE STUDY: Mumbai, India

Mumbai—until 1996 known as Bombay—is a massive city of more than sixteen million people set on a peninsula off the west coast of the Indian subcontinent. Mumbai has been the capital of its region since India's independence from Great Britain in 1947, and the capital of Maharashtra State since 1960. The area was first settled by Koli fisherfolk who immigrated south from Gujarat more than two millennia ago, and was subsequently ruled by Hindu and then Muslim kingdoms. The entry of a series of foreign forces, beginning with the Portuguese and culminating with the longtime British colonial presence, insured that this heterogeneous city of people from all over India would become a truly global city. Mumbai is India's most international metropolis, but at the same time it maintains its distinctive local identities. Some neighborhoods are dominated by particular linguistic, ethnic, or regional ties; others are quite heterogeneous.

In sum, Mumbai blends traditions and innovations from every region, city, and village in India. In the southern part of the city is India's Wall Street, Dalal Street, where most of the country's corporations have their headquarters. An industrial capital, Mumbai has a port that accommodates global shipping traffic and serves as India's gateway to the world. Mumbai is also famous as the site of the Hindi film industry, often called "Bollywood," the largest in the world in terms of personnel and number of films produced. Despite Mumbai's wealth, skyscrapers, and extraordinary examples of Victorian and Art Deco architecture, much of its population lives in poverty, many in shacks without plumbing or electricity, in a massive shantytown said to be Asia's largest slum. Others are homeless altogether.

Despite the city's overwhelming size and complexity, the people of Mumbai acknowledge a sense of cohesion and unity. Whatever their different religions, ethnic backgrounds, or economic status, all are Mumbaikars (what used to be called "Bombayites"), a shared identity said to be stronger in Mumbai than elsewhere in India. The two official languages of the city—Marathi and English—are heard alongside Hindi, Gujarati, and Urdu. There is a Hindi saying that "next to Mumbai city, the rest of India is a village"—an example of Mumbai's pride of place and its people. This oneness was severely tested during 1992–1993, when destructive riots grew out of tensions between Hindu and Muslim factions, but the city still maintains its distinctive street dialect, a mixture of the Marathi, Gujarati, and Hindi languages. Much of Mumbai's oneness is manifested in and supported by its musical life.

The Ganesh Chaturthi Festival

Most urban areas have events that celebrate their sense of place. In Mumbai, the ten-day Hindu *Ganesh Chaturthi* festival leads off the pan-Indian festival season every fall. Although Hindus are the majority in Mumbai, there are

Mumbai was originally an island city, with the section south of Mahim Creek and Bay created by draining and filling in what once were seven islands dotting the harbor.

sizeable Muslim and Christian populations, as well as smaller communities of Jain, Buddhists, Sikhs, Parsis, and Jews. Within this multiethnic and multireligious setting, the *Ganesh Chaturthi* Festival was transformed in the late nineteenth century from a domestic Hindu celebration to a community-wide festival promoting solidarity and independence from the British. Today *Ganesh Chaturthi*, which falls at the end of August or the beginning of September, remains a citywide festival that crosses ethnic and religious lines and includes a wide array of musical performances.

The *Ganesh Chaturthi* festival marks the birthday of Lord Ganesh, one of the most popular Hindu deities, the elephant-headed God. According to one of many competing versions of Hindu mythology recorded in the Puranas, a collection of ancient Sanskrit stories, Ganesh was the son of Parvati (also known as Mumba, from whom the city of Mumbai took its name); Parvati was the wife of Shiva, the Hindu God of destruction. One day, when Ganesh kept watch outside as his mother took a bath, Lord Shiva came looking for his wife. Ganesh did not allow him to enter and Shiva became furious, cutting off his head. Finding out afterwards that the guard was his son, Shiva ordered his servant to bring the head of the first living male he encountered; the servant returned with the head of an elephant, and it was joined to the boy's body. "*Gaj*" means elephant and "*anan*" means head, so Parvati's son became known as "Gajanan." Shiva subsequently made him the deity of his armies and thus his name became Ganesh ("*Gan*" = "army", "*Ish*" = "god") or, Ganpati, which means "The Lord of Hosts."

Ganesh is the god of learning and of auspicious beginnings, addressed as the "Remover of Obstacles" ("Vignaharta"). His devotees consider Ganesh the embodiment of both Shiva and Vishnu. It is believed that no new enterprise will succeed unless Ganesh is invoked, and therefore the image of Ganesh is found everywhere in representations mounted on the doorways of houses and pictures reproduced on wedding cards.

During the days of the festival, images of Ganesh made of clay are displayed in homes. These images are worshipped privately both morning and evening, with prayers and offerings of flowers and incense. There are also public performances of *bhajan* (devotional songs) as well as dance, acrobatic, and dramatic presentations in various urban venues.

A procession through the streets of Mumbai during the *Ganesh Chaturthi* festival.

On the tenth day, the clay images are brought out and ceremonially immersed (*visarjan*) in water, whether in the sea, a river, or a nearby well. The festival's final day is one of frenetic activity. From dawn to dusk, the streets are choked with people. Loudspeakers broadcast music, including film songs, electronic remixes of traditional Marathi folk songs, and *bhajans*. During the closing procession, people chant in Marathi, "*Ganapathi bappa Moraya, Pudcha varshi lavkarya*" ("Father Ganpati, Lord of Moraya, come again quickly next year"). Today, both in Mumbai and in the worldwide Indian diaspora, recordings of prayers for Ganesh such as that heard in Listening Guide 22 are widely distributed, having replaced live priests at worship services.

The recording of *Praise Ganesh* in Listening Guide 22 (see page 68) demonstrates the union of local and global musical influences on several levels. The prayer is a traditional Hindi *Aarati* sung at the end of a *puja* (worship service). The name of the prayer, *Aarati*, literally means a worship lamp or candles which are waved during Hindu rituals in front of an image or icon of a deity.[10] Singing the *Aarati* atones for any mistakes or errors inadvertently committed during the ritual. Therefore this recording, which would probably be played at the end of a *puja* devoted to Ganesh, permits Hindus to perform a ritual on their own without a priest while insuring that they maintain appropriate standards. The sounding of the *shankh* (conch shell) and the use of the six-beat rhythm (*dadra tal*) connects the recorded prayer with Hindu worship. The other instruments in the recording, however, including the vibraphone, *sitar,* and especially the *swaramandal* (zither), are familiar from recordings where they provide accompaniment to several types of music, including popular, classical, and devotional music.

Music of Mumbai's Ethnic Communities

Much of the population of Mumbai participates in festivals such as *Ganesh Chaturthi,* but there are many other aspects of musical life that take place within a subset of the larger community.

The Koli community, the first residents of the area, continue to be a presence in Mumbai; the men fish and the women sell their catch at local markets along the docks. Koli fishing communities live today in a vastly transformed environment, surrounded by expensive offices, apartments, and hotels. Aspects of Koli traditional culture, such as the distinctive nine-yard green saris worn by Koli women, their Marathi dialect, and their musical traditions, are actively perpetuated, spurred in part by the interest of tourists. Koli folk songs are widely distributed on recordings and can be heard over loudspeakers in their neighborhoods.

Folk songs in Marathi are heard everywhere in Mumbai; they address universal topics such as love as well as subjects of local concern, such as monsoons, the intense storms that strike Mumbai during the rainy season. Some of

Jay Ganesh ("Praise Ganesh")

Date of recording: 1999

Performers: Sanjeev Abhyankar and Chorus

Form: Hindu *aarati*

Tempo: Recording to be played at end of worship service (*puja*) for Ganesh to rectify any mistakes or faults in the ritual just performed

WHAT TO LISTEN FOR:

- Entry of a series of Indian musical instruments, including the *tanpura* (plucked lute), *swaramandal* (plucked zither), *shankh* (conch shell), *shehnai* (double-reed aerophone), *tabla* (paired membranophones), finger cymbals (idiophones), *sitar* (plucked lute)
- Use of instruments such as *swaramandal* and *sitar,* as well as vibraphone, to provide atmosphere and resonance to recording
- Use of six-beat rhythmic pattern (*tala*) in drum and cymbal
- Repetition of the ritual text by male vocalist and female chorus
- Substitution of the Marathi expression "*Jaki*"(language spoken in Maharashtra, the state in which Mumbai is situated) for the Hindi expression "*Jay ki*" ("praise to"), within this Hindi *aarati*. The same compact disc also includes a specifically *Marathi Aarati*.

STRUCTURE AND TEXT	DESCRIPTION AND TRANSLATION
0:00	*Tanpura* enters and plays constant drone.
0:01	*Swaramandal* enters and provides atmosphere with descending *glissandos*, rapid slides down the scale.

these folk songs are subsequently reintroduced and popularized through electronic remixes that become well-known and then quickly give way to newer entries. One good example is the monsoon song *Dhagala Lagli Kala* by Baba Kandke, which talks about the coming rain as seen through the eyes of a flirting couple.

Mumbai is home to music traditions from all over India, transplanted to the city through migration. Discussion of this process through the lens of one

0:09		*Shankh* (conch shell) enters, signalling connection to Hindu worship.
0:18		Vibraphone enters, provides atmosphere, quickly fades to background.
0:23		*Shehnai* (double-reed aerophone) melody is not set in a particular *rag*. *Tabla* introduces rhythmic cycle (*tala*) of six beats used in devotional music. Finger cymbals play on beats one and four of cycle; open stroke of one cymbal against the other on beat one (letting both ring) and a closed stroke on beat four (cymbals are held against each other, damping the sound).
0:28		*Sitar* enters, traditionally a solo instrument, here in a minor accompanying role.
0:47	Chorus enters *Jay Ganesha, Jay Ganesha,* *Jay Ganesha, Deva*	Praise Ganesh, Praise Ganesh, Praise Lord Ganesh (repeated)
0:56	Male soloist enters *Mata Jaki Paravati,* *Mata Jaki Paravati Pita* *Mahadeva*	Praise his Mother, Paravati, Praise his Mother, Paravati, And his father Mahadeva (the Hindu god Shiva)
1:06	Chorus *Jay Ganesha, Jay Ganesha,* *Jay Ganesha Deva*	Praise Ganesh, Praise Ganesh, Praise Lord Ganesh (repeated)
1:16	*Sitar* interlude	
1:29	Fade-out and track ends.	

soundscape can illustrate both the manner in which new arrivals have transformed musical life in Mumbai and the corresponding impact that the urban area has had on the imported artistic traditions.

Around the time of Indian independence from Great Britain in the 1940s, many dance and music teachers (*gurus*) from all over India began to migrate to urban centers such as Bombay to teach classical music and dance. One of their number was Bipin Singh, a well-known musician who composed dance

The Jhaveri sisters (from left to right, Ranjana, Suverna, Nayana, and Darshana) dance in 1954 wearing Manipur-style sarong dresses called *phanek*, which they modified for different dance dramas by using a variety of non-traditional cloths.

dramas featuring a style of classical dance from Manipur, a state in the northeast of the country. Singh's style of Manipuri dance was associated with a form of Hinduism focusing on devotion (*bhakti*) to the god Vishnu in his several incarnations, known as Vaishnavism. In 1943, Bipin Singh moved first to Calcutta, and then to Bombay, where he became the *guru* of the four Jhaveri sisters (Ranjana, Suverna, Nayana, and Darshana), daughters of a businessman from Gujarat. The sisters became accomplished dancers and in the early 1990s recalled the course of their careers in a series of interviews.[11]

Bipin Singh combined his traditional knowledge of Manipuri dance dramas with new trends from the other dance styles he encountered in Bombay. The Jhaveri sisters were then young teenagers studying several forms of Indian dance at the local dance school at which *Guru* Bipin Singh taught. Ranjana Jhaveri recalled:

He took special interest in us and our artistic talents flowered. Gradually we decided that his dance style suited us, and that we would like to specialize in this dance form. The grace, the liquidity, the fluidity and even the spiritual aspect, attracted us quite a lot.

In 1948, the two eldest Jhaveri sisters travelled to Manipur "to get a real feel of the background of all these dance dramas. . . . We saw how dance and music was a way of life for the Manipuri people," related Ranjana. "It was in the very fabric of their being and we saw that it was unique in every way." In 1956, all the Jhaveri sisters travelled to Manipur together.

After their return from Manipur in 1956, the sisters began to perform the dance dramas publicly and to actively promote Manipuri dance in Bombay. Darshana Jhaveri recalled that they began touring in 1958 and at the same time began to gather manuscripts and oral traditions about the dance.

Over time, the sisters, with the support of their *guru*, made subtle changes in the dance style, as Ranjana recalled:

We did dance dramas for ten years say in the '50s and '60s. Then we found it difficult to take dance dramas—big groups—to different places. At that time we had started travelling a lot all over India, even abroad. . . . So that's how we tried to have solos, duets, groups, within a small group. . . . We performed in and around Bombay and once we even went to Delhi. . . . Solo performances came a little later, seven or ten years later.

The Jhaveri sisters supplemented the dramatic content of Manipuri dance by adapting male choreographic forms such as martial arts movements. They also altered the dance to match the aesthetic preferences of different audiences they encountered, especially when travelling abroad; for instance, Darshana recalled performing more stylized and graceful dances in Paris and London, while emphasizing speed and drumming in Africa and Russia.

The sisters also began to teach dance: "We thought that we must have more students," noted Ranjana. "If we have more students only then would our line be continued. . . . We used to work together. We have three institutions in Bombay, Calcutta, and Manipur and there are nearly three hundred students in the three centres."

After the premature death of their sister Nayana in the 1980s, Suverna gave up dancing entirely. Ranjana continued to dance, and Darshana devoted more of her time to dance research. The sisters also passed on the dance tradition within their own family. Rashana noted that her nieces learned and performed Manipuri dance, and that one had received her Ph.D. from an American university, writing a thesis on Manipuri *rasleela,* the traditional circular dress of Manipuri dance and theater.

Thus the Jhaveri sisters, born in Mumbai of Gujarati descent, transmitted Manipuri dance within the broader urban soundscape of which they were a part. In similar fashion, other musical styles have been transplanted and transformed in Mumbai by others. These include the traditional Gujarati dance *dandia,* a type of "stick dance" which is widely performed during the *Navaratri* Festival, a nine-day fall festival celebrating a military victory of Rama, an incarnation of the Hindu God Vishnu. More recently, *dandia* has been modified to create "*disko dandia,*" its dance rhythm altered to imitate Western disco music.[12]

North Indian classical music is also actively represented in Mumbai. The native scholar-musician Pandit V. D. Paluskar established a music conservatory, Gandharva Mahavidyalaya, in 1911, where students could study Hindu devotional music and culture. Other important figures included Pandit Vishnu Narayan Bhatkhande (1860–1936), who established a music school to perpetuate North Indian (Hindustani) music in early twentieth-century Bombay and published books about the Hindustani musical system and collections of musical compositions. The study of classical Indian music in Mumbai has been maintained both as an artistic pursuit and as an expression of national, ethnic, and religious identity.[13]

Metakix, founded in 1995 as an underground rock band in a Mumbai suburb, has broken new ground in India by following the American custom of releasing a single song in advance of an album. The song, titled *Hand in Hand*, features a patriotic theme and is intended by Metakix to reach listeners in India and abroad.

European classical music has exerted an influence since the arrival of the British in India during the seventeenth century. The nineteenth-century colonial government established educational institutions following British models, founding a university in Bombay in 1857 and later supporting private colleges.[14] The Parsi community, which migrated to India from Iran as early as the seventh century and settled in Bombay beginning in the seventeenth century, became, along with members of the Anglo-Indian community, well known for patronizing European classical music. The National Center for the Performing Arts became in the twentieth century an important venue for Western-influenced ensembles such as the Bombay Chamber Orchestra and visiting Western groups, but also a space for a wide array of North and South Indian (Karnatak) music, dance, and theater. A variety of international popular musics also share performance venues and audiences at clubs and discos in the metropolitan area and are promoted through groups such as the Mumbai Rock Association and events such as "Dire Straits Night."

The Mumbai Film Industry

Film music is everywhere in Mumbai—heard on the street, in shops and stores, on the radio, accompanying loud and colorful wedding processions, broadcast by television music channels, and played in the discotheques and nightclubs. Indian-produced silent films accompanied by live music date back to 1912, and 1930 marked the beginning of Indian-language films with sound, setting the stage for Mumbai to become the center of a new industry. In the early years, singing actors and actresses performed Indian film songs (*filmi git*) on camera; the music was later rerecorded and released on 78-rpm records. These songs became enormously popular with Indian audiences, and their importance increased in 1935, when new technologies made possible the "playback song," prerecorded by a professional singer and lip-synched by an actor in the film.[15]

Over the years, the Indian film industry mushroomed. By mid-century, "Bollywood" specialized in mass-marketed films known as "*masala* movies," featuring stereotyped romantic plots with elaborate interludes of song and dance. Over time, the subject matter shifted in response to changes in Indian society and to the influence of the global film industry, in particular the impact of Hollywood. A distinctive dual star system arose: On-screen actors and actresses became superstars, and the studio musicians, called "playback singers," who performed the songs, were also universally known and lionized. Among the most famous playback singers, beginning in the 1940s and extending throughout the rest of the twentieth century, were Lata Mangeshkar (1929–) and her sisters, who recorded songs in both Hindi and Marathi for thousands of films.[16]

In the early years of the Bombay film industry, films used the closely related Hindi and Urdu languages of Northern India. By the later twentieth century, Hindi-language films became the industry's most lucrative products, although there were other smaller movie industries, such as those who used the regional Marathi dialect. From the beginning, there was a symbiotic relationship between traditional music and film music: Traditional Indian musical genres provided a basis for film music, and traditional repertories such as those performed by wedding bands began to change quickly, incorporating the most recent film songs.

The renowned playback singer Lata Mangeshkar is cited in the *Guinness Book of World Records* for having recorded the greatest number of songs.

One important influence on film music was the Northern Indian Urdu-language song genre, the *ghazal,* which had long been transmitted in several related forms in both religious and secular contexts. The secular *ghazal* art song, a strophic song performed for elite audiences in North India, accompanied by the bowed lute (*sarangi*), the tabla (two-piece drum), and harmonium, gave rise to the "light classical *ghazal*" that dominated Indian films. Over the decades, the film *ghazal* waxed and waned in popularity, returning in new pop forms in the late twentieth century, always widely distributed through recordings.[17]

Popular music from abroad and trends in the international music industry have deeply influenced Indian film music. For instance, the movie *Bombay Boys,* directed by Kaizad Gustad and released in 1998, tells the story of three young men who return home to Mumbai after living abroad, only to run into trouble with the Mumbai underworld. The song *Mum-bhai* (Listening Guide 23; see pages 74–76) reflects the musical style of Western gangsta rap while underscoring its local meaning through a pun on the city's name: *Bhai* means "big brother" and refers to an underworld figure. The text is in a local dialect that contains some English phrases, while the musical content and form of *Mum-bhai* is cosmopolitan; a flexible strophic form is set to a regular quadruple meter. Some elements—the repetitive synthesizer melody first heard in the introduction, two choruses singing the refrain "I am Mum-bhai," and the list of synthesized instrumental sounds just after 2:19—make it clear that

Mum-bhai (rap song)

CD 1
Track 23

Date of recording: 1998 from the film *Bombay Boys*
Composer and performer: Jaaved Jaffery
    Kaizad Gustad, *director*
Form: Strophic, with refrain
Tempo: Moderate, regular quadruple meter

WHAT TO LISTEN FOR:

- Regular quadruple rhythm moving at a steady rate of approximately one beat per second
- Changing vocal articulations, moving from speech to heightened speech, to song
- Multilingual text conveying local images

	STRUCTURE AND TEXT	TRANSLATION	DESCRIPTION
0:00	**Spoken:** *My name is* bhai . . . Mumbhai.	My name is *bhai* (Big Brother, or Don . . .) Mumbhai.	
0:03	**Instrumental introduction**		Gunshot is heard, followed by rhythm track in regular quadruple beat (4/4), at 60 beats per minute, then synthesizer melody.
0:40	**Verse** Mumbhai ekdum *danger place* *Where you survive if you've got the pace* *You've gotta be fast, you've gotta be* tez *You've gotta be* shaana *to win the race.*	Mumbai is a dangerous place Where you survive if you've got the pace You've gotta be fast, you've gotta be quick You've gotta be smart to win the race	
0:49	Chhota-chhota *matter* baney *police case* Bada-bada lafda, gul *without trace* Ghabraane ka nai—*give it in the face* Woh kya bolta hai—haan— jaisa des waisa bhes!	Small-small matters become big police cases Large-large crimes are gone without a trace Don't worry at all—give it in the face What's that they say?—oh yes—When in Rome. . . !	Singer switches from normal mode of speech to heightened, pitched speech.
0:58	Dikhe behti ganga, *pocket* se nikle kanga	See a girl pass by, your comb should whip out of your pocket	

	Dekh ke lena panga nahin to ho jaayenga danga *Some people are* bhala changa, *some are* bhikmanga *Cannot judge anybody* shareef *or* lafanga!	And choose your fights carefully, or there'll be a riot Some people here are good and honest, some are beggars You can't judge which is which—gentleman or hoodlum!	
1:07	Bhaigiri ko chhod sab—? Bakwaas! Bhai ka *under* jo rehta—? Bindaas! Bhai ko denga traas, to hoinga woh khallaas Bahenga uska *blood just like tomato sauce* . . .	Without the Don, everything is? . . . Nonsense! All those under the Don's protection are . . . ? Carefree! Those who will cross the Don, will end up destroyed Their blood will flow just like tomato ketchup . . .	Solo and chorus alternate as call and response.
1:16	Arre Baap re!	Oh my God!	
	Chorus:		
1:18	Khaaneka peeneka marneka jeeneka Chalneka phirneka uthneka girneka *Tension* nai leneka, bhai se poochneka Kasa kai, bara hai, *I am* Mumbhai!	To eat, do drink, to die, to live To walk, to travel, to get up, to fall down— Now don't get tense, but you'll need to ask Don to do any of this! How's it going? Just remember—I am Mumbhai!	The melody is doubled at the lower octave (that is, it is sung simultaneously by a second voice one octave lower).
1:27	Aaneka jaaneka naachneka gaaneka Nahaneka dhoneka hasneka roneka Boom nai marne ka, bhai se poochneka Kasa kai, bara hai, *I am* Mum-bhai!	To come, to go, to dance, to sing To bathe, to wash, to laugh, to cry— Don't say a word, but you'll need to ask Don to do any of this! How's it going? Just remember—I am Mum-bhai!	
1:36	**Rhythm interlude**		
1:44	Beer bar dance bar—Baar baar lagataar! *Note* chhaapne ke liye—*Solid* hai kaarobaar! Bhai ka adda par dikhta hai jo ek baar Udharich reh jaata hai chodke apna ghar baar.	Beer bars, dance bars!— Anytime, all the time! Counterfeit currency notes!— What a solid business! Anyone who is spotted at the Don's lair once Will be in his service forever, leaving his home and family	(continues)

(continued)

STRUCTURE AND TEXT	TRANSLATION	DESCRIPTION
1:53 *Admission- election, telephone connection,* *Construction permission, illegal erection,*	Be it an admission, an election, or a telephone connection, (If you need) construction permission, or an illegal erection,	
Paisa nu collection, paper nu correction *Everything perfection jab bhi leve bhai action*	The extortion of money, or the correction of an exam paper, Everything is fixed to perfection when the Don takes action—	
2:02 *Court mein agar jaaenga to bees saal tak thaamba*	If you choose to go to court, you'll be stuck for twenty years	
Law and order se to paandu bhai ka haath hai lamba	The Don's reach extends much further than the arms of law and order	
Neta-abhineta, ya ho koi builder *Bhai ko dekar supari, karvata hai murder*	Be he a leader, a politician, or even just a builder Anyone can be murdered if you pay the Don enough	
2:11 Haath mein suka *power* hai sab uska aage jhukta Uska khopdi sanak gaya to poora Mumbai rukta!	He is all-powerful, everyone bows to accept his control When he gets mad, all Mumbai comes to a standstill!	
2:17		Silence
2:19 Ae—khatam nahi hua . . . chootiye!	Hey—I'm not done yet, idiot!	Change in rhythm; ostinatos begin. Bass begins to play. Flute starts playing. Banjo plays.
Ae baas gitaal . . . Piplee . . .? Ae *banjo* —chal! Olchestraaa!	Hey, bass guitar . . . Flute . . . ? Hey, banjo—come on! Orchestra!	
2:51 *C'mon baby!* Ha! *C'mon baby!* Ha! "Choras!"	C'mon baby! Ha! C'mon baby! Ha! "Chorus!"	
3:15 Fade-out		

Mum-bhai merges international musical trends with local culture. This song, like the festival and dance music we have discussed from Mumbai, exemplifies the locally flavored yet cosmopolitan musical and cultural syntheses that have long characterized music of that city, even as it moves abroad to reach new and expanding audiences around the world.

CASE STUDY: Boston, U.S.A.

Why Boston?

Having surveyed the complex and distinctive settings for musical life in Accra and Mumbai, we will now take a more nuanced look at a city closer to home—Boston. One of the oldest cities in North America, Boston provides both a long history and exceptional ethnic, institutional, and musical diversity (see **"Looking Back: A Boston Retrospective"** on page 78).

Boston provides a stimulating counterpoint to Accra and Mumbai; all three are ports, and all three still show the impact of British influence. But Boston is also a quintessentially American city, and its idiosyncrasies have imprinted themselves on its musical life.

Music was not always Boston's primary artistic concern. Its first preoccupation, as noted in a biography of the Boston composer Amy Beach, was with "the word, as taught at Harvard and as preached from Boston's pulpits."[18] Only in the nineteenth century did music flower in Boston, thanks to the conviction among upper-class Bostonians that music had the power to uplift, educate, and refine.

Much of Boston's documented musical life in the nineteenth and early twentieth centuries involved an elite in close contact with England and Europe. Major ensembles that are still prominent, such as the Boston Symphony Orchestra, were established during that time. Understanding the background

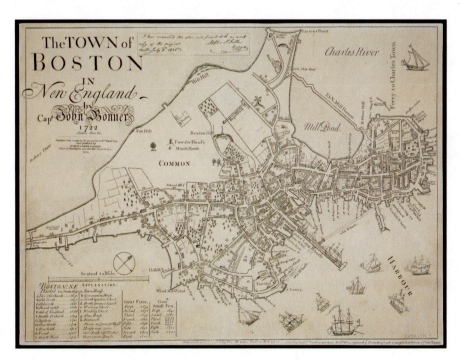

This early map of Boston shows landmarks such as Mill Pond that have not survived as well as those that have, including the Common, Beacon Hill, and Long Wharf.

LOOKING *Back*

A Boston Retrospective

Incorporating Multiple Ethnic Populations

1630	English colonists from Salem, Massachusetts found the city of Boston
1790	Haitian immigrants flee to Boston as a result of revolt against French government in Haiti and establish a French-speaking community
1847	37,000 Irish immigrants come to Boston as a result of famine in Ireland
1870	Portuguese immigrants begin to arrive in Boston
1900	Mass immigration of Italians to United States; 31,000 in Boston by 1910
1990–2000	Soaring minority populations transform City of Boston into a "majority-minority" urban core with several increasingly multiethnic satellite cities

Founding Major Educational Institutions

1636	Harvard University
1852	Tufts University
1861	Massachusetts Institute of Technology
1864	Boston College
1867	New England Conservatory of Music
1869	Boston University
1945	Berklee College of Music
1948	Brandeis University

Making Boston More Musical

1838	Boston public schools incorporate music into curriculum
1881	Boston Symphony Orchestra's inaugural concert
1885	Boston Pops founded
1929	Arthur Fiedler starts the Esplanade Concerts, a summer series held on the east bank of the Charles River
1954	Boston Camerata
1976	Voice of the Turtle
1969	Club 47 becomes Club Passim
1979	Boston Village Gamelan (Javanese)
1981	Boston Early Music Festival and Exhibition
1990	World Music presents world music concerts
1993	*Gamelan Galak Tika* (Balinese)

of musical life in Boston is important not just to unraveling local soundscapes, but also to appreciating Boston's nineteenth-century role in making Western European music and culture prestigious throughout the rest of the United States. Boston is an important springboard for the study of local musics because it exercised so much influence on national musical life in the United States at an early date.

Boston's distinctive physical setting in many ways gives rise to its musical profile. Founded in the seventeenth century, the city is bounded by the Charles River and Boston Harbor. Boston's irregular, winding, narrow streets are similar to those of an English town. Boston's setting is crucial to its cultural life.[19]

The old central area of Boston, known as Beacon Hill, sits alongside the distinctive, five-sided Boston Common and Public Garden, the city's public heart since earliest times. Beacon Hill still retains historic cobblestone streets lit by gaslights and is located on the only one of Boston's hills to survive; the others were leveled in the nineteenth century to provide landfill in the Charles River to create the section of the city referred to as Back Bay. (Interestingly, Mumbai also has a "Back Bay" area that was reclaimed from the ocean by landfill.) Other distinctive neighborhoods abound within the city limits, some with names that do not reflect their actual locations in relation to the central Commons and Public Garden—for example, the South End is not south of the city, nor is the North End north.

Along with their special locales, architectural features, and landmarks, many neighborhoods are home to different socioeconomic and ethnic groups. Boston's population, totaling just under 600,000 for the city and around 3.4 million for the larger metropolitan area, has shifted in its composition in recent decades. The 2000 census shows that for the first time, former minorities within the longtime mainly Euro-American population of the city have become the majority. These changes stem primarily from a surge in immigration; the Latino and Asian communities have increased in size, now totaling 14.4 percent and 7.5 percent of the City of Boston population, respectively. A recent influx of new immigrants from Haiti, Jamaica, and Africa has joined longtime African American residents; almost 25 percent of Bostonians now identify themselves as "black."[20]

A multicultural mixture of peoples from all over the world has transformed and gentrified the South End, once a working-class neighborhood. At the same time, South Boston retains many Irish Americans, Roxbury remains

This aerial shot is a bird's-eye view of the banks of the Charles River, called the Esplanade, transformed into a performance space. At the center is the Hatch Shell, an open-air concert site that was restored and renovated for its fiftieth birthday in 1991. Free performances such as the annual July 4 celebration by the Boston Pops (shown here) are enjoyed by thousands, some listening from boats anchored on the river. The July 4 performance features patriotic choral works, rousing marches, and Tchaikovsky's famous 1812 Overture enhanced by bells from the nearby Church of the Advent and firing of howitzers.

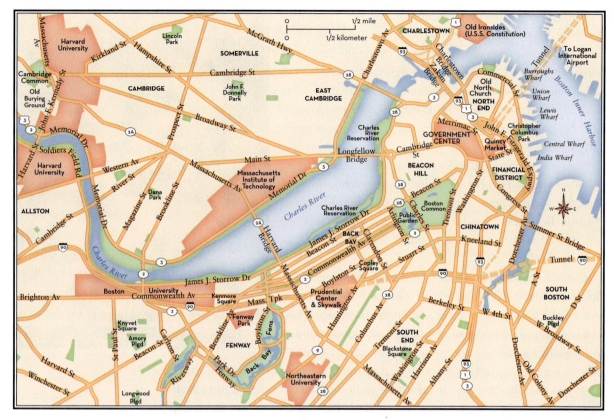

With its relatively compact size and many winding, narrow streets, Boston is best experienced on foot. The completion of the massive "Big Dig" construction project, which has relocated former surface highways underground, has resulted in new parks and public spaces, settings that will undoubtedly have an impact on urban musical life.

heavily African American, and the colonial buildings of the North End still house longtime Italian residents. Moving from Boston proper across the river to Cambridge, we find a uniquely diverse population, reflecting the town's role as the main center for higher education in a metropolitan area that has more institutions of higher learning than any other North American city and more students than any other place of comparable size. We will return later to this important aspect of Boston area life. Other towns adjacent to Boston include Chelsea and Charlestown, as well as nearby Brookline and Newton, each with its own distinctive topography, architecture, and increasingly diverse population.

Boston can be divided according to political boundaries and, to an extent, by economic and ethnic groups, but we can also map the city according to past and present locations of musical life. By 1910, one block of downtown Boylston Street housed so many of Boston's piano dealers, instrument shops, music publishers, and phonograph sellers that it became known as "Piano Row."[21] Some musical monuments are actually noted on street signs. Adjacent to

Symphony Hall, the home of the Boston Symphony Orchestra, is Symphony Road. Nearby is Opera Place, the former site of Boston's original opera house, built in 1908 but torn down in 1958. The present-day Opera House was constructed in 1928 as a grand vaudeville theatre and presented opera performances only from 1978 until 1991. In 2004, Clear Channnel Corporation purchased and restored the Opera House as part of an effort to revitalize the downtown theater district.[22]

But how can we map those segments of the musical life of the city that are not recorded on street signs? And how does music, in turn, map the city? In this case study we will see how an investigation of local music increases our understanding of what makes a particular urban area unique. We start by raising and answering a series of questions about music in the city: What makes up musical life, where is music performed, when is music heard, who makes music, and why?

What Elements Make Up Boston's Musical Life?

We can get an overview, although often a selective one, of musical life in any city through a quick look at the listings in the weekly arts section of a metropolitan newspaper. The *Boston Globe,* which has covered musical events since its founding in March 1872, has a weekly calendar that is a good place to start in mapping present-day musical Boston.

We need to look not just at what musical events are included, but at the manner in which they are organized and presented. On the next page we see a few of the subheadings from the weekly calendar, which in its entirety covers Pop & Rock; Folk, World & Country; Jazz, Blues & Cabaret; Auditions and Rehearsals; Classical; Dance; and the Venues in which music is performed each night of the week.

Note that events are classified not just according to conventional musical categories (classical, folk/world/country), but also by place of presentation—nightspots, museums, and libraries. We need to pay special attention to events that are neglected or excluded from listings. The newspaper listings emphasize Western art music, compressing folk/world/country into a single category. Reading about Boston's musical life in the *Globe,* we might conclude that

MUSIC LISTINGS

VENUE INFO ON PAGE 10

POP & ROCK

THURSDAY 10/7

Axis Kings of Leon, the Features. 7 p.m. $15.

Harpers Ferry The Violet Suns, the Bocks, Rosie Huntress, Chimp Simple, Rachael Cantu. $7.

Johnny D's Kim Richey, Kerri Powers.

Lizard Lounge Dave Tronzo, Club D'Elf. 9:30 p.m. $7-$10.

Lupo's at the Strand Tower of Power. 7:30 p.m. $20-$23.

Middle East
▪ Downstairs: Explosions in the Sky, Adem, Hail Social. 9 p.m. $10-$12. ▪ Upstairs: Bartley's Choice Benefit with Green Magnet School, Slughog, Luca Brasi, Donna Parker. 9 p.m. $10.

Mohegan Sun
▪ Cabaret Theatre: Herb Reed & the Platters with Kenny Vance and the Planotones. $25-$40.

Orpheum Theatre Cake, Northern State. 7:30 p.m. $28.50-$35.

Paradise Rock Club Hothouse Flowers, the Shore. CANCELED.

T.T. the Bear's On Fire, Inouk, Hope of the States. 9:30 p.m.

The Middle East Bartley's Choice Benefit. $10.

The Roxy The Killers, Ambulance LTD, Surferosa. 8:30 p.m. $12.

FRIDAY 10/8

Avalon Alter Bridge, Crossfade, Submersed. 6:30 p.m. $20.75.

Berklee Performance Center Diamanda Galas. 8 p.m. $25-$34.

Harpers Ferry The Young Doublin-ers, Say Hey. $10.

Lizard Lounge Munk, Nikulydin, Count Zero, Specimen 37, IIJ . 9:30 p.m. $7-$10.

Middle East
▪ Downstairs: Fu Manchu, Cougars, the Rolling Blackouts. 9 p.m. $12. ▪ Upstairs: Bartley's Choice Benefit with Kudgel, Red Bliss, the Beatings. 9 p.m. $10.

Mohegan Sun
▪ Cabaret Theatre: Herb Reed & the Platters with Kenny Vance and the Planotones. $25-$40. ▪ Wolf Den: David Cassidy. Free.

Palladium Type O Negative, Amorphis, the Bronx Casket Co. 8 p.m. $25.

Paradise Rock Club Presidents of the United States of America. 9 p.m. $15.

Rock & Shock Centrum Centre, 611 p.m. $20 single-day convention ticket, $49 three-day convention ticket; $99-$149 for three-day convention plus 10/9 Misfits show at the Palladium.

T.T. the Bear's The Subject, Hopewell, Singapore Sling, Lockgroove. 9:15 p.m.

The Middle East Bartley's Choice Benefit. $10. Shows 18 unless noted.

SATURDAY 10/9

Avalon P.J. Harvey, Moris Tepper. 7 p.m. $32.50-$35. 18+,

Berklee Performance Center George Winston. $22-$28.

Harpers Ferry Max Creek. $10.

Lizard Lounge The Ray Corvair Trio. 9:30 p.m. $6.

Lupo's at the Strand Zox, Assembly of Dust. 7 p.m. $10-$12.

Middle East
▪ Downstairs: Throe, Rubikon, Stoic, Drinkfist, Adrenokrome. 9 p.m. $10. ▪ Upstairs: Lamont, Bible of the Devil, Bury the Needle, Chroma. 9 p.m. $9.

Mohegan Sun
▪ Cabaret Theatre: Herb Reed & the Platters with Kenny Vance and the Planotones. $25-$40. ▪ Wolf Den: David Cassidy. Free.

Palladium Misfits, the Deadites. 6 p.m. $25. Discount for advance purchase.

Paradise Rock Club Critters Buggin', Benevento Russo Duo. 9 p.m. $12. Teitur, Tina Dico 9 p.m. at the Lounge. $12.

Rock & Shock Centrum Centre, 11 a.m.-11 p.m. $20 single-day convention ticket, $49 three-day convention ticket; $99-$149 for three-day convention plus Misfits show at the Palladium.

T.T. the Bear's Ovian, Worm is Green, On! Air! Library!, Solex. 9:30 p.m.

The Middle East Throe, Rubikon, Stoic, Drinkfist, Adrenokrome. $10.

Tower of Power Hampton Beach Casino Ballroom, 8 p.m. $20-$24. 18+

SUNDAY 10/10

Harpers Ferry Badfish. $10-$13.

Middle East
▪ Corner: Belly Dancing with Garabed and all the dancers. 8 p.m. Free. ▪ Downstairs: The Mountain Goats, John Vanderslice. 9 p.m. $12. ▪ Upstairs: The Bon Savants, Clickers, Lady of Spain, Shore Leave. 9 p.m. $8.

Mohegan Sun
▪ Cabaret Theatre: Herb Reed & the Platters with Kenny Vance and the Planotones. $25-$40. ▪ Wolf Den: David Foster & the Mohegan Sun All-Stars. Free.

Palladium Insane Clown Posse, Mushroomhead, Mack 10, Anybody Killa. 7 p.m. $32.50. Discount for advance purchase. All-ages shows.

Paradise Rock Club Kings X, Seemless. 8 p.m. $15.

Pearl Street Night Club North Mississippi Allstars, the Dirty Dozen Brass Band, Rising Star Drum & Fife Band. $18. 8:30 p.m. Discount for advance purchase.

Rock & Shock Centrum Centre, 11 a.m.-7 p.m. $20

T.T. the Bear's Radio Nationals, Bloodthirsty Lovers. 9:15 p.m.

Tower of Power Regent Theatre, 7:30 p.m.-10 p.m. $36.

MONDAY 10/11

Avalon Interpol, Secret Machines, Hail Social. 8 p.m. $27.

Harpers Ferry Soulfege, Moneyshot. $5.

Lizard Lounge Pan Nine's Ninth Anniversary. 7 p.m. Free.

Lupo's at the Strand PJ Harvey, Moris Tepper. 9 p.m. $22.50-$25.

Middle East
▪ Corner: Open mike. 10 p.m. Free. ▪ Upstairs: Mr. Airplane Man, the December Sound, Big Digits, the Secret Hearts. 9 p.m. $8.

Paradise Rock Club Marillion, John Wesley. 8 p.m. $30.

T.T. the Bear's Beth Boucher, Dave Alpert, Russell Mofsky, Tom Royal. 8:30 p.m.

TUESDAY 10/12

Centrum Centre Beastie Boys. 7:30 p.m. $30.50-$41. With Talib Kweli.

Harpers Ferry Tablist Tuesdays. $4.

Lizard Lounge Sitar Tabla Power, the Black Eggs. 9:30 p.m. Free.

Lupo's at the Strand Bob Weir and Ratdog, North Mississippi Allstars. 8 p.m. $26.50-$30.

Middle East
▪ Corner: Noche Mexicana with Gustavo and Andres. 10 p.m. $2. ▪ Downstairs: Flickerstick, Brill, Brilliant Misstake. 9 p.m. $10-$12. ▪ Upstairs: Damien Jurado, Richard Buckner, Dolorean. 9 p.m. $10-$12.

Paradise Rock Club Ozomatli, Pressure Cooker. 8 p.m. $18.

T.T. the Bear's Dusky Silo, Mollycoddle, the Crimea. 9 p.m.

The Roxy The Faint, TV on the Radio, Beep Beep. 8 p.m. $15.

WEDNESDAY 10/13

Cumberland County Civic Center Australian Pink Floyd Show. 7:30 p.m. $25-$32.50.

Harpers Ferry The Akashic Sessions with members of Uncle Sammy, Soulwork, and more. $3.

Lizard Lounge Joe Pesci, the Dennis Brennan Band. 7:30 p.m. Free.

Lupo's at the Strand The Faint, the Fever, Beep Beep. 9:15 p.m. $14.

Middle East
▪ Corner: DJ Ali with featured Belly Dancers. 10 p.m. $3. ▪ Upstairs: Will Champlin, Francis Kim, Kevin So, Keren Ann. 9 p.m. $9.

Mohegan Sun Cabaret Theatre: The Rat Pack is Back! $30-$40. 21+

T.T. the Bear's The Concretes. 10:30 p.m.

FOLK, WORLD & COUNTRY

THURSDAY 10/7

Capo's Iain Matthews. 9 p.m. $12.

Club Passim Sarah Lee Guthrie & Johnny Irion. 8 p.m. $14.

Folkal Point Coffeehouse Hewitt Huntwork — Songs from the '50s. 8 p.m.-midnight. $5. Open mike, hosted by Susan Irene Master. Sign-up at 7 p.m.

Iron Horse Music Hall Dan Bern. 7 p.m. $16-$19.

Music for Robin Series Follen Church. 781-862-7837. www.music-for-robin.org Crasdant, with harpist Robin Huw Bowen. 7:30 p.m. $18-$25. Welsh traditional music with master triple harpist, fiddler Stephen Rees, instrumentalist Andy McLauchlin, and guitarist Huw Williams.

FRIDAY 10/8

Bull Run Restaurant Tom Constanten. 8 p.m. $17. Discount for advance purchase.

Capo's Professor Louie & the Crowmatix. 8 p.m. $10. Listening room. Discount for advance purchase.

Club Passim The Nields. 8 p.m. $15.

Coumba Sidibe Cambridge Family YMCA Theatre. 617-388-0413. www.calabashmusic.com 8 p.m. $15-$18. children under 12 $7. West African Massoulou music. Featuring Moussa Traore and Timinandi, Balla Tounkara, Balla Kouyate, Mamadou Sidibe, Mohammed "Joh" Camara, Djeneba Sacko, Abdoul Doumbia, Ali Diabate.

El Bembe Latin Music and Dance Party Jorge Hernandez Cultural Center, Center for Latino Arts. Manguito. 9 p.m. $12. 21+, Complimentary salsa/merengue dance lessons.

Hanneke Cassel, Rushad Eggleston, Christopher Lewis Westford Museum 8 p.m. $15, teens $5, under 13 free. Reservations recommended. Fiddle, cello, guitar.

Iron Horse Music Hall Tony Vacca, World Rhythms. 7 p.m. $15. Wheat, Mount Egypt. 10 p.m. $13.

Pearl Street Nightclub Zox, Averi, Cardinal Direction. 8:30 p.m. $10.

Me & Thee Coffeehouse Tommy Makem. 8:30 p.m. $20.

RUMI: A Turning Night of Stars NEC's Jordan Hall. 617-585-1260. www.houseofonepeople.org. 8 p.m. $25-$75. Coleman Barks, Zuleikha, David Darling, Glen Velez. Poetry of 13th-century mystic Rumi with music, dance, and story. Benefit for Montague conference center.

SATURDAY 10/9

Blackstone River Theatre Hanneke Cassel Trio. 8 p.m. $12. With guitarist and cellist Rushad Eggleston.

Bull Run Restaurant Sonya Kitchell & Band. 8 p.m. $14. Discount for advance purchase.

Cafe Emerson Scott Ainslie. 8 p.m. $12. Bill Morris opens.

Capo's October Project. 7 p.m. $17. Listening room. Discount for advance purchase.

Club Passim Don White. 8 p.m. $15.

Cornerstone Coffeehouse All About Buford. 8 p.m. $12. students $10.

Grange Hall Coffeehouse Lonesome Jukebox. 8 p.m. $12. Seven member band plays roots music.

Iron Horse Music Hall Mark Erelli. 7 p.m. $15. Cordero, Josh Joplin. 10 p.m. $13.

John Michael Montgomery, Andy Griggs & Jeff Bates Lowell Memorial Auditorium, 8 p.m. $45-$55.

Mass MoCA Lucky Ngema. 8 p.m. $13-$16. Nine member band plays Afropop, celebrating 10th anniversary of a free South Africa.

Pearl Street Nightclub Little Brother, the Foreign Exchange, L.E.G.A.C.Y., the Away Team, Yazarah. 8:30 p.m. $18. Discount for advance purchase.

Steeple Coffeehouse Modern Man and Amy Fairchild. 8 p.m. $15. advance $12, seniors and students $10.

Stone Soup Coffeehouse Jess Klein. 8 p.m. $12. Liz Carlisle opens.

SUNDAY 10/10

Capo's Rachel Davis & Friends. 7 p.m. $8. Discount for advance purchase.

Club Passim Mary Gauthier. 8 p.m. $15.

DownDog Weston Public Library 2:30 p.m. Free. Fiddle rock band. Seating limited.

Iron Horse Music Hall 7 p.m. $18. Lucy Kaplansky, Rich Price. 10 p.m. $13. Damien Jurado, Richard Buckner, Dolorean.

Pearl Street Nightclub North Mississippi Allstars, the Dirty Dozen Brass Band, Rising Star Drum and Fire Band. 8:30 p.m. $18. Discount for advance purchase.

The Blue Hill Gospel MCs New Fellowship Baptist Church. 3:30 p.m. $30. seniors $20, children under 12 $10. Performers include the Gospel Four, Eric McKenzie and the Juniors, the Heavenly Angels, the New Gospel Heavyweights, the Fantastic Samaritan Singers, others.

Tricia Elliott Edaville USA. 1 p.m. Free with $5 ($3 children) admission to National Cranberry Festival.

MONDAY 10/11

Livingston Taylor Berklee's Lee & Alma Berk Recital Hall. 10 a.m. Free. With host Kelly Connolly, students from Berklee College and Boston Arts Academy.

Iron Horse Music Hall Magnolia Electric Co., the Court and Spark, Lo Fine. 8:30 p.m. $10.

TUESDAY 10/12

Iron Horse Music Hall 7 p.m. $23. Jesse Colin Young.

WEDNESDAY 10/13

Club Passim Artists Making Progress with Chris Chandler, Sandman and Pete Cassani. 8 p.m. $10.

Emack & Bolio's Eric Balkey. 6:30-9 p.m. With open mike hosted by Jimmy Dorr. sign-up at 6:30 p.m. No cover.

Iron Horse Music Hall Sophie B. Hawkins, Laura Veirs. 7 p.m. $20.

Pearl Street Nightclub Ozomatli, Brazilian Girls. 8:30 p.m. $20.

JAZZ, BLUES & CABARET

THURSDAY 10/7

Steve Coleman New England Conservatory. 8 p.m. Free. Concert of his original compositions.

Paquito D'Rivera in Concert Berklee Performance Center. 8 p.m. $15-$38. Quintet performs as benefit for the South End's La Casa de la Cultura/Center for Latino Arts.

Regattabar Jazz Tribute to Frank Sinatra featuring Hank Jones, Betsyann Faiella, and Jim Dejulio. 7:30 and 10 p.m. $25.

Scullers Jazz Club Keely Smith and Vegas '58. 8 and 10 p.m. $35-$45.

FRIDAY 10/8

James Williams Tribute Concert Ryles Jazz Club. 9 p.m.-1 a.m. $30. Performers include Mulgrew Miller, Donald Brown, Bill Pierce, John Lockwood, Bill Mobley, Greg Hopkins, Andy McGhee, Bill Easley, Javon Jackson, Ron Mahdi, Tony Reedus, Yoron Israel, Ron Savage, John Ramsey. Proceeds benefit James Williams Scholarship Fund at Berklee College.

Johnny D's Milo Z. 9:45 p.m.

MIM (modern improvised music) Series First Congregational Church of Hyde Park. 617-276-3223. Onerous Quartet & Holus-Bolus. Listening room. BYOB. 8 p.m. $8-$10 requested donation.

Marc Rossi Group Depot Square Gallery. 7:30 p.m. $8. With Lance Van Lenten, Bill Urmson, Mauricio Zottarelli.

Regattabar Jazz Tribute to Frank Sinatra featuring Hank Jones, Betsyann Faiella, and Jim Dejulio. 7:30 and 10 p.m. $25.

Scullers Jazz Club Keely Smith and Vegas '58. 8 and 10:30 p.m. $35-$45.

Zeitgeist Gallery Kevin Harris Project. 7-9 p.m. $7. Robert Rivera, Damon Holzorn, and Dan Levin. 9:30

boston.com FOR MORE LISTINGS: WWW.BOSTON.COM/CALENDAR

Listings of musical life in Boston as seen in the *Boston Globe* Calendar, October 7-13, 2004.

Euro-American styles predominate. An alert reader unfamiliar with Boston might be surprised by the entries under one special category—Early Music. For other musical traditions, such as reggae and various Caribbean musical styles, the few scattered listings under Folk, World & Country or Nightspots provide little evidence that Boston, after New York, is the largest reggae market in the United States.[23]

It is clear that newspaper listings provide only a partial map of Boston's active musical scene. Many of the events included are organized by established ensembles or institutions that charge admission. Large free festivals are included, but not smaller music events sponsored by neighborhood or ethnic organizations. We therefore must search beyond newspaper listings to uncover the extraordinary range of music available in Boston. We need to ask where else we should look, and we need to walk or drive through town with our ears and eyes open to musicmaking.

Where and When Is Music Performed?

Many soundscapes are associated with particular places and specific times. For example, the Boston Symphony Orchestra performs most evenings at its majestic Symphony Hall, at the corner of Huntington Street and Massachusetts Avenue.

Boston has many other well-known performance spaces, such as Jordan Hall at the New England Conservatory, most of which not only serve their own resident ensembles but are also rented out regularly to a variety of other performance

Symphony Hall, the home of the Boston Symphony Orchestra, opened in 1900 and celebrated its centennial during the 2000–2001 season. Note the organ pipes mounted on the wall behind the orchestra, with the organ console on the lower left-hand corner of the stage.

groups. Even Symphony Hall is host to a wide array of musical events, particularly during the summer months. Other large performance spaces, such as the Wang Center, showcase musical road shows and other traveling musical offerings.

Boston churches sponsor a great deal of musical activity. Many Bostonians attend Sunday morning services downtown to hear the professional choir at the venerable Church of the Advent (established in 1844) or the renowned weekly performance of the cantatas, famous choral works by Johann Sebastian Bach (1685–1750), at Emmanuel Church. The large Haitian churches in the metropolitan area, such as St. Angela's Catholic Church in Mattapan and the First Haitian Baptist Church of Roxbury, are important sites for Haitian musical performances. Other houses of worship lend their facilities and sponsorship to musical ensembles outside the context of religious observances. For instance, the medieval ensemble Tapestry is in residence at the First Church in Cambridge.

Boston neighborhoods provide venues for many musical events of interest to local communities. Some of the liveliest Caribbean musical events are mounted at settings not intended primarily for musical performance, including parks, cultural centers, and restaurants in areas such as Roxbury and Dorchester, where large Jamaican, Dominican, and Haitian populations reside. To find out the time and location of these events, one needs to speak to residents, keep an eye out for signs and posters in the area, or call a local hotline.

Underground transportation systems provide sheltered performance spaces for buskers, rain or shine. Here Felix (left) and Claudio Silva perform in the Harvard Square T station. Note the large panpipe mounted on a stand so that Claudio can play it and the guitar at the same time.

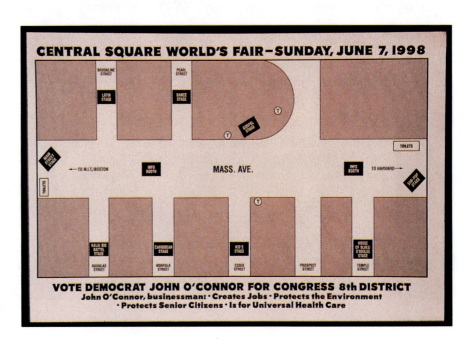

This map of the Central Square World's Fair was widely distributed as part of a program that provided performance schedules. Note the political advertisement at the bottom.

Some soundscapes not only transform the interiors of buildings through changing sounds and rearrangement of space, but reshape the outdoors as well. For instance, Harvard Square in Cambridge is one of the liveliest settings for musical performance. There a wide variety of buskers (street musicians) who ply their trade during the hours that shops and restaurants are open. These include folk singers, accordion players, rock groups, Latin ensembles, Chinese instrumentalists, and West African musicians, most of whom also sell recordings. Various music groups from South America play in the Square. Since the late 1990s, the northern Peruvian group Wayno has performed outside the entrance to the Har-

Girls from the Hellenic American School in Lowell, Massachusetts, perform a traditional dance in celebration of Greek Independence Day (Greece won its independence from the Ottoman empire in 1821) at Boston City Hall Plaza. Eighty-five thousand people attended the parade, including the mayors of Athens and several other Greek cities.

vard Cooperative Society building (known as the "Harvard Coop"), playing traditional Peruvian melodies such as the one heard in Listening Guide 24 (see page 86). Their music features close coordination between two players of the *siku*s (panpipes), aerophones consisting of multiple bamboo tubes laced together. The *bomba* (a large two-headed drum) is joined by a snare drum and an assortment of idiophones, including a rain stick, wind chimes, cymbal, and a rattle.

City streets also provide a venue for special music events that are part of parades and festivals. The music offered by each event may be similar to that found in any large American city, but a closer look can provide insight into the musical preferences of Boston-area residents. At the annual Central Square World's Fair in Cambridge each June, Massachusetts Avenue and the side streets that cross it are closed down. "Mass Ave," as it is known, is lined with booths with ethnic foods and souvenirs for sale. The main street stage houses jazz and rock performances, and on the side streets one finds a range of styles: a Latin stage for salsa, punk mambo, and Cuban *son;* a gospel stage; a stage for acoustic rock, country, and ragtime; a Caribbean stage for *soca,* ska, and reggae; a House of Blues stage; and a dance stage for German folk dance, ballet, modern dance, West African dance, and tango.

Many musical events take place at Boston's Government Center, a complex that includes Boston City Hall. Government Center was previously known as Scollay Square, the site of the famous Lighthouse Pub patronized by President John F. Kennedy during his student days, as well as other landmarks mentioned in *The M.T.A. Song* discussed later. The large concrete plaza in front of City Hall was intended to be spacious enough to accommodate many kinds of musical celebrations.

First Night features so many simultaneous events that participants must keep the multipage program close at hand.

Sikuri (traditional Peruvian melody)

Date of recording: 1995
Performers: Wayno (also known as Nazca)
    Luis Vilcherrez, *producer, composer, sikus* (panpipes), *guitar and vocals;*
    Marco Coveñas *musical director, composer, kenas* (vertical wooden notched
    flute), *sikus, charango* (small lute), *vocals, mandolina, guitar, bomba* (drum)
Form: Three-part (ternary) form (ABA)
Tempo: Moderately quick duple
Function: Entertainment

WHAT TO LISTEN FOR:

- Two panpipes, each with half of the notes of the scale, played by two different performers. In this recording, the two panpipes are recorded stereophonically, so one player can be heard from the left channel and the other from the right.
- A musical form built from two short melodic building blocks, phrases a and b, each of which varies slightly from iteration to iteration
- Various whistles, shouts, and percussion sounds in the background that enliven an otherwise repetitive song

	STRUCTURE	DESCRIPTION
0:00	**Introduction**	Five chords, played slowly and in free rhythm, comprise the introduction. Each chord has three voices: the two panpipes and an aerophone, a bass flute, in a lower range. (This bass flute doubles the top panpipe at the lower octave.) Drum rolls are heard on both the snare and the *bomba*.

The massive, bi-level brick and stone atrium inside City Hall can also be transformed on special occasions by festive decorations and musical performances. Music often marks the beginning and end of civic ceremonial gatherings there.

Even the stately old Boston Common and Public Garden are transformed through musical performance on special occasions, such as the annual "First Night" celebration held every New Year's Eve in Boston since the early 1980s. Boston hosted the original First Night celebration in the United States, featuring performances and exhibitions by over one thousand musical groups and

0:17	**Section A** phrases **a, b**	The melody is played by the panpipes, as the *bomba* plays on some of the strong beats. Phrase **a** rises to the top of the range and is not syncopated except for one pitch near the end of the phrase. Phrase **b**, lower in the range, begins with a catchy syncopation and ends with a quick jumping figure that springs up an octave.
0:27	phrases **a, b**	The two phrases are repeated. The rattle fades into the texture, sounding on every beat.
0:38	phrases **b', b**	The pattern changes here. Phrase **b'** is the same as phrase **b**, except at the ending. The jumping figure of phrase **b** is replaced with a single note at the end of phrase **b'**.
0:46	phrase **b', b'**	Section A ends with two more iterations of phrase **b'**.
0:53	**Section B** phrases **a', b'**	Section B begins with an excerpt from phrase **a**. Phrase **a'** is the same as the second half of phrase **a**. A rain stick can be heard in the background just as section B begins.
0:59	phrases **a', b**	Phrase **a'**, the excerpt from phrase **a**, is repeated. Phrase **b** is played in its entirety, including the jumping figure, as a transition to the next section. Cymbal and wind chime are heard in the background.
1:06	**Section A** phrases **a, b**	Section A returns. From here until the end of the recording, the melody is identical to section A above. The snare drum now creeps into the texture.
1:17	phrases **a, b**	
1:27	phrases **b', b**	The cries and bird calls grow in intensity.
1:35	phrase **b'**	
1:38	recording ends	

artists. Throughout the day and evening, the open Common and the surrounding area are transformed into a variety of performance spaces.

Musical performances at special times in a variety of urban settings reinforce the connections among the diverse populations living within a particular area as well as incorporate them into the broader rhythm of city life. By looking closely at the side-by-side performance of so many music traditions and the transformation of large areas for these musical events, we can better understand the common practice of reimagining local spaces as larger settings for performance.

Who Makes the Music?

The Boston soundscape arises from a complex array of music cultures. In Boston, like most of multiethnic North America, where almost every city or town has some measure of cultural diversity, ties of descent or a shared cultural heritage generate a great deal of musical activity. Boston is home to many ethnic communities, each contributing to the greater urban soundscape. Some ethnic groups, such as the British, Irish, Italians, Haitians, and Cape Verdeans, arrived in New England early, and, swelled by later waves of immigration, have helped build the city into its present form. Others, including many African, Caribbean, and Russian immigrants, have come more recently. Here we will focus on a few communities, including two long-established ethnic groups—the Irish and Portuguese—and one relative newcomer community, the Ethiopians.

Irish

Irish immigrants began to arrive in New England during the eighteenth century; their numbers increased in the mid-nineteenth century because of hardships in Ireland, particularly the great potato famine of the late 1840s. It is estimated that four million Irish arrived in the United States between 1820 and 1900. Musical life in Boston reflects the Irish presence through traditional Irish fiddling in pubs and the sound of bagpipes at many civic and cultural events.

Annual activities such as the Boston College's Gaelic Roots summer festival, discontinued only recently in 2003, helped make Boston the "Irish capital of the

This sign in Gaelic ("Welcome to South Boston") was painted on a Dorchester Avenue building in South Boston. Note the strong references to Ireland, with the four coats of arms from the major regions of the country. The Celtic cross at the center of the sign can be interpreted as an emblem of Irish identity and, given the reference to two major Irish political organizations that sought to end British control of the country (Sinn Fein and Noraid), as a political symbol. The sign has since been painted over.

United States." Home to one of the great concentrations of people of Irish descent, Boston houses important centers for Irish American history, genealogy, and culture at the Boston Public Library and the Burns Library of Boston College.

Not surprisingly, Boston and its Irish inhabitants have been the subject of songs composed and transmitted within the community. Narrative songs, known as *ballads,* commemorate important events and memorable individuals. Many Irish ballads are political in their subject matter, providing a focal point for patriotic sentiments on important anniversaries of Irish history and celebrating the longtime Irish resistance to English rule.

The Ballad of Buddy McClean (Listening Guide 25, see page 90) commemorates composer John Hurley's fellow longshoreman, Buddy McClean, who was murdered after he resisted an effort by organized crime to take over the Boston dockworkers' unions in the 1950s and 1960s. The text of the song, especially in verses 2 and 3, connects the fight for workers' rights in Boston with the fight for independence in Ireland.

The melody is simple and repetitive, which helps both the singer and listeners to remember the ballad, and the guitar accompaniment uses a total of four chords, all fairly easy even for a beginning guitarist to play. These factors enhance the ballad's potential to record and transmit history and thereby to construct and reinforce a sense of identity among Irish Americans, especially those from Boston.

Portuguese

The Portuguese were among the earliest settlers in New England, and a steady stream of immigrants settled in Boston and Cambridge since the mid-twentieth century. These expatriate Portuguese communities came mainly from Portugal itself, as well as from the nearby Portuguese territories of the Cape Verde Islands and the Azores. In recent years, large numbers of Brazilians have swelled the number of Portuguese-speaking Bostonians; between 2000 and 2003, one out of every five new arrivals to Massachusetts was Brazilian, the most of any single immigrant community.[24]

A musical form popular among many Bostonians of Portuguese descent is the *fado* (pronounced "FAH-doe"), a song closely associated with Lisbon, the Portuguese capital. *Fado,* which means "fate," gives voice to nostalgia for the country left behind. In its expression of longing for a homeland, the *fado* became a powerful symbol for both Portuguese immigrants and those of Portuguese descent living abroad. *Fado* is sometimes compared

Senior citizens from the Cape Verdean community perform traditional songs and dances as part of the ensemble Pilon Cola, named after the *cola* (literally, "tail") dance that is performed around a *pilon*, the large wooden pestle shown here, which is used as both a corn grinder and drum. Many Cape Verdeans, who came from an archipelago off the West African coast (under Portuguese rule until it gained its independence in 1970), have lived in New England since the mid-nineteenth century.

The Ballad of Buddy McClean (Irish American ballad)

CD 1
Track 25

Composer: John Hurley

Date of recording: 1998

Performers: Derek Warfield, *voice and mandolin;* Joe O'Rourke, *guitar and chorus;* Des Sheerin, *string bass;* Joe Finn, *uilleann pipes;* Loe Finn, *pennywhistle;* Kefin Sheerin, *accordion;* Joe Cooney, *banjo;* Athena Terais, *fiddle;* Pearse Warfield, *bodhrán* (frame drum) *and chorus;* Peter Wrafter, *chorus*

Form: Strophic ballad with refrain

Tempo: Moderate tempo, triple meter

Function: Commemoration of local hero

WHAT TO LISTEN FOR:

- Vocal style and instruments (guitar, banjo, accordion) typical of American folk music, along with Irish fiddle, frame drum, bagpipes, and pennywhistle, a small flute made of wood or plastic
- Traditional strophic ballad form, with alternation of verse and refrain

STRUCTURE AND TEXT	DESCRIPTION
0:00 **Verse** I'll sing you a song of the deeds that were done, Of the struggles of conflict and tears, Of the men on the run who fought against guns, That brought the community fear. You never wanted the title of hero, Sought fame or great power or acclaim. You had no wealth or might, but you knew wrong from right, And your fight for justice was clear.	Each verse consists of two stanzas. In the first stanza, the melody begins on the tonic (central pitch). We hear three repetitions of a phrase that ascends three scale steps and then drops. The melody then ascends (on the third line of text) and drops to its lowest point on the last note of the stanza. The melody of second stanza is mainly in the singer's upper register, but on the last note of the verse, the singer returns to the tonic.

to the blues because of its heartfelt expression of loss and despair. Said to have originated among Portuguese sailors who spent long periods of time away from home, the *fado* in Lisbon and urban centers abroad is usually performed in clubs and restaurants. The *fado* became less popular after the 1974 Portuguese revolution because of its association with the authoritarian regime of dictator Antonio Salazar, but it slowly recovered its status as a symbol of Portugal in the 1980s and 1990s.

0:38	**Refrain**	The refrain likewise contains two stanzas.

0:38   **Refrain**

Sing away, hills of Boston,
With the spirit of Buddy McClean!
The longshoreman's teamsters are talking
Of their hero now, Buddy McClean.

What greater deed can a man do
Than to lay down his life for his friends?
Winter Hill tells the tale of a strong Irish gale
Who was loyal was pure and was true.

The refrain likewise contains two stanzas. Additional singers can be heard on the refrain, and a countermelody (played first by the flute and then by the violins) becomes prominent. The second stanza of the refrain uses the same melody and harmonies as does the second stanza of the verse.

1:12   **Verse**

Those mobsters of crime said the good would be
        dying
If you did not submit to their ways.
That the fit would be lame if you'd not play their
        game,
And your friends would know more happy days.

Men of liberty, freedom, and courage
Believed that your stand it was true.
And the unions you saved for the homes of the
        brave
And were joined by the faithful and few.

The second verse begins.

1:46   **Refrain**

2:21   **Verse**

The Irish McCleans would kneel to no Queen.
They were proud of the old sod of green.
You were Buddy to all, and you answered the call,
On the waterfront you were the king.

Strong faith and hard work for a living
For your wife and your family and home.
And you bowed to no one whether gangster or
        gun,
And worked for the American dream.

Third verse.

2:55   Refrain and fade-out at 3:00.

Today Portuguese Americans hear the *fado* largely through recordings imported from Portugal, although a new generation of young Portuguese *fado* singers such as Misia and Mariza tour internationally and perform often in the Boston area. But *fado* aficionados constantly compare the young singers to Amália Rodrigues, who before her death in 1999 was the foremost interpreter of the *fado* in twentieth-century Portugal. Thousands of Portuguese poured into the streets of Lisbon for her funeral, and political candidates, out of respect,

The Portuguese *fado* singer Amália Rodrigues had an international following. Here she is seen performing in a Parisian cabaret on January 17, 1972.

halted their campaigning until the funeral services were over.[25] Born around 1920, Rodrigues made her first recording in 1945, releasing more than 170 albums and becoming over the years an international film star.

Today Rodrigues remains a muse and inspiration to young *fado* singers: "Everywhere I go, everybody knows what *fado* is thanks to Amália," the singer Misia has said. "She had that wonderful voice, she inspired many new *fados,* and she wrote beautiful lyrics herself."[26] Some say that the singer Mariza sounds "like the young Amália, with soul." Rodrigues is thought to have personified the *fado,* wearing black clothes of mourning during her performances and once saying that "I have so much sadness in me, I am a pessimist, a nihilist, everything *fado* demands in a singer, I have in me."[27]

In Listening Guide 26 (see page 94), Amália Rodrigues sings a classic *fado* song, *Fado Lisboeta,* which is known for its sophisticated poetry and complex harmony. Rodrigues conveys *saudade* (a feeling of longing or yearning) through her tone color. She also expresses emotion by subtly slowing the tempo of the song near the end of phrases.

Ethiopians

The long histories of the Irish and Portuguese communities in Boston have served to familiarize many in the metropolitan area with Irish ballads and Portuguese *fado,* whereas the music of communities who have arrived in the last two decades has not yet had much of a public impact on the Boston soundscape. But if one watches for local announcements or calls a community hotline, it becomes clear that newer Bostonians are actively making music as well. We can return briefly to City Hall for a glimpse of the gala party and feast mounted by the Boston Ethiopian community each September in honor of their New Year.

Considering that it was not built to house musical events, the City Hall atrium, like the plaza discussed above, is readily transformed for performance. Loudspeakers positioned at the bottom of the imposing staircase in the center of the space amplify the performance by a singer and band standing on the landing above, high enough to be seen as well as heard by the large crowd below. As the pounding beat of the synthesizer's rhythm track encourages people to dance, couples blend Western dance steps with the fast shoulder movements of the Ethiopian dance *eskesta* ("iz-KISS-tah"). Just as dress that evening is divided between traditional Ethiopian garments and Western garb, the music mixes aspects of the Ethiopian homeland and the cosmopolitan musical worlds of Ethiopians abroad. One hears arrangements of traditional folk songs in the Ethiopian language (Amharic) as well as renditions of the latest American popular tunes.

Festive occasions are used by all immigrants to come together and reminisce. In the case of the Ethiopian New Year celebration, many songs recall the Ethiopian homeland, which most remember vividly, having immigrated to Boston in the years since their country's revolution began in the late 1970s. We will return in Chapter 8 to the subject of the process through which Ethiopians and their music moved abroad.

In Listening Guide 27 (see page 96), we hear the poignant song *Hagerei* (pronounced "HAH-gur-rye," meaning "my country") which expresses the singer's homesickness for the beauty of Ethiopia. Mentioning the sights and smells of their motherland arouses a keen awareness of separation from family and the pain of Ethiopian displacement. In its expression of longing for country, this Ethiopian song can be compared to *fado*, despite their different origins and contrasting musical styles.

The nostalgia expressed by the text of *Hagerei* is underscored by the use of a pentatonic melody based in the Ethiopian mode *tizita* (pronounced "TIH-zee-tah"), traditionally associated with longing and loss. The synthesized snare drum accents beats two and five of each six-beat measure, while the drum machine continues to play on the following two half beats, resulting in a syncopated two-against-three pattern Ethiopians call *chik chika* (pronounced "chick chicka"). In this song, text, melody, and rhythm combine to convey a powerful sonic symbol of the homeland.

While both old and new ethnic communities enrich musical life in Boston, many other residents contribute to the soundscape as well. Boston is a magnet for people attracted by opportunities in business and education, many of whom reside in the metropolitan area on a short-term basis. For instance, the special relationship between Boston and its official sister city, Kyoto, Japan, has led to a sizeable Japanese community that has established shops, bookstores, and restaurants and sponsors performances of Japanese music. These events serve not just to bring together Bostonians of Japanese or Japanese American descent, but also to infuse the Boston soundscape with new sounds.

Many music traditions in the Boston soundscape are not sustained by a descent community as part of an ethnic or national heritage. Many people support music cultures which they encounter by chance and to which they are attracted by virtue of the music's sound or setting. For instance, while there is no organized Swiss community of any size in Boston, the widely popular Swiss vocal style called *yodeling* has

The ensemble Kokoo performs an afternoon of *shakuhachi* and *koto* music at Saint Paul's Church in Brookline in 1998, part of an annual concert series sponsored by the Consulate General of Japan in Boston and the Japanese Association of Greater Boston. The instruments, from left to right, include two *koto* (zithers, one with twenty strings and one with thirteen strings) and *shakuhachi,* bamboo flutes.

Fado Lisboeta (Portuguese ballad)

CD 1
Track 26

Date of recording: 1960s, re-released in 1992
Composers: C. Dias and A. Do Vale
Performers: Amália Rodrigues, *voice;* Jaime Santos, *guitar;* Domingo Camarinha, *guitar*
Form: *Fado canção,* a strophic form with refrain
Tempo: Moderate 4/4 meter
Function: Entertainment, personal reflection

WHAT TO LISTEN FOR:

• The ways in which the strophic *fado* text, with alternation of verse and refrain, provides a personal, emotional statement, while simultaneously evoking a nocturnal setting in Lisbon
• Famous *fadista* Amália Rodrigues's expressive vocal style conveying *saudade* (longing or yearning)
• Twelve-stringed Portuguese guitars (*guitarras*) that are finger-picked to achieve a soft timbre; guitarists pluck the individual pitches of a chord (called an *arpeggio*) rather than strum the entire chord at one time
• A subtle interaction between the guitarists and the singer, allowing for expressive changes in tempo known as *rubato,* especially near the end of phrases

	STRUCTURE AND TEXT	TRANSLATION	DESCRIPTION
0:00	**Instrumental introduction**		The guitars establish a syncopated rhythm. The introduction begins in the major mode and ends in minor.
0:10	**Verse 1** **Phrase a** Não queiram mal a quem canta quando uma garganta em ar se desgarra, **Phrase b** porque [y] a mágos já não é tanta se é confissada a uma guitarra.	Don't hold it against one who sings when a voice wells up in challenge, because his pain is not so great when confessed to a guitar.	A rapid syllabic text setting, with three notes (and therefore three syllables) per beat. A complementary ("consequent") phrase responds to the first ("antecedent") phrase.
	Phrase a' Quem canta sempre se ausenta na hora cinzenta de sua amargura,	He who sings always retreats in the ashen hours of his suffering,	The first phrase is repeated with different words.

Phrase c
não sente a cruz tão pesada na longa rua [strada] de desventura.

and the cross he bears doesn't feel so heavy on the long road of misfortune.

This time, a different phrase responds, ending on the tonic. The singer makes dramatic use of *rubato* (flexible, expressive tempo changes) and the guitars emphasize the transition to the refrain.

0:39 **Refrain**
Phrases d-e
Eu só entendo o fado plangente amargurado
na noite a soluçar baixinho,
Phrases f-g
que chega a meu coração tão magoado,
tão frio como as neves do caminho,

I only feel *fado*, plaintive and sorrowful
while I sob quietly in the night.

It touches my heart, so pained

and as cold as the snow on the road,

The guitar melody traces "broken chords," in which individual pitches are plucked separately, called "*arpeggios*." This section begins in the major mode. As in the verse, the phrases in the refrain respond to each other, acting as antecedent and consequent phrases.
The melody at the beginning of the refrain is repeated with different words.

Phrases d'-e'
que chora uma saudade ou canta ansiedade
de quem tem por amor chorado.
Phrases h-i
Dirão que isto é fatal, é natural,
mas é [o] lisboeta, isto é o que é o fado.

that weeps with longing or sings the yearning
of one who has wept for love.

They'll say that this is fateful, that it's only natural,
but this is Lisbon, this is *fado*.

With the mention of "fado," the song switches back into the minor mode.

1:30 **Verse 2**
Phrase a
Oiço guitarras vibrando
vozes cantando na rua sombria,
Phrase b
que as luzes vão se apagando
a anunciar que já é dia.
Phrase a'
Fecho em silêncio a janela,
se ouve na viela rumores de ternura,
Phrase c
surge a manhã fresca e calma,

só em minh'alma é noite escura.

I hear the strumming of guitars and voices singing in the gloomy streets,
as the lights go out announcing the break of day.

Silently, I close the window, sounds of tenderness may be heard in the alleyway,

the morning unfolds fresh and tranquil,
only in my soul is it darkest night.

The second verse has the same musical structure as the first, but with different words.

2:01 **Refrain**

The refrain repeats, this time ending in the major mode at 2:55.

Hagerei ("My Homeland," Ethiopian song)

CD 1
Track 27

Date: 1996
Performer: Ephrem Tamiru
Form: Verses divided by instrumental interludes
Tempo: Moderate 6/8 with syncopation
Function: Popular song expressing a nostalgic longing for home

WHAT TO LISTEN FOR:

- A nasal vocal quality with many ornaments, characteristic of the Ethiopian highland style
- A pentatonic scale and melody, known as *tizita,* that Ethiopians associate with songs of longing
- Influence of international popular music in the instrumentation and use of Western harmony
- Syncopated rhythm, onomatopoetically termed *chik chika* by Ethiopian musicians

	STRUCTURE AND TEXT	TRANSLATION	DESCRIPTION
0:00	**Introduction** ah . . .	Ah . . .	The introduction, while mainly instrumental, includes a brief *vocalise* (wordless song), which is echoed in the synthesized string part.

been taught in the city for decades. Yodeling first spread outside its geographical base in the mountains of Switzerland and Southern Germany when Tyrolean folklore troupes began touring internationally in the 1820s, serenading Swiss and German immigrants abroad who were homesick for their native lands.[28] During the twentieth century, recordings and other media reinforced yodeling circles abroad. Today, people yodel in Boston not as a residue of Central European identity, but, according to some of its practitioners, "for fun" and "to impress people."[29] Many music traditions today are perpetuated by "affinity communities," groups of people who come together to participate in particular forms of music-making. Another good example is the folk dance groups that have spread throughout the Boston area in the last thirty years, bringing people of diverse backgrounds together through dance. We will see below that affinity communities generate some of the most distinctive features of the Boston soundscape.

0:40	**Section A**		
	phrase a		Each of these phrases has a
	endete nesh hagere [pause] ka-semay la-medresh	From earth to heaven, how are you, my land?	pause in the middle and is repeated twice. The first and
1:01	**phrase b**		third lines of each of these
	la-kwelu la-degaw, la-kwelu mederesh	All the surroundings and the neighborhood?	verses are musically identical, as are the second and fourth
1:14	**phrase a**		lines.
	'endemenesh k [?] [pause] anci yetewelede hagere	How are you, the country of my birth?	
1:36	**phrase b**		
	hule ya-metnafeqin kadmasu bashager	The land I miss all the time, from afar.	
1:47	**Instrumental interlude**		
2:01	**phrase c**		
	sereqe lehedenew kadmas basger	I will steal away and leave from far.	
2:18	**phrase d**		
	'alcalem 'anjete (x3) yehagere negr	I cannot bear it, things of my land.	
2:38	**phrase c**		
	zaman tezetasen zewter eyadesew	Time renews memories continuously.	
2:53	**phrase d**		
	tenafeqinales (x3) 'anci hager la-sew	I miss you, land of a people.	
3:14	ah . . .	Ah . . .	Fade-out at 3:20.

Boston's Defining Musical Communities

Distinctive characteristics of Boston, notably the city's history, location, and diverse population, have given rise to three important soundscapes within the broader context of city musical life: campus music, folk music, and early music. All three of these soundscapes have roots in Euro-American history, but each has been transformed by cross-cultural musical connections. Individuals from a variety of backgrounds who today constitute cohesive affinity communities transmit these three soundscapes; many of these participants cross back and forth between two or more of these soundscapes, linking one to the other. Because of their size, internal complexity, and mutual interaction, Boston's campus music, folk music, and early music soundscapes help define Boston's musical profile.

Campus Music

Boston nurtures a rich array of music traditions at the world-renowned institutions of higher education in the metropolitan area. The history of greater Boston can to a certain extent be told through the history of its colleges, universities, and conservatories, starting with the founding in 1636 of the divinity school that shortly thereafter became Harvard University, the establishment of Boston University in 1839, the founding of the Massachusetts Institute of Technology (MIT) in 1861, and the launching of the nation's oldest music conservatory, The New England Conservatory, in 1867. Numerous other institutions with active traditions of musicmaking are located throughout the Boston metropolitan area.

Many of Boston's oldest musical institutions had their roots in campus musical life, and the musical interaction between town and gown was—and remains—close. One notable example is the impact that jazz musicians from the Berklee College of Music have had on Boston club life. Boston clubs such as Wally's Cafe have for more than half a century provided a setting where young jazz students could hone their talents.

Virtually every Boston-area campus is a small city with its own distinctive soundscapes, sustaining a dazzling array of musical activities, ensembles, and music events. Partly because of the increasingly international and multiethnic nature of student populations at these institutions, diverse musical styles have proliferated in recent years. These styles have added to the student orchestras, choirs, and close-harmony singing groups established in the earliest days of many campuses.

Although campus musical life in the past drew mainly on historical Western music ensembles, the later twentieth century has seen the proliferation of groups featuring a range of avant-garde, popular, and international musics. There is little doubt that the broader Boston soundscape has been greatly enriched by the wide array of

This flyer for a Taiwanese Cultural Society meeting at the Harvard University student center blends old Boston images with Taiwanese customs and music.

The Klezmer Conservatory Band, originally composed of New England Conservatory students, gave its first concert in 1980 and continues to receive international acclaim as one of the foremost ensembles performing Eastern European Jewish instrumental and vocal music. Current members of the band include in the front row left to right: Deborah Strauss (violin), Judy Bressler (voice, percussion), Grant Smith (drums); middle row: Jim Guttmann (bass), Hankus Netsky (director and instructor of improvisation at NEC, alto sax, piano, accordion), Ilene Stahl (clarinet), Mark Berney (cornet); back row: Mark Hamilton (trombone), Art Bailey (piano and accordion), Jeff Warschauer (mandolin, guitar, banjo, vocals), and Robin Miller (flute, piccolo).

music traditions easily accessible on area campuses. West African drumming is taught at Tufts University; at Harvard, Gumboot dancers perform and teach the dances of South African miners, and another group teaches Korean drumming and dance; MIT features the study and performance of North Indian and Senegalese music. Widely represented on nearly all campuses are student dance groups, including South Asian, Israeli, Mexican, Chinese, Eastern European, Latin, jazz, funk, and hip-hop dancers.

Among the international music ensembles most prominent on college campuses in Boston and across North America and the world are Indonesian instrumental groups known as *gamelans*. While there are several important Indonesian *gamelan* traditions, two have been widely studied and are today established worldwide. One of these arose first on the island of Java early in the Common Era, and the second later in Bali. Javanese and Balinese *gamelans* are closely related but are distinguished from each other by different instruments, tunings, and playing techniques. Both Balinese and Javanese *gamelans* are active in the Boston metropolitan area on the MIT and Tufts campuses, drawing players from the student population as well as from the community at large. Here we will focus on the Balinese *gamelan* and discuss how this venerable Southeast Asian music tradition has become part of the Boston soundscape (see **"Sound Sources: The Balinese *Gamelan*"** on the following page).

The popularity of *gamelan* music in Boston and on college campuses around the world is a phenomenon with its roots in the nineteenth-century colonial era. However, we can trace the history of the Balinese *gamelan* back to the early sixteenth century, when members of the Javanese court and its musicians fled to Bali. Over the next several centuries, the *gamelan* spread to Hindu temples and to villages across that island. Used in a variety of religious and secular ceremonies, as well as in musical theater, the *gamelan* became a ubiquitous presence in Balinese life. In recent decades, the *gamelan* has assumed an increasingly important role in the Balinese tourist industry as well.

Stamford Raffles, a colonial governor in Java, brought the first Javanese *gamelan* ensemble outside Southeast Asia to England in 1816. The appearance of a Javanese *gamelan* at the 1889 Exposition Universelle in Paris attracted the interest of French composer Claude Debussy and others, as did the performance of a Balinese *gamelan* at the subsequent 1900 Exposition. The Dutch colonial presence in Indonesia also attracted Western scholars to Indonesia, where they worked closely with Indonesian musicians and scholars. During a concert tour of Java in 1919, a Dutch musician named Jaap Kunst became

MIT World Music Weekend

April 3-5, 1998

3 YAMADA-RYU SOKYOKU, Japanese classical chamber music for voice, koto, and shakuhachi; EURASIA ENSEMBLE, Robert Labaree, Director, Turkish classical music performed on traditional instruments. **Friday at 7 PM, Killian Hall. Free.**

4 MITCAN, MIT's African Performance Ensemble, James Makubuya, Director; KINIWE, African Music and Dance Ensemble of the Dept. of Music at Tufts University, David Locke, Director, with guest artist Abukari Lunna, master drummer from Ghana. **Saturday at 7 PM, Wong Auditorium. Free.**

4 SOUTH ASIAN CULTURAL SHOW sponsored by SAAS and Sangam featuring dance, music, drama and other performing arts from India, Pakistan, Nepal, Sri Lanka and Bangladesh. **Saturday at 7 PM, Kresge Auditorium. Adm. $4; MIT students free w/ID.**

5 TRICHUR RAMACHANDRAN, Carnatic vocalist; G. Chandramauli, violin; Umayalpuram Mahalingam, mridangam. Winner of many honors, this distinguished South Indian singer combines a prodigious technique with a graceful and atmospheric presentation. **Sunday at 4 PM, Rm. 6-120. Free.**

The MIT world music weekend brings together aficionados of world music from college campuses throughout the Boston area.

The Balinese *Gamelan*

Although the Balinese *gamelan* includes instruments made of wood and bamboo, including one or two drums, flutes, and a bowed lute called a *rebab* ("reh-BAHB"), gongs and instruments of the xylophone type made of bronze dominate the ensemble's distinctive sound. Here we will focus on the Balinese *gamelan,* with particular attention to the *gamelan gong kebyar,* the most important *gamelan* in twentieth-century Bali. (See the figure on p. 102.)

The metal idiophones (sometimes called metallophones) of the Balinese *gamelan* are divided between keyed and gong instruments struck with different types of mallets. The keyed instruments include the *gangsa* ("GHAHNG-sah") family, each with ten bronze keys suspended on cords hanging over bamboo resonators within a wooden case. In general, the bigger the instrument, the lower the pitch.

The *gangsa* family of instruments expand on and ornament the main melody. The highest-pitched *gangsa* are the four small *kantilan* ("kahn-TEE-lahn"); tuned an octave below them are the four somewhat larger *gangsa pemade* ("puh-MAH-deh"); and another octave lower, one or two tall *gangsa* called *ugal* ("OO-gahl"). The *ugal* usually plays a different musical part from the *kantilan* and *pemade,* and for this reason musicians sometimes talk about the "*gangsa* parts" and the "*ugal* part" separately, even though the *ugal* is technically a *gangsa.*

Several other metallophones with five keys support the *gangsa* and *ugal* parts, and play at a slower rate of speed the core tones that constitute the basic *gamelan* melody. These large instruments include two *calung* ("chah-LOONG") which overlap in range with the *ugal,* and the *jegogan* ("djuh-GOE-gone") which is even larger and is tuned one octave lower than the *calung.* The hammer used for the *calung* and *jegogan* is padded and softer than those used for the *gangsas* and *ugal,* producing a more delicate sound.

intrigued with the *gamelan* and subsequently returned as a colonial official to live in Java and carry out research on the *gamelan* through the mid-1930s.

Kunst's subsequent career as a scholar of Javanese *gamelan* music after his return to Amsterdam inspired others, in particular his student Ki Mantle Hood, an American who later established the first ethnomusicology program in the United States at UCLA. In 1958, Hood purchased for UCLA the Javanese *gamelan* Venerable Dark Cloud, which remains at that institution today. The second half of the twentieth century saw an explosion of scholars

The gongs of the *gamelan* are made of bronze and have a raised boss in the middle on which they are struck with mallets. Different gongs serve colotomic (time-keeping) and melodic functions; the hanging gongs keep the time while most gongs on racks have melodic functions. The number of gongs varies according to the particular *gamelan,* but most use one or two large, hanging gongs (*gong ageng*) to mark the beginnings and endings of melodies. The smaller hanging *kempur* ("kehm-POOR") marks other divisions in the time cycle, as does the *kemong* (also called *klentong*). The *kempli* ("kehm-PLEE"), a single small gong in a wooden frame, keeps a regular, crisp beat that provides a point of reference for all the musicians of the *gamelan.*

Gongs with prominent melodic roles include sets of eight to fourteen pot gongs in frames. This instrument is called a *trompong* when it is played by a soloist, and is termed a *reyong* ("RAY-yong") when played by four people, each attending to a few gongs. The *reyong* is particularly famous for elaborate ornamentation and loud chords. The final metallophone is the *cengceng* ("CHENG-cheng"), which are noisy cymbals, usually set on a wooden base.

A pair of double-headed, cylindrical membranophones called *kendang* lead the *gamelan*. The higher pitched *kendang* of the pair is called the male drum, while the lower pitched is the female, despite their reversal of the range of male and female voices. The lower female drum usually sets the pace and signals upcoming changes to the other musicians.

Bamboo flutes (*suling,* pronounced "SOO-ling"), played with the circular breathing technique, provide another melodic line, as does the tone of the *rebab* ("reh-BAHB") a two-stringed bowed lute that can be heard mainly in quieter passages.[30]

The instruments of the Balinese *gamelan* can be heard in the performance of the dance *Taruna Jaya,* Listening Guide 28 (see page 106).

studying Javanese, Balinese, and Sundanese *gamelan* music and the proliferation of *gamelan* ensembles worldwide, including all over Europe—40 sets in Britain, 150 in North America, and others in East Asia, Australia, New Zealand, Latin America, and even Africa.[31]

Gamelans were imported from Bali and Java to a number of other campuses, including Wesleyan University, the University of Michigan, the University of California, Berkeley, and the Eastman School of Music, to name only a few. As a result, generations of students and community members have played these

Artist's Sketch of *Gamelan Gong Kebyar.*

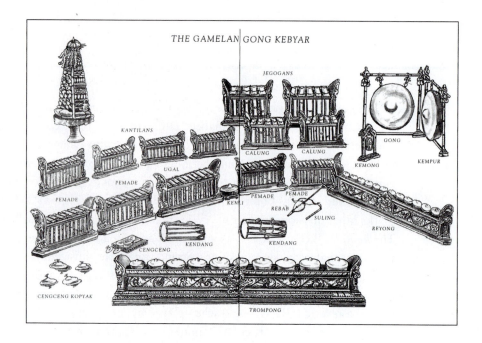

THE GAMELAN GONG KEBYAR

instruments and become aficionados of Indonesian music. In most cases, accomplished Balinese and Javanese musicians have collaborated with local faculty, arriving for visits or permanent positions to teach *gamelan* on college campuses. Many Indonesian musicians, dancers, and scholars have established international careers between the United States and Indonesia, including Hardja Susilo (UCLA), Sumarsam (Wesleyan University), Desak Made Suarti Laksi and I Nyoman Catra (College of the Holy Cross, Worcester, MA), Undang Sumarna (UC Santa Cruz), and others.

The *gamelan* became a symbol of Indonesian culture and national identity during the second half of the twentieth century, and the Indonesian government actively supported the spread of *gamelan* ensembles abroad, establishing performing groups in residence at their embassies and consulates.[32] In the past, *gamelans* have also been presented as official gifts to foreign governments, sometimes remaining in unexpected places, such as the Javanese *gamelan* given to Ethiopia's Emperor Haile Selassie, still preserved at the Institute for Ethiopian Studies in Addis Ababa. The active global life of the *gamelan* has also influenced transmission of *gamelan* music at home in Bali, where one can learn to play through traditional apprenticeships with master musicians or through instruction in Balinese music conservatories.

Historical and political factors have helped shape the international spread of the *gamelan,* but there is no doubt that the sound of the music has been the central attraction. Composers worldwide since Debussy have been drawn to the *gamelan's* sound, many inspired by the experience of Colin McPhee, a

The College of the Holy Cross in Worcester, Massachusetts, home of a *gamelan*, hosted a celebration of Balinese music, theatre, and dance.

FEATURING:

Master Artists from Bali, including:

I Gusti Ngurah Windia
Ida Bagus Gede Mambal
Anak Agung Bagus Sudarma
I Made Suartika
Ni Gusti Ayu Armini
I Ketut Gede Asnawa
I Nyoman Catra
I Nyoman Cerita
I Gusti Ngurah Kertayuda
Desak Made Suarti Laksmi
I Made Lasmawan
I Nyoman Saptanyana
I Nyoman Suadin
I Nyoman Windha

Keynote address by composer/
ethnomusicologist - Michael Tenzer,
University of British Columbia in Vancouver

COMPOSERS:

Shirish Korde
Desak Made Suarti Laksmi
Gerald Levinson
Wayne Vitali
I Nyoman Windha
Evan Ziporyn

GUEST ENSEMBLE:

Boston Musica Viva, under the
direction of Richard Pittman

SPEAKERS AND PANELISTS INCLUDING:

John Emigh
David Harnish
Edward Herbst
Ron Jenkins
Lynn Kremer
I Made Moja
Islene Pinder
Ling Ong
Larry Reed
Farley Richmond

FEATURING VISITING GAMELANS:

Gamelan Lila Muni
Eastman School of Music angklung
Gamelan Galak Tika
Massachusetts Insititute of Technology
(gong kebyar)
Gamelan Dharma Swara
Indonesian Consulate Ensemble, NYC
(gong kebyar)

CONFERENCE COMMITTEE:

Lynn Kremer and Shirish Korde
Conference Co-Chairs
College of the Holy Cross, Worcester, MA

Desak Made Suarti Laksmi
Artistic Director and Luce Assistant Professor of
Balinese Music, Theatre, and Dance
College of the Holy Cross, Worcester, MA

I Nyoman Catra
Artistic Director
Wesleyan University, Middletown, CT

Bethany Collier
Program Coordinator Cornell University, Ithaca, NY

CONTACT INFORMATION:

Bethany Collier
bjc46@cornell.edu
607-339-9779
Desak Made Suarti Laksmi
klaksmi@holycross.edu
508-793-2762
Lynn Kremer
lkremer@holycross.edu
508-793-2462
Shirish Korde
skorde@holycross.edu
508-793-2294

CONTINUITIES AND CHANGE:
A CELEBRATION OF BALINESE MUSIC, THEATRE, AND DANCE
November 21-23, 2003   College of the Holy Cross   Worcester, Massachusetts
CONCERTS ▪ PAPERS ▪ WORKSHOPS
SUPPORTED BY THE HENRY LUCE FOUNDATION, COLLEGE OF THE HOLY CROSS DEPARTMENTS OF MUSIC AND THEATRE, AND WESLEYAN UNIVERSITY MUSIC DEPARTMENT

Canadian composer who heard the first recordings of Balinese *gamelan* music made in the 1920s and who later lived in Bali in the years before World War II. McPhee wrote books about the *gamelan* and his experience in Bali and based some of his compositions for Western instruments on the Balinese *gamelan's* sound and textures. Others have followed in McPhee's footsteps, including

Members of Gamelan Galak Tika rehearse during a trip to Bali in summer, 2005, led by Evan Ziporyn, playing the *kendang* in the foreground.

Michael Tenzer, a leading scholar of Balinese *gamelan* music who established ensembles at Yale and the University of British Columbia, and composer/performer Evan Ziporyn, founder of Gamelan Galak Tika at MIT.

Balinese *gamelan* music is organized according to rhythmic cycles, with the large gong sounding at a point that is simultaneously the end of one cycle and the beginning of the next. It has been suggested that this cyclic way of organizing musical time reflects the Hindu belief in reincarnation and natural harvest cycles. Some instruments mark various parts of the rhythmic cycle, while others play a core melody or variations on it.[33] The complex, many-voiced texture that results from these layers of different rhythms and melodies is, as we have noted in Chapter 1, called "polyphony."

Balinese *gamelan* music does not have a universal standard of pitch. However, the instruments of a *gamelan* are tuned to each other, lending each ensemble a distinctive sound quality; the exact pitches vary slightly from one *gamelan* to the next. One of the most interesting and distinctive aspects of the Balinese *gamelan* is the use of the acoustical phenomenon called "beating tones," a type of shimmering sound that occurs when the same music is played on a pair of similar instruments that are deliberately tuned at slightly different frequencies.

New compositions and innovative combinations of Balinese and Western instruments are part of *gamelan* practice in both Bali and around the globe, but most *gamelans,* such as Gamelan Galak Tika in Boston, continue to perform traditional pieces from the *gamelan* repertory as well as mount programs including theatrical elements and dance. We will take a closer look at *gamelan* innovations and Balinese/American collaboration in Chapter 6. Listening Guide 28 (see page 106) is a lengthy excerpt of a well-known Balinese dance piece, *Taruna Jaya.* The sudden breaks (*angsel*) and strong rhythms so characteristic of the *gamelan gong kebyar* style are reinforced by the dancers as they suddenly assume new poses or change directions.[34]

Beyond their broadly international musical styles, represented by ensembles such as *gamelans,* Boston campuses have folk music clubs as well as organizations that mount performances of a wide array of early music.

Folk Music

The term "folk music" is a complicated one that merits a brief discussion since it encompasses two related but distinct phenomena. The expression "folk music" has been used by scholars since the eighteenth century to refer to music transmitted through oral tradition by non-professional musicians. Traditional folk songs (sometimes called "traditional music") have long been a part of everyday life everywhere, accompanying work, serving to entertain, and providing an expressive outlet for acknowledging and resisting challenging life circumstances. During the late nineteenth and twentieth centuries, in many locales, these orally transmitted folk music traditions were collected and notated by folklorists and early ethnomusicologists. Older songs also began to be revived and performed by professionals and organized groups in settings including cultural organizations, schools and universities, and ensembles organized to represent entire nations.

Folk songs served as informal anthems of various political and labor movements in the United States. During the 1950s, traditional folk songs from a variety of American vernacular and cross-cultural sources as well as newly composed songs in traditional styles became a musical emblem of the young people of that era, providing a traditional sound through which current issues could be addressed. Professional musicians circulated these songs through recordings and other media, attracting a mass audience that was able, thanks to the accessible musical idiom of the songs, to sing along.

Here in *Soundscapes,* we will move back and forth between traditional folk music and the closely associated folk music revivals. Both streams of tradition are present in most urban locales, where folk songs continue to be transmitted by amateurs and to be revived, transformed, and sometimes created anew by professionals.

Since the earliest days of the American folk music revival in the 1950s, Boston has been an important center for the folk music world, and many Boston singer-songwriters and musicians drew on and transformed an enormous stock of music from many ethnic communities. The American folk music revival had its artistic roots in the beatnik phenomenon of the 1950s, centered in the famous alternative lifestyles and artistic culture of New York City's Greenwich Village. Boston's long liberal tradition and the presence of so many young people at area colleges made it a magnet for the young singer-songwriters at the center of the folk music revival. With the increasing momentum of the civil rights movement in the 1950s, followed by the anti-Vietnam war initiative of the 1960s and the simultaneous flowering of the youth movement known as the counterculture, the folk song revival became linked to broader political issues of that period. The civil rights march on Washington held on August 28, 1963, was a watershed event; Joan Baez, Bob Dylan, Peter, Paul, and Mary, and other folk singers performed, implanting songs such as *Blowin' in the Wind* and *If I Had a Hammer* into national and international consciousness.

The independence movement in longtime African colonies during these same years and the growing outcry against apartheid in South Africa brought

Taruna Jaya ("Victorious Youth")

Composer: I Gdé Manik

Date composed: 1940s, with frequent later revisions by composer and others; in 1952 reduced from 55 minutes to 15 minutes

Date recorded: 1996

Performer: Gamelan Galak Tika, Massachusetts Institute of Technology

Tempo: Varies greatly, from fast (*enggal* or *gelis*) to slow (*adeng* or *lambat*)

Mode: *Pelog,* 7-pitch tuning system

Form: *Klasik tari lepas,* a secular, virtuosic composition in which music and dance are tightly coordinated

Function: Composition for Balinese *gamelan* to accompany dance at festivals and competitions; showpiece for dancers and musicians

Dynamics: Closely tied to tempo, with changes ranging from temporary or subtle gradations to incremental changes to interruptions

WHAT TO LISTEN FOR:

- Distinctive shimmering sound of *gamelan gong kebyar,* the *gamelan* most often heard in modern Bali
- Fast-changing combinations of melodies and textures
- Sudden changes in rhythmic patterns and tempos that define large sectional divisions, moving between faster *bapang* sections and alternatively slow and faster paces of *lelongorran.* Tempo changes are led by *kendang* and *ugal,* with *kempli* and other instruments keeping time
- Intense polyphony, including interlocking parts (*kotekan*) played on higher-pitched metallophones (*gangsa*), with their combined rhythm subdividing the beat into two parts
- Dynamics and tempo as two important aspects of ensemble virtuosity and in constant flux, with no trajectory toward a single peak or climax

	STRUCTURE	DESCRIPTION
0:00	**Kebyar I (long)**	Instrumental introduction; literally "to flair up or burst open," with loud, near-unison chords marking irregular rhythms. The *gangsa* play the melody and the *reyong* and *ceng-ceng* punctuate with crashes called *byong;* glissandos are heard in the *gangsa*.

0:49	**Genderan**	Contrasting section with more flowing, polyphonic texture, regular rhythms, omitting pot gongs (*reyong*), drum (*kendang*) and cymbals (*ceng-ceng*) so prominent in *kebyar*. Beat marked by *kempli* and gong, with basic melody in *calung*, elaborated by *gangsa*. Dancer enters during *genderan*, either a young man or, more often, a young woman dressed as a youth.
0:55		*Kotekan* begins, with one part on the beat (*polos*) and the other off the beat (*sangsih*).
1:29	**Bapang I** (refers to a fast and aggressive meter, associated with strong affect or high official)	*Kotekan* stops; fast gong pattern in all gongs, with two *kempur* strokes to one gong stroke; regular tapping pulse in *kempli*. Texture broken by *angsels*.
2:09	**Bapang II**	*Kotekan* begins; regular tapping pulse in *kempli*; melody in *calung*, divided into four-pitch segments.
3:40	**Bapang I**	Each of four *reyong* musicians plays three pots in syncopated rhythm, with *ceng-ceng* punctuation, as *gangsa* plays brief, main melody.
3:51	**Lelonggoran I** (slow, fast)	*Lelonggoran* is based on a 16-beat drumming pattern, called *tari lepas* (hence the name of the piece's form); this section begins quietly and at a slower tempo, as the dancer portrays the reflective, gentle side of impetuous youth, then varies in tempo through nine repetitions of the drumming patterns.
4:01	**Rhythmic cycle #1**	Slows at end of cycle.
4:05	**Rhythmic cycle #2**	Slows then speeds up, with *angsel*.
4:24	**Rhythmic cycle #3**	With *angsel* at 4:28
4:38	**Rhythmic cycle #4**	With *kotekan*
4:47	**Rhythmic cycle #5**	
4:56	**Rhythmic cycle #6**	Transitional, with solo by *ugal* at 5:05
5:09	**Rhythmic cycle #7**	
5:25	**Rhythmic cycle #8**	With *angsel* near end
5:40	**Rhythmic cycle #9**	With *kotekan* and *angsel* near end
5:43	**Kotekan**	
5:47	**Bapang I**	Returns briefly
5:52	Fade-out	Ends at 5:57

new international musical sensitivities and influences to folk music circles. A good example of the way in which African music influenced the folk song movement can be heard in Listening Guide 29 (see page 110). Here a well-known song from the South African *mbube* ("lion," pronounced "em-BOO-bay") repertory, distributed internationally through a 1939 recording, was adapted by the Weavers, a group prominent in the early days of the folk music revival. The Weavers imitated the *falsetto* vocal quality of the original South African singers, but modified the melody, harmony, and rhythm to insure that the song appealed to a Western audience in the mid-1950s.

The folk music revival emerged simultaneously in many urban centers, supported by widely distributed recordings; Boston had a lively folk music scene even before Joan Baez entered Boston University in 1958 (see "**Individual Portraits: Joan Baez**"). By 1960 Boston had become the country's number one folk scene.

Today, two hundred or more venues for live folk music performance are active in the Boston metropolitan area, including Club Passim, the successor to Club 47 in the center of Harvard Square. New clubs are always coming on the scene, such as Irish pubs like Tir na Nog and the Burren, both of which feature newer kinds of contemporary folk music and "roots" music, which draws on a range of American styles from Appalachian fiddling to gospel. The annual Boston Folk Music Festival also provides important public exposure for hundreds of singer-songwriters.

The Folk Song Society of Greater Boston, a non-profit organization of people interested in folk music, was founded during the early years of the folk music

The Weavers, who attained international fame in the folk music revival, were caught up in the political turmoil of 1952 when they were among the many artists accused of being Communists and blacklisted. The group included (left to right) Pete Seeger, Fred Hellerman, Lee Hays, and Ronnie Gilbert.

Joan Baez

Joan Baez was born in Staten Island, New York on January 9, 1941, to a Scottish mother and a Mexican father, both pacifists who took their children with them to Quaker meetings. A minister, research physicist, and consultant to UNESCO, Baez's father eventually moved the family to Boston. At fourteen, Baez began her musical career, accompanying herself on the ukulele (see Chapter 6, "**Sound Sources: The Ukulele**"), singing rhythm and blues songs (such as *Earth Angel*) and country and western songs (such as *Your Cheatin' Heart*). One semester after entering Boston University in 1958, Baez took a job at Club 47—later named Club Passim—and played to standing-room-only crowds who came to hear her "crystal-voiced" renditions of old English and Irish ballads.

Singer Joan Baez performs during a 1965 protest march against the Vietnam war in London's Trafalgar Square.

Performing in coffeehouses and colleges along the East Coast, Baez soon became the "poster girl for folk," making her national debut at the Newport Jazz Festival in 1959. Her performance was released by Vanguard Records in 1960 on an album titled simply "Joan Baez." The festival saw the start of her long working relationship with folk singer/composer Bob Dylan, also then a newcomer.

"I knew that I was the little darling of Newport that year," Baez says now, "I knew that much. That I would be on the front of *Time* magazine within a matter of months, I didn't get that. I didn't have any idea of the magnitude of it." Baez asserts that it was Dylan who turned her into a political folk singer. At the August 28, 1963, March on Washington, Baez sang what became the theme song for the civil rights movement, *We Shall Overcome*. In 1965 she co-founded the Institute for the Study of Nonviolence in Carmel, California, and in 1967 was arrested for civil disobedience during protests against the Vietnam war.

Over thirty albums and countless performances later, Joan Baez still protests against violence, even as her repertory changes. "I never sing *We Shall Overcome* in America anymore," Baez says. "It's just a nostalgia thing here."[35]

LISTENING GUIDE *29*

Wimoweh (South African *mbube*)

CD 1 Tracks 29–30

Date of recordings: **TRACK 29:** 1939
TRACK 30: 1955, recorded at Carnegie Hall
Performers: **TRACK 29:** Solomon Linda's Original Evening Birds, with guitar, piano, and banjo
TRACK 30: The Weavers: Pete Seeger, Fred Hellerman, Lee Hays, Ronnie Gilbert
Tempo: Moderate tempo, quadruple meter
Function: **TRACK 29:** Competition and entertainment; **TRACK 30:** Entertainment

WHAT TO LISTEN FOR:

- *Falsetto,* the "head voice" some male singers use to sing a high pitch with a smooth, light quality
- Western-style harmony, absorbed from Western hymns introduced to Africa by missionaries
- Compare the African model with the Western folk "cover"

TRK 29	STRUCTURE	DESCRIPTION
0:00	Ostinato begins	The basses begin by singing, in unison (monophonically), the repeating patterns in the bassline, called an *ostinato*.
0:10	Call a	The lead singer, or caller, sustains a high pitch and then slides down an octave. More singers join in with a repeating two-part harmony that fills out the polyphonic texture.
0:19		The *ostinato* repeats again, and guitar and banjo enter, heard quite softly in the background. They are largely doubling the two-part repeating vocal harmony. A piano also plays in the background, audible in a few places later in the recording.
0:27	Call b	The caller switches to another call sung in a chest voice a bit lower in his range. Each call is used for two harmonic cycles, or iterations of the *ostinato*.
0:44	Call a	Return to the original falsetto call for two cycles.
1:01	Call b	

1:17	Call a	The caller begins to modify the calls by adding pitches as he moves down the octave at the end of each phrase.
1:34	Call b	This call, too, is modified at the end of the phrase.
1:51	Call a	The singers on the bass and harmony parts switch from the text "uyimbube" to a hum. The hums are accented by the banjo, which attacks each pitch.
2:08	Improvised call c	Instead of call b, as we would expect here, the caller improvises a new melody.
2:16	Call b	One last cycle of call b, with little improvisation, ends the song.
2:29	end of recording	

TRK 30	STRUCTURE	DESCRIPTION
0:00	Ostinato begins	Lee Hays, Fred Hellerman, and Pete Seeger begin by singing, in unison, the repeating *ostinato* bassline, accompanied by Hellerman's guitar and Seeger's banjo to constitute a homophonic texture.
0:08		Hellerman drops off of the bassline and begins singing the two-part repeating harmony with Ronnie Gilbert.
0:16	Call a	Seeger begins calling. Like Solomon Linda, he begins by sustaining a pitch in *falsetto* and then drops an octave into his chest voice. As he repeats the call, he improvises a lip trill (like a rolled 'r', but on the lips instead of on the tongue).
0:32	Call b	Seeger hollers the second call in his chest voice.
0:47	Call a	Returning to the original *falsetto* call for two cycles, Seeger adds improvised ornaments including another extended lip trill.
1:04	Call c	The melody improvised by Solomon Linda at the end of his recording is an essential part of the Weavers' version of the song. This bit of impromptu invention would become widely known as the Weavers popularized the song in the United States. Seeger sings it twice through in *falsetto* here. The banjo crescendos considerably into the next section, signaling to the other musicians that the song will end soon.
1:20	Call b	Two more repetitions of the hollered call b brings the song to a close, called a *cadence*.
1:42	end of recording	

Arabesque Mondays is a monthly event series produced by Karim Nagi Mohammed, featuring Arab and Pan-Eastern music and dance.

The Second Annual
OUD FESTIVAL
featuring
Jon Beberian
Abdul-Wahab Kayyali
Alan Shavarsh Bardezbanian

MONDAY FEB.16 @ 8PM 2004
Club Passim
47 Palmer St. Harvard SQ. Cambridge
$12/ Table Reservations call 617.492.7679

revival in 1958–1959. Today it continues as an active force, issuing a monthly newsletter (*The Folk Letter*) containing a comprehensive listing of all folk music events around town. The Society sponsors concerts, monthly singing parties, informal "midweek sings," and traditional song and tune swaps, where everyone takes turns leading and exchanging songs. Most of the events are held in private homes, and people socialize over refreshments between songs.

The accessible sounds of folk music allow almost anyone to sing along. Folk music performances usually include the audience, which is invited to join in on the well-known refrains of songs. Folk music continues to be attached to a variety of political causes. Mary Travers of the group Peter, Paul, and Mary recalls the social and political associations of folk music from her early days in New York City:

> Folk music was a very integral part of the liberal Left experience. . . . It was writers, sculptors, painters, whatever, listening to Woody Guthrie, Pete Seeger, the Weavers. People sang in Washington Square Park [the "heart" of Greenwich Village] on Sundays, and you really did not have to have a lot of talent to sing folk music. You needed enthusiasm, which is all folk music asks. It asks that you care. . . . So for me it was a social mechanism."[36]

The folk music movement quickly put down deep roots in Boston, and the city itself is memorialized in one of the folk revival's most famous songs. *The*

M.T.A. Song (referring to Boston's Metropolitan Transit Authority) was written for the political campaign of Walter A. O'Brien, Jr., a candidate in Boston's 1949 mayoral race. O'Brien did not win the election—indeed, he finished last—but his catchy campaign song was widely sung by folk musicians and eventually made famous through recordings, radio, and concerts.

The story behind the M.T.A. song (Listening Guide 30, on page 114) is worth recounting here. Candidate O'Brien had objected to a five-cent raise in the M.T.A. fare. Bess Lomax Hawes and Jacqueline Steiner, the campaign workers credited with composing the M.T.A. song, borrowed a well-known melody (taken from an earlier folk song titled *Wreck of the Old 97,* heard in Listening Guide 6) and gave it new lyrics related to the campaign. The process of composing a new song by borrowing an existing melody and providing it with new words is found worldwide, and is particularly common in oral traditions.

During O'Brien's campaign, sound trucks broadcast the M.T.A. song as they traveled through Boston neighborhoods to advertise the campaign. According to his 1998 obituary in the *Boston Globe,* Sam Berman, a musician active in the campaign, recalled: "In those days, political campaigns culminated at a delicatessen in Dorchester, and different campaigns used to try and drown each other out with their sound trucks."

The words of the M.T.A. song map Boston from the perspective of the subway that runs beneath its streets, describing areas of the city that no longer exist. For instance, Scollay Square, mentioned in verse 4, was razed in 1963 to accommodate Boston's Government Center.

The memory of Charlie has been revived recently in Boston with the introduction of the new "CharlieCard," a smart card that can be reused at ticket vending machines and fareboxes, and the "CharlieTicket," a magnetically encoded ticket that contains either stored value or a T pass. In 2005, new equipment was installed throughout the Boston Metropolitan area bus and subway system to accommodate the CharlieTickets and CharlieCards and to ease rider access, a rather ironic commemoration of Charlie, who was never able to get off the train. According to the MBTA website, "A large number of customers suggested CharlieCard. The naming of the card recognizes Charlie's place in Boston's transit history."[37]

The M.T.A. song provides insights into a changing Boston landscape while contributing to its soundscape as well. A third prominent Boston music culture, the early music movement, seeks to revive and perform music traditions from the past.

The underground trains of the Massachusetts Bay Transportation Authority, running on four color-coded lines (red, green, orange, and blue), have been immortalized in *The M.T.A. Song.*

The M.T.A. Song (political campaign song)

CD 1
Track 31

Date of composition: 1949
Composers/lyricists: Jacqueline Steiner and Bess Lomax Hawes
Date of performance: 1959
Performers: The Kingston Trio: Dave Guard, *banjo and vocals*; Bob Shane, *guitar and vocals*; Nick Reynolds, *guitar and vocals, string bass*
Form: Strophic song with refrain
Tempo: Upbeat quadruple meter
Function: Political campaign song; later popularized with new text through recordings and media

WHAT TO LISTEN FOR:

- Catchy refrain and simple strophic form, which ensure that most people who hear the song once or twice can sing along
- Use of spoken text at several points, most notably at the beginning, as well as half-spoken, half-sung *speech-song* in the last verses
- *Blue note*—a flatted-third scale step commonly used in the blues
- References to working-class Boston neighborhoods like Chelsea and Roxbury and once-familiar locations like Scollay Square

STRUCTURE AND TEXT	DESCRIPTION
0:00 **Introduction** **Spoken:** These are the times that try men's souls. In the course of our nation's history, the people of Boston have rallied bravely whenever the rights of men have been threatened. Today, a new crisis has arisen. The Metropolitan Transit Authority, better known as the M.T.A., is attempting to levy a burdensome tax on the population in the form of a subway fare increase. Citizens, hear me out: this could happen to you.	The double-bass sustains long, held pitches by bowing, or shakes the bow to create *tremolo*, while the introductory lyric is spoken.
0:26 **Instrumental introduction**	Guitar accompaniment begins, followed by a syncopated banjo riff on the *blue note*.
0:36 **Verse 1** Well, let me tell you of the story of a man named Charlie On a tragic and fateful day. He put ten cents in his pocket, kissed his wife and family, Went to ride on the M.T.A.	A fairly simple melodic structure makes the tune easy to remember: the first and third phrases of the verse are nearly identical, while the second and fourth are also quite similar to each other.

0:49	**Refrain** Well, did he ever return? No, he never returned, And his fate is still unlearned. He may ride forever 'neath the streets of Boston, He's the man who never returned.	A second singer harmonizes with the lead singer in the refrain. The words "[n]ever returned" are repeated three times in each refrain, and this refrain will itself be repeated five times with small changes. The question-and-answer form of the first line is another effective rhetorical device.
1:02	**Verse 2** Charlie handed in his dime at the Kendall Square station, And he changed for Jamaica Plain. When he got there, the conductor told him one more nickel, Charlie couldn't get off that train.	The singer returns to the blue note at the beginning of the third line and near the end of the fourth line of each verse. In this verse, this occurs on the words "when" and "off that."
1:16	**Refrain**	A third singer adds a comment after the second line of the refrain; this interjection varies with each repetition.
1:29	**Verse 3** Now all night long Charlie rides through the station, Cryin', "What will become of me? How can I afford to see my sister in Chelsea, Or my cousin in Roxbury?"	
1:42	**Refrain**	
1:56	**Verse 4** Charlie's wife goes down to the Scollay Square station Every day at quarter past two; And through the open window, she hands Charlie a sandwich As the train comes rumblin' through!	The singer uses a vocal articulation between speech and song as he shouts out the last two lines of this verse. This technique appears again in verse 5.
2:09	**Refrain**	
2:22	**Banjo solo**	A banjo solo is added to interrupt the regularity of the verse-refrain structure. Syncopation figures prominently in the solo, and the blue note reappears at the end of the solo.
2:35	**Verse 5** Now, ye citizens of Boston! Don't you think it's a scandal, How the people have to pay and pay? Fight for the fare increase! Vote for George O'Brien! Get poor Charlie off the M.T.A.!	Walter O'Brien's name was changed for this recording to avoid any association with his Progressive party. O'Brien was denounced as a communist during the McCarthyite 1950s.
2:48	**Refrain**	The second singer jumps to a higher register to sing a slightly different harmonization for the last repetition of the refrain. The final line is repeated an extra two times to bring the song to a close. Note the spoken "Et tu, Charlie?" at the very end of the track, which concludes at 3:13.

Early Music

The third distinctive Boston soundscape is the lively world of early music, a domain in which musicians play repertories from the past on reconstructed instruments, aspiring to revive the sounds and styles of earlier eras.

Boston provided all the ingredients that allowed early music to flourish. The first center of European music in the United States, the early Boston community supported ensembles such as the Handel and Haydn Society, which was founded by a group of local merchants in 1815 and still survives today.

By the turn of the twentieth century, Boston became a magnet for professional musicians performing European music of earlier eras, many of whom found employment at area educational institutions. Instrument makers such as the harpsichord builder Frank Hubbard and the recorder maker Friedrich von Huene established their workshops in Boston, producing replicas of historical instruments. Musicians began to gravitate to Boston after graduating from music schools elsewhere in the United States and in Europe. Several area colleges, including the New England Conservatory, Boston University, Harvard University, and the Longy School of Music, have offered degrees or certificates in early music, and early music groups are part of the extracurricular musical life on many Boston college campuses. Boston area churches sponsor early music activities as well, particularly sacred music composed in Europe from the Middle Ages through the nineteenth century. Every other June since 1993, The Boston Early Music Festival and Exhibition has attracted thousands for performances, workshops, and exhibitions on all aspects of early music.

The early music movement incorporates music composed at many different times and places in the past, attempting to duplicate how that music might have sounded at the time of its creation. Beyond using reconstructed instruments and playing them in the manner described in historical sources or shown in period paintings, musicians have reinterpreted any musical notation that survives. There is little doubt that many musicians are attracted to the exoticism or "otherness" of the past and enjoy reveling in performances of works that "you read about in history books but never hear."[38] There is a clear paradox involved in the early music culture, since however carefully performers may seek to reconstruct what early music sounded like centuries ago, inevitably their (and their audiences') twenty-first-century ideas and perceptions influence the performance.

Just as we have seen in the case of campus music and folk music cultures, early music ensembles incorporate into their repertories diverse musical styles. The performances heard in

One of Boston's many early music ensembles the King's Noyse brings together a consort of Renaissance stringed instruments with voice. The members include (from bottom, clockwise) David Douglas, Robert Mealy, Scott Metcalfe, Margriet Tindemans, Emily Walhout, and (center) Ellen Hargis.

Listening Guide 31 (see page 118) and Listening Guide 32 (see page 120) of the ballad *Barbara Allen* illustrate how dramatically the early music and folk music cultures can converge.

Barbara Allen is one of the best-loved English ballads, so popular that it has survived until the present in North American oral traditions. The origin of this ballad is unclear, although it may have been a parody of a traditional Scottish ballad, with its text changed to mock in veiled terms the well-known but hated mistress of King Charles II, Barbara Villiers, who died in 1680. Apparently, four basic versions of the text have spread and generated new versions, some influenced by printed English ballad texts called *broadsides,* others transformed as they were transmitted orally in the eastern United States.[39] In Listening Guide 31 you can compare two partial "traditional" versions of *Barbara Allen* recorded in the 1930s by amateur singers and a professional recording from the 1990s by an early music group that seeks to recreate how the ballad might have sounded around the time it was first sung in the seventeenth century. You will hear differences in the texts and tunes of all three renditions as well in their performance styles. Although ballads were often sung without instrumental accompaniment, like the traditional version by Mrs. Bryant in Listening Guide 31 (CD 1/TRACK 32), it was also common to play along with a fiddle (as heard in Mr. Gevedon's rendition in Listening Guide 31, [CD 1/TRACK 33]), banjo, or guitar. In contrast, the early music version in Listening Guide 32, performed by the ensemble the King's Noyse, is accompanied by replicas of instruments dating to seventeenth-century England. Although it is unclear whether such instruments were actually used to accompany ballads in England or Scotland at the time, the King's Noyse has created a version of this ballad that is pleasing to twenty-first-century listeners.

Many early music professionals are interested in cross-cultural musical styles and incorporate them into their performances. For instance, the Boston Camerata has performed and recorded European Christian and Jewish repertories of the Middle Ages and Renaissance, Moroccan musics, and American Shaker music. The director of the Boston Camerata, Joel Cohen, notes, "I'm interested in other cultures besides European, but the only ones in which I'm personally happy is where I can feel like there's something that I share with the other culture."[40]

One of the most interesting examples of the connection between early music and cross-cultural musical styles can be found in the history and *performance practice* (that is, performing style) of Voice of the Turtle, an early music ensemble with deep Boston roots.

This quartet, formally established in 1978, began as part of Quadrivium, an eclectic early music group founded in Cambridge in 1967. Quadrivium's countercultural stance in its early years included all-night sessions featuring close

Barbara Allen (Anglo-American ballad, two traditional, partial performances)

CD 1 Tracks 32–33

Date of recording: **TRACK 32:** 1938
TRACK 33: 1930s
Performers: **TRACK 32:** Mrs. T. M. Bryant, Evansville, Indiana
TRACK 33: Mr. Monroe Gevedon, West Liberty, Kentucky
Form: Strophic ballad
Tempo: Moderate
Function: Entertainment

WHAT TO LISTEN FOR:

- Differences in song text transmitted by oral tradition
- Syllabic text settings, with each syllable of text sung to one pitch
- Distinctive vocal styles without vibrato
- Variations in performance practice, with the second rendition sung slightly faster than the first, with fiddle interludes

TRK 32	TEXT TRACK 32	TRK 33	TEXT TRACK 33	DESCRIPTION
		0:00		introduction in fiddle
0:00	It was in the merry month of May, And the buds on the trees were swelling. Sweet William on his death bed lay, For the love of Barbry Allen.	0:12	Was early in the month of May, When the May buds, they were swelling. Sweet William on his death bed lay, For the love of Barbry Allen.	**TRACK 32** and **TRACK 33:** a a b a phrase structure **TRACK 33:** verse sung without accompaniment
		0:26		**TRACK 33:** Fiddle verse
0:16	He sent his servant into town, To the place where she was dwelling. Saying, "My master sent me here for you, If your name be Barbry Allen."	0:38	He sent his servant to the town, The place where she was dwelling. My master say, "Can you come to quick? If your name be Barbry Allen."	**TRACK 32** and **TRACK 33:** second verse repeats the melody of the first. **TRACK 33:** second verse also sung unaccompanied.
0:33		0:53		Recording ends.

listening coupled with techniques of yoga and meditation. The group's public performances were infused with ritual and heavily choreographed. Initially, the Quadrivium and its offspring ensemble, Voice of the Turtle, performed all types of medieval and Renaissance music as well as folk music of American and European origin. While working on songs of the Spanish Renaissance during 1973–1974, one member of the group came across published versions of Spanish songs still being transmitted in the twentieth century through oral tradition by descendants of late-fifteenth-century Jewish exiles from Spain, known as Sephardic Jews. These songs, with words in Judeo-Spanish dialects, were still sung by Sephardic Jews wherever they lived. Judeo-Spanish songs became Voice of the Turtle's central repertory.

Voice of the Turtle emphasizes the historical Mediterranean roots of their Judeo-Spanish songs by accompanying them on guitar, the Middle Eastern *'ud*, and an array of Middle Eastern string and percussion instruments. The group further attempts to keep vocal and instrumental styles within a range they feel is consistent with those of the Mediterranean and Middle Eastern regions.

Most of the Judeo-Spanish songs were transmitted by women, and the song included here (in Listening Guide 33; see page 122) is sung as a female solo. This traditional Judeo-Spanish lullaby is sung in the "straight" vocal style often heard in the early music movement, without much vibrato. The guitar has been prominent for several centuries in Spain, but its use here was more likely influenced by the American folk music revival.

Barbara Allen (English ballad)

CD 1
Track 34

Date of composition: c. 1660s
Date of performance: 1997
Performers: *The King's Noyse:* David Douglass, *director and violin;* Ellen Hargis, *voice;* Robert Mealy, *violin and viol;* Scott Metcalfe, *viol;* Paul O'Dette, *lute;* Jane Starkman, *viol;* Emily Walhout, *bass viol*
Form: Strophic song
Tempo: Moderately slow; triple meter

WHAT TO LISTEN FOR:

- Adoption of seventeenth-century English pronunciation and a clear, "straight" vocal tone commonly used by singers of early music
- Simple, chordal style of lute accompaniment that varies over the course of the piece, resulting in a homophonic texture
- Use of *viols*, bowed chordophones that were used in Europe from the fifteenth to the eighteenth centuries
- Expressive changes in dynamics and tempos from verse to verse
- Triple meter and phrases that begin just before the strong beat
- *Syllabic* text setting of a poem with *iambic* (short-long) poetic meter

	STRUCTURE AND TEXT	DESCRIPTION
0:00	In Scarlet Town where I was bound, There was a fair maid dwelling, Whom I had chosen for my own, Her name, it was Barbara Allen.	The song is unaccompanied for the first verse, resulting in a monophonic texture. Note the melodic "rhyme" at the end of the second and fourth lines.
0:22	**Instrumental verse**	The same melody is played by viols, with lute accompaniment.
0:42	All in the merry month of May, When green leaves they was springing, This young man on his death-bed lay, For the love of Barbara Allen.	The voice returns, and the viols drop out. The singer is accompanied by a lute, which emphasizes the first and third beats of each measure. The song is strictly strophic, so the musical structure is identical for each stanza of text.

1:02 He sent his man unto her then,
To the town where she was dwelling,
"You must come to my master dear,
If your name be Barbara Allen.

1:21 "For death is printed in his face,
And sorrow's in him dwelling.
And you must come to my master dear,
If your name be Barbara Allen.

1:39 "If death be printed in his face,
And sorrow's in him dwelling,
Then little better shall he be
For bonny Barbara Allen."

1:58 So slowly, slowly she got up,
So slowly she came to him,
And all she said when she came there,
"Young man, I think you're a-dying."

Viols join the lute to accompany the singer. To reflect the meaning of the words, the singer adopts a slightly different vocal quality, the tempo slows down, and the musicians pause slightly before beginning this verse.

2:19 He turn'd his face unto her then,
"If you be Barbara Allen,
My dear," said he, "come pity me,
As on my death-bed I am lying."

2:38 "If on your death-bed you be lying,
What's that to Barbara Allen?
I cannot keep you from your death,
So farewell," said Barbara Allen.

The singer adopts a slightly brighter vocal quality to suggest Barbara Allen's defiance.

2:56 He turn'd his face unto the wall,
And Death came creeping to him;
"Then adieu, adieu and adieu to all,
And adieu to Barbara Allen."

3:18 **Instrumental verse, with fade-out at 3:26.**

Durme, Durme ("Sleep, Sleep," Judeo-Spanish lullaby)

CD 1 Track 35

Date of recording: 1996

Performers: *Voice of the Turtle:* Judith Wachs, *voice;* Jay Rosenberg, *'ud;* Derek Burrows, *guitar*

Source: Arrangement based on a field recording of a Bulgarian Sephardic woman now preserved in the archives of Israeli radio station *Kol Yisrael*

Form: Verse-refrain song form

Mode: Western minor

Tempo: Moderately slow, quadruple meter

Function: Lullaby

WHAT TO LISTEN FOR:

- The unusual combination of voice, guitar, and *'ud,* reflecting early music performance practices incorporating instruments related (however distantly) to the time and place of the song's origin
- A vocal style sometimes described as a "straight tone," with very little vibrato, commonly associated with singers of early music
- Narrow vocal range
- The contrast between strummed chords in the guitar and the melody plucked on the *'ud*
- The sound of the Judeo-Spanish language, also called Ladino, which was spoken by Sephardic Jews who were forced to leave Spain following the Spanish Inquisition. Judeo-Spanish dialects preserve many aspects of fifteenth-century Spanish as well as Hebrew words

Boston's Distinctive Musical Profile

All three of our major Boston soundscapes—college music, folk music, and early music—are both local and international, with deep roots in Boston as well as connections to other places. All three were at some point in their histories derived from European musical styles and institutions, yet came to incorporate the widest array of instruments and repertories from around the world, past and present.

STRUCTURE AND TEXT	TRANSLATION	DESCRIPTION
0:00 Refrain		A brief chordal guitar introduction lasts two measures of four beats each. When the singer enters, she is supported by a simple, strummed guitar accompaniment.
Section A		
Durme, durme, kirido ijiko,	Sleep my beautiful child,	
Durme sin ansia i dolor.	Sleep without worry or pain.	
Uuu, hai, hai, hai.	Oooh, live, live, live.	
Section B		In section B, the lowered pitch on the first syllable of the word *savor* inflects the melody toward a Middle Eastern pitch system.
Serra tus luzius ujikoz	Close your radiant eyes	
Durme, durme con savor.	And sleep comfortably.	
Section B		
Serra tuz luzius ujikoz	Close your radiant eyes	
Durme, durme con savor.	And sleep comfortably	
1:02 Verse		The 'ud enters, adding a melodic "comment" to the end of the first line of this verse. On the third and fourth lines of the verse, the 'ud follows the voice closely in a heterophonic texture. The lowered pitch in section B here falls on the second syllable of the word *ambezaraz*.
Section C		
De la kuna saliraz,	From the cradle you will go,	
A la shkola tu entreraz	Into school you will enter.	
Section B		
I tu ayi, mi kirido iziko,	And there, my beloved son,	
A meldar te ambezaraz.	You will begin to read [Torah].	
1:34 Refrain		
2:26 Instrumental interlude		Fade-out at 2:30.

Of these three soundscapes, the campus music scene is the most heterogeneous; every campus maintains its own diverse and often multicultural world of music. At the same time, manifestations of both early music and folk music are incorporated into the soundscapes of individual colleges.

Most unified in its sound and musical style is the music of the folk revival, with strophic song forms, guitar accompaniments, and catchy melodies well suited to oral transmission and to the abilities of amateur singers. Many of the songs of the folk music revival are closely tied to the moment or place at which they were first sung. These songs have great meaning to many as the music of their youth, as a call to political action, and as a sonic symbol of human rights. At the same time, music from a wide range of cultures has enriched the folk music repertory, just as famous songs and singers that emerged from the Boston folk music scene have become international icons.

The special sound of instruments, vocal styles, and repertories from the past characterize the early music movement, while its boundaries frequently cross over those with folk music and various ethnic music traditions. At the same time, the folk music and early music soundscapes share, along with other campus music traditions, a countercultural edge. Folk music often displays its resistance in the texts of its songs, while the early music movement differentiates itself from standard Western classical traditions by reviving older instruments, exploring historical performance practices, and reviving neglected musical styles. In cross-cultural campus musical ensembles such as the *gamelan*, "difference" is manifested both in novel musical sounds and in the interactive manner of learning and performing that music tradition.

It appears likely that Boston's status as a university town par excellence allowed it to become a congenial home for both folk music and early music. Boston therefore has a distinctive and somewhat paradoxical musical profile; it was the historic center and transmitter of European musical culture in North America, but it has also provided a home for the diverse, alternative, and often resistant soundscapes of the campus music, folk music, and early music worlds.

Conclusion

As you think about the very different soundscapes of Boston, Accra, and Mumbai, consider making some investigations of your own. What are the major soundscapes of the city, town, or campus in which you live and which contribute to a distinctive local musical profile? Which local soundscapes are part of a broader regional, national, or global network?

You can begin to map the soundscapes of your own city or campus musical life by asking the same series of questions (what, who, where, when, why) we used in the Boston case study. To facilitate this process, begin keeping a journal, listing and describing any music traditions you encounter in the course of your daily life.

Studying all the music of a given locality can present a formidable challenge, although the discovery process can provide a wonderful introduction to the place in which you live. Once you are familiar with a place, you will want to focus more deeply on a particular soundscape. In this way, you can come to appreciate more fully the significance music carries in human life, our subject in Chapter 3.

IMPORTANT TERMS

agbadza
atumpan
ballad
beating tones
bhajan
broadsides
buskers
early music
fado
falsetto

filmi git
folk music
folk music revival
gamelan
ghazal
gong kebyar
highlife
interlocking parts
   (*kotekan*)

mbube
playback song/singers
qanun
rhythmic cycle
tizita
'ud
vocalise

Chapter 3

Significance: Music's Meaning in Everyday Life

A Mexican mariachi ensemble plays at a televised tribute to Pope John Paul II, as an empty chair stands at the right of the forecourt of the Basilica of Guadalupe in Mexico City, April 8, 2005. Mexicans gathered at churches around the country to hold masses timed to coincide with the Pope's funeral.

Overview

Main Points

Music's meaning:

- is shaped by the sounds and settings of musical performance.

- can persist across different musical genres and settings.

- is different for different individuals.

- can change over time.

Introduction

Talking about music's significance can spark lively discussions, because music is able to elicit many ideas and emotions at the same time. Music's ability to communicate a range of meanings, to signify, helps shape our perceptions of music's importance in our lives. Significance therefore provides a dual framework for exploring both music's meaning and its importance within and between soundscapes.

Music can convey meaning, or signify, in three different ways.[1] The first is sound's ability to imitate or to refer to other sounds, drawing on sonic characteristics held in common. A good example, discussed in the Introduction, is the ability of a *khoomii* singer, to mimic sounds of the natural environment, such as the bubbling of running water in a stream or the galloping of a horse on the open plain.

Sound can also signify entities or ideas. One example would be the association of a *sabar* drum rhythm, such as the *Lenëën bàkk* (which we encountered in Listening Guide 12 and Listening Guide 16), with a specific family of musicians in Dakar, Senegal. Another example is the association of the sound of the Armenian double-reed aerophone, the *duduk,* heard in Listening Guide 9, with Armenian identity. In both these examples, sound becomes an icon, a likeness of something else related by association to the phenomenon it represents.

Musical sound can also communicate specific meanings within individual cultures or subcultures. This third type of signification is more typical of language, but music can, on occasion, speak as well, as we have seen in the case of the Ghanaian talking drum, the Asante *atumpan,* in Listening Guide 20.

Music most often conveys meaning in the second way, by association, as an outcome of the interaction between sounds as well as between sound and aspects of social and cultural settings existing beyond the music. For an example we can return to the M.T.A. song discussed in Chapter 2 (Listening Guide 30), which carries different meanings depending on the listener's perceptions of the song's sound, knowledge of its performance settings, and familiarity with its history. For instance, one listener might recognize the folk song *Wreck of the Old 97* (see Listening Guide 6) from which the M.T.A. song's melody was borrowed, perceiving the newer song in the light of its traditional roots. Another person might recall the M.T.A. song from its genesis during the 1949 O'Brien campaign in Boston and interpret the song in relation to a political message. A third individual, perhaps a fan of the Kingston Trio or a participant in the folk music revival, may recognize the popular recorded version of the M.T.A. song heard in Listening Guide 30 and simply enjoy the droll story narrated in its text. All of these meanings—and no doubt many more—are potentially conveyed by the song. It is the individual listener who experiences the sound and interprets it in a particular way, ultimately constructing the meaning of the song according to highly variable factors ranging from prior experience to personal idiosyncrasies. The relative importance of the M.T.A. song to an individual listener is to a great extent determined by his or her understandings of the song's meaning, as well as by perceptions of the song's value to others within the same soundscape.

As in our previous discussions of sound and setting, we will again turn whenever possible to musicians for insights into what music means to them. However, our task here is complicated in two ways. First, although music is often casually compared to speech, only in rare instances (such as the Ghanaian drum language heard in Listening Guide 20) is a specific idea linked to a specific musical sound. Music clearly has the capacity to convey meaningful content, but exactly how this is accomplished and what meanings are constructed remain sources of some controversy.

Second, we cannot always depend on language about music gathered during interviews or comments made during performance to explain musical meaning. A great deal of musical knowledge is transmitted nonverbally. Observations of musicmaking and our personal experience as listeners confirm that music has deep significance to participants and listeners alike. But sometimes we are left speechless by a musical experience, unable to articulate its power, let alone describe music's precise meaning in words.

In everyday human experience, sound and setting combine in many different ways to generate musical meaning, as the case studies in this chapter will demonstrate. Shared experiences shape our understandings of music, even when we listen alone to a recording. In this chapter, we begin our discussion by first considering the significance of the South Indian *raga nilambari* across different musical repertories over the course of centuries. In the case of this *raga*, we are fortunate to have extensive historical information and present-day testimony about the significance of these sounds, enabling us to link the music to widely shared notions of its meaning and importance.

We will also explore music associated with a coming-of-age ceremony, the *quinceañera*, which marks the fifteenth birthday of a Latina woman. Here heterogeneous musical content helps convey the multiple significances of this important milestone. In the case of the *quinceañera*, musical meaning emerges from a series of associations aroused by diverse musical ingredients.

The major case study for this chapter discusses the multiple meanings associated with the bagpipe, an instrument popular in many soundscapes around the world. Here we find that the same bagpipe music conveys different meanings in different times, places, and circumstances. In some settings, the distinctive sounds of the bagpipe generate multiple meanings at once, in part through its sheer sonic impact on the mind and body of the listener.

Musical ethnography underscores the difficulty of trying to pin down musical meaning. There may be moments when the significance of music appears clear or unambiguous—for instance, when a country's national anthem is sung at the beginning of a political event, or played during the medal ceremonies at the Olympic Games. Yet even in these circumstances, when music is used to signify national unity or pride, a whole host of hidden historical, political, and personal meanings may be simultaneously evoked, as we will see in a case study of the South African national anthem in Chapter 9. Some of these meanings may be stable over long periods of time and widely shared; others may change rapidly. Certain meanings may be of great importance to some but disputed or rejected by others. In short, we must always take into account music's potential range of meanings and its importance to musicians and listeners alike.[2]

In Chapters 1 and 2, we explored the manner in which sound and setting interact as music is performed. A specific combination of sounds in a particular setting, along with our memories of past hearings and expectations for future performances, triggers our perceptions of music's significance in this moment. Repeated encounters with music under the same circumstances can lead us to associate music with a particular range of meanings.

CASE STUDY: South Indian *Raga Nilambari*

Music sometimes carries such strong associations that it transmits the same meanings across a wide array of music traditions and settings. *Raga nilambari* provides a striking example within South Indian [Karnatak] soundscapes. In Chapter 1, in the discussion of the North Indian [Hindustani] *Rag Des* in Listening Guide 10, we learned that *raga* is the Indian system for organizing melodies according to their distinctive pitch content and their range of associations. *Raga*s vary in their names and musical content between the North and South Indian traditions.

*Raga*s may be associated with the time of day when they are performed (morning, afternoon, or evening *raga*s), or according to the season of the year with which they are linked (the monsoon season, for example). Additionally, each *raga* also has emotional connotations, understood within an aesthetic system known as *rasa,* from a Sanskrit word meaning "juice, essence, or flavor."[3] The sound of a *raga* therefore conveys meanings on both experiential and emotional levels.

Musicians perform a particular *raga* on the occasions with which that *raga* is associated. Our example, *raga nilambari,* is so closely associated with lullabies that it is known as "the lullaby *raga*" in South India and the South Indian diaspora. So close is the association of *raga nilambari* with sleep that any melody in this *raga* may be sung as a lullaby.

Raga nilambari can best be represented in Indian *sargam* notation, which we encountered in our discussion of the North Indian *Rag Des* in Chapter 1 (Listening Guide 10). *Sargam* notation provides names for seven main scale degrees in ascending order—*Sa Ri Ga Ma Pa Dha Ni*—a system similar but not identical to the Western notion of scale. Each scale degree within a *raga* is termed a *svara,* which identifies both its particular place or position within a melody and the way in which it is combined with a type of ornament called a *gamaka.* The *tonic* or first and most prominent *svara, Sa,* and *Pa,* the fifth *svara,* are fixed in their pitch level. In performances with instrumental accompaniment, *Sa* and *Pa* are usually reinforced by a drone, sometimes played by a plucked string instrument called a *tambura.* The remaining five *svaras* are flexible; their precise articulations, attacks and releases, and ornamentation vary according to their position and context in the particular *raga.*

Like many other *ragas, nilambari* has some variation in *svara* order for ascending (*aroha*) and descending (*avaroha*) melodic motion. These characteristic patterns and the emphasis on specific intervals and ornaments signal listeners that they are hearing *raga nilambari.* Note that contrasting melodic patterns differentiate the ascent from the descent—for instance, ascending *nilambari* often skips from *Ma* up to *Dha,* then down to *Pa,* and back up to *Dha* before continuing to ascend through *Ni* to the upper *Sa.* There are two forms of the seventh *svara, Ni,* one lower, the other inflected close to the upper tonic, *Sa.* On the descent, *Dha* is often omitted, creating a gap; note too, that the descending motion often incorporates a move back up to *Ga* before skipping down to *Sa.* The skip from *Ga* to *Sa* on the descent becomes a clear sonic marker for *raga nilambari.*

Ascent: *Sa Ri Ga Ma Dha Pa Dha Ni Sa*

Descent: *Sa Ni Pa Ma Ga Ri Ga Sa*

Raga nilambari is used mainly by those who have a classical music education or who belong to particular classes (castes) of South Indian society. The lullaby heard in Listening Guide 34, (*Araro Ariraro;* see page 132), is performed by Mrs. Jeyalakshmi Sundar, a South Indian Brahmin woman born in Turaviman village, located near Madurai, in Tamil Nadu state. Trained as a teacher, Mrs. Jeyalakshmi has lived in Albertson, New York since emigrating from Madras with her husband in 1984. She sang this lullaby regularly to her two children.

The Tamil word for lullaby is *talattu* (pronounced "TAH-lah-tu"), which means "tongue rocking," an expression borne out by the use of syllables known as vocables that do not convey literal meaning. In this lullaby, the vocables *"araro ariraro"* symbolize the motion of rocking a crying child.

Mrs. Jeyalakshmi describes *Araro Ariraro* as a "folk song that has been heard and sung for generations and generations." She explains:

This was sung by my mother and grandmother for all the children. My mother had thirteen children. It's a giant family, all my brothers grew up hearing this—my brothers, their wives, and children. So we sang for all those years and I sang for my children. And I have two sisters—one lives in Detroit—she also sings the same song and my sister back home, she also sings. But I really don't know how much the other generation will pick up. Maybe my daughter will sing for her children.[4]

Araro Ariraro (South Indian lullaby)

CD 1
Track 36

Composer: Unknown
Date composed: Unknown, but transmitted for at least three generations
Date recorded: June 24, 2004
Performers: Mrs. Jeyalakshmi Sundar
Mode (*raga*): *Nilambari*
Function: Lullaby

WHAT TO LISTEN FOR:

- The vocables "*araro ariraro,*" commonly used for lullabies, imitating the way babies cry
- The free rhythm shaped by meaningful text in the Tamil language
- The melodic content and contours of *raga nilambari,* which differs in its pitch content and order on the ascent and descent (Ascending: Sa Ri Ga Ma Dha Pa Dha Ni Sa; Descending: Sa Ni Pa Ma Ga Ri Ga Sa).

	STRUCTURE AND TEXT	TRANSLATION	DESCRIPTION
0:00	**Phrase a** araro ariraro arirari araro		Vocables
0:13	**Phrase b** arirarira raro		Vocables
	sri ramachandiraro	Sri Ramachandran	The name of the god.
0:31	**Phrase c** arirandum kaveri adan naduve sri rangam	Sri Rangam is located in between the two sections of the river Cauvery	Text begins praise of gods.
0:41	**Phrase d** sri rangamadi kanne ni tiruppar kadaladi	Sri Rangam, rocking, dear, you are "The Great Ocean of Milk" where Vishnu sleeps, rocking	

Araro Ariraro tells of a woman's efforts to conceive a child and the ways in which all the members of her extended family coddle the baby. The lullaby begins with the story of the island town Sri Rangam in Tamil Nadu, located where two sections of the Cauvery River flow together. A place that honors the god Vishnu and where the god is said to sleep, Sri Rangam is described as

0:56	**Phrase a'** mamangamadi ni madurai kadaladi	You are the "Ocean of Madurai" the river Vaigai during Mamangam, rocking	*Mamangam* occurs every twelve years during the full moon in March, when tides are high in all bodies of water; overflowing water is considered auspicious.
1:08	**Phrase b** taipusamadi ni davam ceydu vandaracho	During Taipucam you came, as a result of my having performed austerities	The *Taipucam* holiday honors the god Murugan.
1:24	**Phrase c'** patti adichalo pal pottum sangale	If grandma hits you, it will be with the conch-shaped spoon with which she feeds you milk	Here the text is similar to words of other lullabies.
1:32	**Phrase d** chitti adichalo sirattum kaiyale	If your *chitti* hits you, it will be with the hand with which she demonstrates affection for you	*Chitti* is a maternal aunt or paternal uncle's wife.
1:45	**Phrase a'** mami adichalo mallihaippu sendale	If your *mami* hits you, it will be with a ball of jasmine flowers	*Mami* is a maternal uncle's wife.
1:56	**Phrase b** attai adichalo aralippu sendale	If your *attai* hits you, it will be with a ball of oleander flowers	*Attai* is a paternal aunt.
2:10	**Phrase c''** yar aditta kanniru arayperuharadu	The tears from which who hit you? swell like a river	
2:18	**Phrase d** aray peruhi amellam odaradu	swelling like a river they flow throughout the house	
2:33	End of recording		

"heaven on earth." The song text refers to the *Mamangam,* an observance that takes place every twelve years in March when the full moon causes high tides. At that time, an image of the deity Krishna is placed in a tank of water at the temple, and women who wish to bear children immerse themselves in the tank. The first part of the song recounts the tale of a woman unable to

Jeyalakshmi Sundar discusses the text for the lullaby *Araro Ariraro* during a recording session in June, 2004, at her home in Albertson (in Long Island, New York) with the author and ethnomusicologist Richard Wolf.

C. Saroja and C. Lalitha, known professionally as "the Bombay sisters" since they lived in Bombay (Mumbai) at one point, have published a compact disc of lullabies with the title *Thalattu Paadagal,* "Lullaby Songs"; their recording contains one lullaby in *raga nilambari.*

conceive who immerses herself in the tank and then conceives. The song stresses the image of overflowing water, its connection to fertility, and God's role in the conception of the child whom the mother is now lulling to sleep.

The mother tells the crying child that "After all the penance I did, I got you." She next asks, "Why are you crying?" describing how the baby is always passed around from arm to arm, cuddled, and playfully hit by doting relatives with the conch-shaped spoon used to feed him, as well as with buds of jasmine and oleander flowers. The final verse returns to the image of water from the beginning of the song, again asking the baby why he is crying, and telling him that his "tears swell like a river, flowing through the house."

In South India, lullabies are sung in homes as well as distributed on commercial recordings. While other *raga*s are also used for lullabies, Mrs. Jeyalakshmi says that "if you sing in *nilambari*, it is mostly a lullaby." Thus a particular *raga* is considered to have a specific effect on the body (see page 136, "**Studying Music: The Effect of Music on the Body**").

The strong associations between *raga nilambari* and the act of lulling a baby to sleep extends to South Indian rituals: The *raga* is thought to have the same sleep-inducing impact on deities as it does on humans. Today, *raga nilambari* is played in Hindu temples in South India on the *nagasvaram*, a double-reed aerophone.[5] During rituals in the temple, the *nagasvaram* accompanies moments when the deity is awakened, bathed, or put to sleep.

Outside the Hindu Temple, one can hear *raga nilambari* in many settings, including compositions by South Indian composers with texts that refer to the *raga*'s significance as a lullaby for the gods. For instance, there is a well-known devotional song (termed a *bhajan* or *kirtanam*) in *nilambari* by Tyagaraja (1767–1847), perhaps the most famous composer of South Indian classical music, which describes putting the God Rama to sleep. In Listening Guide 35 (see page 138), we hear a *kirtanam* (also called a *kriti*) composed by Ponniah Pillai in the early nineteenth century, titled *Amba Nilambari,* which is still popular today as a concert piece. This *kriti*'s text praises the deity Amba, to whom the singer pledges undying devotion. *Amba Nilambari* illustrates that the expressive possibilities of *nilambari* extend beyond its use in lullabies or explicit connections with sleep, although it continues to carry that significance on some level for the knowledgeable listener. Indeed, the famous South Indian violinist, Dr. L. Subramaniam, recalls that "his earliest memory of anything" was his mother singing *Amba Nilambari* every day to put him to sleep.[6]

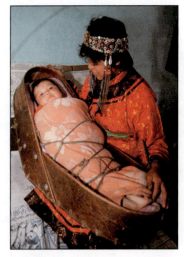

Lullabies are sung in most societies. Here a woman in Shibazhan, China, sings to her son, who is secured in a traditional wooden cradle.

In contrast to the free rhythm of the lullaby *Araro Ariraro* in Listening Guide 34, the rhythmic framework for the classical *kriti* in Listening Guide 35 is a *tala*. *Tala* is an Indian term denoting time cycles consisting of a fixed number of counts. These cycles are subdivided into units with different numbers of beats, sometimes of irregular lengths. The actual rhythms sung or played can vary greatly within a particular *tala* cycle. Listening Guide 35 is in *Tala Adi,* an eight-beat *tala,* one of the most commonly heard *talas* in South India. In *Amba Nilambari, Tala*

T. Viswanathan, the accomplished South Indian flutist heard playing and singing in Listening Guide 35, is seen here performing with his wife, Jody Cormack, who is accompanying him on the tambura. The small black object in the foreground is a *sruti* box, an electrophone which sounds a drone.

The Effect of Music on the Body

As we think about the significance of music within a particular cultural context, it is important first to consider which aspects of musical meaning are shared across cultural boundaries. The lullaby provides a particularly rich example, given its existence in many cultures. Lullabies share many musical characteristics: They are often set in a higher range than other songs, they contain a great deal of internal repetition, and they often incorporate *vocables* within their texts. Lullabies tend to be slow and are commonly sung in combination with rocking motions. In their union of song and bodily motion, lullabies provide an excellent example of *musical entrainment,* an expression used by psychologists to refer to the alignment of bodily motion during the musical experience. Studies have shown that musical entrainment can both help regularize motion and modify a person's physical state. All of us can think of examples of musical entrainment in our own lives, such as using music to enhance repetitive motion during work or workouts, or slowing down our heart rates and relaxing as we drift off to sleep.[7]

Beyond the phenomenon of musical entrainment, there appear to be other factors shaping the effects of lullabies in all cultures. A recent comparative study of maternal singing in several cultures found that lullabies are closely related to speech and replicate the higher pitch, repeating patterns, and slow pace commonly used when talking to babies (so-called "baby talk").[8] Presumably, the historical association of *raga nilambari* with sleep in the South Indian tradition has been enhanced by a performance style demonstrated to induce sleep in all cultures.

Adi subdivides the eight-beat rhythmic units into combinations of 4+2+2 beats, stated and elaborated on by the South Indian double-headed drum, the *mrdangam.* Note that the *mrdangam* provides not just a rhythmic framework, but also subtle alterations of pitch, sounded when the player presses the heel of his hand on the central membrane of the drum. This effect is also enhanced by putting a paste of cream of wheat or similar substance on the center of the drumhead, which lends the drum's sound added weight and depth.

Lullabies share a particular vocal quality, repetition, and a slow tempo, but they also reflect traditions shaped by broader patterns maintained over the course of generations. Thus they transmit images with culturally specific significance within particular ethnic or linguistic communities. But lullabies can also be newly composed by a creative singer or adapted from a popular song, leading to situations in which a song's repeated use as a lullaby may create unique associations within a unit as small as one family. One common example in Christian communities is the use of Christmas carols about the baby Jesus, such as *Away in a Manger* or *Silent Night,* as lullabies.

The lullaby is just one example of music performed to effect a change of mood or consciousness, in this case to calm a child or to induce sleep. Many studies of music have noted its apparent ability to alter mental states or even to induce trance. Some researchers hypothesized that the repetitive nature of musical sound causes brain waves to trigger an altered state.[9] More recently, this theory has been rejected, and trance is now regarded as a culturally conditioned response based on longtime association between a particular musical event and the expectation that it will produce a particular state of body and mind.[10] Although people universally acknowledge music's power to influence emotions, shape behavior, and even heal, scholars have not fully explained how music is perceived and processed within the brain. New technologies and recent advances in psychological research should provide new perspectives on the interaction between the cultural and physiological dimensions of music.

Raga nilambari provides a clear instance of a consistent meaning conveyed by music over long periods of time as well as across different repertories and broad geographical areas; our next case study provides a strong contrast. It focuses on a ceremony in which multiple heterogeneous musical styles without a single historical or aesthetic source become meaningful as a result of their performance on the same occasion by the same musicians, giving rise to shared significance.

LISTENING GUIDE 35

Amba Nilambari ("Oh, Mother Clad in Blue")

CD 1
Track 37

Composer: Sri Ponniah Pillai
Date composed: Early 19th century
Date recorded: March 15, 2001
Performers: T. Viswanathan, flute and voice
    David Nelson, *mrdangam*
    Kala Prasad, supporting vocal
    Susan Tveekrem, *tambura*
Form: *Kriti* with four main sections: *pallavi, anupallavi, citta-svaram, and caranam*
Meter (tala): *Adi tala* (4+2+2)
Mode (raga): *Nilambari*
Function: Devotional piece, also played in concert

WHAT TO LISTEN FOR:

- The four-part polyphonic texture with flute, drum, and voice(s) supported by a drone on plucked lute (*tambura*)
- The melodic content and contours of *raga nilambari,* heard also in Listening Guide 34
- The regular eight-beat cycle of *tala adi,* usually subdivided 4+2+2

	STRUCTURE AND TEXT	TRANSLATION	DESCRIPTION
0:00			Enter *tambura* drone.
0:14			Enter flute.
0:28			Enter *mrdangam,* establishing *tala adi.*
0:38	*Pallavi* begins (sagari) Amba		Enter female voice at a very low decibel level.
0:47	nilam —		Flute stops.
0:50	bari	Oh, mother clad in blue	Flutist (a male voice) joins in singing.
1:00	ananda sagari	Oh, ocean of bliss	

1:10	amba nilam . . .	Oh, mother clad in blue	Repeat of first *pallavi* phrase as transition to *anupallavi*.

1:20	*Anupallavi* begins
	Ambujakshi nidu
	  padambujamula
	  neranammiti
		I take refuge in your lotus feet
		  (i.e I surrender to you)
			Two new lines of text, rhymes with text of *pallavi*.

1:34	(Verse repeated)		Flutist resumes playing; female singer continues, repeating prior verse.

1:47	Ambarishu modalu ninnu
	  pogadaga Adharamaina
	  Brihannaiyaki
		Starting with the sage
		  Ambarisha, you have been
		  universally extolled, oh
		  illustrious leader of the
		  entire world	

2:00	(Verse repeated)		Emphatic drum pattern
2:12	*Citta-Svaram* begins Sa Pa Pa ni Pa Pa ma Ga Pa ma Ga Sa etc . . .		Sung to Indian solfège syllables: (Sa, ri, ga, ma, pa, da, ni). Voice accompanied by flute and drum; melody similar to that of *Pallavi*, rhythm also reflects vocalist's movement.
2:52	Amba nilam—		Voice and flute cadence.
3:03			Instrumental interlude in drum and flute.

3:16	*Caranam* begins
	I dharanu ni sari samanamika
	  ledhanuchu nay gacimari
		Believing you are without
		  equal in the universe	

3:30	(Verse repeated)		

3:43	Madhava sodariyani nay
	  pilachite
		When I call you. Oh sister of
		  Madhava (Krishna)
			Flute stops and flute player rejoins female singer.

	Vinula sunta vinarada	Why do you not listen to me?	
3:56	Fade-out; recording ends at 4:02		

CASE STUDY: The *Quinceañera*

Life is marked by musical occasions. Music and singing enrich our childhood years, providing both entertainment and a pathway to social and cultural knowledge. People in many soundscapes celebrate birthdays with rousing renditions of the song *Happy Birthday to You*, associated with that occasion in the United States since at least the 1920s. The song subsequently spread worldwide, as illustrated by its use in Accra churches to mark members' birthdays. Celebrations mark other special moments, such as religious occasions and school graduations, which are almost always enhanced by familiar music.

The passage through puberty into adulthood is a critical transition celebrated by rituals in virtually every society. All such transitional moments entail a change of status of some sort, but the rites surrounding the physical and social transformations that mark stages of development in the teenage years are particularly significant because they celebrate the future potential—social, cultural, and physical—of a family and a community. These events include music and dance, providing important opportunities for expressing emotion and for celebration. The combination of music and event also gives rise to powerful constellations of meaning.

One celebration with strong musical content is *la quinceañera* (pronounced "la keen-say-on-YEAH-ra"), a tradition celebrated in Latino communities in North, South, and Central America that marks the passage of teenage girls into adulthood. Usually held within a few days of the girl's fifteenth birthday, the *quinceañera* celebrates a chronological passage and acknowledges a particular cultural or ethnic identity and religious affiliation. The ceremony is thought to have had its roots in Aztec society, in which young girls attended schools preparing them for either religious service or marriage, culminating in an initiation ceremony. Following the Spanish colonization of the region, the ceremony merged with Catholic practice to mark a girl's passage into womanhood and entry into the age of courtship.[11]

The central musical event marking the *quinceañera* is a party or ball hosted by the girl's family. Although the event is not a formal religious occasion, the ball is sometimes held in the church hall, and most Latina celebrants have either prepared for or recently received the Roman Catholic sacrament of Confirmation, marking them as adults in the eyes of the Church. Some young women complete short preparatory courses before celebrating the *quinceañera*.

Traditionally, a group of female and male friends act as attendants or a court of honor escorting the young woman into church to receive Communion; they then dance with her at the festive celebration. Color symbolism varies according to family, local, and ethnic traditions—for example, the girl might wear a white gown and a crown of white flowers on her head, while her female attendants wear red dresses and the young men, black tuxedos.

In the context of social change in the twenty-first century, the transformation of Mexican-American family structures, and more equitable gender expectations, some young, urbanized Mexican American women perceive the *quinceañera* not as an initiation into adulthood but as a symbol of historical limitations on women and their choices in society. The strong association of the ceremony with the expectation that the young woman will seek a traditional life as a wife and mother is underscored by the fact that there is no comparable ceremony for young men.[12] Yet for many, the *quinceañera* continues to provide both a marker and celebration of a young Latina girl's coming of age. The *quinceañera* also continues to carry strong social and economic significance, especially in the United States, where it has been compared to debutante balls in certain circles of Anglo-American society. Beyond displaying a family's social status and presenting a daughter on the cusp of adulthood, the *quinceañera* provides a rich example of an event that invokes much of its significance through its musical content.

There is no specific music for the celebration; the choice depends in part on whether the family is of Mexican, Puerto Rican, Dominican, or another background. Although recorded music often accompanies dancing at *quinceañeras* hosted on modest budgets, live music is generally preferred and is seen as a mark of prestige. Members of the Mexican American community hire live *mariachi* bands whenever possible. "If it's a party without *mariachis*, it's not a party," commented one Mexican American woman in New York City, where *mariachis* in 2001 formed an association to meet the increasing demand for their music at events such as *quinceañeras* among the growing population of Mexican descent.[13]

Mariachi is the name for a Mexican and Mexican American instrumental ensemble combining plucked and bowed instruments of various types with trumpets. The ensemble originated in the mid-nineteenth century in the area around Guadalajara. After the Mexican Revolution (1910–1917), *mariachi* musicians arrived in Mexico City as part of a massive migration from rural villages. As a result, *mariachi* music became urbanized, taking on characteristics of the commercialized country music then popular in the radio and film industry. In present-day usage, *mariachi* can refer to a single musician, a type of musical ensemble, or a style of music.[14]

Mariachi bands are common today throughout Mexico and the southwestern United States. The *mariachi* ensemble has also become widespread

Several important stages of a 1994 *quinceañera* celebrated by two friends are shown here. After participating in a Mass at their local church, they don traditional crowns (*diadems*) for a short ceremony marking their coming of age. Afterward, they celebrate with family and friends at a festive party (*fiesta*) with food, music, and dancing.

throughout much of the rest of North America, performing at local Mexican restaurants, community events, and on college campuses. Support from the National Endowment for the Arts and other foundations helped launch the Mariachi Academy of New York in summer, 2003. Mariachi bands were traditionally all male ensembles in Mexico, but about two-thirds of the students in the New York City Academy are girls, reflecting changing gender roles in Mexican American society.[15]

A *mariachi* ensemble can include as few as three players when musicians are in short supply, but traditionally engages more than a dozen musicians playing various Mexican guitars, violins, trumpets, and a harp (see **"Sound Sources: The *Mariachi*"**). *Mariachi* musicians usually dress as *charros,* traditional Mexican horsemen or cowboys; more rarely they wear regional dress. The *mariachi* identity is closely associated with the *charro* costume—the *sombrero* (wide-brimmed hat), short jacket, large bow tie, and tight trousers trimmed with rows of *botonaduras* (silver buttons).

The music played by *mariachis* at *quinceañeras* spans a wide variety of musical styles. Many of the balls feature salsa as well as other popular Latin American and Caribbean musical styles. However, there are some common traditions relating to the order of events and dances performed at the ball celebrating a *quinceañera.* Usually, the attendants enter the dance area and form a corridor through which the young woman and her escort walk, followed by the girl's parents, who carry a pair of white high-heeled shoes. The girl sits down, usually on an elevated chair similar to a throne, and her father places the shoes on her feet. The girl and father next dance together to a traditional waltz. Next the young woman dances with her escort, and then the two take turns dancing with the other attendants. A few songs from the *mariachi* tradition have become associated with the *quinceañera,* including the *Tema para Quinceañera* heard in Listening Guide 36 (see page 144), which is often played as the young woman enters the room with her attendants.

A *mariachi* ensemble performs outdoors on a footbridge in San Antonio, Texas.

The ensemble heard in Listening Guide 36, Mariachi Juvenil, was formed in 1989 by eleven young men from the state of Jalisco in Mexico. Since that time, the ensemble has performed internationally and has issued several recordings. Their music ranges from traditional romantic songs such as the *quinceañera* song heard here to innovative pieces adapting rhythms from salsa and other Latin dance styles to *mariachi* instruments.[16]

Most of the repertory performed at the *quinceañera* is not exclusive to this one occasion.

The *Mariachi*

The *mariachi* ensemble commonly seen today became standardized in the early 1950s. The Mexican *guitarrón* (a large, plucked four- or five-string bass guitar with a large belly) and the *vihuela* (a smaller, strummed folk guitar), alone or with a harp, are the rhythm instruments of the ensemble. Two trumpets and three or more violins usually supply the melody. Although most *mariachi* groups comprise from seven to eleven players, some of whom also sing, smaller or larger ensembles are also common, depending on the needs and financial resources of their patrons.

At the core of the *mariachi* repertory are traditional dances with lively rhythms, including polkas in duple meters and the triple-meter waltz. Today, many types of music are played by *mariachis,* including folk songs, novelty pieces, and bilingual adaptations of pop tunes. *Mariachi* musicians may be hired to accompany events such as birthdays, intimate dinners, and religious services, including funerals.

In the United States, *mariachi* music has spread through growing Mexican American communities and has been quickly adopted into school curricula and university programs. *Mariachi* has also entered Disney World, Hollywood, and the pop music scene, through stars of Mexican descent such as Linda Ronstadt and the late Selena Quintanilla Pérez. Although *mariachi* bands were traditionally male ensembles, women have begun to participate in the United States, a trend taken up in Mexico as well. Dozens of *mariachi* festivals and workshops are mounted every year in numerous places across North America, and in late 2001, more than fifteen *mariachi* bands in the New York area established the Mariachi Association of New York. "You can make your living being a *mariachi* in New York," said Ramon Ponce, Jr., a leader, along with his father, of the New York ensemble called Mariachi Real de Mexico. This group has performed in New York City not only at Mexican weddings and parties for a Mexican population which totaled 187,000 in the 2000 census, but also is in demand for bar mitzvahs and Chinese weddings.[17]

Many of the songs are also performed on the *Día de las Madres* (Mother's Day), another occasion in honor of women that provides *mariachi* bands with regular employment. The *mariachi* band, which also plays at baptisms and weddings, therefore links music of the *quinceañera* to other important occasions in the community's life cycle.

Tema para Quinceañera (*mariachi* song)

CD 1
Track 38

Composer: Nacho Padilla Guerrero

Arranger: Idelfonso Moya

Date of recording: 1995

Performers: Mariachi Juvenil Guadalajara; German Gutierrez Corona, *musical director and trumpet;* Camilo Gutierrez Corona, *trumpet;* Carlos Corona Torres, *guitar;* Noe Ricardo Gonzalez Arias, *vihuela;* Agustín Esparza Sanchez, *guitarrón;* Adrian Humberto Lopez Ortega, Santiago Trujillo Jimenez, Refugio Ortega Acencio, Manuel Ortega Acencio, Jose Alfredo Sigala Damian, and Hector Gonzalez Arias, *violins;* Nacho Padilla Guerrero, *producer and artistic director*

Form: Strophic, but with spoken middle section that suggests a three-part (ABA') form

Tempo: Moderate tempo, quadruple meter

WHAT TO LISTEN FOR:

- Guitarrón and guitars provide a rhythmic and harmonic framework, while trumpets, violins, and the lead singer respond to each other's melodies
- The singer directly addresses the girl celebrating her *quinceañera,* offering advice and reassurance

---

STRUCTURE AND TEXT	TRANSLATION	DESCRIPTION
0:00 Introduction		Trumpets begin the phrase, and violins pick up the melody.
0:16 **Section A** Cuanta felicidad siento verte llegar a tu cumpleaños, Gozando a plenitud tu bella juventud en tus quinceaños.	How much happiness I feel seeing you reach your birthday, Enjoying fully your beautiful youth on your fifteenth birthday.	This section has a four-part internal form (aaba), in which the first, second and fourth stanzas

Through its presence at a range of musical occasions, the *mariachi* ensemble itself enacts the meanings of the *quinceañera* as an important rite of passage. That the musicians play the same songs in an outdoor plaza or at a party in a private home further reinforces the status of the *quinceañera* as one of a series of meaningful events. There is a long-standing tradition that *mariachi* musicians perform at funerals, singing over the dead. Given the *mariachi*'s presence at so many joyous events, it is not surprising that many people want

0:33	Empiezas a vivir, hoy todo es para ti color de rosa Pero hay de comprender que de niña a mujer, ya es otra cosa.	You're beginning your life, today everything is looking rosy, But you have to understand that things change when a girl becomes a woman.	(beginning at 0:16, 0:33, and 1:08), are nearly identical, while the third provides a contrast. The first half of each stanza is sung by the lead singer alone. In the first, second, and fourth stanzas, he is joined by a second voice that sings a parallel harmony. Note the trumpet and violin countermelodies that complement the singer throughout the stanzas.
0:51	Aquí estamos presentes, tus padres y parientes, amigos y hermanos, Para darte un lugar ante la sociedad que forman los humanos	We're all here, your parents and family, friends and siblings, To give you a place in society.	
1:08	Y pedimos a dios que te dé lo mejor toda la vida, Bendiciendo el camino que quieres por andar, hija querida.	And we pray that all your life God may give you the very best, Blessing the road that you want to walk, dear daughter.	
1:27	**Section B (spoken)** Bonita, al cruzar por el sendero de la vida, sigue el camino que te lleve al éxito. Enfrenta con decencia los problemas, sin destruir tu alma por el adverso. Quinceaños para ti son el comienzo de ilusiones que forman mil conceptos. Ya la niña se va, son otros los proyectos. Ahora pensarás como mujer, pero no cambies, no cambies tus nobles sentimientos. Chiquilla.	Beautiful, when crossing the path of life, follow the path that will bring you success. Confront problems with decency, without compromising your soul when faced with adversity. Your fifteenth birthday is the beginning of visions that form a thousand dreams. Now the girl is leaving, the goals are different. Now you will think like a woman, but do not change; do not change your noble feelings. Sweetie.	This section is spoken while the instruments continue playing in the background. The melody and form are the same the first half of section A. A muted trumpet plays the melody for the first stanza, and the violins continue the melody in the second.
2:01	Fade-out		(The second, third, and fourth stanzas of Section A are repeated to end the song.)

the same music to help mark their final passage from life. In the words of one *mariachi* musician from Los Angeles: "People say, 'If I die, I want to hear *mariachi* for the last time at my funeral.'"[18]

The music of the *mariachi,* varied in style and content, performed on vastly different occasions, thus provides an important continuity in the lives of many Mexicans and Mexican Americans. The meaning and content of music at any particular moment is defined by the occasion at hand. In this way, the same

song, performed at times of joy and times of sorrow, gains power with each rendition, accumulating an ever-expanding set of associations for individuals and the communities of which they are part. Here we encounter significance closely linked to music's setting, providing a marked contrast to the one-to-one correspondence between the sound of *raga nilambari* and sleep.

A third case study can help us understand that many musics can have distinctive sounds and yet signify with remarkable flexibility. As these musics transcend any single moment of performance, their meanings proliferate. A particularly rich example is found in the complex traditions connected with the bagpipe.

CASE STUDY: Bagpipe Music

Of the many musical instruments that lend meaning to everyday life, one of the most versatile and ubiquitous is the bagpipe. The bagpipe is a wind instrument whose basic parts are an air reservoir, the bag that is squeezed under one arm; a blowpipe through which the player supplies air for the reservoir either from his mouth or a set of bellows held under the other arm, and one or more sounding pipes fitted with reeds that vibrate to produce the sound. Most wind instruments cannot sustain the sound while the performer takes a breath, but the bagpipe's air reservoir allows the player to keep the sound going continuously. Indeed, most sets of bagpipes are not capable of stopping the sound between pitches. Thus, repeated pitches must be articulated in ways peculiar to the bagpipe.

The history of the bagpipe extends well beyond its Scottish and Irish roots of recent centuries, starting with archaeological evidence of bagpipes in the ancient Middle East (see **"Looking Back: The Changing Settings and Significance of Bagpipes"** on page 148).

The first known mention of a bagpipe by name occurred during the reign of the Roman emperor Nero in the first century CE. The emperor vowed that if the gods saved him from those plotting against him, he would mount a music festival and perform on the *utricularius*. Since this Latin word refers to a bag of skin, this may be the first reference to a real bagpipe, filled with air and used to sound musical pipes.

Currently, many regions of Western and Eastern Europe as well as the Balkans and parts of India have one or more types of bagpipes with widely varying characteristics.

Differences in the construction of pipes can result in markedly different sound quality and volume. Some bagpipes can hardly be heard, even played alone; others can overwhelm any other instrument. In the twentieth century, bagpipe makers have introduced synthetic materials for the bags, pipes, and reeds, mostly to reduce the difficulty of maintaining and tuning the bagpipes. These changes in materials have changed the sound of the bagpipes.

Although Rome has been suggested as a possible source for bagpipes in the British Isles, the pipes may have been invented in the Scottish highlands.[19] Whatever their origin, Scottish and Irish bagpipes assumed distinctive forms by the Middle Ages, certainly by the twelfth or thirteenth centuries, when they were first used in official ceremonies and military affairs. One of the most famous early literary references to the bagpipe occurs in the prologue of *The Canterbury Tales*, where Geoffrey Chaucer (1340?–1400) describes one pilgrim, the Miller, in the following manner:

A baggepipe well cowde [could] he blowe and sowne [sound],
And therewith he brought us out of town.

In recent years, Scottish and Irish bagpipe ensembles have proliferated worldwide. One Internet site lists over two hundred pipe bands, not just in Great Britain or its former colonies, but in such far-flung locations as Finland and Uruguay. The largest number of active pipe bands is not in England, Scotland, or Ireland, but in the United States. There are dozens of Canadian bands and more than one hundred United States bands, ranging from the small-town West Eden Highlanders of Bar Harbor, Maine, to the Red Hackle Pipes and

The Changing Settings and Significance of Bagpipes

The earliest traces of bagpipes

1300 BCE	Earliest Middle Eastern carvings of bagpipes
First century CE	Roman Emperor Nero (died 68 CE) linked to bagpipes

The bagpipe tradition begins in Scotland and Ireland

1200s	Possible beginnings of bagpipe playing in Scotland
1549	First written evidence of the use of the bagpipe by the Highlanders as a battle instrument
Late 1500s	First *pibrochs* composed by Donald Mór MacCrimmon
1700s	The Irish *pìob mhór* (great pipe) dies out and is replaced by the bellows-blown indoor pipe that would become the *uilleann* pipes

Political controversies and resolutions

1747	The Disarming Act outlaws the great Highland bagpipe, considered an instrument of war
1757	Highland regiments in the British army allowed pipers
1782	Repeal of the Disarming Act

New settings for bagpipe competition and performance

1781	The first *pibroch* competition held in Falkirk and run by the Highland Society of London
Late 1700s	Flourishing of the *ceilidh*
Mid 1800s	Possible start of reel and dance music competitions at rural Highland games
1854	Drums added to pipe bands, resulting in the term "pipes and drums"
1930	The Royal Scottish Pipe Band Association established, with one of its primary duties the regulation of band competitions

The emergence and significance of urban and institutional pipe bands

1882	Edinburgh city police establish the first police pipe band in Scotland
1914	The Vancouver police establish the first pipe band in North America
1966	The Simon Fraser University Pipe Band established

This early sixteenth-century engraving of a bagpiper by Albrecht Dürer has been thought to depict an Irish piper who served in Europe with the forces of Henry VIII. The pipes may be Irish war pipes, which were known to have two drones of unequal length and a long chanter, which the player held in front of him.

The strength of the British bagpiping tradition is clear in the legacy it has left in places once part of the British empire, from Hong Kong to India.

Drums in Cleveland, Ohio. The ubiquitous presence of bagpipes in North American cities and towns dates primarily to the late nineteenth and twentieth centuries.

Sound

The instrument most widely played today in Irish and Scottish bagpipe bands around the world is the *Scottish Highland bagpipe,* which is complicated in its construction (see page 150, **"Sound Sources: The Scottish Highland Bagpipe"**). A number of bagpipe tunes are played in both the Scottish and Irish traditions, but they are called by different names. The Scottish bagpipe tune, *Scotland the Brave,* known in the Irish tradition as *The Irishman's Toast,* is played for a variety of occasions (Listening Guide 37; see page 152). Its regular pulse in quadruple meter allows it to serve as a vigorous march at festive parades, and played at a slower tempo, as a majestic memorial during solemn processions. Each phrase consists of four measures of four beats each. In the recording, the bass drums play on beats 1, 2, and 3 of each measure and are silent on beat 4.

In this example, you can also hear several types of characteristic bagpipe ornaments, called *grace notes* or *gracings,* which are very short notes that adorn the otherwise continuous sound of the chanter. The term *cutting* refers to the insertion of grace notes to divide a sustained sound into two or more distinct parts; without the grace note, a continuous pitch would sound.

The Scottish Highland Bagpipe

The Scottish bagpipe has an airtight bag that in the past was made out of the skin of an animal, such as a sheep or goat, but today is more often made of rubber or rubberized cloth. Three kinds of pipes made of wood are inserted into the bag: One is called the *chanter;* the second is the *blowpipe;* and the third kind, of which there are usually three, are *drone* pipes. All the pipes are fastened securely into short wooden sockets called "stocks" sewn into openings of the skin or rubber bag that protect the *reeds* at the end of the pipes.

Each kind of pipe has a different function. The most important is the chanter pipe, with eight finger holes, that plays the melody. The chanter of the Highland bagpipe can play only nine pitches. A chanter can be made of wood, metal, or other materials, and it has a *double reed* that is concealed from view at the end that fits inside the bag.

The drone pipes have no finger holes and sound a single, continuous pitch; in some cases, the pitch has such strong harmonics that a listener may think that extra pipes are being sounded.

The blowpipe, by which the player blows air into the bag, has a non-return valve to prevent air from leaking out. Once the bag is filled with air, the player compresses it with his arm, forcing the air through the reeds of the chanter and drone pipes, causing the reeds to vibrate and the bagpipe to sound. The Scottish Highland pipes have a loud, piercing sound, appropriate for their customary use out of doors.

Playing the bagpipes is a complicated affair, since the same person must blow (or pump) the air, squeeze the bag, and finger the chanter. In the Scottish tradition, in an attempt to isolate the fingering from the other actions, a "practice chanter" has been developed for new students of the instrument and experienced pipers

More complex ornaments consist of several grace notes played in rapid succession. *Doubling* describes a group of several grace notes, one of which has the same pitch as the note being ornamented; in other words, the main pitch is said to be doubled. A *birl* is one type of doubling, an ornament that doubles low A, near the bottom of the chanter's range. *Grips* are several rapid grace notes in the lower part of the chanter's range that sound like the squawk of a breaking voice.

learning new tunes. The practice chanter looks like the chanter of the full bag-pipes, but a cap with a short blowpipe is placed over the chanter reed, allowing the practice chanter to be blown into directly without the bag or drones. This arrangement allows the piper to learn the tunes without filling and squeezing the bag. Bands of great Highland bagpipes often begin rehearsals with their drones "corked"—with stoppers placed in the ends of the drones so that they will not sound—so they can hear the chanters more clearly without worrying about the tuning and blending of the drone pipes.

Pipe bands must often practice indoors, but the *pìob mhór* ("great pipes") is clearly an out-door instrument. Even though there are indoor venues that could accommodate these bands, competitions continue to be held outdoors re-gardless of the weather, testing not only the play-ers' musical skill but also their physical endurance.

The tuning of each bagpipe is fixed, since the player's lips do not touch the reed and the chanter is not blown into directly. In the past, tunings were determined by the traditions of a given locality or region. Today, because most bagpipes are manufactured, the tuning is fixed according to an international standard.

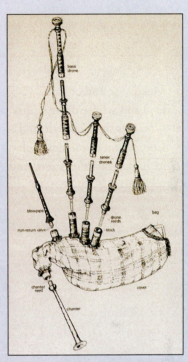

This exploded diagram of a Scottish Highland bagpipe clarifies aspects of bagpipe construction otherwise hidden from view.

Ireland had its own *pìob mhór* ("pee-yab-MORE," "great pipes") until the early 1700s, when they were redesigned for indoor playing. The distinctive Irish bagpipes are smaller than the Scottish Highland pipes, and the air that fills the bag is supplied by a bellows rather than a blowpipe. The distinguishing fea-tures of the great Highland bagpipe are those that make it most suitable for outdoor use and marching—its loud chanter, additional drones to balance the chanter, and the long blowpipe that allows the player to stand upright. In con-

Scotland the Brave (march)

Date of recording: 1996
Performers: The Simon Fraser University Pipe Band
Form: a a' b a' phrase structure
Tempo: Moderate quadruple meter
Function: A march played at parades and other public occasions

---

WHAT TO LISTEN FOR:

- Massive sound of the pipe band, whose chanters have a range of just over an octave and whose drones provide a constant harmonic background
- *Gracings* that separate and embellish pitches
- Compound ornaments, which consist of several grace notes in rapid succession, including *doubling, birl,* and *grips*

	STRUCTURE	DESCRIPTION
0:00	**Phrase a**	Drum rolls and syncopations on the snare drums. The melody begins on low A, the tonic, and by the beginning of the second measure it has risen one octave to high A.
0:11	**Phrase a'**	The first two beats of the first measure, both on the pitch low A, are separated by a *birl*, which sounds like a very quick break in the pipe's sound just before the second beat (0:02, 0:12). In measure two, there are three high A's in a row. Just before the third of those high A's, a *grip* can be heard with its characteristic squawk (0:06, 0:15).
0:21	**Phrase b**	Phrases a and a' are identical except at their cadences. Phrase b contrasts, beginning with several high A's (with *grips* separating a few of them, at 0:23 and 0:25).
0:32	**Phrase a'**	The return of phrase a' is identical to the iteration of a' at 0:11.
0:42		End of recording

trast, the Irish bagpipe's softer sound was suited to more intimate or indoor performances. The "union" or *"uilleann"* ("ILL-in," literally, "elbow") pipes, as Irish pipes are called, declined in popularity until a renaissance of Celtic music during the 1960s and 1970s revived the instrument in both Ireland and the United States. The sound of the *uilleann* pipes is familiar to many today since it was the prominent instrument in the title music of the movie *Titanic*.

Indoor pipes are often distinguished by the term "smallpipes," while the term "bagpipes" generally refers to the Scottish *pìob mhór*. During the mid-nineteenth century, interest in Ireland in the *pìob mhór* resurfaced. By this time, however, the native tradition had been broken and so the Irish adopted the Scottish bagpipes. Some pipe makers modified the Scottish bagpipes, basing their designs on early descriptions of Irish pipes, including the two-drone *pìob mhór*. However, only Scottish-style *pìob mhór* are allowed in international competitions; thus, in competition, Irish bands play the three-drone Scottish pipes.

The distinctive sound of the Scottish pipes is reflected in Scottish and Irish vocal music as well. A vocal style that imitates the pipes is called "mouth music" (*canntaireachd*, pronounced "CAN-ter-rekht," literally "humming a tune"). The recording heard in Listening Guide 38 (see page 154) demonstrates how the voice uses vocables to indicate bagpipe melodies and their gracings. There were several systems of *canntaireachd*, some dating well before the nineteenth century, and most pipers as well as Scottish women were familiar with this singing style.[20] Until the mid-twentieth century, Irish men and women called *lilters* vocalized dance tunes with vocables, a tradition known as *dydeling* or mouth-music.[21]

In Chapter 1, we discussed the tendency among people in many societies to identify certain instruments with either men or women. The bagpipes are among the instruments most strongly associated with men and historically male institutions such as the military. Indeed, many have suggested that strong male gender association of the bagpipes extends to the very shape of the instrument, which resembles male sexual organs. So strong is the association of the bagpipes with male identity that boys begin learning to play the instrument at a young age.

While women were not formally prohibited from playing the bagpipe, in the past they have not often done so. An interesting recent development, along with the revival of the Irish pipes in the second half of the twentieth century, is the emergence of female pipers. In the past, the Irish musical tradition was, like the Scottish tradition, dominated by men, the women largely being restricted to Irish step dancing. By the 1970s and 1980s, however, more women were encouraged to take up instrumental music and to perform in public. In Listening Guide 39 (see page 156), we hear a recording made in 1978 of

LISTENING GUIDE *38*

Canntaireachd (Scottish mouth music)

CD 2
Track 1

Date of recording: 1971 (CD reissue 1992)
Performer: Miss Mary Morrison
Form: Two-part (binary) form
Tempo: Upbeat and lively

WHAT TO LISTEN FOR:

- Vocal technique that uses vocables to imitate bagpipe melody and ornaments
- Range of just about one octave, with the singer imitating bagpipe timbre by using a bright, full chest voice for pitches at the bottom of this range and a lighter head voice for the upper register.

	STRUCTURE	DESCRIPTION
0:00	Section A	A mixture of vowels, nasal consonants, and stops (consonants, like d and p, which stop the airflow) combine to create the impression of a bagpipe. Specific ornaments are imitated—for example, the quick "hm-buh-duh-lum" at the very beginning of this song sounds very much like a *birl*.
0:10	Section A	The first section is repeated. Section A stays mainly in the lower part of the range, except at the very end of the section. It may be divided into two phrases, each of which ends with a moderately high "pee-dee."
0:21	Section B	The contrasting B section uses the upper register more often.
0:33	Section A	Sections A and B are repeated once more.
0:44	Section B	
0:56		The recording ends.

Queen of the Rushes performed by Máire Ní Ghráda, a young woman born in Cork in 1959. As part of a family involved in performance of traditional Irish music, Máire Ní Ghráda first began at age ten to play a small Irish flute (sometimes called a pennywhistle or tin whistle) with six finger holes that plays melodies of limited range. Two years later she began to take piping lessons at the Cork Pipers Club, quickly developing her own sophisticated style. In this recording she plays a set of Irish concert pipes made in Cork.[22]

The revival of the *uilleann* pipes in Ireland has led to new interest in Irish piping among Irish people abroad. But whether a musician plays the Irish or Scottish bagpipes, the sound of the bagpipes is so distinctive that it rarely fails to gain the attention of anyone within earshot. Next we consider aspects of the bagpipes' sound that take us deeper into realms of meaning.

To this point, we have focused mainly on what may be termed a primary level of signification, correlating the way in which sound, through its content and structure, connotes or conveys meaning—for example, the use of the bagpipe to accompany marches, as heard in Listening Guide 37.

There is clearly another level of meaning conveyed through music—music's primal ability to excite, inspire, frighten, and even move us to tears. Here it is worthwhile to speculate on aspects of the bagpipes' sound that affect the listener's body and emotions. We might want to consider first the distinctive timbre and volume of most bagpipes, a sound that, especially in the case of the Scottish pipes, can overwhelm the ear and permeate the entire body. The texture of the sound also commands attention in its subtle complexity and the ongoing relationship between a highly ornamented melody and more stable, unornamented drones. The further ability of the pipes to produce sounds without end counters a basic human physical need to breathe. In sum, the pipes present a distinctive voice that, as we will see below, can express joy or pain.

Máire Ní Ghráda, heard in Listening Guide 39, is seen here with her *uilleann* pipes, which she has played since age eleven; note that the bellows pumping air to the pipes fits under the player's arm. A native of Cork City, Ireland, she lives today near Limerick City and was a founding member of the Limerick Pipers' Club, where she teaches. Máire Ní Ghráda also has a degree in ethnomusicology and teaches Irish Folklore in Limerick.

Setting

Here we will explore three main settings in which bagpipe music is performed, and through which the music gains meaning by association—occasions related to death and commemoration, occasions of entertainment and the dance, and competition and concerts.

Death and Commemoration

Bagpipes have been linked with warfare and death since 1549, when a French military officer observed that "while the French prepared for combat, . . . the wild Scots encouraged themselves to arms by the sound of their bagpipes."[23] As early as the mid-seventeenth century, Highland military companies normally included a piper. Later, small bands of eight or twelve pipers were added to regiments. At war trials following the failed 1745 uprising against England, the bagpipe was called "an instrument of war."

As early as the sixteenth century, a repertory of compositions called *piobaireachd* (pronounced "PEE-ber-rekht"), usually shortened to *pibroch* (pronounced "PEE-brakh"), emerged thanks to the creativity of a famous family of pipers, the MacCrimmons (see page 158, **"Individual Portraits: The Legacy of the MacCrimmons"**).

LISTENING GUIDE 39

Queen of the Rushes (Irish jig)

CD 2
Track 2

Date of recording: 1978

Performer: Máire Ní Ghráda

Form: Jig, with three phrases, each of which is repeated

Tempo: Lively dance in sextuple meter, in which measures of six beats are divided into two groups of three notes each

WHAT TO LISTEN FOR:

- The distinctive quality of the *uilleann* pipes, which are smaller than most Scottish bagpipes and produce more pitches than the Scottish pipes
- Dance rhythms typical of jigs, which generally involve constant movement in a 3-beat or 6-beat meter
- A style of ornamentation somewhat lighter than that heard on the Scottish pipes. The most common on this recording is the *clip*, a quick note heard before the main note, like the *grace notes* in the Scottish examples

	STRUCTURE	DESCRIPTION
0:00	**Phrase a**	The drone begins to sound, and the first two notes of the melody on the chanter are played slowly. On the first strong beat, the lively six-beat meter of a jig is established. This extended first phrase, like all subsequent phrases, is repeated. Note that the repeated phrase includes a minor variation: the low pitches at the end of this phrase are lower on the repeat than they were the first time through.
0:20	**Phrase b**	The next phrase makes use of the *uilleann* pipes' higher register—like a flute, the pipes can produce pitches an octave above those in its normal range. The higher register requires higher air pressure through the chanter, and it is not easily controlled. The chanter can be heard slipping into its lower register on a few pitches.
0:36	**Phrase c**	A long-short rhythm, sometimes termed a "dotted" rhythm because of the manner in which it is written in Western notation, predominates in this phrase, leading into a descending pattern.
0:52	**Phrase a**	The entire jig is repeated.
0:56	Fade-out	

This painting by J. Prinsep Beadle shows Piper James Richardson, V.C., playing the pipes at Regina Trench, Vimy Ridge, as part of the 16th Canadian Scottish Regiment during World War I. The abbreviation V.C. indicates that Richardson received the Victoria Cross, Great Britain's highest military award, underscoring the importance of musicians in battle.

The MacCrimmons are said to have transformed bagpipe music over the course of two hundred years, perfecting the playing style, composing new forms such as the *pibroch* and adding them to the repertory, and raising the status of the bagpipe from a rustic instrument to an artistic venture at the heart of Scottish cultural life.[24]

Individuals associated with the MacCrimmons are also commemorated through *pibrochs* dedicated to them. The *pibroch* in Listening Guide 40 (see page 160) was dedicated to Mary MacLeod (c. 1615–1707), one of the foremost women songwriters and poets in Scottish Gaelic of her time. As the lore goes, MacLeod was banished to the Island of Mull for having offended the Chiefs of Dunvegan and then wrote about her banishment in one of her poetic laments. On her deathbed, MacLeod is said to have regretted having composed a praise song for the Chief who had banished her and later restored her to Dunvegan. MacLeod's innovative poetry is known to have been echoed by pipers in their own medium.[25]

The *pibroch* consists of a ground, or melody, with subsequent extended variations. The ground is always slow and is much longer than a march or dance tune. The melodies, as in the case of the *pibroch* heard in Listening Guide 40, are usually simple, and many of them use fewer than the nine pitches available on the chanter. The basic melody in this *pibroch*, *Lament for Mary MacLeod*, consists of four phrases of sixteen beats each. One pitch, a plaintive high G, first heard in the third phrase of Variation 1 Doubling (at 4:16) is played with a special fingering used only in *pibroch*, not in "light music" such as that for the *ceilidh*, a festive gathering.

The Legacy of the MacCrimmons

"How long have I known about the Mac-Crimmons?" replied bagpiper Gregory Morrow, in response to my question about the famous Scottish piping family. "I knew about the MacCrimmons from day one," emphasized Morrow, who began piping more than forty-two years ago, at age seven, in his home town of Weston, Massachusetts. Beginning in the early 1500s the MacCrimmons were hereditary pipers to the chiefs of Clan MacLeod at Dunvegan Castle, located on the Isle of Skye across Loch Dunvegan from Boreraig, the MacCrimmons' ancestral home. Morrow studied with pipers who had joined the prize-winning Worcester Kiltie Pipe Band (founded c. 1909) after they migrated to Massachusetts in the early 1960s from Lanarkshire, Scotland, a coal-mining district not far from Lockerbie. He first heard about the MacCrimmons when he came across an early LP recording still treasured today by his mother. "On one side of the record there was a *pibroch* titled *Lament for the Children,* Morrow recalled.

Gregory Morrow arranges the drones of his *uilleann* pipes before performing, which he views as a challenge for a longtime player of the Scottish bagpipe. "It's akin to learning a whole different language," says Morrow. "My friends say I play the Irish pipes with a Scottish accent."

"I listened to it and was told a fascinating tale," Morrow continued. "One day Padruig [Patrick] Mór MacCrimmon went to church with his eight sons and within a year, seven of them were dead from smallpox." It is said that Patrick Mór took his inspiration from the heart-rending laments of his grief-stricken wife and composed the *Lament for the Children.*[26]

> I thought about that story, and it grew in my imagination of who the MacCrimmons were and the fact that no one had taught me the *pibroch*. As a piper in America during the 1960s, you didn't have instruction in the *pibroch,* they just ignored it. We played the light stuff, 'the little music' as it is called—marches and strathspeys and reels. In contrast, the *pibroch* is 'great' or 'large' music, which one learns later in life. My teachers were band players, not virtuoso pipers steeped in the solo forms. As a kid, I had 'good fingers' for piping and I was proud of comments about my fingers. I felt I could add expression to the *pibroch*, although I didn't have all the emotions until later.

What we know about the history of the MacCrimmons, the most renowned family of great Highland bagpipers, is based on oral tradition, and the facts surrounding the family's colorful history as performers, teachers, and composers of the *pibroch* are clouded by contradictory tales. The family retained their post for two hundred fifty years, passing it through eight generations of MacCrimmon men. During this time they conceived the *pibroch*, the classical music of the bagpipe. They are also credited with beginning the system of *canntaireachd* ("mouth music"), whereby one could sing the instrumental *pibroch* with syllables representing various pitches and gracings; it was through this system that new *pibrochs* were taught and memorized. Most of the MacCrimmon *pibrochs* are either commemorations or laments for particular people and events, and their attributions and titles have been used to document the MacCrimmons' history. The MacCrimmons also established a college of piping and music at Boreraig, to which chiefs of other clans sent their best pipers for seven years of study to perfect their skills. The college was closed down in 1770, around the time that the position of hereditary piper to the clan ended.

Particularly disputed is the ancestry of the MacCrimmons, which contains tantalizing possibilities of connections to other piping traditions outside Scotland. One history names a native of Scotland (Finlay of Plaid, who begat Iain Odhar MacCrimmon), as the founding father of the MacCrimmons. However, two other tales relate that Iain Odhar came from abroad—either from a family of Norse invaders of Ireland, or from Cremona, Italy. We know that around 1570, Iain Odhar's son Donald Mór was born. The first known composer and possible inventor of *pibroch*, Donald Mór studied with his father and also in Ireland. Donald Mór's son was the composer Patrick Mór (born approximately 1595), who is remembered for the *Lament for the Children* and for his surviving son, the great piping teacher Patrick Og. Patrick Og had two sons, Malcolm and Donald Bàin, who were pipers during the 1745 Jacobite rebellion against Britain. Acting on a premonition, Donald Bàin composed the famous lament *MacCrimmon Will Never Return* a few days before he was killed in a skirmish. Malcolm's sons, Iain Dubh and Donald Ruadh, were the last of the line, and with them died the piping secrets of the MacCrimmons.

Today, although the Worcester Kiltie Pipe Band has disbanded, Greg Morrow continues to play the pipes, moving beyond the great and small Scottish pipes to tackle the Irish (*uilleann*) pipes, which he likes to play for *ceilidhs*. "I am a 'ceilidh piper' as opposed to a 'contest piper'," says Morrow, who has been fortunate to know the best living bagpipe players worldwide and to spend a year working in a bagpipe shop in Glasgow during the mid-1980s. Morrow also says that he has "come to understand the power of bagpipe music. For me, in the *pibroch*, if you play the ground properly, even just a simple variation, it takes you on a journey musically." Yet at the same time, he admits that it can be difficult to explain the music's overwhelming significance. "I can't tell you the number of times when I've seen tears come to peoples' eyes when they hear the bagpipes. There's something very stirring and emotional about [the instrument], and I don't know what it is."[27]

The chanter and top sections of the drones are thought to be all that survive of the pipes that Patrick Mór MacCrimmon played in the seventeenth century. The other parts are replacements.

Lament for Mary MacLeod (Scottish *píbroch*)

CD 2
Track 3

Date of recording: 2005
Composer: Patrick Og MacCrimmon
Performer: Gregory A. Morrow
Form: Ground and variations
Function: Historically performed on occasions of commemoration or mourning; by the late twentieth century, performed by virtuoso pipers at piping competitions
Tempo: Very slow

WHAT TO LISTEN FOR:

- The basic melody, called ground in English, which consists of four phrases (a a b c) of sixteen beats each; the second phrase repeats the first, while the third and fourth phrases contrast the first, each starting the same, but ending differently
- The high G first heard in the final phrase of Variation 1, Doubling, at 4:16, is a highlight of the tune
- The sustained, low drone sounding continuously under the melody
- Subsequent, varied iterations of the four-phrase ground, called variations, incorporate differences in melodic contour, rhythm, and ornamentation. Each variation in a complete performance is "doubled," that is, played a second time increasing the number of pitches at a faster tempo.

The listening guide includes timings for the beginning of each phrase, which can be difficult to hear due to the extremely slow tempo and the absence of breaks between phrases, a consequence of the bagpipes design. A full performance of the *pibroch* with its customary seven variations (including I. Ground; II. Variation 1; III. Variation 1, Doubling; IV. Taorlúath; V. Taorlúath Doubling; VI. Crunlúath; and VII. Crunlúath Doubling), would take more time than available on our CD. The recording heard in Listening Guide 40 is edited to include the Ground, Variation 1, Variation 1 Doubling, and then fades out at the beginning of Variation 2, called the Taorlúath after its characteristic ornament. The recording resumes for the majestic final variation, the Crunlúath Doubling,

STRUCTURE AND TEXT	DESCRIPTION
Ground	
0:00 **Phrase a**	The ground begins with the sounding of the tonic
0:33 **Phrase a repeated**	by both the chanter and the drone pipes in unison.
1:02 **Phrase b**	
1:30 **Phrase c**	
Variation 1	In the first variation changes in ornament and
1:56 **Phrase a**	expression subtly alter the ground.
2:17 **Phrase a repeated**	
2:36 **Phrase b**	
2:59 **Phrase c**	
Variation 1, Doubling	Listen at 4:16 for the high G which is heard for
3:21 **Phrase a**	the first time. The performer describes this
3:37 **Phrase a**	variation as "rounder" in sound.
3:54 **Phrase b**	
4:10 **Phrase c**	
4:35 Taorlúath	Fade out at beginning of Taorlúath, a variation named
	after its signature ornament which features the lowest
	note of the chanter as a grace note.
Final Variation,	Fade in at the beginning of the Crunlúath Doubling,
Crunlúath Doubling	a variation named after its signature ornament,
4:36 **Phrase a**	which is closely related to the Taorlúath, but has
4:57 **Phrase a**	even more pitches.
5:16 **Phrase b**	
5:34 **Phrase c**	
5:53 Return to Original	
Ground	Fade-out; recording ends at 6:05

named after its distinctive ornament which is said to "crown" the series of variations. The *pibroch* ends with a brief return to the first phrase of the ground, which the performer, Gregory Morrow, says is "like the end of a journey."

The haunting strains of the *pibroch* and its longtime use as a lament on the occasion of death has shaped listeners' perceptions of the commemorative significance of the bagpipe. The association of the instrument also moved beyond the battlefield, as many bagpipers began to hold positions in the service of important officials or were hired by towns to play at civic functions. Many towns employed a piper to walk through the streets each morning, playing the bagpipe in order to wake people up, and to make a second round in the evening at bedtime.[28] For these services, pipers received a salary and a free house, called the "piper's croft."

Beyond the boundaries of Scotland and Ireland, and in addition to the military expeditions with which the pipes were associated during the expansion of the British Empire, the civic duties of pipers were eventually absorbed into modern institutional settings. For instance, as many individuals of Irish or Scottish descent became police officers in the United States, bagpipe bands became closely associated with many US police and fire departments.

The distinctive sounds of various American fire and police bands are further enhanced visually by musicians donning Highland dress, particularly the kilt. Like the bagpipe, the kilt is the subject of considerable folklore and provides an excellent example of the "invention of culture" over time.[29] Although the kilt and the association of certain patterns or tartans with particular Scottish clans are popularly thought to be of great antiquity, in fact both the patterns and their associations emerged only in the mid-eighteenth century. Before that time, people tended to wear plaids of many colors, especially browns that were the color of heather, in order to disguise themselves when they needed to bed down outdoors. The sporran, a small leather purse commonly seen worn suspended from the hips of the piper, sometimes decorated with tassels, likely originated as a receptacle for a soldier's provisions while traveling.

The painting on page 163 of the Grant Piper William Cummings illustrates early eighteenth-century formal piping dress. In addition to his kilt with golden yellow, red, and gray stripes, the piper wears a short coat and vest. The bagpipes he holds are quite elaborate, decorated with cord, tassels, and a white banner with red and white fringes. The majestic sound of the pipes and their important role as military and national symbols are underscored by elaborate visual display.

Both the bagpipe and the form of Highland dress associated with it have been subjects of debate; both were banned as symbols of Scottish defiance, notably by the Disarming Act of 1746, not repealed for thirty-six years. Highland dress today draws on and reinvents styles popularized two centuries earlier under political circumstances particular to that time.

In many US cities, bagpipes are commonly played at funerals and other ceremonies of commemoration by pipers in formal dress; the pipes are also played at various civic celebrations. When a police officer or firefighter dies in the line of duty, a group of bagpipers almost always plays at the funeral. In fact, some police bagpipe bands were formed expressly for such solemn occasions.

Following the attacks on New York City and Washington DC on September 11, 2001, the historical role of the bagpipe to signify mourning and commemoration was highlighted in the US

The Emerald Society Pipe and Drum Band of New York City, founded in 1960, follows the Irish tradition of wearing solid-colored uniforms, in this case the blue and gold of the New York City Police Department.

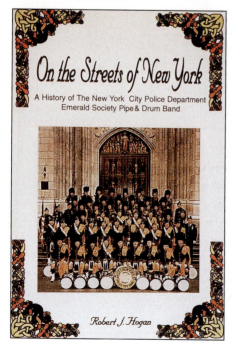

On the Streets of New York

A History of The New York City Police Department
Emerald Society Pipe & Drum Band

Robert J. Hogan

and abroad. When 343 firefighters were lost in the attack on the World Trade Center, the Pipes and Drums squad of the Fire Department of New York City (FDNY) pledged to play at the funeral of every firefighter who had died in the line of duty. Before the tragedy of 9/11, the most formidable crisis faced by these veteran pipers had been the dozen funerals that followed a deadly fire at a Brooklyn supermarket in 1978. "We'd never thought it could get worse than that," noted one.[30] So overwhelming was the number of funerals that one New York City officer talking to a reporter from Boston a week after the tragedy reportedly said, weeping, "You're from Boston? Tell them we need pipe bands. The pipe bands are all booked."[31]

For the members of the New York City Pipes and Drums, the pipes already held a range of deep meanings as an emblem of professional commitment, a reflection of ethnic pride, and an instrument of commemoration. In 2001, the pipes and their music became further imbued with meaning through their ubiquitous presence during a time of national tragedy. For pipers and many others who witnessed the events of September 11, 2001, and its aftermath, the sound most deeply connected with that time is that of the pipes playing *Amazing Grace,* a hymn with its own complex network of associations (to be discussed in Chapter 5).

The tartan worn by the Grant Piper William Cummings, painted by Richard Waitt in 1714, is unlike any Grant tartan worn today.

Entertainment and Dance

The significance of the pipes as an instrument of mourning and commemoration has moved to the forefront since 2001, but it is important to keep in mind that social occasions have long provided another setting and other significances for bagpipe performance. In the past, the duties of the piper included performing at the town's horse races and fairs, playing to honor the election of magistrates, and performing at weddings and harvest festivals. Today the pipes are still heard at *ceilidh*s (pronounced "KAY-lee"), festive gatherings that include music, socializing, and dancing. Here we are reminded of the kinesthetic aspect of bagpipe music and the complex physical engagement of the piper and listener/participant; the sound pervades the body and urges the listener to tap, clap, march, and dance. The internal experience of music is meant to be expressed externally.[32]

The *ceilidh* is rooted historically in public dances that flourished in the eighteenth century, following the Church of Scotland's lifting of decrees that prohibited public dancing. In 1723, the Edinburgh Assembly began to sponsor musical evenings for the gentry to raise money for the poor. These dances, to the accompaniment of the bagpipe or fiddle, at first consisted of basic reels and later gave rise to other forms of country dance. A *reel* is one type of dance music commonly played on the bagpipe, often in combination with a closely related slower dance called the *strathspey*.

Dancers from the Annapolis Valley Highland Dance Association perform at festivals and competitions throughout Nova Scotia and other Canadian maritime provinces. The dancers are tested yearly by examiners from the Scottish Dance Teachers Alliance, Scotland, and have consistently achieved high marks.

During the late eighteenth and nineteenth centuries, the *ceilidh* and its dances flourished. Professional dance masters, known as "Dancie" plus their surnames, plied their trade. Many played the fiddle and taught dances throughout the Scottish countryside. A repertory of dances became popular and associated with the *ceilidh,* including such numbers as *The Highland Scottische,* which entered the bagpipe repertory very early, *The Dashing White Sergeant,* and *The Strathspey and Reel.*[33]

The term *ceilidh* is used today to name any sort of social musical event associated with Scottish or Irish traditions. In the United States, one can attend *ceilidhs* held at Irish taverns in many cities or attend a gathering held at a Scottish arts weekend at a convention hotel in New Jersey. New dances were introduced by creative dance masters throughout the twentieth century, including European and North American regional entries such as *The Swedish Masquerade, The Virginia Reel,* and *The Mississippi Dip.* A variety of tunes are used to accompany the different dances, and the selection may depend on personal taste or local traditions wherever the dance is performed. "Jig" is an umbrella term for several closely related styles of Irish dance. We have already encountered a jig accompanied by the *uilleann* pipes in Listening Guide 39.

Competition and Concerts

Occasions of competition and public display have long been an important part of the history of piping, as the legend of William Cummings, the piper depicted in the painting reproduced on page 163 demonstrates. Cummings, who supposedly composed several *pibrochs,* is said to have died as the result of a wager between his chief at Castle Grant and a local rival at MacIntosh over which had the lustier piper. The two pipers started from the MacIntosh seat at Moy Hall, playing their pipes, and walked to Castle Grant, some hours away. After several hours, the MacIntosh piper was exhausted, but Cummings managed to continue playing until he reached home, whereupon he collapsed, threw his pipes into the fire, and died.

Although the bagpipe's volume and ability to sustain a melody allow it to be played effectively as a solo instrument, bagpipe bands (or pipe bands, as they are often called) were organized and competed in festivals by the twentieth century, especially in the United States and Canada. Each pipe band has its own story and distinctive history. Some have close ties to the Scottish or Irish ethnic traditions, although very few ensembles were founded by individuals immediately after their immigration. Rather, the bagpipe bands in the US and Canada today reflect an eclectic combination of long-time tradition, recent innovation, and the diverse occasions associated with bagpipe music. In many instances, pipe bands were founded as part of civic institutions such as police and fire departments. Another locus for bagpipe bands and competitions emerged in American and Canadian universities.

The recording of *Scotland the Brave* heard in Listening Guide 37 was performed by the Simon Fraser University Pipe Band of Burnaby, British Columbia. The band was formed in 1966, during the university's inaugural year. Since Simon Fraser University was named after a nineteenth-century explorer of western Canada, born in Vermont of Scottish ancestry, the band was founded to give the university "a kind of instant tradition." Today the Simon Fraser pipers consist of a family of five bands with over 150 members. Three are junior bands with players who are under nineteen years of age, organized expressly to train new members. The junior bands include a starter band and two graded ensembles that play increasingly difficult repertories.

The main band, heard in our recording, comprises experienced players who have demonstrated professional achievement as both ensemble and solo players and who have won solo medals in competition, an increasingly important aspect of pipe band culture. Twice in the late 1990s, the Simon Fraser Pipe Band was named World Pipe Band Champions at competitions in Glasgow.

Dressed to honor the Fraser clan in Scottish tartans with decorative sporrans, the pipe bands are a source of great pride for Simon Fraser University, which markets their videos and recordings and sponsors their concerts at venues far from their campus, such as New York City's Carnegie Hall. These performances, which include compositions ranging from marches to *pibrochs*, are occasions for school pride. The band is also featured at alumni reunions and fundraising events.

The world-champion Simon Fraser bagpipe band has since 1966 been a symbol of the Simon Fraser University in Burnaby, British Columbia.

The bagpipe thus sustains a large musical repertory rooted in its history in Scotland and Ireland, but has traveled widely over the last century and a half to many locales around the globe. As increasingly diverse settings support a full range of bagpipe sounds and repertories, the music's meaning has continued to expand as well.

Significance

A wide range of meanings is attached to the soundscapes of Scottish and Irish piping; some are closely connected to the characteristics of the musical sound, such as a lively march or the plaintive strains of the *pibroch* to signal lament or mourning. Many new layers of meaning have been added over the course of time, inspired by the pipes' presence in a range of settings. It is easy for listeners to differentiate the significance of the vigorous march played in a Saint Patrick's Day parade from the same piece played at a slower pace for a policeman's funeral. The pipes and their music have proven flexible; they can be used to perform traditional reels and jigs for entertainment at a party or to play the same selections on a concert stage for a college pep rally. The pipes have also continued to occupy an important role in their players' lives, providing entertainment or solace at unexpected moments in surprising places.

So powerful is the voice of the bagpipe and so strong are its multiple historical associations that it has entered into international popular culture, carrying these multiple meanings to an ever-wider cross section of people, even before the traumatic events of September 11, 2001. While the bagpipe's music can engender many responses and spark the imagination, the music in no way prescribes or limits the range of responses it evokes. Through the bagpipes and its multiple repertories, we can better understand how the "looseness or slippage" between the musical sounds and people's perceptions of their meanings feed debates about music's great power.[34]

An electrician from 103 Pipe and Drum (IBEW Local 103) plays the pipes during his lunch break.

The 1979 film *The Onion Field*, based on Joseph Wambaugh's book, provides a fine example of the multiple meanings of the bagpipes as constructed through the lens of literature and film. The sound of the pipes is used both to advance the movie's narrative and to evoke a range of emotions. The film tells the story of Iain Campbell, a young police officer of Scottish descent who is murdered in an onion field by thugs. A funeral *pibroch* conveys four powerful yet markedly different meanings at four pivotal moments in the film. In the film's opening scene, Campbell performs a *pibroch* on the pipes as a proud expression of his Scottish heritage. The *pibroch* is next heard in the background just before Campbell is murdered in the onion fields, a signifier of impending death. A lone piper next plays the same *pibroch* as a lament at Campbell's funeral. In the final scene of the film, Campbell's mother encounters a young piper playing the *pibroch* at the local Highland games, the pipes and their music signifying both her grief at the loss of her son and the role of the pipes in the community's continuity.

New York City, a major center of the Caribbean diaspora, sustains lively traditions of Caribbean music and dance. Here girls in colorful regalia dance at the Brooklyn Labor Day Carnival, the largest Caribbean event in the United States and Canada, with an annual attendance of over one million people.

The presence of numerous transplanted music traditions in a single place can have a variety of outcomes. Some musics are maintained and performed by those who have migrated and who share kinship and history, while others, as we will see in Chapter 6, attract the attention and participation of individuals who become part of new musical communities based on affinity.

Many of the soundscapes we will study throughout this book are the result of migrations past and present. The stories behind these migrations are rarely simple or straightforward, because people move for different reasons and remain settled for varying lengths of time. Although voluntary migration is commonly assumed to be the norm, forced migration, when circumstances like war or famine compel relocation, is in fact much more common.

In addition to whether migration was voluntary or forced (or a combination of both) other variables—such as the date of the immigration; the conditions under which an individual traveled and arrived; the immigrant's age, ethnic or religious identity, gender, economic situation, and educational background—all influence the *sounds, settings,* and *significances* of immigrant musical life. In the following pages, we will take a close look at the musical outcomes of immigration from four different regions—China, the Middle East, Africa, and Southeast Asia—to the United States, comparing how some musical styles have been maintained after they were transplanted to new locales and how others have been transformed.

Fieldwork Among Immigrant Communities

Although circumstances of immigration vary widely, and migrants come from both rural and urban areas in their homelands, most have ended up relocating in major urban centers in countries around the world.

It is ironic, given the historical importance of cities in immigrant musical life, that ethnomusicologists and folklorists were so slow to acknowledge them as sites for ethnomusicological study. As we saw in our exploration of three major urban areas in Chapter 2, most cities incorporate many immigrant communities, and in fact assumed their present size and influence largely through the influx of immigrants from different places at different times. Immigrants helped build these cities and the railways and roads linking them.

Not only did scholars avoid studying the life of cities, they assumed that people in cities somehow lose the traditions with which they arrived. They assumed this because many countries actively sought to transform or homogenize immigrant cultures. Israel, for example, absorbed a huge number of Jewish refugees from many different places following its founding in 1948, and established "absorption centers" in which most immigrants learned the national language, Hebrew, and a new cultural system, including songs and dances.

In 1968, the folklorist Richard Dorson carried out one of the first studies to show that immigrants in cities do not always abandon their traditions. Before Dorson's research, most scholars assumed that ethnic groups adapted as quickly as possible, leaving behind their original language and customs, especially any that would clearly mark them as foreign. In studying the effect of life in an urban, industrial center on imported cultures, Dorson charted patterns of cultural continuity and change among a number of ethnic groups settled in one metropolitan area—Gary, Indiana. Dorson surveyed cultural life among immigrant communities of African, Serbian, Greek, Mexican, and Puerto Rican descent. To his surprise, he found rich music traditions performed in churches and at various civic celebrations and rites of passage. He approached these urban music traditions primarily as re-creations of those of the original homelands. At the same time, he was aware that these traditions had undergone some changes in the New World and maintained a lively relationship with their homelands.

Although Dorson emphasized ethnic separatism, he also provided evidence of how urban communities shared common experiences of urban life. Dorson then began to document what he termed a new "lore of the city." In the years since Dorson's landmark study, ethnomusicologists have redefined their approaches to the music of ethnic groups in urban areas. They have become keenly aware that the music traditions of immigrant communities change and inevitably differ from those in their homelands.

Voluntary Migration

Voluntary migration is the movement of people into a new region by choice, motivated by an attraction to the new locale. For example, many migrants came to North and South America on a voluntary basis, seeking new religious and economic opportunities. The number of migrants to the United States increased dramatically in the second half of the nineteenth century, when the changeover from sailing ships to steamships around 1860 made ocean crossings faster, safer, and cheaper. During the 1850s, 2.6 million immigrants arrived in the United States; by the 1880s the number had doubled to 5.2 million, and in the first decade of the twentieth century it reached its peak at 8.8 million people. Faster travel allowed migration from areas beyond Europe, and during the late nineteenth and early twentieth centuries the United States saw the arrival of increasing numbers of people from the Middle East and Asia.

Each wave of migration to North America had its musical impact. For example, beginning in the seventeenth century British migrants carried with them *ballads*—strophic songs that tell a story—that found a permanent home in the mountains of Virginia and Kentucky, where they were still transmitted long after they had been forgotten in the British Isles. We encountered an English ballad, *Barbara Allen,* in Chapter 2, where we heard two renditions of the song transmitted orally by musical amateurs (Listening Guide 31) and a professional arrangement performed by an early music ensemble drawing on a version of the ballad text in written sources (Listening Guide 32)

These performances of different versions of *Barbara Allen* provide excellent examples of two important transmission processes we will encounter in many soundscapes—oral and written transmission. *Oral transmission* occurs when music is transmitted from person to person through hearing music performed. Oral transmission can occur both intentionally, between teacher and student, and informally, emerging from casual, repeated hearings of, for example, a lullaby.

In contrast, music can be transmitted through written sources, termed *written transmission.* In addition to the written transmission of song texts, as we saw in the case of the broadsides printing ballad texts in Chapter 2, some cultures have systems for writing music that carry specific information about musical content, including melody, rhythm, form, etc. We will briefly explore and compare some different systems of music writing in subsequent chapters.

Oral and written transmission often overlap. In this chapter, for instance, we will encounter a tradition of Chinese folk songs in which oral transmission is supported by songbooks containing the texts. We will also hear two versions of a famous African American spiritual that was transmitted early through both oral tradition and writing. Since the early twentieth century, recordings have reshaped the processes of musical transmission, inscribing sound within various technological media.

LOOKING *Back*

Turning Points in US Immigration History

1845–1850	"Great hunger" potato famine in Ireland spurs immigration to United States.
1850	Increasing numbers from Latin America, China, and Scandinavia instead of from Great Britain, Ireland, and Germany.
1864	Immigration Act of 1864 encourages immigration to United States; immigrants can apply to US government for financial aid.
Late 1880s	European immigration shifts from northern and western Europe to southern and eastern Europe (Russia, Poland, Greece, Italy).
1921	Quota Act establishes yearly immigration quotas at 3 percent of foreign-born population as of 1910 census.
1924	Immigration Act of 1924 makes national quotas permanent and limits yearly immigration to 2 percent of the US population as of 1890 census; eastern and southern European immigration is sharply decreased, and Asian immigrants are banned.
1948	Displaced Persons Act of 1948 defines those who were victims of Nazi persecution between September 1, 1938, and January 1, 1948, as qualified for permanent residence in United States.
1952	Immigration Act of 1952 provides first fundamental revision of Immigration Act of 1864 and revises the quota system.
1965	Immigration and Nationality Act of 1965 amends Immigration Act of 1924; discontinues quota systems and places a limit of 170,000 on visas.
1986	Immigration Reform and Control Act of 1986 amends basic Immigration and Nationality Act of 1952 to improve control of aliens in United States and increase border control.
1988	Immigration Amendment of 1988 makes additional visas available to immigrants from underrepresented countries to enhance diversity.
1990	Immigration Act of 1990 amends 1986 legislation and revises immigration laws since 1952.
2001	USA PATRIOT Act (Uniting and Strengthening America by Providing Appropriate Tools Required to Intercept and Obstruct Terrorism Act of 2001) contains amendments restricting immigration.

CASE STUDY: The Chinese Migration

Some individuals and communities migrated voluntarily to seek better lives and economic opportunities. However, the idea of the immigrant spurred on by a sense of exploration and a desire for profit is mostly a romantic myth. The decision to immigrate was for most individuals full of conflict and intensely personal. One important example in North American history is the course of Chinese immigration, which can be charted in part through music.

Immigration from China, which began around 1850, was largely voluntary because of the attraction, or "pull," that the United States (called *Jinshan*, the "Gold Mountain") held for many. The first large wave of Chinese immigrants was attracted by the California gold rush; others arrived in the early 1860s to help construct the transcontinental railroad. However, political anarchy, famine, and economic crisis in mid-nineteenth century China were strong "push" (negative) factors that persuaded many to migrate, even though moving to a new country was arduous.

Thousands of Chinese borrowed money for their fares against wages to be earned on arrival, often spending years in indentured servitude in the New World. Soon after their arrival, Chinese migrants encountered serious discrimination and intolerance both in everyday life and in a series of exclusionary laws. (See **Looking Back: Chinese Immigration** on page 179.) Only in the 1960s, were restrictions eased through the Refugee Relief Acts.

This 1850 lithograph of a Chinese immigrant musician from Canton with his family, interpreter, and a young female musician is the earliest surviving image related to Chinese music in the US. The image, produced by Phineas T. Barnum, to whom the musicians were under contract and by whom they were presented as "The Living Chinese Family," is a graphic reminder of mid-nineteenth century practices of displaying so-called "exotic" people in museums and circuses.

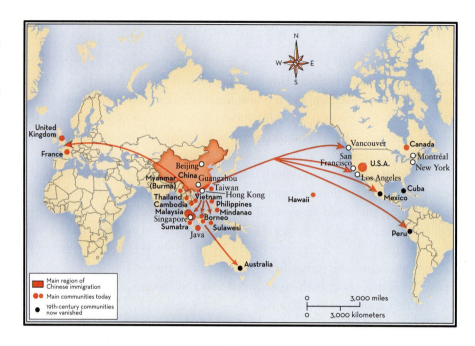

Thus, any discussion of the Chinese American community and its musical life at the turn of the twenty-first century must take into account an episodic and often painful history of migration. The long history of Chinese immigration to the United States also demonstrates the ongoing impact of push and pull factors such as economics and politics long after the initial period of migration, shaping individual responses to both the new home and the ancestral homeland.[3]

Many voluntary Chinese immigrants, particularly during the first half of the twentieth century, considered themselves temporary sojourners in the United States. Most were motivated by economic gain, hoping to return home prosperous. Therefore many sojourners were strongly motivated to maintain the cultural traditions of the homeland to which they expected to return. Though some did return the triumphant homecoming was a dream that most immigrants never realized, and many spent the rest of their lives in North America. Since the 1960s, most Chinese immigrants have come to settle permanently.

The song *Ng Bak Loi Gimsaan* ("Uncle Ng Comes to the Gold Mountain"), Listening Guide 41 (see page 178), relives details of the Chinese migration process through musical performance. This song belongs to a traditional southeastern Chinese genre called *muk'yu* in Cantonese spelling, spelled *muyu* in the pinyin system used today. Ranging in length from a few dozen

LOOKING *Back*

Chinese Immigration

1849–1882	First wave of Chinese immigrants begins shortly after gold rush in California.
1882	Chinese Exclusion Act of 1882 limits the number of Chinese who can enter the United States.
1904	Chinese Exclusion Act is extended indefinitely.
1917	Immigration Act of 1917 excludes all Asians and encourages skilled laborers and professionals only if there is no unemployment in the United States.
1943	Chinese Exclusion Act is repealed and Chinese residents are allowed to become citizens; Chinese quota set at 105 immigrants per year.
1965	Civil Rights Act of 1964 restores basic rights previously denied to Chinese Americans.
1966	Immigration and Nationality Act of 1965 ushers in third wave of Chinese immigrants.

lines to lengthy compositions that can take days to perform, *muyu* are transmitted both by oral tradition and written down in songbooks. Immigration is the subject of five of the twenty *muyu* songs known and sung by Mr. Sheung Chi Ng (affectionately known to his friends as "Ng Bak," or "Uncle Ng"), who migrated to the United States from Taishan County. Even though Uncle Ng arrived in 1979 at the age of sixty-nine, he continued until his death in 2001 to sing of his dream of becoming rich and making enough money to return to Taishan. Ungle Ng therefore maintained the longtime tradition of immigrant Taishanese who felt responsible to their homeland and their relatives there. By the period of Uncle Ng's migration in the late twentieth century, opportunities for Chinese in the United States had expanded and Taishan had lost much of its appeal as a "native place that both needed and valorized overseas Taishanese contributions."[4]

Muyu can be sung by men or women and are performed on a variety of occasions, both public and private. *Muyu* texts, like those of other related Chinese song genres, tell of the concerns of everyday life. *Ng Bak Loi Gimsaan,* composed in 1982, is a typical *muyu,* tracing its composer's experience as a sojourner whose thoughts focus on returning home. Ungle Ng's

Ng Bak Loi Gimsaan (Chinese *muyu*)

Date of composition: 1982

Date of performance: 1989 or 1990

Performer: Sheung Chi Ng, also known as Ng Bak or Uncle Ng

Form: Flexible musical form with rhyming couplets and triplets

Tempo: Moderate; duple meter

Function: Personal narrative song performed alone or at social gatherings

WHAT TO LISTEN FOR:

- Detailed narrative in five parts of Uncle Ng's migration and his experience as an immigrant
- Alternation of lyrics, in boldface in the transliteration below, with vocables, in standard type
- Groups of four, five, or six phrases that are similar in melodic and rhythmic content
- Limited vocal range of about one octave
- Three distinctive types of cadences at the ends of phrases: a long pitch low in the singer's range followed by a descending slide or *glissando;* a long pitch high in his range followed by a *glissando;* and a shorter pitch cut off without a *glissando.* The first of these types ends most sections of the *muyu.*

	STRUCTURE AND TEXT	TRANSLATION	DESCRIPTION
0:00	**Ng bak loi gimsaan jia**	Spoken: Ungle Ng comes to the	Uncle Ng announces the title
	Introduction	Gold Mountain.	of the *muyu.*
	1. wo de **gim mai** ge **dan nan**	1. At this leisure time I have	
	oh shi de **you** wa **dou * xiang**	many thoughts.	Lines 1, 2, and 4 end with a
	2. wo xiang de **xiang eh ge me**	2. Once *muyu* has come to my	cadence near the top of the
	ngo de **gua** ge **diu chang**	mind, I start singing;	singer's range, followed by a
	3. **gei guai ban det** loi you **fei**	3. This piece of *muyu* is about	*glissando.* Line 5 ends with a
	ban da **yang**	nothing else	low pitch, followed by a
	4. wo **you loi wo yan wo** dou	4. But to recall my hometown	*glissando.* In contrast, line
	gok bei yu guan **gai yang**	again.	three ends on a low pitch
	5. wo de **di da** ngo **nan sop shi**	5. This is a long story, hard to	without a *glissando.*
	you jiang	tell in a few words.	
	Life in Taishan		
0:44	6. **shei xi nan dan yu** gok * **gai**	6. Forty years ago my	
	na **fong**	hometown was liberated.	
	7. wo de **gip** da **jiao han** de di	7. A new dynasty came with a	
	yip ge **jiao wang**	new emperor.	
	8. wo de **wa ya shi dan ng jiang**	8. Many other things I'll not	
	wo **ya ng gong?**	talk or sing about.	
	9. **lao lao fo fo** de **qup** ge **soi**	9. But we worked very hard to	
	yang	build reservoirs.	

1:09	10. wo de **soi lei** de **gou gan zang zang** ni ge **wa** ga **miao** la jiao 11. ge **xi bo gep bai** yu **mang liang** ah **sang** 12. wo de **soi gan gei gou** ah de yin gok, lo'a biang 13. **you dan you ma** de you **hao xiang** ah **liang**	10. Once the irrigation works were completed, we produced excellent crops. 11. The granaries were bursting with sweet potatoes and rice. 12. How many people in the world believe 13. That life gets easier when there is money and rice.
1:37	14. ge **liang yao lu lan** yu **gui feng** ah **xiang** 15. **shei yin oh mang** wo de **ci goi gou-eh yang** 16. wo de **jia** ga **yu** a **giang yip** gai **yu** la **mang** 17. wo de **ban wa** gai **niao gan** yu **cuk tiang** ah **kong** 18. wo de **ye loi fan fu** de **shan gui han nong**	14. Yet there were struggles on the political orientation between the two lines. 15. Who wouldn't want to go overseas? 16. I thought during the nights and hoped during the days, 17. On what terms I could go to Hong Kong, 18. It seemed to me just like a mortal wanting to enter paradise.
2:09	*Arriving in Hong Kong* 19. **gei-yu** gai **biang** ah **kong** wo de **yu gui hai** la **bong** 20. **gou lai ai hak jin wei bong** 21. gai **yin zhun wei shou** yu **dan xing** na **song** 22. wa **xiang jia gim song liao lu** zhu **dei bong bong** lao	19. Arrived in Hong Kong, I raised my head looking around. 20. The skyscrapers were majestic and splendid. 21. Good luck makes one happy and full of vigor; 22. I hurried myself on the road going to the Gold Mountain.
2:33	23. **gei yin gong li gok diu** * hai le **han** a **hong** ah 'ei 24. wo de **gu wei gou** yi **fa dou** wo de **yu** ga **gou gei** 25. **wei ya gan no** wa **gui** gui **miu** gah **at** ah ei 26. de **xi huai bon cong fa do** wo de **ya gua mei cei** lao	23. People say that America is paradise. 24. Everybody makes money and becomes rich. 25. If I could reach my destination, 26. It might not be too late for me to have good luck and become rich.
2:57	*Life in the U.S.* 27. wo de **gai** ga **xiang lei hai gan gei loi** de **yin kuai wa** ne **lai** 28. wo de **jia gei lai dong** de ah **gue liang** ah **tai** 29. **Gong** ah **yi** ah **dou** de **loi gui han** ah **gai?** 30. ei **wa ya ti go na** hao wa **lai** de ge **mei gok** wo de **ta** de **sai gai**	27. On the streets I see so many beautifully dressed people. 28. They are in suits and wear ties. 29. They walk on the streets wearing high-heeled shoes. 30. I believed I could enjoy life in America.

The tempo suddenly slows. Note the contrasting musical style and change in pitch level. The *glissando* is heard only at the cadence of the final phrase in this section.

(c o n t i n u e s)

(continued)

STRUCTURE AND TEXT	TRANSLATION	DESCRIPTION
31. wo de **soi jie gei xip** ba **soi nian gan fu** de yep gui yi yong **gai** lao	31. How could I expect that I would still have to endure such hardship at my age?	

	STRUCTURE AND TEXT	TRANSLATION	DESCRIPTION
3:36	32. wo de **gip** ga **sat** da **liang dang bo** ga **xi** la **hei** lao	32. Two meals every day at irregular times.	
	33. wo de **yi** ah **loi ji shi** wo de **ji zhui** la **hong dan nai** ha ge **xip gei sang lei** lao	33. At night I lodge in the *Kangning* building on the twelfth floor.	
	34. wo de **gip** gan **yin** da **han lu** de **doi** gui **gai** la **hong**	34. Every day I walk around wandering in the streets.	
	35. **sang hua diao gan wang gang gong**	35. I wouldn't want to tell my living conditions,	
	36. wo de **yin wei ya ba mm ba me** de **gan ji** de **fong yin** gan **hang** lao	36. Because Uncle doesn't [I don't] have money to deposit in the bank.	
4:14	37. ga **liu** ya ga **bai hei** de **you jing nan** na **wang**	37. New York City is so prosperous.	The tempo gradually increases again.
	38. **gou heng lei ban yin lua luai** la **bong**	38. Traffic is so convenient, and crowds come and go.	
	39. gi **gou lei** ai ha **ding** ding de wa **gai gen cong**	39. There are everywhere skyscrapers and factories.	
	40. **gou** de **gua gai yao huan hung luk** ah **dan?**	40. One has to watch the red and green lights when crossing streets.	
	41. **luk fua leng jiang** go **lo vi hao** de **gu gai hang** lao	41. When the green light is on, one can't cross streets.	
4:44	42. wa **dao wei ha** zang **fu luk** yu **fa yung** ah **cao**	42. In the morning women go back to the factories,	
	43. gan **na ming kei hu** wo de **xiang do cu** wei **fong** lao	43. And men go to work as waiters and cooks.	
	44. wo de **gu wei** go **lai bai cut liang** an **ti** yu **mao cu** wei la **fong**	44. Each week they are given a salary, but there is no place to keep the money,	
	45. wo de **ho** ei **guai fu hai** de **tun yin gan nan** lao	45. So they open an account and deposit money in the bank.	

muyu also provides insights into both the attraction of the United States and the difficult political circumstances at home that led to his migration.

Uncle Ng's *muyu* transmits valuable information about the modern process of immigration, with detailed descriptions of late twentieth-century buildings and cityscapes. At the same time, the song conveys ideas about immigration that reflect the older goal of the sojourner who wishes to return home prosperous and respected.

Time	Transliteration	Translation	Notes
5:13	46. wo de **tan** ah **guan** ah ca lei de yu **mun gai** la **hong**	46. Streets and alleys are full of restaurants and teahouses.	Pause before beginning of section. Sudden slowing of tempo.
	47. wo de **an hua** le **fei wang** wo de **du ou han gong**	47. They are brilliantly illuminated and open until daybreak.	
	48. **ah bak** ge **hua bao** la **mao dan** ge de **mm** kuai **soi gong**	48. Uncle has [I have] no money in his purse; I can't help it.	
	49. wo de **hua bao** lai yu **dan** wo de **ye ye** yu **yin jie** ya **hong**	49. If I had money in my purse, I would go several times a day to the teahouse.	
	50. wo de **yap** yu gei **wai fan** ne ge **wai san cei gyun ng xi** de **gim bei** ah **lao**	50. If I had the opportunity to return to my hometown, Taishan County, Sijui Wushi district, Jinbeilang Township,	
	51. ah **gim san nan yin** loi **gei** de de **jin** hui **wei** ya **wang** lao	51. How glorious and impressive would I be as the returned *gimsaan ke* (the guest from the Gold Mountain).	
5:58	*Imagined return to Taishan* 52. ga **bun diung an** lai **loi gyap** yu giang **loi mang**	52. Brothers from my village would come to welcome me and visit me.	
	53. wo de **gim** ga **hen ai liang fen** de yu **jin nai** la **song**	53. Brothers would be so joyful in meeting each other again.	
	54. wo de **gim ji** yu **but bei** ah **wang**	54. At that time I would no longer be the same person as before.	
	55. an wa **pang** ah **luan gang ji** ge yu **bang ma hong** lao	55. I would first distribute money, then the sesame candies.	
6:25	56. wo de **han** ah ai **ham gan** ni **gong** yu **but** da **ding** la	56. Between brothers we would have so many loving sentiments to tell that the gatherings would be endless.	
	57. wo de **yu loi woi** ga gan **ting yin** ah	57. Thus I am back to my home and see the members of my family again.	
6:37	**Ng bak loi gimsaan jia**	Spoken: "Uncle Ng comes to the Gold Mountain"	end: 6:43

Muyu songs are divided into sections according to the course of their story lines. In *Uncle Ng Comes to the Gold Mountain,* we find the following divisions:

Introduction, lines 1 to 5

Life in Taishan, lines 6 to 18

Arriving in Hong Kong, lines 19 to 26

Life in the United States, lines 27 to 51

Imagined return to Taishan, lines 52 to 57

Written *muyu* have a *fixed form*—seven syllables per line of text, usually divided 2 + 2 + 3, and often rhymed. When performing *muyu,* the singer often adds *vocables* to the text. Generally, the text setting is syllabic, but ornaments can be added so that each syllable is prolonged over three or more pitches (termed a *melismatic* setting).

The relationship between the text and its melody in *muyu* is further complicated because Chinese is a tonal language; that is, it uses different tones or pitches to differentiate the meaning of words. In *muyu,* three linguistic tones can appear at the end of any line of text; correspondingly, each line can end on one of three musical pitches. However, the five main divisions of the song end on the same distinctive low pitch followed by a glissando.[5]

CASE STUDY : Arab Migration from the Middle East

The Chinese migration to the United States was primarily voluntary; other migrations that began as voluntary movements at some later point included forced migration.

Middle Eastern migration provides an example. It has been suggested that immigrants from Greater Syria (including what is now the country of Lebanon) discovered an "entrepreneurial Eden" in America in the late 1870s. Political and economic instability in the Middle East provided an impetus for what is often called the first wave of Arab emigrants to depart. The economic downturn caused by the opening of the Suez Canal in 1869, which disrupted

Over the course of the twentieth century, the large Lebanese diaspora has established major communities in North and South America, West Africa, France, and Australia.

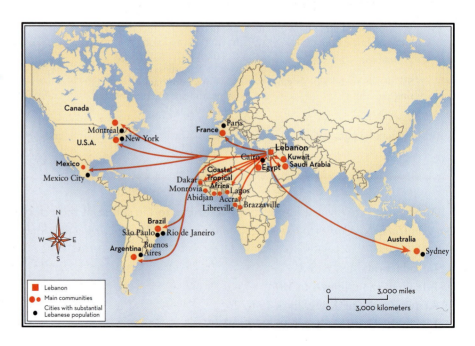

LOOKING *Back*

Middle Eastern Immigration

1875–1918	First wave of Arabic-speaking immigrants arrives, mainly from Greater Syria.
1910s	Dissolution of Ottoman Empire fuels latter part of first wave of Arab immigration.
1950s–1960s	Second wave of Arab immigrants, including those displaced by 1948 Arab-Israeli War.
1960s– present	Third wave of Arab immigration—skilled professionals and unskilled workers—fleeing political instability in Middle East.

longtime overland trade routes, and the breakup of the Ottoman empire in 1917—Turkey became a republic only in 1922—were the final precipitating events, although few were forced to migrate during this period. In contrast, the second wave of Arab immigrants included some who were forced to migrate after being dislocated by the Arab-Israeli conflict in 1948.[6]

Whether Muslims, Christians, or Jews, many Middle Eastern immigrants of the first wave moved as part of extended personal and family networks. Usually termed "chain migration," this process was started by individuals who, on arrival, sent for other family members and encouraged close friends to join them as well. Chain migration contributed to the formation of large Arab American communities in urban areas such as Detroit and New York.

The constant flow of people (until the 1924 immigration restrictions) kept connections with the homeland alive. Immigrants from the Middle East also imported recordings of the latest musical styles and soon began publishing their own recordings. Thus musical styles traveled across great distances back and forth between the new home in the United States and the historical homeland—Syria, Lebanon, Egypt, or elsewhere.

Recordings from the period of Arab migration in the mid-twentieth century supported the transmission of Middle Eastern musical styles to the United States and illustrate the process. Following the end of World War II in the mid-1940s, the Lebanese singer Hanan Harouni (known as Hanan) settled in New York City. Well known for her accomplished

Russel Bunai and Amer Khadaj stand in front of Alamphon Arabic Records around 1950. This store in Brooklyn sold records imported from the Middle East as well as releases by Arab Americans.

This poster advertises a performance by the singer Hanan Harouni, Philip Solomon (violin), Muhammad El-Akkad (*qanun*), and "Rhode Island's hottest darabaka player" at a *Mahrajan*, an outdoor festival lasting two or three days, sponsored by Saint Basil's Melkite Church and held at St. Mary's Church grounds in Cumberland Hill, Rhode Island.

vocal style, Hanan brought to her new country the vocal quality and ornaments typical of Lebanese traditional music.

The recording heard in Listening Guide 42 (see page 186), made after Hanan's arrival in New York, is accompanied by an ensemble of accomplished Middle Eastern musicians, most of whom are also immigrants. The ensemble includes not only Arab Muslim and Christian musicians, but also the Iraqi-born Jewish violinist Hakki Obadia, illustrating the interaction of Middle Eastern musicians of various national and religious backgrounds in the transmission of Arab music. Here, Hanan sings a song called a *mawwal*, a traditional Arab form that alternates sections in free and regular rhythms. During the sections in free rhythm, the soloist repeats words and ornaments the melody, which is set in an Arab mode called *huzam*, one mode in the pan-middle Eastern musical system, termed *maqam*, that we will explore more fully in Chapter 5.[7] The *mawwal* text is colloquial in language and content, commenting on the pain of migration, which by the mid-twentieth century was not just an outflow of people, but an ongoing movement back and forth between homeland and diaspora. The song is accompanied by an ensemble that includes the Middle Eastern lute and zither. (See "**Sound Sources: The 'Ud and the Qanun.**")

Arab Americans continue to have close ties to their homelands, and these connections are reaffirmed and symbolized through song. Live concerts of Arab music featuring famous musicians from the Middle East are often mounted. The most important of these events attract audiences of thousands from all over the United States and receive major press coverage. An example is the appearance in May 1999 of the famous Lebanese singer Fairuz (Nuhad Haddad) at the Garden Arena of the MGM Grand in Las Vegas.

Born in 1934, Fairuz has long represented Lebanon and the Middle East through her musical performances; she is a national heroine and an international star. Fairuz became famous in the 1950s for her performances of songs composed by the Rahbani brothers, one of whom she married. In the 1980s and 1990s, she began singing songs composed by her son Ziyad Rahbani (b. 1956), providing a noteworthy example of musical transmission within a single family.[8]

In her Las Vegas concert, Fairuz was accompanied by ten backup singers and an ensemble that included Middle Eastern instruments (among them, the 'ud and *qanun*) and Western instruments, including nine violins. Such an event reconnects the Lebanese and other Arab Americans with their Middle Eastern

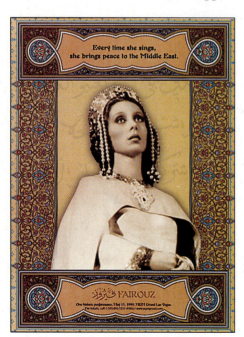

This poster advertising a 1999 Las Vegas concert by Fairuz (also spelled Fairouz or Fayrouz) links diaspora musicmaking to homeland politics.

SOUND *Sources*

The *'Ud* and the *Qanun*

The *'ud* is the principal plucked *chordophone* (string instrument) used in the Arab world. It has a short neck and a large body with a rounded back. Some players describe the shape of the instrument as "half an egg." The rounded sound box is constructed of sixteen to twenty-one ribs made of lightweight wood. Up to three sound holes may be carved into the flat sound-board, which supports the bridge and the strings. The length of the neck varies; tuning pegs anchor the strings attached at the end of the neck. The *'ud*'s ten strings are paired, two to each pitch. A *plectrum,* or pick, sometimes made of an eagle feather, is used to pluck the strings.

Stories about the origins of the *'ud* dating back to the ninth and tenth centuries credit Lamak, a descendant of Cain, with inventing the instrument. According to these myths, Lamak's son had died, and when the boy's remains were hung on a tree, they suggested the original form of the *'ud.* The instrument is believed to bring health benefits to its players and audiences, and its strings are traditionally associated with cosmological elements such as the seasons and the zodiac. While the *'ud* spread east and west through its use in both religious and secular music, it was particularly important as the instrument that accompanied secular songs.[9]

The *'ud* may have different numbers of strings in different places. The highly popular five-stringed (that is, five-course) Egyptian *'ud* has a range of over two octaves. A four-stringed *'ud* is used in Morocco, whereas a six-stringed model is favored from Istanbul to Baghdad. The *'ud* also entered Europe by way of Islamic Spain, where it developed into the lute (*l 'ud*).

Different schools of *'ud* performance have contributed to the establishment of solo repertories, freeing the instrument from its traditional function of accompanying vocal music. Method books for studying the *'ud* incorporating Western theoretical approaches and musical notation have been available since the beginning of the twentieth century. These books depart from the traditional method of oral transmission through individual study with a master.

Another chordophone often heard in Middle Eastern music is the *qanun,* which has a trapezoidal shape and twenty-six courses (sets) of three strings each. The *qanun* player attaches a plectrum to the index finger of each hand to produce music with a heterophonic texture. Both *'ud* and *qanun* are often decorated with mother-of-pearl inlay, lending the instruments extraordinary beauty.

Wakef 'ala shat baher ("Standing on the Shore," Arab song)

CD 2
Track 5

Date: c. 1950
Composer: Zaghul al-Damnour
Performers: Hanan Harouni, *vocalist*; Joe Bedway, *'ud*; Yacoub Ghannim, *qanun*;
  Hakki Obadia and Naim Karakand, violins, drum, wood blocks, and chorus
Form: *Mawwal*, alternating refrains and free rhythm sections
Mode: *Maqam huzam*
Tempo: Moderate duple meter, with sections in free rhythm

WHAT TO LISTEN FOR:

- Classical Middle Eastern instruments, the *'ud* (lute) and *qanun* (zither), as well as the Western violin, which has been played in the Middle East since the nineteenth century
- Vocal style with nasal quality and many ornaments
- A *heterophonic* texture between the voice and the melodic instruments
- An alternation between sections with duple meter and sections with free rhythm
- Text referring to migration, describing a community in motion, carrying news between new home and ancestral homeland.

	STRUCTURE AND TEXT	TRANSLATION	DESCRIPTION
0:00	**Instrumental introduction**		All the melodic instruments play a melody in a heterophonic texture. The melodic structure of the introduction forms an A B A' pattern; the contrasting B section features the violins. The introduction also establishes *maqam huzam*.
	Refrain (Hanan and instruments)		The refrain is sung by Hanan, with the instruments playing the same melody. The first phrase is repeated. A *riqq* can be heard reinforcing the duple rhythm.
0:22	**Phrase a (repeated)**		
	Wa 'if 'ala shatt il-bahr bakkani s-safar	I stand at the seashore, travel made me cry.	
0:36	**Phrase b**		Phrase b contrasts with phrase a as it moves into a slightly higher register.
	Min mitli tlawwa' wa addi natar?	Who like me has suffered and waited as much as I did?	
0:44	**Phrases c and d**		Phrases c and d use a still higher register. It is interesting to note that all of the phrases in the refrain begin on an *offbeat*: that is, the first note of the phrase occurs just after a metrically strong beat. A cadence occurs, followed by a pause.
	Ma'kill mawjih rayihab bib'at salam	With each going wave I send regards	
	Ma'kill mawjih raji'ah bintur khabar	With each returning wave I wait for news	

0:58	**Phrase e**		The sense of meter is disrupted as
	Bintur khabar	I wait for news	the song switches into *free rhythm*.
			The repetition of the text gives
			special meaning to the phrase "I
			wait for news."
	Interlude (free rhythm)		The free rhythmic interlude begins
1:02	**Violin solo**		with an improvised violin phrase
1:14	**Vocal solo**		with no sense of strong or weak
	Min wa 'fet arramlat	When the sand stood still	beats. The *'ud* and violin continue
	'Arfouni Gharib	They knew that I was a	playing heterophonically with the
		stranger	singer throughout all three
	Teshar ma'i najmat	The stars stayed awake with	interludes.
		me	
	We-beterja' tghib	And they disappeared again	
1:43	Wa bkhaf lawla raj'at	And I fear that they will	
		return	
	Wa bkhaf lawla raj'at	And I fear that they will	
		return	
	Min doun lhabib	Without the lover	
	We nrahat lbhar eddami	Then I face the ocean where	
	khatar	danger awaits	

Refrain (chorus and instruments) — The chorus sings the refrain. Note that phrase a is not repeated this time as it was in the first refrain.

	Refrain (chorus and	The chorus sings the refrain. Note
	instruments)	that phrase a is not repeated this
2:03	**Phrases a and b**	time as it was in the first refrain.
2:21	**Phrases c and d**	
2:36	**Phrase e**	

	Interlude (free rhythm)		The *'ud* plays the introductory
2:40	**'Ud solo**		phrase to this section.
2:48	**Vocal solo**		
	Ma kount almah la safinah	I could not see a boat or a	
	wa la felouk	felouca	
	Ma beshouf illa ghyoum	I can only see the clouds	
	jayya men toulou'	coming from the horizon	
	Be yenzalou we ye'abbou	They come and take with them	
	Min 'ouyoun tnour	From the fountainheads that	
		shine	
	We koul sa' a be-ye'malou	Every hour they make a	
	sahbat matar	cloud of rain	

	Refrain (Hanan, chorus and	Hanan can be heard prominently
	instruments)	leading the chorus on this third
3:26	**Phrase a instrumental**	refrain.
3:33	**Phrases a and b**	
3:47	**Phrases c and d**	
4:02	**Phrase e**	

	Interlude (free rhythm)	The *qanun* plays the introductory
4:05	**Qanun solo**	phrase to this section. The voice
4:14	**Vocal solo**	enters, and the recording fades
		out, ending at 4:18.

homelands, evoking deep emotion with songs such as *Take Me (And Plant Me in the Land of Lebanon)*. In the words of a woman who had traveled from Michigan to Las Vegas to hear Fairuz sing:

> My grandmother had a fig tree and grapes, and Fayrouz reminded me of that . . . She sings about things that people used to take for granted: the walls we used to live in, the smell of the air we used to breathe. We just have memories now, and she brought them all back.[10]

Forced Migration

In contrast to voluntary migration, where "pull" factors are an attraction that motivates people to move, forced migration is set into motion by "push" factors beyond individual or community control. Migrations of this sort often result from violent or disastrous events.

There have been many forced migrations throughout history, such as the mid-nineteenth-century mass exodus of the Irish to the United States, discussed in Chapter 2, as a result of the terrible 1845 famine known as the "great hunger." Because people forced from their homes are often nostalgic for the past and maintain music traditions as part of their shared identity, the study of forced migration has emerged as an important area of present-day musical scholarship.

CASE STUDY: African Forced Migrations

Two causes of forced migration—conquest and slavery—continue to reverberate in the background of American life and musical styles. The periods of North American conquest, such as the European settlement in colonial America and the expansion to the western part of the continent, are often celebrated in American popular culture. However, they entailed the forced movement of millions of Africans through the slave trade. In addition, Native American populations were severely reduced through warfare and disease; survivors often found themselves uprooted and their cultures damaged. In the United States, the period of conquest that began in the sixteenth century started a process that shaped the soundscapes of today. New social and legal systems based on those of Europe reshaped the cultural and musical landscape. We will explore the effects of forced migration on musical style and performance, and what these musics mean to performers and listeners alike.[11]

LOOKING *Back*

African Forced Migration

August 1619 First ship carrying African slaves sails into Jamestown, Virginia.
1808 Congress outlaws the international slave trade.
1865 Thirteenth Amendment to the US Constitution abolishes slavery.

From 1619, when the first ship carrying African slaves arrived at Jamestown, the process of African American migration was unique in American history. Many musical repertories show traces of the painful experiences of African Americans during the slave era that followed their forced movement to the US. Among the most influential of these repertories is the black spiritual. Spirituals were the musical expression of slaves converted to New World Christianity, a process that began during the eighteenth century but reached its peak in the early nineteenth. A now lost collection of spirituals may have been compiled as early as 1819, but most of our knowledge of these songs dates from the period around the Civil War.[12] In 1867, the first collection of spirituals, edited by William Francis Allen, was published under the title *Slave Songs of the United States*. Collections such as *Slave Songs* both preserve and romanticize the memory of the slaves' music.[13]

The editors of *Slave Songs of the United States* commented in the 1867 introduction that written notation alone could not convey either the spiritual's

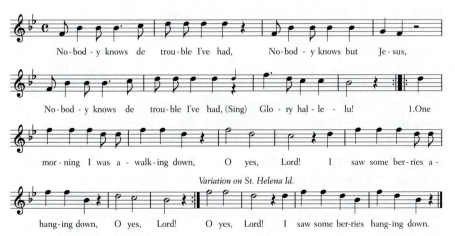

No-bod-y knows de trou-ble I've had,   No-bod-y knows but   Je-sus,

No-bod-y knows de trou-ble I've had, (Sing)   Glo-ry hal-le-   lu!   1.One

mor-ning I was a-walk-ing down,   O yes,   Lord!   I saw some ber-ries a-

Variation on St. Helena Id.

hang-ing down,   O yes,   Lord!   O yes,   Lord!   I saw some ber-ries hang-ing down.

The 1867 collection *Slave Songs of the United States* contains notation for many spirituals, including *Nobody Knows the Trouble I've Seen*. The music includes a variation for part of the verse the authors gathered on St. Helena Island.

distinctive vocal style or the subtle variations in intonation and pitch of the oral renditions. Furthermore, early descriptions of black spiritual singing, such as an 1839 slave owner's diary, mentioned that the spirituals were originally sung in unison. However, Allen's commentary suggests that some spirituals might have been sung in a heterophonic texture or with a soloist and chorus alternating in what is usually termed *call-and-response* style.

> I despair of conveying any notion of the effect of a number singing together. . . . There is no singing in parts, as we understand it, and yet no two appear to be singing the same thing—the leading singer starts the words of each verse, often improvising, and the others, who "base" him, as it is called, strike in with the refrain, or even join in the solo, when the words are familiar.

Clearly, Allen is describing music transmitted through oral tradition, as well as a style that incorporates a great deal of improvisation. As these songs continued to be transmitted within and beyond the African American community, the texts, tunes, and performance styles associated with the spiritual were transformed in the late nineteenth and early twentieth centuries to a style influenced by the Western classical music of the dominant society. The spiritual moved to the concert stage by the late nineteenth century, when the Fisk University Jubilee Singers began to tour the world singing spirituals.

By the early twentieth century, the spiritual was transmitted in many different contexts and in contrasting musical styles. The recordings heard in Listening Guide 43 (see page 192), in folk and concert style, were recorded within

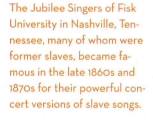

The Jubilee Singers of Fisk University in Nashville, Tennessee, many of whom were former slaves, became famous in the late 1860s and 1870s for their powerful concert versions of slave songs.

five years of each other in the early 1940s. They provide an opportunity to compare the manner in which different pathways of musical transmission and the artistry of individual singers can transform the same song. It is also interesting to compare these two performances to the notated 1867 version of this spiritual presented earlier on page 189.

Folk singers learned spirituals through oral tradition as well as from early recordings. In Listening Guide 43 (CD 2, TRACK 6), we hear *Nobody Knows* performed by Huddie Ledbetter, a great African American folksinger better known as "Leadbelly" (1885–1949). Born in Louisiana near the Texas border, he played the twelve-string guitar, the accordion, and the harmonica from a young age.[14] Ledbetter made his first recordings while he was imprisoned in the Louisiana State Penitentiary for attempted murder. In 1933, ethnomusicologist Alan Lomax visited the prison and recorded Ledbetter: between 1935 and 1940, after Ledbetter's release from prison, Lomax made many additional recordings at the Library of Congress of Ledbetter's large repertory of songs from what has been called "the Texas black song tradition." After some of his recordings were released commercially in 1935, Ledbetter found an audience among jazz and blues musicians in New York, as well as on college campuses.[15]

A contrasting style can be heard in spirituals performed for the concert hall. Inspired by groups such as the Fisk Jubilee Singers, notated sources, and renditions in the oral tradition, black concert artists began to perform spirituals.[16] One of the most famous interpreters of the "classical" spiritual was the singer Paul Robeson (1898–1976). Robeson, the son of a minister, attended Rutgers University and later received a law degree from Columbia University. During his student years, Robeson began acting, and when he was unable to find a job in law because of racial discrimination, made a career in theater. His recording of *Nobody Knows the Trouble I've Seen,* heard in Listening Guide 43 (CD 2, TRACK 7), accompanied by Lawrence Brown, was recorded live in New York City on December 29, 1945, at the Greenwich Village Music Theatre. Robeson's version provides a great contrast in tempo, rhythm, and vocal style to Ledbetter's performance, dramatically demonstrating different channels of transmission for the same song within the African American community. At the same time, both performances give expression to a shared heritage of suffering stemming from slavery, as well as the strong influence of Christian belief.

Paul Robeson rehearses for a performance at Memorial Theatre in London, 1955.

A portrait of Huddie Ledbetter and his wife, Martha Promise Ledbetter, in 1935.

CD 2
Tracks
6–7

Nobody Knows the Trouble I've Seen (African American spiritual in field recording and in concert arrangement)

Date of recording: **TRACK 6:** 1938; **TRACK 7:** 1945
Performers: **TRACK 6:** Huddie "Leadbelly" Ledbetter and Martha Promise Ledbetter;
  TRACK 7: Paul Robeson, *baritone;* Lawrence Brown, *piano and arranger*
Form: Strophic form with refrain
Tempo: **TRACK 6:** Moderate, somewhat upbeat, quadruple meter;
  TRACK 7: Moderately slow, quadruple meter

WHAT TO LISTEN FOR:

- The differences between the two performances. Ledbetter's rendition includes a quicker tempo and more jazzy eighth-note rhythms. The singers use very different vocal timbres and techniques. The chordal piano accompaniment of Robeson's performance contrasts with the simple guitar part played by Ledbetter, consisting of a bass line played on strong beats and chords on the weak beats.
- The call-and-response patterns between Ledbetter and his wife.
- Differences between the texts of the two performances, both in the refrain and in the first verse.

TRK 6	TRK 7	STRUCTURE AND TEXT	DESCRIPTION
0:00		**Introduction**	**TRK 6:** The recording fades in the midst of an instrumental segue, connecting the previous song to this one. Ledbetter being singing after a cadence that confirms the key.

CASE STUDY: The Vietnamese Migration

All cases of forced migration involve a traumatic break with the homeland. Today, forced migrations usually occur when people seek to escape physical, political, or religious persecution. These refugees, who number in the millions, are forced to resettle in unfamiliar and sometimes undesired places. Their

| 0:12 | 0:05 | **Refrain** | **TRK 6:** Ledbetter sings the first two words of the verse, which signals his wife to join in and harmonize. Since Ledbetter sings in a high male register and his wife sings in a low female register, they sing in a very similar range. The refrain is repeated at 0:29. |

Refrain
Phrase a
Oh, nobody knows the trouble I've seen,
Phrase b
Ledbetter: Nobody knows but Jesus.
Robeson: Nobody knows my sorrow.
Phrase a
Nobody knows the trouble I've seen.
Phrase c
Glory, Hallelujah!

0:12 0:05

TRK 6: Ledbetter sings the first two words of the verse, which signals his wife to join in and harmonize. Since Ledbetter sings in a high male register and his wife sings in a low female register, they sing in a very similar range. The refrain is repeated at 0:29.

TRK 7: After a short measure of piano introduction, Robeson begins singing the refrain. The refrain has a phrase structure of a b a c, in which the first line is repeated as the third line.

0:45 0:36 **Verse 1**
Phrase d
Ledbetter: I'm sometimes up, and I'm sometimes down,
Robeson: Sometimes I'm up, sometimes I'm down.
Phrase e
Oh, yes, Lord,
Phrase d
Ledbetter: I'm sometimes almost to the ground,
Robeson: Sometimes I'm almost to the ground.
Phrase f
Oh yes, Lord.

TRK 6: Mrs. Ledbetter sings the verse alone in straightforward fashion. Notice the expressive slide between pitches on "Oh, yes, Lord."
TRK 7: The verse is in a slightly higher part of the singer's range, and the performer takes a slightly faster tempo. The musical phrase structure is similar to that of the refrain, even though the poetic structure is different. Robeson slows dramatically on the final line of the verse, returning to the original tempo.

1:00 1:02 **Refrain**

TRK 6: Mr. and Mrs. Ledbetter sing the first line of the refrain in unison before splitting into harmony. The refrain is repeated at 1:14 and the recording fades out at 1:18.
TRK 7: Recording fades out at 1:37.

migration is the result not of the positive "pull" of a new place, but of the "push" factors of fear or suffering. We will examine the forced migration of Vietnamese to North America to find out how their music was affected by both the circumstances of their departure from the homeland and the paths they followed as they made their way to new places.

This photograph records the plight of the Vietnamese boat people near the shores of Hong Kong in the late 1970s. Refugees have been turned away from Hong Kong as illegal immigrants since 1988.

Bilingual street signs mark Saigon City Mall, just south of the skyscrapers of downtown Houston.

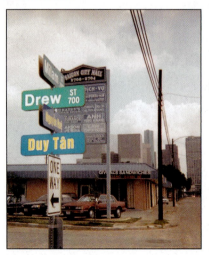

The present-day Vietnamese diaspora has its roots in history, with the entry of French missionaries into Vietnam in the mid-seventeenth century, culminating in French control of the entire country by the 1880s. Beyond the enormous religious, political, and economic impact, the French sought to transform Vietnam by recreating French cultural life in Southeast Asia, including constructing theaters to perform French opera and popular music.[17] The declaration of independence by Ho Chi Minh in 1945 and the subsequent fighting led to the defeat of the French and the division of Vietnam in 1954; Ho Chi Minh was in control in the North and a French-supported ruler, Ngo Dinh Diem, was installed in the South. The continued conflict between North and South Vietnam led to what was to become in the 1960s a disputed chapter in US history—the Vietnam War. The controversial US involvement in Vietnam was largely ended by the 1973 peace talks in Paris. When in March and April of 1975, Saigon, the South Vietnamese capital, fell to the North Vietnamese, two hundred thousand South Vietnamese sought refuge in the United States and other countries. Soon afterward, North and South Vietnam were reunited, and Hanoi became the national capital.

Between 1978 and 1985, half a million people left Vietnam. By the mid-1990s, the Vietnamese diaspora was estimated to number 1.3 million, 70 percent of whom resided in the United States. Other centers for Vietnamese include Paris, where the already established Vietnamese community increased dramatically following 1975. The first wave of Vietnamese immigrants to the United States were the urban elite, many of whom settled in Orange County, California; Washington DC, New York City, and the east coast of New Jersey. By 1978, at least one thousand people a month—the "boat people"—were leaving Vietnam by sea. Many of this second wave of immigrants were less educated farmers and fishermen, and most ended up in refugee camps in the Philippines and elsewhere in Southeast Asia for periods of several months or years.

Over time, individuals filtered through the camps to the United States and established Vietnamese enclaves in places such as New Orleans and Houston; the Gulf Coast region was particularly attractive to immigrants because its climate and landscape are similar to Vietnam.

One finds efforts to preserve homeland traditions as well as changes and innovations in the cultural life of the Vietnamese diaspora. Among the Vietnamese in North America the Vietnamese language is widely spoken. Many of the immigrants maintain their Buddhist religion and most make an effort to observe Tet, the holiday

LOOKING *Back*

Vietnamese Refugees

1953   The Refugee Relief Act of 1953 provides visas for refugees and escapees and establishes a new category of asylum for persons persecuted because of political beliefs.

1962   The Migration and Refugee Assistance Act of 1962 provides appropriations to the UN High Commission for Refugees to assist refugees with transportation, training, and employment.

1975   President Ford authorizes entry of 130,000 refugees from three countries of Indochina after the fall of South Vietnam; over 125,000 are Vietnamese from urban areas of South Vietnam.

1978   The Second wave of Vietnamese refugees, the so-called "boat people," begin to enter the United States in response to Vietnam's implementation of anti-Chinese policies; these primarily rural people with minimal education are funneled through refugee camps in Southeast Asia, especially in 1980–1981.

1980   The Refugee Act of 1980 establishes a uniform basis for assistance to refugees.

in late January or early February that marks both the beginning of the lunar new year and the advent of spring. In refugee camps the observance of Tet lasted for three to six days, but in the United States it is observed on different dates and in various formats depending on the resources and desires of the local Vietnamese community. In one New Jersey community, a traditional ceremony on the afternoon before Tet is followed at midnight by fireworks and traditional dances. Festivities often include a wide range of musical styles, as well as dances and fashion shows in the local school auditorium, an accessible venue for a large crowd.[18]

Since the mid-1980s, Vietnamese diaspora communities in large urban centers have also hosted large popular musical events called *da vu* ("night dance"). One version of the internationally

Members of the Garden City (Kansas) Vietnamese dragon dancers group celebrate Tet, the Vietnamese New Year, at a Garden City elementary school. The Tet festivities for the year 2000 welcomed the lunar year of the dragon.

popular Vietnamese *Paris By Night* concerts was performed at the Houston Coliseum on March 31, 1996, and then distributed worldwide to Vietnamese communities on videotape.

Traditional Vietnamese music is also performed in Vietnamese diaspora communities by residents who maintain the music traditions and instruments of their homeland. Groups of Vietnamese musicians and singers, from California to Minnesota and Virginia, perform southern Vietnamese chamber music in their homes. Their weekend gatherings evoke nostalgia for Vietnam and create a context for ongoing social life in the United States.

Visiting troupes of musicians from Vietnam occasionally visit diaspora communities. The Perfume River Traditional Ensemble from the city of Hue in central Vietnam made a two-week tour of the United States during August 1995. The ensemble performs court, chamber, and folk music of the central Vietnam region. The recording heard in Listening Guide 44 is a type of chamber music, *Ca Hue* (pronounced "ga WAY"), performed for connoisseurs. The song begins with a long section in free rhythm followed by a section with a regular rhythm based on an eight-beat cycle. The text refers indirectly to the mythological princess Tran Huyan Tran (pronounced "chan huyen chan"), who is revered for putting the welfare of her homeland before her personal happiness. The text of the song, telling of the sorrow of a princess living "one thousand miles from home," resonates strongly with diaspora Vietnamese.[19]

The sound of Vietnamese instruments elicits a strong emotional response as well. Among the instruments heard in Listening Guide 44 (see page 198) is the *dan bau* (literally "musical instrument of the people," pronounced "dan boe"),

Phong Nguyen, a Vietnamese immigrant to the United States who received a Ph.D. in Paris and teaches ethnomusicology at Kent State University, is both a scholar and an accomplished performer. The first Vietnamese musician to be awarded a National Heritage Fellowship by the National Endowment for the Arts, Nguyen plays the *dan nguyet,* a moon-shaped lute with two silk strings.

an instrument known as a monochord in cross-cultural terms. The *dan bau* consists of a single string, a resonating chamber, and a small bamboo shaft. The player produces sound by plucking the string with the right hand while moving the bamboo element with the left hand to determine and bend the pitch.

A number of legends surround the history and significance of the *dan bau.* It has been said that the instrument can render all possible sounds, even an imitation of the human voice. A standard textbook used by students at the Hanoi Conservatory describes the *dan bau* as being "like two brothers of the same house." That is, it represents the spirit of solidarity and kinship between two ethnic groups, the majority Kinh and the minority Muong, who are regarded as the ancestors of the Kinh. According to legend, the *dan bau* and the *khen,* a panpipe used by the Muong, have a common origin—each is made from half of the same gourd.[20]

The *dan bau* produces a subtle but resonant sound that can best be heard in a solo performance, as in Listening Guide 45 (see page

200). When played as a solo instrument today, the *dan bau* is often amplified electronically, as is the case here.

The Vietnamese case study provides striking examples of how music is influenced by forced migration. Many post-1975 Vietnamese refugees were traumatized both by their harrowing escape from Vietnam and their subsequent enforced stay in refugee camps in Hong Kong and the Philippines while they awaited resettlement abroad. Very surprising, perhaps, was the presence in refugee camps of many different musical styles, including Buddhist chant, Vietnamese folk and chamber music, and Western popular and classical music. Although people performed and enjoyed music of both the Western and Vietnamese music systems—Western music usually heard in public performances and traditional Vietnamese music played in private settings—any song with a Vietnamese text, whatever its musical style, is considered Vietnamese music.[21] Thus, musical style was not the only factor that determined music's identity, and in the camps, boundaries between formerly distinctive musical categories were blurring.

Finally, people in the refugee camps sang mainly sad songs and love songs, which at first encounter seemed not such surprising choices. However, further investigation showed that love songs and sad songs nostalgic for pre-1975 Vietnam had been prohibited by the Communist regime when it reunified the country in 1975; thus, the singing of these songs in the refugee camps was in fact an expression

The *dan bau* produces a delicate but resonant sound. Here it is played by Bui Huu Nhut, a native of Saigon who immigrated to the United States in 1989.

**CD 2
Track 8**

A Thousand Miles from Home (*Ca Hue*, Vietnamese chamber music)

Date of performance: 1995

Performers: Perfume River Traditional Ensemble

Vo Que, *artistic director;* Thu Hang, *voice;* Manh Cam, *trong* (drum); Thai Hung, *dan nguyet* (two-stringed lute); Le Hoa, *dan tranh* (sixteen-stringed zither); Tran Thao, *dan nhi* (two-stringed fiddle) and *ken* (double-reed aerophone); Si Thoai, *dan bau* (monochord); Ai Hoa, Thuy Van, and Khanh Van, voice and percussion

Mode: *Dieu nam,* a pentatonic mode with three main pitches, *ho, xang* and *xe* (similar to Western scale-steps do, fa, and sol; on this recording, *ho* sounds at the pitch E-flat). Only these three pitches are used for phrase beginnings and endings, and only these three pitches have ornaments such as *vibrato. Nam* usually implies a moderately slow tempo.

Form: A section in free rhythm, followed by a section in fixed rhythm

Tempo: First section in free rhythm; second section in a moderately slow 8-beat pattern

Function: Chamber music performed for connoisseurs

WHAT TO LISTEN FOR:

- Use of *vibrato,* along with sliding between pitches in both string instruments and the voice
- The term *phach* can describe the time period of one beat, the bamboo block that marks the beat, or the tempo. In the second section of this piece, there is a regular cycle of eight *phach* (beats), with a woodblock marking the strong beats 1, 5, and 7 in each cycle.
- Use of a pentatonic mode with three main pitches, *ho, xang* and *xe,* ornamented throughout the piece

STRUCTURE AND TEXT	TRANSLATION	DESCRIPTION
0:00 **Prelude**		The *dan tranh* (zither) plays *arpeggios,* chords broken up and played from bottom to top as individual notes in quick succession.

0:04			The *dan bau* (monochord) joins in, playing a note that is held steady for a moment and then "bent."
0:08			The *dan nhi* (fiddle) enters inconspicuously, in a low register.
0:23			The singer, Thu Hang enters, singing *vocables*. Her voice has a bright, nasal quality.
1:14	Truoc ben Ven Lau chieu o	In the evening at the Van Lau harbor . . .	The text begins, but vocables are also still used. The text often repeats the syllable *ai*, or "who." While the vocables are mostly set *melismatically* (many notes per syllable), the text is mainly set *syllabically* (one note per syllable).
	Truoc ben Ven Lau, Ai ngoi, an cau	At Van Lau Harbor Who is sitting? Who is fishing?	
	Ai sau, ai tham,	Who is melancholy? Who is grieving?	
	Ai thuong, ai cam, Ai nho, ai trong . . .	Who loves? Who feels? Who remembers? Who is empty?	
	Thuyen ai thap thoang ben song Dua cau mai . . . Dua cau mai day	Whose boat appears on the river? A few lines . . . . A few lines from a fisherman's melody	
	Chanh [long] non nuoc non	Fill our hearts with love for our country . . .	
	Non nuoc, nuoc non . . .	For the rivers and mountains of our country . . .	
4:01	**Second section** Ngan dam ra di . . .	A thousand miles from her homeland, she traveled. Her sorrow is masked by makeup to make things appear happy. For O and Ly districts she leaves. It is bitter, because she is in the fullness of youth like the spring. Or is this her fate?	A regular beat is established, using an eight-beat pattern. The recording fades out and ends at 4:21.

Ru (Vietnamese lullaby played on *dan bau*)

Date of recording: 1997
Performer: Phan Kin Thanh, dan bau (amplified monochord)
Form: Solo improvisation
Tempo: Moderate tempo, mainly in free rhythm with no regular meter
Function: *Ru* (lullaby)

WHAT TO LISTEN FOR:

- Bending pitch effects such as slides and *vibrato,* produced by bending the stem (made of water buffalo horn) at one end of the instrument
- Harmonics produced by touching the string lightly with the heel of the hand
- The unique, innovative timbre of the electric monochord
- Melodies based on pentatonic scales, but not confined exclusively to one such scale

	STRUCTURE	DESCRIPTION
0:00	**Introduction**	Introduction in free rhythm on repeated pitch with ornaments, followed by descent.
0:12		Jump of more than an octave, with change of mode. The melody sometimes leaps down an octave and back up; it also moves by step and by small intervals. It is largely based on a pentatonic scale.
0:35		Repeat of motive, but some differences as the section progresses.
1:15		Fade-out

of political ideology. The distinction between pre- and post-1975 Vietnam, when South Vietnam was incorporated into the communist North, became a factor in the choice of musical genres both in the camps and afterward.

Some of the music heard in the camps was that of the composer Pham Duy (pronounced "Fahm Zwee") (see page 202, **Individual Portraits: Pham Duy**), who remains the best-known Vietnamese composer in the diaspora. His songs written before 1975 represent around 90 percent of internationally distributed Vietnamese recordings (both cassettes and CDs) outside Vietnam, and virtually all Vietnamese singers have songs by Pham Duy in their repertories. His newer songs reflect on the situation of exile and the lack of freedom in his former homeland. Pham Duy's life also reflects the changing realities for disapora musicians: In the year 2000, he made the first of ten trips back to Vietnam following twenty-five years in California.[22] In 2005, the 85-year-old composer celebrated Tet in Hanoi where he said, "I hope to return to Vietnam to live the rest of my life with my children."[23]

Many of Pham Duy's songs are patriotic songs based on his role in fighting French colonial forces in the late 1940s and early 1950s; these songs have been banned in Vietnam since 1975. It is not surprising that since Pham Duy's resettlement in California, his music has been performed as an expression of attachment to pre-1975 South Vietnam.

The National Road Song Cycle

Pham Duy's *Con Duong Cai Quan* ("gon duwang gai gwan"), known in English as *The National Road: A Voyage through Vietnam,* is a series of songs, termed a song cycle, incorporating several different streams of musical influence. Conceived in 1954 and completed in 1960, *The National Road* tells of a traveler's journey through Vietnam from north to south.

The song texts celebrate the cultural diversity and regional differences in the country and trace aspects of its history. The musical styles reflect the composer's cosmopolitan musical background and the influence of traditional Vietnamese music, popular Vietnamese song, and the Western classical tradition. *The National Road* is transmitted in Western musical notation prepared by the composer as well as by oral tradition.

Perhaps most surprising to the first-time listener is the hybrid musical language which has both Vietnamese and Western elements. As we have seen, European and Vietnamese musical styles interacted throughout nineteenth- and twentieth-century Vietnam during the French colonial presence. A Westernized Vietnamese popular song tradition emerged

The three regions of the country described in *The National Road* are identified by their major cities: Hanoi in the north, Hue in central Vietnam, and Ho Chi Minh City (formerly Saigon) in the south.

Pham Duy

"In Vietnam, everything—music, poetry—has to do with politics. You cannot avoid it. If you didn't have this situation in Vietnam, you wouldn't have *me*."[24] This observation by the Vietnamese-born composer Pham Duy summarizes a lifetime of musical creativity shaped by Vietnam's turbulent history. His musical career spans the final decades of the French presence, the entry of Americans to Southeast Asia, the Vietnam War, and his forced migration to the United States in 1975.

The composer Pham Duy, who lives in California, during a visit to Paris in 1989.

Pham Duy was born in Hanoi in 1921 and began his career as a member of a traveling musical troupe that performed all over Vietnam in the mid-1940s. His reputation was further enhanced by his performance of new music twice every week for Radio Indochine in Saigon in 1944. Although he studied music in Paris during 1954 and 1955, most of Pham Duy's music education took place in his homeland. A few years before the country was divided, Pham Duy settled in the south and established his reputation as a prolific composer. In addition to his compositions that cut across a variety of traditional, popular, and international musical styles, Pham Duy worked to document traditional Vietnamese music, publishing a book titled *Musics of Vietnam*.

After resettling in Midway, California, in 1975, Pham Duy formed a production company with his son, Duy Cuong, and began to publish and distribute recordings of his own compositions. He and his son are adept in many forms of technology, which has been important to his success and visibility. Pham Duy has discussed the importance of digital technology to the circulation of his compositions in the United States, describing himself as "a computerholic" who composes

between 1920 and 1940, near the end of the French colonial period. Called *tan nhac* ("dan nyac"), this style combined Western instruments and Vietnamese lyrics; occasionally it drew on Vietnamese folk melodies. Popular among young people, *tan nhac* continued to be performed in Vietnam's urban areas and among Vietnamese living abroad. *Tan nhac* features duple and quadruple meters, but performers are also free to improvise, especially in the introductory sections of a song.[27]

using a synthesizer and computer-generated musical notation. In recent years, Pham Duy has increasingly made use of new multimedia technology to enrich and supplement presentation of his music on CD-ROM.

As he explains on his Web site, the composer sees his compositions as divided into distinct categories associated with specific political, humanistic, and moral goals:

- folk songs, which record images of the Vietnamese during the struggle for independence; these songs culminated in his song cycles, which combine several folk tunes to proclaim the greatness of the Vietnamese people.
- heart songs, which aim to awake humanity's conscience, to protest against violence and inhumanity.
- spiritual songs, with a Zen character, which aim to seek the truth.
- profane songs, which tackle head on hypocritical attitudes and phony virtues.
- children's songs, young women's songs, and peace songs, which are songs of joy.

Pham Duy has described his newest works as "refugees' songs" and "prisoners' songs," and continues to rework and recast older compositions. He continues to explore new technologies, and according to a recent article about the composer, he uses technology as a "new way to uphold and to preserve cultural information and memory."[25] When asked why some of his most important compositions, such as *The National Road*, are about roads and travel, Pham Duy made clear the connection between migration and his music:

> I am the old man wandering, the old man on the road. It is my destiny and the destiny of my people—always moving. The Jews and the Chinese went everywhere, but slowly, gradually. The Vietnamese went all at once—in one day, one hour! *Viet* originally meant to cross over—like an obstacle—to overcome. So this is the essence of the Vietnamese spirit. Now *Viet* just means "people," though its real meaning is "the people who overcome, who cross over."[26]

Although *The National Road* is shaped in part by the Western music system as funneled through *tan nhac*, many of its songs draw on traditional Vietnamese melodies. Most of the melodies in *The National Road* are set within the pentatonic scales widely used in traditional Vietnamese music.

The National Road consists of nineteen songs grouped in three sections. The first represents the north; the second, central Vietnam; and the final part, southern Vietnam.

On his Web site, the composer writes of his reasons for composing *The National Road*:

> I wanted to make a musical journey. What can be more pleasurable than traveling through one's country with song cycles? *Con Duong Cai Quan* . . . was conceived in 1954, when Vietnam was divided by the world powers into a nationalist and a communist zone at Geneva. I was then studying music in Paris, and this song cycle was my protest. The work was completed in 1960.[28]

We will focus on the middle section, Part Two: *Through the Central Regions*. Vietnam's central region, with its capital city Hue, is known for its distinctive musical styles. We will discuss Pham Duy's compositions in light of the traditional songs that inspired them, such as the music of Hue, heard in Listening Guide 44, and the lullaby heard in Listening Guide 45.

Listening Guides 46 (see page 206) and 47 (see page 208) are two songs from the middle section of *The National Road*. Performances of songs 8 and 9 from Part Two of *The National Road* (Listening Guide 46, TRACK 10 and Listening Guide 47, TRACK 12) are drawn from live performances recorded in the early 1990s by the Ngan Khoi ("Vast Ocean") Chorus, an organization based in southern California founded to promote choral singing among Vietnamese in America. The compact disc from which these excerpts are taken is sold in Vietnamese record stores throughout the United States. The notes accompanying the recording say that its producers hope to "bring you a taste of Vietnamese music through choral works sung by Vietnamese refugees in memory of their homeland." We will first focus on the sound of the songs.

The Ngan Khoi Chorus of Garden Grove, California (see Listening Guide 47), performed its debut concert in 1989. The group, which promotes choral singing among Vietnamese Americans, founded a children's choir in 1994. In addition to issuing recordings and videotapes of Vietnamese music, the group performs works by American composers such as Randall Thompson's *Frostiana*, settings of poems by Robert Frost, and excerpts from Aaron Copland's opera *The Tender Land*.

Sound

Song 8, *Come to Hue,* for solo female voice, is sung at a relatively slow speed in free rhythm. The song never establishes a regular pulse, leaving its pace to the interpretation of the singer.

The melody of the song is based on a pentatonic scale, with a brief shift (*modulation*) in the middle of the second verse, at "Toward father's village," to a second, higher pentatonic scale. Almost immediately, the song shifts back to its original pentatonic scale. The harmony supports the pentatonic sound by moving in intervals of fourths and fifths. The overall form of the song is straightforward, with the opening phrase returning four times and three verses in between each repetition.

Song 8 is adapted from lullabies of Central Vietnam called *ru* (pronounced "roo"). The rhythm of each lullaby is determined by the meter of its poem, and lines are frequently extended with vocables. *Ru* are also commonly sung in a pentatonic scale. An instrumental rendition of a *ru,* was played on the *dan bau* in Listening Guide 45.

Song 9, *Who Is Walking on the Endless Road,* provides a strong contrast to *Come to Hue;* it is a duet between the villagers who are pounding harvested rice to separate the grains and the traveler who passes them in their fields as he is hurrying through the area. The rhythm of Song 9 depicts its text, establishing a strong quadruple meter appropriate to both the pounding of the rice and the quick pace of the traveler. This song is performed enthusiastically by both chorus and soloist, in contrast to the subdued lullaby that preceded it.

Song 9 has three main sections. The first, Section A, returns after the contrasting second section, Section B. Song 9 also reverses the order of the pentatonic scales heard in the lullaby. That is, Section A of *Who Is Walking on the Endless Road* begins with the higher pentatonic scale heard briefly in the middle of Song 8, and then moves briefly in Section B to the lower pentatonic scale heard throughout most of Song 8.

The B section of Song 9 presents a contrast in texture to its A section, with a duet between the male traveler and a female soloist. Here the male voice sings the main melody, while a competing melody, called a *countermelody,* sung by the woman results in an interesting, polyphonic *texture.*

Who Is Walking on the Endless Road immediately signals its roots in tradition as it opens with the combination of the word *ho* (pronounced "haw"), which means "to raise the voice," and vocables. In traditional Vietnamese music, *ho* are popular songs sung by workers to sustain themselves through hard manual labor. *Ho* can also be used to refer to singing without words or vocalizing in contexts outside of the workplace. In this case, however, the song is sung loudly to the rhythm of the work.

Ai Vo Xu Hue Thi Vo ("Come to Hue, Come"), Song 8 from Part Two of *The National Road* (lullaby in the fashion of a *ru*; excerpt from a Vietnamese song cycle)

CD 2
Tracks
10–11

Two versions: TRACKS 10 and 11
Date of composition: 1960
Composer: Pham Duy
Source: Adapted from lullabies of Central Vietnam called *ru* (pronounced "roo")
Form: Verse-refrain form
Tempo: Slow, free rhythm
Date of performance: **TRACK 10:** Early 1990s, Garden Grove, California;
　　　TRACK 11: 1984, Woodbridge, New Jersey
Performers: **TRACK 10:** Solo female voice, Ngan Khoi ("Vast Ocean") orchestra;
　　　TRACK 11: Amateur singer accompanied by piano
Function: **TRACK 10:** From a song cycle for concert-hall performance;
　　　TRACK 11: Celebration of Tet, the Vietnamese New Year

WHAT TO LISTEN FOR:

- Free rhythm, with no regular pulse, determined by poetic meter of the lullaby text
- Melody based on pentatonic scales, built on the pitch A (A-B-D-E-F#) in the refrain and first verse, and shifting (or *modulating*) to a pentatonic scale built on D (D-E-G-A-B) in the second verse, followed by a shift back to the original scale
- Lines extended by *vocables*

TRK 10	TRK 11	STRUCTURE AND TEXT	TRANSLATION	DESCRIPTION
0:00		Instrumental introduction		TRK 10: A chordophone and two flutes provide a short introduction. TRK 11: This version has no introduction.

The lyrics of *ho* often also refer to love, as in Song 9 with its reference to the mythological princess Tran Huyen Tran, who sacrificed herself to unite Vietnam. Thus the combination of a work song and a love song is a traditional element that Pham Duy maintains.

Another aspect of Song 9 based on tradition is the division between male and female voices in the B section. In folk practice, the *ho* is usually sung

0:09	0:00	**Refrain** A a o a a a a o i		**TRK 10:** and **TRK 11:** The refrain is sung using *vocables*.
0:19	0:10	**Verse 1** Ai vo xu Hue thi vo Cho so Truong Nha Ho Cho so Pha Tam Giang	Come to Hue, come Don't be afraid of the wilds of Nha Ho And the lagoon of Tam Giang	**TRK 10:** A pair of flutes responds to the singer after the first line; an oboe does the same after the second line. **TRK 11:** The piano supports the singer by repeatedly playing a single chord. The chord changes once at the end of this section.
0:47	0:29	**Refrain** A a o a a a a o i		**TRK 10:** Each time the refrain recurs, it is introduced by a chord sustained by two flutes.
0:57	0:38	**Verse 2** Ngo ra que cha duong xa song rong Ngo ve que me nui long deo cao	Toward father's village the road is so long, the river so wide Toward mother's village the mountains and passes are all so high	**TRK 10:** and **TRK 11:** A brief modulation occurs, as the melody shifts to a lower pentatonic scale. **TRACK 10:** Strings provide a chordal accompaniment. **TRACK 11:** The piano moves to a different chord to accommodate the modulation.
1:11	0:52	**Refrain** A a o a a a a o i		**TRK 10:** and **TRK 11:** The melody returns to the original pentatonic scale.
1:21	1:01	**Verse 3** Nhung con oi con ngu ngu sau Cho noi lai nhip cau Cho da co nguoi di!	But sleep well, my child Build a bridge So that we can travel	**TRK 10:** and **TRK 11:** The melody of this section is the same as that of Verse 1, above.
1:52	1:21	**Refrain** A a o a a a a o i		**TRK 11:** ends at 1:33 **TRK 10:** ends at 2:04

loudly by a group in call-and-response style. The one who sings the main verse is the lead caller (or "mother"), while the rest are known as chorus callers (or "children"). In traditional *ho* performance, the call is divided into parts—a male part sung by a leader and a female part sung by a chorus. Note that Pham Duy has incorporated this male-female alternation, perhaps reflecting the fact that when *ho* songs of this type are sung at recent festivals, boys and

CD 2 Tracks 12–13

Ai Di Tren Dam Duong Truong, ("Who Is Walking on the Endless Road"), Song 9 from Part Two of *The National Road* (work song in the fashion of a *ho*; excerpt from a Vietnamese song cycle)

Two versions: TRACKS 12 and 13
Date of composition: 1960
Composer: Pham Duy
Source: Based on traditional Vietnamese work songs called *ho*
Form: Three-part (ternary) form, A B A' with introduction
Tempo: Moderate, quadruple meter
Date of performance: **TRACK 12:** Early 1990s; **TRACK 13:** 1991
Performers: **TRACK 12:** Ngan Khoi ("Vast Ocean") Chorus, *soloist, orchestra;*
   TRACK 13: Duy Cuong, *synthesizer*
Function: **TRACK 12:** Concert performance; **TRACK 13:** Synthesizer arrangement for distribution on CD

WHAT TO LISTEN FOR:

- The composer's creative use of various aspects of the *ho* song tradition
- The strong quadruple meter of the song, representing both the regular pounding of the rice and the quick pace of the traveler
- In the synthesizer version (**TRACK 13**), the absence of text permits the expansion of the otherwise highly-structured three-part form
- Varied textures, including homophonic choral parts, call-and-response between soloist and chorus, imitation between voices, and the use of countermelodies
- Use of pentatonic scales related to those in *Come to Hue, Come,* in Listening Guide 46, CD 2, **TRACK 10,** but deployed in a different order

TRK 12	TRK 13	STRUCTURE AND TEXT	TRANSLATION	DESCRIPTION
0:00	0:00	**Instrumental introduction**		**TRK 12:** Horns and other aerophones establish a majestic mood, with tympani (pitched drums) heard prominently at the end of the introduction. **TRK 13:** The arranger expands the introduction considerably, making use of an array of textures and synthesized instruments.

0:16	0:36	**Section A - The Villagers:**
		Ho ho ho ho oi ho!
		Ai di tren duong la dam
		  duong
		Di mo ma voi va A Cung la
		  ho khoan.
		Ho ho ho khoan
			Who is walking there on
			  the endless road
			Why are you hurrying thus
				TRK 12: After the full choir sings the first line homophonically, a polyphonic texture is heard as the women of the choir sing the verse, and the men of the choir add a countermelody repeating the first and fourth lines of text.
				TRK 13: A synthesizer with a reedy quality plays the melody. The countermelody is eliminated, but other musical responses are added, particularly at the ends of phrases.

0:33	0:54	Ho ho ho ho oi ho!
		Khoan khoan toi moi la
		  moi ban
		Vui hop doAn hom nay chu
		  la A nay.
		Ho ho ho khoan.
			Please join us, my friend
			
			In our celebrations tonight.
				TRK 12 and TRK 13: The second half of section A uses melodies similar to those we have just heard, but at a higher pitch. The end of this verse modulates back to the original.

0:50	1:12	**Section B - The Traveler:**
		Nam te trong luc sang
		  Xuan
		Toi theo Cong Chua Huyen
		Tran toi len duong
		Duong mau xuong da lam
		  oan thuong
		Doi sa huong lay coi giang
		  son
			That year when spring
			  came
			I set out in the footsteps of
			  Princess Huyen Tran
			On this road built on bones
			  and full of sorrow
			She exchanged her beauty
			  for land.
				TRK 12: Reference is made to the mythological princess Huyen Tran, who sacrificed herself to unite Vietnam.
				TRK 12: A solo male voice portrays the traveler, accompanied by a light orchestral part.
				TRK 13: A synthesized violin section takes the melody. The last melodic line is extended and repeated by several instruments as the tempo slows and the section comes to an end.

1:07	1:41	Toi di theo buoc ai tinh
		
		Di cho tram ho duoc hoa
		  binh am no
		Deo nui cao nghe gio vi vu
		Thot phan son bay toi kinh
		  do
			I follow in the footsteps of
			  a love
			To ensure the peace and
			  prosperity of many
			On the hills the wind blows
			Bringing her perfume to the
			  capital city.
				TRK 12: The choir now takes over the role of the traveler in a polyphonic texture.
				TRK 13: As in the A section, the countermelody is eliminated. A synthesized woodwind plays the melody lyrically. Note the drumroll leading into the next section.

(continues)

(continued)

TRK 12	TRK 13	STRUCTURE AND TEXT	TRANSLATION	DESCRIPTION
1:23	2:11	**Section A' - The People of the Center:** Ho ho ho ho oi ho! Anh di tren duong la gap geng Mau mau di keo loa chuyen ting nuoc non Ho ho ho khoan.	You who walk on the bumpy road Hurry, the country's task remains to be done.	**TRK 12 and TRK 13:** The music for this section is virtually identical to that of the A section.
1:39	2:29	Ho ho ho ho oi ho! Mau mau Di keo la keo lo Cau chuyen tinh nam xua la tinh a xua Ho ho ho khoan.	Hurry, or you'll be late For the love story of yore	**TRK 12 and TRK 13:** Note the dramatic slowing during the last line. **TRK 13:** The instrumentation is slightly different from that of the A section, as strings are added.
2:00		**TRK 12 ends**		
2:46				**TRK 13:** A brief tag or *coda* is added to give a sense of closure.
	3:00			**TRK 13 ends**

girls are divided into two groups to sing in call-and-response style as they compete for prizes.[29]

Pham Duy's song cycle is widely distributed on recordings and is performed in polished renditions as heard in Listening Guide 46, CD 2, TRACK 10 and Listening Guide 47, CD 2, TRACK 12 by the Ngan Khoi Chorus. Songs from the cycle are also performed by amateur musicians and transmitted in electronic formats. Here we encounter another traditional Vietnamese musical principle: The composer provides a musical skeleton to be varied and embellished by the performer. The flexibility of Pham Duy's compositions allows for transformations of their musical sound, depending on the settings in which they are performed.

Setting

Pham Duy's compositions, like most Vietnamese music, are intended to provide a basis for interpretation, easily adapted to different performance contexts. Additional recordings of Song 8 and Song 9 illustrate the different *settings* in which songs from *The National Road* are performed and the resulting transformation of each song's sound.

In Listening Guide 46, CD 2, TRACK 11, an amateur singer and pianist perform the lullaby *Come to Hue* at a 1984 Tet celebration in Woodbridge, New Jersey. The event, which attracted a mainly Vietnamese audience numbering more than 1,000, featured a complete performance of *The National Road* as its centerpiece. The singer's performance of the song heard here lacks the ornaments and interpretive flair of the more polished performance of the same song in Listening Guide 46, CD 2, TRACK 10; similarly, the piano part provides only a basic chordal accompaniment. Yet *Come to Hue* remains clearly recognizable. That the producer made the effort to mount a live performance of the entire *National Road* cycle with non-professional musicians at a local Tet celebration underscores its symbolic importance within diaspora Vietnamese community life.[30]

The other live music at the celebration was popular dance music presented by a local family combo with electric guitars, keyboards, drum set, and singer. Their repertory included a range of popular songs as well as Latin American dance music, most sung with Vietnamese texts. The musicians considered these songs, even Latin American tangos, to be part of their Vietnamese musical and cultural heritage because they brought this music with them from Vietnam.[31]

A second recording of *Who Is Walking on the Endless Road*, arranged and performed in a symphonic version for synthesizer by Pham Duy's son, Duy Cuong, is heard in Listening Guide 47, CD 2, TRACK 13. Duy Cuong works in a sophisticated studio at his father's home in Little Saigon (Midway City), California, using sound editing programs on a Macintosh platform. Little Saigon is the center of the Vietnamese American media that includes worldwide distribution of CDs and cassettes as well as Internet projects that unite this widely dispersed community. In the case of *The National Road*, Pham Duy and Duy Cuong have employed the synthesizer to "bridge the gap" between Vietnamese immigrants and their children born in diaspora; Duy Cuong emphasizes that he uses a variety of technologies "to preserve the musics of the past *and* to bring that music into the present." In fact, the composer has said that he would have preferred a symphony orchestra, but acknowledges that "as a refugee, I don't have that kind of money, and therefore, had no choice but to use computer as a means to compose. The software helps us to acquire all acoustic sounds, ethnic sounds and electronic sounds."[32]

Significance

The National Road has powerful significance for the composer and evokes a deep response from diaspora Vietnamese. *The National Road* grew out of the specific experience of the composer, who devoted much of his life to efforts to reunify his country following its partition in 1954, only to be forced to emigrate when Saigon fell in 1975. Although the music of Pham Duy is universally known and sung by Vietnamese people in the diaspora, it is not performed openly today in Vietnam. Pham Duy recalls that he has walked the route traced in *The National Road* four times, first as a singer with a drama and music troupe, and later in various political or military efforts. Pham Duy has used music as a form of political resistance since the 1940s, when he broadcast songs about a free Vietnam from a cave outside Hanoi. Yet *The National Road*, which he intended to be a musical realization of a unified, independent Vietnam, survives only abroad as an important musical symbol of the deep divide between Vietnamese at home and those in the diaspora. In 2005, Pham Duy sought permission of the authorities to perform some of his songs in Vietnam.[33]

Conclusion

The musical progress of the traveler through Vietnam evokes memories of the sounds and sights of different regions. Every time *The National Road* is performed, it reenacts the composer's journey through Vietnam. Today, *The National Road* has also become an ironic symbol of the process of forced migration and dispersal shared by the Vietnamese community abroad. In the diverse performances of *The National Road*, we hear the texts and sounds of Vietnamese music transformed within changing settings, through the piano accompaniment played at a Tet celebration in New Jersey, or in a recorded synthesizer version. Although the musical sound continues to change and is adaptable, it still carries a great deal of meaning as it is transmitted through oral and written tradition.

The National Road is an example of music from a homeland that gives expression to the experience of migration as it has been transformed through that process. The musical vocabulary of *The National Road* reflects its traditional and Western backgrounds; it embeds traces of Western influence in Southeast Asia and the continuation of traditional Vietnamese values in the United States. It is not surprising that *The National Road* has led a lively life abroad among Vietnamese expatriates. Wherever and in whatever arrangement it is performed, *The National Road* is highly charged with meaning, its Westernized musical sound masking a meaning that is intensely Vietnamese.[34]

The impact of migration continues to reverberate through the music traditions of many communities, as we have seen in case studies of Chinese, Middle Eastern, African American, and Vietnamese communities. The experience of migration never entirely recedes for those who have experienced it, as push and pull factors continue to exercise their power long after the initial period of displacement. People rebuild their lives in new ways, engaging in an ongoing dialogue with the new local and global networks of which they are now a part. Musical transmission plays a vital role in this process, providing a stabilizing factor that can at once ground individual and community experience within the realm of the familiar and provide a channel for adaptation to new settings and challenges. At the center of the process of musical transmission within the contexts of migration, memory plays a central role. We will explore the role of memory in musical transmission in Chapter 5.

Which immigrant communities live in your area? Check newspaper listings to see what public musical events the communities sponsor and try to attend one. If there are no public performances, visit local shops or cultural centers and inquire if recordings are available. Check out community bulletin boards or local newspapers for advertisements for ethnic music or dance lessons. Try to find out if music is transmitted by many within the community or by a few musical specialists. Do you see any evidence of oral or written transmission of music through the presence of recordings, sheet music, or other materials?

Once you have located a musical event or recording, watch for references to the community's homeland. Does music allude to the process of migration? See how much you can learn about a community and its migration history through musical ethnography.

IMPORTANT TERMS

ballad	*ho*	quadruple meter
broadside	*maqam*	*ru*
cadence	melismatic text setting	song cycle
call-and-response	melody	spiritual
countermelody	modulation	syllabic text
diaspora	*muyu*	*tan nhac*
duple meter	polyphonic texture	*'ud*
heterophony	*qanun*	

Music and Memory

This painting shows the Sakka family of Aleppo, Syria, gathered around their phonograph. Recordings were an important part of Middle Eastern musical life by the first decade of the twentieth century.

Overview

Main Points

Performing and listening to music enable us to:

- transmit memories of people, places, and events;

- commemorate people and events;

- reconcile the past with the present.

Introduction

Musical transmission is dependent on the process of remembering. At the same time, music enhances memory by helping us to recall aspects of our life experience. First, song texts and melodies can remind us of people, places, and events.

Second, through repeated performances over time and in different settings, music draws on a partly subconscious bank of memories, sometimes triggering recollections—and emotions—long forgotten. Third, the physical processes involved in musicmaking call on what has been termed "habit memory," the ability to dance or play a musical instrument without consciously thinking about every movement. Thus music, through its content and through the physical act of performance, can bring our past into the present, even when we have long forgotten the occasions of which they were a part.

Despite popular notions that memories are stored intact in our brains like photographs in an album, research has shown that each memory consists of fragments or traces scattered throughout the brain and must be reconstructed each time the memory is recalled. Thus a memory, if it has not been forgotten entirely, is vulnerable to being transformed intentionally or accidentally. Music is a particularly powerful carrier of memories because of the active role it plays in so many settings and the ways in which it is associated with complicated texts and events and helps to transmit them over long periods of time.

Music can be transmitted informally through frequent exposure. Here, children of leaders of the African Star Dancers in Accra, Ghana, play the drums while older drummers and dancers take a break from their daily practice sessions, providing an example of casual musical transmission.

Music is furthermore rich in emotional impact, deriving its power from its ability to evoke again and again the feelings experienced at the moments during which the music was first heard. The creation of a musical memory begins the instant music is first heard or performed; the memory may be transformed through subsequent encounters, whether music is transmitted informally or through formal teaching.

When we participate in or hear a musical performance, we experience a moment similar to the moment when a memory was first generated. Thus a musical memory is cued and retrieved the next time the music is encountered; each subsequent hearing adds new layers of associations, enriching and altering the memory over the course of time. An example is the song *Auld Lang Syne,* which dates back to eighteenth-century Scotland and is sung today throughout the English-speaking world on New Year's Eve at the stroke of midnight.[1] Each performance of *Auld Lang Syne* marks the passing of another year and joins each new performance with memories, both joyful and sad, of similar moments in the past.

Musicmaking depends on individual and shared ("collective") memories. An individual may compose a song, but it will last only if it is transmitted by others in a community. A song cannot survive if it is not performed, although as we have begun to appreciate, music notation and recordings make possible the transmission and survival of music beyond the life span and location of its human carriers (see page 218, "**Studying Music: Technologies of Transmission**").

In this chapter, we will explore the interaction of music and memory in several different soundscapes. A number of song traditions preserve historical memories of royal families or important events. The epic songs of West Africa, Southeast Asia, and the Balkans are well-known examples. Although epic songs are lengthy and are usually performed by musical specialists, shorter songs, such as ballads, also contain stories of great interest and importance. We encountered an example in the ballad *Barbara Allen* in Chapter 2. Here we will see how historical events have been remembered in *corridos,* ballads composed and transmitted in Mexico and within communities of Mexican descent, especially along the Mexico/US border. The *corrido* has long preserved the memory of specific historical moments and documented the lives of important individuals in Mexican and Mexican American history.

The *corrido* is designed to record a historical or political event and may commemorate the individuals involved. There are other strong music traditions for commemorating an individual at the time of death. One very moving form is the New Orleans jazz funeral, although some of the music associated with this event is also used in other contexts. We will explore the jazz funeral later in this chapter.

Technologies of Transmission

Various forms of music notation have long served as memory aids in the transmission of music traditions. But remembering music of the past century has been greatly helped by recording technology. In Chapter 1, we discussed the role of recordings in preserving fleeting musical moments. Here we will explore further the role of recording technology in the process of musical transmission. The cylinder phonograph, with its recording and playback capabilities, was first marketed commercially in 1888, initiating a new age of musical transmission mediated by technology.

Changes in technology divide the history of transmitting music through recordings into four eras. The first period, from 1888 to 1940, can be termed the "phonograph era," since during this time a series of phonographs and gramophones were developed to record and play wax cylinders and 78-rpm discs. Recording companies throughout Europe, Africa, and Asia fed what by the 1920s had become a thriving "ethnic record" market. Immigrants brought with them recordings of music from their homelands and could order such recordings by mail. No longer were immigrants forced to rely on their musical memories or on live performances in their new locales. The emergence of radio in the 1920s provided another new technology for transmitting music and reinforcing it in memory.

After the disruption of World War II, the "LP era" began in 1948, followed a year later by the first commercial magnetic-tape machines. The new vinyl LPs not only greatly improved the fidelity of the sound; they also contained much more music per side—thirty minutes of uninterrupted music. Now listeners could enjoy performances of works that in the days of 78s had to be divided into five-minute segments that fit on one side of a record. The increasing portability of tape recorders also helped people doing fieldwork to record music, thereby feeding the growth of musical scholarship and facilitating the publication and distribution of

Our major case study in this chapter will investigate the manner in which song can bind together seemingly incompatible strands of cultural history and memory, reflecting, reshaping, and even transforming perspectives of the past. *Pizmonim* are songs sung by Jews whose ancestors emigrated from Aleppo, Syria, to establish new communities across the Middle East, Europe, and the

music from around the world. Music traditions once known only within local communities now could move quickly into the international domain.

A third transition took place in the late 1960s with the advent of the cassette tape recorder. Cassette technology allowed anyone anywhere to record and play back sound at very little expense. At the same time, the cassette made it easy for individuals and communities to share music, transforming processes of musical transmission. The wide availability and reasonable cost of cassette players, and, eventually, the Walkman, caused a further shift from public consumption of live music to private listening to recordings.

The introduction of digital recording in the last decade of the twentieth century is a fourth technological innovation that has assisted musical memory and has even affected the sound of the music it encodes. Remastering recordings of earlier eras has allowed us to hear clearly music formerly obscured by limited earlier technologies and thus to juxtapose unrelated traditions in new contexts.

The development of recording technology has enabled music of the past to live on into the future beyond the workings of human memory, has allowed music to be separated from live performance settings, and has provided music with an afterlife in venues such as living rooms and sound archives. Recordings have served music as devices of tremendous power that can replace human memory and make a people's musical heritage impossible to forget.

This staged reenactment of a recording session during the first decades of the twentieth century shows an Edison disc recorder and a Stroh violin fitted with a horn to amplify the sound. The artists include Zinka Milanov and Giovanni Martinelli.

Americas. These songs that set sacred Hebrew words to popular Arab melodies show how musical performance can accommodate memories difficult to express in other situations. These same songs also carry different streams of memory, sacred content in their texts and secular associations in their tunes, insuring music's persistence in different areas of long-term memory.

Remembering through Music

CASE STUDY: The Corrido

The Mexican *corrido* (ballad) displays the ability of music to convey memories of particular places, people, and events. As noted previously, the ballad is a strophic song that tells a story, usually a historical narrative, real or mythical. In the case of the ballad, hearing a strophic text sung to the same melody makes it easier for us to learn and recall the words. The melody helps us remember phrases, line lengths, stress patterns, and emphases, especially when that melody is simple, symmetrical, and repetitive. Most ballads have simple, catchy tunes and repetitive structures. In the *corrido* (as in most other ballads) memories are carried primarily in the text, while the melody supports that text and helps the singer recall it during a performance. (In the Syrian case study we will see examples in which the melody itself sustains important historical memories.)

The *corrido* first emerged in the second half of the nineteenth century as a song genre shaped by intercultural conflict between Mexicans and Anglo-Americans in the border region. Following the independence of Mexico from Spain in 1821 and the 1835 declaration by American settlers in Texas of independence from Mexico, culminating in the heavily mythologized battle of the Alamo in 1836, the United States annexed Texas, resulting in the Mexican-American War of 1846–1848. Interethnic relations remained strained through the rest of the century, fueled by discrimination against the Mexican minority by the dominant Anglo-American majority. Music, especially the *corrido*, became a medium through which Mexicans and Mexican Americans were able to respond to American political, economic, and social domination. Subsequent shifts in ethnic and political relations were reflected in changes in musical repertories and style. The *corrido Gregorio Cortez,* a famous example of this repertory, portrays detailed memories of an early stage of the on-going conflict.[2]

Corridos of the late nineteenth and early twentieth centuries focused on the actions of important individuals. So common is the portrayal of larger-than-life Mexican figures in the *corrido* that songs such as *Gregorio Cortez* have been termed "*hero corridos.*" The *corrido Gregorio Cortez* also exemplifies a song genre in which a Mexican man defends his rights.[3]

This famous *corrido* recounts the story of Gregorio Cortez, who, on June 12, 1901, shot and killed the Texas sheriff Brack Morris. The sheriff had just shot Cortez's brother while trying to arrest the men for a crime they had not committed. Gregorio Cortez fled, justifiably fearing that he would be lynched. In the course of his flight on foot and horseback toward the Rio Grande and the safety of Mexico, Cortez eluded search parties trying to capture him. During this period he killed a second Texas sheriff named Glover and was also accused of murdering a constable.

Cortez was finally captured near the border town of Laredo. The resulting trial galvanized the support of Mexican Americans. Following a legal battle that lasted three years, Cortez was acquitted of murder in the deaths of Sheriff Morris and the constable, but was sentenced to life imprisonment for the death of Sheriff Glover. In 1913, Cortez was pardoned by Texas governor O. B. Colquitt. The *corrido Gregorio Cortez* records this dramatic story and marks in song what proved to be a milestone in Mexican Americans' struggle for civil rights and social equality.[4] The performance of *Gregorio Cortez* heard here (Listening Guide 48; see page 222), from one of the many "ethnic records" distributed on 78-rpm discs in the 1920s and 1930s, was recorded in San Antonio by singers performing in two-part harmony, accompanied by two guitars.

Classic *corridos* such as *Gregorio Cortez* have been passed on through oral tradition for nearly a century; new types of *corridos* have been composed and transmitted widely as well. Following the popularity of the *hero corridos* in the 1910s and 1920s, the genre entered a period of decline and transformation. The texts about heroes were replaced by what have been termed "*victim corridos*," which emerged just as Mexican American society was becoming in the 1930s part of an urban, Americanized culture. As Mexican Americans began to challenge the dominance of Anglos, especially through new civic and political organizations such as the League of United Latin American Citizens (LULAC, founded in 1929), they continued to use song to inspire their own community to take collective action on the victims' behalf.[5]

Throughout the later twentieth century, the *corrido* continued to change in dialogue with shifting social relations and particular political events. For instance, a new repertory of "*revolutionary corridos*" arose, commenting on the social and economic hardships experienced during Carlos Salinas de Gotari's term as President of Mexico (1988–1994).[6] Mexican rock bands and singers performed updated versions of older *corridos* to protest the political situation in the 1990s, distributing these songs widely through recordings and films.

Popular as well are the so-called "*narco-corridos*," or "drug ballads." Sometimes compared to African American *gangsta rap*, these late twentieth- and twenty-first-century *corridos* tell tales of powerful drug lords and are particularly popular in the border area. The *narco-corridos* are widely performed by groups such as Los Tigres del Norte (The Tigers of the North), based in San Jose, California. Their lead singer, Jorge Hernández, has said that the drug ballads are intended as "constructive criticism, not praise. We sing about what people want to hear, about their lives," he continued. "If that happens to be about drugs, there has to be a deeper, positive message attached." Many of the

Gregorio Cortez in a photograph taken as a joke after his release from prison, perhaps enacting verses of the ballad.

Gregorio Cortez (Mexican American *corrido*)

CD 2
Track 14

Date: Early 1930s

Performers: Trovadores Regionales: Pedro Rocha and Lupe Martînez

Form: Strophic song

Tempo: Moderate, triple meter

Function: Ballad transmitted by oral tradition and, beginning in 1920s, on ethnic recordings distributed on 78-rpm records

WHAT TO LISTEN FOR:

- The narrative flow of the text, recounting the story of Gregorio Cortez
- Regular rhymes between the second and fourth lines of each verse and a mostly syllabic text setting
- A melody with a very narrow range and mainly conjunct (stepwise) motion
- Consistent harmony in thirds

	STRUCTURE AND TEXT	TRANSLATION	DESCRIPTION
0:00	En el condado del Carmen miren lo que ha sucedido. Murió el sherife mayor quedando Román herido.	In the country of the Carmen look what has happened. The main sheriff died, leaving Roman wounded.	The guitar provides a two-measure introduction before each verse. The voices re in parallel motion: although they sing different pitches, they ascend and descend at the same time.
0:21	Otro día por la mañana cuando la gente llegó Unos a los otros dicen no saben quien lo mató.	The following morning when the people arrived Some to the others said they don't know who killed him.	Parallel thirds (that is, two voices in parallel motion separated by the interval of third) provide a common way of harmonizing a melody in many kinds of Western music. Tempo speeds up.
0:35	Se anduvieron informando como tres horas despúes Supieron que el malhechor era Gregorio Cortez.	They were investigating and about three hours later They found out that the wrongdoer was Gregorio Cortez.	
0:50	Insortaron a Cortez por toditito el estado. Vivo o muerto que se aprenda porque a varios ha matado.	Cortez was wanted throughout the state. Alive or dead may he be apprehended for several he has killed.	

1:04	Decía Gregorio Cortez con su pistola en la mano, "No siento haberlo matado al que siento es a mi hermano."	Said Gregorio Cortez with his pistol in his hand, "I'm not sorry for having killed him, it's for my brother that I feel sorry."	
1:18	Decía Gregorio Cortez con su alma muy encendida. "No siento haberlo matado la defensa es permitida."	Said Gregorio Cortez with his soul aflame, "I'm not sorry for having killed him, self-defense is permitted."	
1:32	Venían los americanos que por el viento volaban, porque se iban a ganar tres mil pesos que les daban.	The Americans came, like the wind they flew, Because they were going to win the three thousand pesos reward.	
1:46	Siguió con rumbo a Gonzáles, varios sherifes lo vieron, no lo quisieron seguir porque le tuvieron miedo.	They continued toward Gonzales, several sheriffs saw him, They did not want to follow him because they were afraid.	
2:00	Venían los perros jaundes venían sobre la huella Pero alcanzar a Cortez era alcanzar a una estrella.	Came the hound dogs, they came on his trail, But to reach Cortez was to reach a star.	
2:14	Decía Gregorio Cortez "Pa' que se valen de planes si no pueden agarrarme ni con estos perros jaundes."	Said Gregorio Cortez, "What's the use of plans If you can't catch me even with those hound dogs."	At the end of this verse, the guitarist plays a *cadence* (a phrase or verse ending), as if to end the song. Since this recording was originally made on a 78-rpm disc, the musicians were limited to around 3 minutes per side. The cadence and pause in the middle of the song allowed the listener to flip the record and continue listening.
2:34	Decían los americanos "Si lo vemos que le haremos, si le entramos por derecho muy poquitos volveremos."	Said the Americans, "If we see him what shall we do to him, if we face him head on very few will return."	
2:50	En el redondel del rancho lo alcanzaron a rodear, Poquitos mas de trescientos y allí les brincó el corral.	In the corral of the ranch they managed to surround him. A little more than 300 men and there he gave them the slip.	
3:05	Allá por el Encinal a según por lo que dicen Se agarraron a balazos y les mató otro sherife.	There around Encinal from all that they say They had a shoot-out and he killed another sheriff.	During this period, Cortez killed a second Texas sheriff named Glover and was also accused of murdering a constable.
3:19	Decía Gregorio Cortez con su pistola en la mano, "No corran rinches cobardes con un solo mexicano."	Said Gregorio Cortez with his pistol in his hand, "Don't run, you cowardly rangers, from one lone Mexican."	
3:33	Giró con rumbo a Laredo sin ninguna timidez, "¡Síganme rinches cobardes, yo soy Gregorio Cortez!"	He turned toward Laredo without a single fear. "Follow me, you cowardly rangers, I am Gregorio Cortez!"	(continues)

(c o n t i n u e d)

	STRUCTURE AND TEXT	TRANSLATION	DESCRIPTION
3:47	Gregorio le dice a Juan en el rancho del Ciprés, "Platícame que hay de nuevo, yo soy Gregorio Cortez."	Gregorio says to Juan at the Cypress Ranch, "Tell me what's new, I an Gregorio Cortez."	
4:01	Gregorio le dice a Juan, "Muy pronto lo vas a ver, anda háblale a los sherifes que me vengan a aprender."	Gregorio says to Juan, "Very soon you will see him, go on and talk to the sheriffs that come to arrest me."	
4:16	Cuando llegan los sherifes Gregorio se presentó, "Por la beuna si me llevan porque de otro modo no."	When the sheriffs arrive Gregorio presented himself, "It's best that you take me, because there is no other way."	Gregorio Cortez was finally captured near Laredo, and the resulting trial galvanized Mexican Americans.
4:29	Ya agarraron a Cortez, ya terminó la cuestión, la pobre de su familia la lleva en el corazón.	Now they caught Cortez, Now the case is closed, His poor family he carries in his heart.	
4:43	Ya con esto me despido con la sombra de un ciprés Aquí se acaba cantando la tragedia de Cortez.	Now with this I take my leave in the shade of a cypress, Here we finish singing the tragedy of Cortez.	Recording ends at 4:57.

songs of Los Tigres del Norte speak to the difficult lives of Mexican immigrants to the United States, such as *El Mojado Acaudalado* ("The Wealthy Wetback"), which describes the conflicts and disillusionment of illegal immigrants who succeed financially in the United States but live in constant fear of being deported.[7]

The *corrido* continues to chronicle major events, ensuring that they are remembered through music. Recent *corridos* include a song titled *Black September* by Filogonio Contreras, commemorating the attacks of September 11, 2001, and *The Ballad of Osama bin Laden* by Rigoberto Cardenas Chávez adapts the classic *hero corrido* format to interrogate the motives of "a dragon" that has arisen, marking "the beginning of the end of the world."[8]

Jorge Hernández (on left), lead singer of Los Tigres del Norte, salutes the crowd at a concert in November 2000, in Puebla, Mexico. The group plays a musical genre known as *norteño*, a northern Mexican and border musical style which features the accordion.

Corridos are composed to sustain memories of a particular individual or event; many other music traditions have used music in distinctive ways to honor the memory (commemorate) individuals at the time of death. Commemoration is a common function of the close relationship of music and memory, as we see in the jazz funeral.

Commemorating through Music

CASE STUDY: The Jazz Funeral

In Chapter 3 we encountered two examples of the manner in which music is used to commemorate individuals: *mariachi* music and bagpipe laments, both of which are played at funerals. Here we will explore the music of the jazz funeral, which marks the death of a musician or some other person of note.

When the famous jazz musician Louis "Satchmo" Armstrong died on July 6, 1971, he was given two funerals. One, a conventional ceremony, was held at the Corona Congregational Church near his New York City home. A second, two days later, was an old-fashioned jazz funeral in New Orleans, the city of his birth. These contrasting funerals illustrate different styles of commemoration common in different cultural arenas.

Louis Armstrong was one of the stars of the New Orleans jazz style during its emergence in the early decades of the twentieth century. His 1960 trip to Africa provided inspiration to many there at a period when a number of African countries were gaining their independence from colonial powers.

Reports of Armstrong's tours in newspapers and on early television broadcasts also caught the attention of many at home in North America, bringing jazz a new, domestic white audience.[9] That Armstrong was a major force in popularizing jazz nationally and internationally, attracting huge audiences, accounts for the public events preceding his New York funeral: Some twenty-five thousand people lined up to pay their respects to Armstrong's coffin at the Seventh Regiment Armory on Park Avenue in Manhattan before the church ceremony and burial in a Flushing, New York cemetery.

At the same time, Armstrong had maintained his local ties and was fondly remembered in his hometown; this attachment inspired the second funeral in

Processions are an important part of many African ritual observances for the living and the dead. Here Louis Armstrong is carried in triumph in a procession at Brazzaville's Beadouin Stadium after a 1960 concert in the Congo.

New Orleans. Armstrong's jazz funeral included a large parade of musicians and fans, with the Onward Brass Band leading the procession as it marched through town.

The jazz funeral features the signature instruments associated with early New Orleans jazz: a small ensemble, known as the *jazz band,* which improvised on both the melody and accompanying parts of well-known popular songs. Armstrong began his career playing the trumpet with the Creole Jazz Band led by another famous New Orleans jazz musician, Joseph "King" Oliver (1885–1938); recordings such as King Oliver's *Dippermouth Blues* (1923) popularized the "wah-wah" sound of the cornet played with a mute and also launched Armstrong's career (see **"Sound Sources: The New Orleans Jazz Band"**).

The jazz funeral in New Orleans was sparked by the history of the brass band with which it was closely associated. After the Civil War, street bands were employed by African Americans for parades, at dance halls, and for advertisements called "ballyhoo."[10] At the same time, black funeral societies, strikingly similar to the funeral societies we discussed in Accra, Ghana, offered burial insurance, as well as other forms of assistance to their members. The main obligation of these funeral societies was to sponsor a funeral for their dues-paying members, which included the active participation of a brass band.

In the classical jazz funeral that emerged in the early twentieth century, the band leads a procession, followed by a hearse carrying the coffin, mourners, and members of the funeral association.

During the events preceding the burial at the cemetery, the band plays *hymns* (sacred songs used for worship) and *dirges* (instrumental laments played at a slow tempo) outside the church or home where the funeral sermon is preached. The band then leads the procession to the graveyard and plays hymns or spirituals at graveside. After the internment, the band performs celebratory music in marked contrast to the earlier music. By shifting to faster paced, lively repertory, the band gives voice to the African American belief that the funeral is not just a farewell, but also a celebration of the person's life and a time for rejoicing. The music performed during the return from the cemetery conveys this mood of celebration, incorporating improvisation and accompanying dancing.

On the return from the cemetery, the band and mourners follow a route passing the home, workplace, or other

The Olympia Brass Band marches slowly through the streets of New Orleans on the way to a church or funeral home, its music establishing a solemn mood. The men at the front of the procession wear sashes to mark their status as marshals of the band's lodge or social club. The band, led by Harold Dejan and heard in Listening Guide 49 (see page 230) was founded around 1960.

The New Orleans Jazz Band

Brass, woodwind, string, and percussion instruments make up the jazz band. To understand the choice of instruments for the jazz band, we must trace the history of several types of bands in New Orleans, the birthplace of jazz in the early twentieth century.

During and after the American Civil War, marching street bands, termed "tonk" bands, were common in poorer districts of the city. Many important performers, such as Louis Armstrong and Jelly Roll Morton, got their start playing in these bands. At high-society events in the wealthier parts of town, another type of band, called the "society" band, played waltzes and sentimental ballads. A third kind of band, the New Orleans dance band, performed for general dances, advertisements, and picnics. All of these bands—tonk, society, and dance bands—influenced the early jazz band.

Between 1900 and 1915, these various brass bands evolved into the classic New Orleans jazz band. Driven by the social demand for jazzy dances such as the foxtrot and the Charleston, occasional marches, hymns, and popular songs, the New Orleans jazz band played a diverse repertory. In addition to funeral processions, the jazz band also played in many other settings.

There are anywhere from five to fourteen instruments in the New Orleans jazz band: cornets or trumpets, trombones, violin and string bass, snare and bass drums, clarinets, and alto or tenor saxophones. The style of the music often reflects the outdoor settings of its performances: loud volume, a penetrating quality, and wide *vibrato,* all woven into a dense polyphony. The drums provide the beat while the trumpets, clarinets, violin, and trombones take turns carrying the melody. A solo trumpeter often improvises at the final chorus of the piece. In general, bands with a maximum of three melody instruments feature more improvised passages than those with four or more, which are likely to play arrangements.

Within the first two decades of the century, jazz bands began to tour the country, resettling on the West Coast and in New York and Chicago. Yet through its many transformations, the jazz band remained similar enough to nineteenth-century American brass bands that it still can be said to reflect a 1917 description of the Original Dixieland Jass Band as "a brass band gone crazy!"[11]

Brass bands, such as this ensemble of German immigrants in an 1879 painting, were commonly heard in the streets of American cities during the last decades of the nineteenth century. Brass bands strongly influenced the development of the jazz band.

Beyond its use at military and jazz funerals, the sound of a bugle or a trumpet, as seen here, playing *Taps*, marks the lowering of the US flag.

sites associated with the deceased; in this way, the memory of the individual is inscribed on the spaces he frequented during life. In this way, too, the procession can memorialize an individual, such as Armstrong, even when he is not actually buried in that locale.

The jazz funeral also underscores the collective identity of members of the funeral society, an important aspect for individuals, especially poor musicians, who stand outside the traditional halls of power. During the return from the cemetery, onlookers join *"the second line,"* a crowd that follows behind the band and mourners as they process through the streets. The second liners dance, encouraging others to join the procession as it moves along. Members of the second line wear ribbons, banners, and laminated pins inscribed with the name and face of the departed. In some recent New Orleans jazz funerals, second liners have worn memorial T-shirts printed with a large color photograph of the deceased and a caption including the person's nickname as well as birth and death dates, the latter termed "sunrise" and "sunset."[12]

Just as there are customs associated with the jazz funeral that link one such event to another over time, the music is drawn from familiar songs and hymns. A march in a medium tempo generally accompanies the initial procession to the funeral home or church. At the church the band plays an appropriate hymn chosen by the church or the family in a solemn style and homophonic texture. When the procession arrives at the cemetery, the band moves aside, forming a double rank to create a corridor through which the hearse passes, and the snare drummer plays a long roll. This moment, when the band signals the conclusion of the processional segment of the funeral, is called "turning the body loose." The band next plays a hymn at graveside, after which the minister preaches and people sing hymns. A trumpeter from the band often plays *Taps* as a solo.

Outside the cemetery, it is customary for the band to regroup. At this point the snare drummer tightens his snares, which had been muffled for the dirges and hymns, signaling the transition to celebration. Louis Armstrong once spoke about the roll of the snare drums as marking the climax of the jazz funeral:

> Them old time drummers, they just put a handkerchief under the snare on their drums and it go *tunk-a, tunk-a,* like a tom-tom effect. And when that body's in the ground, man, tighten up on them snares and he rolls that drum and everybody gets together and they march back to their hall playing *When the Saints* or *Didn't He Ramble*. They usually have a keg of beer back there and they rejoice, you know, for the dead.

The lively marches or popular tunes that the band plays once it is a respectful distance from the cemetery contrast to the solemn hymns they played on the way out. During the somber procession leading from church to cemetery, well-known hymns such as *Amazing Grace,* heard in Listening Guide 49 (see page 230), are performed. *When the Saints Go Marching In,* is a standard number for the celebratory return from the cemetery.

In addition to its religious significance and power to commemorate belief in a powerful way, *Amazing Grace* contributes additional layers of historical memory to any occasion on which it is performed. Its text was probably written by an eighteenth-century English evangelist and reformed slave trader named John Newton. The tune to which Newton's text is sung today, known as *New Britain,* was transmitted through William Walker's *Southern Harmony,* a songbook published in Tennessee in 1835 and still used today in the southern United States. The hymns in Walker's songbook were printed in *shape-notes,* a system of notation devised to make hymn tunes easier to read.

By the second half of the twentieth century, the hymn was heard in a variety of American settings. Its powerful theme of redemption struck a chord in the 1960s during the civil rights movement and the American folk music revival.

> Amazing Grace, how sweet the sound
> That saved a wretch like me.
> I once was lost
> But now I'm found
> Was blind, but now I see.

In the remastered recording of *Amazing Grace* performed at a New Orleans jazz funeral in the late 1960s (Listening Guide 49), we hear Dejan's Olympia Brass Band, one of New Orlean's oldest active brass bands. Founded in the 1960s by Harold Dejan, the band includes around ten instruments, including cornets, trombones, tenor and alto saxophones, clarinet, bass horn (a type of tuba or sousaphone), snare drum, and bass drum.

New Britain, from *The Southern Harmony*

Shape-note notation, also called *fasola,* is a system that uses different shapes to indicate the notes of the Western scale also represented by the syllables do, re, mi, fa, sol, la, and ti.

Amazing Grace (hymn)

CD 2
Track 15

Date of recording: Late 1960s, reissued in 1998
Performers: Dejan's Olympia Brass Band; Milton Batiste, *director*
Form: Strophic
Tempo: Moderately slow, triple meter

WHAT TO LISTEN FOR:
- The relationship between a lead instrument, carrying the melody of the hymn, and other instruments in a supporting role
- The repeating harmonic structure, which can be heard as the sousaphone plays the same bass line in each verse
- Repeating melodic elements within each verse

	STRUCTURE AND TEXT	DESCRIPTION
0:00	**Introduction**	By way of introduction, a cornet plays the last phrase of the verse, in free rhythm, accompanied by a sousaphone.
0:11	**Verse – instrumental**	The cornet continues playing the melody, while the rest of the band provides harmonic support by playing long, sustained chords. The verse consists of four phrases, each of which corresponds to a line of text. (In this instrumental performance, of course, the text is not heard.) Each phrase consists of four measures, and each measure contains three beats. Each phrase begins on the third beat of the measure a weak beat. The bit of melody on that weak beat is sometimes called a *pickup*. In this hymn, the first syllable of each line is a pickup.
0:50	**Verse – instrumental**	While the cornet maintains the lead, it improvises on the melody.
1:28	**Verse – instrumental**	All instruments drop out except two saxophones, sousaphones, and percussion. One of the saxophones takes over the melody, while the other harmonizes.
2:05	**Verse – instrumental (fade-out)**	Recording ends at 2:12.

Amazing Grace is classified as a *hymn,* which can be loosely defined as a song praising God. Hymns are almost always strophic, with simple, easily remembered tunes that aid singers in remembering multiple verses. The cornet plays the closing phrase as an introduction, varying the melody in the first two verses before the saxophone takes over in the third. In this performance, the hymn is played as a dirge, sounding the melody clearly at a very slow tempo. The rhythm is maintained by the bass drum, as well as by slow rolls and single beats on the snare and bass horn line. Like most dirges, this performance of *Amazing Grace* emphasizes the middle range, with a high cornet solo. The more upbeat mood and faster tempo of *When the Saints Go Marching In* is habitually used for the celebratory return of the funeral procession, as noted earlier in the comment by Louis Armstrong.

Although there has been a tendency in popular and scholarly writings to represent the jazz funeral as a relic of the distant past, recent inquiry suggests that "not only is the tradition surviving, but it is a dynamic form, constantly being reappropriated and revised for new circumstances."[13] The devastating impact of Hurricane Katrina on New Orleans in late August 2005, has provided an unprecedented test for the city's jazz community. In mid-November, members of the New Orleans Jazz Orchestra returned home and performed free concerts and jam sessions, including a jazz funeral procession mounted to mourn the city's losses and celebrate its rebirth.[14]

Indeed, like many of the music traditions we have explored, the jazz funeral is being transmitted in striking new contexts, including tourism. One notable early example of the popularization of the jazz funeral in the media is its inclusion at the beginning of the 1973 James Bond film *Live and Let Die.*[15] The music and traditions associated with the jazz funeral have also inspired groups outside New Orleans, such as "The Second Line Social Aid and Pleasure Society Brass Band" (SAPS) of Boston, which aims "to please if the cause is true and the time is right," performing for "populist, grass-roots events associated with political action." While SAPS does not play for jazz funerals and performs a wider and more eclectic repertory than the traditional jazz band, it takes its inspiration from the "second line, the people who followed the band . . . to give the band a riotous neighborhood performance."[16]

Whatever the setting, we find remarkable resilience in the sound of the jazz funeral, an effective and versatile musical means for memorializing departed individuals while reaffirming the cohesive nature of a community. The power of music to look backward in commemoration while insuring the future of its transmission marks many soundscapes, as we shall see in the following case study of the Syrian Jewish *pizmon.*

Reconciling Memories through Music

CASE STUDY: The Syrian Jewish *Pizmon*

Sometimes music sustains memories that seem to be at odds with the present-day settings for the music. Such is the case with the songs we will study next. When Jews left Aleppo, Syria, in the early twentieth century and established communities abroad, they brought the *pizmon* with them. The term *pizmon* (plural *pizmonim*) literally means "adoration" or "praise," and most of these hymns consist of Hebrew texts set to melodies borrowed from Middle Eastern Arab music.

Over the years, Syrian Jews have continued to sing these hymns and have composed new *pizmonim*. The union of sacred Hebrew texts with melodies drawn from popular Arab music may seem ironic to outsiders, especially given the twentieth- and twenty-first-century conflict between Arabs and Israelis. However, the Syrian Jewish community treasures these songs as part of its unique Arab-Jewish heritage. The following case study deals with a colorful example of music that conveys memories that conflict with present-day realities.

The Sound of the *Pizmon*

The *pizmon* tradition had its beginnings in the late Middle Ages, when Jews began to borrow melodies from the gentile world around them to set new sacred Hebrew texts (see "**Looking Back: Memories of the Syrian Jewish Past**").

Creating a song by setting a new text to an existing melody has a long and lively history in many music traditions. The song that results from this process is termed a *contrafactum* (plural *contrafacta*). The use of a well-known, pre-existing melody ensures, of course, that the new text will be remembered more easily. Indeed, it seems likely that *contrafacta* are widespread precisely because the familiar melody helps us recall the new words.

Jewish religious tradition deems it acceptable to borrow melodies from non-Jewish sources. Setting sacred Hebrew texts to these tunes is thought to render them holy, to bring out a melody's "holy spark." Syrian Jews borrowed the music they heard daily, the Arab songs

Syrian Jews preserve the culinary traditions of their homeland and patronize local grocery stores that stock Middle Eastern foods. The main Syrian Jewish shopping area in New York is in Brooklyn, near Ocean Parkway.

LOOKING *Back*

Memories of the Syrian Jewish Past

Jewish Life in Aleppo

c. 1000 BCE	Jews said to have arrived in Syria during reign of King David.
834 CE	First archaeological evidence of a Jewish community in Aleppo, Syria.
c. 1500	Jews expelled from Spain (Sephardic Jews) during the Inquisition arrive in Aleppo.
1500s	First publications of Jewish hymns (*pizmonim*) with borrowed melodies and sacred Hebrew texts.
1850	Revival of *pizmonim* in Aleppo by Rabbi Raphael Taboush.
1869	Opening of Suez Canal decreases use of overland trade routes and causes economic decline of Aleppo.
1881	Economic strains trigger first wave of Middle Eastern emigration abroad.

Establishing Syrian Jewish Communities Abroad

1901	Syrian Jews found Great Synagogue Ades in Jerusalem.
1903	Syrian Jewish community established in New York City.
1911/1912	Syrian Jews in New York establish a synagogue on the top floor of a tenement building on the Lower East Side.
1912	Taboush's students leave Aleppo and immigrate to Mexico and New York.
1914	Annual immigration to the United States from Greater Syria peaks at 9,023.

The Brooklyn Era

1919–1920	First Syrian Jewish families move from Manhattan to Bensonhurst, Brooklyn.
1920s	Syrian immigration to the United States restricted by Immigration Acts of 1921 and 1924.
1930s	Syrian Jews settle in Flatbush, Brooklyn.
Early 1990s	Virtually all Jews remaining in Aleppo and Damascus immigrate to Brooklyn.

popular in their community. Living in Aleppo, where Jews and Arabs had regular contact and congenial relations, Syrian Jews acquired Arab tunes through oral tradition, hearing the songs in coffeehouses and concerts. Many *pizmonim* from the nineteenth century, set to Arab melodies popular at the time, are still sung today.

Most *pizmonim* borrow their tunes from Arab songs, and so are based within the Arab musical system of *maqam*. The concept of *maqam*, which is at the core of Arab music, is described by one Syrian Jewish musician as the "science behind Arab music" and the "bottom line of the entire culture we have absorbed and used."[17] Each *maqam* (plural *maqamat*), is a category of melodies that share pitch content, range, and characteristic ornaments. There are at least a dozen categories of *maqamat,* each distinguished by its *pitch content* and the way in which those pitches are ornamented and developed within the song. In Western musical terminology, a category of melody distinguished by its pitch content and ornamentation is called a *mode* (discussed in Chapter 1).

The number of *maqamat* and their names have differed over time and in different geographical areas of the Arab world. Even within the same locale, the number of *maqamat* varies according to whether closely related *maqamat* are considered part of the same family or independent. Present-day Syrian Jews usually count eight *maqamat* as the most important.

Twentieth-century Arab music theory defines a *maqam* as a basic scale divided into two sections of four pitches each, called *tetrachords.* Musicians learn to recognize a *maqam* by the distinctive intervals between the four lower pitches (the lower tetrachord, the bottom pitch of which is the *final* or *tonic*) and those between the four upper pitches (the upper tetrachord). Syrian Jews share Arab *maqam* theory, and further emphasize that the "nucleus of a *maqam*" can be found by identifying its final pitch and the two preceding pitches. One can also recognize *maqamat* through practice and experience; musicians learn to listen to the end of a time and match it to the *maqam* of a song they already know. This process works especially well with *maqamat* that have distinctive lower tetrachords.

In their Sabbath morning rituals, Syrian Jews prescribe a *maqam* to be emphasized each week. Selected *pizmonim* and important prayers are sung in the weekly *maqam*. The *pizmonim* we will study in this unit are in *maqam ajam* and *maqam nahawand.*

We encounter *maqam nahawand* first, in a late nineteenth-century *pizmon, Attah El Kabbir* (Listening Guide 50; see page 238). This *maqam* has remained popular until today; it is clear that some *maqamat* became more popular than others because they were widely circulated on recordings. In addition, *maqam nahawand* was particularly attractive and memorable after the migration to the new world because it sounds similar to the minor scale of Western music. The spread of Western musical notation has also helped standardize many of the *maqamat* across the Middle East.

Attah El Kabbir represents a particularly interesting case study of musical transmission. We can trace its path from its composition in late nineteenth-century Aleppo to its performances today all over the Syrian Jewish diaspora. In the course of the intervening century, *Attah El Kabbir* was periodically forgotten and then remembered again.

Attah El Kabbir was composed in Aleppo by Rabbi Raphael Taboush (see page 236, "**Individual Portraits: Remembering Great *Pizmon* Composers**"). The Hebrew text of *Attah El Kabbir* calls on God to have mercy on his chosen people, alluding to Jews exiled among strangers. Its melody derives from a forgotten Arab song that must have been popular in the late nineteenth century; otherwise, it would not have been heard by Taboush nor set as a *pizmon*.

Attah El Kabbir evidently spread quickly as Syrian Jews migrated from Syria to other places. A transcription made by an early ethnomusicologist of the *Attah El Kabbir* melody confirms that it was sung in Jerusalem before 1910. The *pizmon,* like the Arab song on which it was based, is in duple rhythm and proceeds at a spirited pace. The performance in Listening Guide 50 (see page 238) by a soloist and chorus accompanied by an *'ud* (see "**Sound Sources: The *'Ud* and the *Qanun*"** in Chapter 4), results in a *heterophonic* texture; the voices and instrument play the same melody with slightly different ornaments. There is a brief, improvised vocal introduction in *maqam nahawand* that introduces the *pizmon.* Called a *layali,* this type of introduction is used in Arab vocal music to help establish the *maqam.* Although it may sound as if the soloist is singing vocables, the text is derived from the Arabic word *la yahl* ("oh, night") which give the introduction its name.

Although the text of the original Arab song on which *Attah El Kabbir* is based has been forgotten, the *pizmon* melody maintains its well-known Arab form, called a *muwashshah.* A three-part form, the *muwashshah* has a clearly recognizable melody at the beginning that returns after a contrasting middle section.

Attah El Kabbir also traveled to Syrian communities outside the Middle East. Around 1912, disciples of Raphael Taboush who immigrated to Mexico City introduced the song there. At the same time, Cantor Moses Ashear and other Taboush students brought the song to New York City. But in the decades after the death of Cantor Ashear in 1940, *Attah El Kabbir* was forgotten in New York. Some longtime residents who know many *pizmonim* remember learning the song in the 1960s, when it was reintroduced by Israeli cantors

Remembering Great *Pizmon* Composers

"That's what my grandmother told me," said eighty-year-old Gracia Haber during an interview in Brooklyn. Haber recounted many colorful stories about her great-uncle, Rabbi Raphael Taboush (c. 1850–1918), the beloved composer of *Attah El Kabbir* and many other *pizmonim* in late nineteenth-century Aleppo.

> He had tunes in his head, and every time there was a wedding, or there was a *bar mitzvah*, or a circumcision, he used to, in Hebrew, translate the words. The music is in Arabic, but the wording was Hebrew. And that's how we start the *pizmonim*. And for every occasion, there is another *pizmon* he used to make.

While the names of Raphael Taboush and his student, Moses Ashear, are remembered as the composers of *pizmonim*, and their Hebrew *pizmon* texts continue to circulate in books published within the Syrian Jewish community, most of what we know about both men comes from memories transmitted orally by their families. While Syrian men transmit details about the meaning of *pizmon* texts and tales about the people to whom the songs are dedicated, Syrian Jewish women also transmit memories that would otherwise be forgotten. Women arrange the various religious and social settings at which the *pizmonim* are performed in homes and synagogues. In the past women did not generally learn to read or write Hebrew, but they sang the Arab songs that became *pizmon* melodies. Perhaps most important of all, women transmit tales about the composers of *pizmonim* and their songs.

Gracia Haber remembered otherwise forgotten details about Raphael Taboush's life and career, recalling that he learned Arab music from hearing it performed by his Arab neighbors in Aleppo. Raphael loved Arabic songs and used to go to places where he could hear them and learn them. Gracia noted that "every time they heard there's a wedding or a party by the Arab, he used to go there. He had some friends that went with him."

An image of Rabbi Raphael Taboush, about whom many tales still circulate in Syrian Jewish oral tradition. They say he had a wonderful ear and could repeat a melody at first hearing. "Very, very smart and very fine at singing," Taboush startled people with his ability to compose *pizmonim* on the spot.

who moved to New York around that time. *Attah El Kabbir* was evidently forgotten in Syria as well and was reintroduced to Damascus through cassette tapes sent from Israel around 1980.

Today, *Attah El Kabbir* is very much alive in Israel, where it is sung in every Syrian Jewish synagogue in Jerusalem. It is also heard regularly in Mexico City

At an early age, Raphael went blind, but he continued to listen to Arab music whenever it was performed. He subsequently became known throughout Aleppo as a "thief" since he "stole" the melodies from songs he heard only once and used them for *pizmonim*.

Living at a time when many of his community were leaving Aleppo for destinations abroad, Taboush was concerned that his students remember the *pizmonim*. He taught his students hundreds of songs, which they carried with them when they moved abroad. Taboush's most famous student was Moses Ashear, who was born in Aleppo in 1877 and was mentored by Taboush after he lost his father as a child. Ashear migrated to New York in 1912, where he worked as a cantor and composer of *pizmonim* until his death in 1940. Cantor Ashear's son recalled that his father, unable to hear live Arab music as his teacher Taboush had done in Aleppo, used to listen for hours to recordings of Arab music imported from the Middle East on 78-rpm discs. Moses Ashear is said to have died as he was straining to remember the melody of an Arab song that had long ago been made into a *pizmon*.

The memories of Taboush and Ashear are kept alive through oral tradition as well as through their *pizmonim*. The names of both Taboush and Ashear are encoded in the texts of many of the songs they composed. For instance, in Raphael Taboush's *pizmon Attah El Kabbir* (Listening Guide 50; page 238), the first letters of each Hebrew verse, read down, spell out the words, "I am Raphael." Similarly, in Moses Ashear's *pizmon Mifalot Elohim* (Listening Guide 51; see page 242), the first letters of each verse spell the name Moses. Around 1900, while both men were still living in Aleppo, Taboush composed a *pizmon* in honor of Moses Ashear's wedding. This song is still sung in Syrian Jewish communities today, serving as a musical commemoration of a composer, his student, and a significant occasion in the life cycle.

After his immigration to New York City, Cantor Moses Ashear officiated at Syrian synagogues in lower Manhattan and later in Brooklyn, but continued to work as a bookkeeper in order to support his family.

and New York during prayers in the synagogue, at life-cycle events, at parties, and at concerts. Thus, *Attah El Kabbir* has traveled the world with Syrian Jews over the course of the last century. In light of its reintroduction to New York City and its subsequent return to Syria by cassette, we see that musical memories can be refreshed and transmission begun anew.

Attah El Kabbir, ("You, God, Are Mighty," Syrian Jewish *pizmon*)

CD 2
Track 16

Date of composition: c. 1900
Composer: Raphael Taboush
Date of performance: 1989
Performers: Moses Tawil and Ensemble, Brooklyn, New York
Form: Three- part Arab *muwashshah* (lit., "encircled, ornamented") preceded by
 layali (improvised introduction, lit, "oh night")
Function: Sung in many contexts, including social gatherings and prayer services
Tempo: Brisk, with regular quadruple meter

WHAT TO LISTEN FOR:

- Setting of a deeply religious Hebrew text to a lively melody of popular Arab origin
- Contrast between the free rhythm of the improvised introduction, or *layali,* and
 the regular quadruple meter of the *muwashshah* that follows
- Three-part *muwashshah* form containing a refrain (A) and a contrasting middle
 section (B), both of which have their own internal structures
- Heterophonic texture in which voices and instruments sing and play the same
 melody and rhythm at the same time with slight deviations

STRUCTURE AND TEXT	TRANSLATION	DESCRIPTION
0:00 *Layali*		A brief solo vocal improvisation accompanied by *'ud,* with one sung response by ensemble. The *layali* establishes *maqam nahawand,* which is similar to the Western minor scale with some subtle differences in the third and seventh pitches in the scale.

The Settings of *Pizmon* Performance

Most *pizmonim* celebrate joyous life-cycle occasions such as the birth of a
child, a *bar mitzvah* (held when a boy turns thirteen and officially becomes an
adult), or a wedding. For such occasions, a family may commission a new
pizmon, with the father of the newborn baby or groom sometimes suggesting

Time	Section/Phrase	Text	Commentary
0:40	*Muwashshah* **Section A (Refrain)** **Phrases a and a'** Attah el kabbir rachum shimkha rachem al am segullah	You, God, are mighty, your name is merciful, Have pity on a chosen people,	This line is sung twice by the ensemble to the same melody (a and a'). The repetition (a') has a slightly different ending that leads directly into the second half of the refrain.
1:04	**Phrases b and c** Ki rabbim rachemekha le-eyn kets vetikhlah.	For your compassion is abundant, Without end and without limit.	The second line of text is sung twice by the ensemble to new melodies (b and c) that round out the four-phrase refrain.
1:27	**Section B** **Phrase d** Nafshi todekha bekhol et uvkhol zeman **(Phrase d repeats)**	My soul shall thank you, every moment and at all times.	The middle section, with contrasting melody and register, is led off by the soloist with ornamentation at the end of the first phrase on the word "zeman." The line is repeated by the ensemble to the same melody.
1:54	**Phrase e (with repeat)** She-eh mahalali ne-e-man **Phrase f** Chon a-lai be-chemlah **Phrases e' and f'**	Accept my faithful praise! With pity act upon me graciously.	Phrase e is sung by the soloist and then repeated by the ensemble. (Note that phrase e has the same melody as the beginning of phrase d.) Phrase f is then sung by the soloist. The ensemble and the soloist repeat these texts in phrases e' and f', although the melodies are somewhat different.
2:20	**Section A (Refrain)** **Phrases a and a'** Attah el kabbir rachum shimkha rachem al am segullah	You, God, are mighty, your name is merciful, Have pity on a chosen people,	
2:44	**Phrases b and c** Ki rabbim rachemekha le-eyn kets vetikhlah.	For your compassion is abundant, Without end and without limit.	
3:05	**Section B**		Return of middle section with new text and soloist. Fade out at 3:08.

to the composer that he set the melody of a particular popular song. The composer then invents a Hebrew text to fit the melody, including references to the occasion and the names of important family members and friends. This new *pizmon* is first performed at the synagogue ritual at which the baby, young boy, or the engaged couple are blessed. If the *pizmon* becomes popular,

Any occasion can provide a setting for music making. Here musicians play *qanun*, *'ud,* violin, and drum (*darabukkah*) at a house-warming party in the Syrian Jewish community of Deal, New Jersey.

it may continue to be performed at subsequent events and enter the chain of musical transmission. In this way, over time, a song linked to a particular family transcends its original association and becomes part of the broader community's collective memory.

One important setting for *pizmon* transmission is a Sabbath afternoon songfest called the *Sebet,* held by Syrian Jews to celebrate special occasions. One member of the Syrian community describes the *Sebet* as follows:

When a groom is going to get married, they give him the honor by calling him up to the reading of the scrolls . . . and then they go home and they make a little party. They call that "Sebet." "Sebet" is in Arabic . . . the Sabbath. They invite all their close friends. Sometimes they have over a hundred people. And they have very nice food prepared for them and they spend about two or three hours singing. . . . They have all types of songs. They sing, sometimes they dance. They do the same thing when they have an engagement, when they have a *bar mitzvah,* or when they have a new child, whether it be a boy or girl.

Moses Ashear is said to have introduced the *Sebet* to early twentieth-century New York. The *Sebet* is a festive affair, with families clearing their public rooms of furniture and setting up long tables and folding chairs. Plates of food and bottles of cold drinks are set out on each table and replenished often while the men sing. The women, in addition to serving, traditionally gather in the dining room, where the table is filled with buffet dishes and chairs line the walls. Recently, however, these traditions have begun to change, and many families now employ professional caterers. Young women who have learned *pizmonim* in Jewish schools have also started to participate in the singing in some households. Because Jewish law prohibits playing instruments on the Sabbath, the *pizmonim* are performed unaccompanied at the *Sebet.*

The *Sebet* has played a major role in Syrian ceremonial life, providing a regular time for musicmaking in which the entire family can participate. The *Sebet* also serves to reinforce memories of Syrian social life. Community member Moses Tawil observes that:

It is a very necessary part of our, you might say, socializing. We can't use instruments, we don't use any other electrified type of music. So what do you do really in a social affair? Outside of talking, talking, talking, talking to someone? We sing! And you come, we put the very nice table, we put the drinks, and we start singing the *pizmonim*. So we want . . . our younger people to grow into it, to be familiar with it, so that they do not feel estranged and feel "What kind of oddball would do it?" And they have grown into it. So this is the way we train them? . . . And they still go for this in a big way. They like it very much. This is the way.

Another Syrian Jewish community event features music—the party known by the Arabic word *haflah*. Held any evening except the Sabbath in a local auditorium or club, the *haflah* celebrates special occasions such as anniversaries. It is customary to hire a singer and professional musicians, often bringing together Middle Eastern musicians from Jewish, Christian, and Muslim communities. Rather than singing *pizmonim* with Hebrew texts, musicians at a *haflah* perform the original songs from which the *pizmon* melodies have been taken, complete with their Arabic texts. Thus, the *haflah* features songs in Arabic with instrumental accompaniment by a synthesizer, violin, *qanun*, *'ud*, flute, and drum, whereas the *Sebet* includes only unaccompanied *pizmonim* sung in Hebrew. The performance of the same melodies in these different settings with different texts reinforces the process of musical transmission and enhances musical memories.

Musical Sources for Diaspora Pizmonim

Over the years, *pizmon* melodies have been drawn from many sources, including the music traditions Syrian Jews encountered in their new homelands. For instance, Moses Ashear, who settled in New York City, based a *pizmon* on the popular Italian song, *Santa Lucia*. Composed by a nineteenth-century Neapolitan musician, *Santa Lucia* was transmitted by Italian immigrants who lived in Lower Manhattan near Syrian Jews. Ashear, the story goes, one day heard *Santa Lucia* from his apartment window played by an Italian organ grinder and decided on the spot to use the tune for a *pizmon* he was composing in honor of a newborn baby girl.

Sometimes melodies were borrowed for *pizmonim* without full knowledge of their origins. For

An organ grinder like this one (left), with a dancing monkey, photographed on a New York City street in the early 1900s, played *Santa Lucia* outside Cantor Moses Ashear's apartment window.

Mifalot Elohim ("The Works of God," *pizmon*)

CD 2
Track 17

Date of composition: c. 1920

Composer: Moses Ashear

Source: School song of High School 62, Brooklyn, itself borrowed from the German
Christmas carol, *O Tannenbaum*

Date of performance: 1985

Performer: Hyman Kaire

Form: Strophic song

Tempo: Brisk, with regular triple meter

Function: Wedding *pizmon* composed for Samuel Aharon Franco

WHAT TO LISTEN FOR:

- Hebrew text set to popular melody best known as a Christmas carol
- Alteration of *O Tannenbaum* melody and form from four phrases (aaba) to five phrases (aaaba)
- *Maqam ajam,* which sounds like the Western major mode

example, *Mifalot Elohim* was commissioned during the early 1920s in New York City on the occasion of a wedding. At the request of the groom, Moses Ashear set the wedding *pizmon* to the melody of the groom's high school song. The melody was easily remembered and *Mifalot Elohim* became a popular *pizmon* (Listening Guide 51). However, neither the groom nor the composer realized at the time that the high school had borrowed the melody from the Christmas carol *O Tannenbaum*. Composed more than a century before the school song, *O Tannenbaum* had apparently failed to cross ethnic and religious boundaries and was not known by Syrian Jews at the time the *pizmon* was composed. As the years went by, Syrian Jews heard the Christmas carol and began to associate the *pizmon* melody with Christmas. As a result,

STRUCTURE AND TEXT	TRANSLATION	DESCRIPTION
0:00 **Phrase a** Mifalot elohim chazu, Lo shitu libkhem shichu	Gaze upon the works of God, Pay attention and speak aloud.	The melody of the first phrase is repeated to set the text of two more phrases.
0:09 **Phrase a** Shiru lo bemakhelot, Besimchat chatanim kalot	Sing to Him in choirs, In the happiness of brides and grooms.	Composed on the occasion of a wedding, the verse of the song text refers to brides and grooms.
0:15 **Phrase a** Lo levad hathelot, Ye-otu lo ye-otu	To Him alone are the adulations, they suit him, they suit.	
0:22 **Phrase b** Harem yah tsur olamim, Bet aharon haramim	Rock of the world, raise the lofty House of Aaron,	This phrase is set to a contrasting melody.
0:22 **Phrase a** Loveshei urim vetummim, Bakkodesh yasharetu	Those who don the Urim and Thumim, They serve you in holiness.	The fifth and final phrase returns to the first melody to round out the song. "Urim and Thumim" refer to the High Priest's twelve precious stones, representing the twelve tribes of Israel, mentioned in Biblical descriptions of the Jerusalem Temple.
0:37		Example ends.

Mifalot Elohim is rarely sung today in Syrian Jewish circles, since memories of the Christmas carol from which it derives have replaced the older associations with the school song. The melody of this *pizmon*, by the way, is classified by Syrian Jews as *maqam ajam* even though the melody is not an Arab song. Since *maqam ajam* is very similar to the Western major scale, Western major melodies borrowed for *pizmonim* are included within the *maqam ajam* category.

While *pizmon* composers such as Taboush in Aleppo and Ashear in New York City heard and remembered melodies from live performances in coffee houses and other public places all around them, Syrian Jews in diaspora came to depend in large part on records imported from the Middle East as a source for new melodies from the Arab tradition.

Continuing Use of Arab Melodies

Although composers of *pizmonim* have borrowed melodies from a wide array of music traditions, they continue to depend most heavily on the Arab music tradition despite the passage of nearly a century since the departure of Syrian Jews from the Middle East. We will now investigate the relation of one *pizmon* composed in the late twentieth century to the Arab song from which its melody was borrowed. Through a close look at its sound, setting, and significance, we will see how the text and tune of the *pizmon* sustain two different but complementary channels of memory.

The *pizmon Ramach Evarai* was composed for the *bar mitzvah* of the junior Moses Tawil, which took place on May 23, 1982. The song was first sung as the youth was called forward to read from the *Torah*, the Five Books of Moses.

On the occasion of his 1987 *bar mitzvah*, another grandson of Moses Tawil, Alan Nasar, carries the *Torah* scroll dedicated five years earlier by his grandfather (standing at left) at the *bar mitzvah* of Moses Tawil.

Louis Massry displays his *'ud*, imported from Damascus, handsomely decorated with mother-of-pearl inlay.

This *pizmon* also celebrated a second event that took place on the same day—the dedication of a newly copied *Torah* scroll that had been donated to the synagogue by the youth's grandfather, the senior Moses Tawil. *Ramach Evarai* commemorates both a young boy's coming of age and the philanthropy of his grandfather, a respected community leader. This *pizmon* was even more of a family affair than most; the composer was Louis Massry, the grandfather's brother-in-law, a businessman who is both a Hebrew scholar and a player of the *'ud*.

The text of the *pizmon* embeds memories important to the Tawil family as well as memories of the religious community as a whole. At the same time, the melody is connected with Arab popular culture.

The melody chosen for the *pizmon Ramach Evarai* was borrowed from *The Wheat Song*, composed in 1946 by the famous Egyptian musician Muhammad 'Abd al-Wahhab (1910?–1991). *The Wheat Song* was composed for a scene in an Egyptian film, *Lastu Malakan* ("I Am Not an Angel"), in which Egyptian peasants are harvesting wheat. The song is light and short by Arab standards; it is a strophic form with a refrain. The original text is a poem in colloquial Arabic celebrating the harvest.

Muhammad 'Abd al-Wahhab was known for his striking innovations in Arab musical style, particularly in his film songs, where he used a large instrumental ensemble that combined traditional Egyptian and Western instruments.[18] The original 78-rpm recording of *The Wheat Song*, transferred to audio cassette, is heard here in Listening Guide 52 (see page 246) with 'Abd al-Wahhab performing as soloist.

The Wheat Song begins with an eight-beat rhythm played three times by the drums at a moderate pace. When the rhythm is repeated, a solo piccolo enters, playing a melody based on the flute theme from the second act of Tchaikovsky's *Nutcracker* ballet. 'Abd al-Wahhab was known for frequently quoting from a wide variety of Western classical compositions he learned from recordings.

Next, the instruments establish the pulse underpinning the song proper, a duple rhythm with an accent on the second beat. The song is set in *maqam ajam*, but here again, 'Abd al-Wahhab looks West and strongly implies a Western major scale. The nod to Western music is further enhanced by the presence of Western harmony instead of the traditional Middle Eastern heterophonic texture, and by the entrance of European singers, borrowed from the Cairo Opera Company, performing a high countermelody.

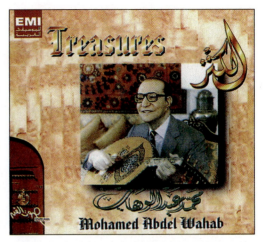

The music of Muhammad 'Abd al-Wahhab (1910?–1991), who made innumerable recordings during his long career, was popular across ethnic and religious lines throughout the Middle East.

Many Syrian Jews know and love *The Wheat Song*, which was so widely circulated through recordings that most are unaware that it was originally composed for a film. The *pizmon's* composer, Louis Massry, chose the melody of *The Wheat Song* for *Ramach Evarai* (Listening Guide 53; see page 252) because it was a "catchy tune, not a deep song, but a light, catchy song a lot of people could sing." He knew the melody well because *The Wheat Song* is often played at parties on account of its "excellent tempo," which is "beautiful for dancing." Massry's concern that the melody be "catchy" (memorable) is an aesthetic value echoed by others in his community. As another person put it, "the poem depends on the music that he's putting in his community. As another person put it, "the poem depends on the music that he's putting words to. It's the music that controls the words that are being said."

The long lag between the composition of the original Arab song and the composition of the *pizmon,* some thirty-six years, is unusual. But composer Louis Massry explained that like many in the Syrian community, he remembered the song from recordings: "I have every record and tape of 'Abd al-Wahhab; as soon as a new one came out, I would buy it."

Ramach Evarai is a *contrafactum* that follows precisely the form, melody, and rhythm of the original *Wheat Song*. However, note that it substitutes a new instrumental introduction for 'Abd al-Wahhab's original and eliminates the women's chorus. The omission of the original introduction makes sense

The Wheat Song (Egyptian film song)

CD 2
Track 18

Date: 1946

Composer: Muhammad 'Abd al-Wahhab

Performers: Muhammad 'Abd al-Wahhab, *voice*

Cairo Opera Chorus

Instrumental ensemble including *tiran* and *riqq* (frame drums), *qanun* (zither), six violins, cello, bass, piano, and piccolo

Form: Egyptian *ughniyah* (strophic song with refrain)

Function: Composed for the film *Lastu malakan* ("I am not an angel") to accompany a scene during which Egyptian peasants harvest the wheat crop

Tempo: Moderate

WHAT TO LISTEN FOR:

- Combination of traditional Arab with Western instruments, and the use of a Western-style opera chorus
- Contrast between melodic and rhythmic context of the instrumental introduction and that of the song
- Overall song form with refrain sung to the vocable "ah." Note the melodic contrast and asymmetrical structure of verses 1 (a a b) and 2 (c c a b)
- Reference to a classical Western melody from Tchaikovsky by the piccolo in the introduction
- Inflection of *maqam ajam* toward C major throughout the song and at the final cadence

STRUCTURE AND TEXT	TRANSLATION	DESCRIPTION
0:00 **Instrumental introduction** **Cycles 1-3 (frame drums)**		Three large frame drums (*tiran*) play three rhythmic cycles. Each cycle, named *'iqa masmudi kabir,* is eight beats long and can be represented as an 8-beat pattern. (The drums accent beats 1-3-5-7 of the cycle.) At the third cycle, a fourth frame drum (*riqq*) joins in.

0:12	**Cycles 4-6 (piccolo melody with string response)**		On the fifth beat of cycle 4, a solo piccolo enters playing a melody borrowed and transformed from the well-known "Chinese flute" theme in the second act of Tchaikovsky's ballet, *The Nutcracker*. The piccolo melody overlaps the beginning of cycle 5, with the strings responding at the end of that fifth cycle.
0:24	**Cycles 7-9 (repeat of above)**		Cycles 7-9 repeat cycles 4-6.
0:35	**Cycles 10-11 (string melody with piccolo response)**		At the beginning of cycle 10, the strings enter with a melody that matches the length of the eight-beat cycle. The piccolo responds with its own melody at the beginning of cycle 11.
0:43	**Cycles 12-13 (repeat of above)**		Cycles 12-13 repeat cycles 10-11.
0:51	**Cycles 14-15 (string melody)**		Strings conclude the introduction with a fast descending melody that drowns out the percussion accompaniment. The introduction ends with the main pitch of the *maqam ajam*.
0:59	**Refrain (instrumental)**		The instruments accelerate into the refrain, which is set to a duple rhythm named *krakoviak*. The piccolo plays a high countermelody above the other instruments.
1:16	**Refrain (instrumental)**		
1:32	**Verse 1** **Phrases a and a'** El amhil laila el laila lailot 'iidu, Ya rabb tibarik tibarik witzidu,	Tonight is the celebration of the wheat, May God bless it and let it increase,	Verse 1 begins with two related melodic phrases, a and a', sung solo by the composer. These verses are then repeated.
1:40	**Phrases a and a' (repeated)**		
1:48	**Phrase b** Ya rabb tibarik, ya rabb itbarik, ya rabb tibarik witzidu.	May God bless it, may God bless it, may God bless it and let it increase.	The strings interrupt the melody twice with short echoes where the commas occur in the text.

(continues)

(c o n t i n u e d)

	STRUCTURE AND TEXT	TRANSLATION	DESCRIPTION
1:56	**Transition (instrumental)**		The strings provide a transition that foreshadows melody c.
1:59	**Verse 2** **Phrases c and c'** Luli wimfattah 'ala 'udu (ah, ah, ah, ah) widdunyaw gudha min gudu (ah, ah, ah, ah).	Pearly and clustered on the stem, the existence of life comes from its existence.	The soloist sings phrases c and c', with choral response on "ah."
2:07	**Phrases c and c' (repeated)**		
2:15	**Phrases a and a'** 'Umru mabyikhlif ma wa 'idu (ma wa 'idu), Ya rabb itbarik witzidu (witzidu).	It never misses its coming time? The existence of life comes from its existence, May God bless it and let it increase.	Verse 2 continues with the return of phrases a and a', with an echo by the chorus.
2:23	**Phrase b** Ya rabb itbarik (tibarik), ya rabb itbarik (tibarik), ya rabb itbarik witzidu.	May God bless it, may God bless it, may God bless it and let it increase.	Verse 2 ends with the return of phrase b. This time, the chorus interrupts the phrase (instead of the strings) with echoes of the soloist's melody.
2:31	**Refrain (choral)**		The chorus sings refrain on the vocable "ah." High female voices sing a countermelody.
2:46	**Refrain (choral, repeated)**		The refrain has a cadence with harmony implying a C major scale. In the original recording of *The Wheat Song* on 78-rpm discs, the song continues on a second disc with a third verse set to a contrasting melody. This contrasting melody is heard earlier in the *pizmon Ramach Evarai,* where it is named x.
3:07	End		

given the limited instrumental resources available in Brooklyn, and the borrowed Tchaikovsky flute melody would not be recognized by most of the *pizmon*'s listeners.

Although the melody of *Ramach Evarai* is remembered by Syrian Jews as borrowed from *The Wheat Song*, thereby carrying memories of Middle Eastern life and the other works of 'Abd al-Wahhab, the Hebrew text establishes an entirely Jewish framework, with references at its core to Jewish law and custom.

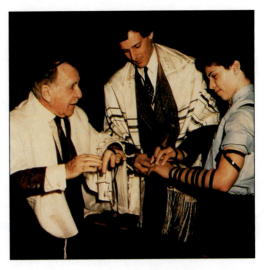

Following the traditions mentioned in the text of the *pizmon Ramach Evarai,* Alan Nasar dons *tefillin* (phylacteries) for the first time, for prayers during the week before his *bar mitzvah.*

This *pizmon* text, like most of them, is filled with hidden meanings. For example, the three Hebrew letters that spell the first word, *ramach,* can be added together as numbers, totaling 248, symbolizing the number of parts in the human body, according to Jewish tradition, and the number of positive commandments (thou shalt's) enumerated in the Torah. The metaphorical meaning is that the young man's entire body should be devoted to the service of God. The text also contains numerous references to liturgical custom. For example, it mentions the *tefillin*—scriptural passages enclosed in black leather boxes that are strapped on one arm and the forehead during weekday morning prayer services.

The reference to Moses' encounter with the burning bush is particularly meaningful, since this is the name of both the elder grandson and his grandfather. Finally, the "secrets of the Torah" revealed to Moses allude to Jewish mysticism and to the Torah scroll dedicated that day by the senior Moses Tawil.

Along with numerous references to Jewish ritual, literature, and folklore, included in the *pizmon* text are the names Abraham and Moses, representing four generations of Tawil men. That Abraham and Moses were prominent biblical figures brings additional honor to the family and meaning to the song. The name "Hannah" found in the text does not refer to anyone in the family, but to the city of Hannah, mentioned in Joshua 19:14.

The melody of a *pizmon* such as *Ramach Evarai* carries memories of musical trends that Syrian Jews share with the broader Middle Eastern community around the world. It also brings to mind the many occasions on which *The Wheat Song* was heard, live or recorded, at parties in the Syrian Jewish community. Simultaneously, the *pizmon* text incorporates allusions to Jewish prayers and psalms, weaving in the names of family members taking part in a meaningful life-cycle event. The content of this *pizmon* thus contains the residue of a dual Jewish and Arab identity. We should recall that prior to the twentieth century, when political conflicts in the Middle East deeply divided Jews and Arabs, these peoples shared for centuries both a music tradition and

Music, Memory, and the Senses

We already learned that we perceive music not just in the ear but also throughout the body. Some individuals, when hearing music, actually experience sound as a color, taste, or smell, a phenomenon known as "synesthesia." Many musical memories draw on images that cross sensory boundaries. In the Syrian *pizmon,* we encounter an unexpected network of connections between music and food.

Some of the associations between music and food arise because many of the occasions at which *pizmonim* are sung—life-cycle events in the home, parties—involve the consumption of special foods.

Food carries symbolic meaning in Syrian Jewish life, and publications such as the *Syrian Festival of Holidays Recipe Book* prescribe in detail the foods to be used in celebrating the important Jewish holidays. For instance, at the Jewish New Year (*Rosh Hashanah*), blessings are sung while people eat special foods. These foods include Swiss chard or spinach used to protect against enemies; a special candy called *hilu,* made from squash, syrup, and nuts, eaten to insure that God will guard the community with prayer; and a combination of black-eyed peas and lubiah fish thought to help the community "propagate and multiply like the fish in the sea and the abundance of peas."

This page from the *Syrian Festival of Holidays Recipe Book* presents the menu of traditional foods for the Jewish New Year (*Rosh Hashanah*) among Syrian Jews. The preliminary blessings (*berachot*) are accompanied by fruits, vegetables, meat, and fish. The main course includes ground meatballs (*kibbe geraz*), vegetarian meatballs (*kibbe naya*), stuffed grape leaves (*yebra*), and stuffed Swiss chard (*yebra sileet*).

a way of life. The *pizmon* incorporates this hybrid identity and continues to sustain it as part of a remarkable Jewish-Arab heritage, decades after Syrian Jews left their homeland.

The *pizmon* also arouses conflicting emotions. Songs are not only heard, they reverberate in the other senses as well, adding other layers of meaning (see **"Studying Music: Music, Memory, and the Senses"**).

Strains of a familiar *pizmon* can transport listeners back to important moments in their lives. Songs can also elicit powerful memories of a deceased

In the Arab music tradition shared by Syrian Jews, food metaphors are liberally applied to music. Each *maqam* is said to have its own "flavor," which can be "sweetened" by ornamentation and improvisation. Syrian Jews extend this metaphor by prescribing that both the *pizmonim* and the food should be "sweet, not sour." The book containing Syrian *pizmonim* is dedicated to the memory of "the sweet singer of Israel" (Moses Ashear) and to the holy songs, "which are sweeter even than the honey and the honeycomb." In this way, the memory of song is reinforced and strengthened by invoking a food with which it shares settings and associations. The following comment from a Syrian woman shows how completely music and food are intertwined:

> Everybody knows everything, what they do on holidays, they have certain foods on different holidays. On Purim, we make *kibbeh*—meatballs—with mushrooms. We always have that, they are best on Purim. And we used to sing, get drunk. Oh there's a lot of songs. I used to know them all. . . . For Rosh Hashanah we used to make rice and sweet sauce, you can't make a sour sauce. Everything sweet, you know. And different songs. Every holiday has a song. . . . And the funny part is, on Saturday, when they sing the songs, they bring in the melody that goes in with the time.

Although the *pizmonim* are composed by men and performed by men, food is the domain of the women. Women prepare and serve the traditional foods at home rituals while the men sing. Just as the men passed on *pizmonim* by oral tradition and reinforced their memories through written *pizmon* collections with blank pages to accommodate new songs, the women have transmitted recipes in cookbooks with blank pages at the end of each section so that "everyone can add her own recipes."

relative or some other experience of loss by recalling occasions with an individual no longer present or a place no longer visited. That songs continue to be sung in situations similar to those in which they were first performed and heard sets in motion the highly charged process of reminiscence. For the performer as well as the listener, *pizmonim* recreate events and arouse emotions. These songs also keep alive for twenty-first century Syrian Jews memories of their history in the Middle East and their pride in the traditions of earlier times and different places.

Ramach Evarai ("Let My Whole Being Testify," *pizmon*)

Date: 1982
Composer: Louis Massry
Performers: Moses Tawil, Sr., and Ensemble, *voices*
    Louis Massry, *'ud*
    Ezra Ashkenazi, *darabukkah*
Form: Strophic song with refrain, adapted from popular Arab *ughniyah*
    (see Listening Guide 52)
Function: Composed for the *bar mitzvah* of Moses Tawil, grandson of Moses
    Tawil, Sr.
Tempo: Brisk, with regular pulse in changing meters

WHAT TO LISTEN FOR:

- The tuning of the *'ud,* which deviates from Western major mode and contrasts with the Western intonation of the voices
- The organization of the regular pulse into groups (*measures*) of different length
- References within the text to the *bar mitzvah* ceremony for which the song was written, as well as inclusion of names of the family members to whom it is dedicated
- Interaction between soloist, chorus, and the instruments
- The differences in the overall form from that of *The Wheat Song,* on which *Ramach Evarai* is based. *Ramach Evarai* substitutes a different introduction, and uses an additional melody (x) in verse 2. The overall form of the song is: Refrain / a a' b / Refrain / x x c c' a b / Refrain / x x c c' a b / Refrain

STRUCTURE AND TEXT	TRANSLATION	DESCRIPTION
0:00 **Solo *'ud* introduction**		The introduction opens with a brief solo *'ud* section, based on variations of phrases that become important later in the song.
0:12 **Refrain melody begins**		The *darabukkah* enters just after the *'ud* introduces the
0:14 ***Darabukkah* (drum) enters**		melody of the refrain, reinforcing the rhythm. Conversation can be heard in the background.
0:28 **Refrain**		Chorus sings the refrain, set to the vocable "ah."

	Verse 1		
0:45	**Phrases a and a'**	Let my whole being testify	The verse begins with two
	Ramach evarai ya-idu en	that there is none other	phrases (a and a') that are
	bilado yah ram tevarekh	besides Him Who dwells	similar. The second, beginning
	tevarekh ushlach lo.	in the heaven above.	with the words *yah ram*, mimics
0:53	**Phrases a and a' (repeated)**		the content of the first at a
			slightly lower pitch level.
1:01	**Phrase b**		
	Et birkat avraham umosheh	Bless and send him the	Phrase b concludes the first
	ben amram yah ram	blessing of Abraham, and	verse. It is based on the refrain
	tevarekh ushlach lo.	Moses the son of Amram,	melody and contrasts with
		yes bless and send him.	phrase a.
1:09	**Refrain (instrumental)**		The *'ud* plays the melody of the
			refrain.
	Verse 2		
1:25	**Phrase x**	In honor of the *bar mitzvah*,	The second verse begins with a
	Likhvod chatan bar mitsvah	let them sing the song in	new melody, phrase x, sung twice
	yashiru et hashirah be-ir	the glorious city of Zion,	by the soloist. The *'ud* echoes the
	tsiyyon hannimah kirat	and the city of Hannah.	melody at the end of the phrase.
	channah.		
1:34	**Phrase x (repeated)**		
1:41	**Phrases c and c'**	Bind the words of *Shema* on	Phrases c and c' each end with an
	Koshrem al yadkha (Ah, ah,	your hand (Ah, ah, ah,	echo by the chorus. Notice how
	ah, ah) ulot yehi lekha	ah), and let it be for you a	phrases c and c' are related to the
	(Ah, ah, ah, ah)	sign (Ah, ah, ah, ah).	refrain melody, but with a
1:49	**Phrases c and c' (repeated)**		slightly different rhythm.
1:56	**Phrases a and a'**	To Moses his servant, the	Phrase a and a' return. There is a
	Ulmosheh avdo sod torah	secrets of the Torah he	new text for phrase a, while a'
	gillah lo, yah tevarekh	revealed to him, Yes bless	retains its original text.
	tarekh ushlach lo.	and send him.	
2:05	**Phrase b**		
	Et birkat avraham umosheh	Bless and send him the	Both the melody and text of
	ben amram yah ram	blessing of Abraham, and	phrase b return to round out the
	tevarekh ushlach lo.	Moses the son of Amram,	second verse.
		yes bless and send him.	
2:13	**Refrain**		
	Verse 3		
2:29	**Phrase x**	Gladden the hearts of your	Phrase x returns with new words
	Aneg kabbed horekha	parents and honor them,	and is repeated.
	ushmor mitsvat borekha	and observe the	
	ya'arikhu yamekha birkat	commandments of your	
	horim	Maker, and this precept	
2:37	**Phrase x (repeated)**	will lengthen your days.	(c o n t i n u e s)

(continued)

STRUCTURE AND TEXT	TRANSLATION	DESCRIPTION
2:45 **Phrases c and c'** Avi simah alai (Ah, ah, ah, ah) tefillin ben enai (Ah, ah, ah, ah)	Father place upon me (Ah, ah, ah, ah) the *tefillin* between my eyes (Ah, ah, ah, ah).	The soloist sings phrases c and c' with a new text, and then repeats these two phrases.
2:53 **Phrases c and c' (repeated)**		
2:59 **Phrases a and a'** Ehgeh battorah eshmor mitsvotecha vesas anokhi ai kol mimrateha.	I will meditate upon the Torah and keep its commandments and rejoice in all its words.	
3:09 **Phrase b** Tsiyyon la-ad tivneh el ram shokhen seneh nahgem vechesed uvrachamim	Zion will be rebuilt forever, and whose presence was even in the burning bush, lead them in love and compassion.	
3:17 **Refrain**		Tempo slows down at end and Western harmony (a Western major chord) is heard at the final cadence. (End at 3:39)

Conclusion

As we learned earlier, bonding a text to a melody establishes a durable memory that can more easily be recalled; think of our ability to sing complete songs many years after we first heard them. In part because music—especially song—embeds itself so readily in memory, songs have been used to help people remember. For this reason, too, music is used to commemorate events and to memorialize individuals.

In this chapter we encountered examples of the ways in which music and its performances are linked to memory. The *corrido* and hymns such as *Amazing Grace* are preserved in memory through the supporting sound of a repetitive melody. In contrast, the setting of the jazz funeral adds layer of meaning to music heard in other sacred and secular contexts, such as *Amazing Grace*. Finally, the *pizmon* tradition borrows existing melodies for reuse in situations where their original identity is also remembered, a compositional technique used to sustain memory across cultures.

The transmission of music depends on individual and collective memory; the case studies in this chapter demonstrate that music in turn enhances memory. Musical transmission is further shaped by a variety of factors besides memory, including practical aspects of economics, politics, and individual initiative, as we will see in Chapter 6.

What information have you learned by connecting it with music? Many English speakers learn the alphabet by singing it aloud to a simple melody. Do you remember the *Alphabet Song*? Note that the melody of the *Alphabet Song*, particularly memorable to the Western ear, is based on the children's song *Twinkle, Twinkle, Little Star*.

IMPORTANT TERMS

brass band	jazz funeral	*pizmon*
contrafactum	*layali*	second line
ethnic records	*maqam*	shape-note/*fasola*
hero corrido	mode	synesthesia
hymn	*muwashshah*	*'ud*
jazz band	phonograph era	

Chapter 6

Music, Mobility, and the Global Marketplace

The search for a global market and ways to sell music traditions across cultural divides is not a new one. Here we see an advertisement dating from about 1900 for Hohner, a popular manufacturer of harmonicas, seeking to attract a multicultural market for the instrument.

Overview

Main Points

- Music, an important signifier of place, helps sustain and enhance travel and tourism.

- New technologies and performance venues give rise to new musical vocabularies and hybrid musical styles.

- Economic and political forces shape the transmission of music.

Introduction

In Chapters 4 and 5, we discussed processes of musical transmission. Chapter 4 focused on the ways communities that share aspects of descent (ethnicity, religion, or national identity) have transmitted and transformed music as they resettled in new places. In Chapter 5, we took a close look at how individual and collective memory interact to transmit music over long periods of time as well

An image of members of the brass band of Claflin University, a historically African American university in Orangeburg, South Carolina, was part of an exhibit on African American life at the Paris Exposition of 1900.

as across great distances. In this chapter we will explore music's increasing mobility through the global pathways that have emerged in twentieth- and twenty-first century musical life, including travel, tourism, concert tours, festivals, and new technologies.

The deep-seated Western notion that the arts exist in a purely aesthetic arena of emotion and beauty has diverted attention from the social and economic factors that bring twenty-first-century music traditions to new audiences. Individual initiatives and creativity, economic considerations and corporate decisions all play a role in shaping aspects of musical life. The work of agents and presenters has brought unfamiliar music traditions to far-flung localities and has shaped new musical communities of affinity that would not otherwise exist.

Over the course of the last century new settings for musical performance—international educational exchanges, recordings, broadcasts, and festivals—have opened new channels of musical transmission. We find the historical roots of this trend in the nineteenth century colonial era and the exhibition culture that emerged in Europe and the United States in the mid-nineteenth century. For example, the first American Exposition in 1853 displayed live Native Americans for profit, entertainment, and public education. Later exhibitions reproduced native villages and scenes from daily life, including musical performances. The World's Columbian Exposition (Chicago, 1893), which featured musical performances by Kwakiutl Indians of the Northwest Coast and others, has been termed "an early form of touristic consumption."[1]

The opening ceremony of the 1939 Golden Gate Exposition in San Francisco featured dozens of bands including a Chinese drum and bugle corps (center).

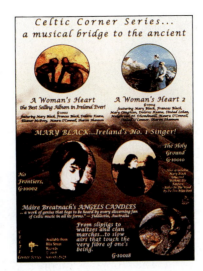

Recent advertisements have represented "exotic"—that is, unfamiliar or foreign—cultures as links to an ancient past depicted as a primitive stage of cultural development. These advertisements, intended to validate these musics, are in fact based on popular misconceptions of social evolution.

Many of these displays at early fairs and festivals presented so-called "exotic traditions" in reconstructed scenes from daily life. These were the first panoramic exhibitions that an observer could walk into and interact with—early ancestors of theme parks such as Disneyland.

Other presentations adopted a "panoptic" or all-seeing approach; the viewer watched from a distance, commanding a supreme vantage point.[2] Concepts underlying these early panoramic and panoptic exhibitions are still detectable in present-day musical presentations and performances, at festivals or in concert halls, raising many issues for those who mount, perform, attend, or study these musical events (see page 262, **"Studying Music: Presenting Music and Musicians"**).

The juxtaposition of music traditions within the same setting has resulted not just in the introduction of music to new audiences, but also in exchange between musicians who formerly did not interact but now have been brought together. Musicians from one tradition now borrow from other musics and combine music traditions in new ways.

How do we study such musical interactions and take into account the wide variety of factors at work around the world that shape and transmit music? Scholars have proposed frameworks for examining the forces that influence present-day musical production, performance, and reception. One approach has been to focus on "micromusics," "small musical units within big music cultures." This approach includes situating all micromusics within three overlapping levels called subculture, superculture, and interculture.[3]

Presenting Music and Musicians

"Think Globally, Listen Locally," advised the February 4, 2000 headline of a *New York Times* article celebrating the fifteenth anniversary of the World Music Institute, a major presenter of world music in New York City. As we have seen throughout *Soundscapes*, today it is possible to travel only a few minutes from your living room to attend concerts of musics from around the world. Therefore it is important to analyze through ethnomusicological investigation the channels through which music reaches us in our daily lives.

Over the last century and a half, great changes have taken place in the presentation of music. Following the exhibitions that first brought global styles to local settings, the presentation of public concerts was dominated throughout much of the twentieth century by impresarios (organizers) who managed—and sometimes mismanaged—musicians' careers.

During the second half of the twentieth century, an increasing number of nonprofit organizations began to contract with musicians for performances. The World Music Institute is an example of a relatively recent major institution that now organizes musical tours. Many universities, museums, and cultural organizations present live performances. As we saw in Chapter 2, many cities and towns also sponsor festivals that feature both local and imported musical talent. Presentation is organized on the national level in many countries, as in the Smithsonian Institution's National Folklife Festival, which brings together musicians from many sectors of American and international musical life.

Most performances by artists from traditions that lack mass audiences are sponsored by nonprofit organizations that underwrite expenses through a precarious

With the Capitol building in the background, His Holiness the Dalai Lama waves to the crowd at the Smithsonian Folklife Festival on the Mall in Washington DC on July 2, 2000. Approximately forty thousand people came to watch the Nobel Peace Prize winner preside over a Great Prayer Ritual led by Tibetan monks. The 2000 Smithsonian Festival featured a celebration of Tibetan culture, including the performance of ritual dances; the creation of traditional Tibetan Buddhist sand mandalas and butter sculptures; the construction of a twenty-eight-foot Buddhist monument ringed by thirty prayer wheels; and the celebration of a secular Tibetan festival, including performances of Tibetan opera. The performance seen here is panoptic in its orientation; at the same time the spectators become participants in the panoramic presentation of the larger festival.

combination of ticket sales, private donations, corporate support, and grants from agencies such as the National Endowment for the Arts. But the world of musical presentation is changing radically. In particular, new kinds of corporate involvement are transforming the promotion, production, and presentation of musical events.

In the first years of the twenty-first century, Clear Channel Entertainment (CCE) became a major force in presenting music, theater, and dance events in the United States and worldwide. A network of companies that spanned the entertainment industry and produced and promoted musicians as diverse as Britney Spears and TLC, CCE became the world's largest producer and promoter of live entertainment. What distinguished CCE from earlier presenters, such as record companies that have long sponsored national and international tours by their artists, is that CCE contracted with artists and also operated the largest network of performance facilities. A subsidiary of the radio corporation Clear Channel Communications, by the spring of 2004 CCE owned, leased, or booked 125 performance venues in North and South America and Europe. CCE holdings included performing sites such as Houston's Compaq Center, the Aerial Theater at Bayou Place, and Boston's Wang Center. According to CCE's own figures, 69 million people attended 32,000 CCE events during the last year, including concerts, theatrical shows, family entertainment, and motorsports shows. Although CCE's shows tended to focus on the most marketable musicians, they also mounted "second stages" at many of their events to bring less well-known musicians to new audiences.

The activities of CCE in consolidating the live entertainment industry raised deep concerns in many sectors. Nonprofit organizations who support musical diversity cannot compete with the resources and scope of major corporations like CCE. Many musicians and listeners have also voiced concern about corporate control over performance and its impact on existing traditions as well as on new artistic directions, in the name of marketability. On April 29, 2005, in a move sparked in part by a drop in revenue, Clear Channel announced that by the end of 2005 it would spin off its entertainment division (Clear Channel Entertainment) from its radio and TV groups and not retain any ownership in the entertainment company. It was subsequently announced that the new company would be named Live Nation and headquartered in Los Angeles.[4]

Although we have touched on many important issues relative to music's role in the world throughout *Soundscapes,* the new and powerful corporate presence in the presentation and marketing of musical events is exactly the type of change that demands thoughtful and informed study and discussion.

Throughout this book so far, we have generally situated each music tradition within its *subculture,* which includes local, personal, familial, occupational, and community networks. It is within individual subcultures that most of the music traditions we have explored, from the *fado* (Chapter 2) to the *pizmon* (Chapter 5), have been created and transmitted, even as they have become available to outsiders through recordings and live performances.

The second sphere of musical interaction is the *interculture.* Subcultures influence each other through economic or commercial connections, proximity, or affinity. We encountered intercultural interaction in the remarkable worldwide dispersion of the Scottish bagpipe, spread through British colonial and military presence but also adapted to numerous local settings (Chapter 3). We will encounter further examples of intercultural connections in Chapters 7 and 10 in case studies involving the accordion, an instrument spread by migration and commerce through many musical subcultures and incorporated into diverse musical styles.

The case of the bagpipe also illustrates a third, overarching sphere of musical interaction termed the *superculture,* which is shaped by the power of the state and by the national and global economy.

In subsequent chapters, we will encounter several musical practices that began locally, were spread through intercultural exchange, and were then further transformed through the influence of the superculture. These include the music traditions associated with the *tango* (Chapter 7), *reggae* (Chapter 9), and *karaoke* (Chapter 10).

The following chart is another way of looking at how local music traditions are subject to complex societal forces. This approach sets forth in detail the complex interactions of the superculture, interculture, and subculture, located at the top, middle, and bottom of the chart. The chart incorporates the impact of national policy, the music industry, the media, and international economic forces on the creation and transmission of music. This framework emphasizes the institutional forces such as national arts organizations, the music industry, the music business, and educational entities, including schools and universities. Read horizontally, the chart provides a summary of factors, organizations, and areas of activity; read vertically, it moves from international to local entities.

In this chapter, we will explore the forces shaping soundscapes through three contrasting case studies. We will look first at the impact of travel and tourism on musical transmission within the Hawaiian tradition. Next we study intercultural transmission and cross-cultural collaboration between composers in Bali and the United States that have produced new, hybrid musical styles. Finally, we will investigate a large-scale musical endeavor, The Silk Road Project, which has created a new, global community of participants and audiences from various subcultures, influenced by forces of the interculture and superculture to create an international soundscape of great economic impact.

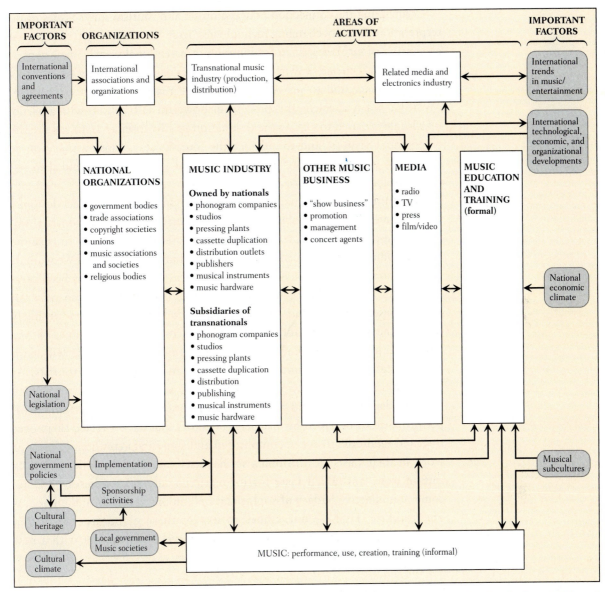

The chart contains the following labels:

IMPORTANT FACTORS | **ORGANIZATIONS** | **AREAS OF ACTIVITY** | **IMPORTANT FACTORS**

- International conventions and agreements
- International associations and organizations
- Transnational music industry (production, distribution)
- Related media and electronics industry
- International trends in music/entertainment
- International technological, economic, and organizational developments

NATIONAL ORGANIZATIONS
- government bodies
- trade associations
- copyright societies
- unions
- music associations and societies
- religious bodies

MUSIC INDUSTRY

Owned by nationals
- phonogram companies
- studios
- pressing plants
- cassette duplication
- distribution outlets
- publishers
- musical instruments
- music hardware

Subsidiaries of transnationals
- phonogram companies
- studios
- pressing plants
- cassette duplication
- distribution
- publishing
- musical instruments
- music hardware

OTHER MUSIC BUSINESS
- "show business"
- promotion
- management
- concert agents

MEDIA
- radio
- TV
- press
- film/video

MUSIC EDUCATION AND TRAINING (formal)

- National economic climate
- National legislation
- National government policies
- Implementation
- Sponsorship activities
- Cultural heritage
- Local government Music societies
- Cultural climate
- Musical subcultures

MUSIC: performance, use, creation, training (informal)

This chart by Roger Wallis and Krister Malm maps the world of everyday musical life. One reads the chart by following the arrows, all of which are bi- or multi-directional, reflecting the complex interaction of organizations and other entities across and between levels of society.

Travel and Tourism

In studying the presentation of music, it is necessary to consider the impact of the travel and tourism industries. Musical performances are important attractions in most locations and are actively marketed to draw visitors. We need think only of the lure of the Grand Ole Opry in Nashville, of steel bands playing at many Caribbean island resorts, and of Broadway musicals in New York City.

Confronting the connection between music and tourism raises issues of interpretation. Rapidly changing technologies, from the steamship to the newest generation of airplanes, have revolutionized recreational travel. The financial impact of tourism has spawned entire industries designed to draw tourists to a particular place and to provide a range of recreational activities for them. Music plays a vital role in this process: its powerful associations with a particular locale are used to signify the destination in advertisements, to sell the site to potential visitors, and to enhance the tourist's stay. Close association of music and place as reinforced through tourism can then be extended to sell other products as well.

Many musical performances presented to tourists have been designed both to entertain and to shape their perceptions of the place. Music traditions have probably been transformed, translated, or shortened to ease the understanding and enjoyment of those unfamiliar with the place. We want, if possible, to identify the ways in which a musical performance has been carefully calibrated or constructed—for example, the musicians who play the steel drums every weekend at a hotel bar in a Caribbean resort are likely hired by the management for regular appearances, carefully costumed for the audience's pleasure, and encouraged to perform a repertory that will mesh with the taste of white, middle-class, American and European tourists. At the same time, we must also be careful not to assume that a performance's apparent lack of historical anchors or authenticity robs it of meaning. All performances are shaped by a variety of factors that have affected them over time and retain the traces of complicated and sometimes conflicting forces at work in their pasts. Anthropologists have self-consciously noticed that "a certain irony and allied taste for incongruous cultural syntheses" can become "unreflective badges of sophistication" among travelers and ethnographers alike.[5] That is, one comes to expect these elaborate—and often exoticized—musical displays as part of the traveler's encounter with a new place.

CASE STUDY: Transmitting the Hawaiian Sound

New technologies made travel easier and more affordable by the middle to late twentieth century, but the exhibition and sale of music as part of tourism became a lucrative industry in many places long before that. For instance, in Hawaii, the distinctive sounds of the steel guitar and ukulele, as well as the swaying movements of the hula dance, became a part of the burgeoning Pacific tourist trade early on. By the end of the first quarter of the twentieth century, these sounds and sights came to signify Hawaii whenever and wherever one encountered them (see page 266, "**Sound Sources: Steel Guitar and Ukulele**").

One of the ironic aspects of the story of Hawaiian music is that some of the foremost performers responsible for the global marketing of Hawaiian music were not born in the islands and spent most of their adult lives abroad. An example is the Moe family, who performed Hawaiian music around the world for over a half century. The four Moe brothers were born in Samoa, moved to Hawaii at an early age, and married there. With their wives and other musicians, they became known as the Royal Samoan Dancers and in 1928 left Hawaii for a tour of the Far East.[6]

Eventually, the brothers split up into separate ensembles. Tau Moe continued to perform with his family, establishing his headquarters in Brussels. Pulu Moe and his wife, Louisa, joined with a third musician, Kaili Sugondo, to constitute the Pulu Moe Trio; Louisa sang, danced the hula, and played the ukulele, while Pulu played a steel guitar and also performed a Samoan knife dance.

After spending a few years in London, they were signed in 1941 by the impresario Felix Mendelssohn (not the famous German composer who lived in the nineteenth century), for whom they made their first recording. As a result of that recording, the group became well-known in Europe and Asia. Both the Pulu Moe and Tau Moe ensembles sometimes played with other bands under Mendelssohn's management and kept busy with broadcasting and recording. Mendelssohn managed the Pulu Moe ensemble, arranging the details of its shows, costumes, and publicity. Mendelssohn promoted the Pulu Moe ensemble vigorously, riding a wave of European fascination with foreign and exotic traditions.

Following the devastation of World War II, Mendelssohn fell on hard times and eventually declared bankruptcy in the late 1940s. Here we see the direct impact of economic pressures; after Mendelssohn's death in 1952, the Moe Trio disbanded. Pulu Moe worked in a factory in London until he returned to Hawaii in 1962. The Tau Moe family, however, continued to tour and lived in Brussels until they returned to Hawaii when they were in their eighties.[7]

After their return to Hawaii, the Tau Moe family reissued some old recordings and made several new ones with younger musicians. *Samoan Moon*, heard in Listening Guide 54 (see page 268), demonstrates the distinctive

The Pulu Moe Trio, including (left to right) Kaili Sugondo (guitar), Louisa Moe (ukulele), and Pulu Moe (steel guitar), performing in Copenhagen in May 1951.

Steel Guitar and Ukulele

Several lively oral traditions exist regarding the development of the lap steel guitar. Some say the Hawaiians adopted the instrument from Mexican herders who arrived on the island around 1830. Others credit Joseph Kekuku with the invention of the steel guitar after he experimented with pulling a comb or penknife across the strings of an ordinary Spanish guitar.[8] A third account credits a young stowaway from India who applied playing techniques used on Indian zithers to the guitar while en route to Hawaii in 1884.

Bob Brozman plays the steel guitar.

The player produces the characteristic sounds of the steel guitar—a pronounced *vibrato* and slides up or down to a pitch—by using the left hand to slide a steel bar across a string on the neck of the guitar or, on recent models of the instrument, by using a pedal. Picks, called plectra, on the thumb and first fingers of the right hand pluck the strings or can be drawn across all the strings to produce a *glissando*. *Vibrato* on individual pitches is produced by vibrating the hand holding the steel bar. The lap steel guitar is played like a zither, held flat on the lap.

It is easy to produce harmonics on the lap steel guitar by flattening strings at certain places with the palm of the hand; the resulting overtones are called "palm harmonics" or "chimes." Formal characteristics of steel guitar music are given colorful names by insiders; the repeated final phrase of a verse, for instance, is called the "turnaround."

A second chordophone closely associated with Hawaii is the ukulele. Resembling a small guitar with four strings, the ukulele is a descendant of the Portuguese *braguinha* that was brought to Hawaii in the late 1870s by immigrants from the island of Madeira. The name *ukulele* means "leaping flea" in Hawaiian, and according to local legend, this strange name refers to either the diminutive and lively English ukulele player Edward Purvis, or the movements of a skilled player's fingers.

Soon after its introduction to Hawaii, the ukulele gained popularity because of the efforts of its early makers and royal patronage. Augusto Dias, Manuel Nunes, and José do Espirito Santo, who established shops to make and repair ukuleles in the 1880s, were active promoters of the instrument. The ukulele was also King David Kalakaua's favorite instrument and played a prominent role in many cultural events within the royal palace.

By the beginning of the twentieth century, the ukulele had become a media symbol for the Hawaiian Islands' fledgling tourism industry. The 1915 Panama-Pacific International Exposition in San Francisco introduced the instrument to the American mainland. Its portability, simple playing technique, and low cost made it instantly popular nationwide. Even Hollywood movies capitalized on the ukulele's associations with idyllic island life, featuring grass-skirted beauties strumming ukuleles on moonlit beaches. Celebrities such as Elvis Presley and Tiny Tim played the instrument, and it was used to sell products ranging from Listerine to Dole pineapples.

The ukulele is traditionally made of koa wood, a tree of the acacia family that grows in Hawaii. Ukuleles come in a variety of sizes and shapes and may be decorated with elaborate inlaid mother-of-pearl designs or paintings. Although the instrument is relatively easy to learn, it takes a virtuoso to master the ukulele. A recent revival of interest in Hawaiian culture has led to an increased demand for ukuleles and lessons as well as an annual ukulele festival in Honolulu's Kapiolani Park. In 1999, the Island Ukulele Company, a producer, distributor, wholesaler, and retailer of Hawaiian-made ukuleles, opened in the Waikiki Hyatt Regency Hotel. The shop offers free introductory ukulele lessons and sells its products worldwide, with particularly heavy sales in the mainland United States, Southeast Asia, and Japan.[9]

Today vintage ukuleles are collector's items. Beginning in the 1920s and 1930s, some instrument makers decorated their ukuleles with everything from Hawaiian scenes, as here, to pineapples.

Samoan Moon (Hawaiian song)

CD 2 Track 20

Date of recording: 1989
Performers: Tau Moe family with Bob Brozman
Form: Strophic song with instrumental interlude
Tempo: Moderately slow triple meter

WHAT TO LISTEN FOR:

- Effects particular to the lap steel guitar, including slides and harmonics. The harmonics are produced by touching the string lightly at its mid-point while it is plucked.
- Vocal techniques including yodeling, in which the singer intentionally produces a break in her tone as she switches from chest voice to head voice.

STRUCTURE AND TEXT	DESCRIPTION
0:00 **Introduction**	The steel guitar carries the melody. At the cadence, the guitar's harmonics are used to play an *arpeggio* (broken chord), ascending to some very high pitches.
Instrumental 0:08 **Phrase a**	This instrumental section is based on two melodic ideas, here labeled phrase a and phrase b. The ukulele strums on each beat, outlining fairly simple Western harmonies. In the melody, the beat is often subdivided into three equal parts (triplets), or into long-short (swung) rhythms. A triple meter that is further subdivided into triplets can be described as being in 9/8.
0:23 **Phrase a'**	
0:39 **Phrase b**	
0:55 **Phrase b'**	

acoustic properties and playing styles of the lap steel guitar and ukulele still strongly associated with Hawaii. The characteristic sound of the steel guitar with *vibrato*, slides up and down to pitches and occasionally the production of audible overtones, led one ethnomusicologist to suggest that these ornaments alone can signify Hawaiian music to listeners outside of Hawaii.[10]

The popularity of the steel guitar and the ukulele spread to North America during the ukulele craze of the 1920s and 1930s, and was then revived

Verse

1:10 Back home, across the sea
That's where I long to be,
In my dear old grass hut by the sea.

When the singers enter, the melody is that introduced in phrase b, above. The steel guitar drops out except for occasional ornaments, such as the *arpeggio* played on the harmonics at the end of the first line of text. A female voice leads with the melody, while the other members of the family sing under the leader homophonically: one singer can be heard outlining a bassline, and the others fill in the inner harmonies.

1:23 Back home, across the sea,
That's where I used to be,
On the deep Samoan moon with you.

Instrumental

1:43 **Phrase c**

A new melodic idea is introduced in the steel guitar. Listen for *tremolo* in the steel guitar, rapidly and repeatedly plucking the same pitch.

1:59 **Phrase c'**

Verse

2:14 Back home, across the sea
That's where I long to be,
In my dear old grass hut by the sea.

While the family sings homophonically as before, the lead singer improvises a *descant* (an ornamental melody sung above the main melody) using vocables and yodels.

2:30 Back home, across the sea,
That's where I used to be,
On the deep Samoan moon with you.
On the deep Samoan moon with you.

Note the repetition of the final phrase, called a "turn around."

3:01 Recording ends

through LP recordings in the 1950s. Early television personalities such as Arthur Godfrey, who played the ukulele, contributed to the international popularity of Hawaiian music as well. More recent influences in spreading Hawaiian music have been record labels such as George Winston's Hawaiian Slack Key Guitar Masters series, which has released more than thirty albums since 1994, and Michael Cord's Hana Ola label, which specializes in restoring and remastering historic Hawaiian recordings.[11] The ukulele has also made

The image shows a Web page from the Ukulele Hall of Fame Museum, with a main menu on the left side listing: HOME, INDUCTEES, UPCOMING EVENTS, UKE EXPOS, HOW TO JOIN, MUSEUM SHOP, REFERENCE, and PERSONNEL. The central portion displays "Ukulele Hall of Fame Museum," a non-profit organization dedicated to the preservation of ukulele history, along with the journal "Uke Said It" and a portrait of King David Kalakaua, the Ukulele Hall of Fame Inaugural Inductee.

Ukulele culture is a living tradition, as we can see from the range of activities announced on the Web site of the Ukulele Hall of Fame.

inroads into popular music, such as the recent CD titled *Manuia* released by the Ukulele Club de Paris, a group guided by guitarist Dominique Cravic.[12]

Hawaii has witnessed a resurgence of interest in its indigenous music and hula dance traditions since the 1970s. Former island residents living abroad have continued to practice these traditions, transmitting them to others who have no personal ties to the islands. It is estimated that in addition to numerous hula schools in Hawaii, the continental United States, and Canada, there are 40 hula schools in Holland, more than 600 in Mexico, and about 1,000 in Japan.

Hawaiian music and dance, especially the hula, have become enormously popular among young Japanese women. There were several earlier waves of popularity of Hawaiian music in Japan, beginning before World War II.[13] In the 1960s, Japanese bands played Hawaiian music and took Hawaiian-style names such as "Setsuo Ohashi and His Honey Islanders." Nearly two million Japanese tourists each year visit the Hawaiian Islands, a relatively short and reasonable trip from Japan. Today ukulele lessons are aired on Japanese television, and it is estimated that there are between 20,000 and 30,000 students studying the hula in Japan. Each year, many Japanese women fly to Honolulu to participate in the King Kamehameha competition, an important annual event staged since 1974 by the State Council on Hawaiian Heritage.[14] Thus the global transmission of Hawaiian music has reinforced its performance at home as well.

Today Hawaiian music is found in surprising locales. For instance, the city of Indianapolis has since 1988 held a hula workshop known as "Dancers Dream Weekend," bringing together nearly two hundred dancers from Hawaii and places all over the United States and Europe. Ukulele and hula dancing are also taught in San Antonio, Texas, by a woman who fell in love with the music forty years ago while living in Hawaii: "We came back to the mainland and there wasn't any hula in Texas, so I started teaching. I love everything Hawaiian," she said.[15] Of interest to students of musical transmission is the fact that while most dance groups in Hawaii focus entirely on the hula, many of those in the continental United States teach and perform many Polynesian dances, including those of Tahiti and New Zealand.[16]

The wide array of international Hawaiian music and dance traditions testifies to the impact of tourism on music. These diverse examples also demonstrate that transmission processes initially spurred by fleeting contacts and economic gain can spark deep involvement and innovative musical activity that become an important part of peoples' everyday lives.

New soundscapes sometimes emerge from unexpected contacts, as we saw in the Introduction in reference to outsiders' encounters with Tuvan *khoomii* singing. Next we return to the subject of boundary crossing in the Balinese *gamelan* tradition, which has been transmitted through multiple channels ranging from tourism to national politics and has spawned new soundscapes at home and abroad. We will explore ways in which musical mobility transforms the musical creativity of individuals living half a world apart.

The American Folklife Center of the Library of Congress presents

FREE AND OPEN TO THE PUBLIC

HOMEGROWN 2003

Traditional music and dance "homegrown" in communities across the United States

Hālau o nā Maolipua
Hawaiian *mele hula*
A program celebrating Asian Pacific American Heritage Month

Wednesday, May 21, 2003
12 Noon - 1:00 PM
Neptune Plaza,
west front steps of the
Jefferson Building, Library of Congress, Washington, D.C.

Cosponsored with the Kennedy Center Millennium Stage
The Smithsonian's National Museum of the American Indian and the Folklore Society of Greater Washington
With support from the Office of Hawaiian Affairs
A part of "I Hear America Singing," a Library of Congress project celebrating America's music.

Intercultural Transmission and Boundary Crossing

CASE STUDY: New Music for Balinese *Gamelan*

In Chapter 2 we discussed the worldwide spread of the *gamelan,* supported by the desire of the Indonesian government to represent the country's music traditions abroad and the interest of Western composers and ethnomusicologists entranced by the *gamelan's* sound. Some composers such as Colin McPhee, who lived in Bali during the 1930s, had firsthand exposure to *gamelan* music; other Western composers were inspired by recordings and performances by touring Balinese musicians. The Indonesian *gamelan* even inspired some composers to design and build their own *gamelans* and compose innovative music for them.

But what about the *gamelan* tradition in Bali and the impact of innovations introduced by composers there? In Chapter 2, we looked briefly at *gamelan gong kebyar* in Bali, which emerged in the first two decades of the twentieth century as a revolutionary musical style characterized by sudden, intense bursts of sound and discontinuity in its structure.[17] The *gong kebyar* style was performed by a new *gamelan* that replaced many older ones, some of which were melted down and recast as new *gong kebyar* instruments.

Almost immediately, these new Balinese *gamelans* began to attract attention abroad. Their reputation was established in part through distribution of recordings issued in 1928 by the German labels Odéon and Beka, a project

Traditional Hawaiian *mele hula* (chants accompanied by dance) were perpetuated as oral traditions by female master artists long before a popular version of the historical dance became institutionalized as an emblem of Hawaiian culture and tourism. One prominent *hula* school was founded in 1976 by Alicia K. Keawekane Smith, a fourth-generation *kumu hula* (*hulu* master) pictured here with her students. Chosen to carry on her family's legacy as customary in this line of matrilineal descent, Keawekane Smith says that "Hula is my life, a heritage I humbly and honorably carry deep within me."

Composer Lou Harrison (bearded, in plaid shirt) rehearsing in 1982 with Gamelan Si Betty for a performance at the Cabrillo Music Festival. Named for its benefactor, Betty Freeman, the gamelan was built in 1979 by Lou Harrison and William Colvig. Modeled on the court gamelan of central Java, Gamelan Si Betty is one of the largest American-built gamelans.

facilitated by a German painter and musician named Walter Spies, who lived in Bali from the early 1920s until his death in 1942. Numerous travelers wrote about Bali, and Balinese dancers and musicians performed to great acclaim at the International Colonial Exposition in Paris in 1931. Bali quickly became a "chic tourist spot" in the 1930s, and by 1937, it was said that "Bali has become the fashion" in distant places such as New York City, where there was "an invasion of Bali bars and Bali bathing suits and Bali songs."[18]

One *gamelan gong kebyar* ensemble, which played throughout the 1930s at the Dutch-run Bali Hotel in the center of Denpaser, the largest city in Bali and the capital after Independence, became famous locally and internationally. Performing in this new, touristic context resulted in changes—a more rigorous rehearsal schedule, new teachers, new compositions, elaborately decorated instruments, and coordinated dance costumes. The income from these performances and the growing enthusiasm of a constituency abroad also encouraged competitions between Balinese *gamelans* and additional public exposure. The impact of tourism over time helped shape a new musical style, making *gamelan gong kebyar* "the emblem of a rapidly changing way of life.

Following Indonesian independence in 1945, Balinese culture was pushed to the fore as an international symbol of Indonesia. A *gamelan gong kebyar* was installed at the Presidential Palace in Bali, and lengthy dances such as *Taruna Jaya* (Listening Guide 28) were shortened to accommodate the briefer attention span of foreigners.

In the 1960s, the settings for the transmission of *gamelan gong kebyar* were altered; two government-sponsored schools for music, dance, shadow puppetry, and visual arts were established in Bali. At the beginning the teachers were drawn from village *gamelan* masters, but over the next decades the schools employed increasing numbers of Balinese musicians trained abroad. These institutions served to perpetuate a variety of local musical styles, became sites for innovative composition and choreography, and provided an institutional setting for global transmission of Balinese music. Interestingly, a recent study of *gamelan gong kebyar* music stresses that even with these new institutional settings, a single, coherent style did not emerge. Rather, the music continues to be multidimensional and embodies the contradictions, continuities, and instability of twentieth-century Balinese history.

One well-known Balinese composer is I Nyoman Windha (born 1956), a faculty member at Institute Seni Indonesia (Institute of Indonesian Arts). Trained at the new Indonesian music schools during the 1970s and 1980s, Windha first made his reputation as an accomplished *ugal* player. He began composing in 1983 and has produced numerous works well-known both in Bali and abroad. From the late 1980s on, Windha traveled between Indonesia, the United States, and Germany; many of his compositions from this period were composed for American and German ensembles. In 2003, Windha moved to California, where he worked closely with *Gamelan Sekar Jaya* and began to study for a master's degree in composition at Mills College.

Composer I Nyoman Windha plays the *ugal* while leading Balinese conservatory students and faculty in rehearsal for a recording.

Windha has remarked that "the first thing I think about when I compose is *desa, kala, patra,*" a phrase from a Balinese saying meaning "everything in its proper place, time, and context." In his composition *Kembang Pencak* ("Flowering Pencak"; Listening Guide 55, page 276), composed in the mid-1980s, one finds "in their proper place" traditional and innovative elements. *Kembang Pencak* was composed by Windha at the request of dancer and choreographer I Nyoman Catra for a Balinese festival held in memory of Walter Spies.[19] (In addition to his work sponsoring early recordings of *gamelan* music, Spies supported Balinese music and arts through the 1920s and 30s, played *gamelan* instruments, transcribed repertory, and performed piano duets with Colin McPhee in local concerts.)[20]

Pencak is a type of martial arts from Indonesia and *kembang* means "blooming" or "outgrowth," implying that an artistic flowering has grown out of the *pencak* movements.[21] Cast in the genre *kreasi baru* ("a new artistic creation"), Windha's *Kembang Pencak* combines diverse ingredients, has unstable and asymmetrical sections, and changes textures and tempos with dizzying speed. Innovations include hitting cymbals with sticks rather than crashing them together and an unaccompanied section for a male chorus doubling as dancers. Windha's works in the *kreasi baru* genre have been described as follows:

> He delights in complexity, lights up in praise of musical *keberanian* ("guts"), but does not value them for their own sakes; he wants to baffle musicians and audiences, but not beyond the point of surprise and beguilement where they are drawn to the music's challenge.

Successful compositions often set the stage for further innovations by the composer and others. I Nyoman Windha and his compositions had a direct impact on an American composer in 1989, when Windha joined Berkeley's gamelan *Sekar Jaya* for a yearlong residency. There he met American composer Evan Ziporyn (See page 278, **Individual Portraits: Evan Ziporyn**) and *Kembang Pencak* became the model for a new piece, titled *Kekembangan*.

In addition to the musical dialogue between I Nyoman Windha and Evan Ziporyn, *Kekembangan* presents a commentary on the differences between Balinese and American music systems and ways of hearing. This composition also raises important issues in musical transmission and musical ownership by challenging the boundaries between the traditions.[22]

Kekembangan (Listening Guide 56; see page 280) emerged through a combination of circumstances. Berkeley's *Gamelan Sekar Jaya* wanted to shift its focus from playing Balinese classics such as *Taruna Jaya* to performing newer repertory, including Windha's compositions. Windha wanted to learn more about

Western music and worked closely with Ziporyn, who taught him to read Western notation and to play the piano. During this period of exchange, Windha and Ziporyn had long discussions about differences in the Balinese and Western music systems, debating such issues as whether it was possible to replicate in an aesthetically satisfying way the Balinese tuning system *pelog* on certain white notes of the piano. In the end, Windha decided that the simulated Balinese piano scales were "*masih kurang,*" "still lacking."

The aesthetic issues were in fact only the surface concealing much deeper matters: What should be the role of an American *gamelan* of considerable skill and reputation, admired even in Bali? Could an American *gamelan* rightfully take the same liberties with Balinese music as contemporary Balinese composers and performers did? Could *Sekar Jaya* face the fact that by the late 1980s they were not just perpetuating traditional Balinese music, but had already established a two-way relationship with Balinese music and musicians? Ziporyn and Windha decided that they should acknowledge all of these realities. The result was the collaborative composition *Kekembangan*.

Kekembangan builds on Windha's composition *Kembang Pencak* but substitutes a saxophone quartet for the male singers. This substitution of Western instruments for Balinese voices intentionally blurs the boundaries between sound sources and musical styles.

According to Ziporyn, the role of the saxophones continually changes. Sometimes the saxophones blend with the *gamelan* parts, helping the Western listener to hear the Balinese phrases in a Western framework; at other times, the saxophones act as Balinese percussion instruments; at other moments, the saxophones play pitches clearly not part of the Balinese music system. Ziporyn says:

> Saxophones and *gamelans* are not so different; they're actually inversions of one another, if you think about it: *gamelan* metallophones work by striking metal and letting the sound resonate through bamboo tubes, while saxophones work by striking bamboo (the reed, with the tongue) and letting the sound resonate through metal tubes (the instrument itself). This became for me a perfect, secret metaphor for alternate traditions (secret in that I never discussed it with Windha): the same activity (organized sound), on the same materials (pitch, rhythm, timbre, etc.), producing radically different results.

In the end, Ziporyn believes he and Windha produced music "that was neither a *gamelan* piece with saxophones, nor a saxophone piece with *gamelan* accompaniment, but rather a piece equally informed by both traditions. . . . That Windha and others may hear the composition differently reflects the reality that individual listeners are free to construct their own meanings."

Kembang Pencak ("Flowering Pencak" composition [*gending*] for *gamelan* and male chorus)

CD 2
Track 21

Date of composition: Late 1980s

Composer: I Nyoman Windha

Date of recording: late 1980s

Performers: ASTI Gamelan, Denpasar
  I Nyoman Windha, *pemimpin (leader)*

Genre: *Kreasi baru,* a "new artistic creation" for *gamelan,* male dancers, and singers

Form: Based on traditional five-part structure, of which the first three are heard here, with expanded and innovative percussion sections

Tempo: Variable, moderate to fast

Tuning system: *Pelog*

WHAT TO LISTEN FOR:

- A traditional *kebyar* opening section played by the entire *gamelan*
- Prominence of five-note melodies in *pelog* introduced by flute and varied by other *gamelan* instruments
- The use of an unaccompanied (*a cappella*) male choir for part 2, punctuated by a *jegogen* solo
- Return to large ensemble for part 3, which is *Lelambatan Pengawak,* a slow central part of the composition not heard in its entirety here

---

	STRUCTURE AND TEXT	DESCRIPTION
0:00	**Part 1**	*reyong* introduction
0:05		enter entire *gamelan*
0:30		flute (*suling*) solo introducing *pelog* melody

0:44		entire *gamelan* returns
0:52		*kemong* (small gong) plays off beat, with *kendang* (drum) heard underneath
1:00		entire *gamelan* returns
1:06		repeat solo flute section first heard at 0:30
1:20		*reyong* entry
1:27		*Damped kempur* (a special gong used for *pencak* practice imported for this piece) plays "pur pur"
1:34		entire *gamelan*
1:43		repeat solo flute section from 1:06
2:03		long percussion section, with large gong; *damped kempur* plays "pur pur" in alternation with *kemong,* and extended *kendang* solo
2:41		closing section to Part 1 by entire *gamelan,* with *kebyar* and pause at end
2:54	**Part 2**	unaccompanied male chorus begins singing in unison
3:12		*jegogan* (large five-key metallophone in *gangsa* family) solo
3:22		chorus unison, with subtle *jegogan* accompaniment
3:43	**Part 3 (*Pengawak*)**	section begins with *gangsa* and drum
3:58		flute solo
		fade-out and ends at 4:03

Evan Ziporyn

We began to sketch a portrait of composer Evan Ziporyn in Chapter 2, where we encountered a Balinese *gamelan* founded and directed by Ziporyn in residence at the Massachusetts Institute of Technology. Born in 1959, Ziporyn received his graduate degrees in composition from the University of California, Berkeley, where he became an early member of *Gamelan Sekar Jaya,* founded by Michael Tenzer, Rachel Cooper, and I Wayan Suwekca, a Balinese drummer and composer.

Composer Evan Ziporyn with his clarinet.

Ziporyn had become involved with Balinese music while an undergraduate at Yale, where he first heard recordings of Balinese *gamelan* music and had what he terms a "conversion experience." Ziporyn began to study Balinese drumming and jazz along with his main instrument, the clarinet. Following his graduation from Yale in 1981, Ziporyn spent a year in Bali studying under I Madé Lebah, a famous Balinese musician from the town of Peliatan. Here we encounter an extraordinary link in the chain of musical transmission: Lebah went to Paris in 1931 with a *gamelan* to perform in the Colonial Exposition and subsequently worked in Bali as a musical associate and companion to composer Colin McPhee.[23]

Ziporyn has incorporated a deep knowledge of Balinese *gamelan* techniques and trends into his own compositions. He strongly believes that

> by working cross-culturally we can make new musics, musics previously unimaginable, which ideally can speak to people in both traditions, saying different but comprehensible things in all languages.

His compositions seek to communicate across cultures. *Luv Time* (1984) anticipates *Kekembangan,* since three saxophones play against a background of piano and Balinese percussion. Ziporyn's work *Tire Fire* (1994) blends a quartet of electric guitars and synthesizers with a traditional Balinese *gamelan*.[24]

Ziporyn has also composed dramatic works inspired by Balinese theatrical forms. His chamber opera *Shadow Bang* (October 2001) is inspired by the Balinese *wayang kulit* (puppet theatre) and was a collaboration with Balinese puppeteer I Wayan Wija. Ziporyn has also collaborated by writing music for Western theatrical performances, including a 2004 production of Sophocles' *Oedipus* at the American Repertory Theatre. Instruments used for *Oedipus* include a synthesizer, Western string instruments (both traditional and retuned), Balinese gongs, Tibetan bowls, and Chinese drums and cymbals. The musical ensemble included an international array of singers as well—an early music specialist; natives of Kazakhstan, Poland and Turkey; people with experience in Balkan and Russian singing styles; and one male singer accomplished in Balinese vocal style.

A virtuoso clarinet player, Ziporyn has a parallel career as a performer and composer of experimental works for the Bang on a Can Ensemble. Working in so many capacities and across so many boundaries of culture and genre has been deeply satisfying for Ziporyn not just as a musician, but also as a human being. He says that he has learned from performance, noting that, for example, apart from its virtuosity, playing *kotekan* allows one to connect with another player and to achieve what one cannot play by oneself. Ziporyn perceives Balinese music—and by extension, his own compositions—as modeling social interaction, with instruments having special functions and their music marking occasions that delineate the life cycle. "The Balinese like to fill space," Ziporyn comments, comparing the Balinese tendency to elaborate and fill in melodies to the process of carving wood. "Everyone plays all the time," he observes. "They learn together, a musical process becoming a social process."

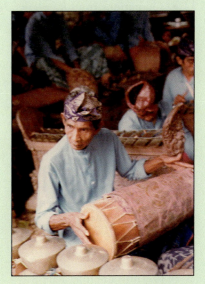

I Madé Lebah playing the *kendang* in 1982.

Kekembangan (composition [*gending*] for *gamelan*)

CD 2
Track 22

Date of composition: 1990

Composers: Evan Ziporyn and I Nyoman Windha

Date of recording: 1990

Performers: *Gamelan Sekar Jaya* (northern California)

Genre: Quotation *gending* in which most of the materials of a preexisting composition are adapted for *gamelan gong kebyar*, transforming the original composition and surrounding it with contrasting materials

Source: Draws on *Kembang Pencak* for *gamelan* and male chorus by I Nyoman Windha

Form: Five-part structure, of which the first three sections are heard here: Introduction (*gamelan* with saxophone ornaments), *A Cappella* (saxophone quartet), and *Pengawak* (*gamelan* and saxophone in harmony)

Tempo: Variable, moderate to fast

Tuning system: *Pelog*

WHAT TO LISTEN FOR:

- Quotations from *Kembang Pencak* at the opening of the piece, followed by new, contrasting materials
- Saxophone quartet added to the *gamelan gong kebyar,* using alternate fingerings to produce pitches approximating those of the *gamelan*
- Prevalence of five-note melodies in saxophones based on *pelog* as played by *gangsa* metallophones

---

	STRUCTURE	DESCRIPTION
0:00	**Introduction, Part A**	*Gamelan gong kebyar* provides an introduction.
0:05		Drum (*kendang*) and *cengceng* enter.
0:27	*Theme 1*	*Gangas* (metallophones with ten keys, played with hammers, that flesh out and ornament the melody) introduce theme 1.
0:34	**Introduction, Part B** *Theme 1*	Saxophone quartet joins the *gamelan* with theme 1; *reyong* and *cengceng* punctuate texture; note that saxophones are used percussively.
0:50	*Theme 2*	Saxophones play theme 2 in imitative texture.

0:59	*Transitional Theme*	*Gangsas* play a descending pattern. *Reyong* plays melody and *cuks* (pronounced "chucks"), non-pitched rhythms, sometimes joined by *cengceng,* which fills out the percussion.
1:07	**Introduction, Part B'** *Theme 1*	
1:24	*Theme 2*	
1:32	*Transitional theme*	*Gangsa* descending pattern with *reyong cuks* and *cengceng* percussive sounds.
1:41	**Introduction, Part B''** *Theme 1*	
1:58	*Theme 2*	Saxophone with *cengceng,* drums, *jegogan* and gong moving into . . .
2:33		transitional descending pattern by *gangsa,* with *reyong* and *cengceng cuks.*
2:37		Acceleration leading to end of introduction.
2:43		*Kebyar* (explosion) and pause.
2:46	**A Cappella**	Saxophone quartet without *gamelan;* repeated pitches, ostinatos, and extended section of polyphonic interweaving saxophones somewhat similar to *kotekan.*
4:09		Repeated jazzy chords by saxophones.
4:25		Close intervals between pairs of saxophones replicate "beating tones" between pairs of *gamelan* instruments.
4:48		Melody emerges in high saxophone.
5:00		Tempo slows.
5:10		Final saxophone statement.
5:15	***Pengawak***	*Gangsa* and rest of *gamelan* enter, joining saxophones in harmony at end of transition; saxophones play along with *gangsas.*
5:41		Fade-out and recording ends.

Music as Art and Commodity

Mobility has long been a fact of global musical life, as demonstrated by the case studies of Hawaiian and *gamelan* music; it is also clear that in many settings music is both an artistic expression and a commodity. Music exists as a form of expression that gives voice to human emotions and aspirations and is used to promote social and political causes; it is equally true that music has often been created and marketed for economic advantage.

Music certainly has value to the person who conceives and performs it, and many music traditions are considered to be the common property of a family,

clan, or community. We saw examples of familial ownership of music in the *bàkks* (rhythms) of the Senegalese Nder family in Chapter 1 and the bagpipe laments composed by the MacCrimmons in Chapter 3. Concepts of music's value and the dimensions of personal control over musical resources vary considerably from culture to culture. In Europe and the United States, ownership of music is conceived as an individual's right, although clearly this notion is challenged by creative processes such as the Ziporyn/Windha collaboration on *Kekembangan*. In many instances, music is formally protected by copyright, the legal protection of intellectual property. However, it is certainly more difficult to apply notions of ownership to musical sound than to a literary text, especially if the music is not notated and is transmitted as an oral tradition. Similarities between musical compositions have led to famous court cases, such as the successful challenge to the copyright held by former Beatle George Harrison for his song *My Sweet Lord,* which was proven to have been borrowed from Harrison's unconscious memory of the 1963 song *He's So Fine,* composed by Ronald Mack and performed by The Chiffons.[25]

Western intellectual property laws become even more problematic when assumptions of individual composition are applied to music across cultures. For example, when music is considered to have sacred origins, to have been inspired through revelation, or to be the property of an entire clan or community, the ownership issues at stake are both ethical and economic. Complex situations arise—for example, when Native American sacred songs are borrowed without permission, transformed, and marketed by individuals from outside a particular First Nation (Native American) community.

There are discount airlines named "Jazz" and "Song," suggesting that a travel experience is an appealing way to move through time.

Recording technology has further complicated the issue of the commercial value of intellectual property, since electronic production and reproduction of sound reduce the distance between an original and a copy, making it much easier to disregard property rights. It is clear that new methods for digitizing music will continue to complicate and to transform musical transmission.

Music is not only a commodity—property that can be bought or sold; it is also used to sell other products. "If coffee were music, blends would be our symphony," reads a recent Starbucks advertisement. Today, advertising has moved beyond using music to accompany visual images to using music as a metaphor for a well-blended beverage, a smooth and exhilarating airplane flight, or a cosmopolitan life style.

The wide circulation of music has enormous economic consequences. The increasing presence of corporations raises questions, as we have seen in the case of Clear Channel Corporation (see **Studying Music: Presenting Music and Musicians** on page 260), but can also provide opportunities for innovation. Our next case study focuses on a soundscape that makes clear music's dual role as art and commodity, enabled by the workings of the global marketplace.

CASE STUDY: Traveling the Silk Road

Among the endless examples of musical mobility, the historical Silk Road, a series of overland trade routes established millennia ago and stretching from East Asia to Europe, provides an extraordinary tale of extensive human and musical movement, crossing vast geographical areas over thousands of years (see page 286, "**Looking Back: The History of the Silk Road**").[26]

The Silk Road, with its heritage of trade and exchange, has often been invoked as a metaphor for travel. At the beginning of the twenty-first century, we encounter a particularly colorful revival of the Silk Road with a musical focus in concerts, recordings, and other musical gatherings. We can begin to explore this present-day Silk Road through the lens of a festival held in 2002.

This gold Buddhist head ornament decorated with images of musical instruments was carried along the Silk Road during the Tang Dynasty (800–900 CE).

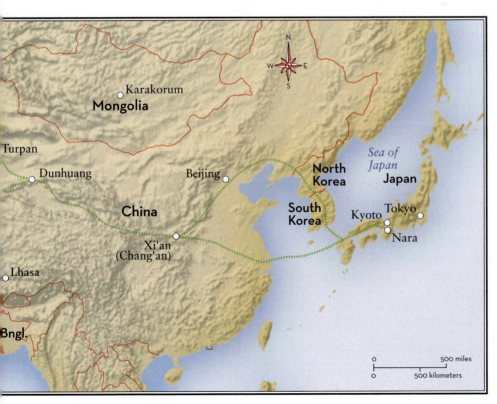

The Silk Road extended from Japan to Italy, winding its way across China and Inner Asia, where it divided into several routes, terminating in Venice and Rome.

LOOKING *Back*

The History of the Silk Road

The Genesis of the Silk Road(s)

c. 4000–5000 BCE	Fragments of silk cloth and a cup carved with silkworm design survive from the Yangzi River Valley in Southern China, suggesting the early origin of sericulture, the process of making silk.
2nd millennium BCE	Trade, beads, and languages begin to move back and forth across Inner Asia.
500 BCE	Evidence of trade in ancient Chinese silk found in Inner Asia excavations, today in Afghanistan.
206 BCE–220 CE	Silk becomes an important trade item for the Han dynasty, used for gifts and tribute.
200 BCE	Sericulture enters Korea from China.

The First Silk Road

2nd century BCE	Chinese envoy journeys into Inner Asia in search of horses and allies.
1st century BCE	Silk first reaches Rome, initiating trade between China and Rome.
552 CE	Two Assyrian Christian monks visit China and smuggle silkworms back to Constantinople, beginning a local silk industry; around this time, Persians acquire knowledge of silk production; Damascus becomes a silk center.

The Second Silk Road

618–907	The Tang Dynasty develops the Inner Asian silk trade, increasing movement of ideas, literature, artistic production, and religion across the Silk Road.
751	The battle of Talas results in the transfer of Chinese weavers as prisoners of war to Iran and Mesopotamia.
1096–1200s	The Christian Crusades in the Holy Land.

| 1271 | Venetian merchant Marco Polo (1254–1324) begins twenty-four-year trip across Asia, living in the Chinese court of Kublai Khan for seventeen years. |
| 13th century | "Pax Mongolica"; descendants of Genghis (Chinghis) Khan close the major land routes across Eurasia from Black Sea to the Pacific. |

The Third Silk Road

13th–14th centuries	Competition and conflicts spread across Eurasia; Chinese silk supplanted by gems, spices, precious metals, horses, and armaments.
1325	Muhammad Ibn Batuta (1304–1368?) travels from Morocco to Mecca, continuing on to India and China.
14th–15th centuries	Silkmaking becomes an important art in northern Italy.
17th century	Europe enters into the trade; Jean-Baptiste Tavernier (1605–1998) makes six journeys to India and Inner Asia; mulberry trees and silk-worms are sent with settlers to Jamestown.
	Silk production becomes industrialized with punch cards programming patterns.
Early 1800s	George IV of England builds Brighton palace in Persian style, decorated with Chinese furniture.

The Modern Silk Road

1869	The opening of the Suez Canal begins the decline of overland trade routes.
1877	The term "Silk Road" is coined by German geologist and explorer Baron Ferdinand von Richthofen to define the exchange of products across Eurasia from China to the Mediterranean.
1877	Queen Victoria is declared Empress of India; the Orientalist period begins.
1998	Cellist Yo-Yo Ma founds "The Silk Road Project" to celebrate and foster traditional music cultures and musical creativity along the historical Silk Road.

The Silk Road's New Settings

On June 26, 2002, the thirty-sixth annual Smithsonian Folklife Festival opened on the National Mall in Washington DC. Titled "The Silk Road: Connecting Cultures, Creating Trust," the festival attracted a record-breaking 1.3 million people who came to experience the music, artistic production, crafts, and food from countries located on the historical Silk Road. The Festival brought together approximately four hundred artists, vendors, musicians, and scholars from more than two dozen nations, speaking more than thirty languages.[27] Following in the tradition of the major international gatherings discussed at the beginning of this chapter and the thirty-five annual events previously sponsored by the Smithsonian Institution, the festival featured sites including reconstructions of architectural monuments from different areas of Asia and stages for musicians performing everything from Chinese opera to *khoomii* singing.

Although the historical Silk Road was a trade route that over the course of centuries generated an unprecedented amount of cross-cultural contact and exchange, this twenty-first-century reenactment was conceived by a single individual, the cellist Yo-Yo Ma. In 1998, Ma launched "The Silk Road Project" to study "the historical and present-day flow of culture and ideas along the trans-Eurasian trade routes." He writes:

> I believe that when we enlarge our view of the world we deepen our understanding of our own lives. Through a journey of discovery, the Silk Road Project hopes to plant the seeds of new artistic and cultural growth, and to celebrate authentic living traditions and musical voices.[28]

Yo-Yo Ma himself provides a model for musical mobility; he is a twenty-first-century musician with a global career who performs in a growing range of musical styles, crossing frequently and deliberately between soundscapes. Born in Paris to Chinese parents in 1955, Ma moved to New York City when he was seven. He studied at several schools, including the Professional Children's School and Juilliard, where he studied with Leonard Rose, and after graduating from Harvard University in 1976, he quickly distinguished himself in international music competitions.

Throughout his career, Yo-Yo Ma has collaborated with other musicians, notably the classical pianist Emmanuel Ax. In the early 1990s, Ma began to perform with musicians from other musical styles. His 1992 album *Hush*, with singer Bobby McFerrin, was listed as a "Top Classical

In his festival booth, Armenian instrument maker Hakob Yeritsyan displays a *qanun* (rear), *'ud* (on table) and violin, which are among the musical instruments transmitted in both directions along the historical Silk Road. The *qanun* originated in the Arab Middle East, the *'ud* is the ancestor of the European lute, and both the Chinese *pipa* and the European violin may be related to Inner Asian horsehead fiddles.

Crossover Album" in *Billboard* magazine. Ma went on to win one of his over fifteen Grammy awards for an album titled *Soul of the Tango*. Although he continued to record Western classical music and to produce an innovative series of recordings and films of Johann Sebastian Bach's Six Suites for Solo Cello, Yo-Yo Ma continued to reach out; recently he collaborated with Cuban and Brazilian musicians to produce the album *Obrigado Brazil*.[29]

Connecting Silk Road Sounds and Significances

In 1998, Ma launched a new cross-cultural project with two goals: He wanted to present music and musicians from music cultures along the ancient Silk Road, and he wanted to commission new music from composers from these regions. Yo-Yo Ma's Silk Road Project emerged from his own expanding interests in different music traditions. He has described his efforts as "pushing the envelope . . . I'm seeking to join, to connect things, that were not precisely joined together: from Bach to the Kalahari [desert in southern Africa] to music along the Silk Road, to country fiddling and the tango."[30] In these projects, Yo-Yo Ma becomes an active force in initiating musical transmission.

The Silk Road Project began as a global musical initiative, but one drawing heavily on subcultural and intercultural musical resources. The project has many aspects, including sponsoring concert tours by traditional musicians identified through the project, producing recordings, and collaborating with institutions such as the Smithsonian to produce festivals on the theme of the Silk Road. Ma engaged a team of scholars, including ethnomusicologists, to provide the necessary expertise in musical and cultural

The 2002 Smithsonian Folklife Festival included panoramic reproductions of famous sites from the historical Silk Road, such as "The Istanbul Crossroads," seen here with festival patrons walking through it.

Yo-Yo Ma, violinist Mark O'Connor, and bassist Edgar Meyer kick off their Appalachian Journey Tour at the Grand Ole Opry House in Nashville on March 30, 2000. Their collaborations, exploring the common ground between American classical and folk musics, have been recorded on audio and video.

content. The Silk Road Project required considerable financial resources, most obtained through a group of global corporate sponsors. The main funder was the Aga Khan Trust for Culture, an outgrowth of the Aga Khan Development Network, which has helped societies challenged by war, drought, and famine in the Central Asian part of the Silk Road since 1992. The Foundation financed efforts to preserve and promote the music traditions of the Silk Road region, underwriting concerts and master classes featuring compositions commissioned from area composers. The Foundation further supported a compact disc of traditional music issued by the Smithsonian's Ethnic Folkways label.[31]

This two-CD set titled *The Silk Road: A Musical Caravan* embeds the notion of travel in both its visual and musical content. The first disc contains recordings united under the title *Masters and Traditions,* concentrating on court and art musics of the region; the second, *Minstrels and Lovers,* features vernacular musics. The challenge of representing music traditions stretching from China to the Black Sea was, in the words of editors Ted Levin and Jean During, "a daunting task." Challenges included insuring historical and musical accuracy, which the editors believe they achieved by focusing on the central portion of the Northern Silk Road as a coherent musical realm. The editors also selected music that was "less known in the West than that from other regions," thus largely excluding India and the Middle East. The recordings include many tracks from the private collections of the editors, both of whom are ethnomusicologists. This recording provides a fascinating window on the careful balance of opportunities and dilemmas raised by projects of this sort. Scholarly insights and sensitivities are carefully balanced with pragmatic considerations related to sponsors, the potential audience, and the global market (see page 292, "**Studying Music: Ethical Considerations**").

Yo-Yo Ma notes that an important goal of The Silk Road Project was to bring attention to diverse music traditions from places along the historical Silk Road. While many of the musicians included on the recording are new to international audiences, several are not, including the Chinese musician Wu Man, a virtuoso player of the Chinese plucked lute, the *pipa.* The *pipa* is derived from Central Asian lutes that traveled to China on the Silk Road.

Smithsonian Folkways Recordings

THE SILK ROAD
a Musical Caravan

2 CD SET

No less well-traveled than this instrument is Wu Man herself, born in China and trained at the Beijing Central Conservatory.

In the early 1990s, well before the launching of The Silk Road Project, Wu Man was already established on the global musical scene. She moved to the United States, where she has collaborated with a wide range of musicians and ensembles, including Brian Eno, the Kronos Quartet, the New York Philharmonic, the composer Tan Dun (for the soundtrack of the film *Crouching Tiger, Hidden Dragon*), and of course, Yo-Yo Ma. Wu Man has published her own recordings in a wide range of styles. In addition to two earlier albums, *Posture of Reality* (Asian Improv Records) captures a live jazz concert Wu Man gave with a string bass virtuoso in 2002, while the recording *Pipa: From a Distance* (Naxos World Music Series) presents her playing an electrified *pipa* with a Western bow, collaborating with instruments ranging from an Australian *didjeridoo* to a bicycle horn. *Pipa: From a Distance* also includes several tracks based on traditional Chinese dances and songs, illustrating her ability to bring together traditional and experimental elements.[32] On *The Silk Road: A Musical Caravan,* Wu Man is heard playing a nineteenth-century Chinese instrumental piece titled *High Little Moon,* played with little improvisation in a traditional style (Listening Guide 57; see page 294). Wu Man's career provides insight into the changing world of many Inner and East Asian musicians, who well before the advent of The Silk Road Project had established themselves beyond the borders of their homelands.

As artistic director of the Silk Road Project, Yo-Yo Ma has worked to commission and perform new music. In July 2000, he invited fifty-eight composers and musicians to attend a nine-day workshop at Tanglewood Music Center in western Massachusetts to rehearse new works commissioned by the project. These musicians have performed at festivals and cultural institutions across the United States, Europe, and Asia, including the Amsterdam Concertgebouw in 2002. A network of partner cities was also recruited to host a series of concerts and cultural events. As a result, some presenters of the ensemble incorporated the Silk Road theme during their 2001–2002 concert seasons. To insure that these collaborations would do justice to the musicians and repertory they presented, beginning in fall 1999, The Silk Road

Wu Man, the *pipa* player heard in Listening Guide 57, has performed in many cross-cultural collaborations. Here she plays in the world premiere of a composition for *gamelan* and *pipa* by composer Evan Ziporyn.

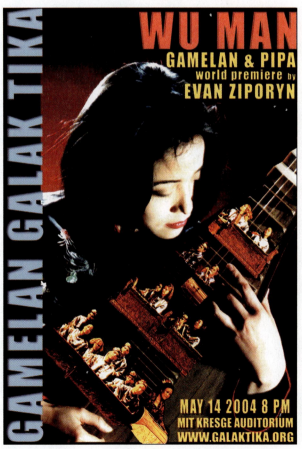

Ethical Considerations

Professional ethics have always been an issue for ethnomusicologists carrying out fieldwork and publication. As we study musical mobility and evaluate the factors that have impinged on musical presentation and transmission, we need to keep in mind that many of these same factors have also shaped the study of music. Ethnomusicology, like the closely related fields of anthropology and folklore, emerged during the late nineteenth century, when European colonization of Africa and Asia was at its height. By the early decades of the twentieth century, ethnomusicologists were able to carry out fieldwork abroad precisely because of the residual power and resources of colonial institutions such as universities and government agencies.

The Silk Road Project involves a complex set of issues related to the impact of research and publication on local music traditions expanded to an unprecedented global scale. These same issues, on a less grand scale, occupy all ethnomusicologists. Even when conducting research in the field at home, one encounters economic, political, and personal challenges.

Among these issues are the following: In what ways should ethnomusicologists mediate between musicians and the broader public, whether in the classroom or in other public performance contexts? In what ways does the scholar intentionally or unwittingly join in the politics of exhibition and display when he or she presents a musician to an audience of insiders or outsiders? How does transforming music into a commodity by publishing a book or recording contribute new variables to already fast-changing sounds, settings, and significances?

Many ethnomusicologists who have published recordings as part of their scholarly research have worked to insure economic equity for the participating musicians. Some have assigned royalties to the musicians with whom they worked, whether at home or abroad.

Beyond the important economic issues, most ethnomusicologists feel an obligation to work for the welfare of the musicians whose musics they study. These concerns were at the heart of The Silk Road Project, originally conceived by Yo-Yo Ma in order to promote "connectedness." In his introduction to the Smithsonian Folkways recordings, Yo-Yo Ma writes:

> As human culture-producers, we have much more that connects us than separates us, and of all the arts, music surely offers one of the most vital ways to feel the glow of connectedness—to loved ones and friends, community and nation. But

what about connecting to strangers, and to cultures we might consider alien, impenetrable, or even uncivilized? Might we also better understand them by listening to their music? In doing so, might we come to see, hear, and ultimately trust them in a more intimate and human way? My answer is a resounding "yes." If I'm familiar with your music, that's the beginning of a conversation, and now more than ever, we cannot afford not to know what other people are thinking and feeling—particularly in the vast and strategic regions of Inner Asia linked to the Silk Road.[33]

More and more, scholars seek to collaborate with their research associates, building resources within communities to ensure that traditions are conserved and represented in a manner consistent with the desires of the people who transmit them. Research and presentation have the potential to aid transmission, helping to sustain and document music traditions that might otherwise be lost. In some cases, musical research has led to new understandings about social relations with regard to race and gender or provided new insights about the history of a community. In all cases, ethnomusicologists seek both to memorialize the musicians who have shared their traditions with them and to ensure continued access to the materials they transmit. Whether we study and present music traditions or consume the products of the studies of others, it is vital that as we seek cross-cultural understanding and knowledge, we carefully consider the impact of our activities.

Many early recordings of Native American music traditions have been repatriated to the tribes from which they came. This photograph shows a recording session at the Smithsonian Institution in 1913.

Xiao Yue Er Gao ("High Little Moon")

CD 2
Track 23

Date of composition: 2001
Performer: Wu Man
Form: Short, sectional form
Tempo: Moderate duple meter

WHAT TO LISTEN FOR:

- Pentatonic melodic content emphasizing a central pitch (tonic) sounded at three different octaves from high to low (T2, T1, T)
- A variety of subtle ornaments distinctive to this four-stringed plucked lute: (1) brief grace notes sounding above a pitch, usually a tonic; (2) fingered *tremolo* (the repeated, fast plucking of the same string); (3) *glissando* (a slow and blurred descent produced by plucking a string repeatedly with right hand while sliding a finger of the left hand down the string to gradually change the pitch); (4) bending of a pitch by stretching a string slightly; and (5) a high harmonic produced by touching a string lightly.

	STRUCTURE	DESCRIPTION
0:00	**Section A**	Repeated sounding of tonic pitch at octaves T2 and T1; brief grace notes sounded on octave pitches T2 and T1.
0:09		Fingered *tremolo* begins.
0:26		Section A cadences on T1.
0:28	**Section B**	Contrasting section begins with melodic motion in lower register between tonics in octaves T1 and T; *tremolo* prominent throughout; section cadences on tonic at T.
0:54		Bending of final three pitches in descent to cadence on T.
0:57	**Transitional section**	Motion back and forth between T and T1.
1:09		*Tremolo*
1:15	**Varied repeat of section A**	Ascent and repeated sounding of octaves T2 and T1, slightly varied.
1:24		Slide up, then *glissando* down to cadence on T1; abrupt stop.
1:31	**Extension of section A**	
1:32–1:36		Harmonics
2:00		Final cadence on T1, with *tremolo*, leading to descending *glissando*.
2:06		Brief closing section (*coda*), with final descent to tonic bending final three pitches toward major scale. Ends at 2:17.

Project hosted a series of forums for European presenters to grapple with "the complex issue of how to represent non-Western musics in a manner that would not exoticize or essentialize them."[34]

As part of the activities of The Silk Road Project over the course of several years, these accomplished musicians in various combinations played concerts and led workshops, eventually calling themselves "The Silk Road Ensemble."

In August 2001, twenty-four of the musicians met in New York City to produce a CD issued by Sony Classical titled *Silk Road Journeys: When Strangers Meet.*

Yo-Yo Ma and the Silk Road Ensemble played with the Kazakh folk-rock group Roksonaki on the Venice Pianna stage at the festival.

The recording, according to the introductory notes by Yo-Yo Ma, "is what happened when twenty-four strangers supported by scores of others behind the scenes met, developed trust, learned from each other, and eventually devised a common language that allowed them to be creative together." The selections on this CD are intended for an international audience and include both old and new compositions from Eastern and Western composers, as well as arrangements of traditional pieces. Nine instrumentalists, including Yo-Yo Ma and Wu Man, combine forces in a lively arrangement of *Mido Mountain,* a traditional piece named after a village in China's Yunnan Province (Listening Guide 58; see page 296). In addition to the cello and *pipa,* we also hear a *sheng,* a Chinese mouth organ made of bamboo pipes, played by Wu Tong, a young Chinese musician who is both a rock star and a performer on traditional instruments. Yo-Yo Ma said about these jam sessions:

We had a huge amount of fun. No one knew exactly what was going to happen. We had an amazing mix of instruments, and people just figured out what to play and where to fill in. I think that's the way people have always made music. Part of being artistic is being prepared to ask questions to which you don't have the answers. It's something that happens inside you—something that's very private, very intimate, but if you locate your question and if you're able to make it come alive in a musical form, and somebody else receives it and it comes alive within them, you can get pretty connected to another person. I think that's a beautiful way to communicate.[35]

Mido Mountain (folk song arrangement)

Date of recording: 2001

Performers: Members of the Silk Road Ensemble: Yo-Yo Ma, *cello;* Wu Man, *pipa* (Chinese lute); Wu Tong, *sheng* (Chinese mouth organ); Xu Ke, *erhu* (Chinese bowed lute); Edgar Meyer, *bass;* Joel Fan, Joseph Gramley, Mark Suter, Shan Shanahan, *percussion;* Sandeep Das, *tabla* (North Indian drum)

Form: Three-part (ternary) form built on an *ostinato*

Tempo: Moderate quadruple meter

Function: Concert performance and recordings

WHAT TO LISTEN FOR:

- Melodies and harmonies built on a pentatonic scale
- A unique juxtaposition of Western cello with an Indian membranophone (*tabla*), Chinese chordophones (*pipa* and *erhu*), and a Chinese aerophone (*sheng*)
- An energetic, virtuoso performance that is marketable and accessible to many different audiences

---

STRUCTURE AND TEXT	DESCRIPTION
0:00 **Section A**	The *ostinato* theme is introduced by the *pipa,* each phrase punctuated by *claves,* a pair of cylindrical wooden sticks struck together. The *pipa* uses *vibrato* and short slides at the ends of phrases. The *ostinato* repeats every 10–11 seconds in section A.
0:11 **Phrases a and a'**	As the *pipa* continues playing the *ostinato,* the *erhu* chimes in with a two-phrase melody. On the next *ostinato* cycle, as phrases a and a' are repeated, the cello and bass join in.
0:21 **Phrases a and a' repeated**	
0:32 **Transitional passage**	A brief transitional passage includes several instruments playing the same melody in parallel octaves. This melody, based on a repeating three-note motive, has a complex rhythm. After the transition, the *sheng* comes to the fore, accompanied by the *tabla* and the *pipa ostinato.*
0:47 **Phrases b and b'**	The *erhu* and cello now play a single melody in parallel octaves. The *pipa* and *tabla* continue in the background.
0:57 **Phrases b and b' repeated (with countermelody a and a')**	The texture grows more complex and polyphonic. The cello continues playing the phrases b and b', while the *erhu* plays phrases a and a'. The *pipa* stops playing the *ostinato* and joins the cello.

1:06	**Transitional passage**	Another brief transitional passage, in which the *erhu* and cello imitate each other's trills, leads into another section highlighting the *sheng*. This time, the *sheng* and the cello share a motive.
1:22	**Variations on phrases a and b**	The texture becomes more polyphonic as the various instruments diverge, each playing a different melody. Many of these melodies recall those heard earlier.
1:41	**Transitional passage**	Another transitional passage. The constant rhythmic energy of the *ostinato* ceases, and long-held notes predominate. *Erhu* and cello briefly quote the imitative trilling passage from 1:06.
1:57	**Section B Phrases c and c'**	A new *ostinato* is established, in a much slower tempo. A frame drum and the *pipa* play the *ostinato* cycle. The *sheng* plays a melody based on the pentatonic scale, which is repeated.
2:32	**Phrases d and d'**	The *sheng* presents a contrasting phrase which is repeated with a slightly different cadence. The ensemble pauses briefly at the end of the section.
3:04	**Section A' Phrases b and b'**	The energetic first section suddenly returns. Phrase b, originally presented by *erhu* and cello at 0:47, is again played by the same instruments. On phrase b', the *sheng* introduces a new countermelody.
3:13	**Phrases b and b' repeat (with countermelody a and a')**	The cello continues playing phrases b and b', while the *erhu* plays phrases a and a' as a countermelody. The tempo and volume gradually increase, and other instruments add layers of polyphony.
3:22	**Phrases b and b' repeat twice more**	
3:37	**Closing passage**	The instrumentalists suddenly quiet down. The melody, a repeating three-note motive, is the same as that at 0:32. A large *crescendo* takes place, from softest to loudest, as the tempo continues to accelerate.
3:51	recording ends	

Conclusion

Music, which has always been important in signifying place, has become even more prominent in the context of travel and tourism. As people move and encounter new locales, different modes of musical presentation and the ways in which they are marketed can convey important information not just about the nature of musical life in various places, but also about how individuals, communities, or institutions present themselves and wish to be perceived. The ubiquitous presence of music, flowing through channels including conventional radio, live performance, and rapidly changing digital formats, insures that sound continually reshapes our perceptions of a wider world. Musical sound is innately mobile, and infuses each of us with a type of virtual mobility even when we are in our home environments; today, we can at any moment travel an imagined musical Silk Road through internationally distributed recordings, festivals, and concerts.

Musical mobility raises similar issues in each of the case studies we explored in this chapter. In every case, we encounter a type of translation process as music traditions flow from one soundscape into another. No single music tradition is simply recreated within the sounds and settings of another. Rather, as music travels, it may go through processes of appropriation, parody, revision, or fusion. As music travels, its significance almost always shifts as well, often giving rise to an outcome in which the original is transformed into a version that emphasizes the translator's own agenda.[36]

We explored the complex world of Hawaiian music and dance, tracing the historical appropriation of Hawaiian music in the service of tourism and the subsequent spread of traditional hula schools in Hawaii and abroad. The movement of Balinese *gamelan* music presents a contrasting example of musical mobility: It accommodates the collaboration of I Nyoman Windha and Evan Ziporyn, two native speakers of different musical languages, each gaining fluency in the tradition of the other and choosing to play out their own understandings—and misunderstandings—of musical differences in a collaborative composition. Finally, we traveled Yo-Yo Ma's Silk Road, a project intending to support traditional musicians while at the same time transforming aspects of their musical heritage. The Silk Road Project highlights the symbiotic relationship between music produced as artistic expression and the marketplace. Indeed, none of these case studies provides a simple picture, and each provides ample material for debates about the pros and cons of musical mobility and the global reach of formerly local soundscapes.

Musical mobility is a fact of twenty-first century musical life. It can bring us moments of unexpected exhilaration and examples of patent exploitation. There is no doubt that through music we can experience the changing worlds

Advertisements can spread music traditions to wider audiences.

around us and imagine ourselves in different places. On occasion a new musical experience can perplex and confuse us, but there are moments when an unexpected musical encounter enables us to fashion new ways of hearing and understanding the world. Music in fact "composes" much of our experience in everyday life in ways that will be sketched in the next part by exploring music's role in dance, ritual, politics, and identity.

Who presents concerts of diverse music traditions in your community? What arts organizations, institutions, or promoters are involved? How are the events marketed, and to whom? What are the issues (musical, political, economic) surrounding the presentation and performance of music in your local areas?

Is one particular type or style of music or dance associated with the place in which you live? Take into account your region, city, town, and college campus. Does music play a role in the local economy? Is it a factor in public entertainment or tourism?

IMPORTANT TERMS

bimusicality
copyright
hula
impresario

kreasi baru
palm harmonics or chimes
panoptic/ panoramic

saxophone
slide
steel guitar
ukulele

PART III
Understanding Music

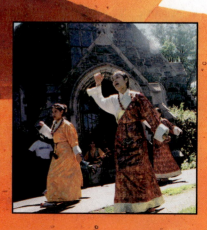

*W*hat would life be like without music? Can you imagine a day without listening to the radio or humming a tune? Consider how dull a party would be without a band or DJ. Worship services would become monotonous recitations of texts. Now that we have learned how to approach music's sound, setting, and significance, and have traced the pathways through which music travels, it is time to discuss important domains of human experience of which music is a vital part.

In Chapter 7, we will study music's role as the constant partner of dance, a universal form of bodily expression. We will explore ways in which music and motion combine to allow even casual participants to engage in musical performance in a meaningful way.

Chapter 8 presents case studies of music within belief systems, exploring music as an indispensable part of all religious experience.

Music's frequent union with politics and its use in the contexts of political repression and resistance is the subject of Chapter 9.

Finally, Chapter 10 caps our inquiry with an exploration of the role music plays in the construction of identity, both for individuals and for groups.

The epilogue brings out study full circle as we study a soundscape that unites a surprising array of music traditions.

Chapter 7

Music and Dance

The 1914 color lithograph by French artist George Barbier (1882–1932) depicts a couple dancing the tango dressed in the latest fashions of the day. Like other art and architecture of the art nouveau ("new art") movement that flourished from the late nineteenth century until World War I, Barbier's lithographs have flowing lines, sensuous curves, and background patterns of leaves and branches. Barbier, who produced many other illustrations of music, theatre, and fashion of his era, must have encountered the tango soon after it was introduced in Paris around 1907.

Overview

Main Points

- Dance transforms a basic rhythm into a distinctive set of physical movements.

- Dance invites anyone to participate who can master its basic movements, whatever their cultural background, social experience, or musical expertise.

- Dance accommodates a wide variety of meanings, from recreational to political.

- Dance illustrates different views of gender and sexuality in different societies.

Introduction

Like music, dance exists in time and space. Dance consists of patterned movements that join with organized sound to express the values and emotions of a soundscape. During the moment of performance, dance transforms the most basic physical unit—the pulse—into rhythmic patterns that can be seen and

Pandit (Master) Chitresh Das performs *kathak*, a classical northern Indian dance, considered a fusion of Hindu and Muslim cultural aesthetics. It is rooted in the traditions of the hereditary Hindu caste of Kathaks in the northwestern Indian state of Rajasthan. During the later Moghul era, female courtesans performed *kathak* in the Muslim courts and for wealthy patrons. As the local nobility lost their resources and prestige during the British colonial era, many *kathak* dancers came to depend on British patronage. Some dancers, such as Chitresh Das, moved to Calcutta, the capital of British India, and later migrated abroad. Today both men and women perform this solo dance form.

heard. Body movements coordinate closely with the underlying rhythmic organization of the accompanying music, sometimes replicating specific musical rhythms in a dancer's footwork, as in the Latin-derived chachachá, at other times linking a series of shorter rhythmic units into larger, graceful groupings, as in the Argentine tango. Whether we prefer to waltz or salsa, or simply to watch the ballet, the body in motion—with music shaping its rhythms—captures our imaginations and makes us want to move.

Dance and the music that accompanies it are so closely joined that both are often known by the same name, as we will see in our studies of *bhangra,* polka, and the tango. The precise relationship of music and movement varies widely among music traditions. In some cases, a dancer follows the flow of the music and interprets it in flexible ways, as in Western modern dance. In other styles, such as the North Indian *kathak* dance, the instrumentalists follow the rhythms sounded by a solo dancer's feet and the jingle of the bells tied around his or her ankles.

Dance plays an important role in communicating a wide range of emotions and ideas. Some dances tell a story of replicate a familiar scene, sometimes drawn from literature or mythology. Dances can transmit important historical narratives, exemplified by the National Dance Company of Ghana's reenactment of scenes from the historical slave trade (Chapter 2). Some dances, such as the North Indian *kathak,* incorporate both narrative and abstract sections.

Dance almost always makes a statement about the time, the place, and the people who are performing it, conveying who they think they are and who they would like to be. Dance can affirm the status quo, as when aristocrats of the eighteenth-century French society danced the minuet:

> Well-bred gentlemen and ladies danced with refinement and the restrained classical values of clarity, balance, and regularity as part of their formalized social

exchanges. Manuals explained the rules and intricate steps which precluded individual expressiveness, and dancing masters spent hours with aristocratic students before they could perform in public. Since dance protocol reflected the performers' social rank, hosts for minuets carefully researched the background of each guest to determine who would open the ball and in what order each guest would step out into the floor. With highly controlled vitality and disdain for revealing inner feelings, as well as ordered equilibrium and weightlessness, couples moved away and together again and again, usually keeping their focus on each other.[1]

At other times and places, dance has challenged social and political hierarchies, as when South Africans spontaneously performed the rousing *toye-toye* dance during demonstrations against apartheid. Through its motions, then, dance can reinforce norms of polite behavior or challenge social conventions.

Even when they are abstract, dances reflect and express a wide range of emotions. For instance, dances performed at joyous events such as weddings can simultaneously celebrate a couple's union and affirm the national or ethnic background of the pair. Guests at a Jewish or Arab wedding joining in a Middle Eastern line dance or friends dancing *bhangra* at the union of a couple of South Asian descent celebrate the particular moment and also its contribution to the future of particular ethnic, religious, and national traditions. On the other hand, people may dance a Middle Eastern line dance at an Indian wedding or *bhangra* at a Jewish wedding, providing evidence of intercultural contact and exchange.

The *macarena* fad began with a Spanish song of the same name, released in a recording by the Seville singing duo Los del Río. The song topped the international charts and became a staple of North American wedding celebrations, cutting across ethnic and religious boundaries. Here, delegates to the 1996 Democratic National Convention in matching patriotic hats and sunglasses dance the *macarena*.

Notation can capture only a small part of dance's complexity. This is an example of Labanotation, which uses symbols on both sides of a vertical center line to represent dance movements. Symbols on the right side of the line are for the right side of the body; those on the left, for the left side of the body. Each symbol indicates which part of the body moves in what direction and at what speed. The notation here indicates that the figure on the right, who is standing with a flexed back leg and retreating posture, should step backward with a double bounce on each foot.[2]

In general, dance enacts the most important values of a soundscape and also communicates and reinforces these ideas. For instance, the jazz funeral discussed in Chapter 5 incorporates lively dancing by the second line to transform grief into joyous celebration. Through dance, individuals convey both artistry and feelings while bringing people together in close coordination, whether for simple pleasure or on behalf of a cause.

Despite the fact that all of us have at some point danced, either during lessons as children or in various social settings, the study of dance in academia has been marginalized. Some music schools and conservatories incorporate dance into their curricula, but dance studies are usually housed within recreational or physical education programs. As a performance art grounded in bodily movement, dance has had to surmount more hurdles than any of the other arts to be taken seriously. Dance has no doubt suffered from the longtime separation of the mind and body in Western philosophical thought and study. Additionally, before the advent of film and videotape, students of dance had difficulty documenting and interpreting a phenomenon that is so ephemeral.

A group of scholars known as dance ethnologists has specialized in dance studies, some focusing on *choreological approaches,* emphasizing the classification and description of dance steps and styles, while others have pursued *contextual approaches,* stressing what dance tells us about a society. We will draw on both approaches to illuminate the ways in which dance's union with music communicates the social values of various soundscapes (see page 306, **"Studying Dance: Interpreting Performance of Sexuality and Gender"**).

In order to preserve details of dance form and structure, dance ethnologists have developed methods to document dance. One of the most important is a system of dance notation named after its creator, Rudolf Laban. Labanotation uses diagrams to describe dance motion in great detail.

In recent years, film and videotape have been used to document dances, enabling one to view a particular movement repeatedly. Utilizing these technologies, the ethnomusicologist Alan Lomax developed a method for comparing movement styles. Termed "choreometrics," this system measures many types of movement, including arm and leg motion, posture, dynamic qualities, use of space, movement flow, group organization, leadership roles, choreography, step style, and others. It is useful to keep these categories in mind when describing and comparing dances.

Scholars of dance in recent decades have also become more concerned with the meaning of dance. Like music, dance can signify different things to participants and observers; it can also accrue new layers of meaning over time, as we will see with the case studies in this chapter. The web of meanings surrounding dance is further enhanced by dance's accessibility to a wide array of participants.

Dance traditions are often open to participation and observation. In American or British neighborhood parks and plazas at dawn on the annual summer and winter solstices, you may encounter Morris dancers costumed in white, with bells attached to pads strapped to their legs, dancing to the music of a fiddle, bagpipe, accordion, or pennywhistle. Today this dance is about socializing and recreation, but it grew out of open-air processions in late medieval England that may have even older roots in Druid traditions. Morris dancing was revived and spread around the world during the twentieth century, arriving in the United States around 1915 with the founding of the Country Dance and Song Society. Here Morris dancers are seen performing at Quoddy Head State Park, Maine.

The constant presence of dance during ceremonies, celebrations, and concerts, and at other important moments in all cultures underscores that dance is an indispensable medium of human expression and a worthy subject for study.

Hearing and Feeling the Dance

Dance's regular rhythms enable anyone who is motivated to join in without the ability to play an instrument or to sing a song text. Group dances are particularly welcoming to beginners who perform only a fixed set of motions, anchored by a regular and recurring rhythmic pattern. As we will see below, dance is often a medium for intense competition, perhaps because of its ability to empower both individuals and groups.

Interpreting Performance of Sexuality and Gender

Dance's wide range of movements can engage all parts of the body from the head to the toes. As we explore dances, we find that each incorporates multiple postures and movements that carry multiple significances. A dance can entertain at the same time as it conveys a political message; dance also embodies attitudes toward sex and gender relations. In this chapter, we will discuss three dances that provide insight into different attitudes toward sexuality and gender. In order to understand what dance conveys, we must consider the following three issues.

First, we need to consider the use of space and the relationship between the dancers. A Middle Eastern line dance, for instance, deploys multiple dancers side by side or in a horizontal sequence, whereas a couple dance brings together two people face to face within an intimate space. The restriction of participants in many line dances to one sex, and the limitation of physical contact between dancers to the touch of a hand mirror the physical separation of the sexes in other aspects of daily life. In contrast to the line dance, most dances of Western European origin not only unite the two sexes on the dance floor, but also put them in a posture resembling an embrace. That the spatial configurations of couple dances are a result of what European cultures consider proper relationships between men and women may seem obvious; however, note that sometimes these spatial arrangements idealize or even transgress social norms about gender.

Second, we need to observe how repetition of stereotyped movements or postures in a dance can parody or challenge gender norms. We will encounter a striking example in the tango, in which a powerful and dominant male advances

Most dances are performed to music with a strong pulse. Dance music usually features regular groupings of beats; the frequency of duple and quadruple rhythms probably stems from the easy match of these musical patterns to movements of feet and legs. However, some dances, such as the waltz, are based on three-beat patterns. Whatever their meter, the underlying beat structures of most dances remains constant and is easily sensed by the body.

toward and leans over his female partner. Early controversies about the tango focused on the dance's overt representation of sexuality. For instance, when the tango was first performed in Europe around 1914, Vatican officials publicly condemned it as an "offense against God," while a Catholic cardinal in Paris called the tango "a sin."[3]

Third, any study of a dance must take into account its distinctive dress, props, and setting. One cannot interpret the classical ballet, for example, without considering the ballerina's costume of tutu and toe shoes; furthermore, the ballerina performs on a stage which accentuates her frail, idealized feminine beauty. The classical *pas de deux,* an extended duet between the female ballerina and leading male dancer, draw on these conventions of costume and choreography that transmit strong messages about sexuality and gender roles. The relationship of the male and female dancers in ballet, whose bodies intertwine as they move through a sequence of graceful motions and lifts, has been interpreted as a "type of refined love affair." Additionally, the male dancer, who balances the ballerina as she spins and anchors her often precarious positions, replicates the cultural ideal of the "gallant gentleman" who supports a woman and "endures hardships for her comfort."[4]

Writers about dance have noted its presence in all societies, speculating that choreographed movement may have served humans as a primary mode of communication. There is no doubt that patterned movement is a part of all rituals, from courtship to religion, in all cultures. By studying the spatial relationships, movements, and contextual aspects of the dance, we can understand better the ways in which bodies in motion represent the most basic aspects of life experience.

CASE STUDY: Moving through Time and Space with *Bhangra*

Bhangra, a tradition today associated with South Asian diaspora communities in Great Britain and North America, is an accessible dance style. Its strong rhythms and quadruple meter are emphasized throughout by percussion instruments and vocal accents.

Magat Ram, a fifth-generation *dhol* player who has represented Punjab at national and international events, poses with his *dhol*. Ram is famous for his encyclopedic knowledge of *bolis*, patterns associated with the *dhol*. "As a boy, it was my passion to play the *dhol* for hours and never repeat a *boli*. I know hundreds of them," he says.[9]

The historical roots of *bhangra* lie in the Punjab region of South Asia, which was partitioned in 1947 between India and Pakistan. *Bhangra* originally referred to the rhythms played by the *dhol* drums at events such as the harvest festival (*baisakhi*) in rural Punjab. The term was later extended to the dance performed by men to the drums.[5] The related dance for Punjabi women, known as *giddha,* was accompanied by handclaps rather than drums.[6]

The *dhol* is a two-headed drum made of mango wood, with lacings securing the heads. The left head, named *dhamma,* has a coating on the underside to give it a heavier sound. The right head, *purha,* is untreated and sounds a higher pitch. The *dhol* is beaten with slightly curved sticks. Brightly colored tassels are often attached to the drum, and a sash secures the drum to the player's body, freeing both hands. The beat of the *dhol* signals festivity and dancing, and it is always played by a man.

In Listening Guide 59 (see page 310), we hear an excerpt of a traditional *dhol* rhythm, *jhummar,* that originated in the Punjab. According to Punjabi oral tradition it was danced at night during the rainy season along river banks and for Sufi rituals, and it was incorporated into the *bhangra* repertory only after Indian Independence.[7] However, another source identifies *jhummar* as a women's circular dance and song repertory accompanied by *dholaki,* the smaller, feminine version of the *dhol.*[8] Whatever the precise origin of the *jhummar* rhythm in rural Punjabi culture, it plays a prominent role in modern *bhangra* and lends its name to a common motion in *bhangra* choreography, as illustrated on the next page.

The *dhol* used to be the only accompaniment for traditional *bhangra,* but today it is often heard in combination with other instruments. In Listening Guide 59, the ensemble includes a monochord (*bugdu*), a double flute (*algoza*), and an idiophone (*chimta*). The *bugdu* is a single-pitch string instrument; the string is anchored within a sound box made from a gourd or wood covered with skin. The player tucks the sound box under his arm and holds a weight attached to the string with the same hand, plucking the string with the other hand to produce a humming sound. The *chimta* and *algoza* are pictured on the bottom of the next page.

Bhangra would have remained a regional harvest dance in India had rural Punjabis not migrated in large numbers to the British Isles beginning in the early 1950s. The majority of these immigrants were of the Sikh religion and from the Jat caste of landlords or farmers accustomed to hearing *bhangra* at harvest celebrations and weddings. These early immigrants, at first mainly

J hummar, a common *bhangra* motion coupled with the rhythm heard in Listening Guide 59, is performed with the arms raised and one leg lifted. The hands are thrust upward, with index fingers straight and thumbs held touching the other fingers. The dancers jerk their shoulders on drum beats one and three; they jerk the raised leg on beats one, two, and three, and bring it to the ground on beat four.

men, later joined by their families in the 1960s, were soon followed by another wave of Punjabis who had lived for years in East Africa. The latter had different caste backgrounds and were more religiously diverse than the earlier wave of Sikh immigrants. All became part of a burgeoning and heterogeneous British South Asian community in urban and suburban England. Musicians soon began to perform *bhangra* for weddings in their new homeland. By the 1960s, *bhangra* helped South Asian youths affirm their identity in a positive way within a hostile and exclusionary British culture.

By the late 1970s, there were a number of amateur Punjabi musicians who performed traditional *bhangra* at weddings and other community events in the British diaspora. The British musical scene was at that time alive with new sounds from other immigrant communities, notably reggae, soul, and rap, all of which influenced what came to be called "*bhangra* beat." The major transition in *bhangra* style and the emergence of an expanded audience took place in

The sound of the *chimta* depends on the size of the metal discs attached to the iron strip. *Chimtas* with big discs are used at rural festivities; those with smaller discs are used to accompany *bhangra* dancers and hymn singers.

Mangal Singh Sunami, one of Punjab's best known *algoza* players, also makes and decorates his own instruments. Here he is seen in traditional dress with a set of lavishly decorated *algoza*.

**CD 2
Track 25**

Jhummar (Traditional *bhangra* rhythm)

Date: Between 1995 and 1998

Performers: Ravi Kumar, *dhol*; Mangal Singh Sunami, *algoza*; Jagdish Jagga, *bugdu*; Rajvinder Dhindsa, *chimta*

Form: Drum roll followed by several variations of *jhummar*

Tempo: Moderate

Function: To accompany dancing at night during rainy season along river banks and for Sufi ceremonies; incorporated into *bhangra* after Independence (1947)

WHAT TO LISTEN FOR:

- Repeated eight-beat rhythmic patterns produced by the *dhol* and accompanying instruments, which shift subtly through the course of the example. Each beat of the eight-beat pattern can be counted as four fast beats.
- The two heads of the *dhol* drum producing high (right) and low (left) sounds.
- The double flute (*algoza*), sustained by circular breathing; only the repeated eight-beat phrase can be heard; the drone of the second flute is drowned out by the volume of the drum.
- The subtle humming sound of the *bugdu*.
- The sharp, clanging sound of the *chimta* (literally "tongs"), a long iron strip bent double around the neck and intersected across the chest with a crossbar, often with attached metal discs.

	STRUCTURE	DESCRIPTION
0:00	**Introduction**	6-beat drum roll by *dhol*.
0:04	**Short drum break**	4-beat *dhol* pattern (x2) with *chimta* entering at end of the first beat.
0:10	***Jhummar* Break 2**	8-beat *dhol* pattern; flute enters at end of third beat (x7).
0:41		4-beat *dhol* pattern (x2).
0:46	***Jhummar* 2**	10-beat *dhol* pattern (x7).
1:26		fade-out and end of recording

1984. A commercial recording of a *bhangra* band known as *Alaap* became a best seller, combining traditional *bhangra,* urban black musics, and modern technology fused with Punjabi lyrics. By late 1987, *bhangra* beat received a great deal of publicity and began to be performed outside South Asian clubs, attracting broad audiences in London and other cities.[10]

By the early 1990s, new *bhangra* styles had emerged in Great Britain as well as abroad and had crossed over into the mainstream. *Bhangra* was featured on United Kingdom radio shows and had an impact on British society and musical culture.[11]

The 4 x 4 Bhangra Dancers perform the dance step *chaal* at the Milk Cup Festival at Ballymoney, Northern Ireland, in July 2000. Shown from left to right are the dancers Billu Bains, Gurdish Sall, Sunny Sandher, and Marni Dhinsa, with Bill Sandher at the rear playing the *dhol.*

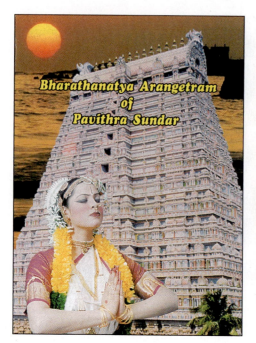

Pavithra with Gurus

Other Indian dance styles, such as the historical South Indian *bharata natyam* tradition, are transmitted within South Asian communities worldwide as markers of ethnic identity. Many young South Asian American women study *bharata natyam* for years with local *gurus*, and finally present a formal, public performance called an *Arangetram* to celebrate their achievement. The *Arangetram* has a traditional structure, with multiple sections displaying the knowledge, grace, and stamina of the young dancer. The invitation reproduced here announces the *Bharathanatya Arangetram* (*Bharata Natyam* recital) of Pavithra Sundar (which took place in Flushing, New York, on July 26, 2003). Pavithra Sundar, wearing traditional dress and ornaments poses in front of a backdrop of a South Indian temple. On the back cover of the invitation, Pavithra Sundar is flanked by her *gurus* Saavitri Ramanand (left) and Aarati Ramanand (right).

In North America, *bhangra* performance spread to schools and college campuses. By the early 1990s, for instance, the South Asian *desi* ("local") community in Toronto developed its own *bhangra* scene; teenagers skipped school to attend daylong dances in suburban clubs.[12] *Bhangra* gave young people of South Asian descent an opportunity to celebrate their shared heritage and participate in increasingly popular musical competitions.

The team aspect of North America *bhangra* performance emerges from the complicated history of the dance and also transforms it. Many campuses now have *bhangra* clubs that host annual intercollegiate dance competitions, such as the *Bhangra* Blast held at the Massachusetts Institute of Technology (2003). Some of these competitions have philanthropic goals—for instance, the *Bhangra* Blowout held at George Washington University in 1998 sought to establish a South Asian scholarship and to "bring together the South Asian community in the hope of promoting unity and awareness of its vast and diverse culture."

Many students view participation in *bhangra's* updated, technologically sophisticated form as a way to construct their own relationship with the traditions of their parents. Deepi Sidhu, exposed to traditional *bhangra* by her immigrant father as a child in Indianapolis, speaks about the shifts in her personal experience with *bhangra* over the years: "Growing up, I was always pretty fond of it," Sidhu remembered, but "when you get to the junior high school age, you become too cool for it, because it was like 'That's my parents' music.'"

After turning to classic rock and hip-hop, Sidhu got interested in the new *bhangra* styles through recordings made in England that were played at local weddings. "The music sounded completely different from anything I had ever heard," Sidhu recalls. "The lyrics sounded like something my dad would listen to. But the music—there was scratching and reggae." Sidhu began listening to the recordings of Bally Sagoo, Heera, and other South Asian artists prominent on the popular music scene. A decade later, she finds that she also has renewed interest in "good, old-time *bhangra* . . . Now I find myself going back and listening to the more traditional stuff to kind of fill in the blanks for myself."[13]

The sound and choreography of *bhangra* may seem straightforward on the surface, but both lead us to a soundscape of considerable complexity. For instance, the sound of *bhangra* music places it within the musical context of modern urban dance styles, while the texts shed light on conflicting currents of tradition and innovation within South Asian communities. Many post-1985 *bhangra* styles, including varieties such as rock *bhangra,* house *bhangra,* and *bhangramuffin,* use new technology and sampling combined with acoustic instruments. However progressive its sound and the subtle references to gender and sexuality in its texts, *bhangra* movements continue to represent traditional South Asian notions of clear gender roles and often separate male and female teams at competitions. Even in diaspora social contexts as opposed to heavily choreographed competitions, the dance is usually performed by groups of either men or women; the dancers replicate its most characteristic movements and *bhangra* dancers wear traditional Indian dress.

Our example is the song *Aao Nachiye,* heard in Listening Guide 60 (see page 316), a *bhangra* hit of the mid-1990s. It is performed by the Sangeet Group, an ensemble founded in 1989 by eight musicians from Punjab who met after moving to Northern California. The group's name means "sweet music" and, according to Sangeet Group's Web site, combines "a limited number of pitches in different melodic sequences with traditional Indian bodily gestures to emphasize its rhythmic or melodic design." In 1996 the group issued an album titled *Bhangra Roots* containing the wedding song *Aao Nachiye,* which became

Moving with Chitresh Das and Indian *Kathak* Dance

Around the time that *bhangra* began its migration to Indian diaspora communities, other Indian dances also traveled abroad. Although they did not become part of global popular culture as did *bhangra*, these dances have had a continued impact in India and its diaspora communities. The paths of these solo dances can be tracked through a look at the lives of the individuals who transmitted them to new settings. We will consider the career of Chitresh Das, a virtuoso *kathak* dancer born in Calcutta (now Kolkata) several years before the 1947 declaration of Indian independence. "I am that part of India that is always traveling," said Chitresh Das. "I am a pioneer, the Johnny Appleseed of *kathak* dance."[14] Chitresh Das's career provides an example of the response of a *kathak* dancer and his art to change.

As a child, Das studied with his parents, accomplished dancers who founded a school for Indian classical and folk dance in Kolkata. At age ten, Das was formally "tied" to the *kathak guru* Pandit Ram Narayan Mishra and trained with him until leaving India for the United States in 1972.

Das introduced *kathak* dance to California, where since 1973 he has taught in the San Francisco Bay Area and established one of the largest schools of Indian classical dance in North America. *Kathak* involves intensive footwork and sounds are produced by bare feet slapping the floor and by the bells, or *ghungroo*, tied

an international hit. *Aao Nachiye* was later featured in the wedding scene in the 2001 film *Monsoon Wedding*, directed by Mira Nair.

The double-headed Indian drum (*dhol*) is one ingredient of a stylistic fusion that draws on technologically enhanced musics such as disco, reggae, techno, and rap. *Aao Nachiye* is typical in its use of synthesizers and electronic manipulations. Following a brief *dhol* introduction, a regular quadruple meter is established.

Despite its upbeat sound, *Aao Nachiye* retains a number of traditional elements. The text is in a colloquial style that might be heard in a village, including a reference to Heer, a fictional beauty in Punjabi culture. The text mentions the *bolis,* short solo phrases played and sung at the beginning of songs. The listener is invited to join the *giddha,* the dance performed by Punjabi women as the equivalent to the male *bhangra*. The phrases translating

around the dancer's ankles. Both men and women perform this predominantly solo dance, and every dancer is expected to portray male and female characters with equal ease. When teaching in America, Das focuses first on the rhythmic and technical capabilities that he considers to be objective measures of talent, compensating for the fact that many of his American dance students do not "look Indian."[15]

While Das's style of teaching, athletic and fluid, is arguably more orthodox and conservative than that found in his homeland, he also advocates innovation within the tradition. Das has developed a practice known as *Kathak Yoga,* in which a dancer sings and recites the rhythmic cycle (*tala*) while dancing. Taking on the role of accompanist makes the dance much more complex and physically demanding. With so many things going on at once, the dancer's mind must detach from the particular moment, hence the term "yoga."

Although he has now lived more than half his life in America, Chitresh Das has a continuing relationship with India. He and his American students (the Chitresh Das Dance Company) have presented his unique style of *kathak* in India through annual tours and teaching at the Kolkata-based *kathak* school he opened in 2002. Das has also been honored for his contributions to the San Francisco dance community. Both worlds meet in Das's choreography, as in his dance *Gold Rush,* (1990), in which scenes of the California Gold Rush are used as a metaphor for his Western journey from India.

"the yarn is spun" and "the milk is churned" were included to enhance the rhyme within the Punjabi text and have no other connection with the theme of the song.

Aao Nachiye contains a suggestive sexual metaphor referring to the groom as "my beloved *dhol* player." The word *"valikan,"* derived from an Urdu word meaning "master," in Punjabi slang signifies the United Kingdom or the West in general. A textual element that links this rendition of *Aao Nachiye* to an American setting is the use of the vocables *"yo, yo, yo"* by the chorus in addition to the more common Punjabi expression *hoye, hoye.*

Bhangra has in recent years moved beyond college campuses to enter the professional "Indipop" scene. Famous stars such as Daler Mehndi (the *badshah* or "emperor" of *bhangra*) perform in concerts, movies, and television commercials. Since the late 1990s, *bhangra* has also been performed regularly at

Aao Nachiye ("Come Let's Dance," *bhangra*)

**CD 3
Track 1**

Date: 1996

Performers: Sangeet Group: Anoop Cheema, *lead vocals;* Amarjit Dulai, *lead vocals;* Ranjit Dhaliwal, *keyboard;* Lal Singh Bhatti, *dhol;* Bobby, *dholaki;* Suresh Kumar, *drums;* Tommy, *bass guitar;* Karan Bajwa, *back-up vocals;* Sukie Uppal, *president / sound engineer*

Form: Two main sections (A and B) contrasting in performance style and melodic content, flanked by instrumental introduction and conclusion

Tempo: Lively tempo with regular groupings of four-beat units

---

WHAT TO LISTEN FOR:

- The complex mix of vocal articulations (song, shouts) and textures (call and response; unison singing; heterophony between voices and melody instruments) that lend variety to repetitive melodic content
- The use of off-beat accents, particularly emphasizing the second and fourth beats of a four-beat grouping to add rhythmic interest and syncopation to an otherwise regular metric structure
- The inclusion of traditional instruments, including *dhol, dholaki,* and *chimta*

	STRUCTURE AND TEXT	TRANSLATION	DESCRIPTION
0:00	**Introduction**	Hoye (x8) Yo (x8) (repeated)	Begins with *dhol* roll and "*bulande bakre,*" the sound produced by loosely rolled lips to call goats in the Punjabi countryside. Shouts on 2nd and 4th beats of each 4-beat grouping
0:14			Unison strings with dhol accompaniment. The melody is divided into four phrases (a a b c). Phrase a is repeated, then phrase b is at a higher pitch level, and phrase c descends to conclude the phrase, overlapping with chorus shouts.
0:33		Yo (x10)	

0:43	**Section A** *Aaj an gaya ve aa ke mera veer vai* (x2) *Bhabo lagadi syalan di koi heer vai* (x2) *Mukh punya da chand aai phulan di sugandh jadon vehre vich pair bhabo paia* *Giddhe de vich...*	Hey Today my brother has come home. Sister-in-law looks gorgeous like the legendary Heer of the legendary Siaal clan. Her face beautiful like the full moon and her fragrance like flowers, she steps into the courtyard. In *giddha*....	Ascending *glissando*. Call-and-response on each phrase between soloist and chorus, same melody repeated and varied. Strings parallel vocal lines in close heterophony.
1:00		*Hoye* (x4)	*Dhol* lead-in and chorus shouts.
1:04	**Refrain** *Giddhe de vich aao nachiye; aao nachiye* *Veer mera ghar aaia; giddhe de vich aao nachiye*	Come, let's dance in the *giddha*, let's dance! Brother has come home, let's dance in the *giddha*!	Call-and-response.
1:12	**Brief instrumental bridge**		Brief instrumental bridge leads into section B.
1:14	**Section B** *Saade tan vehre vich tana buninda* (x2) *UK di kuri, munda valikan suneenda* *Jori tan phab ve he gai*	In our courtyard the yarn is spun. The girl's from the UK and the guy's said to be from the West. And this couple looks good together.	Unison chorus repeats same melody.
1:36	*Jori tan phab ve he gai* *Ve loko, jori tan phab ve he gai*	This couple looks good together. Yes, O folks, this couple looks good together.	Descending bells lead into unison chorus.
1:46	**Instrumental interlude**		Similar to 0:14, with variation.
2:13	**Section A** *Hoian purian umeedan aaj aaian* (x2) *O nach lahonian ve reejhan aaj aaian* (x2) *Apan bahn bahn toli, pauni bolian te boli pata lagoon kidan veer vihaia* *Giddhe de vich ...*	All our wishes have been fulfilled today. And today we'll dance to our hearts' fill. Dancing in groups and singing *boli* after *boli*. We'll show that brother has gotten married. In *giddha* ...	Call-and-response on each phrase
2:30		Yo (x4) Hey	*Dhol* lead-in and chorus shouts. Ascending glissando.

(c o n t i n u e s)

(continued)

	STRUCTURE AND TEXT	TRANSLATION	DESCRIPTION
	Refrain		
2:34	*Giddhe de vich aao nachiye; aao nachiye*	Come, let's dance in the *giddha*, let's dance!	
	Veer mera ghar aaia; giddhe de vich aao nachiye	Brother has come home, let's dance in the *giddha*!	
2:42	**Brief instrumental interlude**		
2:44	**Section B**		
	Sade tan vehre vich chale madhani ve (x2)	In our courtyard the milk's churned.	Unison chorus.
	Dil da tu Raja tere, dil di main	You're the king of my heart, and	
	Rani ve	I'm the queen of yours.	
	Ban ke tu sada mera rahin	I want you to stay mine	
3:06	*Ban ke tu sada mera, rahin ve dholna*	I want you to stay mine forever, o my *dhol* player.	Descending bells lead in.
	Ban ke tu sada mera rahin	I want you to stay mine forever.	
3:16	**Instrumental prelude**		Descending bells. String postlude similar to intro and interlude, varied slightly.
3:34			Fades out and ends at 3:36.

Translation by Usha Verma and Rajwinder Singh

clubs in England and in urban North America, at places such as New York City's S.O.B. (Sounds of Brazil) and Basement Bhangra. One of the DJs and producers responsible for *bhangra's* high profile in England, Bally Sagoo, has said:

> You can't run away from the bhangra beat. It's an ethnic drum sound that makes you dance and incorporates a whole lot of ingredients. . . . It's progressed to where 50,000 screaming people are at Daler Mehndi shows—with more and more non-Asians.[16]

Bhangra has also had a long-running conversation with African American hip-hop and has proven a lively partner in creating new hybrid styles. An example is Panjabi MC (Rajinder Rai), who grew up in Coventry, England, listening to his parents' LPs of traditional Punjabi music and to rap. Rai was inspired by a 1997 hit, *Fire It Up,* that sampled the theme from the television show *Knight Rider;* Rai borrowed this sample, combining it with *dhol* drums and a vocal line from a Punjabi song by a Bollywood singer named Labh Janjua. The resulting song, titled *Mundian to Bach Ke,* was released in 1998 and became a hit over the next three years. By 2001 hip-hop musicians had begun to draw on *bhangra,* sampling Indian instruments. In 2003, rapper Jay-Z heard Rai's song *Mundian* in Switzerland and decided to rap over it; the result was the international popularity of Panjabi MC and Jay-Z's song titled *Beware of the Boys,* a rap remix of the Panjabi MC's *Mundian to Bach Ke.*[17]

The popularity of *bhangra* with non-Asians and its success in crossing over to forge new styles has surprised members of the Punjabi diaspora community. Monica Dandona, a student at Rice University in Houston, remembers when she first heard *bhangra* outside the South Asian community: "I immediately called my brother and said, 'They are playing Indian music on the radio.' It was shocking to realize that Indian music made it into American culture."[18]

Bhangra's move beyond the borders of the South Asian community and its recent transformations by diaspora Punjabi young people have not always been well received by elders in the community, who have questioned the music's departure from its historical roots and sounds. The cultural politics of performing and participating in new forms of *bhangra* has opened debates within South Asian communities that are acknowledged as "much more than a discussion of the music and dance form; rather, it is a struggle over the definition of authenticity, tradition, cultural values, and above all, sexual mores." Ironically, in this conflict between elders and youth about new types of *bhangra,* both generations claim tradition as part of their agenda.[19] The ongoing dialogue about *bhangra* has been aired publicly, as in the video *The Bhangra Wrap* (1994) directed by Nandini Sikand, which deals with *bhangra* in Toronto and New York.

In summary, *bhangra*'s stereotyped, repetitive movements, such as *jhummar,* which both amateurs and experienced performers can do, coupled with the strong, regular *dhol* rhythms and Punjabi texts, have become this dance's most defining characteristics. *Bhangra* is not defined by fixed melodic content or form, but adjusts comfortably to settings including the wedding hall and the dance hall and is able to partner with new sounds such as reggae and rap. Because of its range of sounds, choreography, and settings, *bhangra*'s meaning is also quite flexible, varying not just from audience to audience, but from person to person. The malleable nature of *bhangra*'s sounds and steps may lend it

Bally Sagoo was born in New Delhi, India, and as an infant moved with his family to Birmingham, England. There he started as a deejay and producer on the *bhangra* club dance scene. Sagoo's albums include *Star Crazy* and *Hanji.*

American-born *dhol* players of Punjabi descent, Sandeep Sulhan, left, and Chris Adlakha form the "Dhol Collective," which plays at Indian weddings and parties in Houston, Texas. Here they perform at a "Bayou *Bhangra*" party hosted in 2003 at the Lotus Lounge in downtown Houston.

extra power as a force for social cohesion and a lively subject of debate. In our next case study, the polka, we encounter a dance that has traveled as widely as *bhangra* and is equally flexible in its meaning but more stable in its musical content.

CASE STUDY: The Polka

The polka originated in Central Europe among the Czech-speaking people of Bohemia. For more than one hundred and fifty years, it has been popular in many countries. We will explore the polka as a dance particularly effective at crossing national and ethnic boundaries, keeping its musical content and its characteristic physical motions intact. The polka has also been a powerful but flexible symbol of national and ethnic identities. Over the years, it has also had strong working-class associations in European and American societies.

The polka first appeared in Prague in 1837. The origin of its name is uncertain. It may be connected to a Czech word for "half" (a reference to its signature step), or the name may derive from *polska*, the Czech term for a Polish girl. From its beginning, the polka was a dance style in duple time performed by couples and cultivated in urban ballrooms. Polka tunes, written down and published in colorful collections, were either newly composed or adapted from popular songs of the time; all of them shared a strong duple rhythm.

The polka quickly became popular throughout Europe, then spread east to Calcutta, India, where British colonial officials danced it in 1845 at a ball in honor of Queen Victoria. The polka also arrived early on in Norway, where it persists until the present, although known by different names in different places.[20] The polka was danced in Mexico City during the reign of Emperor Maximilian (1864–1867), and quickly spread to provincial regions of that country as well.[21] The polka was one of the European dances that entered Mexico during a period of intense pressure for Europeanization. By the turn of the twentieth century, the polka was played throughout Mexico.[22]

By 1844, the polka was also known in the United States, where it became the source of jokes related to the name of the 1844 presidential candidate, James K. Polk. The migration to the American Midwest (including Wisconsin, Nebraska, Iowa, and Minnesota) of nearly 400,000 Czech and other eastern Europeans between 1848 and the beginning of World War I had a major impact on musical life of that region as the immigrants brought polka music and dance.[23] The name of the polka, as well as its popularity in Polish communities in the Midwest, gave rise in the 1920s to the close association of the polka with Polish culture and identity.

A large number of Czechs also migrated to Texas, which still has more Czech Americans in its population than any other state.[24] Many settled near Highway I-10 (called by insiders the "Polka Road") which links Houston and Dallas. Polish and German immigrants who settled further west also performed the polka, reinforcing the widespread popularity of the dance among Mexicans and Mexican Americans in the region.

This photograph, taken in 1927 on a farm in Getzville, New York, shows the typical posture for the polka, a close embrace by the dancing couple. The dance, accompanied by saxophone, violin, and a button accordion, is performed outdoors in a field. The photograph also provides interesting evidence of gender flexibility in partnering; two men dance on the left and a man and woman on the right.

The Accordion

The accordion, first developed in early nineteenth-century Europe as a byproduct of the Industrial Revolution, revolutionized music the world over. The instrument spread quickly thanks to mass marketing in the 1830s, which, along with the grass-roots polka craze, made musicians throughout Europe aware of the accordion's loud volume, full sound, portability, and low cost. European immigrants brought the instrument with them to the New World; various types of accordions were adopted within a wide range of music and dance traditions, including the polka and the tango. By the late nineteenth century, the instrument had spread around the world, giving rise to accordion soundscapes in unexpected places. The European colonial presence, for example, brought the instrument to Africa. Throughout the twentieth century, the instrument continued to travel, becoming established in locales as diverse as Japan and Cape Dorset in Nunavut, Canada. Although the piano is generally considered the instrument that spread Western music to the world outside Europe, the accordion deserves considerable credit as well.

The accordion consists of a bellows with a headboard on each side. Both headboards have multiple holes containing reeds of a type known as "free reeds" that sound in response to the entry or exit of air, controlled by the motion of the bellows. (The visible reeds used on a number of other wind instruments, such as oboes and clarinets, are termed "beating reeds," since they are set into motion and stopped by the mouth of the player.)

The player controls the volume of the instrument by inflating the bellows quickly or slowly, a process that also shapes musical phrases. In addition to sustaining a high volume of sound over a long period of time, accomplished accordionists can achieve special effects, such as an intense vibrato termed "bellows shaking."

Button accordions, including the *bandoneón* used for the tango, have bass buttons on the left and melody buttons on the right. The piano accordion has a keyboard on the right side and has been manufactured in two sizes, a regular "male" instrument, and a small "ladies'" size, with the keys set closer together. Complex in their construction, accordions can also be elaborate in design; the color and decoration of their cases are important artistic and visual symbols of cultural identity.

In the 1950s and 1960s, the instrument became a regular fixture on Lawrence Welk's TV show. Frank Yankovic, in 1948 crowned "the Polka King," popularized the accordion until his death in 1998, accompanying famous singers and winning a Grammy Award. The accordion has even inspired literature: E. Annie Proulx's 1996 novel *Accordion Crimes* traces the path of a small green accordion, brought along by its late nineteenth-century Italian maker when he immigrated to New Orleans from Sicily and played over the course of the next century by musicians of different ethnic backgrounds and musical styles.

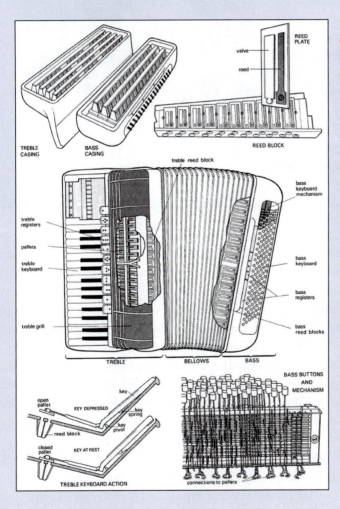

In this illustration, the parts of the accordion that are normally hidden are visible and labeled. The performer plays the melody on the treble (high-pitched) side of the instrument, which has either a piano keyboard, as seen here, or buttons. The bass (low-pitched) side, which always has buttons, is used to play supporting harmony. The figure also shows how the treble keys and bass buttons work differently to open and close the reed blocks hidden within the cases on both sides. The treble keyboard action, illustrated on the lower left, opens and closes pallets controlling each reed on the reed block. The bass buttons, illustrated on the lower right, are attached to their pallets through rods and levers. Air pushed through from the bellows sounds the open reeds.

The Accordion (continued)

While the accordion—nicknamed the "squeeze box"—has been the butt of many jokes, it may have had the last wheeze. According to the National Association of Music Merchants, accordion sales were up 30 percent in the mid-1990s, and accordion schools report increasing enrollments. Musicians as diverse as Madonna, Barenaked Ladies, Sinead O'Connor, and Luciano Pavarotti have used the accordion as accompaniment. From zydeco to Tex-Mex to polka, an accordion revival is under way. According to Carl Finch, an accordionist for Brave Combo, an alternative polka band from Texas, "We look at the accordion as just another cool instrument."

Women of Brazzaville in the Congo adopted the accordion from Europeans who colonized their country in the late nineteenth century.

The accordion was associated with the polka whenever and wherever the dance was performed (see page 322, **Sound Sources: The Accordion**). An instrument that originated in early industrial Europe, the accordion traveled together with the polka wherever Europeans migrated. Brass bands supplemented by an accordion usually accompanied the polka; lower brass instruments such as the sousaphone emphasize the strong duple meter.

The polka is characterized by the distinctive polka step, a heel-and-toe half step associated with the duple meter. Any rollicking (usually strophic) tune played by accordion and/or brass band in duple meter can be used to accompany the polka, but some pieces were composed expressly for the dance and became strongly linked to its performance. The *Beer Barrel Polka* (Listening Guide 61; see page 327) is the most famous of the early twentieth-century polkas that are still part of the polka repertory. Composed by Jaromir Vejvoda (b. 1902) under the title *Skoda Lasky* and also known as the *Rosamunde Polka,* the *Beer Barrel Polka* was first recorded in Germany by Will Glahé's Musette Orchestra and was distributed in North America in 1935 or 1936.

The *Beer Barrel Polka* is a notable example of the success of the polka within and outside the Central European communities of its origin and the European ballroom setting. Although the early transmission of the polka in and beyond Europe predated the invention of recording by decades, recordings enabled numbers such as the *Beer Barrel Polka* to reach an even wider cross-section of people and communities. The *Beer Barrel Polka* became part of United States popular culture thanks to a best-selling recording with English words made by the Andrews Sisters in the late 1930s.

The *Beer Barrel Polka* became a landmark polka because of its appearance on jukeboxes, machines that played songs chosen from a list of well-known offerings of the time. Alvin Sajewski, son of the Polish immigrant who in 1897 founded the famous Sajewski Music Store in Chicago, traces the history of the song:

Label from a 78-rpm recording of the *Beer Barrel Polka* released by Victor in 1935.

> *Beer Barrel Polka* really started things going, and they never slowed down after that. It started the whole polka thing. It was just as the jukeboxes were coming out. The jukeboxes were in the taverns. *Beer Barrel Polka* came out in the spring, so all the doors were open, and all the taverns with jukeboxes put them right in the door and blasted away. That was a shot in the arm. People were getting jobs, and all of a sudden there was new life completely. You could get a big twenty-six-ounce stein of beer for a dime, and things were really rolling.[25]

Jukeboxes and radio brought the polka to working-class people of a wide variety of ethnic backgrounds; they also reinforced the popularity of the polka among Mexican Americans, who since the nineteenth century had danced the polka on both sides of the border. The recording of the *Beer Barrel Polka* heard in Listening Guide 61 is performed by Valerio Longoria, a prominent Mexican American accordion player who spent much of his life in San Antonio, Texas.

Longoria was born in 1924 to a family of poor migrant laborers: "My father was following the work in the fields. He always worked in the fields," he recalled.[26] Longoria started playing the accordion at age seven and made his first public appearance performing at a wedding when he was eight years old.

Following service in the US Army during World War II, Longoria became a professional musician. His button accordion was the lead instrument in a group that also included a guitar, bass, and drums. Both the ensemble and its musical style were called *conjunto* (literally "united" or "connected," pronounced "con-hoon-toh"). An instrumental style featuring the accordion that emerged along the Texas-Mexico border beginning in the 1930s, *conjunto* music included polkas and waltzes in its core repertory of up-tempo, lively dances. In the mid-1950s, Longoria and his *conjunto* ensemble recorded the rendition of *Beer Barrel Polka* heard in Listening Guide 61.

Every community that has performed the polka has made adaptations, and Longoria was no exception. An innovative musician, he is credited as the first to use a drum set for *conjunto* in 1948, instead of having the guitar and bass emphasize the rhythm.[27] Longoria was also known for altering the reeds on his button accordion, retuning one of the two reeds that produced each note so that it would sound an octave lower. These and other innovations were said to have given Longorio's accordion—and his music—a distinctive "*sonido ronco*" ("hoarse sound").

Polkas continue to be performed at weddings and have even been played during the Roman Catholic Mass since 1972.[28] The practice of incorporating the polka into the Mass on special occasions, accompanied by a live polka band, is well received by many but considered controversial or even blasphemous by others. The polka Mass keeps the traditional texts, but adds new texts sung to familiar popular melodies. For instance, *Let the Sun Shine In,* from the musical *Hair,* became *Let the Son Shine In* in the polka Mass. The practice of using *contrafacta* in the polka Mass is justified by its positive effect on the community, as opposed to the justification for singing Syrian *pizmonim* in sacred contexts discussed in Chapter 5. As one priest noted when discussing the use of sacred covers of popular songs for the polka Mass: "What is sacred music? It's anything that raises your mind to God. It's anything that unites a congregation—the people and the priest—in praising God."[29]

Valerio Longoria, who died in 2000, is seen here playing his button accordion flanked by his sons Valerio Jr. (on right, with guitar) and Flavio (on left, with alto saxophone) and grandson Valerio IV, who plays the drums (in the center).

Beer Barrel Polka

CD 3
Track 2

Composer: Jaromír Vejvoda
Date of composition: Late 1920s or early 1930s
Performer: Valeria Longoria
Date of recording: Mid-1950s, reissued 1997
Form: Strophic
Tempo: Upbeat duple meter

WHAT TO LISTEN FOR:

- The sound of the *conjunto* ensemble, with accordion as the main melodic instrument; guitar, electric bass, and drums provide strong rhythmic support.
- Accented second beat of each duple measure, reflected in the short heel-and-toe half steps of the dance
- Variations and extensions of the main theme as it is repeated

	STRUCTURE	DESCRIPTION
0:00	Fade in	
	Main Theme (4 phrases)	
0:02	phrase a	Melody in accordion; guitar plays chords; drum
0:10	phrase a'	accentuates off-beat accompaniment.
0:18	phrase a''	
0:26	phrase b	
	Main theme repeat, with extended phrases	
0:34	phrase a	At the end of the third phrase, the accordion
0:47	phrase a'	elaborates with conjunct scales that obscure the
0:55	phrase a''	melody.
1:02	phrase b	
1:10	**Transitional (B) section**	Call-and-response between accordion and guitar.
1:22	**Main theme** spoken: "All right" and "cold beer"	Similar to strophe at 0:34 in its ornamentation.
1:55	fade out	Recording ends at 1:58.

In the early 1970s, some Roman Catholic churches began occasionally celebrating Mass to the accompaniment of a live polka band. The words of traditional or newly composed hymns are set to melodies of familiar polkas. Here, Father Wally Szcypula, an accordion embroidered on his vestments, celebrates a polka Mass in Rosemont, Illinois.

Polka—the dance and the music—has had a long life, although its popularity has ebbed and flowed over the years. In recent years, performance of the polka among people of German and Polish descent in Milwaukee, once known as the polka capital of the United States, diminished and shifted to smaller towns in the Midwest, notably around Green Bay. Today, polka festivals are held in northern and central Wisconsin, and the influence of country and western styles can be heard; in 1994, the polka was named Wisconsin's official state dance. The polka also continues to thrive in Polish-American clubs across the nation, as well as in recordings; polka music has been recognized by the Grammy Awards as a separate category since 1985.

In contrast with *bhangra*, polka has not crossed over into the mass youth market, nor has it radically transformed its musical style. It has accommodated various national, regional, and ethnic inflections with ease. One key to the polka's wide distribution as well as its musical continuity may be its longtime transmission by way of musical notation, in contrast to *bhangra*'s movement through oral tradition. For the last century, of course, recordings have also spread the polka throughout the world. Yet while the polka has interacted with other styles to enrich its musical vocabulary and expand its audience, it continues to be closely associated with the sound of the accordion, to maintain its strong duple rhythm, and to display everywhere its signature dance step.

Walter "Li'l Wally" Jagiello, known as the "Polka King," has performed for the pope and the US president. Here he plays the concertina, a type of button accordion, in his North Miami Beach studio.

Dance Styles and Their Multiple Meanings

We sometimes assume that the nature of dance as physical movement makes it impossible to explain its meaning in words. The famous dancer Isadora Duncan once remarked, "If I could tell you what I mean, there would be no point in dancing!" The nonverbal aspects of dance performance encourage not only variations in choreography but also multiple constructions of dance's meaning. As we have seen with *bhangra,* the flexibility of dance enables its meanings to shift at different times and in different places.

Despite the fact that participation in a dance is the most direct route to understanding its form and meaning, dancers have developed terms to describe dance's qualities and explain them. Many dances have insider terminology to describe and cue motion as well as to define movements. A familiar example is the "do-si-do," a crossover between partners seen in square dances. Frequently, dance steps become known by the name of the dance with which they are associated, as we have noted in the case of the heel-and-toe "polka step," which has been incorporated into many other dances.

Although on one level we need to approach dance as structured motion shaped by and giving form to music, we must also consider the range of settings in which dances take place and the multiple meanings of dance. We will take a close look at the rich tradition of the tango and the manner in which its sound, setting, and significance have been maintained and transformed over time.

CASE STUDY: The Tango

In the case of the tango, we encounter a group of closely related soundscapes that share many aspects of sound and meaning while retaining their individual settings and historical frameworks. The sounds and movements of today's tango music and dance have their roots in the slums of late nineteenth-century Buenos Aires, where rural Argentinean *gaucho* (cowboy) and African influences joined with the creativity of European immigrants (see page 330, **"Looking Back: The Tango"**).

The early tango emerged in Argentina with the introduction of the *bandoneón,* a type of button accordion. Brought by German immigrants, the *bandoneón* slowly displaced the guitar in tango ensembles. Its distinctive sound merged with the syncopated rhythms of traditional *gaucho* and African styles that gave the music and dance its distinctive rhythmic sense. Vivid description of life's hardships in the slums of the *arrabal* (outskirts) of Buenos Aires pervade the lyrics of tango songs. At the center of the tango's musical style and choreography, however, is the myth and the exaggerated postures of the *compadrito* (literally, "a man who has come to less"), a type of urban *gaucho,* both lover

LOOKING *Back*

The Tango

Tango's multiple roots and influences

1870	Influx of immigrants to the Río del Plata region of Argentina.
1880	Fusion of indigenous music traditions of Río del Plata region with those of immigrants from Europe.
1887	Carlos Gardel born, possibly in France.
1890s	First tangos composed in Buenos Aires.
1900	*Bandoneón* introduced into tango ensembles.

Tango's transnational journey

1902	Earliest recordings of tango.
1907–1908	Tango first introduced in Paris, where Camille de Rhynal, dancer and dance teacher, modifies abrupt tango movements considered too crude for ballroom dancing.
1911	Columbia Records make first tango recording.
1912	Tango first introduced in London.
1913–1915	Argentinean tango comes to Europe as a ballroom dance.
1917	Samuel Castriota composes *Mi Noche Triste* ("My Sorrowful Night"); the lyrics by Pascual Contursi introduce a mood of pessimism, melancholy, and nostalgia into tango lyrics.
1917	First film devoted entirely to tango, *El Tango de la Muerte* ("The Tango of Death"), produced in Argentina.
1921	Rudolph Valentino performs the first Hollywood tango in film *The Four Horsemen of the Apocalypse*.
1920s–1940s	Golden Age of tango worldwide.

Tango confronts and adapts to a changing world

1929	At height of political turmoil, Ministry of Navy in Argentina bans protest tangos (*tangos de protesta*) from Argentinean radio.
Early 1930s	Great Depression reinforces acceptance of tango as misery, bitterness, and resentment expressed by dance.
1932	Addition of vibraphone, viola, cello, percussion, and harp to tango ensemble.
1936	Wind instruments incorporated into tango ensembles.
1950s–1960s	New concert tangos.
1980s	*Tango Argentino* opens on London's West End and New York's Broadway, and goes on world tour.
1990s	Tango reenters global popular culture.

and pimp, dressed in a tight black suit and high-heeled shoes. The straight, un-bending upper body of the tango dancer is said to be the characteristic stance of the *compadrito*; the smooth pattern of the steps reflects patterns in knife duels, and the forward tilt of the man's body is attributed to his high-heeled shoes. The formalized interaction of the male and female dancers is distinctive: The man moves forward, dominating the woman so that she is forced to retreat.

Sounds and Steps

The musical foundation of the tango is quadruple meter, strongly emphasized in the bass. Other rhythms, particularly stress on the second half of the second beat, may be superimposed on the quadruple framework. In contrast to the quadruple framework and rhythmic variations in the instrumental parts, the physical motions of the dance usually stretch across two of these four-beat units, resulting in a pattern that is counted out as slow-slow-quick-quick-slow (2+ 2 +1 +1 +2).

The strong quadruple beat is often embellished in the instrumental accom-paniment with a long-short rhythmic pattern, consisting of a long beat fol-lowed by one that is half its duration. This pattern is sometimes termed the "*habanera* rhythm," after the Cuban rhythm from which it was derived.

The tango is a circular dance that moves counterclockwise. Needless to say, tango dancer must have command of "floor craft" to avoid collisions with a partner or with other couples on the dance floor.

Within the parameters of this rhythmic pattern and circular motion, the tango includes a number of standard motions, called "steps" or "figures." Many of these steps have become part of the tango (and broader ballroom dance) oral tra-dition. These include the basic starting stance called the "promenade position," and other common moves such as the "swivel," a sliding turn on one foot.

Some steps, including the "fan," in which the female partner is swung out to one side by the male, are also used in Latin dances such as the chachachá and rumba. It is important to realize that steps with the same names may be inter-preted differently depending on the dance and context, and can vary even with different tango styles. The names of some movements have been the same for a long time. For instance, the following passage from a 1914 dance manual describes a classic tango step sequence called the "Single Cortez":

Two common tango steps: the swivel (left) and the back corté (right).

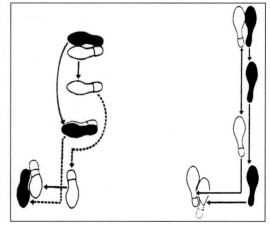

> The man starts backward with his left foot and the lady for-ward with her right. The man steps and counts as follows: One, backward on the left; two, backward with the right and "brush" [a short, quick motion with the toe]; three, forward on the right; four, bend. Repeat four times. The reverse of the above for the lady . . . After completing the Single Cortez as described above, take eight walking steps, the man backward and the lady forward.[30]

La Cumparsita (tango)

Date of composition: 1917

Composer: Gerardo Matos Rodríguez

Date of recording: Early 1930s

Performers: Orquesta Típica Francisco Canaro; Francisco Canaro, *director; two bandoneones, two violins, piano, bass*

Form: *Tango-romanza,* which can be either instrumental or vocal

Tempo: Moderate quadruple meter, with characteristic tango rhythms

Mode: Minor

Function: Classic orchestral tango, performed for dancers and for listeners

WHAT TO LISTEN FOR:

- Classic *orquesta típica,* a type of ensemble popular until the 1940s
- Strong and regular rhythm meant to accompany dancing
- Modified verse/refrain form

STRUCTURE		DESCRIPTION
0:00	Section A (refrain)	The *bandoneón* plays short *staccato* notes on each of the four beats of the measure. This staccato pattern recurs throughout the piece. In the second half of this first section, the *bandoneón* plays ascending and descending *arpeggios.*

During its early years around the turn of the twentieth century, tango music was an instrumental form to accompany the dance, played by ensembles consisting of a piano, violin, and *bandoneón.* This "*orquesta típica*" soon became larger, eventually including up to four *bandoneones;* a string section with violins, a cello, and a double bass; and a piano.[31] In Listening Guide 62, we hear a recording of the classic tango *La Cumparsita,* recorded by an *orquesta típica* in the early 1930s. Gerardo Hernán Matos Rodríguez composed *La Cumparsita* ("The Little Carnival Procession") in 1917 as a march in duple meter. Soon thereafter, Roberto Firpo arranged the piece as a tango in quadruple meter with the characteristic long/short rhythms. The form of *La Cumparsita* is an early example of the *tango-romanza,* with two alternating main sections (A and B). A third section, which appears once at 1:33, is reminiscent of an earlier three-part tango form.

Around 1910, the tango is said to have moved "from the feet to the mouth," and tango music now was sung.[32] The poetry that circulated during

0:30	Section B	A melodramatic contrasting theme is played by violins, with the *bandoneón* continuing its elaborate ornamentation. This theme is repeated. One of the violins jumps to a very high register, where its vibrato can be heard clearly.
1:02	Section A	The *bandoneón* plays a melody that includes a special effect produced by repeatedly and rapidly striking a single key. Trills can also be heard. The supporting harmonies are the same as in the first section.
1:33	Section C	This section features a motive similar to the beginning of section B, but the whole orchestra plays it homophonically with breaks near the ends of each phrase. In the second half of this section, a polyphonic texture returns, and an unusual scratchy sound can be heard in the bass, produced by striking the strings with a percussive bow technique.
2:05	Section A	A violin comes to the fore, playing at the very bottom of its range. The *bandoneón* plays ascending and descending accompaniments.
2:37	recording ends	

the early years of the tango was melancholy and depressing, reflecting the difficult socioeconomic conditions from which the tango emerged. Unlike the instrumental form of the dance, which maintains a constant tempo, the sung tango is more irregular, slowing down and speeding up for dramatic purposes. In Listening Guide 63 (see page 336), we hear one of the best-known examples of the tango song; this is a vocal performance of *La Cumparsita,* recorded in 1924, when Pascual Contursi and Enrique Pedro Maroni added lyrics to the famous orchestral tango heard in Listening Guide 62.

The song is performed by the singer most responsible for the internationalization of the tango, Carlos Gardel (1887–1935). In this recording, we hear the standard tango ensemble accompanying Gardel, including a prominent *bandoneón* and violin. The singer slows down and speeds up to express the meaning of the words.

The form of *La Cumparsita* is traditional—an instrumental introduction, a simple statement of the main melody (A), a contrasting theme/verse (B), and

Carlos Gardel sings over NBC radio in 1934.

the return of the main melody as a refrain, dramatized and embellished (A'). Note that when the main theme returns, a solo violin plays a separate melody, termed a *countermelody*. The underlying rhythmic pulse, in typical tango fashion, emphasizes the second half of the second beat in the four-beat measure.

The lyrics of the song express "views of love and life in highly pessimistic, fatalistic, and often pathologically dramatic terms."[33] The words seem to contradict the male's domination of the female that is implied by the dance.

Gardel is an integral part of the tango legend. The son of an immigrant Frenchwoman, Gardel grew up in Buenos Aires and became a famous singer, the embodiment of all the dreams and aspirations of the Argentinian lower class. After World War I, Gardel was a major force in popularizing the tango in Paris as well as in Argentina through nightclub performances at home and abroad, and also through the new electronic media, including recordings, radio, and film.[34]

Settings

The early home of the tango was the cafés and bordellos of the slums of Buenos Aires. Tango lyrics drew on the *lunfardo,* a lower-class dialect of Buenos Aires.[35] The settings were early tango songs were performed are described in melancholy texts such as *Cafetín de Buenos Aires,* by E. S. Discépolo.[36]

> How could I forget you in this lament,
> café of Buenos Aires,
> if you are the only part of my life
> which reminds me of my mother?
> In your miraculous mixture
> of know-it-alls and suicides,
> I learned philosophy, dice, and gambling
> and the cruel poetry
> of no longer thinking of myself.

Organ grinders (*organitos*) also played tangos throughout the streets of the *arrabal*. Because of these connections to the slums of Buenos Aires, the tango was widely associated in early twentieth-century Argentina with poverty, low social class, and ill repute. Only the migration of the tango to Europe—first to Paris, and then to other cities—gave it respectability in Argentina. Through the sponsorship of Argentine beef barons, the dance debuted in elite Paris circles; its simultaneous introduction by sailors in the French port city of Marseilles insured that it became rooted in European music culture. In their histories, the tango resembles the polka, which also became popular in Paris in the mid-nineteenth century.

When the Argentine government closed the brothels in 1919, the tango slowly began to attract an elite audience in Argentina, and Buenos Aires followed Paris's lead in welcoming the tango to upper-class cabarets and theatres. By the 1930s, as it was accepted into higher social circles at home and becoming popular abroad, the tango became a symbol of Argentinean national pride.

The varied settings and the paradoxical mixture of associations with poverty, nationalism, and cosmopolitanism were sparked in part by Gardel himself. At home in Argentina he performed the tango in elegant, European attire at chic nightclubs; in his performances in Europe he dressed as a *gaucho*.[37]

The tragic death of Carlos Gardel in a plane crash in 1935 generated adoration for the musician and his music that verged on religious veneration.[38] The dates of Gardel's birth and death began to be commemorated and his portrait—in a tuxedo, bowtie, striped shirt, and hat—was widely displayed. This event marked a turning point in the tango's role in Argentine national culture.

New Sounds for the Concert Hall

As the tango assumed a greater role as Argentina's national music during the first half of the twentieth century, musicians introduced innovations that demonstrated its versatility. By the 1950s, as the popularity of the traditional tango of the 1920s and 1930s began to diminish, Astor Piazzolla created a purely instrumental "new tango," one intended not for dancing, but for the concert hall.

Piazzolla's new tango retained the sound of the traditional tango ensemble while expanding the rhythmic and harmonic complexity of the music. Thus, Piazzolla revived the early role of the tango as instrumental music and reshaped its sound to span the gulf between popular and classical music. Piazzolla popularized arrangements of tangos for large ensembles including several *bandoneones*, strings, and percussion instruments, as well as piano.

One of Piazzolla's most famous tangos is the beautiful *Adiós Nonino*, composed in 1959 in memory of his father, who died that year. The performance heard in Listening Guide 64 (see page 340) is by Piazzolla's *Quinteto Tango Nuevo*, including *bandoneón*, violin, piano, guitar, and bass.

Adiós Nonino is a substantial expansion of the traditional tango form, with more repetitions of its themes than we heard in *La Cumparsita*. *Adiós Nonino* begins with an extended introduction for solo piano introducing the main theme (A). Next, the *bandoneón* and ensemble play a rousing rendition of a lively second theme (B), followed by a restatement of the first theme played by the solo violin and ensemble. At this point, where a traditional tango would end, *Adiós Nonino* continues with a restatement of the first theme in the violin and then a restatement and development of the second theme performed by the entire ensemble. The piece concludes with a final appearance of the first theme played first by the *bandoneón* and then by the entire group.

Western classical music, particularly sonata form with its restatement and development of both themes, clearly influenced *Adiós Nonino*. Piazzolla's

LISTENING GUIDE *63*

La Cumparsita (tango song)

Date: Early 1930s
Performers: Carlos Gardel, *voice*
    bandoneón, strings, double bass, piano
Form: Modified verse/refrain form
Tempo: Moderate quadruple meter, with characteristic tango rhythms
Mode: Minor
Function: Classic vocal tango, performed for listeners live and on recordings

WHAT TO LISTEN FOR:

- Melancholy lyrics expressing a pessimistic view of life.
- Rhythmic patterns typical of the tango including *syncopation* (accentuation of beats that are normally unaccented). One archetypal tango rhythm includes an accented note on the second half of the first beat of each measure, and another has an accented note on the second half of the second beat of each measure.
- Shifting roles of voice, *bandoneón,* and strings, each of which is prominent at some points but not at others.
- Dramatic changes in tempo to play up the dramatic, theatrical qualities of the text.

	STRUCTURE AND TEXT	TRANSLATION	DESCRIPTION
0:00	**Introduction**		The *bandoneón* carries the melody during the introduction, with piano and violin emphasizing the second half of the first beat and the third beat of each measure. *Glissandi,* or slides, can be heard in the violin. All the instruments play a slow, descending line ending with a pause.
0:26	**Section A (refrain)** Si supieras que aún dentro de mi alma conservo aquel cariño que tuve para ti.	If you only knew that in my soul I still keep that affection that I had for you.	Gardel begins singing. The *bandoneón* accompanies with staccato chords on each beat. The strings punctuate the singer's phrases with countermelodies in parallel octaves.

0:41	Quien sabe si supieras que nunca te he olvidado, volviendo a tu pasado te acordarás de mí.	Who knows if you'll ever know that I've never forgotten you; if, returning to your past, you'll remember me.	
0:57	**Section B** Los amigos ya no vienen ni siquiera a visitarme, nadie quiere consolarme en mi aflicción.	My friends don't even come anymore to visit me; Nobody wants to comfort me in my grief.	Gardel moves to a slightly higher register, with a corresponding increase in intensity. In the first line of this stanza and the first line of the next stanza, the strings and *bandoneón* heighten the tension by accenting chords on beats 2 and 4.
1:13	Desde el día que te fuiste siento angustias en mi pecho, decí, percanta, ¿que has hecho de mi pobre corazón?	From the day you left I've felt anguish in my chest. I said, grieving, "What have you done to my poor heart?"	After the second and third lines of each of these stanzas, the solo violin and *bandoneón* play more intricate countermelodies.
1:31	**Section C** Al cotorro abandonado ya ni el sol de la mañana asoma por la ventana como cuando estabas vos,	To the abandoned bedroom now not even the morning sun shines through the window as it did when you were there,	The next verse begins another new section, with new musical material and a more subdued mood.
1:48	Y aquel perrito compañero que por tu ausencia no comía, al verme solo el otro día también me dejó.	And that little dog, our partner, that because of your absence would not eat, on seeing me alone the other day also left me.	The end of section C features a dramatic *ritardando,* or slowing, and a vocal *glissando* into the refrain.

2:09	**Section A (refrain)**
	Si supieras que aún dentro de
	    mi alma
	conservo aquel cariño
	que tuve para ti.
		If you only knew that in my
		    soul
		I still keep that affection
		that I had for you.
			Although the melody and text of the refrain are the same as at the beginning of the song, the tempo is much slower and the instrumentation much lighter. A violin counter-melody is prominent.

2:26	Quien sabe si supieras que nunca te he olvidado, volviendo a tu pasado te acordarás de mí.	Who knows if you'll ever know that I've never forgotten you; if, returning to your past, you'll remember me.	Another effective *ritardando* by the *bandoneón* and voice ends the song.
2:52			End of recording.

Astor Piazzolla

The life and career of the tango composer and *bandoneón* player Astor Piazzolla reflects the ways in which music and musicians have crossed boundaries. "My music is a popular chamber music that comes from the tango," he wrote. "If I do a fugue in the manner of Bach, it will always be 'tanguificated.'" Born of Italian descent in Argentina on March 11, 1921, Piazzolla moved to New York City with his parents in 1923. There he first heard the tango on 78-rpm recordings. Piazzolla's father gave him a *bandoneón* for his ninth birthday, and by age thirteen Piazzolla was already proficient enough to play for the legendary tango singer Carlos Gardel, when Gardel visited New York.

In 1939, Piazzolla returned to Argentina, giving up his accounting studies and devoting his life to music. While playing his *bandoneón* "in every cabaret in Buenos Aires," he maneuvered a meeting with the famed pianist Arthur Rubinstein, who arranged for the ambitious young musician to study with the Argentinean composer Alberto Ginastera. By the early 1940s, Piazzolla had learned to compose music in classical styles. He wrote prodigiously, eventually producing the 1953 piece (*Sinfonía*) that won him a scholarship from the French government to study in Paris. There, Piazzolla studied with the legendary teacher Nadia Boulanger, who had already taught many famous composers. In an interview with the journalist Gonzalo Saavedra during Piazzolla's last visit to Spain in 1989, Piazzolla recalled that Boulanger led him to realize that his distinctive voice as a composer was found not in the standard Western classical compositions, but in the tango. One day, after Piazzolla finally admitted to Boulanger that he played the *bandoneón*, she asked him to perform one of his tangos for her. After hearing some of his music, Boulanger "suddenly opened her eyes, took my hand and told me: 'You idiot, that's Piazzolla!'"

From that time on, Piazzolla composed in his own distinctive style, and in 1955 he returned to Argentina to found a tango ensemble. Then he developed his "new tango" that experimented with rhythm, harmony, and form. At first his new tango was not well received, and Buenos Aires radio stations refused to play his music. By 1960, however, along with his Quinteto Nuevo Tango ensemble, Piazzolla became the leading performer and composer of a new type of tango—the "listening tango." Piazzolla eventually received many honors in his native Buenos Aires, where he was named a Distinguished Citizen of the City. He toured internationally and released many recordings before his death in 1992.

In addition to his skill as a composer, Astor Piazzolla was a virtuoso *bandoneón* player who had an active performing career with his ensemble Quinteto Tango Nuevo.

Classic tango collections rereleased on CD include performances by (top row, left to right) Carlos Gardel; Ricardo Tanturi, Alberto Castillo, and Enrique Campos; Trollo and Roberto Goyeneche; (bottom row) Juan D' Arienzo; Tita Merello; Astor Piazzolla and Gary Burton.

orchestration is also quite complex, passing the melodies from piano to violin to *bandoneón* and back, and using colorful instrumental techniques such as *glissandos.* Piazzolla's first and second themes contrast with and complement each other; the first theme is lyrical, and the second has a distinctive rhythm. *Habanera* rhythms can be heard in the background throughout the work, setting off the lively harmonies drawn from twentieth-century Western classical music and Latin jazz.

Following World War I, well before Piazzolla's "new tango," European classical composers such as Igor Stravinsky had incorporated the tango into their compositions. But then Carlos Gardel transformed the tango into a truly popular form, and by the middle of the twentieth century it had spread beyond Europe through Asia to Japan, as well as throughout North America. The worldwide financial depression of the 1930s and World War II made the tango's pessimistic and despairing themes relevant to the period.

During the second half of the century, the tango began to appeal to a new audience and became part of the rapidly growing middle-class ballroom culture. Amateurs learned the dance and practiced to recordings. As the tango spread, three distinct dance styles developed: the Argentine style; the International style, originally developed in France and Great Britain; and the American style. The styles are differentiated by their postures; the Argentinian tango is performed in a close embrace, with contact in the upper torso. Ballroom tango divides into the International style and the American style, neither using the close embrace. The

The worldwide spread of the tango extends to Japan, where the tango has long been popular in social and competitive circles.

Adiós Nonino (new tango)

Date of composition: 1959
Composer: Astor Piazzolla
Date of performance: 1984
Performers: *Quinteto Tango Nuevo*
    Astor Piazzolla, *bandoneón*
    violin, low strings, piano, guitar, bass
Form: Double three-part (ternary) structure: two sections, each ABA, with introduction and coda
Tempo: Sometimes slow with liberal *rubato,* sometimes energetic and faster
Mode: Mainly minor, but theme A begins in major
Function: Performed in concert hall, combining aspects of traditional tango dance music, Western concert music, and jazz

WHAT TO LISTEN FOR:

- Instrumentation similar to the traditional tango *La Cumparsita,* but using an expanded harmonic language that draws on jazz.
- A formal structure that expands on the verse-refrain form found in the traditional tango.
- Dramatic *rubato* like that heard in the traditional tango.

	STRUCTURE	DESCRIPTION
0:00	**Introduction** piano solo	The pianist uses chords and techniques commonly heard in jazz piano music, giving the impression of an improvisation, but does not present any thematic material (that is, melodies that will be revisited later in the piece). An arpeggio and scale lead directly into the exposition of the first theme.
1:36	**Main (First) Section** piano solo, theme A	Theme A, a melodious, songlike tune that begins in the major mode, is presented with simple accompaniment but with dramatic, expressive *rubato* and occasional trills. The

International style is simpler than the Argentinian tango, and is highly choreographed for competitions. The American style is a social dance, although it is used for competitions as well. Riding the revival of ballroom dancing and increasing interest in Latin American dances beginning in the 1970s, the tango became an increasingly popular focus of dance clubs and competitions. In the

		pianist builds tension by expanding his range and increasing volume as he cadences, leading into the next section.
2:47	*bandoneón* and ensemble, theme B	Theme B, with its assertive dissonance and distinctive rhythm, contrasts with theme A. It is presented by the *bandoneón*, accompanied by the ensemble. The violin answers the *bandoneón*'s phrases with *glissandi*, or slides. The violin takes over the melody.
3:33	violin and ensemble, theme A	The violin returns to theme A with a sentimentality characteristic of the tango. At 4:07, the accompaniment changes and the syncopated tango rhythm returns, with an accent on the second half of the first beat. The cadence at the end of this section includes an extended trill, at 4:26.
4:34	**Extension (Second) Section**	The violin ascends an octave to present the theme in its upper register. From 5:05 to 5:15, a homophonic texture predominates.
5:15	*bandoneón* and ensemble, theme B	The guitar plays theme B with the *bandoneón* and violin. The ensemble develops the theme and modulates several times, at 5:30, 5:44, and 5:58, each time raising the key by one semitone. This section contains many *glissandi*. A special, scratchy-sounding bass technique, also heard in the *orquesta típica* performance of *La Cumparsita,* is used beginning at 5:59.
6:22	*bandoneón* and ensemble, theme A	The *bandoneón* presents theme A, coming full circle by recalling the simplicity of the first (solo piano) presentation of the theme. In the accompaniment, the string bass plays *glissandi* and the piano and guitar play a countermelody. The tempo starts slow and gradually gets slower.
7:28	**Coda** ensemble, theme A	(Literally, "tail," a closing section) As the violin and *bandoneón* improvise on theme A, the piano and bass accompany with an energetic tango rhythm, with an accent on the second half of the second beat. The tempo gradually slows as the piece ends, with the violin and the piano moving to progressively higher registers.
8:40	recording ends	

1990s, ballroom clubs proliferated in urban areas and on college campuses, many of them training teams to compete in different styles and competition networks. Throughout the second half of the century, the tango also appeared in Broadway musical numbers such as *Hernando's Hideaway* from *The Pajama Game,* in 1990s touring shows such as *Forever Tango,* and in films.

The dancers Carolina Zokalski and Diego Di Falco star in *Tango Magic,* aired in 1999 on public television stations.

Significance

The significance of the tango, given its roots in the Buenos Aires slums and its heavy sexual overtones, remains in dispute in Argentina. The lore of the tango has had a long life, and twenty-first-century students of the tango are still told tales of its roots as a dance of "lust and anger." These themes of open sexuality and male dominance are embedded in the choreography of the dance, based on the mannerisms and style of the Argentinean *compadrito* in late-nineteenth-century Buenos Aires—a skilled fighter, bully, dandy, and hero. The body language of the tango—especially the aggressive posture of male over his female partner—incorporates and perpetuates notions of masculine dominance.

As the tango spread from Argentina to Europe and beyond, it was considered to be exotic and was exploited as a commodity in what has been called "the economy of passion."[39] Others explain exoticism as a market-driven phenomenon by which Western culture appropriates other cultures and then profits from exploiting them. In Argentina, the tango has played a central role that moves beyond issues of gender and sexuality, evolving from a comment on poverty and class resistance into a symbol of Argentinean national pride.

Today, the tango holds great significance for its many aficionados who are enthralled with the grace and rhythm of the dance itself, in whatever version they have learned it. Whether in Argentina, Germany, or Japan, they belong to tango clubs that sponsor frequent *milongas,* social and dance events named after an Argentine dance that was a predecessor of the tango. They participate in tango teas. They become involved in the tango lifestyle and the tango world, which provides everything from a social network to tango videos and recordings, and even proper tango shoes. For tango devotees, whether dancers or spectators, the tango holds great significance and appeal as an intricate art of sensual, physical expression. They enjoy the sound of the music and the challenge of coordinating dramatic bodily movement to its fluid rhythms.

Conclusion

Our case studies of *bhangra,* the polka, and the tango provide three examples of dances whose histories both overlap and diverge. All three dances have long and complicated histories, mixing indigenous elements from their home environments with aspects of other soundscapes. *Bhangra* and the polka migrated with their communities of origin, becoming new and broader practices in diaspora. The tango did not travel through mass migration, but, like the other two dances, flowed through channels of technology and travel. All three dance styles have played a role in politics as well as in the artistic marketplace.

Receptive to innovations in their sounds and settings, all three dances have taken on new meanings. They have all proven adaptable, moving from restricted ethnic or local settings into the lives of middle-class dance amateurs and professionals around the world.

All three dances have marked gender and sexual associations, and each dance acts out clear gender hierarchies. For the first time since our discussions of the voice in Chapter 1, the body takes center stage as the main instrument. It is used very differently in *bhangra,* polka, and tango.

Scholars of dance have suggested that children first experience a sense of power through their control of their own bodies. Memories of these early perceptions, it has been proposed, provide "potent, dramatic, and easy-to-recall sources of images that influence their responses to dance as participant or observer. Using the signature key of sexuality, essential for survival and desirable for pleasure, dance resonates universal instincts and particular concerns. The medium is part of the dance message."[40]

This chapter has added the world of physical motion to our repertory; actually, music is rarely played or experienced without some sort of movement. The worldwide popularity of dance must be due in part to the power of its rhythms as they become part of our bodily memories and help shape music's participation in our everyday lives. In the next chapter, we will continue our exploration of music as lived experience through a close look at the role of music in contexts of worship and belief.

What dances do you know? How did you learn them? Do you know any special terms associated with these dances? Are they associated with one style of music or one song, or are they more versatile?

Are you aware of any dances that have become popular recently?

Many communities have centers where dances from many traditions are taught. What dance resources can you locate in your area? Is there one dance style that dominates in your community?

IMPORTANT TERMS

accordion	*dhol*	new tango
bandoneón	figures	polka
bellows-shaking	*giddha*	polka-step
bhangra	glissando	sonata form
compadrito	*habanera*	syncopation
conjunto	jukebox	tango
countermelody	*kathak*	
development	*milonga*	

Chapter 8

Music and Ritual

Dating to the fourteenth century, this Tibetan mandala shows the deity Buddhakapala, "Skullcup of the Buddha," embracing his consort and assuming the dancer's pose over the body of a corpse (at center). He presides over the twenty-five deities who appear on the concentric petals of an open lotus and guard the mandala's four gates. This mandala was once part of a set illustrating teachings transmitted by Indian and Tibetan masters, who are represented at the top and bottom borders of the painting and by the four figures encircled by scrolling vines just beyond the mandala's circle.

Overview

Main Points

Music serves in ritual settings to:

- shape and order the rituals that celebrate belief;

- enact and convey ritual's symbolic power and meaning;

- empower the participants.

Introduction

Throughout history, the public celebration of belief has provided an important setting for music. It is scarcely possible to imagine religious rituals without music, which has long shaped ritual form and marked off ritual time. Through

Much of the power of rituals rests with our ability to bracket time in special ways, for example, by donning elaborate vestments or using substances such as wine or incense. Here, an Elvis Presley impersonator sings as part of a ceremony marking the renewal of a couple's marriage vows at Graceland Chapel, Las Vegas, Nevada.

song, instrumental music, and dance, rituals deeply impress our senses and signify communication with deities.

We usually think of rituals in connection with religious practice, and that is the sense in which they are discussed in this chapter. But it must be understood that rituals extend well beyond the boundaries of religious belief. Many of their formal characteristics—an established sequence of events, participants with clearly defined roles, and features including special dress, sound, and movement— can also be found in secular settings such as parades, sporting events, concerts, and operas.

In popular usage, we find the words *ritual, sacred service, liturgy,* and *liturgical order* used interchangeably to refer to public acts of worship. All such terms refer to formal events that are performed in specific contexts at particular times. The parts of rituals typically occur in a set order and serve to connect the individual to a broader community.

Whatever their specific textual and musical content, rituals share a common structure. Most rituals—especially those marking life-cycle events, such as initiations and funerals—incorporate a symbolic process or an actual change of state that consists of three stages: separation, transition, and incorporation.[1] For example, a wedding ceremony is a rite of passage that separates the bride and groom from their single status, takes them through a brief transition, and finally incorporates them into the society of married couples.

Music, sometimes alternating with periods of silence, provides clear markers of the stages in a rite of passage. The jazz funeral in Chapter 5 provides a good example, with the slow hymn played during the procession to the cemetery to mark separation, a break in music during interment, and a celebratory piece on the return marking incorporation.

Rites of passage also can incorporate several layers of meaning. For instance, wedding ceremonies mark the official union of a couple or of two families, but in the context of royal lineages, they symbolize new national and political alliances. Rituals transcend the moment at hand to speak at once to the past and the future. Here we can recall the Syrian Jewish *bar mitzvah* ceremony discussed in Chapter 5, which not only marked a thirteen-year-old boy's official passage from childhood to adulthood, but also honored his ancestors, especially his grandfather, and celebrated the future of the community through the dedication of a new *Torah* scroll. These multiple layers of meaning are almost always marked in rituals through texts, music, and related bodily movements.

Building on the view of ritual as a process, we see that ritual guides participants through time in special ways, bringing about the perception of an important experience shared with others.[2] The power of a ritual to achieve its goal and to be truly efficacious often rests directly on the impact of its performance. This is especially the case when religious rituals are performed in archaic or esoteric languages little understood by most of their participants, like the Catholic Mass, which was until recently performed in Latin. In these cases, music and movement are crucial to expressing what cannot be conveyed through words. Moreover, music's role in the ritual process is vital to producing a sense of transcendence, a feeling that the moment has special significance that extends beyond the limits of everyday experience.

The ability of ritual to evoke a strong emotional and physical response is shaped through different means in different cultures. Ritual participants in some soundscapes experience transcendence through strong drum rhythms and dance; an example is the *Santería* tradition discussed later. Others find meaning and move into an altered state through more subdued performances, as in the case of Tibetan Buddhist chant. There is no single musical pathway to transcendence; in some traditions, decorum and quiet trigger transcendence, while in others heightened sound and movement have the same effect. The ritual process can also have very different outcomes, ranging from perception of a personal connection with a deity to a feeling of moving beyond the self to merge with a broader community—a sensation that anthropologists have termed "communitas." The experience of an altered state of consciousness is an important part of the ritual process in many cultures and is sometimes referred to as "trance." The use of music to achieve a state of "trance" or "deep listening," is a culturally conditioned response to certain sights, smells, and sounds that leads an individual to feel that he or she is in contact with a spiritual realm and/or is endowed with special physical or mental powers.[3] There are many forms of trance cross-culturally; within religious settings it can be used to communicate with deities or other spirits, to enlighten, and to heal.

Although rituals are performed in a manner that emphasizes their separateness from daily life, their content and significance are much more closely tied to secular concerns than we might imagine. We will take a close look at rituals with prominent musical content that are currently celebrated within three distinct religious systems. Religious pluralism is common today in many localities worldwide as an outgrowth of large-scale migration and other forms of cultural mobility enabled by new technologies and travel. Recent research in world religions indicates that the increase in multireligious environments has resulted in changes within denominations and exchanges between them. For example, Buddhist communities that originated in Cambodia, Thailand,

The *stupa* on the roof of the Buddhist Church of San Francisco contains relics of the Buddha; it was presented in 1935 as a gift from Thailand to the Jodo Shinshu Buddhist Mission of America.

China, Japan, Korea, and Tibet have migrated and have given rise to communities of "new Buddhists" in many locales, joining with individuals of other ethnic, racial, and religious backgrounds who have "come to Buddhism through its meditation practices and ethics." In the United States, for instance, one finds the Buddhist Sangha Council of Southern California, the Buddhist Council of the Midwest, and the Texas Buddhist Association, examples of a new "ecumenical Buddhism."[4] In this chapter, we will explore three contrasting religious traditions from far-flung homelands that are active today in diaspora settings. We will explore the different ways music has served to sustain belief and accommodate strong forces of change.

The Centrality of Chant

There is no better place to begin our discussion of music and ritual than with the quintessential musical form associated with rituals of belief—chant, also called plainchant or plainsong. Chant is a type of vocal expression in which clarity and the precise articulation of the sacred words are of utmost importance. We encountered an example of Western Christian chant in Chapter 1, Listening Guide 15.

CASE STUDY: Tibetan Buddhist Chant

Chant may sound simple, but its musical surface can mask extraordinary depths of meaning. Tibetan Buddhist chant provides an example of such complex significance; Buddhists believe that performing chant moves the singer through the ritual process to a transformed state. Once again we encounter, as we did with *khoomii* singing in the Introduction, a distinctive vocal style that generates a deep, fundamental pitch that produces audible harmonics. It has been suggested that Tibetan monks may have learned this technique through contact with Inner Asian *khoomii* singers.

Buddhism entered Tibet over the course of many centuries, during which four Buddhist sects became established there. We will hear a chant sung by

Buddhist monks of the Gyuto monastery (one of the Gelugpa sect, from which the Dalai Lama is chosen), an institution that was founded in Tibet during the fifteenth century.

The Buddhist chant in Listening Guide 65 (see page 350) is an excerpt from a ritual meditation text (called a *sadhana*) that evokes the sacred and helps the monk visualize and unite with the deity. It is believed that the act of chanting—which includes recitation of a *mantra* (a ritual phrase or formula), prayers, and vocables—shapes this transcendent experience by connecting sound, breathing, and mind. The quality of the chant should, in the words of an early Tibetan Buddhist musical treatise, "be 'pleasant to hear' (*snyn-pa*), with sweetness, a relaxed character and clarity of enunciation."[5]

Monks of the Gyuto Tantric University pose for a photograph by Mono Lake, California.

This chant is part of a ceremony dedicated to the deity Mahakala, a wrathful force worshipped as a protector. We hear a brief excerpt from a long, elaborate ritual comprised of sustained sections of chant (*dbyangs*) accompanied by cymbals, drums, and horns. The instrumental ensemble accompanying the chant is known as the *rol mo* (pronounced "ro-mo") (see Listening Guide 65).

The melody of the chant is organized around simple melodic patterns, which can be difficult to hear even in a full-length ceremony because they vary in length. Some are short, others stretched out over long periods of time to declaim a combination of vocables and sacred texts.

In Listening Guide 65, the biphonic vocal style of the monks includes a low fundamental in the bass as well as a harmonic high above it. This type of biphonic singing is sometimes called "the Tantra voice" (referring to its use in rituals associated with Tantric belief and philosophy) or, more colloquially, "the *mdzo* voice," said to take its name from a cross between a yak and a cow.[6] The higher sound is actually two harmonics, the fifth and the tenth, which combine to form the impression of one overtone sounding two octaves and a third above the fundamental.[7]

The fundamental, which hovers around the pitch C, slowly rises and falls throughout the *Mahakala* ritual, moving gradually up to C-sharp and down to B, characteristic of this Tibetan chant style. Following about eleven minutes of chant accompanied by cymbals and drum (only the end is heard here), additional drums, horns, and a bell play an instrumental interlude, after which the monks begin a new chant.

Melody for *Mahakala* (Tibetan chant, excerpt)

**CD 3
Track 6**

Date: 1996
Performers: Gyuto monks of the Gyuto Tantric College, Dalhousie, Himachal
Pradash, India
Form: Alternating instrumental and vocal sections
Tempo: Varies
Function: Chant for a ceremony dedicated to the deity Mahakala

WHAT TO LISTEN FOR:

- A deep fundamental pitch that hovers around the pitch C, slowly rises one half-step to C-sharp, and then gradually sinks to B
- Soft but audible harmonics above the fundamental tone
- The afterbeats following each cymbal beat, with subtle differences in each; note louder afterbeats at transition prior to instrumental interlude at 1:08

DESCRIPTION

0:00   Voices, drum, cymbals, chant on mantra "Om" accompanied by two cymbal beats with afterbeats; drum beat following first cymbal beat; chant melody ascends the ornamented interval of a third at end of phrase 1.

0:11   Phrase 1 repeated. Afterbeats begin more loudly on first cymbal beat and increase in speed; slower on second beat; chant melody ascends at end of phrase.

While most interest in Tibetan Buddhist chant has focused on its singing style and its function as a pathway to ensure transcendence, here we will consider the rhythmic organization of the chant. An ethnomusicological study of the *rol mo* repertory has shown that it contains a complex mathematical organization of rhythmic structures, demarked by the cymbal beats. The cymbal motions (the ways in which rims of the instruments are rubbed together as well as the direction of this motion) and sounds during the *Mahakala* ritual symbolically represent the form of the *mandala,* a diagram used in Buddhism and Hinduism to map various levels of reality, from the cosmic to the personal.[8]

These rhythmic complexities require training and experience to perform and perceive; the novice listener can focus on the end of each phrase or verse of the chant text, marked by a melodic cadence or short pause for breath

0:18   Vocal phrase 2 on single pitch without cymbal and drum. Break at 0:24.

0:24   Vocal phrase begins, sustaining single pitch.

0:25   Cymbals and drum reenter; chant sustains single pitch. Cymbals play 6 beats, speeding up on beats 3, 4, 5, with slight pause before beat 6.

0:36   Voices sustain single pitch, with slight ascent at end of phrase.

0:43   Voices take breath and sustain single pitch, with slight ascent at end of phrase.

0:54   Voices take breath and sustain single pitch.

0:57   Cymbals and drum return, overlapping chant. Afterbeats increase in speed and dynamic level, then diminish. Cymbals play 6 beats, with elaborate afterbeats on beat 6, continuing as accompaniment to trumpet.

1:05   Voices drop out.

1:08   *Rol mo* interlude. A pair of trumpets (*rag-dung*) can be heard playing two pitches, approximately a fifth apart. The entire ensemble plays; trumpet repeats a two-pitch pattern eight times, with slight variations on patterns 4 and 8, followed by brief silence.

1:39   The trumpets and frame drum stop playing, leaving only the cymbals, playing five cymbal beats with afterbeats; fade out.

1:50   Fade out and end of recording at 2:04.

followed by a series of cymbal beats that begin slowly and increase in speed. From the Tibetan perspective, a beat (*brdung*, pronounced "dung") is not a single sounding of the cymbal, but is composed of accelerating, unequal pulses, generated by the manner in which the instrumentalist brings together and then moves the rims of the cymbals against each other. That is, each beat, or sometimes, a grouping of two or more beats (sometimes up to 180-beat groups), includes what are termed "afterbeats," counted as part of the preceding beat. The afterbeats are usually shorter and softer than the preceding main beat; at times, especially at the end of a rhythmic pattern, the afterbeats may begin softly, grow louder, and then grow soft again. These rhythmic properties of Tibetan chant, found in the playing of the cymbals as well as in the larger structure of entire rituals, do not correspond to the Western definition of beat

as a single pulse, nor does their broader organization fit comfortably within any of the categories of rhythmic systems we have encountered to this point. The rhythms of Tibetan chant are not metered, cyclical, or regular. They can best be described as free rhythmic patterns that expand the notion of the beat. They stretch and contract time in a novel and flexible manner, following broader mathematical proportions that are meaningful within Buddhist belief.[9]

Although Buddhist chant was traditionally performed only in religious settings in its Tibetan homeland, since the 1959 exile of monks from Tibet to India, chant has occasionally been presented in public performance.

In 1986, the monks of the Gyuto Tantric choir visited the United States for the first time, presented concerts, and released a recording authorized by the Dalai Lama. It is noteworthy that despite changing performance settings, the Gyuto monks continue to sing in a traditional vocal style. They also want their chant to be heard as sacred sound whenever and wherever it is performed. A note on their recording states that the chanting heard there is prayer, not performance, and that each time the recording is played its prayers are "effectively said anew."

Tibetan chant is adaptable to different settings. It can be performed by one singer or by a group, and it can be part of private prayer or a public ritual. The chant has also been performed in recent years to gain political and financial support for Tibetans in exile. In 1991, the Gyuto monks returned to the United States and performed widely. As a result, Tibetan chant has won an increased following and is now associated with the cause of Tibetan independence. The sound of Tibetan chant and the Gyuto monks' distinctive type of harmonic singing has become well known internationally, and many outside the tradition listen to and buy recordings. Tibetan chant is so familiar to a broad cross-section of North Americans that it has been used in a range of popular contexts, including car commercials on television.

Monk Tenam Lama accepts a 2004 Grammy Award in the best traditional world music category for the album *Sacred Tibetan Chant: The Monks of Sherab Ling Monastery.* Sherab Ling is the seat of Tai Situ Rinpoche, a monk of the Karma Kagyu sect, which has a monastery in the Indian Himalayas.

The Changing Contexts of Ritual Performance

CASE STUDY: *Santería*

Tibetan chant is not the only ritual music to move from a religious setting to public performance and to acquire new meanings in the last century. Another notable example is the music of *Santería,* an Afro-Cuban religion derived from the Yoruba cult, incorporating southwestern Nigerian language and practices that were transplanted to the Caribbean and combined with aspects of Catholicism. In Cuba, large numbers of Africans were imported in a final wave of slavery in the mid-nineteenth century to work in sugar plantations, "revitalizing, replenishing, and influencing the religious knowledge of the existing slave population."[10]

Although conditions varied from one sugar plantation to another, slaves in Cuba created social institutions that perpetuated and transformed the traditions they had brought with them. Most important were the *cabildos,* organizations established by various linguistic and cultural groups as mutual aid societies and centers for entertainment. These societies, in which slaves were at first allowed to worship their gods and perform their music, were increasingly regulated by the Cuban government over time and banned by law in 1888. However, many individuals continued to practice these traditions in secret, assuring the transmission of the Lucumi cult, the name by which Yoruba beliefs came to be known in Cuba.

Members of the Lucumi cult and similar traditions from other regions of West Africa worshipped African deities combined with Catholic saints called *orishas* or *santos.* The union of each *orisha* with a specific Catholic saint meant that these rituals were easily hidden. *Santería orishas* are diverse in their natures, origins and personality traits; each is associated with particular herbs and plants, and with his or her own chants, drum rhythms, and dance movements. At the center of *Santería* religious practice is the performance of music, drumming, and dance as part of complex rituals that seek to achieve divination and trance. (See **"Sound Sources: Sacred Drums."**)

The goal of *Santería* worship is to establish a relationship with the *orishas,* to consult them, and to offer them animal sacrifices in hopes of obtaining their help with the problems of daily life. The worshipers of the *orishas* came to be called *santeros,* and their religious practice became known as *Santería.*

Felipe García Villamil, a master drummer, instrument maker, and *santero* (practitioner of *Santería*), who arrived in the United States from Cuba in 1980, teaches *batá* drumming to his son Miguel and another drummer. Villamil has received a National Heritage Award from the National Endowment for the Arts.

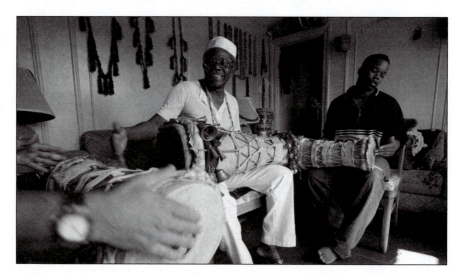

S O U N D *Sources*

Sacred Drums

In this chapter, we encounter two types of sacred drums: the *batá* drums of *Santería*, which are played in sets of three instruments of different sizes, and the *kebaro* of the Ethiopian Christian church, which can be played alone or together with similar drums.

These *batá* drums are strung with laces, unlike most modern sets, which have metal tuning fasteners.

Both the *batá* drums and the *kebaro* have a drumhead at each end. The shape of the *batá* drum resembles an irregular hourglass, with a larger drumhead ("the mouth") and a smaller head ("the butt"). *Batá* drums are considered to be owned by the *orisha* Changó, and their shape is said to represent Changó's thunder axe. The *batá* ensemble is made up of three drums. A large drum, called *iyá*, is decorated with brass bells strung around the heads. It is the lowest-pitched drum, and it leads with the most complex rhythms. The middle drum, the *itótele*, plays in regular conversation with the *iyá*. The smallest drum, the *okónkolo*, performs mainly ostinatos.[11]

The oval-shaped Ethiopian *kebaro* is held so that the large head, or "voice," can be played with the right hand, while the smaller head, called "rapper" or "knocker," is assigned to the left. The larger heads of both the *kebaro* and the *batá* drums have deeper, more penetrating sounds than the smaller. The heads of the *batá* drums are connected by tension chords that control the pitch, which is carefully tuned within each ensemble; the *kebaro* heads, secured by laces, are untuned.

The *kebaro*, associated with the music of Saint Yared (discussed later), is typically covered with brightly colored, flowered cloth under the lacings. The *kebaro* accompanies the final, jubilant repetitions of the chants that accompany liturgical dance and plays fixed rhythmic patterns. The large *kebaro* is used only within the church; a smaller version is used for secular music and dance.

Ethiopian churches patronized in the past by the aristocracy often had *kebaro* covered in silver. Here is the drum played by musicians at one of the rock churches in Lalibela, a town named after the emperor who is said to have built the churches there during the twelfth century.

At the end of the 1950s and during the 1960s, following the Cuban revolution, a number of *santeros* fled Cuba and entered the United States. Many settled in New York City. As they established *Santería* there, individuals from other ethnic and religious communities began to adopt the religion and to split into different groups or *Santería* "houses."

Within the rituals of *Santería*, *batá* drums summon the *orishas*. Only people initiated as a *santero* or *santera* are possessed or "mounted" by *orishas*. Possession is regarded as dangerous for those who are not "spiritually developed," including novices and children. If an uninitiated or inexperienced individual shows signs of possession, such as frenzied motions or a catatonic state or seizure, they are immediately taken out of the room where the drums are playing.[12]

In addition to the drums, chanting is an important part of the *Santería* rituals. The chants, sung with or without instrumental accompaniment, are almost always performed in call-and-response style. Like the drum rhythms, a chant is identified with a particular *orisha*; some chants are secret and may be performed only at ceremonies reserved for initiates. Chants differ in their content and function; some criticize or even joke with the *orisha*. Singers of chant are valued not for the beauty of their voices, but for their ability to be heard over the drums, their capacity to engage listeners, their success in engendering *communitas,* and their power to communicate with the divinities—"to bring the *orishas* down."

As the *Santería* belief system was adopted by a diverse community in diaspora, some of its Catholic practices were abandoned, and heightened emphasis was placed on the African aspects of the rituals. But the greatest impact on musical content resulted from new performance settings, as some practitioners opened traditionally secret rituals to the public. One scholar who has studied *Santería* in New York City tells how he handled the issue of secrecy:

> As a researcher, I did not aggressively pursue ritual information that was beyond what I had the right to know at any given time. To have done so would have compromised, if not violated, the relations of trust and reciprocity that bind practitioners together in ritual kinship groups. . . . For example, there were many occasions when my questions about the meaning of a ritual practice or belief would be greeted with the response, "That's something you shouldn't know yet, you're not ready to understand that." On another occasion, a *santera* whom I had interviewed the day before telephoned me that her *orisha* had told her through divination that I should not include the interview in my dissertation.[13]

The transmission of the *Santería* music tradition through public performances has been documented in the activities of the New York-based ensemble Eyá Aránla.[14] Headed by Milton Cardona, a professional drummer of Puerto

Rican descent, the group performed *Santería* music—by request—for various organizations in New York City, including the Public Theater and the Museum of Modern Art. The ensemble also participated in international festivals and eventually made the recording *Bembé*, from which the musical example in Listening Guide 66 (see page 358) is taken.

Cardona is the only professional musician in Eyá Aránla; the other members are drawn from a variety of ethnic and religious backgrounds in the *Santería* community. The ensemble does not rehearse, according to Cardona's notes for the recording: instead, its members "just make believe you went to a Bembé [traditional *Santería* celebration] and you're singing, and it works."

The percussion parts are performed by a trio of *batá* drums. The rhythmic patterns played by the three drums interlock, producing a "conversation" with the *orisha*. In Listening Guide 66, we also hear the rattling of brass bells attached to the drums. What results is a complex polyrhythmic texture in which the drums and bells play different rhythms simultaneously, accompanying the call-and-response of the vocal chant.

The selection in Listening Guide 66 is based on a *Santería* rhythmic pattern called *toque*, from the Spanish verb meaning "to touch" or "to play an instrument." The *Santería* liturgy includes many *toques*, each associated with a different *orisha*. In this example, the rhythmic call of the *toque* addresses the *Santería orisha* named Changó, who represents virility, strength, sexuality, and thunder.

The chant, sung by a soloist and chorus in call-and-response style, implores Changó to descend, in order to join the congregation, and to mount one of the musicians or dancers so that the individual will be possessed by the deity. A more detailed translation of this text is not available. Chant texts, transmitted mainly by oral tradition, have been particularly vulnerable to change outside Cuba, especially when performed by singers who are unfamiliar with their complex mix of Yoruba, other African dialects, Spanish words, and vocables.

Santería provides a rich example of the use of drumming, dancing, and chant to achieve transcendence and attain trance. It also shows how music with liturgical roots can be adapted and taken outside the boundaries of religious practice. The music retains its significance to *Santería* practitioners, who, in performance and recordings, seek to translate the music tradition for interested outsiders.

Santería has over the course of its history been the target of intolerance and persecution, in part because many *santeros* were active as healers and herbalists. Some outsiders regarded these practices as sorcery or witchcraft. Beginning in the early twentieth century, under Cuban governmental pressure for modernization, many *cabildos* were raided, religious paraphernalia confiscated, and practitioners arrested.[15]

Changó (*toque* from a *Santería* service)

CD 3
Track 7

Date: 1986
Performers: Milton Cardona and his ensemble, Eyá Aránla
Form: Call-and-response
Tempo: Moderate quadruple meter overlaid with complex layers of drum rhythms
Function: *Toque* to call out the *orisha* Changó at a Santería Bembé

WHAT TO LISTEN FOR:

- Three *batá* drums: the large *iyá*, the "mother" drum with its brass bells, the mid-sized *itótele*, and the small *okónkolo*. In this recording, the resonant *iyá* and the *okónkolo* are heard on one channel (or speaker), while the *itótele* is heard on other channel. Play the recording several times, focusing on one drum each time.
- Call-and-response formulas in which the group repeats what the leader sings. Note that the group knows the melodies beforehand, and that their rendition differs slightly from what the leader sings.
- The text of the chant, transcribed according to sung pronunciation.

STRUCTURE AND TEXT

Section A

0:00	**Call:** e oba lube, oba lube oba e, oba lube, oba lube oba e, oba e, oba yana yana	The first call is without accompaniment until the last words. The *batá* drums enter: the first few strokes are on the small *okónkolo*. A quadruple meter is established, with the *itótele* marking every beat.
0:14	**Response:** oba lube, oba lube oba e, oba lube, oba lube oba e, oba e, oba yana yana	The two heads of the *iyá* can be heard, the larger, deeper head on beat one of each four-beat pattern, and the smaller head in a syncopated pattern just before the second and fourth beats. The rattle, called *atchere*, also keeps the beat.
0:26	**Call:** e oba lube, oba lube oba e, oba lube, oba lube oba e, oba e, oba yana yana	
0:38	**Response:** oba lube, oba lube oba e, oba lube, oba lube oba e, oba e, oba yana yana	At around 0:42, the *iyá* and the *itótele* break their regular pattern.

Section B

0:49	**Call:** e, oba i sere, chango iworo, oba i sere chango iworo	The *iyá* soon returns to the established pattern, while the *itótele* switches to a less regular rhythm. The *okónkolo*, meanwhile, provides a faster pattern; it often plays two-stroke groups with the second stroke on a beat and the first stroke just before it. Changó's name is invoked.
0:56	**Response:** oba i sere, chango iworo, oba i sere	
1:01	**Call:** e, chango iworo	
1:04	**Response:** oba i sere, chango iworo, oba i sere	

Section C

1:09　**Call:** e, kawo e, alado, kawo e, alufina, kawo e, kavie sile o

1:17　**Response:** kawo e, kawo e, kawo e, kavio sile o

1:23　**Call:** e, kawo e, alado, kawo e, ala afrika, kawo e, kavie sile o

The text refers to Africa.

1:31　**Response:** kawo e, kawo e, kawo e, kavio sile o

Section D

1:38　**Call:** e, selemina in yode, selemina in yode

1:42　**Response:** selemina in yode, selemina in yode

1:46　**Call:** chango, selemina in yode, selemina in yode

Changó's name is invoked.

1:50　**Response:** selemina in yode, selemina in yode

Section E

1:53　**Call:** e, alagada ni w' oba, orisa lewa o, alagada ni w' oba, orisa lewa o

2:00　**Response:** alagada ni w' oba, orisa lewa o, alagada ni w' oba, orisa lewa o

2:06　**Call:** chango, alagada ni w' oba, baba orisa lewa o, alagada ni w' oba, orisa lewa o

The *itótele* breaks its pattern here, playing several quicker strokes in succession.

2:14　**Response:** alagada ni w'oba, orisa lewa o, alagada ni w' oba, orisa lewa o

The *iyá* responds to this change.

2:20　**Call:** chango, alagada ni w' oba, baba orisa lewa o, alagada ni w' oba, orisa lewa o

As the dialogue between *itótele* and the *iyá* grows in complexity, the *okónkolo* also breaks its pattern, playing triplet (three equal pitch) patterns and other rhythms with increased intensity.

2:28　**Response:** alagada ni w'oba, orisa lewa o, alagada ni w' oba, orisa lewa o

Section F

2:35　**Call:** lewa e lewa o
　　　Response: a, o se lewa
　　　[repeated several times]

As the chant is repeated by the singers, the dialogue between the *batá* drums continues to develop. Each drum comes to the fore in its turn.

2:55　

Ululation (high-pitched trill) by women

3:06　**Section G**
　　　Instrumental

The *toque* changes substantially, shifting to a new (but related) "conversation." This change is termed a *viro* or *vuelta* ("turn"). The *itótele* plays a three-note pattern (*ostinato*) which repeats throughout. The *okónkolo* joins in with a short-long pattern like a gallop, which evolves into a rapidly repeating short-short-short triplet pattern. Meanwhile, the *iyá* joins in, playing a pattern of two low notes followed by one high note and then a rest.

Fade out at 3:30; recording ends at 3:38

Cardona believes that his public performance of *Santería:*

> helps the religion 'cause there's so many negative things written about it . . . this is what happens at a Bembé [religious feast], behind closed doors, so they [the public] can see that this is a religion and that it can't be that bad. We have a feast, people are enjoying themselves, singing and dancing . . . and the chants are beautiful.[16]

CASE STUDY: Ethiopian Christian Chant

Another rich chant tradition that has spread around the world since the 1970s is the ritual music of the Ethiopian Christian Orthodox Church. One of the oldest Christian denominations, the Ethiopian Orthodox Church was founded in the Horn of Africa in the early fourth century (see "**Looking Back: The Ethiopian Orthodox Christian Church**").

Although the Ethiopian Church always maintained close relations with the Coptic Church of Egypt, even having a Coptic Patriarch, the Ethiopian Christian sacred language (Ge'ez, pronounced "GUHZ-uhz"), liturgy, and music tradition grew out of its own creativity in a unique cultural context. From its beginning the church stood at the center not just of Ethiopian religious life but also of its political and cultural life; the emperor also headed the church.

The overthrow of Haile Selassie, the last Ethiopian emperor, during a revolution that began in 1974, diminished the status of the church. The subsequent years of civil unrest, drought, and famine forced millions to leave Ethiopia and the surrounding region. As a result of these natural and manmade disasters, Ethiopians established diaspora communities in far-flung locales, including Italy, Sweden, and Israel. North America also became one of the largest and fastest-growing locations for Ethiopians abroad.

Ethiopian Christian chant in the diaspora provides a rich case study of the surprisingly flexible relationship between music and worship. Of particular interest are the changes that have taken place within this music tradition over the last quarter century. Although Ethiopian chant continues to be associated with the rituals expressing Christian belief and is regarded by the community as intrinsically meaningful, some centuries-old practices and associations have shifted as a result of political and economic pressures.

Many of the changes in music and worship over the course of Ethiopian history have been shaped by events outside the religious domain, especially by tensions

Ethiopia's location in the rugged plateau of the Horn of Africa protected it from invaders and helped preserve its independence, except during a sixteenth-century invasion from the south and the Italian occupation of 1935–1941. The region along Ethiopia's Red Sea coast, Eritrea, became an independent country in 1992 following a long civil war.

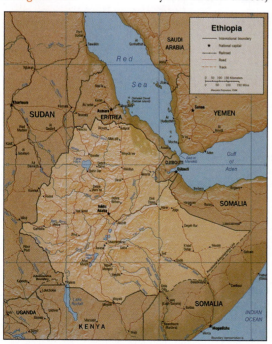

The Ethiopian Orthodox Christian Church

Entry and expansion of Ethiopian Christianity

332 CE	Entry of Christianity to Ethiopia with the conversion of King Ezana.
Late 400s–500s	Syrian missionaries arrive in Ethiopia and establish monasteries.
600s–700s	Consolidation of Ethiopian Christian liturgy by St. Yared.
Before 1200	Churches carved from stone at Lalibela.
1270	Founding of "Solomonic dynasty" of Ethiopian emperors.
Early 1300s	Establishment of Bethlehem monastery to train church musicians.
1434–1468	Consolidation of church and expansion of empire under Emperor Zara Ya 'qob.

Political crises and musical innovation

1529–1541	Muslim invasion of Ethiopia and destruction of churches and monasteries.
1540–1559	Abba Gera and Abba Ragu'el introduce the *melekket* (notational signs).
1635	Gondar becomes Ethiopian capital and site of literary and musical activity.
1800s	Innovation in Ethiopian dance and instrumental traditions.

Colonialism, occupation, and revolution

1887	Addis Ababa becomes Ethiopian capital.
1890	Italy establishes colony in Eritrea.
1930	Haile Selassie crowned emperor of Ethiopia after more than a decade as Regent Ras Tafari.
1935–1941	Italian occupation of Ethiopia.
1950	First native-born Ethiopian patriarch (head of the church) appointed.
1952	Federation of Ethiopia and Eritrea.

A church divided

1974	Beginning of Ethiopian revolution.
1987	Holy Cross Square in Addis Ababa renamed Revolution Square.
1992	Abuna Paulos installed as patriarch of Ethiopian Orthodox Church; Ethiopian Orthodox Church in America declares independence from mother church in Ethiopia. Eritrean independence and separation of the Eritrean Orthodox Church.

between ritual practice and everyday life. However, ritual provides a context in which old symbols can be given new meanings and into which new symbols can be incorporated. Such is the case with Ethiopian Christian chant, which has brought longtime practices and values into the present while providing a creative setting for innovation and new meanings.

Ethiopian Chant in Its Historical Homeland

To understand musical changes in the Ethiopian diaspora, we must be familiar with the heritage of the Ethiopian Church's proud past. The creation of Ethiopian Christian chant, called *zema* (pronounced "ZEH-mah," literally "a pleasing sound," "a song," or "a melody"), is attributed to Saint Yared (pronounced "YAH-rehd"), a holy man said to have lived in the sixth century, working under divine inspiration, composing the chants and organizing them into service books.

This icon portrays the transcendent qualities of Ethiopian chant. Saint Yared (right) performs chant before the Ethiopian emperor Gabra Masqal and is so transported by the singing and dancing that he does not notice the emperor's spear, which has accidentally pierced his foot.

Although the texts of the Ethiopian liturgy were written down in the Ge'ez language in parchment manuscripts, church musicians learned and transmitted the chant through oral tradition. When Muslim forces from the south invaded Ethiopia in the sixteenth century, two musicians of that time, Gera and Ragu'el, invented a system of musical notation to help transmit liturgy and music amid the destruction (see page 364, **"Studying Music: Systems of Music Writing"**).

In Western church history the Mass is the Christian ritual with the most elaborate musical content, but in the Ethiopian tradition the Mass is chanted simply, without accompaniment, by an ordained priest rather than a trained musician. The main setting for elaborate chant performance in the Ethiopian church is the ritual called the Hymnary, performed before the Mass on Sundays and festivals. The musicians, traditionally men, were obligated by church law to learn the nearly two dozen types of chants in the Ethiopian Christian Hymnary. The lengthy and demanding education of these musicians is described in "**Individual Portraits:** *Liga* **Berhanu Makonnen, Ethiopian Church Musician**" (see page 368).

Sound

Ethiopian chants fall into three categories of melody (or *mode*) named *Ge'ez* (the same name as that of the sacred language), *Araray* (pronounced "AH-rah-ra-ee") and *'Ezl* (pronounced "UH-zuhl"). The legend of Saint Yared ascribes associations to each mode: *Ge'ez* is linked to God the Father, *Araray* symbolizes the Son, and *'Ezl* represents the Holy Spirit. The *Ge'ez* mode is used in chanting the Hymnary and is not associated with a particular occasion, the *Araray* mode is used for daily morning services, and the *'Ezl* mode is used mainly for Holy Week and Easter.

The Ethiopian Christmas chant in Listening Guide 67 (see page 366) is one of a group of chants in the *Ge'ez* mode named *engergari* (pronounced "AHN-guh-gah-ree," literally, "excitement"). Called *Yome fesseha kone* (pronounced "YO-muh FESS-suh-hah KON-nuh") after the opening words of its text, it is always sung as part of the ritual for Christmas, because it refers explicitly to the birth of Christ. *Liga* Berhanu Makonnen sang this solo version, in a style called *qum zema* (pronounced "KOOM zeh-mah," "plainchant"), during an interview.

Because the rhythm of the chant follows that of the text, the words may be clearly heard. At the phrase where the text describes the Wise Men bowing before the baby Jesus, the melody descends by the interval of an octave, symbolizing their deep bow. This chant is set in the *Ge'ez* mode, which can be confirmed by its frequent and distinctive vocal slides, called *rekrek* (pronounced "RUCK-ruck"). Like most Ethiopian melodies, this chant emphasizes a pitch known in secular Ethiopian musical terminology as the "returning tone," repeated at phrase endings and cadences. The Ethiopian notation for chant *Yome fesseha kone* is given in the figure on page 365 and is "translated" into Western staff notation in a figure on page 370.

The performance of *Yome fesseha kone* during Ethiopian Christmas rituals is more elaborate than the solo version heard in Listening Guide 67. In the liturgical setting, the chant is preceded by the singing of *hallelujah* and is performed by two *dabtaras* singing in alternation, called *antiphonal style*.

This Ethiopian Christmas chant can help us understand how differently pitch is perceived in different cultures. As we said, each notational sign (a

STUDYING *Music*

Systems of Music Writing

Ethnomusicologists often use Western musical notation to write down or transcribe the oral traditions they hear so they can study and analyze them. Many systems of music writing developed outside the West, including two that belong to soundscapes encountered in this chapter.

The system for notating the Tibetan *dbyangs* is found in songbooks termed *dbyangs-yig* (literally, "written account of the song"), or *yang-yig* (see illustration below). Tibetan chant, written from left to right in two or three horizontal lines, indicates the name of the song, its author, the meaning of the song, and introductory drum beats. Directions for performance style are sometimes indicated, in one case instructing the singer that a song should "be chanted like the sound of the wind." The text syllables are placed below the notational curves. Black and red ink are used to differentiate between text syllables and instructions for their performance.

The notational system used in the Ethiopian church, developed in the late sixteenth century, contains several types of signs. The most important and largest number of signs are the *melekket* (literally "signs," pronounced "MILL-uh-kit"), some six hundred and fifty in all, each consisting of one or more characters from the Ge'ez alphabet, which is actually a syllabary; each symbol combines a conso-

The Tibetan notation shown here has been annotated to help readers. The numbers in circles indicate where each song begins and ends; dotted rings (or ellipses) are placed around syllables in Tibetan to differentiate them from vocables, which extend the sound of the main syllable.

melekket) represents a short melody; several melodies are linked together to constitute a phrase of the chant. Thus the melody represented by each *melekket* is the smallest musical unit transmitted by Ethiopian church musicians. Although it is possible to transcribe Ethiopian chant in Western musical notation (as we see in the figure on page 370) and to describe it in the same

nant and a vowel. Placed between the lines of the prayer texts, each *melekket* is an abbreviation of the word or phrase that represents a specific short melody. The *melekket* are themselves divided into three categories, each of three sets of signs representing the melodies of a single mode.

An additional dozen signs consisting of dots, dashes, and curved lines regulate aspects of rhythm, pace, and vocal style. They tell the singer when to slow down or when to cut off the tone abruptly at the end of a phrase. These signs must be combined with the *melekket,* a challenging task that takes years of practice. Performing a chant from Ethiopian notation is possible only for a musician who already knows the music from oral tradition.

Ethiopian notation for the Christmas chant *Yome fesseha kone,* discussed in Listening Guide 67. The manuscript reads from left to right, and the chant notation begins about two-thirds of the way across on the top line. A small character that looks like eyeglasses marks the start of the chant text. The *melekket* (signs) are found between the lines of text. Above the third line in the manuscript, a double line of *melekket* begins, indicating that the words from that point ("He is Jesus" in the English translation) to the end should be repeated with a different melody. This repeat is not always taken, however, and the singer in our recording does not perform it.

way we do Western melodies, Ethiopian *dabtaras* do not hear or conceive a chant melody as consisting of a series of individual pitches. Rather, an Ethiopian church musician learns an entire chant by hearing it in a service and practices it by repeating short phrases, each represented by a notational sign, in sequence after his teacher.

Yome fesseha kone ("There Is Joy Today," Ethiopian Christmas chant)

CD 3
Track 8

Date: Recorded in an interview, 1975
Performer: *Liga* Berhanu Makonnen
Form: *Angergari* (literally, "excitement") prayer for Christmas morning
Function: Required chant in Christmas Hymnary ritual
Musical Setting: *Ge'ez* mode
Tempo: Moderate

WHAT TO LISTEN FOR:

- Christmas chant sung solo as *qum zema* (plainchant) during an interview
- Vocal slides (*rekrek*), which are heard only in the *Ge'ez* mode
- Note how the chant is divided into short phrases, with phrase endings and the final cadence emphasized through a repeated pitch.

STRUCTURE AND TEXT	TRANSLATION	DESCRIPTION
0:00 *Yome fesseha kone*	There is joy today	The opening words of this chant are so indelibly associated with its melody that the first notational symbol for this melody is called *yome*.

Ideally, a musician memorizes an entire chant. According to *Liga* Berhanu:

> The student puts his book far from the teacher and the teacher must sing without looking. If he looks he is a weak teacher. Everything must be taught orally by the teacher—he should know it by heart and so should the student. They should have it all by memory.

However, should the student forget, he can consult a notated manuscript. Therefore, Ethiopian chant is conceived, learned, performed, and heard by Ethiopian musicians in a manner different from that of most outsiders, especially Westerners who conceive of melody as a sequence of individual pitches.

In churches in Ethiopia, when a large number of *dabtaras* are present, a chant is sung additional times following an antiphonal performance. It is

0:08	*be-ente ledetu lekristosse*	because the birth of Christ	
0:14	*emqeddeste dengele*	from the Holy Virgin	A vocal slide (*rekrek*) occurs on the word *dengele.*
0:19	*We-etu iyyesuse krestose*	He is Jesus the Christ	
0:27	*zelottu*	before whom	
0:31	*seb-e segele*	the Magi	
0:35	*segedu lottu*	prostrated themselves.	The melody descends to portray the Magi's low bow. Another *rekrek* occurs on the syllable *lo.*
0:41	*Emane*	Truly	
0:43	*menkere sebhete ledetu*	the glory of his birth is wonderful.	
0:51	Recording ends.		

accompanied by each musician waving his prayer staff rhythmically while chanting, and then is sung again accompanied by the sounding of the *sistra,* small idiophones shaken in patterns of three, four, five, or more beats. The drums (*kebaro*) accompany subsequent repetitions of the chant, playing their own rhythmic patterns overlapping polyphonically with the *sistra*. As the pace of the drumming increases, the *dabtaras* put down their prayer staffs and *sistra* and begin to dance, in a distinctive formation described by *Liga* Berhanu:

> Rows of twenty-four men each face each other—this is the optimum number, but you can have six, or even three, in each line. It is called the twenty-four priests of heaven. Twenty-four, in one line, walk forward, and the others walk backward. They take four steps forward and four steps backward. On each side there is one man with a *kebaro*. It is necessary to drum and dance—or it would not be a holiday.

Liga Berhanu Makonnen, Ethiopian Church Musician

Berhanu Makonnen recalls his career:

I studied for thirty-one years, beginning when I was ten years old in Gojjam Province. Next I went for twelve years to the Bethlehem Monastery at Debra Tabor, where the government supported my studies. After I got my diploma, they asked me to stay there and teach, but after two-and-one-half years, I wanted to go home to Gojjam. Later, after more studies to become a priest and to specialize in all areas of chant and instruments, I came south to Addis Ababa, where I became the Vice-Administrator in charge of music in all the churches. I have taught more than 100 students and the head of music at the Bethlehem Monastery today was my student as well.[17]

Liga Berhanu Makonnen (wearing cape) stands at the center of a group of *dabtaras,* many of whom hold prayer staffs and liturgical umbrellas. In front of the group sits the *kebaro,* the church drum.

The personal experience of *Liga* ("chief" or "learned man") Berhanu Makonnen tells us about the life and education of an Ethiopian church musician, the *dabtara* (pronounced "deb-TARE-uh"). Among the most highly educated musicians in the world, *dabtaras* must undertake years of study beginning in early childhood and then enter a series of chant schools (literally, a "*zema* house"), to master chant melodies, the notational system (*melekket*), instruments, and liturgical dance.

Like most *dabtaras, Liga* Berhanu came from a family of church musicians and priests. "My father and grandfather were leaders of the *dabtaras,*" *Liga* Berhanu reminisced. "I am the third generation. Usually our family becomes priests, but I am more specialized." *Liga* Berhanu is proud of his vocal skill and extraordinary liturgical knowledge: "When there is a holiday and I join the singing, everyone is surprised because my voice is so experienced. I know many chants and no one's voice can dominate me," he adds.

During their student years, *dabtaras* sometimes work as merchants, particularly in the butter trade, to support themselves and their families. Because of their reading and writing skills in a country where only a minority of the population is literate, some *dabtaras* write special scrolls on parchment that are used by Ethiopians to heal the sick. The scrolls can be hung on the wall or carried rolled up in leather pouches. The healing powers of the *dabtara* are so respected that they are patronized beyond the Christian community by peoples of other religions who believe in the *dabtara*'s ability to protect them against spirits and devils thought to cause illness and misfortune.

As we will hear in Listening Guide 67, Berhanu Makonnen sings in the vocal style of the Bethlehem monastery, the most prominent of several distinct styles of liturgical singing named after important monasteries in northern Ethiopia. Vocal style provides a clue to a *dabtara*'s background and social status, as we learn in a story transmitted by *dabtaras* about three sons. One was the son of the king, the second the son of an aristocrat, and the third the son of a poor man. The son of the king sang in the Bethlehem style, but the son of the aristocrat and the poor man sang in two other regional styles.

The overthrow of the Ethiopian monarchy and the church's loss of prestige have reduced the power of the Bethlehem monastery: "It is said that Saint Yared sang in the Bethlehem style. But there is not as much honor today to teach there as there was in the past," *Liqa* Berhanu commented.

With the nationalization of church land and revenues in 1975 during the Ethiopian revolution, the position of the clergy lost much of its appeal and more *dabtaras* sought employment outside the Church. One leading *dabtara* noted that "Now they are ready to work everywhere the government asks," suggesting that the future of these musical specialists and healers will be very different from their past.

An Ethiopian magic scroll (*asmat*) is usually cut to the height of the person for whom it is made. Each scroll is decorated with motifs, drawings, and sections of prayers and incantations written in Ge'ez, the Ethiopian liturgical language. This detail from an early twentieth-century scroll shows checkered patterns and faces; the full faces usually represent the king of demons, whereas the seven pairs of half-hidden faces depict either demons or angels.

This transcription of the Ethiopian Christmas chant melody, performed in Listening Guide 67 translates the traditional Ethiopian notation into Western staff notation. Notational signs (*melekket*) placed above words in the Ethiopian manuscripts are represented by alphanumeric formulas. For example, the number representing the first *melekket*, G259, indicates that it is the two hundred fifty-ninth sign in a comprehensive list of Ge'ez *melekket*. The transcription shows the location of the notational signs (*melekket*) above the words in Ethiopian manuscripts. The short phrases sung in Listening Guide 67 are the musical equivalent of one, two, or three notational signs; the chant is transmitted and learned in these short textual/melodic segments.

In Listening Guide 68 (see page 372), you can hear these different performance styles in an excerpt from the Christmas liturgy performed by a large group of *dabtaras* in a church in Addis Ababa. The example begins with chant accompanied by *sistra*, followed by the entry of the drum, later joined by clapping and ululation, the high piercing cries of joy vocalized by women in the congregation. The recording captures the growing sense of excitement conveyed by the music, drumming, and dancing which will culminate in a burst of activity at double speed, ending abruptly in complete silence. This final, transcendent moment of silence, in which all participants experience something approaching an altered state, is not captured in the recording, but is vividly described by an Ethiopian writer:

As the lines of the *debteras* approach nearer to one another, the atmosphere becomes electrical. Then comes the climax: suddenly the sound and movement stop, with the sticks, faces and bodies of the *debteras* straining towards the sky. The whole scene is surcharged with devotion. It appears that the assembly of priests and people has been blessed by the Supreme.[18]

Ethiopian Chant in the North American Diaspora

Since the period of the revolution in the late 1970s, the Ethiopian Christian Orthodox Church has established itself outside Ethiopia, including throughout the United States. Many urban areas house several Ethiopian congregations. Most lack their own meeting spaces and depend on the generosity of other denominations to provide room on Sundays and major holidays. One exception is the Ethiopian community in Seattle, Washington, which has constructed its own church building.

Ethiopian Christian musicians dancing during a performance of the Hymnary while pounding their prayer staffs (*maqwamiya*) on the floor and playing *sistra* (*senasel*). Ethiopian liturgical dance is said to have been inspired by biblical accounts of King David and the people of Israel dancing around the Ark of the Covenant.

Challenges confront diaspora Ethiopians seeking to continue their religious and musical practice in North America. The Ethiopian community, like the Vietnamese community we encountered in Chapter 4 came here recently, beginning in the mid-1970s. Many of its members were forced migrants who arrived in the United States only after periods of imprisonment or other hardships. More than forty-six thousand immigrants from Ethiopia entered the United States between 1971 and 1994; the community grew from around three thousand prior to 1974 to a total in 1990, including Eritreans, estimated at fifty thousand to seventy-five thousand people. The community has increased rapidly since that time.

Ethiopian Americans have established community organizations and extensive social networks. Restaurants present a public face for the Ethiopian community in large cities, and the widely circulated *Ethiopian Yellow Pages* documents a community with its own accountants, attorneys, and dentists, and a group that maintains its culinary and cultural traditions by patronizing special groceries, restaurants, and stores. A large number of compact disc and video recordings, many recorded here, are sold in these shops.

Although many diaspora Ethiopians have made successful transitions to new careers in academia, the professions, and industry, the majority are struggling, working-class people who hold service jobs in hotels, parking lots, taxi companies, and similar enterprises.

Priests and *dabtaras* celebrated the final stages of construction of the Ethiopian Orthodox church of Saint Gabriel in Seattle, Washington, in 1999.

Excerpt from an Ethiopian Christian Christmas ritual

CD 3
Track 9

Date: 1965
Performers: *Dabtaras* of the Bahta Church, Addis Ababa
Function: Festive performance of the Christmas liturgy
Form: Repetition of a chant in different performance styles
Tempo: Accelerates as performing styles change, doubling the tempo at the end

WHAT TO LISTEN FOR:

- Changing performance styles, moving from chant accompanied by *sistrum* alone (this section termed *nus senasel*), *sistrum* and *kebaro* (termed *shubshubbo*), and finally *kebaro* and clapping (termed *safat*).
- Increasing intensity and sense of excitement as the chant is repeated.
- Intensity in the vocal parts that obscures the Ge'ez text of the chant, which has two main phrases, each repeated three times.

	STRUCTURE	DESCRIPTION
0:00	**Phrase a**	Unison chant accompanied by *sistra*. Each repetition of the melody is accompanied by approximately six strokes of the *sistrum*.
0:14	**Phrase a^1**	
0:29	**Phrase a^2**	
0:43	**Phrase b**	Pitch level shifts higher and melodic contour changes. Again, there are about six *sistrum* strokes per phrase.

These circumstances have made it difficult to gather the funds necessary to support Ethiopian Christian worship.

Ethiopian churches in North America also face a severe shortage of qualified clergy. There are no schools for training Ethiopian priests or musicians in North America, and since the revolution in Ethiopia, fewer clergy have been trained there as well.

The scarcity of clergy places the Ethiopian church's music traditions at risk in the diaspora, where a congregation is fortunate if it can obtain the services

0:57	**Phrase b^1**	
1:05	**Phrase b^2**	
1:21	**Phrase b (repeated twice)**	Soft beats by *kebaro* sound at 1:38, signaling its entry in the next section.
1:56	**Phrase a (repeated three times)**	*Kebaro* enters, accenting alternate beats to *sistrum*. Note increasing heterophony in vocal parts.
2:17		Women ululate.
2:37	**Phrase a (repeated twice)**	
3:11	**Phrase b**	
3:23		Two loud beats in *kebaro* signal final melodic repetition before change of performance style.
3:28	**Phrase b**	
3:40		Additional, louder *kebaro* beats begin, now doubling the *sistrum* beats.
4:11	**Phrase a**	
4:16		The *sistra* drop out before the musicians clap and dance.
4:23		Clapping and ululation accompany the dance.
4:48		Recording ends.

of a single priest who must officiate at all liturgical functions. If a priest is not available, some congregations worship with the aid of recordings imported from Ethiopia. Churches address this problem by importing musicians for important holidays such as Christmas and Easter.

Ethiopian Americans have additionally sought to bring their liturgy closer to the practice of other American Christian denominations. The unique Ethiopian Hymnary with its elaborate musical content is now performed mainly on special occasions such as annual holidays; even then, it is generally shortened.

Record stores selling music imported from Africa and recordings of African music produced in the US are found in many American cities. This shop is located in the Adams Morgan area of Washington DC, a neighborhood where many thousands of immigrants from Ethiopia, Eritrea, and other African nations now live.

Yome fesseha kone is still sung in an antiphonal style at the Christmas ritual in diaspora churches, but these performances, generally by knowledgeable congregants, lack the polish of the version we heard in Listening Guide 67. Beyond the less elaborate and faster performance of this chant, few other portions from the traditional Hymnary are sung. As the complete rituals fall into disuse, fewer chants are remembered and they are no longer perceived in the traditional way.

Sunday Mass in most Ethiopian American churches attracts a lively congregation; most of the women and a few men wear traditional Ethiopian dress. In most churches, the prayers are still sung in Ge'ez, but the sermon is in the Ethiopian language that the congregation understands. The clergy use books imported from the Ethiopian capital, Addis Ababa. Few members of the congregation own service books, but photocopied texts in English transliteration are sometimes distributed.

The Impact of Changing Settings on Liturgical Music at Home and Abroad

Church music has clearly changed among Ethiopians of the diaspora. The Hymnary is performed only on special occasions, and the Mass has gained importance. As a leader of one Ethiopian church in the United States noted, "It's easy to translate the Mass" and, in any event, "there is no one to do the music of the Hymnary."

In some diaspora churches, the Hymnary is not performed at all, except at concerts on holidays. These events can attract a sizable audience. One Christmas gathering at an Ethiopian church in New York City transformed the sacred ritual into a concert; a banner announced a performance of "Yared Music." Each chant was introduced and explained in English by a knowledgeable member of the community, who mediated between young members of the audience who do not understand Ethiopian languages and the musicians, who were flown in from Ethiopian communities around the world and who speak little or no English.

Other changes within the ritual have taken place. In pre-revolutionary Ethiopia, women did not participate in Ethiopian Christian liturgical performance other than to clap or ululate at important points in the ritual. Ethiopian women stood in a separate area of the church, separated from the male congregants, musicians, and priests.

In the early 1990s, women began to participate in diaspora Ethiopian Christian church music, and youth choirs began to sing hymns before and after Mass. We might assume that these changes, like the new emphasis on the Mass, have been shaped by the constraints of the diaspora setting. Certainly, power has shifted from the clergy to the congregation, where women play increasingly important roles. The growing popularity of Pentecostalism among Ethiopian Americans, with its emphasis on lively strophic hymns, congregational participation, and clapping, may have also encouraged these changes. Still, the presence of choirs and the participation of women actually have come from an unexpected source—changes in Ethiopia.

During the traumatic early years of the Ethiopian revolution, young people sought refuge in churches by attending Sunday school classes. Late-night church services were hindered by urban violence, political surveillance, and restrictive curfews. In contrast, the Sunday schools brought students together to study the Bible, church history, and the music of the Hymnary and the Mass. These sessions also provided a venue for solidarity and resistance to disturbing political events. As Sunday schools spread in the 1980s, youths began to organize choirs. They also composed hymns—not in Ge'ez but in the vernacular language, Amharic—and began to circulate their music on cassettes.

By the early 1990s, a new sacred musical style had emerged. A young musician remembers that not only were the texts in Amharic, but "the sound had changed." Today, in both Ethiopia and the diaspora, these new hymns are called "Sunday school songs." They differ from chant, but congregants still consider them closely related to older music traditions and feel that they honor the memory of Saint Yared.

The Sunday schools also opened a pathway for women to become active in Ethiopian Christian worship. Although women cannot be ordained priests or serve as *dabtaras,* they can now participate in liturgical performance and play the *kebaro.*

From Los Angeles to Washington, we find women participating regularly in Ethiopian Christian worship and music. Since the mid-1990s, women have stood alongside the clergy during rituals, held prayer staffs and *sistra,* and drummed the *kebaro.* Choirs of children and

Members of the Ethiopian Youth Choir sing and drum at the Festival of the True Cross (*Masqal*) at River Park in Cambridge, Massachusetts, in September 1999. Note the prominence of the Ethiopian flag.

Kasamay waradat ("He Descended from Heaven," Ethiopian Sunday School song)

CD 3
Track 10

Date: 1990s

Performers: Women's Choir, St. Mary's Ethiopian Orthodox Tewahedo Church, Los Angeles, with *kebaro* (drum). (The voice of a male deacon or congregant can be heard intermittently singing along.)

Form: Strophic hymn

Function: Ethiopian post-revolutionary congregational hymn

WHAT TO LISTEN FOR:

- Strophic structure, with internal repetition in each verse, including a brief restatement of all three melodic phrases to bring each verse to a close
- Regular *kebaro* pattern and clapping on alternate beats
- Melody, which is largely pentatonic (C-D-E-G-A) until phrase b'

	STRUCTURE AND TEXT	TRANSLATION	DESCRIPTION
	Verse 1		
0:00	**Phrases a and a'**		
	Kasamay waradat,	He descended from Heaven,	Drumming begins at
	Kadengel mareyam tawaladat,	Born from the Virgin Mary,	phrase a'.
0:09	**Repeat phrases a and a'**		Clapping begins when these phrases are repeated.

women have been founded in most churches to sing newly composed strophic hymns dedicated to the Virgin Mary. In Listening Guide 69, we hear a choir of women from St. Mary's Ethiopian Orthodox Tewahedo Church in Los Angeles singing a Sunday School song. This strophic hymn is sung in unison, accompanied by the *kebaro*, clapping, and ululation.

The new hymns, most of which commemorate the Virgin Mary, have proven very popular. Although most are still imported from Ethiopia, transmitted by oral tradition and cassette, young Ethiopians in North America are now beginning to compose their own songs.

Significance

Changes in rituals, musical content, and performance styles—as well as in church administration—have brought additional shifts in meaning within

0:16	**Phrases b and b'**		
	Endihonan beza,	So that he would be a Redeemer,	
	Endihonan beza	So that he would be a Redeemer	

0:23	**Phrase c**		
	La'alam hullu	For the whole world,	
	Labisu yamareyamin tsegga	What grace has Mary put on.	

| 0:28 | **Phrase a''** | | The restatement of phrase a is shortened and sung without text. |

| 0:32 | **Phrases b and b'** | | |

| 0:39 | **Phrase c** | | |

| | **Verse 2** | | Verse 2, and subsequent verses, |
| 0:44 | **Phrases a and a', with repeat** | | repeat text and melody of verse 1. |

| 0:52 | **Repeat phrases a and a'** | | Women ululate during the repetitioin of phrases a and a'. |

| 0:59 | **Phrases b and b'** | | |

| 1:05 | **Phrase c** | | |

| 1:11 | **Phrase a''** | | Women ululate |

| | **Phrases b and b'** | | |

| | **Phrase c** | | |

| | Fade out at 1:27; recording ends at 1:33 | | |

Ethiopian Christianity. Continuity in ritual music enables Ethiopians in diaspora to adjust to changing political and social conditions while expressing their beliefs in a familiar way. But as the Ethiopian Christian Church becomes an international ethnic church, it must be flexible enough to accommodate two different streams of tradition—one based on long-standing practices, the other making room for innovation. At the center of this dilemma is the universal search to make liturgical content and practice relevant to everyday life.

Changes in Ethiopian worship cannot be attributed to new settings alone; new musical practices and the new genre of Sunday School songs emerged in large part because of political pressures in Ethiopia. Ritual and its musical content have been reshaped by the continuing interaction of homeland and diaspora.

Earlier we learned that a sixteenth-century invasion of Ethiopia spurred the development of a system for writing sacred music; in the late twentieth

Ethiopian women have brought their traditional music to a broader audience. Here, Aster Aweke, a leading Ethiopian singer now living in Washington DC, performs at the Charlotte, North Carolina Jazz Festival. Aster fuses traditional Ethiopian songs and styles with American musical idioms, including rhythm and blues, jazz, and other repertories.

century, revolution and political oppression gave rise again to musical creativity. In the words of a young Ethiopian who lived through this revolutionary period in Ethiopia and today teaches and sings the Sunday School songs in the United States, the new music "was the response of youths to the politics of the regime. The reaction was for youth to join churches. They became the backbone of the church. And women now play the drum."

Sacred music remains a vital part of the life in the Ethiopian diaspora. Some of the music traditions that sustain belief have been maintained with great care and at great sacrifice; at the same time, changes in the sound and concept of performance have been accepted. Familiar chants are retained but in shortened forms and modified styles, sung by musicians new to their practice. Chant performance has also moved from ritual to concert, as secular performers adapt chants for purposes of entertainment and commemoration. Strikingly, Ethiopian chant also continues to influence music in the popular realm, inspiring musicians to draw on Ethiopian chant, psalm texts, and vocal styles as the inspiration for new compositions. The composer Mulatu Astatke has since the 1960s innovated a distinctive style called "EthioJazz," which includes songs such as one titled "Lent" with a vocal part inspired by Ethiopian Christian chant. In recent years, Mulatu Astatke's music has circulated internationally through recordings and his soundtrack for Jim Jarmusch's 2005 film *Broken Flowers*.[19]

Conclusion

Clearly, it takes care and sacrifice to maintain the music traditions that sustain belief. To keep these traditions alive, there must be an institutional structure in which musicians are trained and music can be regularly performed. In all three of our case studies—Tibetan chant, *Santería*, and Ethiopian church music–migration has prevented the establishment of secure institutional settings. Thus, although Tibetans and Ethiopians have sought to sustain ties with their past through ritual music, the meaning of that music is surprisingly vulnerable to change. Change raises questions—will new and abbreviated rituals still be able to effect transcendence? Ongoing ties to the historical homeland, whether broken, as in Cuban *Santería* and Tibetan Buddhism, or once again accessible, in Ethiopian Christianity, are an important factor in the practice of diaspora religious and music traditions.

Over time, the settings of rituals have shifted and the musical styles of chants have changed. The heirs of Saint Yared now include women as well as men; *Santería* incorporates women in ritual chanting and drumming, domains once reserved exclusively for men. Ethiopian churches in diaspora have now divided according to ethnic and linguistic communities that have long been adversaries in the homeland. The Eritrean church has also been separate since Eritrea became an independent country in 1992.

One aspect of traditional ritual performance that has been enthusiastically maintained by the *Santería* and Ethiopian communities is dance, the single area of traditional rituals in which all can participate, whatever the congregants' grasp of the liturgical language or knowledge of its musical system. Here we must acknowledge again the power of dance, in union with music and sacred text, to incorporate individuals into a larger community.

All three case studies vividly demonstrate the impact of political events on the transmission of rituals and their music. The displacement of the Cuban *santeros,* Ethiopian *dabtaras,* and Tibetan monks from their homelands in the face of political upheaval and revolution serves as a reminder of the influence of politics on all aspects of life, including music. Music and politics will be our subject in Chapter 9.

———

Which religious traditions are celebrated in your community? Try to attend a ritual of a religious tradition with which you are unfamiliar. What language(s) are used in the service and the music? Is there prominent musical content and how is this music performed? Does the congregation participate in the ritual or its musical content? Are books or other technologies used to help musicians or the congregation remember texts or music?

IMPORTANT TERMS

afterbeats	*kebaro*	*rol mo*
batá	liturgy	*sadhana*
call-and-response	Lucumi	*Santería*
Changó	*melekket*	*sistra* (sing. *sistrum*)
chant, plainchant	mode	Sunday school songs
dabtara	*orisha*	*toque*
dbyangs	*rekrek*	ululation
Ge'ez	ritual	*zema*

Chapter 9

Music and Politics

The cover art and advertising copy for the 1986 CBS reggae anthology
Rhythm Come Forward puts the focus on the power of rhythm.

Overview

Main Points

- Music is frequently used for symbolic communication in political contexts.

- Music can convey official ideologies, as in national anthems.

- Music can convey what cannot be spoken publicly, giving voice to political resistance.

Introduction

The subject of music and politics is not a new one in *Soundscapes*. We have already encountered many examples of music's link to political events, such as the historical role of bagpipes as instruments of war or songs that recall the pain of forced migration. In these instances, music provides a mode of expression for individual and collective political action.

On the level of national and international politics, music is consistently invoked in overt and deliberate ways. Music has always been an integral part of displays of political power, conveying national identity and official ideologies

African American protesters sing during a protest march for equal employment in the American south.

through symbolic acts, such as the singing of a national anthem. Here we must recognize the difference between open and coded political messages. Open musical displays of power, termed *public transcripts,* affirm and perpetuate an existing power structure. The term *hidden transcripts,* on the other hand, describes musical performances and repertories that embed messages through metaphorical or coded terms. Although hidden transcripts are often used to oppose the dominant culture of political establishment, the powerful also have hidden transcripts representing the aspects of their rule that cannot be openly acknowledged.[1] Conversely the forces of opposition can have public transcripts expressing open opposition, as in the song *We Shall Overcome,* first sung by striking African American workers during the 1940s, which twenty years later became the musical emblem of the Civil Rights movement.

Music is crucial in helping us understand how power is enforced and how it is challenged. In this chapter, we will take a close look at the genesis and significance of the new national anthem of South Africa, which combines public and hidden musical transcripts from the past that have been transformed to symbolize a new political order. We will then explore reggae, which has always had a dual life as music of protest and entertainment. Our major case study is music of the Native American powwow, in which a complicated mixture of social commentary and political resistance is embedded in aspects of music and dance within large-scale performance events. The three case studies of disparate traditions in South Africa, the Caribbean, and the United States demonstrate the manner in which music empowers people while being used and transformed in different contexts.

Musics of Power and Resistance

A song can incorporate many layers of meaning, partly because music can convey what cannot be spoken or what might not be heard in everyday speech. We have seen that music can express different channels of memory through melody, rhythm, and textual content. Because of its ability to communicate in

subtle ways, music has historically been a way to assert power and also to give voice to overlooked groups or suppressed issues. Frequently, resistance is couched in language and musical styles understood only by insiders.

Musical styles are extraordinarily flexible; they can begin within a sound-scape as an emblem of resistance, then move to broader audiences as vehicles of popular entertainment. African American hip-hop music is an example of this flexibility, since it began as a hidden transcript of urban black resistance to oppressive institutions.[2] Hip-hop has remained an important medium of political expression while becoming entertainment for a broader audience and influencing the styles of other musics. A similar process can be seen in the history of reggae music, which we will trace from its inception as a music of resistance through its move into the popular mainstream.

Some traditions contain aspects of both resistance and conciliation. We will explore these seemingly contradictory tendencies in the music of the Shoshone powwow. The powwow provides a musical transcript that both masks and reveals, at once celebrating and protesting the historical and present-day situations of Native Americans.

CASE STUDY: The Birth of a National Anthem

Music can challenge inequitable power relations. One such example is the South African song *Nkosi Sikelel' iAfrika* ("Lord, Bless Africa," pronounced "EN-koe-see see-ka-LEL ee-AF-ri-ka").

The choirmaster Enoch Mankayi Sontonga composed *Nkosi Sikelel' iAfrika* and conducted performances of the song by his choir until his premature death in 1905. On September 24, 1996, Sontonga's grave in Johannesburg, South Africa, was declared a national monument, and a memorial was unveiled on the site by President Nelson Mandela.

Nkosi Sikel' iAfrika originated little more than a century ago as a Christian hymn, was quickly transformed into a musical emblem of political resistance, and in the 1990s, became an official national anthem. Over the course of its history, this song inspired resistance against *apartheid* (literally "separation," the official laws of racial segregation enforced in South Africa until 1990) and became an international symbol of victory in the fight for racial equality.

The story of *Nkosi Sikelel' iAfrika* begins with Enoch Mankayi Sontonga (1873–1905), a choirmaster of Xhosa descent who was a teacher at a Methodist mission school near Johannesburg, South Africa.

In 1897, Sontonga composed *Nkosi Sikelel' iAfrika* as a hymn, and it was first performed at the ordination of a minister in 1899. Sontonga composed only the melody, first verse, and chorus of *Nkosi Sikelel' iAfrika*. Seven more verses were added later by the South African poet S. E. K. Mqhayi; the full English text was published in 1927. However, the text is sung in several different South African languages and is further varied by singers during performances. The first verse of the text is in Xhosa or Zulu, while the second verse is in Sesotho; there is no standard version or standard translation.

There is considerable internal repetition within the melody and rhythm of the five phrases of the song's refrain. This repetition is characteristic of indigenous South African melodies, which usually consist of short, repeated segments; melodies constructed in this manner are sometimes termed *iterative forms*. Despite its overall strophic structure, the performance occasionally includes the call-and-response common in many regions of Africa.[3]

Like other South African music, *Nkosi Sikelel' iAfrika* was also influenced by Western music and harmony introduced to the country by Western missionaries. Around the time of the hymn's composition in the 1890s, black South Africans educated by the missions founded touring choral groups that performed Western hymns, ragtime, minstrel music, and Zulu dance and wedding songs.[4] Terms derived from English for the four voice parts in Western harmony entered the South African music vocabulary: *bes* (bass), *thena* (tenor), *altha* (alto), and *fast pathi* (first part, or soprano). The primarily homophonic texture of *Nkosi Sikelel' iAfrika* in this field recording reflects this strong Western influence.

By 1912, *Nkosi Sikelel' iAfrika* was sung at meetings of the organization that would later become the African National Congress. The ANC, whose leader for much of the second half of the twentieth century was the imprisoned Nelson Mandela, led the fight against apartheid. Over the years, the song *Nkosi Sikelel' iAfrika,* like the liberation movement it symbolized, became a focus of controversy and a target of repression, banned by the South African government as subversive.

Following the official end of apartheid in the early 1990s and the 1994 election of Nelson Mandela as South Africa's first black president, the nation needed a new anthem. Since 1957, an Afrikaans song, *Die Stem van Suid Afrika* ("The Call of South Africa"), had served as the South African national anthem. Afrikaans is derived from the Dutch dialect spoken by European settlers in South Africa since the seventeenth century. The text of *Die Stem van Suid Afrika* was written as a poem by C. J. Langenhoven in 1918; the melody was composed in 1921 by Reverend M. L. de Villiers. The song was well known to the public, since it was played daily (along with *God Save the King*, as South Africa was part of

the British Commonwealth until 1961) to close South African radio broadcasts. However, *Die Stem* became the official national anthem only in 1957.[5]

After Nelson Mandela assumed the South African presidency, *The Call of South Africa* and *Nkosi Sikelel' iAfrika* were for a period of time designated dual national anthems. The use of the two songs was a first step toward reconciliation after a deeply divided history. In an official publication on the national symbols of the Republic of South Africa, Mandela described the two national anthems as "a manifestation of the desire to achieve a national consensus."[6] During this period, *Nkosi Sikelel' iAfrika* continued to be viewed as an anthem of freedom and independence throughout Africa, also becoming the official national anthem of countries such as Tanzania and Zambia.

By 1996, the use of two separate anthems had become increasingly awkward for South Africa, and with reconciliation between the races moving forward, the government approved a single, composite national anthem. The new combined song was composed by two men from Cape Town—Edmund Bourne, a teacher, and John Hendricks, a part-time traffic officer. Bourne, who holds a degree in music from the University of Cape Town, said that he had been "experimenting on the piano" one day and joined sections of the two songs. "From a musical point of view, both are incredible pieces of music," Bourne noted. Hendricks, a poet who had previously written church hymns, wrote the new lyrics in one day, emphasizing reconciliation and unity. The two men submitted the song as a proposal for a new national anthem and "were definitely taken by surprise" when it was chosen.[7]

The new South African national anthem consists of four verses in four different languages: Zulu and Sesotho in two versions of the chorus from *Nkosi Sikelel'*

Nkosi Sikelel' iAfrika (South African hymn)

**CD 3
Track 11**

Date of composition: 1897

Composer: Enoch Mankayi Sontonga, of the Mpinga clan of the Xhosa nation

Date of performance: 1984

Performers: Congregation of St. Paul's Church, Soweto

Form: Strophic hymn with verse and refrain

Mode: Western major mode

Tempo: Moderate quadruple meter

Function: Hymn; later, national anthem

WHAT TO LISTEN FOR:

- Religious text and harmony reflecting the influence of Christian missions
- Words from several South African Nguni languages: Zulu, Xhosa, and Sesotho
- Predominantly homophonic texture, with prominent use of Western harmony
- The influence of indigenous South African singing traditions, including call-and-response sections and vocal slides
- Parallel motion between the low (bass) and high (soprano) voices

STRUCTURE AND TEXT	TRANSLATION	DESCRIPTION
Zulu language		
Section A		
0:00 **Phrases a, b, and c**		Phrase a is sung by a female soloist, and the full choir responds homophonically in four-part harmony.
Nkosi, sikelel' iAfrika,	Lord, bless Africa,	
Maluphalkanyisw' uphondo lwayo;	May her spirit rise high up;	
Yizwa imithandazo yethu	Hear thou our prayers	
0:15 **Phrases d and d'**		
Nkosi sikelela,	Lord, bless us.	
Nkosi sikelela.	Lord, bless us.	
Section A (repeated)		
0:25 **Phrases a, b, and c**		The verse is repeated by the full choir. The final phrases of the verse, phrases d and d', have a slightly different text this time. The tempo speeds up.
0:40 **Phrases d and d'**		
Nkosi sikelela,	Lord, bless us,	
Thina lusapho lwayo.	Your family.	

	Section B		
0:50	**Phrases e and e'**		The women sing a call in
	Call/Response: Woza Moya	Descend, O Spirit,	unison, a descending motive
	Call/Response: Woza Moya	Descend, O Spirit,	to which the men respond
1:00	**Phrase f**		homophonically. At phrase f,
	Woza Moya, Oyingowele.	Descend, O Holy Spirit,	the men and women rejoin in
1:09	**Phrases d and d'**		a single homophonic group.
	Nkosi sikelela,	Lord, bless us,	This section ends with phrases
	Thina lusapho lwayo.	Your family.	d and d', which serve to close
			several sections of this hymn.

	Sesotho language		
	Section C		
1:20	**Phrases g and h**		The choir switches to the
	Morena boloka setjhaba sa	Lord protect our nation,	Sesotho language. Although
	heso,		the melody is similar to that
	O fedise dintwa la	And end the wars and	at the beginning, this section
	matshwenyeho.	tribulations.	has a substantially different
1:30	**Phrases g and h repeat**		structure. The tempo
			increases.

	Section D		
1:40	**Phrases i and i'**		Another call and response
	Call/response: O se boloke	Protect us, our entire nation,	section, in which the women
	Call/response: O se boloke		sing an ascending motive and
1:50	**Phrases d'' and d'**		then the full choir (including
	Setjhaba sa heso,	Our nation.	the women) responds. The
	Setjhaba sa heso,		vocal style here includes slides
			characteristic of traditional
2:01	**Section D (repeated)**		Zulu song. The final lines of
			this section are musically
			similar to the final lines of the
			first and second sections.

	Section E		
2:24	Ma kube njalo,	Let it be so,	The text here is closely related
	Ma kube njalo,		to the "lesser doxology" that
2:33	Kude kube ngunaphakade.	Forever and ever.	ends many Christian prayers.
	Kude kube ngunaphakade.		The tempo slows.
2:47	**End of recording**		

iAfrika, and Afrikaans and English from *The Call of South Africa.* Although it has been South African government policy to sing only the new, combined anthem since 1997, the new anthem has not been accepted in South Africa without controversy and protest. At a memorial service for Walter Sisulu (1912–2003), longtime leader of the African National Congress and anti-apartheid movement who was imprisoned by the government for decades, the singing of the new anthem elicited criticism at the event as well as editorial protest:

> The two anthems represent opposite and opposing ends of our history as a country and people, one good and the other bad. For them to continue to be sung together, nine years into the democratic SA, is baffling. . . . It is high time that the ANC government stopped compromising on issues that define the national identity of SA, such as the national anthem.[8]

Over the years, *Nkosi Sikelel' iAfrika* has continued to accrue multiple layers of meaning—as a Christian hymn, a song of resistance, and finally, part of a new national anthem. Beyond its role within South Africa's new political order, the song has had a second life as a worldwide anthem for racial equality and human rights.

CASE STUDY: Reggae

The fight against apartheid dominated international news about Africa in the last decades of the twentieth century. Songs such as *Nkosi Sikelel' iAfrika* became familiar to a global audience through concerts organized to free Nelson Mandela from prison. During the first half of the twentieth century, however, another African leader captured the imagination of people of color in North America and the Caribbean—Ethiopia's Ras Tafari, who became regent in 1916 and assumed the throne as Emperor Haile Selassie in 1930. Ethiopia's successful fight for independence, and the courage of its emperor when its autonomy was challenged by the Italian invasion in 1935, provided a symbol for the Rastafarian political and religious movement that became closely associated with the musical style known as reggae.

The Rastafarian movement had its philosophical roots in Marcus Garvey's "Back to Africa" movement of the 1920s, which sought to reclaim black pride through a return to Africa. In 1927, Garvey was deported from the United States and returned to his homeland, Jamaica. There he and others predicted that the crowning of a black king in Africa would presage deliverance for all black people, pointing to passages in the Book of Revelation that forecast the rise of the Lion of Judah. References comparing Biblical Israel (Judah) to a lion are found first in the Book of Genesis 49:9 and elsewhere throughout the Bible. Later, Christ is called "the Lion of Judah." The coronation of Ethiopian Regent

Ras Tafari as Haile Selassie I, the Lion of Judah, was greeted by many as a fulfillment of these prophecies. In the West Indies, new groups were formed—some called Ethiopians, others called Rastafarians—to support the new Ethiopian emperor.[9] The accession of Ras Tafari to the Ethiopian throne was thought to herald the downfall of "Babylon" (white colonial powers) and the subsequent deliverance of oppressed blacks.[10]

Rastafarianism developed powerful rituals and symbols. These new traditions, established within a short time, are a good example of what has been termed the "invention of tradition." Invented traditions are characterized by the fast pace at which they are conceived and adopted, and by their association with a network of symbols.[11] The symbols of Rastafarianism include the green, yellow, and red colors of the Ethiopian flag, dreadlock hairstyles, and the use of mind-altering substances.

At first, no single musical style was associated with Rastafarianism. Rather, several Jamaican musics, including the drumming of the Afro-Jamaican Burru and Kumina cults and rural *mento* music (a local tradition related to calypso), influenced the styles that emerged in Jamaican urban areas in the 1950s and 1960s. Musical influences from outside Jamaica, including jazz and rhythm and blues, also fed into the mix.

By the early 1960s, groups such as Toots and the Maytals were playing a predecessor of reggae called *ska*, based on an indigenous Jamaican rhythm that emphasized the off-beats in a quadruple rhythmic pattern.[12] Ska was followed in the mid-1960s by *rock steady*, characterized by a much slower tempo than ska, anchored by a drum and bass line; the texts of rock steady discussed freedom and equality.

In 1968, *reggae* came on the scene, taking its name from a song by Toots and the Maytals entitled *Do the Reggay*.[13] The lead singer of the Maytals, Frederick "Toots" Hibbert, is said to have coined the word "reggae," defining it as follows:

> Reggae just mean comin' from the people, an everyday thing, like from the ghetto. When you say reggae you mean *regular*, majority. And when you say reggae it means poverty, suffering, Rastafari, everything in the ghetto. It's music from the rebels, people who don't have what they want.[14]

Reggae singer Bob Marley performs in front of a backdrop emblazoned with the image of the Ethiopian emperor Haile Selassie.

Symbols of Rasta life and culture printed on T-shirts include the green, yellow, and red of the Ethiopian flag overlaid with images of Bob Marley, marijuana, and the Lion of Judah.

The New South African National Anthem

Date of composition: 1996

Source: composed by Edmund Bourne and John Hendricks; based on *Nkosi Sikelel' iAfrika* (1897) and *Die Stem van Suid Afrika* (*The Call of South Africa*, 1921)

Date of performance: 1998

Performers: The Kuumba Singers

Form: Combination of two strophic hymns

Tempo: Lively

WHAT TO LISTEN FOR:

- Verses sung in four different languages. The first two verses, in the indigenous languages Zulu and Sesotho, are from *Nkosi Sikelel' iAfrika.* The last two are choruses from *Die Stem van Suid Afrika,* sung in Afrikaans and English.
- Homophonic singing in the style of hymns

STRUCTURE AND TEXT	TRANSLATION	DESCRIPTION
0:00 **Section A - Zulu** **Phrases a, b, and c** Nkosi, sikelel' iAfrika, Maluphalkanyisw' uphondo lwayo; Yizwa imithandazo yethu **Phrases d and d'** Nkosi sikelela, Thina lusapho lwayo.	Lord, bless Africa, May her spirit rise high up; Hear thou our prayers Lord, bless us, Your family	The choir sings the first verse homophonically. The slow tempo and full volume give the performance a feeling of breadth and grandeur. The arrangement is similar to that heard on the field recording from Soweto in Listening Guide 70, but the harmonies vary somewhat.

Many musicians were important in developing reggae's musical and political profile, including the controversial Peter Tosh (Winston Hubert McIntosh, 1944–1987). Throughout his short life, Tosh was on the front lines protesting inequality through political action or through his performances. His most famous protest music includes the song *Get Up, Stand Up* (Listening Guide 72; see page 394) and the albums *Legalize It* (1977) and *No Nuclear War* (1987).

Rhythm is essential to the Rastafarian reggae tradition and is a metaphor for the idea of resistance in the lyrics. The reggae term *riddim* is derived from the

0:29	**Section B - Sesotho**		
	Phrases g and h		
	Morena boloka setjhaba sa heso,	Lord protect our nation,	The choir increases the tempo and decreases the volume.
	O fedise dintwa la matshwenyeho.	And end the wars and tribulations.	The rapid declamation emphasizes the syllabic text setting with few long notes.
	Phrases g and h repeat		
0:45	**Section C**		
	Phrases i and i'		
	Call/response: O se boloke	Protect us, our entire nation,	As in the version from Soweto, the women call the
	Call/response: O se boloke		ascending motive. In this
	Phrases d" and d'		version, the responses include
	Setjhaba sa heso,	Our nation,	a dramatic increase in volume
	Setjhaba sa South Afrika.	South Africa.	or crescendo. A smaller ensemble of four soloists sings a transitional phrase repeating the words "South Africa."
1:07	**Section D - Afrikaans**		
	Uit die blou van onse hemel,	Ringing out from our blue heavens,	The small ensemble sings the first phrases of the Afrikaans
	Uit die diepte van ons see,	From our deep seas breaking ground,	hymn.
	Oor ons ewige gebergtes,	Over everlasting mountains,	
	Waar die kranse antwoord gee,	where the echoing crags resound,	
1:27	**Section E - English**		
	Sounds the call to come together,		The full choir responds in English.
	And united we shall stand,		
	Let us live and strive for freedom,		
	In South Africa our land.		
1:49	recording ends		

English word "rhythm"; however, its meaning extends beyond the main beat—and beyond the emphasis on the second and fourth off-beats—to include the tempo, the relationship between the bass and rhythm instruments, and the repeating patterns they form. In contrast to most Western music, with its steady pulse, the ever-changing, syncopated rhythms of reggae and many other African-derived musics are highly symbolic. Much of the subversiveness of the Rasta subculture and its associated soundscape has been coded into its rhythms. Some *riddims* are named, such as "*cordiroy*" (corduroy), "*bangara*"

Singer-songwriter Peter Tosh performing in an undated photograph. Born in Jamaica in 1944, by age twenty-two Tosh was a rising musician in the world of ska, famous for his performances and recordings with Bob Marley and the Wailers. After leaving the group in 1973, Tosh released a number of solo albums before being murdered in 1987 at his home in Kingston, Jamaica. The first Grammy Award for best reggae album was awarded to him posthumously in March 1988.

(from *bhangra*), or "*diwali,*" named after a Hindu festival, which emerged in the late 1990s in the music of Jamaican keyboard player Steven (Lenky) Marsden. Marsden had used the rhythm for years before he started "voicing it"— that is, adding vocals over a pre-recorded rhythm track.[15]

The subversive power of reggae rhythms and the soundscape of which they are a part are captured by the advertisement for a reggae recording seen in the illustration at the beginning of this chapter.

In *Get Up, Stand Up,* we hear the rhythmic characteristics typical of reggae: a strong, regular pulse of twos and fours, crosscut by syncopated counter-rhythms. Rastafarian beliefs in the text address the political situation. Another innovative sound was the electronic organ heard in the background.

Electronic organs were first manufactured in the 1930s; technological innovations in the 1960s led to their widespread use in popular styles such as rock and reggae. This is one of a growing array of electrophones that were increasingly prominent in popular music during the last quarter of the twentieth century (see page 396, **"Sound Sources: From Synthesized Sounds to Scratching"**).

Like *Get Up, Stand Up,* many reggae lyrics connect music, dance, and political resistance. The song *Chant Down Babylon,* from Bob Marley's album *Confrontation,* invokes music ("chanting down") as a way people of color can triumph over oppression:

With music, we chant down Babylon
Music, you're the key,
Talk to who, please talk to me.
Bring the voice of the Rastaman,
Communicating to everyone

Reggae musicians have taken strong political stands through their music. Burning Spear (Winston Rodney), for instance, released songs such as *Marcus Garvey, Slavery Days,* and *Red Gold and Green.*[16] However, Tosh's partner in the Wailers, Bob Marley, since his death in 1981, is the musician most widely associated with reggae and Jamaican music all over the world.

Marley, who was born in 1945 in Jamaica and died when he was only thirty-six, came to public attention in Jamaica when his first single, *Judge Not,* was released in 1962. He gained an international following with the release of the historic 1975 album *Natty Dread*, its title referring to the dreadlocks worn by Rastafarians.

Reggae has always been transmitted throughout the world, but even after various transformations it has maintained its status as a vehicle of political resistance. In one of the most powerful testimonies to reggae's power in new political contexts, on April 18–19, 1980, Bob Marley and the Wailers were invited to celebrate Rhodesia's independence from Great Britain and the

renaming of the country as Zimbabwe. Marley's song titled *Zimbabwe,* which had inspired the Zimbabwe National Liberation Army during the struggle for independence, was scheduled to be performed immediately after the flag-raising ceremony. The performance became an occasion of protest; the start was delayed and a riot broke out when officials tried to make Marley leave the stage after a brief performance. It was reported that the entire stadium full of people sang *Zimbabwe* along with Marley.[17]

Every man gotta right
To decide his own destiny
And in this judgment
There is no partiality
So arm in arm, with arms
We will fight this little struggle
'Cause that's the only way
We can overcome our little trouble . . .
Refrain
Natty dread it in a Zimbabwe
Set it up in a Zimbabwe
Mash it up in a Zimbabwe
Africans a liberate Zimbabwe.[18]

Early reggae came to be known as "roots reggae" as new reggae styles emerged in the 1980s, including "dancehall" in 1983, with synthesizers providing beats and texts focusing more on relationships than Rastafarianism,[19]

Get Up, Stand Up (reggae)

Composer: Peter Tosh

Date of first recording: 1973, by The Wailers

Date of this recording: 1977, on Peter Tosh's album *Equal Rights*

Performers: Peter Tosh, *vocals, guitar & keyboards;* Sly Duunbar, *drums;* Earl Lindo, *keyboards;* Bunny Wailer, *background vocals;* Robbie Shakespeare, *bass;* Al Anderson, *guitar*

Form: Strophic form with refrain

Mode: Minor

Tempo: Moderate quadruple meter

WHAT TO LISTEN FOR:

- A variety of timbres produced by electric guitars, including a bullfrog-like "wah" sound. These qualities are produced by signal processors, developed in the late 1960s, that filter and transform the guitar's electric signal before it is amplified.
- An electronic organ, softly filling in harmonies in the background
- Explicit references to tenets of the Rastafarian religion, setting them in opposition to Judeo-Christian beliefs and framing them as a basis for political action

---

STRUCTURE*	DESCRIPTION
0:00 **Introduction**	The band lays down the pattern that will provide the rhythmic and harmonic framework for the entire song. The rhythm guitar plays a syncopated pattern, playing off the unaccented first beat of the four-beat pattern and accenting the second and fourth beats. The lead guitar improvises a melody that uses bent notes similar to the blue notes used in blues and jazz.
0:14 **Refrain (twice)**	Although each line begins on the first beat, syncopation predominates in the refrain. The refrain is sung staccato by a small chorus singing in parallel octaves. Note that the range of harmonies is exceedingly small; every beat in the song is based on a single chord, the minor chord built on the tonic note. The guitar with the distinctive "wah" sound can be heard after the first and third lines of the refrain.

0:43	**Verse**	The verse has an unusual rhythm. While the band maintains the regular beat, the solo singer's part (Tosh) is so syncopated that it seems almost *rubato*, sometimes ahead of the beat and sometimes behind it. This sensation of rubato is illusory, however, because the singer places his pitches quite precisely at certain points between beats. The reference to "preacher man" in the text of the verse refers to Rastafarians' rejection of traditional Christianity, which is associated with the white race and, by extension, the oppression of blacks. The second half of the verse reflects another central belief of Rastafarianism, the rejection of materialism.
1:10	**Refrain (twice)**	Tosh interjects various calls like "come on," "brothers," and "sisters" in between the lines of the choral refrain.
1:37	**Verse**	Another highly syncopated verse, as the singer continues to give the impression of spontaneous rubato. This quasi-speechlike syncopation, common in reggae, would later influence new popular music styles in the 1980s such as rap and hip-hop.
2:05	**Refrain (twice)**	More interjections are added to the refrain.
2:33	**Verse**	The line "Almighty Jah is a living man" describes another Rastafarian principle. *Jah* is the Rastafarian name for God, and the "living man" is the Ethiopian emperor Haile Selassie.
3:01	**Refrain (twice)**	
3:26	Recording ends.	

*We did not receive permission to reprint the lyrics.
Please refer to the song included on the CD.*

From Synthesized Sounds to Scratching

Reggae's use of electronic organs—and later digitally altered and remixed sounds—is an example of the prominence of synthesized sounds within many soundscapes today. The first instrument that could generate and transform sound with electricity was probably Thaddeus Cahill's "Telharmonium." Completed in 1900, it had two keyboards and produced multiple timbres. Its prohibitively high cost, unwieldy size, and high consumption of energy prevented its commercial success. More experiments in the field led to the invention of new instruments such as the theremin (an electronic instrument that produces a wide range of pitches cued by hand motions) and the Hammond organ. By the mid-1960s, however, the computer began to play an important role in the further development of electronic instruments.

The synthesizer, first marketed commercially in 1964, was used first to compose music in studios; in 1970, Moog produced the first synthesizer designed for performance.[20] The central features of the generic performance synthesizer include "electricity, the ability to combine and modify basic sonic elements, and some degree of programmability."[21]

A synthesizer has a performance interface, programming controls, and a sound engine. A performance interface allows the performer to manipulate the sound

and "ragga" or "ragamuffin," a style from the mid-1980s dominated by sounds produced or reproduced digitally.[24] Another descendent of reggae, "dub," remixes and alters recordings as a backdrop for improvised vocal solos with political texts.

As reggae entered mass culture through recordings, it led a dual life as both cult music and commercial music, similar to the music of *Santería* (Chapter 8). Reggae has also taken on new traits through its interaction with other soundscapes, and since the 1980s has joined with other styles to produce new, hybrid forms. West Indian and South Asian immigrant communities in Great Britain embraced reggae along with *bhangra,* and the resulting styles have dealt with new political issues. For example, the singer Apache Indian (Steve Kapur) has merged reggae, rap, Anglo-American pop, and *bhangra* to produce a style called "bhangramuffin." Apache Indian has also transformed reggae music and Rastafarian beliefs and traditions into a public transcript challenging older

through pitch selectors (such as a keyboard) and controllers (a joystick, foot pedal, etc.). Controls allow the synthesizer to be programmed for editing, mode selection, and program selection. These controls allow the performer to choose the types, tones, and dynamics of sound used in the performance. The engine generates sounds, either by synthesis or sampling, the use of digitally pre-recorded sounds. All the components described above share a number of practical features: an operating system, internal memory, external storage data device, a display, program selection controls, audio connections and controls and MIDI (Musical Instrument Digital Interface) connections. Synthesizers today are usually digital, although some hybrid instruments are both analog and digital. They are also programmable, use both synthesized and sampled sound sources, and have built-in audio effects units, computer editors, and keyboards.

The synthesizer has transformed all aspects of the composition and performance of pop music. Hip-hop DJs since the late 1970s have used record turntables as musical instruments, "scratching" the needle on vinyl recordings to produce short bursts of sound;[22] today a computerized DJ station can synthesize that process. A computer holds MP3 files of songs and connects via a USB port to two turntables that play special records with timecodes on them. In this way the computer knows where the needle is on the record and controls playback of the song, allowing the DJ to scratch the samples as if they were pressed on a record.[23]

notions of distinct British, Asian, and black identities.[25] Apache Indian's recordings have resonated among young Indian Canadians, who interpret his music as "a sign of respect for Indian traditions."[26]

The 1990s also saw the emergence of new kinds of locally generated reggae styles, such as a style of dance music in Puerto Rico, called *reggaeton,* which superimposes Spanish-language rap above a beat derived from dancehall reggae. "To make reggaeton, you need to know about your Puerto Rican music, salsa, and to know about rap, reggae, and the kind of art that makes a difference," said Don Omar, a well-known Puerto Rican reggaeton performer. Reggaeton lyrics deal with drugs, crime, and sex, and the style has been performed mainly by men. Associated with close, slow-grind dancing, in recent years reggaeton has spread to Miami and New York City, where it now is heard in both social and political contexts. Tego Calderon, a leading reggaeton innovator who has moved away from controversial subjects in his lyrics, says that "I've got to do reggaeton in order to make people listen to my social stuff. I'm getting them to dance, and then I'm getting them to think a little bit."[27]

Reggae is a clear example of a soundscape in which music signifies open resistance to social, racial, and economic inequities. Still, we need to be aware that the genre also has many love songs, even if the international audience has identified with its prominent themes of "resistance, repatriation, and redemption."[28] It has also been has suggested that the surface qualities of reggae have been more faithfully adopted by white musicians than its political content. In fact, the reggae-influenced compositions of musicians such as Paul Simon, Paul McCartney, and Eric Clapton, who drew on reggae during its early period, made the mainstream further aware of reggae's commercial potential.[29]

CASE STUDY: The Shoshone Powwow

All the music traditions we have explored so far have traveled far from their place of origin. The Native American music tradition, in contrast, has remained in North America. Yet Native Americans have always been dispersed widely within the continent, originally constituting separate nations (termed "First Nations" in Canada) that were forced to migrate as a result of US and Canadian expansion and policies. One traumatic migration was the removal and forced march of tens of thousands of Cherokee peoples from the eastern United States to what is now Oklahoma in December 1838. Troops under orders from President Andrew Jackson patrolled the march, during which thousands died. Here we will take a close look at the music of the Native American powwow as practiced by Shoshone people of the Wind River Reservation in Wyoming, and the powerful role this music plays in Shoshone political life.

Voluntary and forced migrations have indelibly marked Shoshone history. The Shoshone originally lived in the Great Basin, a desert region of the western United States lying mostly in Nevada but extending into California, Oregon, Idaho, and Utah. One group migrated to the Plains in the 1500s and split into two groups: those who remained on the northern Plains,

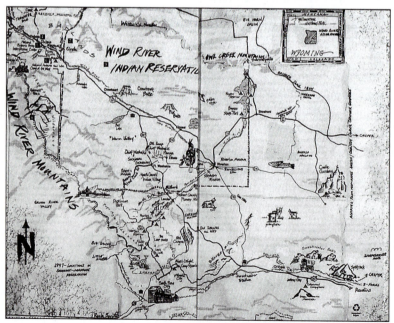

Important sites on the Shoshone Wind River Reservation in central Wyoming.

known as the Eastern or Wind River Shoshone, and those who moved to the southern Plains, today centered in Oklahoma, known as the Comanche.

A group of Northern Shoshone settled in Idaho, while the Western Shoshone remained in their ancestral homeland of the Great Basin. The Eastern Shoshone today live on the Wind River Reservation in central Wyoming on lands formally deeded to them by the American government in 1868. The Shoshone chief Washakie, who negotiated the 1868 treaty, chose to establish the reservation in a region known to the Shoshone as Eu-ar-eye, which means "warm valley."[30]

Although the Shoshone have been classified as people of the Great Basin, present-day Shoshone have been influenced by the Plains Indian horse and buffalo culture of which they were a part for centuries. By the early twentieth century, all the Plains peoples, including the Shoshone, were forced to abandon their traditional pattern of hunting by the pressures of United States expansion and urbanization (see page 400, **"Looking Back: The Shoshone People in American History"**). For Shoshone living on the reservation, life was one of discrimination and poverty, the latter only partially mitigated by income from the mineral and gas deposits found on their lands.

Many changes have taken place in Shoshone society over time. Women developed new roles during the twentieth century, some of which are clear in the musical practices we will explore below (see page 402, **"Individual Portraits: Helene Furlong, Buffy Sainte-Marie, and the Changing Musical Roles and Political Impact of Native American Women"**).

Traditional male roles have also changed in many complex ways. One of the most striking changes is the substitution of military service in place of traditional warrior roles, as we shall see in our discussion of the Shoshone powwow.

LOOKING *Back*

The Shoshone People in American History

The independent Native American past

30,000 years ago	Paleo-Indians migrate to North America from Asia.
By early 1500s CE	Ancestors of Wind River Shoshone migrate eastward, crossing the Rocky Mountains, to the Plains.
Early 1700s	Eastern Shoshones split; one group moves south and becomes known as the Comanche.

Native American dislocation and resettlement in reservations

1828	Forced removal of Native Americans peaks during Andrew Jackson administration.
1848	Treaty of Guadelupe Hidalgo cedes Mexican territory to the United States, including the Great Basin, where the Shoshone live.
1851	Fort Laramie Treaty begins settling Western tribes on reservations.
1868	Treaty of Fort Bridger establishes Shoshone Wind River Reservation.
1878	United States government forces the Northern Arapahoes, traditional enemies of the Shoshone, to resettle on Wind River Reservation.
1890	Wounded Knee massacre of Ghost Dancers on Pine Ridge Reservation in South Dakota.

The Setting of Shoshone Indian Days

The first Native American powwow was held in the late nineteenth century. The Algonquian word *pawwaw*, first recorded in 1827, referred to "religious practitioners" and healing ceremonies. Along with other Algonquian words such as *tomahawk*, *wampum*, and *wigwam*, powwow made its way into American English. By 1900, the word was applied to any type of gathering.

The modern intertribal powwow has its origins in Oklahoma in the 1920s; it was begun as a symbol of "Indianness." The Wind River Shoshone mounted their first powwow in 1957, calling it "Indian Days," following a model popular among Native Americans since World War II. The large, intertribal powwow became widespread over the years, with participants from a variety of tribes and regions traveling great distances to attend.

Reservation life and constraints

1886	Wind River boarding school founded by United States government.
1887	Dawes Severalty Act reallocates parcels of land to individuals ownership, thereby overturning the tribal practice of land collectively held through the maternal line.
1890–1924	United States government bans many Native American religious practices, including the Ghost Dance.
1924	Citizen Act of 1924 grants citizenship to all Indians who had not previously received it; the act is viewed as a first step toward taxation and loss of political and territorial sovereignty.
1925	Indian Defense League of America is formed to "obtain justice for Indian people."
1934	Indian Reorganization Act allows American Indians to participate in aspects of their culture and religion once more.
1968	Indian Bill of Rights, passed as part of Civil Rights Act of 1968, extends Bill of Rights to Native Americans living under tribal self-government.
1990	Supreme Court rules that the "free exercise of religion" clause in the First Amendment does not extend to the Native American church.
1994	President Clinton signs American Indian Religious Freedom Act.

Today, the number of North American powwows is estimated at more than two thousand a year.[31] Powwows are mounted all over North America, mainly during the summer months when weather permits outdoor gatherings (see page 404, **"Studying Music: How to Be Courteous at Powwows"**).

Like most annual Indian Day celebrations, the Eastern Shoshone festival is held on a warm summer weekend, part of the established "powwow circuit" that draws participants from the region and beyond. The powwow is held on the Wind River Reservation, which sits in a fertile valley ringed by the foothills of the Wind River Mountains, whose snow-covered peaks can be glimpsed in the distance.

The powwow takes place in the town of Fort Washakie, the center of Shoshone tribal life, named after the nineteenth-century chief whose skillful leadership ensured the founding of the reservation. Fort Washakie is a small,

INDIVIDUAL *Portraits*

Helene Furlong, Buffy Sainte-Marie, and the Changing Musical Roles and Political Impact of Native American Women

As we have seen in earlier chapters, women often have limited roles within individual music cultures. Gender is frequently a factor determining who will be permitted to acquire musical knowledge and perform music in public. Our knowledge of women in musical life has been further limited until the last two decades by the few existing studies on music and gender.

Native American music traditions provide rich materials for studying the politics of gender in musical contexts. For more than a century women have studied Native American music, among them Alice C. Fletcher (1838–1923), Natalie B. Curtis (1875–1921), and Frances Densmore (1867–1957), but they did not document the activity of female Native American musicians. We are fortunate that while studying ceremonial music at the Wind River Reservation in 1977 and 1978, Judith Vander noticed that women were participating in the powwow and began to inquire about the involvement of Shoshone women in musical life. Vander wrote a book about her observations called *Songprints,* which charts the lives and musical experiences of five Shoshone women of different ages.

In *Songprints,* we hear the singing voice and learn about the musical experience of Helene Furlong, the first Shoshone woman to drum at the Eastern Shoshone Indian Days.

> I've heard a lot of people criticize a woman on this reservation among my own people: "Women can't do that and that." Well, I thought it's about time, you know, women did this. Women never did vote in the first place until one of our own Wyoming ladies. So I thought why not set a trend? So then I thought, well I'll just try it. . . . Instead of waiting two years or longer we came home and picked up our drum sticks.[32]

As a young adult, Furlong also performed the fancy war dance in male regalia and her innovations helped pave the way for the fancy shawl dance.

Women like Helene Furlong have helped reshape musical life within their own communities; other Native American female musicians have had major impact in circles extending worldwide. Some have used their music and fame to support political and humanistic causes. One notable example is the singer Buffy Sainte-Marie, who was born on a Cree reservation in Saskatchewan, Canada. Later

Ethnomusicologist Judith Vander, dressed in traditional regalia, participated in intertribal dances during the Wind River Shoshone Indian Days.

adopted and raised in Maine and Massachusetts, Sainte-Marie has played a prominent role in Indian political and social affairs and is said "to have invented the role of Native American international activist pop star."[33]

Buffy Sainte-Marie in a recording studio in 1969.

Buffy Sainte-Marie was from her early days a political figure, achieving renown as a singer and composer of protest and love songs in the 1960s. Many of her songs, including *Universal Soldier,* an anthem for peace, and *Until It's Time for You to Go,* have been recorded by other artists; *Up Where We Belong* won an Academy Award in 1982 when it appeared in the film *An Officer and a Gentleman.* During the intense debate over the Vietnam War in the late 1960s and early 1970s, Sainte-Marie was the target of an informal blacklist against performers who had protested against the war.

In 1976, Sainte-Marie took a break from the international concert stage and set out in new activist directions, especially concerned about the welfare of Native American children. She appeared on the TV show *Sesame Street* for five years with her young son, Dakota Starblanket Wolfchild, seeking to teach a wider public that "Indians still exist." She used her music on behalf of the aboriginal people of Canada, and worked with the United Nations in 1993 to proclaim the International Year of Indigenous People.

In addition to advancing causes in education and the arts, Sainte-Marie received a Ph.D. in Fine Arts from the University of Massachusetts and became a visual artist. A pioneer in digital art and music, Sainte-Marie likens electronic painting to "painting with light." Her huge digital paintings hang in the lobby at her concerts, always incorporating subject matter relating to "how Indians are alive and thriving even within the digital revolution."

In 1969, Buffy Sainte-Marie founded the Nihewan Foundation for Native American Education, which has over the years supported educational and political causes. Her Cradleboard Teaching Project, named after the flexible, protective child carrier used for Native American infants, provides cultural resources and materials in Native American communities and schools. Buffy Sainte-Marie, speaking about Indian people of all ages, says:

> It hurts to be misperceived all your life. Cradleboard reaches both Indian and non-Indian children with positive realities while they are young. This is the cultural "real deal" that comes out of the Indian community to youngsters half a globe away; in time, we hope to benefit the lives of Indian children who wonder "Who am I? . . . and who do others think I am?"[34]

How to Be Courteous at Powwows

How should you behave at a musical event of a tradition with which you are unfamiliar?

This is a complex question facing anyone studying music, a challenge growing more important as performances of different music traditions proliferate. Ethno-musicologists do a great deal of background research before attending an event they wish to study; they check descriptions of past performances, often consulting a knowledgeable insider for advice on everything from dress to etiquette. What they cannot learn in advance, they try to ascertain on the spot by carefully observing the behavior of those who appear to be regular participants.

As these musical events are now open to outsiders, the sponsors or performers of an event often circulate written guidelines. In Wyoming, where frequent powwows attract many outsiders who have never attended a powwow and who are therefore unfamiliar with expectations for their behavior, the following guidelines appeared in a local newspaper, *The Ranger,* on May 21, 1998, before the beginning of pow-wow season. They provide a valuable guide for outsiders who may wish to attend:

> It is important to be aware of the ways to behave at a powwow.
> Powwows are celebrations, social gatherings and friendly dance competitions, but there are sacred traditions which are part of this coming together.
> Many dances are done in a circle which represents the circle of unity, the circle of life. Dancers often follow the clockwise path of the sun. Some of the regalia and ornaments signify special events in a person's life, religious tradition or legends from the past.
> While most powwows welcome both members of other tribes and non-Indians, it is important to be aware of the ways to behave at a powwow. For instance, when the eagle staff is brought in during the grand entry, everyone should stand, and those wearing hats should remove them.

dusty town, with neighborhoods of modest homes, a historic cemetery, a clinic, and a Shoshone Cultural Center. The official buildings, overshadowed by the imposing Shoshone-Arapaho Tribal Center, are flanked by acres of open fields surrounding the arbor that houses the powwow.

The circular, wooden arbor is the focus of powwow activities. Spectators sit under the shelter of the arbor on permanent wooden bleachers or on folding chairs. The large space in the center, planted with grass, is reserved for

If an eagle feather falls during the dancing, everything stops until the feather has
been properly returned.

The use of cameras varies from powwow to powwow. Flash cameras should not be
used during the dance contests.

Videotaping is often discouraged. Permission should always be asked before taking
an individual's photograph outside the dance.

It is improper to bother the performers or those preparing to sing and dance.

Do not touch the regalia or the ornaments. Many of these are delicate heirlooms,
and many are handmade and highly valuable.

If the master of ceremonies issues the invitation, feel free to join in intertribal dances.

Honor the drug-free, alcohol-free policy of the powwow.

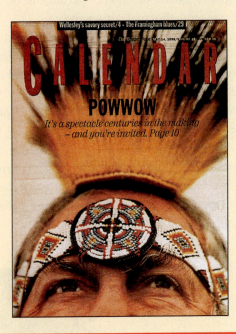

Newspapers carry notices of intertribal powwows in urban and rural locations throughout North America.

dancers. In the middle stands a large pole that has no ritual significance; it
supports speakers to broadcast the narration by the master of ceremonies and
the music of the drum groups that accompany the dancing.

Around the periphery of the arbor are refreshment stands and small shops
selling T-shirts, clothing, jewelry, cassettes, and other goods. In the fields
beyond, tipis and campers house those who remain at the grounds for the
three days of the gathering.

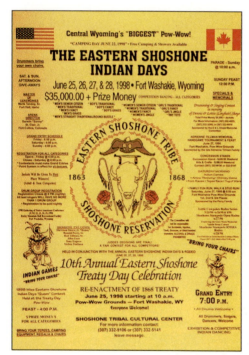

A poster advertising Eastern Shoshone Indian Days, 1998.

Each day during the evening hours, dance competitions are held. A major powwow such as the Eastern Shoshone Indian Days draws participants from throughout the West, including Wyoming, Montana, Colorado, and Idaho.

The modern intertribal powwow features several drum groups that take turns accompanying the dancers. Each group sets up its bass drum under a different section of the arbor, and four to six drummers gather in a circle around the large drum. A microphone amplifies the playing of each group. Most drum groups at the Eastern Shoshone Indian Days come from other reservations in the region, but a few travel from area institutions, including universities. Most leaders and participants are Native Americans, but many groups contain players of other ethnic backgrounds. Although drummers are still predominantly male, female drummers participate on occasion and there are several all-female drum groups.

Indian Days celebrations follow similar patterns. People camp out in the vicinity of the powwow grounds. They socialize during the day and participate in organized games such as foot races, tugs of war, tipi-raising contests, and hand games. The families of girls who have been crowned "powwow queens" plan "giveaways," celebrating their good fortune by presenting gifts to others attending the powwow. This important ceremony, with its own special song and dance, emphasizes Native American cultural values of generosity and public honoring.

The evenings of Indian Days are given over to the powwow ceremonies; here, intertribal dances open to all visitors, including non-Indians, are interspersed with dance competitions restricted to contestants in tribal regalia

The Wind River Shoshone arbor is a wooden structure that shelters spectators and drumming groups from the sun and rain during the long hours of dancing and competition at powwows.

A concession trailer at the Shoshone Indian Days flies a US flag with a Native American face superimposed on it. The adjacent campground, with tents and tipis, can be seen in the background.

displaying official, numbered badges. Competition plays an important role—the youngest dancers compete for cash prizes during the early evening hours, and older dancers move to center stage as the evening goes on. The dance and music competitions are critical to the powwow's success, and prizes can be quite substantial. Beyond their importance to the content of the powwow, the dances provide an index of change in the powwow ceremony. Powwow dances fall into three main categories: (1) competitive dances performed by registered participants in full regalia; (2) special dances for public entertainment and display such as "hoop dances"; and (3) intertribal dances open to all attendees, even those in street clothes.[35] Most dancers progress clockwise around the circumference of the arbor, marking the tempo of the drum with step patterns that carry hidden meanings:

> Footwork is the same at the most basic levels of competitive and intertribal dancing. For men, each foot alternates in extending forward and tapping twice, more light on the first drumbeat. The dancer's weight shifts forward onto the foot for the second step. The legs alternate as the body moves forward. According to one tradition, the step honors the "four-leggeds" (various mammals) that taught Indians how to dance by imitating an animal's four-legged gait. . . . Another belief is that the ability to dance—to pray using motion—is a gift to Natives from the Creator.

Women's basic footwork is closer to a stylized walk, with a step corresponding to every other drumbeat, although women can use the same step as men if they wish.

Competitive dances are usually divided into traditional and fancy styles, the former reflecting older choreography and practices, the latter a more flamboyant and free form, with faster tempos requiring more athletic skill. The history of the various dances is complex and varies between the Northern and Southern plains, as well as from one tribal community to the other.[36]

Most prominent among the competitive dances are the Traditional and Fancy War Dances for men. The main difference between them is the added spins and twirls in the Fancy War dance. There is some difference in regalia as well—for the Traditional War Dance, men wear a small feathered bustle, along with eagle feathers and a breastplate. For the Fancy War Dance, they usually wear two large bustles decorated with feathers and ribbons.

In the past women did not dance the War Dance, but some do so today.[37] Most women dance either the Traditional or Fancy Shawl Dance, a circular dance performed wearing a basic dress, moccasins, and leggings. Traditional Shawl dancers carry a shawl over their arm, as seen in the photograph of Judith Vander on page 402, while Fancy Shawl dancers drape the shawl over the shoulders, freeing their arms for more expansive motions.

The traditional dances have lost some of their popularity, since younger people are attracted to the more athletic Fancy War and Fancy Shawl Dances. Other dances and their regalia are also prominent in the powwow. The Grass Dance, marked by distinctive outfits decorated by fringe resembling grass, has characteristic steps that mimic a motion flattening the grass.

In recent years the Jingle Dress Dance has become very popular. Young girls wear dresses covered with jingles, made in the past from shells or animal bone, today fashioned from pieces of metal or the tops of chewing-tobacco tins. The Jingle Dress Dance has a strong association with healing through the sound of the jingling ornaments, a meaning maintained even in the secular powwow.

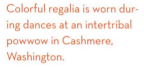

Colorful regalia is worn during dances at an intertribal powwow in Cashmere, Washington.

Among the many stories about the genesis of the Jingle Dress Dance is one relating that when a young girl was ill, her father had a vision that she should perform a dance in a dress with jingles attached. The father made the dress, the daughter danced while wearing it, and she was miraculously cured.

The focus of most powwows today is the dance competitions. Some powwows, such as the huge event mounted by the Mashantucket Pequot Tribal Nation, last several days, include more than two thousand dancers, and offer more than $850,000 in prize money.[38] Generally, the Fancy War Dance carries the largest cash prize.

During the powwow, the emcee announces the various events and offers commentary on everything from the performances of visiting drum groups to current political issues. Shoshone Indian Days includes speeches by dignitaries on inspirational and historical subjects, referring to past injustices and calling for equal rights and opportunities for Native Americans. A study of the emcee discourse at Southern Plains powwows suggests that these spokesmen are accomplished verbal artists and vital links in transmitting a sense of Indian identity. The emcee also provides a connection to older traditions that revered oratory and speechmaking among Native Americans. The emcee's task is to mediate between Native participants drawn from different tribes and the tourists and other non-native observers who are present. Remarks by the emcee run the gamut from straightforward description of the events to ironic commentary on social and political issues. At one recent powwow, asked to announce that a lost tribal identification card had been found and turned in, the emcee announced that "they had found the man's I.D. card; the government had spent a lot of money making them into Indians, so would he please come and get the card."[39]

In other aspects of the powwow, the political message is less open and is embedded in musical performance and dance. Here we will consider two important frameworks for communicating overt and hidden political messages—the flag ceremony and the war dance.

A dancer wears a traditional ojibwa jingle dress decorated with multicolored ribbons and tin cones; she also holds an eagle feather and wears beaded moccasins.

The Flag Song's Sound and Significance

Every powwow begins with a Grand Entry—a procession of all the contestants in regalia, who dance single file around the perimeter of the dance area. This display is followed by the formal presentation of the colors. Veterans carry in the American flag, the state flag, and banners of the Veterans of Foreign Wars, and move straight across the arena. This flag presentation is accompanied by a special song, called a Flag Song, signaled by a slow drum rhythm. The Flag Song is performed with great solemnity, filling a sonic space that in other American contexts would be reserved for the national anthem. Participants and spectators remove their hats and stand during the performance of the Flag Song.

The Flag Song heard in Listening Guide 73 (see page 412) was recorded during the Wind River Shoshone Indian Days in 1977. The singers, Helene Furlong and her brother Wayland Bonatsie, adapted this Shoshone song from a Cheyenne Flag Song they heard in Lame Deer, Montana, at the Northern Cheyenne Reservation. Transmission of songs from one community to another is quite common as powwows incorporate the musics of many tribes. We hear the slow, deliberate tempo typical of the Flag Song, punctuated by the drum on every other beat. A series of drumbeats is called "honor beats" by many Native Americans, a clue to the importance of the sound of the drum. A sliding drum and voice flourish is heard at the end of this flag song, followed by ululation.

Helene Furlong sings in a high register an octave above her brother, entering after him and "seconding" his vocal line. The text consists of vocables, mainly set in syllabic style. According to Furlong, some individuals use slightly different vocables, although patterns are widely shared.

As we discuss the Flag Song and other Native American music, we need to be aware that while Native Americans share much of the Western musical vocabulary, they use some terms in a distinctive manner.[40] We have already defined the special terms "honor beats" and "seconding." The term "melody" generally has the same meaning as in Western practice, but Wind River Shoshone musicians describe the wide range of the Flag Song's melody in ter-

Native Americans have made important contributions to the American military, including the ingenious use of their languages as codes during World War II. On June 6, 1994, Native American veterans participated in a commemoration of the D-Day landing at Omaha Beach in Normandy fifty years earlier.

minology that is visual and linear. Songs have curves and dips that can be straightened, smoothed out, made more curvy, and zig-zagged.[41]

The high, tense vocal quality allows male singers to sing clearly for long hours during a powwow. Northern singers also place their vocables or words between drumbeats (termed "singing off the beat") whenever possible, to make their voices more audible.[42] In the past it was conventional to "stretch" (lengthen) a song, a practice that has fallen off in recent years. It has also been traditional to repeat whole songs. The English expression "push-ups" is used to indicate the number of times a song is repeated. The term push-ups has been traced to the Sioux, who used the word *pawankiye,* meaning "to push the voice upward."[43] Origi-nally, "push-ups" referred to the repetition of the opening call of a song; today Shoshone and other powwow singers use the term in its broader sense.

The Shoshone repertory contains many Flag Songs for the presentation of the Colors. The Flag Songs convey several different political messages; most important, they honor particular people and events, or offer formal respect for the flag, country, and veterans.

The Flag Song replaces the American national anthem, *The Star-Spangled Banner.* The Flag Song has great significance for Native American veterans of the armed services, who compose new Flag Songs to commemorate the con-flicts in which they have served. For example, the Flag Song for Desert Storm,

A local Veterans of Foreign Wars post in Riverton, Wyoming, salutes powwow season.

Helene Furlong, seen here singing and playing the drum with her brother, Wayland Bonatsie, has lived most of her life in Crowheart, a small community forty miles north of Fort Washakie. A Head Start teacher educated both on and off the reservation, Furlong learned Shoshone songs from her father and grandfather and was one of the first women to partici-pate in the war dance. Her family drum group, no longer active, was known as the Big Wind Singers.

Shoshone Flag Song

Date of recording: 1977 Wind River Shoshone Indian Days

Performers: Helene Furlong and Wayland Bonatsie

Function: To salute the presentation of the flag following the Grand Entry, which begins every powwow

Source: Adopted by Shoshone singers from a Cheyenne flag song heard in Lame Deer, Montana, at the Northern Cheyenne reservation

Form: Iterative verses

Tempo: Moderately slow

WHAT TO LISTEN FOR:

- A wide vocal range, each singer covers nearly a two-octave ranges. Furlong "doubles" or "seconds" Bonatsie, singing the same melody an octave higher.
- Bonatsie sometimes uses the falsetto register to sing the highest notes
- A slow, deliberate tempo appropriate for a flag ceremony
- The use of vocables, and ululation at the conclusion of the song

	STRUCTURE	DESCRIPTION
0:00	**Verse 1** E ai ya we he e	The drum begins, accenting every other beat. Bonatsie begins singing the melody. The vocables, transcribed for the first verse, are repeated throughout the song.
0:13	we ai hai ya we hai hai ha he ha we hai hai ya yai we hai ya we he hai ya we hai ya we ya hai ya we hai ya we yo we yo we yo we yo	Furlong seconds Bonatsie, singing the same melody an octave higher. This melody begins quite high in their ranges, descends in several jumps, ascends somewhat, and then descends further, ending with the lowest note they sing.
1:06	**Verse 2**	Bonatsie begins singing and Furlong joins him a few seconds later.
1:48	**Verse 3**	The complete verse is repeated one more time.
2:14	**Conclusion**	The piece concludes with a drum roll while Furlong ululates.
2:20	Recording ends	

heard in Listening Guide 74 (see page 414), is one of many composed by Native American veterans of that conflict. This song, intended to be sung during the Grand Entry, honored tribe members recently returned. Unlike the Shoshone example we heard earlier, this newer Flag Song has a faster tempo, perhaps reflecting generational differences.

Honoring Warriors in Song: The War Dance

Another integration of past with present is the War Dance. Twentieth-century wars—World Wars I and II, Korea, Vietnam, Desert Storm—have reinforced traditional Native American cultural practices such as the War Dance that otherwise would have atrophied. Songs and dances celebrate the heroic actions of Native American soldiers, thereby preserving these cultural forms and encouraging tribal pride.

Like Flag Songs, War Dance Songs make an overt political statement, especially since they were once performed for armed conflict. In the twentieth century, however, the warrior-fighter has given way to the warrior-dancer and present-day War Dances mimic traditional fighting movements.[44] Some of the motions illustrate the War Dance's connection to the Wolf Dance, in which the dancer mimics a wolf stalking its prey.[45]

Wayland Bonatsie and Helene Furlong learned the War Dance song (Listening Guide 75; see page 416) from powwow singers of the Blackfoot tribe. Midway through the song, Helene Furlong picks up a set of the large bells that war dancers tie around their knees and begins to shake them in time to the song. At the end of the song there is a short additional section called a *nduah* (literally, "son" or what other Plains singers call the "tail").

In this War Dance Song, we hear how customary gender roles shape performance style; women traditionally enter after the opening section and then sing all the way through. The male vocal style alternates loud and soft pulses on an unbroken tone. Finally, as in most War Dances, the song ends with a decisive final drumbeat.

Beyond its historical and political significance, the War Dance is also connected to nature. Helene Furlong makes this connection through the sound of the powwow drum, as she explains:

And I think the style of dancing is adopted from nature—the sage chicken. Have you ever seen a sage chicken dance? It's beautiful. There's one type of War Dancing—I forget what they call it now—it's one beat at a time, almost like a stomp, and it's a slow kind of War Dance. I guess it's similar to a Chicken Dance of today. That's the reason why it's called that because of the sage chickens. And if you happen to be around a place where the sage chickens are, like in March, and then before the sun is just beginning to come up, that's when you notice these. If

Flag Song for Desert Storm (Blackfoot Flag Song)

CD 3 Track 15

Date of recording: 1992
Performers: Black Lodge Singers of White Swan, Washington, powwow drum
Function: To salute the flag following the Grand Entry
Form: Iterative
Tempo: Moderately fast

WHAT TO LISTEN FOR:

- A formal organization similar to that of the Shoshone Flag Song
- A faster tempo, supported by a regular drumbeat
- A text that honors veterans of the 1991 Gulf War

	STRUCTURE	DESCRIPTION
0:00	**Introduction**	The drum begins beating. One singer sings an introductory phrase, a fragment of the main melody, which is repeated by the group.
	Verse	
0:16	**Phrase a**	The main verse begins. Like the Shoshone Flag Song, it begins high in the singer's range and gradually descends. The verse
0:29	**Phrase b**	consists of two phrases with the text "Our Indian boys have returned from Desert Storm." The two phrases begin in similar fashion, but they diverge as they go on. Some syncopated rhythmic patterns between the voice and the drum rhythm recur several times within the phrases.
	Verse	The verse is repeated by the group.
0:45	**Phrase a**	
0:59	**Phrase b**	
1:13	**Transition**	The transition passage is identical to the introductory passage. The same fragment is sung, first by the leader and then by the ensemble.
	Verse	
1:25	**Phrase a**	The entire verse is repeated again.
1:38	**Phrase b**	
	Verse	
1:53	**Phrase a**	As the next iteration of the verse begins, the recording fades out.
1:56	recording ends	

you creep up on 'em, you see these sage chickens dancing. Every once in a while you'll hear "mphhh" and then "boom." Just like a regular Indian drum, you know, going "boomph, boomph." And that's their whole chest bag. It comes out and then it hits and then the back end of their feathers spread out just like a bustle. Beautiful! And then when part of their feathers touch the ground it makes that noise, just beautiful noise. . . . It just really makes you feel good to see it. I know a lot of these dances have been adopted from nature.[46]

The War Dance Song is the centerpiece of the powwow, sung and drummed during both the traditional War Dances and the more recent "Fancy" War Dances. The War Dance Song repertory changes quickly; songs appear and disappear from year to year.

What makes a good War Dance Song? According to Wayland Bonatsie, "It depends on how many get up and dance to that song."[47]

As we have seen, Shoshone singers often borrow songs from other groups, including the Cheyenne and the Blackfoot. Indeed, the social interaction at the intertribal powwow encourages musical borrowing. There are, however, clear protocols relating to the transmission of powwow songs:

> When you sing a song, you're supposed to know what you're singing, what the words are, where it came from, who [composed] it, and got permission to sing that song. That's the proper way to do things.[48]

A young dancer performs a war dance during intermission at an athletic competition, 1998.

At a powwow, drummers listen attentively to others as well as to recordings as they mentally rehearse and learn new songs while awaiting their turn to perform. Some songs borrow from non-Native American sources, although these are not common and require replacing the original text with vocables. For instance, one Shoshone war song borrows the melody of the hymn *Amazing Grace*. Although this War Dance Song originated in Albuquerque, New Mexico, Helene Furlong learned it from a friend's tape in the mid-1970s. Furlong comments that this is "a white man's song," but that only certain singers in the white man's world "make it beautiful."[49] Her aesthetics find a song beautiful when it is sung "high." As a War Dance Song, this tune is not widely sung, although the manner in which it was transmitted—by personal contact and tape recording across regional boundaries outside the setting of the powwow—is quite common. The use of *Amazing Grace* for a War Dance Song adds another layer of significance to a melody that in other American contexts, such as the jazz funeral, signifies commemoration.

War Dance Song No. 9 (Shoshone War Dance)

CD 3 Track 16

Date of recording: 1977
Performers: Helene Furlong and Wayland Bonatsie
Function: Song to accompany the war dance
Source: Learned by Shoshone singers from relatives in the Blackfoot tribe
Form: Song with a b b a b b form, followed by a *nduah,* literally "son" or "tail"
Tempo: Moderately fast

WHAT TO LISTEN FOR:

- Pulsation in the male vocal style, alternating loud and soft pulsations without breaking the tone
- The female singer's part, which enters after the opening call and continues to the end
- Loud final drumbeat that ends the war dance

STRUCTURE	DESCRIPTION
0:00 **Phrase a** E he he ha e he he	This phrase begins with Bonatsie, in his falsetto register, singing vocables. (Vocables are transcribed only for the first verse)
0:07 **Phrase b** Ye	

The Changing Settings of Powwow Music

The music of the powwow has also shifted to new settings such as special performances at rodeos and football half-time shows and lecture-demonstrations on college campuses. In addition, the powwow and its songs have also begun to reach new audiences through various forms of mass media.

Groups such as the American Indian Dance Theatre, which includes members from nearly a dozen Native American communities, perform widely at dance festivals. They present traditional dances, such as the Shawl and Hoop Dances, as well as new choreography. References to other music traditions and their political agendas are also incorporated; one performance of a modern Fancy Dance by the American Indian Dance Theatre featured a dancer wear-

0:09	hai hai ya e hai ya he ya hai ya he yoi	Furlong joins in just after Bonatsie begins the second phrase, singing an octave above him.
0:18	**Phrase b** Ya e i hai hai ya he hi ya hai ai ya We hai ha ya he	Furlong picks up a large set of bells, worn by war dancers around their knees, and shakes them in time with the drum. This time, Furlong sings the complete phrase with him.
0:28	E hai e hai ya (repeated)	Furlong drops out, and Bonatsie sings the falsetto opening phrase. The phrase is repeated, with Furlong singing the same melody in the same range with him.
	Phrase a	
0:39	**Phrase b**	Furlong joins the second phrase an octave higher just after Bonatsie begins the phrase.
0:49	**Phrase b**	The phrase is repeated, with Furlong singing the complete phrase.
0:59	*Nduah* **(Phrase b)**	The drum stops just before this final section, called a *nduah*. The drum pattern changes, for a time striking only every other beat. A strong drumbeat marks the end of the final phrase of a war-dance song.
1:10	Recording ends	

ing black gym clothes in a reference to the Gumboot Dance, a dance of resistance performed by South African miners.

The powwow is a remarkable example of an event with many layers of meaning. Not only does the powwow provide an opportunity for socializing and celebrating Native American identity, it also reaffirms the vitality and political strength of the community and its institutions. The powwow transmits and affirms Native American power both inside and outside the immediate setting. The dual nature of the event is evident in the clear division between intertribal and contest dances, as well as the narration of the emcee who speaks to insiders and also translates for visitors.

As we can see in this CD cover art, Native American musicians such as Brulé have adapted their own traditional music for wider audiences.

Conclusion

The music and dance of the powwow provide opportunities for making a variety of political statements, some public, others hidden. The powwow explores the relationship of Native Americans to white society and celebrates the Indian Nations. In contrast, the song *Nkosi Sikelel' iAfrika* and reggae music are open markers of—and rallying points against—social, racial, and economic inequities.

The counterpoint to mainstream culture signified by the Flag Song in place of the national anthem is evident also in the powwow's requirement that contest dancers be Native Americans. Other statements of community strength and pride include the display of colorful traditional regalia and the maintenance of traditional rituals.

Still, the powwow thrives today in part because its boundaries are porous. The borrowing of melodies from the outside world, such as *Amazing Grace,* are seen as a transformation that enhances the beauty of the borrowing. Musical commemoration and reenactment of historic battles through war dances pay tribute to modern Indian veterans of American wars as well as warriors of the past.

We find equally porous boundaries in the case of reggae; a versatile music style has served both Rastafarians and a much broader audience around the world. Likewise, the song *Nkosi Sikelel' iAfrika,* which emerged from indigenous creativity and intercultural musical influence, has signified the struggle for equality both as the national hymn in the fight against South African apartheid, and as an international call for human rights.

The music of all three case studies in this chapter combines elements that define and defy past and present political realities. Like so many of the soundscapes we have encountered in previous chapters, all testify to the importance of individual and community identity. It is to music and its role in shaping and expressing identity that we turn in our concluding chapter.

———

Do you know any songs that comment on politics or have been the subject of controversy? What are the controversial issues and how did they arise? Has the meaning of the song changed over time?

IMPORTANT TERMS

Fancy Shawl Dance	national anthem	*riddim*
Fancy War Dance	*nduah* / "tail"	Shawl Dance
Flag Song	powwow	War Dance
Grass Dance	"push-ups"	
Jingle Dance	reggae	

Chapter 10

Music and Identity

The Southwest Louisiana Zydeco Festival began in 1982 as a small local event on the outskirts of the city of Opelousas, a short distance north of Lafayette, and grew to become the "world's largest zydeco festival," featuring concerts and many other associated events. Opelousas escaped the severe destruction caused by Hurricane Katrina on New Orleans and southeast Louisiana. Indeed Lafayette, located two hours northwest of New Orleans, has served as a refuge for musicians displaced by the 2005 storm.

Overview

Main Points

- Music can signify many aspects of identity, including nationality, place, ethnicity, race, class, religion, and gender.

- Music constructs the identities of individuals and groups.

- Text, melody, vocal style, instrumentation, and body motion contribute to the performance of identity.

Introduction

Among the many elements that define our identities are ethnicity, race, class, gender, and religious orientation. National or regional heritage, language group, political affiliation, and occupation also contribute to our perceptions of who we are. Although identity is experienced differently by each individual, it is almost always constructed in relation to groups that we wish to be part of or seek to avoid.

The British barbershop quartet Matrix performs in downtown Montreal on July 3, 2003, as part of the 65th annual convention of the international Barbershop Harmony Society, an organization that seeks to "build a better world through singing." Over 10,000 singers and fans from around the world participated in this convention, which featured competitions by singers in chorus, quartet, senior, and college categories.

Many of the identities we are slowest to recognize and define are the ones that are so familiar that they are invisible to us. We can compare identity's transparency to Muzak, the customized, recorded music used as background in public spaces, designed to remain below the threshold of focused attention—elevator music. Muzak is heard passively, not listened to actively, because it provides a continuous stream of simple arrangements of music familiar to most Western listeners.[1] Aspects of identity can be masked in similar ways; whether by design or circumstance, they are so familiar that they simply fade into the background, leaving us unaware of their presence.

Some identities, especially those of majorities within the societies in which we live, are so ubiquitous that we have tended to overlook them. For instance, scholars have only recently begun to study "whiteness" as a category of racial identity with its own associated forms of cultural and musical expression. Interest in "whiteness" has affected studies of the twentieth-century revival of the barbershop quartet, explaining that tradition as "a quest to reconstruct a space of privilege for white American middle-class males based on nostalgia for unchallenged and exclusive sociability and camaraderie located in the adolescent memories of middle-aged men."[2]

Identities are complex formations that rarely stay static. Each of us is also a mix of competing and interacting identities. Depending on the situation, we may choose to emphasize or play down one or more of these aspects of identity. Of course, identity is not nearly as flexible for racial minorities within a society, whose choice of identity is much more constrained.

Whatever identity we give preference to at a given moment, it is often expressed or reinforced through music. Whether we sing *pizmonim* or listen to jazz recordings, our musical choices serve as a guide to who we think we are and who we wish to be. Our musical choices also provide a guide to how we perceive others in relation to ourselves and how our perceptions of cultural difference shape our lives.

Many music traditions are associated with communities that share a background and a history. With the exception of gender, most other aspects of identity—race, class, religious orientation, and descent—often fall under the broad umbrella of ethnicity. An ethnic group is composed of people within a larger society who have (or think they have) common ancestry, memories of a shared historical past, and elements in common, such as kinship, religious affiliation, language, or some combination of these.[3]

The definition implies that although many aspects of ethnic identity are shaped by descent, others are freely chosen through affiliations. We find a similarly mixed picture when we try to define musical identity. Many traditions are transmitted through biological families and communities linked by descent; our case study of Native American music in Chapter 9 provide an excellent example.

In some cases the music that symbolizes identity maintains strong links with the past or with an original homeland. In other cases newly invented musical styles convey equally important meanings. We noted in Chapter 9 that the phrase "invention of tradition" describes the way identities can be constructed without reference to actual historical realities. Generally, however, the situation is fluid; traditions from the past are continually enriched and transformed through new experience and exposure.

Among the most colorful invented traditions we have encountered is the bagpipe, which became a marker of Scottish identity, along with the kilt, only in the late seventeenth century. The kilt and the bagpipe were adopted as symbols of protest against the Union with England and as a "distinguishing badge" of highland society.[4] The bagpipe case study (see Chapter 3) also demonstrated how traditions are often reinvented in diaspora, where the instrument has found a new life in cities around the globe and in international competitions. Ironically, in case such as these, traditions are invented in order to provide a sense of history and to buttress ties to the past.

In this chapter we will explore how people create their identities through music and how music communicates aspects of identity that are difficult to express otherwise. We will hear the voice of individual identity in the flute concerto of Reza Vali, a composer of Persian descent living in the United States. We will also explore the surprisingly deep national and cultural associations of *karaoke* music—music rooted in Japanese society that has distinctive forms elsewhere in Asia and in popular culture worldwide.

One challenge in charting identity and its expression through music today is the increasing separation of identity from place. Scholars have long assumed that people and their traditions are grounded in specific geographic locales. Throughout *Soundscapes* we have carefully considered the importance of setting, geographic location being one of the important contextual factors that define a soundscape. Music has a striking ability to retain the traditions of a particular place, despite the movement of people and their music far from their home. We will see an example in this chapter's major case study of Cajun and Creole musics, both associated with southern Louisiana, where many

Music is often transmitted to children within ethnic communities, who may begin acquiring instrumental skills at an early age. Here, three-year-old Louis Ancelet, son of the Cajun folklorist and radio show host Barry Ancelet, demonstrates what he has learned about the accordion from the musicians around him.

French-speaking people resettled after long periods of displacement. As these Cajun and Creole styles interacted with each other and other musics—including African American traditions—they gave rise in the second half of the twentieth century to a new Creole style called *zydeco* music. Both traditions have moved well beyond southern Louisiana. For this reason, Cajun and zydeco music provide a rich study of music and identity; they celebrate deep historical and geographic roots and accommodate newfound affinities.

Expressing Individual and Group Identities through Music

At its most basic level, music becomes a symbol of identity and attains meaning through its sound and settings. The multiple channels of text, tune, dance, instrumental practice, and performance style produce further layers of meaning. We will explore the expression of individual identity conveyed through the flute concerto of Reza Vali, a composer of Iranian descent who today lives in Pittsburgh, Pennsylvania. We will also explore ways in which Vali's compositions shed light on issues relating to musical styles that intentionally cross cultural boundaries.

CASE STUDY: The Music of a Persian Composer

Reza Vali was born in Iran (formerly known as Persia) in 1952, but as a child he was not educated in the techniques of Persian music (see **"Individual Portraits: Reza Vali"**). As he grew up, Vali was schooled in the Western classical music tradition, a common occurrence in Iran. From the nineteenth century until the Revolution in the late 1970s, Iranian rulers supported Western music. A conservatory was founded in Tehran during the 1930s under the Iranian Ministry of Culture and Arts; the Tehran Symphony Orchestra, founded in the late 1930s, performed standard Western repertory and newly commissioned work. The Iranian capital also had an opera house, a ballet troupe, and an orchestra maintained by the National Iranian Radio and Television.[5]

Thus, Vali's knowledge of Western musical instruments and styles was acquired at home in West Asia and further developed in Europe, well before the composer settled in the United States. Although his interest in Persian music began when he was a teenager in Iran, his early involvement focused on ethnomusicological work rather than transmitting or performing traditional styles.

Here we will explore Vali's flute *concerto* (a work for orchestra and soloist), in which elements from the composer's diverse background and musical experience come together. The Concerto for Flute and Orchestra was commissioned by the Boston Modern Orchestra Project and was first performed on February 13, 1998. At first glance, the instruments appear to be standard Western orchestral instruments (see **"Sound Sources: The Western Orchestra"**); Vali employs a scaled-down ensemble called a chamber orchestra, rather than a full-sized orchestra. In addition to the soloist, the score calls for a second flute doubling on alto flute and piccolo; an oboe doubling on English horn; a clarinet doubling on bass clarinet; a bassoon doubling on contrabassoon; two French horns; trumpet; trombone; tuba; harp; a battery of percussion instruments; and strings.

A closer look reveals evidence of Iranian musical influence as well. The flute soloist is instructed to hum while playing a Western flute to produce a sound resembling the end-blown Persian flute, the *ney*. The Persian *ney*, one of a large family of related Middle Eastern end-blown flutes, takes its name from the Persian word for the reed or bamboo from which it is made.[6] The power of the *ney*'s sound was described by the thirteenth-century poet Mowlânâ Jalâleddin Rumi:

> Listen to the *ney* how it tells a tale,
> Complaining of separations
> Saying, "Ever since I was parted from the reed-bed,
> My lament hath caused man and woman to moan."[7]

The plaintive sound of the *ney* is enhanced by the distinctive manner in which it is played, blown through a mouth-hole carved with a beveled edge or rim, often covered in brass. In Iranian folk music, the instrument is held between the lips. Iranian classical music, however, uses a more complex method termed the "Isfahan technique," named after the city in which a famous school of *ney* players originated in the nineteenth century. In the Isfahan technique, the player anchors the end of the *ney* between the front teeth at a 10- to 20-degree angle to the chin and directs a stream of air toward the instrument's opening. Reza Vali says:

> I tried to imitate the sound of the Isfahan school, which is today predominant in Persian classical music. This is why the Persian sound is so distinct. When the *ney* is held in the front teeth and the lips closed, the sound vibrates in the mouth, against the teeth, and through the sinus cavities. You can especially hear the second and third partials [harmonics] (specifically, the octave and fifth above it). I tried to imitate this sound.

Reza Vali

Born in Ghazvin, Iran, a town about 300 kilometers north of Tehran, Reza Vali grew up in the foothills of the Alborz mountains. He attended the Conservatory of Music in Tehran, where he studied trumpet and trombone. Following additional studies at the Academy of Music in Vienna, he came to the United States, where he earned a Ph.D. in music theory and composition from the University of Pittsburgh in 1985.

Vali became interested in Persian music when, as a teenager in Iran, he learned that the composer Béla Bartók had listened to, recorded, and transcribed folk music in his native Hungary. Vali began to collect and transcribe Persian music. To study Persian classical music, which he describes as "unbelievably rich and extremely complex," he created a computer program to re-create the melodic system, called *dastgah,* that is unique to Persian music.[8]

From his early years as a composer, Vali was influenced by Persian music. He composed fifteen cycles of Persian folk songs between 1978 and 1999, for many different combinations—voice and piano, voice and orchestra, and instrumental ensemble without voice. Other compositions include a cello concerto titled *The Dervish and the Magus* (1994), and a piece called *Deylàman* for large orchestra, Persian lute, and Persian flute (*ney*) (1995).

The flute concerto explored in this chapter has a particularly deep meaning for the composer, who says that it marks a transition in his compositional style.

> The flute concerto is a very important piece for me. After the flute concerto, I have changed my aesthetic and have left the Western system altogether. I started using the Persian *dastgah* system as a basis of my compositions. I believe that the Persian *dastgah,* with its use of tetrachords (called *daang*), had a great influence on the development of Middle Eastern *maqam.* I want to go to the very roots of *dastgah.*

Vali's compositions after the concerto, such as *Calligraphies No. 1, No. 2, and No. 3* for string quartet, as well as other new works, are solidly based in *dastgah.* These pieces also use what Vali terms "mixed tunings," incorporating intervals that differ in size from both Western and Middle Eastern intervals. Vali recently composed a concerto for *ney* and orchestra, to be premiered early in 2006 by the Persian *ney* master Khosro Soltani and the Boston Modern Orchestra Project. "After all I have created for the Western flute," he commented, "I thought now I have to do it for the *ney.*"

Today, Vali is a member of the music faculty at Carnegie Mellon University. His compositions, which have been performed all over the world and can be heard on numerous recordings, include music for orchestra, string quartet, piano and voice, electronic and computer media, and chamber ensembles.

In 2000, Reza Vali returned to Iran for a six-week visit after an absence of twenty-seven years. He spent time in the north at the Caspian Sea, traveled to Shiraz and Isfahan to see the famous architecture, and lingered a month in Tehran. The trip gave Vali a deepened sense of the sights and sounds of his homeland, which he had missed during his formative years because of Iran's policy of westernization. He is aware of changes in himself and in his former homeland:

> It was very emotional, a wonderful trip. As a kid, I used to look at and climb the mountains. Today, the Iranian combination of desert meeting lush mountains reminds me of Washington State. And it used to take two-and-one-half hours to travel by car from my hometown of Ghazvin south to Tehran. Today there is a highway that cuts the trip to an hour and a half.

NAXOS

21st Century Classics

DDD
8.557224

Reza
VALI
Flute Concerto • Deylámân
Folk Songs (Set No. 10)
Almarza • Mgrdichian • Baty
Boston Modern Orchestra Project • Gil Rose

The cover of the Naxos CD for Reza Vali's Concerto for Flute and Orchestra shows an adobe shrine in the foreground and imposing Mount Damavand of the Alborz chain in the background. The image was selected by the composer, who grew up in the foothills of the Alborz mountains. "The image reminded me of the calm at the beginning of my flute concerto. The image also shows the plateau and great Alborz mountain range, which at once links Iran to the Caucasus in the east and to the Hindu Kush in the West."

The Western Orchestra

Although the term *orchestra* is used to describe a wide variety of large instrumental ensembles, in the Euro-American tradition it refers to an organized body of bowed stringed instruments (chordophones) with several players to a part; wind and brass instruments (aerophones); and percussion (idiophones and membranophones). The word *orchestra* comes from the Greek, literally meaning "a dancing place," referring to the semicircular space where the Greek chorus sang and danced. The Western orchestra originated with small groups (termed *consorts*) of instruments formed for ceremonial and entertainment purposes in sixteenth-century courts. Consorts grouped sets of like instruments, such as strings or winds, in different sizes and ranges, and over the course of time these consorts combined, leading to the Western orchestra of strings, brass, woodwinds, and percussion.

By the 1720s, new instruments had been added, such as the double bass. Over the course of the eighteenth century, stringed instruments grew in importance and became the backbone of the ensemble. As a result of the Industrial Revolution, technical improvements to the brass and woodwind instruments made them more versatile in volume and quality.

By the end of the eighteenth century, a standard orchestra had strings divided into five parts (first violins, second violins, violas, cellos, and basses) and included two each of the following: flutes, oboes, clarinets, bassoons, trumpets, horns (sometimes there were four), and timpani. In the nineteenth century, this configuration varied according to function and location. Small chamber ensembles were hired for events in private homes, and larger groups served the concert halls. Nineteenth-century composers expanded the wind and brass sections. The orchestra expanded in size during the nineteenth century; composers such as Anton Bruckner, Gustav Mahler, and Richard Strauss required orchestras of one hundred or more players.

Although the *ney* is used in the classical Persian orchestra, it is usually played as a solo instrument. The *ney* heard in Listening Guide 76 (see page 432) is improvising within the Persian musical system known as *dastgah*. *Dastgah* resembles other music systems we have studied, such as Middle Eastern *maqam* and Indian *raga;* it comprises a number of distinctive categories of melody distinguished by pitch content, melodic contours, and ornamentation.

In Listening Guide 76 the *ney,* which has a range of two and one-half octaves, improvises within *dastgah homayoun,* a mode that the Western listener

In the twentieth century, economic constraints imposed by the two world wars led to smaller ensembles such as chamber orchestras and modified orchestras for new works. In addition, the orchestral sound of the twentieth century has been enriched by an enormous increase in the number and variety of percussion instruments, many borrowed from outside the West. The use of new and innovative performance techniques on traditional orchestral instruments has been another outcome of the ways in which the Western orchestra has borrowed and domesticated cross-cultural musical resources. In this way, Reza Vali's Concerto for Flute and Orchestra reflects recent trends in both musical composition and playing techniques of the modern orchestra.

The Minnesota Symphony Orchestra, showing the standard orchestral seating arrangement; the strings are deployed in a semicircle fanning out from the conductor; woodwind, brass, and percussion instruments are in the center and the back.

hears as having its second step subtly lower than that of the corresponding tone of the Western scale. The melodic contours (each short melody is termed a *gushe*, pronounced "goo-SHAY") within a *dastgah* are distinctive and identify the *dastgah* for the knowledgeable listener. Here the player uses a *gushe* called *shushtari*, which emphasizes the first, second, and fourth steps of *dastgah homayoun*. Traditionally, improvisation begins in a low register of the *dastgah*, slowly moving up to a higher range.[9] In Listening Guide 76 the player begins low, then jumps up an octave in the second section of the piece.

Behzad Faruhari plays the Persian *ney* during a concert by the Iranian Ava Ensemble at the Asia Society in New York City, September 1998.

Although Vali uses Western instruments and the Western harmonic system in his flute concerto (Listening Guide 77; see page 433), he adds Persian color through the unusual flute effects. "I discovered that if you sing and play the flute at the same time, it creates an effect similar to the Persian *ney*," recalls Vali. "This is a very difficult technique on the Western flute, but the soloist (Alberto Almarza) is fabulous."

Vali began experimenting with this flute technique in 1987, in a composition titled *Song* for solo flute. In that piece the flute player sings and plays in polyphony, the voice and the flute creating separate melodies. Vali says:

The flute concerto is much easier than *Song*. "I wanted to use the technique of simultaneous singing and playing in an easier way in order to produce the sound of a *ney*. So in the flute concerto, the flute player sings and plays the same melody.

In the percussion section, in addition to various Western idiophones and membranophones (xylophone, marimba, chimes, timpani, glockenspiel, cymbal, tom-toms, bass drum), Vali also calls for Persian drums, including an hourglass-shaped drum (called *darabukkah* across the Middle East, known in Iran as the *tombak*) plus the Persian frame drum (*daf*). The drums play a prominent role at the beginning of the second movement.

The flute concerto is influenced by Persian classical and folk music as well as by the Persian visual arts. It also has been subtly shaped by the composer's exposure to other soundscapes beyond the borders of the Western art music tradition.

The first movement is written for flute, strings, harp, and percussion. However, the composer says that he conceives of these instruments not as a single group, but as three separate ensembles playing together. The first is described by Vali as a "quasi *gamelan*" ensemble consisting of two chimes, the harp, and vibraphones. The second group is a chorus of strings, four solo violins along with the first chairs (that is, the leading players) of the viola, cello, and bass sections. The third incorporates the rest of the strings playing parts that interlock, according to Vali, "like strands in a Persian carpet."

The pitch content and melodies of the first movement draw on the Persian *dashti* mode, a small or satellite *dastgah* that is part of the larger *dastgah shur* family. "*Dashti*," according to the composer, "is a very beautiful mode used in folk music which has a somber sound and is often played by the *ney*. That's why I used it."

The form of this movement is intended to replicate a Persian carpet or the mosaic patterns decorating a mosque, in which a variety of details form an overall design. The composer calls this musical technique "mosaic elaboration." Its effect is static, as opposed to Western techniques of elaboration or

LISTENING GUIDE *76*

Dastgah of Homayoun (Persian music for *ney*)

Date of recording: 1966, reissued on CD in 1991
Performers: Hassan Kassayi, *ney*
Mode: *Dastgah Homayoun*
Tempo: Moderate

WHAT TO LISTEN FOR:

- The timbre and range of the *ney*
- The melodic pattern or *gushe* heard here, called *Shushtari*. It emphasizes the first, second, and fourth steps of *Dastgah Homayoun*.

STRUCTURE		DESCRIPTION
0:00	Section A	The first phrase begins on the first and second steps of *homayoun,* and at 0:12 the phrase ends on the fourth step. In the next phrase, the fourth step is repeatedly ornamented by quickly touching on the fifth step. These melodic patterns recur several times throughout this improvisation.
0:49	Section B	After an extended pause, the player produces a sound an octave higher and less breathy than before. The same melodic patterns can be heard in this section; the first phrase of this section, for example, has virtually the same shape as that at the beginning of section A.
1:17	Recording ends	

development, which are linear, with strong climactic moments. The result in the first movement is a constantly shifting polyphonic texture in which multiple melodies interweave with no single line dominating. The unusual flute technique, which brings out additional harmonics and alters the sound of the Western instrument, reflects the Western avant-garde's interest in ear-catching new sounds, but Vali does not consider the first movement a Western composition. Rather, he feels that it extends "Persian polyphony" from an implicit to an explicit level. Vali considers the second movement of the concerto, which draws on rhythms that resemble cycles in medieval Persian music (a brief excerpt is heard in Listening Guide 77, CD 3, TRACK 19), to be more Western in its conception.

The interweaving of instruments in the concerto may sound random or improvisatory, but Vali has left very little to chance or to the discretion of the musicians. In the notated music (score) for the work, the beginning of which is reproduced in the following figure, the flute player is given explicit instructions to sing and play simultaneously.

Rehearsal numbers are placed in the score by the composer to facilitate starting and stopping in rehearsals for both the conductor and instrumentalists; these numbers are reproduced next to the timings in Listening Guide 77.

Instructions to the flute player as well as rehearsal numbers 1 and 2 can be seen in this excerpt from Vali's score for the flute part to his concerto. Note that the first staff above where the flute enters is blank, except for markings letting the flute player follow the timing of the orchestral introduction.

CD 3
Tracks
18–19

Concerto for Flute and Orchestra
(Movement 1 and excerpt from movement 2)

Date of composition: 1998

Composer: Reza Vali

Date of performance: 1998

Performers: Boston Modern Orchestra Project; Alberto Almarza, *flute soloist;*
   Gil Rose, *conductor*

Form: Concerto in two movements. **TRACK 18:** First movement for flute, strings, harp, and percussion. **TRACK 19:** Second movement for full orchestra with flute solo and special percussion.

Function: Concert music

WHAT TO LISTEN FOR:

- A special flute technique in which the soloist plays and hums the melody at the same time, imitating the sound of the Persian *ney*
- Wide variety of percussion instruments, including the *darabukkah,* the hourglass-shaped Middle-Eastern drum
- Melodies that make use of slides and quarter-tones, pitches that fall between those of the Western scale
- Movement form based on "mosaic elaboration"; sections are numbered according to the composer's rehearsal numbers
- Use of an orchestra divided into three ensembles

	STRUCTURE	DESCRIPTION
0:00	**Movement 1 [TRACK 18]**	Harp and strings slowly play a series of pitches, mainly using descending stepwise motion, sustaining each pitch for some time. Although the conductor is marking a regular beat pattern, the listener cannot perceive any sense of the beat because nearly all of the pitches are placed irregularly between the beats.
1:07	1	The flute soloist begins playing. Strings and the "quasi *gamelan*" group (chimes, harp, and vibraphone) continue sustaining notes as before.
1:53	2	Various instruments, including violin and vibraphone, come to the fore and then fade back into the texture.
2:31	3	
2:52	4	A pair of stones are played by a percussionist, accelerating and then decelerating.

(c o n t i n u e s)

(continued)

	STRUCTURE	DESCRIPTION
3:10	5	The strings and "quasi *gamelan*" gradually grow in volume, playing fragments of scales and bits of melodies more insistently.
3:46	6	A *crescendo*. Imitation occurs as the violins copy bits of the flute part. The flute moves up to a high register, and the humming effect is no longer heard.
4:00	7	The orchestra pauses for breath, and the strings and flute play ascending scales.
4:29	8	The flute trills, and the rest of the orchestra plays a *sforzando* (a burst of volume), followed by a crescendo from softest to loudest.
4:42	9	The strings and flute drop out, leaving only the "quasi *gamelan*." As at the beginning of the movement, the rhythms are so irregular that no real beats are perceived.
5:24	**Recapitulation**	The harp and violins, then the rest of the strings, gradually reenter with a stepwise melody nearly identical to that at the beginning of the movement.
6:09	10	The flute enters with the humming technique. The melody is a variation of the original flute theme, at 1.
6:48	11	
7:13		The flute soloist changes to an alto flute. Meanwhile, another flutist in the orchestra plays a second alto flute using the same humming technique.
7:25	12	The stones are heard again, though less loudly than at 4. The flute soloist begins playing the alto flute.
8:09	13	"Quasi *gamelan*" drops out, leaving only the solo flute and strings. These instruments begin hovering around a single pitch; some play pitches slightly higher, and some slightly lower, using regular Western pitches as well as quarter-tones. They change pitches at seemingly random (but actually carefully timed) intervals.
8:46	14	The music seems to shimmer as different clusters of tones appear. Gradually, the instruments drop out, beginning with the flute and ending with a viola playing the central pitch, B-flat.
9:30	**End of movement 1**	There is a segue into movement 2, with no break between movements. The second movement is composed for full orchestra with flute solo.
0:00	**Movement 2 [TRACK 19]**	
	15	A horn joins the viola on the B-flat, and the viola drops out. A short ascending three-note motive appears in the string bass and is repeated, adding instruments and volume as it goes. As the motive builds, the pause between repetitions gets shorter and

shorter until it disappears. The full orchestra crescendos. After a sudden break and a pause, the solo flute presents a new motive, rising and falling, which is imitated by woodwinds (piccolo, oboe, clarinet, and bassoon).

0:38	17	The dialogue between the soloist and the woodwind section develops, accelerating and growing louder. There is a pause.
1:02	18	An ascending motive based on the last three notes before the pause is tossed from clarinet to flute to bassoon, back to flute, and then to piccolo.
1:19	19	The full orchestra does another large crescendo and plays an ascending scale.
1:25	20	The *darabukkah* begins a fast-paced solo. The solo is sharply rhythmic, but the meter is unusual; the *darabukkah* plays two measures of five beats each, followed by one measure of seven beats, then two measures of five, one measure of seven, etc. This irregular pattern makes the meter difficult to hear.
1:32	21	The solo becomes a duet as a solo piccolo sounds high above the *darabukkah*. The meter of the flute part is different from that of the *darabukkah* and even more irregular; measures containing 2, 4, 5, 6, 7, and 8 beats are mixed together without any discernible pattern. The piccolo and *darabukkah* solos accelerate into a trill.
2:05	22	The string section takes over the role of the *darabukkah*, as it plays a single chord rhythmically in a rhythmic pattern based on 5+5+7. The music in section 22, then, is the same as that in 20, but the instrumentation changes.
2:10	23	All the woodwinds play the same melody heard in 21. The string section continues with the *darabukkah* pattern, repeating the first half of 21 with a different instrumentation.
2:21	24	The high woodwinds (piccolo, oboe, clarinet) continue playing the piccolo melody, as in the second half of 21. The rest of the orchestra ceases the *darabukkah* pattern, instead playing homophonic chords in a rhythmic pattern based on the piccolo (now woodwind) part.
2:33	25	
2:45	26	Trombones and trumpets enter loudly, just as the high woodwinds build to a trill like that at the end of 21. The rest of the orchestra also crescendos.
2:54	27	The orchestra suddenly falls silent, except for a percussion solo that begins on bongos, moves briefly to tom toms, and finally to the *darabukkah*. The solo has the same 5+5+7 metric pattern as before.
3:07	28	A flute solo joins the *darabukkah*, which soon drops out.
3:26	Recording ends	

Rehearsal numbers are often placed at changes of texture or structurally important points as can be seen and heard at rehearsal number 1, where the flute solo enters.

Vali clearly draws inspiration from Persian music and his music represents the complex identity of a Persian expatriate. A listener familiar with Persian folk and classical music would recognize the Persian sounds and rhythms; "Persian listeners would certainly identify the *dashti* mode," says Vali. For Persians who migrated from Iran and settled in Paris or Los Angeles, the Vali concerto evokes memories of musical life in Iran, where Western symphonies existed alongside Persian traditional music. Vali's music perpetuates a century-long, hybrid soundscape that grew out of the interaction between Persian and Western musics.

Reza Vali's experience in drawing on Persian musical sources and his commentary on the dialectic between Western and world musics move us beyond issues of individual and community identity to consider broader questions regarding music and intercultural identities. Since the colonial era, European and American composers have drawn freely on the music traditions of people their societies have ruled. The Western listener might interpret Vali's flute concerto within the Western orchestral soundscape, hearing the mixture of elements as typical late twentieth-century exotic or experimental music.

During the last two decades there has been increasing sensitivity among scholars and composers about the significance and ethics of musical borrowing. Many have argued that these borrowings are not benign, but exploit traditions as they use and transform culturally significant sounds. Controversies over musical borrowing and hybrid musical styles cut across all types of music, from classical to world pop. For example, a heated debate arose surrounding Paul Simon's use of South African musics and musicians such as the Ladysmith Black Mambazo ensemble in his popular *Graceland* album, a process Simon conceived as collaborative, but which others have criticized as exploitative.

Indeed, Reza Vali has questioned Western ideas of Persian music, especially resisting the notion of heterophony. Vali states:

Heterophony derives from an Orientalist vision of the Middle East. What Westerners perceive as heterophony is actually polyphony, just not explicit. It's more subtle, emerging from the interactions between, say, a voice and instrument. When a Persian singer improvises with an instrumental accompaniment, subtle time delays between the musicians occur which result in a special type of horizontal polyphony. Westerners like to claim that the West has invented polyphony, and we have as a result looked at the music of Asia from a perspective that has distorted the view. In my opinion, heterophony is a myth.

The music of Reza Vali guides us back to the issues of musical exchange and synthesis we have encountered in previous chapters, providing yet another perspective on this complex issue. We have seen instances of musical exchange shaped by close study and cooperation with the music tradition in question; the music of Evan Ziporyn and his collaboration with Balinese composer I Nyoman Windha, discussed in Chapter 6, are models of cross-cultural musical dialogue. Some composers have incorporated music they encountered through live performances or recordings, as we heard in the compositions of David Hykes, presented in the Introduction, who uses the biphonic singing styles of *khoomii* and Tibetan chant in his music. Astor Piazzolla composed music informed by lifelong activity as a player of the *bandoneón* and lover of the tango of his native Argentina, as we learned in Chapter 7. The Vali flute concerto provides more nuance as we encounter a composer who draws on soundscapes from his national background while operating within and questioning the aesthetic frameworks and institutional settings of modernist twentieth-century composers.

Reza Vali's music is an example of informed musical synthesis, drawing on processes of descent, affinity, and close study, to attain another variation on "the ways in which art musics have drawn upon . . . popular, non-Western, and ethnic musics, and what these relations mean in cultural and political terms."[10] This case study suggests that the creation of musical hybrids extends well beyond the arena of musical sound to provide insight into personal and collective identity. Reza Vali's music tells us a great deal about how he perceives himself, but also about how he conceives of himself in relation to others, even others with whom he shares historical, national, and creative connections. As Reza Vali muses: "I cannot go back to being a traditional Persian musician. The other part of me is the Western. It is through the two conflicting aesthetics in one that my music comes to life. For me, the contradiction between the Persian and the Western systems is what I am."

CASE STUDY: The Multiple Meanings of *Karaoke*

Some music, such as the Vali concerto, is a personal statement that has significance for broader communities; other musics belong to a group, even when performed by individuals. One such music tradition, known as *karaoke,* carries a range of ethnic and national associations.

Karaoke—the Japanese word literally means "empty" (*kara*) "orchestra" (*oke*)—originated in 1972 at a snack bar in Kobe, Japan.[11] It is a form of technologically mediated performance that quickly spread throughout Japan, from there to the rest of East Asia, and then became popular internationally.

Karaoke has been discussed by scholars on several levels—as a performance medium grounded in technology; as a setting-specific musical genre; and as a ritualized form of musical behavior.[12] *Karaoke* is dependent on machines—a microphone and playback equipment that amplifies the amateur singer's live performance of the main vocal part and mixes it with the song's instrumental tracks. Typically, a video screen displays the lyrics of the song, although technologies of *karaoke* vary widely and are changing rapidly.

Karaoke is closely associated with specific settings, especially places such as restaurants and clubs with music and drink. From its beginning *karaoke* was performed in nightclubs and bars, where it substituted for live performers, but it has also had an active life at dinner parties and in private homes.[13]

Wherever it is performed in Japan, the social and musical behaviors associated with *karaoke* are quite formalized and patterned. *Karaoke* is generally performed in a group setting; one person takes the microphone at a time. Rules for *karaoke* performance circulate formally in *karaoke* journals and informally through oral tradition. Variants of a popular list of seven taboos in *karaoke* include the following rules: (1) Do not sing when you are drunk; (2) Do not sing too loudly; (3) Do not abuse the echo effect too much; (4) Do not monopolize the microphone; (5) Do not sing songs written for the opposite sex unless you want to surprise the audience; (6) Do not sing songs composed by very gifted writers (because they are usually too difficult for lay persons); and (7) Do not be too narcissistic.[14] These rules are intended to regulate politeness in public spaces and maintain traditional gender hierarchies. Additional hidden rules— an individual ought not sing two songs in succession nor repeat a song that another person has already sung—guarantee decorum and minimize competition.[15] In general, *karaoke* provides a congenial, if formalized, setting for repetition of well-known songs and imitation of beloved singers. It also reveals connections to an important Japanese aesthetic principle.

A ten-year-old boy sings *karaoke* with his family at home in Tokyo.

Karaoke draws on the traditional Japanese value of *kata* ("patterned form"), which pervades the Japanese arts, including the tea ceremony, flower arranging, dance, and the martial arts. All of these forms are composed of precise, named patterns. Form is considered more important than original content, and deviations from the established pattern are discouraged. In learning to replicate songs, dances, or tea ceremonies, the individual becomes part of a historical continuum linked together through rituals of repetition.[16]

An excellent example of the *kata* principle in a historical musical style is *kabuki* theater, dramatic entertainment that first emerged in seventeenth-century Japan and is still performed today. In *kabuki, kata* guides everything from the actor's vocal expression and physical movements to costuming, makeup, and scenic effects:

> Some *kata* are ephemeral and pass as quickly as they are created. But other *kata* of "patterned acting" have been polished and perfected over generations, and these form the foundation of kabuki performing art. When the best actors perform traditional *kata*, we are strongly reminded of . . . [Japanese] woodblock prints, in the economy of means, strong visual design, and vividness of execution.[17]

Just as there are *kata* through which actors convey different emotions and choreograph their movements, there are *kata* shaping musical expression. Music accompanies every scene in *kabuki* theater, performed by an onstage ensemble termed the *debayashi* and an offstage ensemble for sound effects, called the *geza*. The music of both ensembles is constituted of musical patterns that signal the progression of the highly structured *kabuki* play.[18]

In Listening Guide 78 (see page 440), we hear the passage *kata shagiri*, a well-known *kata* pattern played by the *noh* flute and *taiko* drum before or after the performance of famous compositions or dances within a *kabuki* performance.

In the *kata shagiri*, following an introduction by the *taiko* drum punctuated by the cries (*kakegoe*) of the drummer, the *noh* flute enters with a high, piercing pitch heard at the beginning and end of the first musical pattern; the same pitch returns at the end of the entire *kata shagiri* passage. The highest pitch on the flute is used to signal the beginning and end of a section of *kabuki* dance. This pattern is so standard that when an audience familiar with the style hears this passage and the high flute sound, it begins to applaud and the curtain starts to close even before the piece ends. Thus the *kata shagiri* is constructed of a series of small musical patterns or formulae, which together constitute a short passage that marks a juncture within larger divisions of form in the *kabuki* play.

Revelations of self are thought to occur within such highly patterned forms, their repetitiveness engendering trust, empathy, and intimacy. *Kata* provides the aesthetic framework for repeating a well-known pattern, an aesthetic that reverberates through *karaoke. Karaoke* also draws on a long tradition in Japan of communal, public singing in which the act of participation was considered to be more important than the quality of the performance. *Karaoke* originated in male-dominated nightclubs, where conviviality was expressed through participatory activities such as singing. Speech was thought to be variable and unpredictable; song was valued for its structure and pattern.

Kata Shigiri (prelude or postlude for Japanese *kabuki* theater)

CD 3
Track 20

Date of recording: 1956
Performers: *Noh* flute and *taiko* drum of the *hayashi* (ensemble)
Form: *Hayashi* interlude
Function: Short, formulaic piece performed before period theatrical pieces or dance
Tempo: Irregular

WHAT TO LISTEN FOR:

- The piercing quality of the *noh* flute and blurring of pitches through the use of slides
- Variation throughout of two shifting rhythmic patterns sharply delineated by the *taiko* drum
- The cries of the drummer, called *kakegoe,* which serve to mark the time and hold together the flexible rhythmic structure and overlapping patterns of flute and drum

---

STRUCTURE AND DESCRIPTION

0:01   The section is introduced by a woodblock, struck twice, followed by the drummer's cry "ho." The *taiko* begins playing, followed by the flute playing a six-pitch pattern, with alternation between adjacent pitches. We will call this pattern a, which has a contour like this: Ν

0:14   The flute plays a short melodic pattern three times; it consists of a stepwise ascent followed by a descending skip. This pattern is repeated while the *taiko* plays a regular rhythm. We will call this pattern b. The rhythm becomes asymmetrical during the third playing of pattern b.

0:34   The rhythm becomes more dense and complex as a melodic pattern begins, pattern a', which reverses pattern a. (Pattern a' has a contour like this: Ν) This is followed by a short pattern, b', which is based on the end of b. Both are then repeated, with an extra b' at the end (a' b' a' b' b').

0:53   The musicians accelerate as the flute plays a third pattern, c, related to what came before. A final pattern, similar to b but extended, rounds out the passage. The high pitch on the flute, the final drummer's cry, and the two strong *taiko* beats mark the cadence and close this short piece, signaling the rise or fall of the curtain.

1:09   Recording ends.

One Japanese popular song genre, called *enka,* is closely associated with *karaoke.* This nostalgic style is well known and especially meaningful to the generation of Japanese who came of age immediately following World War II. Some Japanese musicians compare *enka* music to the tango; both have melodramatic themes of love and the capacity to bring listeners to tears. *Enka* is based on stylized formulas on multiple levels—formulas for its processes of production and formulas to ensure the emotional impact of its performances.

The *karaoke* singer of *enka* must not only reproduce the song's words and music, but also must imitate the original singer's style. Thus, the performer has a model in mind and imitates the soloist whose voice is absent in the *karaoke* version, which contains only accompaniment. For this reason, the *karaoke* song repertory tends to be accessible to amateur performers, predictable in style, and centered around a small group of popular singers.

In Listening Guide 79 (see page 442) we hear a classic *enka* song sung by Hibari Misora, the singer known as "the Queen of Enka" and "the Lark." Misora, whose music is revered in Japan, was often compared during her lifetime to the famous tango singer Carlos Gardel, known as "the Thrush." The Japanese tango singer Abo Ikuo composed a tango titled *The Thrush and the Lark,* which seeks to convey the affinity between the songs performed by these singers, who in fact never met. The similarity of the *enka* and tango repertories in both affect and subject matter probably accounts for the popularity of both genres in Japan and among Japanese abroad.[19]

This *enka* song, *Ringo Oiwake,* (Listening Guide 79) is the poignant reminiscence of a girl from the north part of Japan (Tsugaru) who became a pack-horse driver in the years after World War II. The song's nostalgic text, typical of the *enka* genre, is a meditation on the transience of natural beauty and conjures memories of the girl's mother, who died in Tokyo. The song, its rhythm mimicking the horse's gait, evokes nostalgia for a simpler, rural past in striking contrast to the technologically sophisticated, urban environment in which *enka* was composed, recorded, and performed. Through nostalgia for an imagined past, performed within the social setting of *karaoke, enka* highlights shared values and forges group identity.

Karaoke has deep roots in traditional Japanese values and also maintains broad-based popularity in Japan supported by an active *karaoke* culture. Monthly magazines list the most popular songs—the texts are available in booklets for purchase—and a Japanese television series airs *karaoke* singing lessons. Individuals often join *karaoke* clubs or circles and compete in contests in which participants attempt to emulate the moves and mannerisms of famous singers. Although performed by millions across various national and cultural boundaries, *karaoke* derives its significance from intimate settings for individual performance within a specific group.

Hibari Misora's meteoric career as an *enka* singer is memorialized through recordings and by a museum dedicated to her in Kyoto, Japan.

Ringo Oiwake (Japanese *enka*)

**CD 3
Track 21**

Date: 1945
Composers: Masao Yoneyama, music
Fujio Ozawa, text
Performer: Hibari Misora
Form: Repeated A B A' (ternary), with introduction
Tempo: Moderately slow, duple meter
Mode: Pentatonic melody, based on a mode of Japanese folksong with Western harmony

WHAT TO LISTEN FOR:

- Melancholy, sentimental, and theatrical lyrics typical of *enka,* especially popular in the decades following World War II
- Combination of Western and Japanese modalities in harmony and melody
- Melismatic ornaments called *kobushi* ("little melodies"), particularly at cadences, and often using a vocable "ah" or "e"

STRUCTURE AND TEXT	TRANSLATION	DESCRIPTION
Section A		
0:00 Ringo no hana biraga kaze ni cit-ta yo na Tsuki yo ni, tsuki yo ni sot-to e —	Apple blossoms falling in the wind. Quietly on a moonlit night, moonlit night, e—	The first phrase traces the pentatonic scale upward. The melody then descends on *"kaze ni cit-ta yo na,"* meaning "falling in the wind." In the next phrase, "moonlit night" is sung twice in the lower part of the singer's range, and the phrase ends with a long, arching melisma on the vocable "e."

A casual observer might dismiss *karaoke* as a simple or homogeneous form of popular entertainment, but it actually encompasses many different styles, is performed in varied social contexts, and carries strong meaning for many of its performers and audiences. During the late twentieth century, *karaoke* spread first throughout East Asia, and changes were introduced in different

Time	Japanese	English	Commentary
	Section B		Section B modulates to a different, though related, pentatonic scale. When section A returns, the final phrase is replaced with a short melisma on the vocable "ah."
0:53	Tsugaru Musume wa na i ta to sa	A Tsugaru girl cried	
	Tsu ra i waka re wo na i ta to sa	For the hard farewell.	
	Section A'		
1:03	Ringo no hana biraga kaze ni cit-ta yo na	Apple blossoms falling in the wind,	
	Ah—	Ah—	
	Spoken narration		An oboe plays the melody of the entire A section as the singer narrates. The combination of speech and song dates at least as far back as the earliest examples of *enka,* which were political songs during the Meiji period of the late nineteenth century.
1:30	(Section A)		
	Oiwaki yama no tep-penwo	When over the top of Mount Oiwaki,	
	Wata mi té é na shiro i kumo ga	A cloud like cotton	
	Poc-cari, poc-cari na ga re te yu ki	Slowly floats and	
	Momo no hana ga sa ki sa ku ra ga sa ki	Peach blossoms, cherry blossoms,	
	So I ka ra haya zaki no ringo no hanac-co ga sa ku ko ro wa	And then, early apple blossoms bloom,	
	Orataci no iciban ta ne shi i ki setsu da na ya	It has been our favorite season.	
	Da do mo Jip-pari mu jō no amekosa fut-té	But as it rains incessantly and	
	Shiro i hana bi ra wo ci ra su ko ro	The white petals fall,	
	Ora a no ko ro to kyo Tokyo sa de shinda	I remember my mother	
	Okācian no ko to omo i da shi té	Who died in Tokyo, and	
	Ora ora . . .	I, I . . .	
	Section B		
2:18	Tsugaru Musume wa na i ta to sa	A Tsugaru girl cried	
	Tsu ra i waka re wo n i ta to sa	For the hard farewell.	
	Section A'		
2:28	Ringo no hana biraga kaze ni cit-ta yo na	Apple blossoms falling in the wind,	
	Ah—	Ah—	
2:58	Recording ends		

national settings. For instance, although Japanese *karaoke* is performed in public restaurants and in private homes, Korean *karaoke,* termed *no rae pang,* is usually performed by groups of friends in private rooms at restaurants.[20]

In the 1980s *karaoke* spread among the Chinese in Taiwan, Hong Kong, and China and was exported to diaspora Chinese communities. By 1988,

karaoke was established in a Chinese restaurant in New York City. An ethnographic study of Chinese *karaoke* in the United States suggests that *karaoke* functions in different ways among different segments of the Chinese American community. The study found that Cantonese immigrants from Hong Kong in New York City used *karaoke* for reinforcing cultural connections among themselves and for translation of their customs to outsiders; Taiwanese immigrants in New Jersey used *karaoke* mainly as a status symbol; and Malaysians of Chinese descent living in Queens used *karaoke* as an escape from the pressures of everyday life.[21]

Others worldwide have adapted *karaoke* to a variety of settings, including concerts, life-cycle occasions, and home performances. In addition to its role as an international form of popular entertainment, *karaoke* has grown and diversified to construct identity within many different social settings. *Karaoke* singers are keenly aware of differences between *karaoke* styles, describing them in terms of ethnic and national sensibilities. The owner of several *karaoke* clubs on the East and West Coast in the United States says that "Japanese singers like to sing alone to show off their voice. Americans like to sing together, loud, chorus style and with dancing."[22]

Other music traditions are transformed over time, proving flexible enough to incorporate new styles and settings. Next we will take a close look at the multiple identities expressed by soundscapes that originated in the Gulf Coast regions of Louisiana and Texas.

CASE STUDY: Multiple Identities in Cajun and Zydeco Musics

The closely related Cajun and zydeco music cultures illustrate several issues that relate to identity in the twenty-first century through their relevance to place, ethnicity, class, race, and gender. The two musical styles share the same geographical base and spring from closely related historical roots that they continue to celebrate through music. As we will see, Cajun and zydeco musics and the people who perform them are defined by their similarities as well as through their differences.

The French Heritage of Creoles and Cajuns

The Creoles and the Cajuns share the same language—French—and the same geographical space—Southwest Louisiana. Although their cultures and musics developed side by side and display many common features deriving from a shared French heritage, present-day Creoles, in particular, go to great lengths to point out the distinctions between the two groups.

The Creole and Cajun traditions can be traced back to the French-speaking people who arrived in Louisiana during the sixteenth and seventeenth centuries (see **"Looking Back: Creole and Cajun History"**). Before the Creoles and Cajuns, the Spanish and then the French colonized the region; the French became dominant when the area became a French colony in 1731.

The people termed Creoles, a heterogeneous group of mixed French, Spanish, and African or Afro-Caribbean descent, began arriving in New Orleans in the early 1600s, while the Cajuns arrived later, beginning in 1755. Cajuns come from a community of French refugees who lived in Acadia, the region off the eastern coast of Canada later called Nova Scotia and who were expelled by British troops and forced to migrate once again. Some settled in the northeastern United States, but the majority migrated south to the French territory of

The map locates south Louisiana Cajun towns such as Eunice, Mamou, Basile, Gueydon, and, of course, Lafayette.

LOOKING *Back*

Creole and Cajun Histories

The background of Creole identity

1600s	Term *Creole* first used to describe people of African, French, Spanish, or Portuguese descent living in the West Indies and present-day southern United States.
1718	New Orleans (la Nouvelle-Orléans) founded.
1719	Wholesale importation of slaves from Africa to Louisiana begins.
1724	Promulgation of *code noir* ("black code"), a social system with a free black class that enjoyed legal rights and privileges but not the social status of whites.
1779	Term *Creole* first used in Louisiana documents in reference to persons of color.
1780s	Louisiana imports African and Creole slaves from the West Indies.
1791–1809	10,000 free blacks and slaves flee insurrection in Santa Domingo and go to New Orleans.
1803	Haitian refugees arrive in New Orleans.
Late 1803	Louisiana Purchase.
1809	6,000 French refugees flee the West Indies for Louisiana.

Acadian migration and emergence of Cajun identity

1604	Samuel de Champlain founds Acadia in present-day Nova Scotia, populated by French-speaking settlers from coastal France.

Louisiana. The name "Cajun" derives from the adjective *acadien,* meaning a person from Acadia.[23]

Although many Creole people preceded the Cajun migration into the region, the present-day musical style most closely associated with Creole identity—zydeco music—emerged only in the mid-twentieth century. For this reason, we will begin our discussion with the Cajun music tradition, which predates zydeco, and then discuss the Creole music tradition.

1713	Treaty of Utrecht cedes Acadia to Britain, turning Acadia into a British colony.
1745	Acadians refuse to take oath of allegiance to King of England.
1755	Expulsion of 1755, marking forced migration of French people from Acadia mainly to south Louisiana.
1763–1776	2,400 Acadians arrive in Louisiana.
1785	Second group of Acadians arrive in Louisiana.

Creole and Cajun reconciliation and interaction

1929	Creole accordionist Amédé Ardoin and Cajun fiddler Dennis McGee record *Eunice Two-Step,* a landmark bringing the music of Cajuns and Creoles together.
1930s	The accordion becomes the instrument of choice for early zydeco musicians.
1950s–1960s	Surge of Cajun pride as music reaches mainstream audience.
Early 1970s	Cajun renaissance movement.
1980s	Shift toward English lyrics in zydeco.
1982	First annual Southwest Louisiana Zydeco Festival in Plaisance, Louisiana.
1987	Popularization of zydeco music in commercial films (*The Big Easy*) and recordings (Paul Simon's *Graceland*).
1990s	New zydeco groups formed across the United States and around the world.

Settings: Musics of Place

Shortly after the Cajuns settled in Louisiana in 1762, control of the area was ceded to Spain. Unwelcome in Spanish-dominated New Orleans, many Cajuns moved to the tidal flats and lived alongside the bayous (inland channels with thick vegetation) of what is now southwest Louisiana.

There they kept their French traditions and language and came into contact with a number of other peoples, including Spanish, Native Americans, European

Bayous are found throughout much of the state of Louisiana and range from small, slow creeks to swampy inlets along the Gulf Coast. Bayou communities such as the one shown here were particularly hard-hit by the storm surge and floodwaters caused by Hurricane Katrina in August 2005.

Americans, and African Americans. The mix gave rise to a rich, distinctive culture and musical style that came to be known, along with the people themselves, by the term "Cajun."

Evidence suggests that long before their music became popular in the late twentieth century, the Cajuns contributed to other well-known American musical styles. The Cajuns kept horses in Louisiana, and it appears that their cowboy songs later spread to Texas and the West. John and Alan Lomax, who made recordings among the Cajuns from the 1930s onward, noted that one Cajun song had a French-derived refrain, *"Hip and Tiyo"* (*Taïaut*), which may have inspired the cowboy song "hipiyaye, tipiyayo." Whatever its origin and influence, the refrain *Hip and Tiyo* was certainly in wide circulation among Cajun singers. In a song recorded in 1934, the Cajun musician Joe Falcon sings of two dogs named Hip and Taïaut who stole a sled.

The Cajun accordionist Joe Falcon performed with his first wife, Cleoma, a guitarist (pictured here), and with his second wife, Theresa, a drummer. The importance of Cajun music to family and ethnic identity is underscored by the presence of young Lulubelle Falcon, standing between her parents.

Joe Falcon's 1928 version of the song *Allons à Lafayette,* accompanied by his wife Cleoma Breaux, is generally considered the first recording of a Cajun song (Listening Guide 80; see page 452). This recording started a thriving ethnic record business within the Cajun community (see page 450, **"Studying Music: Ethnic Recordings and Ethnic Identities"**).

The song heard in Listening Guide 80 was recorded live at the Triangle Club in Scott, Louisiana, in 1963 and released after Falcon's death. Joe Falcon plays accordion and sings; his vocal style and French dialect are distinctive, as are the instruments. In addition to the accordion, the ensemble includes fiddle, guitar, triangle, and drums, the latter played by Falcon's second wife, Theresa Falcon. Women usually performed Cajun music publicly only in the company of their husbands. The fiddle traveled with the Acadians when they were forced to migrate south. The accordion, introduced into Cajun music by German immigrants to Louisiana during the second half of the nineteenth century, dominated Cajun music during much of the twentieth. In the late twentieth century, the electric guitar and drum set were incorporated into Cajun bands.

The text of the song pays homage to Lafayette, an important Cajun center and one of many South Louisiana towns featured in Cajun music. Note that the Cajun French lyrics of *Allons à Lafayette* are pronounced in a slurred manner. Unlike other ballads we have examined, such as *Barbara Allen*, the words in *Allons à Lafayette* do not recount long narratives; the only consistent theme is the journey to Lafayette, retold at the beginning of each verse. As with many songs transmitted through oral tradition, the text of this song exists in multiple versions.

We might wonder at the widespread popularity of a song with such thin and variable textual content; the emphasis here is on the *sound* of the words. Cajun French has declined dramatically; until the late twentieth century, it was illegal to teach the language in Louisiana schools. Young people were discouraged from learning or speaking Cajun so that they might better fit into mainstream society. Cajun song was one of the few means of preserving the special Cajun French dialect, and, by extension, Cajun identity. Cajun music has recently been at the center of efforts to revive Cajun culture by a generation that has lost the ability to speak the language. The emphasis on language as sound, termed "cajunization," evokes a certain nostalgia, since through music one can still "speak Cajun." This perspective comes through in a description of the important Cajun fiddler Dennis McGee, who is said to have used words for their rhythm and sound, not simply to tell a story.[24]

The button accordion is at the heart of the Cajun sound, making songs longer by what Cajuns refer to as "turning the verses," repeating the tune between verses.[25] A single accordion or fiddle might suffice for a small private dance in a home, but the grand ball of Cajun society, called the *fais-dodo,* requires a full band. The name *fais-dodo* (literally, "go to sleep"), which refers to both the ball and the building in which it was held, comes from the old custom of bringing along small children who would be lulled to sleep by the music.

In addition to Cajun music's important role in reviving a language rarely spoken and its distinctive sound, the music was also performed in settings that ensured its close association with Cajun family and social life. The association of Cajun music with dance has played an important part in keeping the music

Ethnic Recordings and Ethnic Identities

Between 1900 and 1940, the major record companies (Victor, Columbia, and Edison) sent out teams to discover new musics among ethnic communities. Because of the large immigrant population in its cities, the United States became a center for these recording efforts, and a new American genre of "ethnic recordings" was born.[26] Directed at ethnic communities united by shared national, linguistic, racial, or religious backgrounds, these records were produced and distributed on 78-rpm discs. In the century since the first discs were issued, ethnic records have become one of our most valuable resources for studying ethnic identity as expressed through music.

In general, ethnic recordings were characterized by their small runs of about one thousand copies. They spanned a wide variety of musical styles. A very popular subset of ethnic recordings of the 1920s and 1930s, known as "race records," consisted of music performed by and for African Americans. Many of the earliest jazz recordings were race records.

An oral history of the first Cajun record in 1928, Joe Falcon's *Allons à Lafayette,* explains how the Cajun community supported the recording and the importance of the recording to Cajun identity.

> George Burrow, a jewelry store owner in Rayne, persuaded Falcon to go to New Orleans with him to make some records to be sold in Burrow's Rayne store. "We went over there," Falcon recalled. "They looked at us—we was but two, just myself and my wife Cleoma Breaux, she played the guitar—but they were used to

alive. A variety of dances are performed to Cajun music, ranging from country square dances to waltzes and polkas, usually in counterclockwise motion around the dance floor. Both the "Cajun jitterbug" and the "Cajun two-step" are performed in distinctive ways in Cajun communities in Louisiana and elsewhere.

> They use a slightly deeper knee and ankle bend on the second and fourth beats of each measure, cued by the backbeat usually played on the snare drum. The net effect of this characteristic, distributed over most of the couples on a dance floor, is a sea of heads gently bobbing together in time to the music, regardless of variations in footwork and arm orientation. In the two-step, many dancers also execute the so-called "double bounce," in which smaller sinking movements on

recording with orchestras. 'That's not enough music to make a record,' they said. So George had 250 records paid for before I even went to make them. So George started talking: 'We got to run it through because that man there,' he said, pointing to me, 'is popular in Rayne; the people are crazy about his music and they want the records.' But they said, 'We don't know if it's going to sell.' They then turned around and asked him, 'How much would you buy?' He told them he wanted 500 copies as the first order. 'Ah,' they said, '500! When are you gonna get through selling that?' 'That's my worry,' he said, 'I want 500.' And he made out a check for 500 records. They started looking at each other. 'Well,' they said, 'you go ahead and play us a tune just for us to hear.'"[27]

In those days ethnic recordings did not have to sell by the thousands to satisfy the companies. In that same interview, Falcon recalled that Cajun people were impressed and proud that one of their own had cut a record: "Even some of the poorest country fellows, they buy as high as two records. They ain't got no Victrola, but they buy and go to their neighbor's and play it!"

Despite its success, the ethnic recording industry declined in the great economic depression of the 1930s and World War II. By the late 1950s, independent companies had taken over the recording of ethnic music on LPs, paving the way for the world music record market that proliferated in the last quarter of the twentieth century. But the vintage ethnic records still survive today, the originals preserved in sound archives and the songs reissued on cassettes and compact discs, providing a rich resource for scholars and for individuals and communities seeking to revive the music of their pasts.

beats one and three are added to the pronounced sinking movements on beats two and four, which means that all of the dancer's upward movements happen between the beats, in constant syncopation with the music.[28]

By the middle of the twentieth century, with the advent of the radio and the phonograph, new influences shaped Cajun music. Through recordings, touring musicians, and festivals, the music also began to spread beyond the immediate community. Among the outside influences on Cajun music were country and western tunes, which many Cajun musicians borrowed to supplement the repertory of traditional Cajun songs. This modeling on "American" musical styles reflects the Cajun culture's gradual move into broader American society and the slow transformation of Cajun identity.

Allons à Lafayette ("Let's Go to Lafayette," Cajun song)

CD 3
Track 22

Date of performance: 1963; first recording of this song made in 1928
Performers: Joe Falcon, *accordion and voice;* Lionel Leleux, *fiddle;* Theresa
    Falcon, *drums and voice;* Allen Richard, *bass guitar*
Form: Strophic song
Tempo: Moderate two-step duple meter

WHAT TO LISTEN FOR:

- The distinctive Cajun French dialect and pronunciation
- Instrumental improvisations that provide variety within the strophic structure by building on the original melody
- The spontaneity of a live performance at the Triangle Club in Scott, Louisiana, including cries from Joe Falcon and background noise from the audience

---

	STRUCTURE AND TEXT	TRANSLATION	DESCRIPTION
0:00	**Refrain** **Phrase a** Allons à Lafayette c'est pour changer ton nom. **Phrase b** On va t'appeler madame, Madame Canaille Comeaux.	Let's go to Lafayette for to change your name. They're going to call you madame, Madame Canaille Comeaux.	Falcon sings the verse; the fiddle plays a more ornamented version of the melody in a low register. The bass guitar and drums provide harmonic support and keep the beat. These background instruments are sometimes referred to as the *rhythm section.*
	Phrase a Petite, t'es trop mignonne pour faire ta criminelle! **Phrase b** Observe moi bien, mignonne, tu vas voir mais pour toi-même **Phrase a** Que moi mais j' mérite pas tous ça mais t'après faire! **Phrase b** Si loin comme moi j'su' d'toi, mais ça, ça m'fait pitier!	Little one, you're too cute to do me wrong! Look me over, my beauty, you'll see for yourself. That I don't deserve all the things you're doing! So far as I am from you, why, it's pitiful!	The phrase structure is simple: there are two contrasting phrases, a and b, which repeat in alternation. Within each phrase, there is also a two-part *antecedent-consequent* structure; the first half of each phrase poses a question (*"Allons à Lafayette"*), which the second half of the phrase answers (*"c'est pour changer ton nom"*).

0:32	**Instrumental section** **Fiddle solo**	The instrumental section uses the same chord structure as the refrain—that is, the rhythm section plays the same pattern of harmonies, but occasionally extends a harmony for a few extra beats. Meanwhile, the soloists improvise a fiddle melody that fits with that harmonic pattern. After playing once through the complete chord pattern, the fiddle plays a new countermelody.
1:10	**Fiddle solo continues, lower register**	The fiddler drops into a lower register as he improvises, based more closely on the original melody of the refrain.
1:32	**Accordion solo**	Next, the accordion takes a solo. Falcon (who plays accordion in addition to singing) bases his improvisation rather closely on the original melody of the refrain. Some calls by Falcon, probably to the dancers, are heard.
2:17	**Refrain**	Falcon sings the refrain again without much variation from the original.
2:27	**Recording ends**	

"Rendez Vous des Cajuns" is a radio show broadcast every Saturday evening from the Liberty Theatre in Eunice, Louisiana. The audience includes local fans and visitors from out of state, as families come to celebrate their Cajun heritage. Because the show is completely in French, visitors often turn to local people sitting near them to ask questions, establishing a context through which outsiders learn about Cajun music and identity and insiders validate their heritage. Here Ally Young and the Basile Cajun Band (bass player Claudia Wood, accordionist Ally Young, guitarist Erroll Guilbeau, drummer Eston Bellow, and fiddler Lee Manuel) play as audience members dance. Longtime host Barry Ancelet sits on a stool at the far left.

At the same time, these borrowed tunes were "cajunized" by blurring the clear declamation of their words and instead emphasizing the "feeling of loss and longing" through the sound of the text.[29] New instruments such as the pedal steel guitar and techniques such as new styles of fiddling entered Cajun music as well.

Throughout its history, Cajun music has benefited from musical cross-fertilization, but of all the influences that shaped it, the Creole zydeco tradition has had the greatest impact.

Sound and Significance: Singing Ethnicity, Race, and Class

People do not define their identities in a vacuum but establish them in relationship to the identities of others. For the French-speaking peoples of Louisiana and the Gulf Coast, music became a reflection of the distinct identities of two groups in particular—Cajuns and Creoles—who shared the same language and economic hardship, but came from different racial backgrounds.

The relationship between Cajuns and Creoles has been complicated and still is, perhaps because Cajun and Creole cultures have had much in common. Scorned by urban whites, poor Creoles of color and Cajun whites worked side by side in the same fields. This prolonged period of cultural exchange resulted in the blending of culinary and linguistic traditions. Spicy Creole *gumbos*

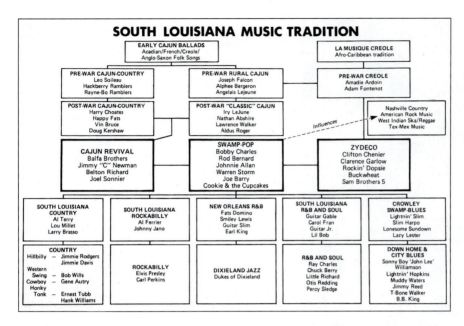

SOUTH LOUISIANA MUSIC TRADITION

EARLY CAJUN BALLADS
Acadian/French/Creole/
Anglo-Saxon Folk Songs

LA MUSIQUE CREOLE
Afro-Caribbean tradition

PRE-WAR CAJUN-COUNTRY
Leo Soileau
Hackberry Ramblers
Rayne-Bo Ramblers

PRE-WAR RURAL CAJUN
Joseph Falcon
Alphee Bergeron
Angelais Lejeune

PRE-WAR CREOLE
Amadie Ardoin
Adam Fontenot

POST-WAR CAJUN-COUNTRY
Harry Choates
Happy Fats
Vin Bruce
Doug Kershaw

POST-WAR "CLASSIC" CAJUN
Iry LeJune
Nathan Abshire
Lawrence Walker
Aldus Roger

Influences →

Nashville Country
American Rock Music
West Indian Ska/Reggae
Tex-Mex Music

CAJUN REVIVAL
Balfa Brothers
Jimmy "C" Newman
Belton Richard
Joel Sonnier

SWAMP-POP
Bobby Charles
Rod Bernard
Johnnie Allan
Warren Storm
Joe Barry
Cookie & the Cupcakes

ZYDECO
Clifton Chenier
Clarence Garlow
Rockin' Dopsie
Buckwheat
Sam Brothers 5

SOUTH LOUISIANA COUNTRY
Al Terry
Lou Millet
Larry Brasso

SOUTH LOUISIANA ROCKABILLY
Al Ferrier
Johnny Jano

NEW ORLEANS R&B
Fats Domino
Smiley Lewis
Guitar Slim
Earl King

SOUTH LOUISIANA R&B AND SOUL
Guitar Gable
Carol Fran
Guitar Jr.
Lil Bob

CROWLEY SWAMP-BLUES
Lightnin' Slim
Slim Harpo
Lonesome Sundown
Lazy Lester

COUNTRY
Hillbilly — Jimmie Rodgers
 Jimmie Davis
Western
Swing — Bob Wills
Cowboy — Gene Autry
Honky
Tonk — Ernest Tubb
 Hank Williams

ROCKABILLY
Elvis Presley
Carl Perkins

DIXIELAND JAZZ
Dukes of Dixieland

R&B AND SOUL
Ray Charles
Chuck Berry
Little Richard
Otis Redding
Percy Sledge

DOWN HOME & CITY BLUES
Sonny Boy 'John Lee'
 Williamson
Lightnin' Hopkins
Muddy Waters
Jimmy Reed
T-Bone Walker
B.B. King

This chart shows the complex interchange between Cajun and Creole traditions over time. Some styles, such as swamp pop, which emerged in the late 1950s, blend Creole and Cajun styles with others such as rhythm and blues.

(stews) combined French, African, and American ingredients, and the Cajun dialect of French took on distinctive local features. At times Cajun and Creole musicians even played together, as in the famous duets in the 1920s and 1930s between Cajun fiddler Dennis McGee and Creole accordionist Amédé Ardoin.

But Ardoin was brutally beaten after playing for a Cajun dance, and he never recovered. Racial tension pervaded the history of these two communities. There is one story that a black Creole accordionist playing for a dance was forced by lighter-skinned Creole dancers to don white gloves, stand outside a window, and reach into the room so that only the gloves and his instrument were visible from inside.[30]

The division between Cajuns and Creoles extends to their names for the places they share. Many Creoles take exception to the Louisiana state legislature's decision to label the region Acadiana and refer to it instead as Southwest Louisiana. "The Cajuns have done a good job of promoting their culture," according to one Creole musician, "but I'm not a Cajun. I'm Afro-American Creole, black Creolo—whatever you want to call me other than a Cajun."[31]

Out of these complicated musical, cultural, and racial interactions, a distinctively Creole music that came to be called *zydeco* emerged after World War II. Much more than Cajun music, zydeco has interacted with other African American and Caribbean traditions, including the blues, rhythm and blues, and reggae, adopting the bass guitar, percussion, and even the saxophone. Although zydeco was influenced by Cajun music at first, the tables turned in the second half of the twentieth century, and zydeco began to influence Cajun musicians.

Zydeco musician Clifford Alexander is known for playing the rub board (*frottoir*) in live performances and on recordings, appearing with C. H. Chenier (the son of zydeco king Clifton Chenier) and the Red Hot Louisiana Band as well as with Steve Riley and the Mamou Playboys, who incorporate both Cajun and zydeco styles.

Zydeco uses the same core ensemble as Cajun music: voice, fiddle, accordion, electric guitar, and sometimes piano. Zydeco musicians, led by Clifton Chenier, also began using the keyboard accordion instead of the old button accordions, although button accordions were revived by some in the 1980s.

Zydeco's distinctive sound, however, came in large part from a "found" instrument—a steel washboard or "rub board" (*froittoir*), against which a bottle opener, spoon, or other implement is rubbed. Clifton Chenier is credited with inventing the usual form of the instrument seen today, a corrugated steel plate extending from a collar draped over the player's shoulders, that covers the chest.

The story is that Chenier used an old washboard tied by a string around his neck, but found it awkward and asked a friend at the Gulf Oil Refinery near Houston to design a new arrangement. The close fit of the rub board allows the player not only to keep the rhythm, but also to move around and lead the dancing that accompanies zydeco music.

In Listening Guide 81 (see page 458), we hear the song that gave zydeco its name. The word *zydeco* is said to derive from a French expression, *les haricots* ("the beans"), alluding to a metaphor popular among Creole peoples of color that "the beans are not salty," that is, they are not flavored by the salted meat that is too expensive to buy during hard times. The well-known phrase was first recorded in a musical context by the Lomaxes in 1934 as part of the lyrics to an old French song at a Church in Port Arthur, Louisiana. It was only in 1965, when accordionist Clifton Chenier recorded a piece called *Zydeco Sont Pas Salé,* that the term became permanently attached to the Creole musical style.

This recording captures the fast syncopated rhythm; Chenier's accordion chords stress the second beat of each pair. The chordal accompaniment and bass line are played by the buttons at the player's left hand, while the melody and an occasional chord are played on the piano keyboard at the player's right hand. The distinctive scratching sound of the rub board provides another layer of rhythmic accompaniment.

In Creole society, as in Cajun circles, music long flourished in *bals de maison* ("house dances"). For these parties, young people borrow the home of an elder and clear away the furniture. They eat gumbo, drink, and—most important—dance. Music at these *bals* was a catalyst for social interaction, as it is at a Cajun *fais-dodo*. As zydeco recordings became popular, zydeco became a regular feature of concerts and dance clubs throughout the United States and elsewhere.

Zydeco's Kings and Queens

The use of the titles "king" and "queen" by famous zydeco musicians derives, according to Cajun lore, from Joe Falcon, who called himself the "Famous Columbia Record King." But the first "king of zydeco" was Clifton Chenier. Although there are conflicting stories about how Chenier got his crown—some suggest it was just a publicity gimmick—Chenier claimed in an interview that he became the king of zydeco by winning an accordion contest in Europe

"King" Clifton Chenier plays a keyboard accordion at the Cajun Music Festival in Lafayette, Louisiana, in the mid-1970s.

in 1971: "They had a lot of accordion players, but they couldn't capture my style. But I could play their style, so that's how I walk out with that crown.[32] Whatever the source of Chenier's crown, the image of zydeco kings became a standard part of zydeco culture. When Chenier died in 1987, his crown was buried with him.

Zydeco kings ruled this male-dominated tradition, and only a very few women were able to make a career as zydeco musicians. Ida Guillory is a marked exception (see **"Individual Portraits: Zydeco Queen Ida Guillory"**).

Queen Ida's music embodies all the hallmarks of zydeco style while showcasing her virtuosity on the accordion. Many of her songs comment on aspects of her identity as a zydeco musician with roots in south Louisiana (*Zydeco, Home to New Orleans*), her unusual status as a woman in the largely male world of zydeco musicians (*Hard-Headed Woman*), and issues of race (*Hey Negress*).

Queen Ida's *C'est Moi* (Listening Guide 82; see page 462) is a bilingual song in English and French comparing her personal background in south Louisiana with the reality of her life as a female musician on the road. The song is strophic, with a verse and refrain typical of zydeco music. The rub board provides the rhythm and backup characteristic of zydeco. In this recording Queen Ida plays a three-row button accordion in straight-out zydeco style, with little reference to the Latin or rock-and-roll influences heard in many of her other songs.

Zydeco Sont Pas Salé ("The Beans Are Not Salty," zydeco song)

CD 3
Track 23

Date of recording: 1964, reissued in 1997
Performers: Clifton Chenier, *accordion and voice*; Cleveland Chenier, *rub board*; and members of the Red Hot Louisiana Band
Form: Iterative form
Tempo: Lively, fast

WHAT TO LISTEN FOR:

- The fast, syncopated rhythm with accordion chords stressing the second beat of each pair
- The distinctive scratching sound of the rub board
- A regularly repeating chord progression, a four-measure harmonic pattern, underlying the various melodies

	STRUCTURE AND TEXT	TRANSLATION	DESCRIPTION
0:00	**Introduction** chord progression a		The accordion begins with a dotted (short-long) rhythm. The rub board and drum join in the midst of the first measure. A four-measure chord progression is established: two measures on the tonic, one measure on the dominant, and one measure on the tonic (T T D T).

Raising Voices Together: Uniting Cajun and Zydeco

After a long period of racial tension extending from the period after the Civil War to the twentieth-century civil rights movement, interaction between Cajuns and Creoles is once again evident. New bands are now bridging the racial and musical gap. One such band is Filé, which incorporates elements of Cajun and zydeco and includes musicians from both traditions. Filé plays both traditional Cajun repertory and newer zydeco songs, keeping traditional instruments such as accordion, fiddle, and guitar but adding a keyboard and harmonizing the vocal parts. The cymbals of the drum set replace the traditional rub board. The innovative music of Filé is heard in Listening Guide 83 (see page 464).

Time	Structure	French	English	Commentary
0:10	**Instrumental** chord progression a			The chord progression is repeated, with some modifications to the melody. Syncopation is added in the third measure of the progression.
0:21	**Verse** chord progression a' (shortened)	O Mama! Quoi elle va faire avec le nègre?	Oh, Mama! What's she going to do with the man?	The accordion stops providing the main melody and drops into a chordal accompaniment pattern as the singer enters.
0:28	chord progression a	Zydeco est pas salé, zydeco est pas salé. T'as volé mon traîneau, t'as volé mon traîneau.	The beans aren't salty, the beans aren't salty. You stole my sled, you stole my sled.	Just before the verse begins, the chord progression drops one measure, so the harmony changes to the dominant sooner than expected.
0:38	chord progression a	Regarde Hip et Taïaut, regarde Hip et Taïaut. Regarde Hip et Taïaut, regarde Hip et Taïaut.	Look at Hip and Tiyo, look at Hip and Tiyo. Look at Hip and Tiyo, look at Hip and Tiyo.	*Hip et Taïaut*, the two sled-stealing dogs, are mentioned.
0:48	**Instrumental** chord progression a			The accordion resumes its role as a melody instrument. The melody is closely related to that in the introduction. The accordion suddenly stops its rhythmic chordal accompaniment. Using only the right-hand keyboard, the accordion sustains a single chord—almost a cry—and the singer shouts in response.
0:58	**Break** chord progression a			
1:08	**Instrumental chord** progression a			The accordion's rhythmic accompaniment resumes. The recording fades out.
1:14	Recording ends			

The song contains traditional Cajun and zydeco references, naming places on the Gulf Coast, alluding to "bayou culture," and naming traditional food such as candied yams and turnip greens. The ensemble's name derives from food—filé means an herb mixture containing sassafras and other ingredients.

The song text mentions a "down home" girl, signaling that it draws on an old style of Southern ("down home") country blues, a clear sign of the influence of African American music and identity on the zydeco tradition. We hear this influence in the way that *One Foot in the Bayou* adopts, expands, and varies the traditional blues form. Traditional blues songs have a standard form—*twelve-bar blues* form—in which each verse consists of three lines. The

Zydeco Queen Ida Guillory

Ida Guillory was born in 1930 to rice-farming parents in Lake Charles, Louisiana. She spoke French until she was seven and learned English when she went to school. In 1940, her family moved to Beaumont, Texas, and seven years later to San Francisco. Following her marriage to Ray Guillory, Ida raised three children and drove a school bus. Her mother, an accordionist, passed on the instrument to her daughter. Ida played the accordion for recreation, until one day in 1975 when she sat in with her brother's band, which needed an accordionist for a Mardi Gras fundraising festival. Ida had never played in public before, since "it wasn't feminine for a girl to play any instrument unless it was a piano or violin."

Newspapers picked up word of this performance, and soon Queen Ida and the Bons Temps Band were performing regularly. Within a year, she had a record contract. She quit her job as a bus driver in 1977 to perform full-time and in 1982 won a Grammy for the best ethnic/folk recording.

An interesting aspect of Queen Ida's career and the zydeco tradition as a whole is the close connection between music and food. Queen Ida published a cookbook in 1990 with the same name as one of her albums—*Cookin' with Queen Ida*. The cookbook features Creole recipes such as gumbo, jambalaya, boudin, and shrimp creole that she brought from Louisiana to California. According to Queen Ida, "there's little difference between Creole and Cajun cuisines. . . . Like zydeco, Creole cooking is just a bit spicier."

Queen Ida's ensemble incorporates members of her family, including her brother, Wilbert Lewis, who plays rub board, and her son, Myrick "Freeze" Guillory, who plays accordion and does vocals. On occasions when her brother can't play, Queen Ida drafts her daughter.

When Queen Ida and her family are not touring, they live in a San Francisco suburb where they participate in the active zydeco music and dance scene in the Bay area. Among the trips she deems particularly memorable were her visits to five former French colonies in Africa. "For me it was like going back to Louisiana, where the people speak French, or going to France or Switzerland," Ida explains. "It gave me a chance to speak my *patois* with the people there. They understood me better than I understood them."[33]

Ida Guillory became known as "Queen Ida" after she won a crown at a Mardi Gras celebration in the San Francisco Bay area in 1970. Her musicmaking has always been a family affair; she performs with her brothers Al Rapone and Willie Lewis and her sons Ronald and Myrick "Freeze" Guillory.

second line usually repeats the first, and the third serves as a kind of punch line. Each line is set to four measures (bars) of music, and each of the twelve-bar verses is accompanied by the same sequence of harmonies. *One Foot in the Bayou* expands the blues form to sixteen bars by adding as a refrain a fourth four-bar phrase.

Conclusion

All of the musicians discussed in this chapter construct and express multiple aspects of their identities—ethnic, national, regional, race, class, gender—through their music. In every case, the sound itself contains distinctive markers of identity, providing entry into soundscapes rich in meaning. Sound conveys a sense of place and past through unique instruments such as zydeco's rub board; through rhythms imitating the steady clip-clop of the packhorse's gait in an *enka* song; or through special flute-playing techniques in a concerto. Words play a central role as an integral part of sound preserving unique dialects. The words also refer to places and times that evoke nostalgia—the Louisiana cities and bayous in Cajun lyrics or of the seasons of the past recalled in the *enka* song.

The setting of each of the musical styles also contributes immeasurably to the meaning of the sound. In a concert hall, a restaurant, a dance club, or a home, all these musics come to life only when linked to people, places, and the

C'est Moi ("It's Me," zydeco song)

Date: 1989
Performers: Queen Ida and her Zydeco Band: Queen Ida Guillory, *voice and accordion*; Myrick "Freeze" Guillory, *voice, accordion, and rub board*; Wilbert Lewis, *rub board*; Dennis Geyer, *guitar*; Terence Buddingh, *bass guitar*; Ben Holmes, *drums*; Bernard Anderson, *saxophone*; James Hurley, *violin*
Form: Strophic song with refrain
Tempo: Moderate tempo, quadruple meter

WHAT TO LISTEN FOR:

- Rub board rhythm and backup vocals characteristic of zydeco
- Important role of instruments in introduction, interlude, and conclusion
- Queen Ida's three-button accordion played in a straight-out zydeco style
- Queen Ida's statements of personal identity

STRUCTURE AND TEXT	DESCRIPTION
0:00 **Instrumental introduction**	The introduction begins with a *pick-up* on the accordion, notes played on the weak beats just before the first strong beat. The pervasive long-short rhythmic pattern is sometimes termed a *swing rhythm*, evoking a boogie-woogie blues or early jazz style.
0:16 **Verse 1** Listen to my story, I come from Louisian'. I play my music on an old accordion. *Ooh la la, je suis comme ça.* ("Oo la la, that's the way I am")	Queen Ida sings. Each verse has the musical form A A B A A B; the four A's represent lines of text set to the same music and the two B's represent the repeated line *oo la la, je suis comme ça*, a miniature refrain. Notice the backup singers harmonizing the beginning of this line. The poetic form of each verse is similar: it has two rhyming couplets in addition to the repeated miniature refrain: a a B, c c B. Backup singers harmonize the phrase *Ooh la la*.
0:31 Hotel rooms, I've seen 'em all before. My favorite room is the dance hall floor. *Ooh la la, je suis comme ça.*	

0:45	**Refrain**	The second statement of the phrase *c'est moi* in
	C'est moi, c'est moi, oh, je suis comme ça.	each line of the refrain is performed as speech-song.
	C'est moi, c'est moi, oh, je suis comme ça.	The two lines of the refrain are musically identical.
	("That's me, that's me, oh, that's the way I	Backup singers sing all of the refrain except the
	am.")	interjection "oh." Two trumpets can be heard
		supporting and filling out the sound of the backup
		group and sustaining a note at the end of each line
		of the refrain.

1:01 **Verse 2**
Oh there was a time, I had myself a man.
He didn't realize, he didn't understand.
Ooh la la, je suis comme ça.

The second verse is based on the same music as the first, so the song is strophic. Though the rhyme scheme is repeated, the rhymes themselves are new.

1:15 That's the way I am, it's everything I know.
Playing with the band and singing zydeco.
Ooh la la, je suis comme ça.

1:29 **Refrain**

The refrain is repeated as before.

1:45 **Instrumental break**

The lead accordion takes a solo, emphasizing the swing rhythm. Another accordion fills in harmonies, like a rhythm guitar in a rock band. The instrumental break has the same length as one complete verse and is based on the same harmonic structure as the verse.

2:14 **Verse 3**
You have to put it down, everybody say.
This won't last, some day you'll walk away.
Ooh la la, je suis comme ça.

2:28 That's the way I am, goin' to work at nine.
Three in the morning is about my suppertime.
Ooh la la, je suis comme ça.

2:42 **Refrain**

The refrain is lengthened by adding one repetition of the line.

3:00 Fade out; recording ends at 3:10

One Foot in the Bayou (Cajun/zydeco song)

Date of recording: 1996

Performers: Filé; David Egan, *piano and vocals;* D'Jalma Garnier, *guitar;*
Peter Stevens, *drums;* Kevin Shearin, *bass;* Ward Lormand, *accordion*

Form: Expands on and varies standard 3-line (a a' b), 12-bar blues (3 × 4 bars)
form to a 4-line, 16-measure form with a refrain in line 4

Tempo: Up-tempo, quadruple meter

WHAT TO LISTEN FOR:

- Expansion and variation of the standard twelve-bar blues form
- Feeling of syncopation between the voice, percussion, and other instruments
- Use of cymbals of the drum set to replace the traditional zydeco rub board
- Traditional Cajun and zydeco references to places on the Gulf Coast, bayou culture, and local foods

---

	STRUCTURE AND TEXT	DESCRIPTION
0:00	Instrumental introduction (4 measures)	
0:08	Chorus 1, Vocal solo (16 measures):	
	Phrase a:	
	Diamond rings, limousines, down home girl, uptown dreams.	A melodic line is introduced.
	Phrase a':	
	Penthouse suites, Broadway shows, just don't move her like the zydeco.	The first melodic line is repeated, but with different words.
	Phrase b:	
	She done gone up to the city, now she don't know what to do.	A second melodic line is introduced.
	Refrain:	
	She got one foot in New York City and one foot in the bayou. Spoken: All right!	The refrain uses the same melody as Phrase b.
0:38	Interlude by instruments (4 bars)	

0:46	**Chorus 2, Vocal Solo:**
	Phrase a:
	Taxi cabs, traffic jams, sure do miss her candied yams.
	Phrase a':
	She packed her bags, you should a seen, the big suitcase full of turnip greens.
	Phrase b:
	She done gone up to the city, still got mud on her shoes.
	Refrain:
	She got one foot in New York City and one foot in the bayou.
	Spoken: All right!

This verse uses same structure as in the first, but with different words.

1:16	Interlude by instruments (16 bars)

This interlude contains the complete 16-measure form that appears in verses 1 and 2. Without the words, one can more easily hear the harmonic changes. Also note the "stride" style piano playing, another signal of the blues influence.

1:46	**Chorus 3, Vocal Solo (24 bars)**
	Phrase c:
	Well, if she's gone, I wish her well, she might come home, you just can't tell.
	Phrase c':
	But if she runs out of luck, I'll drive right up and get her in my truck.
	Phrase b:
	'Cause she done gone up to the city, now she don't know what to do.
	Phrase b':
	Born and raised in Morgan City, still got mud on her shoes.
	Refrain:
	She got one foot in New York City and one foot in the bayou.
	She got one foot in New York City and one foot in the bayou.

More harmonic changes can be heard throughout the third verse.

A new melodic phrase is introduced.

Note the return to one of the same melodic phrases as in verse 1 and 2.

2:30	Postlude by instruments (4 bars)
2:44	Recording ends

broader stream of tradition. To step into a musical setting—whether a *fais-dodo, bal de maison, karaoke* bar, or concert hall—is to be surrounded by associations emerging from the musicmaking and the social interaction. In the case of Cajun music and zydeco, the ever-present dancing means that the music is not just sounded, but embodied.

Musicians are linked to a group through live performance and to a broader public through recordings. Today the sounds of *karaoke* and zydeco have moved from private and local realms to public and worldwide contexts, transmitted by the mass media well beyond the boundaries of a single community or place. Country singer Hank Williams had a hit titled *Jambalaya* ("On the Bayou"), and films such as *The Big Easy* feature scenes of Cajun and zydeco music and dance.

Although many people deplore the impact of the mass media on the identity of groups such as the Cajun and Creole communities, sometimes a broader audience reinforces musicians' commitment to their roots. Take the case of Dewey Balfa, a beloved Cajun fiddler. Mr. Balfa was invited as a last-minute replacement to perform in the 1964 folk music festival at Newport, Rhode Island. His local newspaper described his decision to play Cajun music in this public context as "an embarrassment, especially to those trying to put their country roots behind them." His daughter Christine remembers that her father "had never seen more than 200 people together at one time before. And 17,000 people gave him a standing ovation after the first song. And that changed his life. He became a strong advocate for Cajun culture."[34]

Beau Jacques and the Zydeco High Rollers perform at the Southwest Louisiana Zydeco Musical Festival in September 1992.

As we have seen in this chapter, music can support both traditional and rapidly-transforming identities. Through its sound and settings, music can preserve values from the past while providing a lifeline for those struggling to redefine themselves in the present. Whether in the most private moments, or in the most public of contexts, music gives voice to the intensely human search for definition and meaning. It is in the search for identity that the content and form of organized sound enable people to understand their place in the world and to explore new possibilities for the future.

Think carefully about the identities that define you. Which are most important in your life? What musics do you associate with these identities?

Consider your ethnic, racial, and national background. Do any of these categories overlap or converge in your experience? Does one clearly outweigh another in your life at the present moment? What music do you associate with your own background, place of residence, or homeland?

Think about music that has been transmitted through your family or community. Does it reinforce a heritage that you find personally meaningful? Can you recall any music associated with family identity, such as songs sung together on important holidays or at other shared moments?

Is there an identity you have been reluctant to accept? Is there a music tradition associated with this identity in which you do not participate?

As you review other important aspects of your own identity, don't forget to consider the music of your generation. Think about the significance of music in your school or college. Is there any aspect of your personal identity that you have arrived at in part through exposure to a new soundscape?

IMPORTANT TERMS

accordion	*enka*	*ney*
Cajun/Acadian	*fais-dodo*	Persian (Iranian) music
chamber orchestra	fiddle	rub board
concerto	flute	triangle
Creole	*karaoke*	Western orchestra
darabukkah	*kata*	zydeco

Epilogue

Our journey has taken us through more than thirty case studies, surveying soundscapes that emerged in different regions of the globe and extend worldwide today. All are present today in the United States, where they continue to reach wider audiences, transmitted through individuals, groups, or the media. Many soundscapes continue to interact and change in the new locales they inhabit, conveying a complex collection of sounds with a rich variety of meanings. New soundscapes emerge as indivudals or communities orchestrate their musical lives in new settings.

Music can reinforce or blur the boundaries of belief, identity, or imagination. The twenty-first century is rich in musical diversity, through which a record of the past and the conflicts of its present join together, sung, played, and danced. Music traditions maintain their complexities of sound, setting, and significance, while traveling in ways that would have been impossible in another age. They create a new musical pluralism, a global musical environment defined more by its multiple styles than by any single dominant tradition.

The larger musical memory charted by *Soundscapes* is constructed of shared sounds and meanings. We find shared sound sources such as the accordion sustaining repertories as different as tango and zydeco. This instrument, with its roots in the European Industrial Revolution, participates in a variety of styles that cross soundscapes.

Many soundscapes share settings and are juxtaposed at civic events and festivals. This circumstance has led to new musical communities born of affinity, as individuals hear and participate in previously unfamiliar music traditions. As a result, musicians have carried songs from soundscape to soundscape. The hymn *Amazing Grace* is an example. We encountered this eighteenth-century hymn in settings as diverse as bagpipe performances, jazz funerals, and Native American powwows. Since 2001, we have witnessed this hymn performed as an important emblem of mourning and commemoration.

Although the settings and style of the hymn vary, inevitably it marks solemnity and remembering.

We have seen that music is deeply entwined with movement—of immigration, forced migration, displacement, and travel. All music has the potential to move, and transplantation is a theme cutting across every tradition we have encountered. Whether celebrating travel or mourning displacement, music's motion through time and space affirms the present in relation to both the past and future. Transplantation, a constant theme of song texts, transfers music traditions into new settings and helps people accommodate such changes. Through music individuals can travel instantly to times and places in their past, such as a home left behind in China or a moment retained in the mind and ear through a lullaby.

Despite the reality of music's movement, sounds closely associated with particular settings continue to carry great significance over time. Syrian *pizmonim* gain meanings as they are sung at life-cycle events, generation after generation. Shoshone war-dance songs may change over the years, but they continue to reinforce the powwow. Music's constant transformations are vital to traditions that expand to unite insiders and outsiders. Sound and its settings can temporarily persuade us that we are Cajun or Creole in southern Louisiana, not just an enthusiast delighting in the beat.

Music is the site of constant creativity, as musicians combine sounds to innovate or delight. Encountering *khoomii* or Ethiopian chant in unexpected contexts challenges the ear and forces the listener to assimilate new sounds.

Music serves to reinforce boundaries, but it can also encourage us to sing and dance across barriers of class, region, race, or gender. At times multiple styles merge into new creations, weaving such remarkable conflations as the Vietnamese *karaoke* tango heard in Listening Guide 84. Introduced by a musical nod to nineteenth-century European romanticism, the song has a Vietnamese text that unites Vietnamese experience at home and in diaspora. Vietnamese musical memory views the tango as a legacy of the French colonial era infused with new life through international popular culture in the twenty-first century. The worldwide dispersion of *karaoke* has entered into the rhythms of everyday Vietnamese life abroad, and has been transformed in ways distinctive to Vietnamese social life and identity. The resulting song, *Bai Tango Cho Em*, brings together all of these streams of tradition.

Bai Tango Cho Em is sung in Vietnamese and exists in different *karaoke* versions: one constructs a visual narrative of life in the old Vietnam of memory, while another follows a teenage couple in suburban Long Beach, California.[1]

Here the classic tango rhythm underpins a story of travel—both departure and return. This song is engraved in memory through its uncanny ability to transcend time and space, to cause the voice to sing, the body to dance, to allow the spirit to soar—the quintessential qualities of any soundscape.

Bai Tango Cho Em ("A Tango for You," Vietnamese *karaoke* song)

CD 3
Track 26

Date: **Late 1980s or early 1990s**
Performer: **Elvis Phuong and Ai Van,** *voice*
Form: **Ternary form (A B A) with introduction and repetition**
Tempo: **Moderate quadruple meter**
Function: *Karaoke* **song popular among Vietnamese Americans**

WHAT TO LISTEN FOR:

- A sense of melancholy in the lyrics common to many Vietnamese love songs as well as traditional tangos.
- A violin theme based on the famous melody of *Liebestraum No. 3* by Franz Liszt.
- Musical references to tango: characteristic rhythms and the sound of an accordion.
- A catchy melody and repetitive musical form that allows listeners to learn the song quickly and sing along.

	STRUCTURE AND TEXT	TRANSLATION	DESCRIPTION
0:00	**Introduction** (violin solo)		The violin plays the melody of *Liebestraum* with an accompaniment that has straight, unsyncopated rhythms.
0:22	**Section A** **Woman** Tu' ngay co em ve nha minh tran anh trang the.	Since you came back to me, My house is filled with moonlight.	Piano and electric bass can be heard prominently in the accompaniment while the singer presents the song's main melodic theme.
	Dong nhac tinh da tat lau.	Love was absent from my heart for a long time,	
	Tuon trao, ngot ngao nhu giong suoi.	And now it overflows like a rushing stream.	
0:38	**Man** Anh yeu phut ban dau, dep nghieng nghieng dang em sau.	I loved you the first moment I saw you move in sadness	The piano is less prominent, but an accordion can be heard playing a chordal accompaniment. A violin weaves bits of countermelody into the male singer's solo.
	Trong mat em buon ve mau.	With sadness quickly clouding your eyes.	
	Anh o'i co khi nao, lan gap day cho mai sau	Could this meeting last forever?	

0:54	**Section B** **Woman** Tieng dan hoa em ai	The sound of music, harmonious and soft,	The accordion plays the countermelody. The accordion evokes traditional tango.
	Nhip bu'oc em them la lo'i,	As you move ever more gracefully,	
	Cung dieu buon cho'i vo'i,	The sad melancholy tune hovers in the air,	
	Doi tam hon rieng the gio'i.	Our two souls are lost in their own world.	
1:10	**Man** Minh diu sat di anh, De nghe lan ho'i chay, trong tim nong nan.	Hold me tightly as we dance, So I can feel the burning of your passionate heart.	Although the melodies in section B are different from those of section A, there are many similarities between the two sections. For example, the male solo and duet here may be compared with the male solo in section A, at 0:38. The accompaniment includes a pattern of two chords in rapid succession followed by a rest (at 1:12) that echoes tango rhythms.
1:17	**Duet** Tiec th'o'ng chi, khi tro'i rong thenh thang. Vu'o'ng van de roi, mot do'i cu'u mang.	Why regret anything when the sky is limitless? Why harden ourselves with any cares, for they will remain with us all our lives?	
1:26	**Section A'** **Woman** Gio' mingh co nhau roi, **Man** do'i dep vi tieng em cu'oi,	Now that we're together, Your laughter makes life beautiful,	Section A' has the same melodic and harmonic elements as section A, but with different words.
1:34	**Duet** Vu'ot ngan trung, qua be kho'i.	We'll journey a thousand miles and cross a deep ocean	Section A' also redistributes the text between the voices, with most of this verse sung as a duet in parallel octaves. The accordion often answers vocal statements.
	Dat diu cung ve can nha mo'i.	And hand in hand we'll enter our new home.	
	Ta xay vach chung tinh,	We'll build a wall of everlasting love.	
	Nhieu chong gai co tay ming, Xin ca'm o'n do'i con nhau, Ghi sau phut ban dau,	We'll overcome all obstacles. We're thankful to be together, We'll engrave the memory of our first meeting on our hearts,	
	Bang bai Tango cho em.	With this tango dedicated to you.	
1:58	**Repetition** **Introduction** (violin solo)	as at 0:00	The piano accompaniment features a tango rhythm, with a syncopated accent on second half of the first beat of each measure. This accompaniment differs subtly from that in the introduction at the beginning of the song.
2:21	**Section A**	as at 0:22	The rest of the repetition is nearly identical to the first rendition.
2:25	Recording ends		

Appendix
Classifying Musical Instruments

The Sachs-Hornbostel system for classifying musical instruments comprises five categories, each subdivided according to different principles, that accommodate most musical instruments in existence.[1]

I. IDIOPHONES

Idiophones (from the Greek for "self" and "sounds") are instruments made of sonorous materials. These instruments do not require any additional attachments, such as strings or drumskins, to produce sound. Idiophones are set into vibration by the action of the player.

A. Concussion idiophones are struck together or against another surface. Instruments in this category sometimes exist in pairs, such as clapping hands and stamping feet; cymbals, such as those used for Tibetan Buddhist ceremonies; and castanets.

B. Struck idiophones consist of individual pieces of wood, metal, stone, bamboo, or glass that are struck with a stick or mallet. Examples are xylophones, gongs, bells, and many of the instruments in a *gamelan* (most of which are termed *metallophones* because the material struck is bronze).

C. Stamped idiophones are boards placed over pits, on which people stamp their feet. The pit serves as resonator.

D. Stamping idiophones include instruments, such as the Ethiopian prayer staff, that the musician pounds on the ground.

E. Shaken idiophones are rattles of various sorts, such as a gourd or hollow tube containing seeds or other materials that make noise when shaken. Some shaken idiophones, such as the *sistrum,* have the rattling parts strung on rods.

F. Scraped idiophones are notched objects, such as shells or bones, that are scraped with a stick or some other rigid item; for example, a stick scraped along the notched surface of a zydeco rub board.

G. Plucked idiophones have flexible metal or bamboo strips attached to a frame, which are then plucked by the fingers or another implement. Examples include the African *mbira*, a small wooden box to which metal tongues are attached, and the European music box, in which the carefully tuned "teeth" of a steel comb are plucked by studs on a revolving cylinder.

H. Rubbed or friction idiophones produce vibrations through the friction arising between two rough surfaces, such as sandpaper. Rubbing the rims of wine-glasses with moistened fingers is a method of producing sound that dates from at least the seventeenth century and that gave rise to the most famous friction idiophone, the glass harmonica, invented by Benjamin Franklin in 1761.

II. AEROPHONES

Aerophones, often called "wind instruments," have a tube enclosing a column of vibrating air. What sets the air into vibration can be the compressed lips of the player (as in the trumpet), the movement of an open reed (oboe) or an enclosed reed (accordion, bagpipe, organ), or the edge of a mouthpiece (flute). Aerophones are arbitrarily subdivided into three main categories.

A. Trumpets and horns are usually grouped together because over time they have combined despite their separate histories. Trumpets were originally made from hollowed-out tree branches or tubes of bamboo. The player blows into the mouthpiece with vibrating lips, usually producing a brilliant sound. Horns were originally just that—curved animal horns. They have a wider passage for air and a more mellow tone than trumpets. The mouthpiece on trumpets and horns may be at the upper end of the tube (end blown) or pierced into the side of the instrument (side blown). If the lower end expands, it is called a bell. Western trumpets and horns of various types, such as the trombone and the cornet, are commonly termed "brass instruments" because most are made of brass.

B. Plain pipes and reed pipes are also grouped together. Like trumpets and horns, they are hollow tubes into which the player blows, but without vibrating the lips.

1. Plain pipes, called flutes, are tubular with finger holes that the player covers or uncovers to determine the pitch. Flutes can be either open or closed at the lower end. Less common are globular flutes, molded from clay or fashioned by cutting holes in a dried fruit shell or gourd; an example is the ocarina.

End-blown flutes are classified as "vertical," side-blown flutes as "transverse." Panpipes are sets of small flutes, each pipe producing one pitch, that are tied together in bundles.

2. Reed pipes use one or more reeds to produce sound. The reed may be set in motion directly by the lips—as in the clarinet, which has a single beating reed, or the oboe, which has double reeds—or indirectly, as in the bagpipe, which has an enclosed reed, also called a free reed.

C. Free aerophones do not enclose a column of air, but act directly on surrounding air. The Australian bullroarer, for example, is a thin board that the player whirls overhead by an attached cord, producing a roaring or wailing sound. Mouth organs and accordions are free aerophones that have a single reed for each pitch.

III. MEMBRANOPHONES

Membranophones, or drums, produce sound when a vibrating membrane stretched over an opening is set in motion. Drums can be played singly, in pairs, or in sets, like the *batá* drums (Chapter 8). In the Sachs-Hornbostel system, drums are not classified; rather, they are described, using the following characteristics:

A. Materials (wood, coconut, gourd, bamboo, clay, and metal, among others)

B. Shape

  1. Tubular drums
      a. Cylindrical (straight tube)
      b. Barrel (bulging tube)
      c. Conical (tapered tube)
      d. Hourglass (cup-shaped ends with a narrower waist in between)
      e. Footed (large and stationary, with one end shaped to form a foot)
      f. Goblet (footed but small and portable)
      g. Handle (having one or more loop handles)

  2. Kettledrums, which have a vessel-shaped body, are termed hemispheric if the largest diameter is at the top, as in the timpani, or egg-shaped, if the largest diameter is below the top, as in the *kebaro* (see Chapter 8).

  3. Frame drums have a frame instead of a solid body.

C. Number of membranes (also called skins or heads): A drum with one membrane is referred to as single-headed, one with two membranes as double-headed.

D. How the membrane is fastened to the body: It may be glued, nailed, buttoned, neck-laced (tie with a circular cord near the head), or braced (also called "laced"). Braced fastenings are laced either directly through holes in the edge of the membrane, or indirectly through hoops that can be either open or concealed.

E. The drum's playing position: It may be positioned on the ground or on a stand, or the player can hold it in place with his hand, arm, or legs; a drum may also be suspended from the ceiling, from a stand, or from the player's body.

F. How the drum is played (either by striking or rubbing) and what the player uses to strike or rub it (bare hands, sticks, mallets, among other objects). A drum can have a friction chord or stick that passes through a center hole in the membrane.

IV. CHORDOPHONES

Chordophones are instruments whose sound is produced by vibrating strings. The strings may be made of fiber, gut, horsehair, silk, metal, or other material, and can be strung singly, in pairs (double strung), or in threes (triple strung). Some stringed instruments, such as some North Indian instruments, have additional, thinner strings called "sympathetic strings" attached below or behind the main strings to add extra reverberation and resonance. The strings may be plucked with bare fingers, fingernails, or a plectrum (a guitar pick, for example); bowed with a bow of horsehair or other material; or struck with sticks.

The main structural sound box, or resonator, for the instrument is called the body. The flat or curved front of the body, which receives and reflects vibrations from the strings, is usually made of wood or skin and is called the soundboard. The wooden crosspiece that holds the strings away from the soundboard is called the bridge. Sound holes are sometimes cut into the soundboard to improve the acoustics and to decorate the instrument. The fingerboard against which strings are pressed (or "stopped") by the player's fingers is called the neck, or handle. Some instruments have small ridges, called frets, along the fingerboard to mark off pitches of the scale. Players tune stringed instruments by turning dowels at the top of the neck, called tuning pegs.

Chordophones are classified by shape and by the relationship of the strings to the body of the instrument.

A. In this system, lutes comprise all stringed instruments with a neck that allows the strings to be stretched beyond the top of the body. Lutes may be plucked or bowed. This category includes the Western violin family, the Middle Eastern 'ud, the guitar, and many other familiar instruments.

B. Zithers are instruments in which the strings are stretched between opposite ends of the body, which also serves as a resonator.

1. Stick zithers have sticks in place of bodies and have an additional resonator attached, as in the Vietnamese *dan bau.*

2. Tube zithers have a tube as a resonating body to which strings are attached lengthwise.

3. Board zithers have strings stretched over a soundboard and glued into a box. Examples include the piano, *qanun,* dulcimer, and harpsichord.

4. Long, narrow zithers, such as the Japanese *koto,* fall between tube and board zithers.

C. The harp is the only chordophone in which the strings are stretched at an angle away from the soundboard. Most harps have numerous strings, which are plucked. The bodies of most harps are angular (that is, with the body and neck at an angle to each other), but there are examples of arched harps, in which the body is elongated at one end into an arched neck.

D. Lyres are similar to lutes but are differently constructed: in place of a neck, they have a yoke with symmetrical or asymmetrical arms, the upper ends of which are connected by a crossbar. The strings are attached to the front of the body and run up to the crossbar, to which they are fastened. Most lyres are plucked.

V. ELECTROPHONES

A. Electromechanical instruments, such as the Hawaiian steel guitar, produce vibrations mechanically and then transform them into electric oscillations, which are amplified and reproduced by electric speakers.

B. Radioelectric instruments are those in which the oscillations of electric circuits are transformed into audible vibrations by electric speakers. They are often referred to as "analog electric instruments" because the electric oscillations are analogous to the acoustic vibrations created by the speaker. A common example is the analog synthesizer.

C. Digital electronic instruments, such as the digital synthesizer, are those in which a specialized computer emulates acoustic patterns. These digital simulations are converted into electric oscillations, which are then amplified and transformed into audible vibrations by electric speakers.

Although the Sachs-Horbostel system for classifying musical instruments has inconsistencies and flaws and other methods of instrument classification have been proposed during the later twentieth century, most museums and writings about instruments continue to use this framework.

Notes and Additional Sources

Introduction

In the Introduction, I drew on the expertise and publications of the ethnomusicologist Theodore Levin, whose work forms the backbone of the discussion in this Introduction about the significance of Tuvan music. The different styles that reflect the contours of the Tuvan landscape ("steppe" and "mountain," "nose" and "chest," and so on) are described in detail and can be heard on the CD *Tuvanian Singers and Musicians,* No. 21 of the World Network Series. Information on the Harmonic Choir is based in part on my participant-observation with David Hykes and the Harmonic Choir between 1979 and 1981.

Notes

[1] Stephen Blum, "European Musical Terminology and the Music of Africa," in *Comparative Musicology and the Anthropology of Music,* ed. Bruno Nettl and Philip V. Bohlman (Chicago: University of Chicago Press, 1991), pp. 4–9.

[2] R. Murray Schafer, *The Soundscape: Our Sonic Environment and the Tuning of the World* (Rochester, VT: Destiny Books, [1977] 1994), pp. 274–75.

[3] Theodore C. Levin, "Music in Tuva," in *The Garland Encyclopedia of Music, The Middle East,* eds. Virginia Danielson, Scott Marcus, and Dwight Reynolds (New York and London: Routledge, 2002), Vol. 6, pp. 932–84.

[4] Theodore C. Levin, "Tuvan Music," in *The New Grove Dictionary of Music and Musicians,* 2nd ed., ed. Stanley Sadie (London, Macmillan, 2001), Vol. 25, p. 938.

[5] Carole Pegg, "Overtone-singing," in *New Grove,* 2nd ed., Vol. 18, p. 822.

[6] Ibid.

[7] Levin, "Tuvan Music," p. 938.

[8] Pegg, "Overtone-singing," p. 822.

[9] Theodore C. Levin, Program Notes for Huun-Huur-Tu concert, World Music, Sanders Theater, Cambridge, MA, March 2, 1997.

[10] David Hykes, Concert Notes, New York, May 20, 1981.

[11] Gurdjieff's best known work is the autobiographical *Meetings with Remarkable Men,* revised translation (E. P. Dutton: New York, 1969).

[12] Hykes, Concert Notes.

[13] Ibid.

Additional Sources

Books and Articles

Hykes, David. Flyer advertising the Harmonic Choir's 1981 Spring Concert Series.

Leedy, Douglas. "David Bond Hykes." In *The New Grove Dictionary of Music and Musicians,* 2nd ed., ed. Stanley Sadie (London: Macmillan, 2001), Vol. 12.

Levin, Theodore C., and Michael E. Edgerton. "The Throat Singers of Tuva." *Scientific American* 281, no. 2 (September 1999): 80–87.

Myers, Helen, ed. *Ethnomusicology: Historical and Regional Studies.* New York: W. W. Norton, 1993.

Nettl, Bruno. *Theory and Method in Ethnomusicology.* London: Free Press of Glencoe, 1964.

Chapter 1

A number of individuals have provided advice and information and aided with gathering sound examples for this chapter. I am particularly grateful to Sandra Graham, Tomie Hahn, Nazir Jairazbhoy, David Lyczkowski, Scott Marcus, Sarah Morelli, Jean-Jacques Nattiez, Pauline Oliveros, Helen Rees, Lara Setrakian, Patricia Tang, and Lamine Touré.

Notes

[1] John Blacking, *How Musical Is Man?* (Seattle: University of Washington Press, 1973), p. 27.

[2] Jean-Jacques Nattiez, "Some Aspects of Inuit Vocal Games," *Ethnomusicology* 27 (1983): 457–75; p. 459.

[3] Jean-Jacques Nattiez, "Inuit Throat-Games and Siberian Throat Singing: A Comparative, Historical, and Semiological Approach," *Ethnomusicology* 43 (1999): 399–418.

[4] Bruno Nettl, "Music," in *The New Grove Dictionary of Music and Musicians,* 2nd ed., ed. Stanley Sadie (London: Macmillan, 2001), Vol. 17, p. 425.

[5] Karl Hutterer, "Southeast Asia in Prehistory," in *The Garland Encyclopedia of World Music,* Terry E. Miller and Sean Williams, eds. (New York and London: Garland Publishing, 1998, Vol. 4: *Southeast Asia,* pp. 32–40.

[6] Gage Averill, personal correspondence, June 14, 2005.

[7] Carole Pegg, "Mongolia," in *New Grove,* 2nd ed., Vol. 16, p. 924.

[8] Ashenafi Kebede, "The Bowl-Lyre of Northeast Africa. Krar: The Devil's Instrument," *Ethnomusicology* 21 (1977): 379–95.

[9] Margaret Kartomi, "Instruments, Classification of," II, III, and V, in *New Grove,* 2nd ed., Vol. 12, p. 420.

[10] Jeremy Montagu and John Burton, "A Proposed New Classification System for Music Instruments," *Ethnomusicology* 15 (1971): 49–70.

[11] Kartomi, "Instruments," *New Grove,* 2nd ed., Vol. 12, p. 420, crediting a suggestion of Dale Olsen.

[12] Patricia Tang, "Masters of the Sabar: Wolof Griots in Contemporary Senegal," Ph.D. dissertation, Harvard, 2000, pp. 201–202.

[13] Michael Tenzer, *Gamelan Gong Kebyar: The Art of Twentieth-Century Balinese Music* (Chicago: Chicago University Press, 2000), p. 345.

[14] Tenzer, *Gamelan Gong Kebyar,* p. 347.

[15] Joep Bor, ed., *The Raga Guide: A Survey of 74 Hindustani Ragas* (Netherlands: Nimbus, 1999).

[16] Bor, *The Raga Guide,* vii–viii.

[17] Tang, "Masters of the Sabar," pp. 201–202, 248–50.

[18] Faruqi, Lois Ibsen al-, *An Annotated Glossary of Arabic Music Terms* (Westport, CT: Greenwood Press, 1981), p. 292.

[19] Allan Marett and Linda Barwick, eds. Notes by Alan Maralung to accompany *Bunggridj-Bunggridj: Wangga Songs from Northern Australia,* Traditional Music of the World 4, International Institute for Traditional Music (Washington DC: Smithsonian Folkways, 1993).

[20] Quotations by Pauline Oliveros are drawn from www.pofinc.org/EIShome.html and media.hyperreal.org/zines/est/intervs/oliveros.html

Additional Sources
Books and Articles

Charron, Claude. "Toward Transcription and Analysis of Inuit Throat-Games: Microstructure." *Ethnomusicology* 22 (1978): 245–59.

Hood, Mantle. *The Ethnomusicologist.* New York: McGraw-Hill, 1971.

Knopoff, Steven. "Didjeridu." In *The New Grove Dictionary of Music and Musicians,* 2nd ed., ed. Stanley Sadie, Vol. 7. London: Macmillan, 2001.

Lawrence, Mary Lawrence and Peter Yoo, eds. Notes to accompany *Mademoiselle, Voulez-vous Danser? Franco-American Music from the New England Borderlands.* Washington DC: Smithsonian Folkways Recordings, 1999.

Lomax, Alan, and Anna Lomax Chairetakis, eds. Notes to accompany *Deep River of Song. Bahamas 1935. Chanteys and Anthems from Andros and Cat Island.* Cambridge, MA: Rounder Records, 1999.

Malm, William P. *Japanese Music and Musical Instruments.* Rutland, VT, and Tokyo: Charles E. Tuttle, 1959.

Myers, Helen. "Trinidad and Tobago." In *The New Grove Dictionary of Music and Musicians,* 2nd ed., Vol. 25.

Nooshin, Laudan. "Improvisation as 'Other': Creativity, Knowledge and Power—The Case of Iranian Classical Music." *Journal of the Royal Musical Association* 128 (2003): 242–96.

Oliveros, Pauline. *Deep Listening: A Composer's Sound Practice.* New York, Lincoln, Shanghai: iUnivers, Inc., 2005.

Pegg, Carole. "Mongolia." In *The New Grove Dictionary of Music and Musicians,* 2nd ed., Vol. 16.

Rees, Helen. Notes to accompany *Naxi Music from Lijiang. The Dayan Ancient Music Association.* London: Nimbus Records, 1997.

"Sitar." *The New Grove Dictionary of Music and Musicians,* 2nd ed., Vol. 23.

Chapter 2

For the overview of music in Boston, I have drawn on a combination of ethnographic research, documentary sources, and Web sites. My experience confronting the distinctive musical profile of Boston after thirteen years of intensive fieldwork in New York City sparked my interest and guided my fieldwork in Boston, including research with members of the local Ethiopian community.

Much of the material on campus musical life was gathered with the help of students in my 1996 Harvard University seminar Music of the City. The overview of early music derives in large part from a research seminar on the Early Music movement I taught jointly with my Harvard colleagues Carol Babiracki and Thomas Forrest Kelly. I also acknowledge our teaching assistant, Jen-Yen Chen, and the five students whom I advised in a project documenting the Voice of the Turtle: Judah Cohen, Caprice Corona, Hubert Ho, David Lyczkowski, and Judith Quiñones. I thank Millie Rahn and Betsy Siggins Schmidt for advice and materials on Club Passim and the folk music movement. Michael Washington and Lara Pellegrinelli provided useful insights on the Boston jazz scene.

The work of the urban geographers Downs and Stea provided a wealth of insights in their publications and useful maps of greater Boston. Michael Tenzer and Evan Ziporyn generously provided information on the Balinese *gamelan*.

A fieldtrip to Accra during January 2004 provided the basis for my musical profile of that city. For their help before, during, and after my stay in Ghana, I sincerely thank Emmanuel and Ruth Akyeampong. For research assistance in Accra, I am grateful to Setor Amuzu and Godsway Abotsi. A number of colleagues in both the United States and Ghana generously extended advice and assistance that extended well beyond the boundaries of their publications cited here, including J. H. Kwabena Nketia, Daniel Amponsah, Daniel Avorgbedor, David Locke, and Steven Friedson. I received valuable information about Ghanaian music traditions from Dr. F. Nii Yartey, Herman Kwei, Lucas Tagborlo, Simon Zigah, Isaac Abonkwah, Moses Abonkwah, Simon Zigah, and Mawule Yao Semevo. Charles Boateng's knowledge of Accra proved an immense help. David Kaminsky assisted with analysis of the *agbadza* example.

I thank "Richie" Neeraj Banerji for initial research assistance in Mumbai. Amy Bard, Richard Wolf, and Sarah Morelli provided helpful advice and materials on all aspects of the Mumbai musical profile.

Notes

[1]Ruth H. Finnegan, *The Hidden Musicians* (Cambridge: Cambridge University Press, 1989), pp. 306–307.

[2]John Collins, *Musicmakers of West Africa* (Washington DC: Three Continents Press, 1985), pp. 1–2.

[3]H. N. A. Wellington, "Kewewele, Kpokpoi, Kpanlogo: A Random Search for Accra's Urban Quality in a Sea of Globalisatiion," in *Visions of the City: Accra in the 21st Century,* ed. Ralph Mills-Tetey and Korantema Adi-Dako (Accra: Woeli Publishing, 2002), pp. 79–80.

[4]A. M. Jones, *Studies in African Music,* 2 vols. (London: Oxford University Press, 1959); Vol. 1, p. 162.

[5]Daniel Avorgbedor, "Rural-Urban Interchange: The Anglo-Ewe," in *The Garland Encyclopedia of World Music,* Vol. 5, *South Asia: The Indian Subcontinent,* ed. Alison Arnold (New York: Garland Publishing, 1998).

[6]*Bethel Epistle,* the Voice of Kwabenya Prayer Camp, Bethel Prayer Ministry International, No. 003, October 2003 (Accra: A Media Line Production, 2003).

[7]J. H. Kwabena Nketia, personal letter.

[8]Atta Annan Mensah, "Compositional Practices in African Music," in *The Garland Encyclopedia of World Music,* Vol. 1, *Africa,* ed. Ruth Stone, pp. 208–31 (New York: Garland Publishing, 1998), pp. 220–21.

[9]Statements by Nketia are drawn from a conversation between him and the author in Accra on January 12, 2004, as well as from subsequent correspondence.

[10]Bansi Pandit, *The Hindu Mind* (Glen Ellyn, IL: B & V Enterprises, 1993), p. 427.

[11]All statements by the Jhaveri sisters are taken from C. S. Lakshmi, *Seven Seas and Seven Mountains,* Vol 2: *Mirrors and Gestures: Conversations with Women Dancers* (New Delhi: Kali for Women, 2003), pp. 195–243.

[12]Gordon R. Thompson, "Regional Caste Artists and Their Patrons," in *The Garland Encyclopedia of World Music,* Vol. 5, p. 405.

[13]Andrew Burton Alter, "Institutional Music Education: Northern Area," in *The Garland Encyclopedia of World Music,* Vol. 5; Stephen Slawek, "The Classical Master-Disciple Tradition," in *The Garland Encyclopedia of World Music,* Vol. 5, p. 466.

[14]Alter, "Institutional Music Education," p. 443.

[15]Teri Skillman, "The Bombay Hindi Film Song Genre: A Historical Survey," *Yearbook for Traditional Music* 18 (1986): 133–44.

[16]Alison Arnold, "Film Music: Northern Area," in *The Garland Encyclopedia of World Music,* Vol. 5, pp. 538–39.

[17]Peter Manuel, *Cassette Culture: Popular Music and Technology in North India* (Chicago: University of Chicago Press, 1993), pp. 92–94.

[18]Adrienne Fried Block, *Amy Beach, Passionate Victorian* (New York: Oxford University Press, 1998), p. 105.

[19]The following description of Boston draws on Roger M. Downs and David Stea, *Maps in Minds: Reflections on Cognitive Mapping* (New York: Harper & Row, 1977).

[20]Stephanie Ebbert, "For 2nd Time in Two Decades, A City on Rise," *The Boston Globe,* March 22, 2001, B7; Rick Klein, "Census 2000: Massachusetts by the Numbers: City, State Take on New Cast, Political Clout Shifts Toward Boston, Cape," *The Boston Globe,* March 22, 2001, A1; "American Housing Survey for the Boston

Metropolitan Area," 1998, based on 1990 census data; www.census.gov/prod/2000pubs/h170-98-3.pdf

[21]Susan Diesenhouse, "564 Beds, w/park view: Emerson College Tower to Close Gap on City's Old Piano Row," *The Boston Globe,* April 10, 2004, C3.

[22]Charles P. Pierce, "Golden Opportunity," *The Boston Globe Magazine,* March 14, 2004, 30–33, 44–46, 50–52; pp. 33, 50–51.

[23]Vanessa E. Jones, "Caribbeantown," *The Boston Globe,* January 4, 2001, D1.

[24]Johnny Diaz, "Do we fit here?" *The Boston Globe,* July 17, 2005, C11.

[25]Marco Werman, "Mariza's Youth Reinvigorates Portugal's Fado," *The Boston Globe,* July 5, 2002, D10 and D12.

[26]Johanna Keller, "Drawing Tears in Any Language," *The New York Times,* July 7, 2002, AR 27–28; p. 27.

[27]Jon Pareles, "Amalia Rodrigues, 79, Queen of Fado, Lisbon's Sad Songs," *The New York Times,* October 7, 1999, C 23.

[28]Bart Plantenga, *Yodel-Ay-Ee-Oooo, The Secret History of Yodeling Around the World* (New York and London: Routledge, 2004), p. 182.

[29]Jim Metzner, "You're Hearing Boston: Yodeling," Radio WEEI-FM Boston, 1976–1979.

[30]Michael Tenzer, *Balinese Music* (Berkeley: Periplus Editions, 1991), pp. 33–39; *Gamelan Gong Kebyar: The Art of Twentieth-Century Balinese Music* (Chicago: University of Chicago Press, 2000), pp. 40–51.

[31]Maria Mendonca, "Gamelan," in *The New Grove Dictionary of Music and Musicians,* 2nd ed., ed. Stanley Sadie (London: Macmillan, 2001), Vol. 9: 505–506.

[32]Mendonca, "Gamelan," p. 506.

[33]Michael Tenzer, *Balinese Music.*

[34]Listening Guide 28 is adapted from Tenzer, *Gamelan Gong Kebyar;* p. 364, with emendations by Christine Southworth.

[35]Baez quotes from Scott Alarik, *Deep Community: Adventures in the Modern Folk Underground* (Cambridge, MA: Black Wolf Press, 2003), p. 84.

[36]Mitchell Fink, ed., *Off the Record: Stories Told to Joe Smith, An Oral History of Popular Music* (New York: Warner Books, 1988; London: Pax, 1990).

[37]www.mbta.com/projects_underway/easyway/easyway.asp#isback

[38]Anthony Tommasini, "Even at Birth, Opera Wed the Stirring and the Silly," *The New York Times,* June 14, 1997, Arts and Leisure, p. 13.

[39]Charles Seeger, "Versions and Variants of the Tunes of 'Barbara Allen,'" in *Selected Reports in Ethnomusicology,* Vol. 1, No. 1. Los Angeles: University of California at Los Angeles, 1966, pp. 120–67.

[40]Kay Kaufman Shelemay, "Towards an Ethnomusicology of the Early Music Movement: Thoughts on Bridging Disciplines and Musical Worlds," *Ethnomusicology* 45 (2001): 1–29; p. 18.

Additional Sources
Books and Articles

Alarik, Scott. "Folk Kicks Up Its Heels." *The Boston Globe,* April 29, 1999, Calendar, p. 10.

"All Set for Shaggy," *The Mirror* (Accra), Saturday, January 3, 2004, 27.

Barfield, Thomas, ed. *The Dictionary of Anthropology.* Oxford Malden, MA: Blackwell Publishers, 1997.

Berman, Sam. "With a Politician's Passing, Memories of 'Charlie on the MTA.'" *The Boston Globe,* July 9, 1998, B1.

Boston History Collaborative. "Boston Family History: Fenway/Kenmore." 2002. www.bostonfamilyhistory. net/neighborhoods/neigh_fenw.html

Briggs, Philip. *Ghana: The Bradt Travel Guide,* 2nd ed. Guilford, CT: The Globe Pequote Press, 2001.

Broyles, Michael. *Music of the Highest Class: Elitism and Populism in Antebellum Boston.* New Haven: Yale University Press, 1992.

Byrne, David. "I Hate World Music." *The New York Times,* October 3, 1999, Section 2, p. 1.

Diagram Group. *Musical Instruments of the World: An Illustrated Encyclopedia.* New York: Facts on File, 1976.

Diamond, Jody. "Out of Indonesia: Global Gamelan." *Ethnomusicology* 42 (1998): 174–83.

DjeDje, Jacqueline Cogdell, "J. H. Kwabena Nketia." In *The New Grove Dictionary of Music and Musicians,* 2nd ed., Vol. 18. Edited by Stanley Sadie. London: Macmillan, 2001.

Erlmann, Veit. Notes to accompany Solomon Linda's Original Evening Birds, *Mbube Roots, Zulu Choral Music from South Africa, 1930s–1960s.* Cambridge, MA: Rounder Records, 1987.

———. *Nightsong: Performance, Power, and Practice in South Africa.* Chicago: University of Chicago Press, 1996.

Foerster, Robert Franz. *Italian Emigration of Our Times.* Cambridge, MA: Harvard University Press, 1919.

The Folk Letter, a publication of the Folk Song Society of Greater Boston. Vol. 31, no. 3, March 2004. Somerville, MA: FSSGB, Inc.

Fuld, James J. *The Book of World-Famous Music,* 4th ed. New York: Dover, 1995.

Greene, Paul D. "Film Music: Southern Area." In *The Garland Encyclopedia of World Music,* Vol. 5,

South Asia: The Indian Subcontinent, ed. Alison Arnold. New York: Garland Publishing, 2000.

Handlin, Oscar. *Boston's Immigrants: A Study in Acculturation.* Cambridge, MA: Belknap Press of Harvard University Press, 1979.

Hood, Mantle. "Jaap Kunst." In *The New Grove Dictionary of Music and Musicians,* 2nd ed., ed. Stanley Sadie. Vol. 14. London: Macmillan, 2001.

———, and Hardja Susilo. *Music of the Venerable Dark Cloud.* Los Angeles: Institute of Ethnomusicology, 1967.

Impey, Angela. "Popular Music in Africa." In *The Garland Encyclopedia of World Music,* vol. 1, *Africa,* ed. Ruth Stone. New York: Garland Publishing, 1998.

Koetting, James. "Analysis and Notation of West African Drum Ensemble Music." *Selected Reports* 1, no. 3, pp. 115–46. Los Angeles: University of California, 1970.

Low, Setha M. "Theorising the City: Images for the Future." In *Visions of the City: Accra in the 21st Century,* ed. Ralph Mills-Tettey and Korantema Adi-Dako, 48–55. Accra: Woeli Publishing Services, 2002.

Manuel, Peter. *Popular Musics of the Non-Western World.* New York and Oxford: Oxford University Press, 1988.

———. "Pop Music and Audio-Cassette Technology: Northern Area." *The Garland Encyclopedia of World Music,* Vol. 5, *South Asia: The Indian Subcontinent,* ed. Alison Arnold. New York: Garland Publishing, 2000.

McArdle, Nancy. *Race, Place, and Opportunity: Racial Change and Segregation in the Boston Metropolitan Area, 1990–2000.* Cambridge, MA: Harvard University, Civil Rights Project, 2002.

McPhee, Colin. *A House in Bali.* New York: John Day, 1946.

———. *Music in Bali: A Study in Form and Instrumental Organization.* New Haven: Yale University Press, 1966.

Nketia, J. H. Kwabena. "Asante Music." In *The New Grove Dictionary of Music and Musicians,* 2nd ed., Vol. 2.

O'Connor, Thomas H. *The Boston Irish: A Political History.* Boston: Northeastern University Press, 1995.

Pellegrinelli, Lara. "A Guided Tour of America's Most Fascinating Jazz Clubs." *New Music Box* 9 (January 2000). www.newmusicbox.org/archive/index

Plotkinoff, David. "Joan Baez: A Legend in Search of Listeners." *Philadelphia Inquirer,* January 24, 1993.

Ranade, Ashok. "Music and Bombay." *Journal of the Indian Musicological Society* 27 (1996): 80–83.

Reyes Schramm, Adelaida. "Explorations in Urban Ethnomusicology: Hard Lessons from the Spectacularly Ordinary." *Yearbook for Traditional Music* 14 (1982): 1–14.

Rubin, Cynthia, and Jerome Rubin. *Comprehensive Guide to Boston.* Newton, MA: Emporium Publications, 1972.

Schmidt, John C. *The Life and Works of John Knowles Paine.* Ann Arbor, MI: UMI Research Press, 1980.

Twum-Baah, Kwaku A. "Population Growth of Mega-Accra—Emerging Issues." *Visions of the City: Accra in the 21st Century,* ed. Ralph Mills-Tettey and Korantema Adi-Dako, 231–38. Accra: Woeli Publishing Services, 2002.

Vecoli, Rudolph J., et al., eds. *Gale Encyclopedia of Multicultural America.* Detroit: Gale Research, 1995.

"World Urbanization Prospects: The 2001 Revision." United Nations Population Division. New York: United Nations. un.org/esa/population/publications/wup2001/WUP2001report.htm

Web Sites

Joan Baez:
www.vanguardrecords.com/Baez/Home

Berklee College of Music:
www.berklee.edu

Boston College:
www.bc.edu/cwis/aboutbc

The Boston Early Music Festival:
www.bemf.org/2003/about.html

Boston Lyric Opera:
www.blo.org

Boston Symphony Orchestra:
www.bso.org/genC/genCone.jhtml?id=cat20058&area=bso

Boston University:
www.bu.edu/admissions/explore/about.html

Brandeis University:
www.brandeis.edu/overview/historical.html

Club Passim:
www.clubpassim.org/history

Folk Song Society of Greater Boston:
www.fssgb.org

Handel and Haydn Society:
www.handelandhaydn.org/learn/learn_home.htm

New England Conservatory of Music:
www.newenglandconservatory.edu

New Music Box:
www.newmusicbox.org

Tufts University:
www.tufts.edu/source/about.html

Chapter 3

The case studies for this chapter are based on a combination of sources. I thank Richard Wolf for suggesting the *raga nilambari* examples as a provocative case study, for helping to obtain the recordings, and for assistance with the text and listening guides. I thank Jeyalakshmi Sundar for performing, translating, and discussing the lullaby *Araro Ariraro*. Robin Carruthers brought the lullaby study by Trehub et al. to my attention. Caprice Corona and Norma Cantú provided some helpful information on the *quinceañera*. Daniel Sheehy located the *mariachi* musical example heard here. The bagpipe is remarkably well documented in the written sources listed below. Robert J. Hogan of New York City generously supplied piping manuals and recordings and shared his extensive experience as a piper and band leader. Charles Starrett, who began research on American bagpipe bands during the summer of 1999, sorted out the complicated history of the MacCrimmons and helped deepen my discussion of the pipes and the settings in which they are played. Gregory Morrow provided information on piping and recordings of uillean pipes from his own collection. He also selected and performed the *pibroch* heard in Listening Guide 40. In this chapter, as in others, I have drawn on *The New Grove Dictionary of Music and Musicians* and the *New Grove Dictionary of Musical Instruments* for discussion of musical instruments. For my discussion of significance, I have drawn on *Music and Cultural Theory* by John Shepherd and Peter Wicke.

Notes

[1]John Shepherd and Peter Wicke, *Music and Cultural Theory* (Cambridge: Polity Press, 1997), pp. 205–206.

[2]Timothy Rice, "Reflections on Music and Meaning: Metaphor, Signification and Control in the Bulgarian Case," *British Journal of Ethnomusicology* 10 (2001): 19–38.

[3]Richard Widdess, "Rasa," in *The New Grove Dictionary of Music and Musicians,* 2nd ed., Vol 20, p. 834.

[4]Jeyalakshmi Sundar sang the lullaby and discussed it at great length in an interview at her home with the author and Richard Wolf on June 24, 2004.

[5]Richard K. Wolf and Zoe C. Sherinian, "Tamil Nadu," in *The Garland Encyclopedia of World Music*, Vol. 5, South Asia: The Indian Subcontinent, ed. Alison Arnold (New York: Garland Publishing, 2000).

[6]www.raveindia.com/bir/version1/html/subramaniam.htm

[7]Tia DeNora, *Music in Everyday Life* (Cambridge: Cambridge University Press, 2000), pp. 78–79.

[8]Sandra Trehub, Anna M. Unyk, and Laurel J. Trainor, "Maternal Singing in Cross-Cultural Perspective," *Infant Behavior and Development* 16 (1993): 185–95.

[9]Andrew Neher, "A Physiological Explanation of Unusual Behavior in Ceremonies Involving Drums," *Human Biology* 4 (1962): 151–60.

[10]Gilbert Rouget, *Music and Trance: Relationship Between Music and Possession,* rev. and trans. by Brunhilde Biebuyck (Chicago: University of Chicago Press, 1985).

[11]Bert Watters, "Quinceañera: The Mexican-American Initiation Ritual for Young Women," in *The American Ritual Tapestry: Social Rules and Cultural Meaning,* ed. Mary Jo Deegan (Westport, CT: Greenwood Press, 1998), 145–58; p. 151.

[12]Watters, "Quinceañera," p. 149.

[13]Seth Kugel, "Neighborhood Report: New York Sounds; Mexican Musicians Are Uniting to Meet Mariachi Shortage," *The New York Times,* December 16, 2001, Section 14, 4.

[14]Daniel Sheehy, "Mexican Mariachi Music: Made in the U.S.A.," in *Musics of Multicultural America,* ed. Kip Lornell and Anne K. Rasmussen (New York: Schirmer Books, 1997), 131–54.

[15]Miroya Navarro, "Old Mexico for a New Generation: A Tiny Academy Teaches Children the Joys of Mariachi," *The New York Times,* January 28, 2003, B1.

[16]Ramiro Burr, *The Billboard Guide to Tejano and Regional Mexican Music* (New York: Billboard Books, 1999), p. 78.

[17]Kugel, "Neighborhood Report," p. 4.

[18]Don Terry, "Mariachi Musicians Sustaining Their Traditions," *The New York Times,* October 31, 1997, A14.

[19]Francis M. Collinson, *The Bagpipe: The History of a Musical Instrument* (London: Routledge and Kegan Paul, 1975), pp. 39–60.

[20]Francis M. Collinson and Peggy Duesenberry, "Scotland," in *New Grove,* 2nd ed., Vol 22, p. 916.

[21]Nicholas Carolan, "Ireland" II, in *New Grove,* 2nd ed., Vol. 12, p. 563.

[22]P. J. Curtis, Notes for "The Pipers Rock: A Compilation of Young Uillean Players" (Mulligan Music, LUNCD 023/LC 4779, 1978).

[23]Collinson, *The Bagpipe,* p. 140.

[24]Collinson, *The Bagpipe,* pp. 141–54.

[25]Dr. William Donaldson, Aberdeen, Scotland, November 2002; "Beautiful and Melodious Airs . . . An Exploration of the Piobaireachd: Series III," *Piper & Drummer Magazine,* 2000–03).

[26]Alexander John Haddow, *The History and Structure of Ceol Mor: A Guide to Piobaireachd, The Classical Music of the Great Highland Bagpipe* (M. R. S. Haddow, 1982), p. 99.

[27]Beth Potier, "The Big Picture: Greg Morrow, Piper," *Harvard University Gazette,* March 18, 2004, p. 5.

28Collinson, *The Bagpipe,* p. 98.

29Eric Hobsbawm, "Introduction: Inventing Traditions," in *The Invention of Tradition,* ed. Eric Hobsbawm and Terence Ranger (Cambridge: Cambridge University Press, 1983).

30Seth Stern, "In the Aftermath of Tragedy, FDNY Bagpipers March On," *Christian Science Monitor,* November 17, 2001, p. 14.

31Anne Barnard and Beth Daley, "A Community of Loss," *The Boston Globe,* September 19, 2001, pp. 1 and A37.

32Shepherd and Wicke, p. 279.

33Robbie Shepherd, *Let's Have a Ceilidh: The Essential Guide to Scottish Dancing* (Edinburgh: Cannongate, 1992).

34Shepherd and Wicke, p. 115.

35Shepherd and Wicke, p. 183.

Additional Sources
Books and Articles

Adam, Barbara. "Perceptions of Time." In *Companion Encyclopedia of Anthropology,* ed. Tim Ingold. London and New York: Routledge, 1994.

"Bagpipe." In *New Harvard Dictionary of Music,* ed. Don Randel. Cambridge, MA: Belknap Press of Harvard University Press, 1986.

Baily, John. "Music and the Body." *The World of Music* 37, no. 2 (1995): 11–30.

Baines, Anthony. *Bagpipes.* Oxford: Oxford University Press, 1960.

Barry, Dan. "The Pipes are Calling, Calling Still." *The New York Times,* March 17, 2002, p. 33.

Bodley, Séóirse, and Breandan Breathnach. "Ireland." In *The New Grove Dictionary of Music and Musicians,* Vol. 9.

Breaking the Waves (film). Written and directed by Lars von Trier. London: Faber, 1996.

Buckley, Martin J. *Scarlet and Tartan.* Sydney: Red Hackle Association, 1986.

Campbell, Archibald. *The Kilberry Book of Ceol Mor,* 3rd Edition. Glasgow: John Smith & Son Ltd., 1969. Distributed on behalf of the Piobaireachd Society.

Campsie, Alistair Keith. *The MacCrimmon Legend: The Madness of Angus MacKay.* Edinburgh: Canongate, 1980.

Cannon, Roderick D. *The Highland Bagpipe and Its Music.* Edinburgh: John Donald, 1988.

Cantú, Norma. "*La Quinceañera:* Toward an Ethnographical Analysis of a Life-Cycle Ritual." *Southern Folklore* 56, no. 1 (April 1999): 73–101.

Clayton, Martin. "Introduction: Towards a Theory of Musical Meaning." *British Journal of Ethnomusicology* 10, no. 1 (2001): 1–17.

Cocks, William A., Anthony C. Baines, and Roderick D. Cannon. "Bagpipe." In *The New Grove Dictionary of Music and Musicians,* Vol. 2.

———. "Bagpipe." In *The New Grove Dictionary of Musical Instruments,* ed. Stanley Sadie. Vol. 1. London: Macmillan, 1984.

Cullen, Kevin. "Gaelic Column Bags Top Award in Ireland." *The Boston Globe,* March 18, 1997, B2.

Dean-Smith, Margaret. "Jig." In *The New Grove Dictionary of Music and Musicians,* 2nd ed., Vol. 13.

Dunbar, John Telfer. *History of Highland Dress.* Edinburgh and London: Oliver & Boyd, 1962.

Dunbar, J. Telfer. "Early Tartans." In *Old Irish and Highland Dress,* 2nd ed., ed. H. F. McClintock. Dundalk, Scotland: Dundalgan Press, 1950.

Ewart, David, and May Ewart. *Scottish Ceilidh Dancing.* Edinburgh and London: Mainstream Publishing, 1996.

Fabbri, Franco. "A Theory of Musical Genres: Two Applications." In *Popular Music Perspectives,* ed. David Horn and Philip Tagg. Papers from the First International Conference on Popular Music Research, Amsterdam, June, 1981. Göteborg and Exeter: International Association for the Study of Popular Music, 1982.

Grimes, Ronald L. *Deeply into the Bone: Re-inventing Rites of Passage.* Berkeley: University of California Press, 2000.

Hogan, Robert J. *The Irish-American Manual of Bagpiping Instruction.* New York: Robert J. Hogan, 1996.

Johnson-Hanks, Jennifer. "On the Limits of Life Stages in Ethnography: Toward a Theory of Vital Conjunctures." *American Anthropologist* 104 (2002): 865–80.

Moloney, Mick. Notes for *Fathers and Daughters: Irish Traditional Music in America.* Ho-Ho-Kus, New Jersey: Shanachie Records Corp., 1985.

Monaghan, Peter. "Simon Fraser's Pipers Blow Away Competition." *Chronicle of Higher Education,* July 18, 1997, A8.

"Mrdangam," *The New Grove Dictionary of Music and Musicians,* 2nd ed., Vol. 17.

Nicol, Angus. "Highland Laments Ring Out." *Times* (London), August 10, 1999.

Podnos, Theodor H. *Bagpipes and Tunings.* Detroit: Information Coordinators, 1974.

Powers, Harold S., and Richard Widdess. "India," III 1-5. In *The New Grove Dictionary of Music and Musicians,* 2nd ed., Vol. 12.

Radano, Ronald M. "Interpreting Muzak: Speculations on Musical Experience in Everyday Life." *American Music* 7 (Winter 1989): 448–60.

Rao, T. K. Govinda, compiler and editor. "Compositions of Muddusvāmi Dīkshitar." In *National and International Scripts*. Indiranagar, Chennai, India: Ganamandir Publications, 1997.

Rodriguez, Cindy. "Coming of Age, Latino Style." *The Boston Globe*, January 5, 1997, C1.

Saaduddin, Abul H. "Bangladesh." In *The New Grove Dictionary of Music and Musicians*, Vol. 2.

Seton, Sir Bruce Gordon, and Pipe-Major John Grant. *The Pipes of War* (new introduction by Major General Frank Richardson). East Ardsley, England: EP Publishing: New York: British Book Centre, 1920 and 1974.

Tanenbaum, Susie J. *Underground Harmonies: Music and Politics in the Subways of New York*. Ithaca, NY: Cornell University Press, 1995.

Terry, Don. "Mariachi Musicians Sustaining Their Traditions." *The New York Times*, October 31, 1997, A14.

Trevor-Roper, Hugh. "The Invention of Tradition: The Highland Tradition of Scotland." In *The Invention of Tradition*, ed. Eric Hobsbawm and Terence Ranger. Cambridge: Cambridge University Press, 1983.

Web Sites
Bagpipes:
news://rec.music.makers.bagpipe
www.hotpipes.com
www.carnatica.net/cgi-bin/rasikaforum_technical/
messageviewN_technical.pl?topicid=94

Chapter 4

For the discussion of Chinese *muyu*, I have drawn on Su Zheng's study published in 1992 and in forthcoming materials. I thank Meredith Schweig and Andres Su for transliterating Uncle Ng's Chinese text. For the discussion of Arab American migration, I have drawn on the recording and articles of Anne Rasmussen (1991, 1992), as well as my own fieldwork and publications on Syrian Jews from Aleppo now living in the United States. Ronald Radano provided helpful advice regarding spirituals.

For the Vietnamese case study, in addition to a brief trip to Houston's Little Saigon and the superb resources provided by the *Gale Encyclopedia* and the *Penguin Atlas of Diaspora*, I am indebted to the publications and advice of Adelaida Reyes, Pham Duy, and Deborah Wong. Pham Duy graciously supplied scores and readings of *The National Road*, and Andrew Talle gathered and translated information on Vietnamese instruments and Vietnamese texts. Terry Miller kindly provided copies of *Nhac Viet*.

Notes

[1] Judith T. Shuval, "Diaspora Migration: Definitional Ambiguities and a Theoretical Paradigm," *International Migration* 38 (2000): 41–56.

[2] David Morley, "Belongings: Place, Space, and Identity in a Mediated World," *European Journal of Cultural Studies* 4 (2001): 425–448.

[3] Sunil Bhatia and Anjali Ram, "Locating the Dialogical Self in the Age of Transnational Migrations, Border Crossings, and Diasporas," *Culture and Psychology* 7 (2001): 297–309; p. 305.

[4] Madeline Y. Hsu, "Migration and Native Place: *Qiaokan* and the Imagined Community of Taishan County, Guangdong, 1893–1993," *The Journal of Asian Studies* 59 (2000): 307–31; pp. 310–28.

[5] Su De San Zheng, "From Toisan to New York: *Muk'yu Songs in Folk Tradition*," *CHINOPERL PAPERS* 16 (New York: Conference on Chinese Oral and Performing Literature, 1992/93). See also Zheng forthcoming. Note that Zheng uses Mandarin spelling for the song's title (*Ng Bok Lai Jinshan*); we have used a phonetic system for transliterating the Taishanese text, representing the sound of the words as sung (*Ng Bak Loi Gimsaan*).

[6] Alixa Naff, *Becoming American: The Early Arab Immigrant Experience* (Carbondale, IL: Southern Illinois University Press, 1985).

[7] Lois Ibsen al-Faruqi, *An Annotated Glossary of Arabic Musical Terms* (Westport, CT: Greenwood Press, 1981), p. 179.

[8] Ali Jihad Racy, "Fayrūz," in *The New Grove Dictionary of Music and Musicians*, 2nd ed., Vol. 8.

[9] Margaret J. Kartomi, *On Concepts and Classifications of Music Instruments* (Chicago: University of Chicago Press, 1990).

[10] Neil MacFarquhar, "This Pop Diva Wows 'Em in Arabic," *The New York Times*, May 18, 1999, E1.

[11] Thomas Sowell, *Migrations and Cultures: A World View* (New York: Basic Books, 1996).

[12] Dena J. Epstein, *Sinful Times and Spirituals: Black Folk Music to the Civil War* (Urbana, IL: University of Illinois Press, 1977), p. 323.

[13] Ronald Radano, "Denoting Difference: The Writing of the Slave Spirituals," *Critical Inquiry* 22 (1996): 506–44.

[14] Kip Lornell, Notes to "Nobody Knows the Trouble I've Seen," Leadbelly (Rounder Records, 1994).

[15] Paul Oliver, "Leadbelly," in *New Grove*, 2nd ed., Vol. 14.

[16] Paul Oliver, "Spirituals. II. Black," in *New Grove*, 2nd ed., Vol. 18.

[17] Michael E. McClellan, "Performing Empire: Opera in Colonial Hanoi," *Journal of Musicological Research* 22 (2003): 135–66.

[18] Phong T. Nguyen, "Vietnamese Music in America," in *Transcending Boundaries: Asian Music in North America,* ed. Yoshitaka Terada (Osaka: National Museum of Ethnology, 2001), 113–22; p. 118.

[19] I thank Andrew Talle for transcribing the Vietnamese text for the first section of this song and for supplementing the English translation presented in Phong Thuyet Nguyen and Terry E. Miller, Notes for *Music from the Lost Kingdom: Hue, Vietnam,* the Perfume River Traditional Ensemble (New York: Lyrichord 7440, 1998).

[20] Van Giang, *Vietnamese Traditional Music in Brief,* trans. Andrew Talle (Saigon: Ministry of State in Charge of Cultural Affairs, c. 1970).

[21] Adelaida Reyes Schramm, *Songs of the Caged, Songs of the Free: Music and the Vietnamese Refugee Experience* (Philadelphia: Temple University Press, 1999), p. 95.

[22] Tran Quang Hai, "Vietnamese Music in Exile," *The World of Music* 43 (2001): 103–112.

[23] Thanh Hang, "Pham Duy Hopes to Settle Down in Vietnam," www.ThanhNienNews.com, February 5, 2005.

[24] Deborah Wong, "Plugged in at Home: Vietnamese American Technoculture in Orange County," in *Music and Technoculture,* ed. René T. A. Lysloff and Leslie Gay (Hanover, NH: Wesleyan University Press, 2003), p. 135.

[25] Wong, pp. 144–45.

[26] Wong, pp. 147–48.

[27] Jason Gibbs, "Reform and Tradition in Early Vietnamese Popular Song," *Nhac Viet: The Journal of Vietnamese Music* 6 (Fall 1997), 5–33.

[28] http://kicon.com/phamduy/TievSu/index2.html

[29] Pham Duy, *Music of Vietnam,* ed. Dale R. Whiteside (Carbondale, IL: Southern Illinois University Press, 1975).

[30] Adelaida Reyes Schramm, "Tradition in the Guise of Innovation," *Yearbook for Traditional Music* 18 (1986): 84–89.

[31] Reyes Schramm, p. 89.

[32] Wong, p. 125–52; pp. 132–37; p. 142.

[33] Thanh Hang, "Pham Duy Hopes to Settle Down."

[34] Reyes Schramm, pp. 91–101.

Additional Sources
Books and Articles

Allen, William Francis, Charles Pickard Ware, and Lucy McKim Garrison. *Slave Songs of the United States.* A. Simpson & Co., 1867; New York: Books for Libraries Press, 1971.

Arana, Miranda. "Modernized Vietnamese Music and Its Impact on Musical Sensibilities." *Nhac Viet: The Journal of Vietnamese Music* 3 (1994) 1, 2: 91–110.

Bankston, Carl L. "Vietnamese Americans." In *Gale Encyclopedia of Multicultural America,* ed. Judy Galens, Anna Sheets, and Robyn V. Young. Detroit: Gale Research, 1995.

Bragg, Rick. "Vietnamese Refugees in New Orleans Find a Little Peace." *The New York Times,* October 2, 2000, A18.

Chaliand, Gérard, and Jean-Pierre Rageau. *The Penguin Atlas of Diasporas,* trans. A. M. Berrett. New York: Viking, 1995.

Dictionary of the Vietnamese Language 1997 (Tu Dien Tieng Viet 1997). Hanoi and Da Nang: Nha Xuat Ban Da Nang [Da Nang Publishing House], 1997.

Dorson, Richard. "Is There Folk in the City?" In *The Urban Experience and Folk Tradition,* edited by Américo Paredes and Ellen J. Stekert. Austin, TX: University of Texas Press, 1971.

Gall, Susan, ed. *The Asian American Almanac.* Detroit: Gale Research, 1995.

Gargan, Edward A. "Trading Fame for Freedom: Chinese Opera Stars Find Haven, and Hardship, in US." *The New York Times,* June 21, 1998, 25.

Haiek, Joseph R., publisher. *Arab American Almanac 1992,* 4th ed. Glendale, Calif.: News Circle Publishing House, 1992.

Henretta, James A. *America's History to 1877.* Chicago: Dorsey Press, 1987.

Kartomi, Margaret J. *On Concepts and Classifications of Musical Instruments.* Chicago: University of Chicago Press, 1990.

Lee, Gary. "Detroit Area is the Unlikely Capital of Arab America." *The Boston Sunday Globe,* February 6, 2000, M17.

Loan, Nguyen Thuy. *Lich su Am nhac Viet Nam* (History of Vietnamese Music). Hanoi: Nha Xuat Ban Am Nhac Viet Nam (Music Publishing House of Vietnam), 1990.

Lysloff, Rene T. A. and Leslie C. Gay, Jr., eds. *Music and Technoculture.* Middletown, CT: Wesleyan University Press, 2003.

Miller, Ruby M., and Willard E. Miller. *United States Immigration.* Santa Barbara: ABC-CLIO, Inc., 1996.

Nguyen, Phong T. *Searching for a Niche: Vietnamese Music at Home in America.* Kent, OH: Viet Music Publications, 1995.

———, and Patricia Shehan Campbell. *From Rice Paddies and Temple Yards: Traditional Music of Vietnam.* Danbury, CT: World Music Press, 1990.

Norton, Mary Beth. *A People and a Nation: A History of the United States,* 4th ed. Boston: Houghton Mifflin, 1994.

Poché, Christian. "'Ud." In *The New Grove Dictionary of Musical Instruments,* ed. Stanley Sadie. London: Macmillan, 1984. Vol. 3.

Radano, Ronald M. "Soul Texts and the Blackness of Folk." *Modernism/Modernity* 2, no. 1 (1995): 71–95.

———. "Denoting Difference: The Writing of the Slave Spirituals." *Critical Inquiry* 22 (1996): 506–44.

Rasmussen, Anne K. "Individuality and Social Change in the Music of Arab Americans." Ph.D. dissertation, University of California, Los Angeles, 1991.

———. "An Evening in the Orient: The Middle Eastern Nightclub in America." *Asian Music* 23 (1992): 61–88.

Seeger, Charles. "Versions and Variants of *Barbara Allen*" (with "Comment on the Words," by Edward Cray) *Selected Reports* 1, no. 1 (1966): 120–67.

Slobin, Mark. "Music in Diaspora." *Diaspora* 3 (1994): 243–51.

Vecoli, Rudolph J., et al., eds. *Gale Encyclopedia of Multicultural America*. Detroit: Gale Research, 1995.

Wong, Deborah. "'I Want the Microphone': Mass Mediation and Agency in Asian American Popular Music." *Drama Review* 38 (1994): 152–67.

Zheng, Su. *Claiming Diaspora: Music, Transnationalism, and Cultural Politics in Chinese/Asian America*. Oxford University Press, forthcoming 2006.

Zheng, Su DeSan. "Music and Migration: Chinese American Traditional Music in New York City." *The World of Music* 32 (1990): 48–67.

Recordings

The Music of Arab Americans: A Retrospective Collection. Research and documentation by Anne K. Rasmussen. Rounder CD 1122, 1997.

Seeger, Charles, ed. *Versions and Variants of Barbara Allen*. Washington, DC: Library of Congress, 1964.

CD-ROM

Pham Duy. *Truong Ca Con Duong Cai Quan (Voyage Through the Motherland)*. San Jose, CA: Coloa, Inc., 1995.

Chapter 5

Much of the introductory material on music and memory as well as the case study on the *pizmonim* is drawn from my book *Let Jasmine Rain Down*, which is based on more than a decade of fieldwork among Syrian Jews in New York, Mexico, and Israel. Américo Paredes's classic study of the *corrido,* updated by analysis from Manuel Peña, provided documentation on the famous ballad *Gregorio Cortez*. Vernel Bagneris's extraordinary images and sounds of the jazz funeral were valuable resources, as was Schafer's detailed description of the jazz funeral. Robert Rumbolz and Ingrid Monson provided details that enhanced the information Roe-min Kok had gathered on the jazz band, and Justin Linam lent me unpublished material on the jazz funeral. Details regarding the *Wheat Song* came from Nabil Azzam; I am also grateful to Moses Tawil, Louis Massry, Joseph Saff, Sheila Schweky, and the late Sophie Cohen for interviews about the *pizmon Ramach Evarai*; for translations I thank James Robinson and Joshua Levisohn; for information on the *'ud,* I thank Roe-min Kok and Mark Kligman.

Notes

[1] See *The Burns Encyclopedia* for details of the song's origin and transmission: www.robertburns.org/encyclopedia/AuldLangSyne/5html

[2] Manuel H. Peña, *Música Tejana: The Cultural Economy of Artistic Transformation* (College Station, TX: Texas A&M University Press, 1999), pp. 34–36, 40.

[3] Américo Paredes, *With His Pistol in His Hand: A Border Ballad and Its Hero* (Austin, TX: University of Texas Press, 1958).

[4] Paredes, *A Texas-Mexican Cancionero: Folksongs of the Lower Border* (Urbana, IL: University of Illinois Press, 1976), pp. 30–31.

[5] Peña, p. 77.

[6] Mark A. Hernández, "Remaking the *Corrido* for the 1990s: Maldita Vecindad's 'El Barzón,'" *Studies in Latin American Popular Culture* 20 (2001): 101–116; pp. 101–102.

[7] Marion Lloyd, "Mexican Immigrants Find Musical Voice, Mixed Message," *The Boston Sunday Globe,* January 28, 2001, A6.

[8] Simon Romero, "Terrorism's Troubadours," *The New York Times,* November 18, 2001, A6.

[9] Laurence Bergreen, *Louis Armstrong: An Extravagant Life* (New York: Broadway Books, 1997), p. 494.

[10] William J. Schafer, *Brass Bands and New Orleans Jazz* (Baton Rouge, LA: Louisiana State University Press, 1977). Schafer's discussion on pp. 50–98 provides details of the jazz funeral on which this summary draws unless otherwise indicated.

[11] Schafer, p. 56.

[12] Helen A. Regis, "Blackness and the Politics of Memory in the New Orleans Second Line," *American Ethnologist* 28 (2001): 752–77; pp. 762–64.

[13] Regis, p. 767.

[14] Keith Spera, "Jazz Therapy," the *Times-Picayune,* Friday, November 11, 2005, p. 15.

[15] Regis, p. 752.

[16]Lesley Bannatyne, "Making a Joyful Noise, with a Purpose," *The Boston Sunday Globe,* November 16, 2003, City Weekly, 13.

[17]Kay Kaufman Shelemay, *Let Jasmine Rain Down: Song and Remembrance among Syrian Jews* (Chicago: University of Chicago Press, 1998). All quotations in this case study are drawn from this book unless otherwise indicated.

[18]Nabil Salim Azzam, "Muhammad 'Abd al-Wahhab in Modern Egyptian Music," Ph.D. dissertation, University of California, Los Angeles, 1990, pp. 114, 123, 129.

Additional Sources
Books and Articles

Bagneris, Vernel, ed. *Rejoice When You Die.* Baton Rouge; LA: Louisiana State University Press, 1998.

Brunn, H. O. *The Story of the Original Dixieland Jazz Band.* Baton Rouge, LA: Louisiana State University Press, 1960.

Chase, Gilbert. *America's Music,* 3rd ed. Urbana, IL: University of Illinois Press, 1987.

Collier, James Lincoln. "Armstrong, Louis." In *The New Grove Dictionary of Jazz,* ed. Barry Kernfield. London: Macmillan, 1998. Vol. 1.

———. "Bands." In *The New Grove Dictionary of Jazz,* Vol. 1.

———. "Jazz." In *The New Grove Dictionary of Jazz,* Vol. 2.

Dean, Roger T. "Jazz, improvisation and brass." In *The Cambridge Companion to Brass Instruments,* ed. Trevor Herbert and John Wallace. Cambridge: Cambridge University Press, 1997.

Dweck, Francine, and Sheila Haber. *Festival of Holiday Recipe Book,* Brooklyn, NY: Sephardic Community Center, 1987.

Farmer, H. G. "Qanun." In *The New Grove Dictionary of Musical Instruments,* ed. Stanley Sadie. London: Macmillan, 1984. Vol. 3.

Fuld, James J. "Twinkle, Twinkle, Little Star (ABCDEFG; Baa, Baa, Black Sheep; Schnitzelbank)." *The Book of World Famous Music: Classic, Popular, and Folk,* 4th ed. New York: Dover, 1995.

Gushee, Lawrence. "A Preliminary Chronology of the Early Career of Fred 'Jelly Roll' Morton." *American Music* 3 (1985): 389–412.

———. "Oliver, King." In *The New Grove Dictionary of Jazz,* Vol. 3.

Hazen, Margaret Hindle, and Robert M. Hazen. *The Music Men: An Illustrated History of Brass Bands in America, 1800–1920.* Washington DC and London: Smithsonian Institution Press, 1987.

Idelsohn, A. Z. "Die arabische Musik." In *Hebraisch-Orientalischer Melodienschatz,* Vol. 4: *Gesänge der Orientalischen Sefardim.* Jerusalem-Berlin-Vienna: Benjamin Hart Verlag, 1923.

Kinzer, Stephen. "Blues Giant Leaves the Stage in a Grand Old Jazz Funeral." *The New York Times,* May 1, 2003, A22.

Marco, Guy A., ed. *Encyclopedia of Recorded Sound in the United States.* New York: Garland, 1993.

Par, C. F. "The Alphabet." In *The New Blue Book of Favorite Songs,* edited by John W. Beattie. Chicago: Hill and McCreary, 1941.

Rubin, David C. *Memory in Oral Traditions: The Cognitive Psychology of Epic, Ballads and Counting-out Rhymes.* New York and Oxford: Oxford University Press, 1995.

Schacter, Daniel L. *Searching for Memory: The Brain, the Mind, and the Past.* New York: Basic Books, 1996.

Schafer, William J. "Brass Band." In *The New Grove Dictionary of Jazz,* Vol. 1.

Schuller, Gunther. *Early Jazz: Its Roots and Musical Development.* New York: Oxford University Press, 1968.

Shelemay, Kay Kaufman. "Recording Technology, the Record Industry, and Ethnomusicological Scholarship." In *Comparative Musicology and the Anthropology of Music,* ed. Bruno Nettl and Philip Bohlman. Chicago: University of Chicago Press, 1991.

———. *Let Jasmine Rain Down: Song and Remembrance among Syrian Jews.* Chicago: University of Chicago Press, 1998.

Tick, Judith. *Ruth Crawford Seeger: A Composer's Search for American Music.* New York: Oxford University Press, 1997.

Vecoli, Rudolph J., et al., eds. *Gale Encyclopedia of Multicultural America.* Detroit: Gale Research, 1995.

Wald, Elijah. "The Ballad of a Mexican Musical Tradition." *The Boston Globe,* January 18, 1998, K1.

———. *Narcocorrido: A Journey into the Music of Drugs, Guns, and Guerillas.* New York: Rayo, 2001.

Wilkie, Curtis. "A Funeral for the 'Chicken Man': Shrunken Heads, Incense and Jazz." *The Boston Sunday Globe,* January 31, 1999, A5.

Williams, Martin, ed. *The Smithsonian Collection of Classic Jazz,* 3rd ed., Notes. Washington, DC: Smithsonian Institution, 1973.

———. *The Smithsonian Collection of Classic Jazz,* rev. ed. Washington, DC: Smithsonian Institution, 1987.

Chapter 6

The addition of the Hawaiian case study was suggested by a brief discussion of the Moe family in James Clifford's *Routes* and a memorable night I spent at a performance by the traveling Ukulele Hall of Fame.

I thank Evan Ziporyn for his assistance with all aspects of the Balinese *gamelan* case study, for discussions of his work, for providing a hard-to-find recording of *Kembang Pencak*, and for sharing an unpublished paper that provided details of his collaboration with I Nyoman Windha. I Nyoman Catra kindly provided information, advice, and contacts. Christine Southworth was an indispensable help in guiding musical analysis of *Kembang Pencak* and *Kekembangan* for the listening guides. The work of Michael Tenzer, especially his book *Gamelan Gong Kebyar*, provided the central source for my discussion of the history and musical style of *gamelan gong kebyar*. Philip Yampolsky graciously aided with contacts for copyright.

The Silk Road Project provided an ideal case study for this chapter, which was further enhanced by the Silk Road residency at Harvard beginning in 2005. I thank Richard Kurin for inviting me to the opening ceremony at the Smithsonian Festival and for providing useful materials. I also thank Ted Levin, Yo-Yo Ma, and Laura Freid for their assistance.

Notes

[1]Curtis M. Hinsley, "The World as Marketplace: Commodification of the Exotic at the World Columbian Exposition, Chicago, 1893," in *Exhibiting Cultures: The Poetics and Politics of Museum Display*, ed. Ivan Karp and Steven D. Lavine (Washington DC: Smithsonian Institution Press, 1991), p. 363.

[2]Barbara Kirshenblatt-Gimblett, "Objects of Ethnography," in *Exhibiting Cultures*, ed. Karp and Levine, p. 413.

[3]Mark Slobin, *Subcultural Sounds: Micromusics of the West* (Hanover, NH: Wesleyan University Press, 1993).

[4]Katy Bachman, "Clear Channel Spins Off Unites," *Mediaweek*, April 29, 2005; L. M. Sixel, "Live Nation Is Going to L.A.," *Houston Chronicle*, December 23, 2005, D4.

[5]James Clifford, *Routes: Travel and Translation in the Late Twentieth Century* (Cambridge, MA: Harvard University Press, 1997), p. 182.

[6]George S. Kanahele, ed., *Hawaiian Music and Musicians* (Honolulu: University Press of Hawaii, 1979), pp. 241–49.

[7]Clifford, p. 26.

[8]Mantle Hood, "Musical Ornamentation as History: The Hawaiian Steel Guitar," *Yearbook of Traditional Music* 15 (1983): 141–48; p. 144.

[9]Heather Tang, "Waikiki Ukulele Retailer Tunes Into Locals and Visitors Alike," in *Pacific Business News,* December 3, 1999, p. 38.

[10]Mantle Hood, p. 141.

[11]John Berger, "Hawaii: Hawaiian Islands are home to music that travels well," *Billboard,* May 12, 2001, 30–34.

[12]Mike Zwerin, "Adopting the Uke Attitude," *International Herald Tribune,* January 13, 2004, p. 9.

[13]Amy Ku'uleialoha Stillman, "Globalizing Hula," *Yearbook for Traditional Music* 31 (1999): 57–66.

[14]Yumiko Ono, "Hawaii Is Beckoning: Lovely Hula Hands from Distant Isles," *Wall Street Journal* (Eastern edition), July 20, 1999, A1.

[15]Amy Dorsett, "Sounds of the Pacific: Ukulele lovers stage musical luau monthly," *San Antonio Express-News,* August 2, 2003, Metro/South Texas, 1B.

[16]Stillman, pp. 58–59, 62.

[17]Michael Tenzer, *Gamelan Gong Kebyar* (Chicago, University of Chicago Press, 2000), pp. 87–89; information and quotations about *gamelan gong kebyar* are drawn from Tenzer unless otherwise indicated.

[18]Carol J. Oja, *Colin McPhee: Composer in Two Worlds* (Washington DC: Smithsonian Institution Press, 1990; Urbana, IL: University of Illinois Press, 2004), pp. 60, 63, 121, 146.

[19]I Nyoman Catra, e-mail correspondence, August 28, 2003.

[20]Oja, p. 124.

[21]Evan Ziporyn, e-mail correspondence, March 31, 2005.

[22]This account of the genesis of *Kekembangam,* including quotations, is based on Evan Ziporyn, "One Man's Traffic Noise: A Case Study in Cross-cultural Collaboration," an unpublished paper presented at Berkeley, CA, c. 1992.

[23]Oja, p. 90.

[24]Kyle Gann, "Ziporyn, Evan," in *The New Grove*, 2nd ed., Vol. 27, p. 850.

[25]Joseph C. Self, "The 'My Sweet Lord'/'He's So Fine' Plagiarism Suit," *The 910 Magazine*, 1993; reprinted on www.abbeyroad.best.vwh.net/mysweet.htm

[26]This box is constructed primarily from information in *The Silk Road: Connecting Cultures, Creating Trust,* ed. Carla M. Borden (Washington DC: Smithsonian Institution, 2002).

[27]Richard Kurin, "Director's Talk Story," *Smithsonian Talk Story* 21 (Fall 2002), pp. 2–3.

[28]Yo-Yo Ma, "A Journey of Discovery," in *The Silk Road*, p. 7.

[29]Keith Powers, "Yo-Yo's World Music," *The Improper Bostonian,* Sept. 10–23, 2003, p. 23.

[30]Janet Tassell, "Yo-Yo Ma's Journeys," *Harvard Magazine,* March-April 2000, pp. 43–51, 207.

[31]Luis Monreal, "The Silk Road Today," in *The Silk Road,* ed. Carla M. Borden, pp. 8–9.

[32]Richard Dyer, "Pipa Player's New CDs Cross Cultures," *The Boston Sunday Globe,* July 6, 2003, N3.

[33]Yo-Yo Ma, "A Word from Yo-Yo Ma," in notes to the Smithsonian Folkways recording.

[34]*The Silk Road News* (New York: The Silk Road Project, Fall 2000).

[35]Notes for *Silk Road Journeys: When Strangers Meet* (Sony Classical SK 89782, 2001), p. 11.

[36]After Yunte Huang, *Transpacific Displacement: Ethnography, Translation, and Intertextual Travel in Twentieth-Century American Literature* (Berkeley: University of California Press, 2002).

Additional Sources
Books and Articles

Appadurai, Arjun. "Introduction: Commodities and the Politics of Value." In *The Social Life of Things: Commodities in Cultural Perspective,* ed. Arjun Appadurai. Cambridge: Cambridge University Press, 1986.

Beloff, Jim. *The Ukulele: A Visual History.* San Francisco: Miller Freeman Books, 1997.

Davies, Hugh. "Hawaiian Guitar." In *The New Grove Dictionary of Musical Instruments,* ed. Stanley Sadie. London: Macmillan, 1984. Vol. 2.

Farhi, Paul. "See It, Hear It, Read It—Buy It?" *Washington Post,* November 28, 1995, D1.

Hafner, Katie. "In Love with Technology, as Long as It's Dusty." *The New York Times,* March 25, 1999, G1.

Harris, Ron. "New Technology Could Reshape Music Industry." *Star Tribune* (Minneapolis), December 12, 1998, D1.

Horner, Bruce. "On the Study of Music as Material Social Practice." *Journal of Musicology* 16, no. 2 (1998): 159–99.

Ma, Yo-Yo. "A Word from Yo-Yo Ma." Liner Notes, *The Silk Road: A Musical Caravan.* Smithsonian Folkways Recordings, 2002, 4.

Nettl, Bruno. "The Dual Nature of Ethnomusicology in North America." In *Comparative Musicology and the Anthropology of Music,* ed. Bruno Nettl and Philip Bohlman. Chicago: University of Chicago Press, 1991.

Odell, Jay Scott. "Ukulele." In *The New Grove Dictionary of Musical Instruments,* vol. 3. Edited by Stanley Sadie. London: Macmillan, 1984.

Pareles, Jon. "Think Globally, Listen Locally." *The New York Times,* February 4, 2000, B1.

Wallis, Roger, and Krister Malm. *Big Sounds from Small Peoples.* New York: Pendragon Press, 1984.

Recording

Brozman, Bob. *Traditional Hawaiian Guitar.* Woodstock, NY: Homespun Video, 1993. Videocassette.

Chapter 7

In addition to the many secondary sources listed below, I am grateful to Samantha Chaifetz and Mike Bortnick of the Harvard Ballroom Club and Team for lessons, demonstrations, and explanations regarding the version of the tango used in competitive ballroom dancing. David Lyczkowski and Sarah Morelli helped mine a wide range of secondary sources on the dance and found contacts in the world of tango and *bhangra*. A seminar on *bhangra* and a performance by the MIT *bhangra* team provided a useful introduction to *bhangra* on American college campuses, as did attendance at a *Bhangra* Blowout in Boston in 1999. Sarah Morelli drafted a biography of Chitresh Das, which I have drawn on for the Individual Portraits Box in Chapter 7, and provided details on traditional *bhangra*.

Jesse Johnston generously provided many useful references on the polka. For information on Morris dancing, I drew on my observations of groups such as the Newtowne Morris Men, who frequently dance in Harvard Square, and earlier encounters with Morris dancers in locales as diverse as Bath, England and New Haven, Connecticut.

Notes

[1]Judith Lynn Hanna, *Dance, Sex, and Gender* (Chicago: Chicago University Press, 1988), pp. 162–63.

[2]Judith Lynn Hanna, "Dance," in *Ethnomusicology: An Introduction,* ed. Helen Myers (London and New York: Macmillan and W. W. Norton, 1992), p. 321.

[3]Hanna, *Dance, Sex, and Gender,* pp. 164–65.

[4]Hanna, *Dance, Sex, and Gender,* p. 167.

[5]Iqbal Singh Dhillon, *Folk Dances of Punjab* (Delhi: National Bookshop, 1998), pp. 80–89.

[6]Gerd Baumann, "The Re-Invention of Bhangra: Social Change and Aesthetic Shifts in a Punjabi Music in Britain," *The World of Music* 32 (1990): 81–95.

[7]Sarah Morelli, fieldnotes from presentation by Punjabi Lok Versa, November 1, 2003.

[8]Alke Pande, *From Mustard Fields to Disco Lights: Folk Music and Musical Instruments of Punjab* (Ahmedabad: Mapin Publishing, 1999), p. 125.

[9]Pande, p. 59.

[10]Baumann, pp. 82–84; Rahinder Dudrah, "Drum'n'dhol: British Bhangra Music and Diasporic South Asian Identity Formation," *European Journal of Cultural Studies* 5 (August 2002): 363–83.

[11]Sanjay Sharma, "Noisy Asians or 'Asian Noise'," in *Dis-Orienting Rhythms: The Politics of the New Asian Dance Music,* ed. Sanjay Sharma, John Hutnyk, and Ashwani Sharma (London: Zed Books, 1996), p. 39; Rupa Huq, "Asian Kool? Bhangra and Beyond," in *Dis-Orienting Rhythms,* pp. 78–79.

[12]Jacqueline Warwick, "'Make Way for the Indian': Bhangra Music and South Asian Presence in Toronto," *Popular Music and Society* 24, no. 2 (Summer 2000): 25–44; p. 41.

[13]Tara Dooley, "Bhangra Bounces Back," *Houston Chronicle,* November 16, 2003, 1E.

[14]Marilyn Tucker, "A Tame Indian's Take on the Golden West: Chitresh Das," *The San Francisco Chronicle,* Sunday Edition Section, 48.

[15]Sarah Morelli, "Individual Portrait: Pandit Chitresh Das," unpublished essay, 2004.

[16]Jim Bessman, "Bhangra Beat Transforms Indipop Scene," *Billboard* 3, no. 39 (1999): 100–101.

[17]Sasha Frere-Jones, "Hip-Hop is a Guest at the Indian Wedding," *The New York Times,* August 3, 2003, Section 2, 23.

[18]Dooley, 9E.

[19]Ketu H. Katrak, "Changing Traditions: South Asian Americans and Cultural/Communal Politics," *Massachusetts Review* 43 (Spring 2002): 75–88; p. 76, 78

[20]Egil Bakka, "The Polka Before and After the Polka," *Yearbook for Traditional Music* 33 (2001): 37–47.

[21]Ramiro Burr, *The Billboard Guide to Tejano and Regional Mexican Music* (New York: Watson-Guptill Publications, 1999), p. 169.

[22]Manuel Peña, *The Texas/Mexican Conjunto: History of a Working-Class Music* (Austin, TX: University of Texas Press, 1985), pp. 21–22.

[23]James P. Leary, "Czech American Polka Music in Wisconsin," in *Musics of Multicultural America: A Study of Twelve Musical Communities,* ed. Kip Lornell and Anne K. Rasmussen (New York: Schirmer Books, 1997), pp. 30–31.

[24]Leary, p. 30.

[25]Richard Spottswood, "The Sajewski Story: Eighty Years of Polish Music in Chicago," in *Ethnic Recordings in America: A Neglected Heritage* (Washington DC: American Folklife Center, Library of Congress, 1982), p. 150.

[26]Peña, p. 82.

[27]Ben Ratliff, "Valerio Longoria, 75, Conjunto Musician," *The New York Times,* December 19, 2000, A32.

[28]Robert Walser, "The Polka Mass: Music of Postmodern Ethnicity," *American Music* 10 (1992): 183–202.

[29]Walser, p. 187.

[30]Caroline Walker, *The Modern Dances: How to Dance Them* (Chicago: Saul Brothers, 1914).

[31]Gerard Béhague, "Tango," *New Grove,* 2nd ed., Vol 25, p. 74.

[32]Donald S. Castro, "The Massification of the Tango: The Electronic Media, the Popular Theatre, and the Cabaret from Contursi to Peron, 1917–1955," *Studies in Latin American Popular Culture* 18 (1999): 93–115; p. 93.

[33]Béhague, p. 74.

[34]Castro, p. 94.

[35]Chris Goertzen and Maria Susana Azzi, "Globalization and the Tango," *Yearbook for Traditional Music* 31 (1999): 67–76; p. 67.

[36]Julie M. Taylor, "Tango: Theme of Class and Nation," *Ethnomusicology* 20 (1976): 273–91; p. 277.

[37]Goertzen and Azzi, p. 68.

[38]Taylor, p. 287.

[39]Marta E. Savigliano, *Tango and the Political Economy of Passion* (Boulder, CO: Westview Press, 1995).

[40]Hanna, "Dance," p. 323.

Additional Sources
Books and Articles

Banerji, Sabita. "Ghazals to Bhangra in Great Britain." *Popular Music* 7, no. 2 (1988): 207–13.

Barrand, Anthony G. "But America for a Morris Dance!" *Sing Out!* 33, no. 4 (1988): 14–21.

Barrella, Humberto. *El Tango después de Gardel, 1935–1959.* Buenos Aires: Corregidor, 1999.

Carroll, Dennis J. "In Wisconsin, the Polka Beat Goes On." *The Boston Globe,* November 29, 1996.

Černušák, Gracian, and Andrew Lamb. "Polka." In *The New Grove Dictionary of Music and Musicians,* ed. Stanley Sadie. London: Macmillan, 1980. Vol. 15.

Cohen, Judah. "Bhangra, Asian Beat Music of the Asian Diaspora: An Exploration of a Transforming Gender Space." Unpublished paper, 1998.

Collier, Simon. *Tango! The Dance, the Song, the Story.* New York: Thames and Hudson, 1995.

———, and María Susana Azzi. *Le Grand Tango: The Life and Music of Astor Piazzolla.* New York: Oxford University Press, 2000.

Connerton, Paul. *How Societies Remember.* Cambridge: Cambridge University Press, 1989.

De Buenosaires, Oscar. *Tango: A Bibliography.* Albuquerque: FOG Publications, 1991.

Flores, Rafaelo. *El Tango, desde el Umbral Hacía Dentro.* Madrid: Euroliceo, 1993.

Gorin, Natalio, ed. *Astor Piazzolla: A Manera de Memorias.* Buenos Aires: Editorial Atlantida, 1990.

Gronow, Pekka. "Ethnic Records: An Introduction." In *Ethnic Recordings in America: A Neglected Heritage.* Washington, DC: American Folklife Center, Library of Congress, 1982.

Hall, Edward T. *The Hidden Dimension.* Garden City, NY: Doubleday, 1969.

Hanna, Judith Lynne. *Partnering Dance and Education: Intelligent Moves for Changing Times.* Champaign, IL: Human Kinetics, 1999.

Harrington, Richard. "Piazzolla and the Newfangled Tango: An Argentine Composer's 30-Year Quest for Respect." *Washington Post,* May 7, 1988, C1.

Ingalls, Zoë. "The Tango: a Scholarly History of a 'Very Passionate Dance'." *The Chronicle for Higher Education,* April 18, 1997, B8–9.

Kaeppler, Adrienne L. "American Approaches to the Study of Dance." *Yearbook for Traditional Music* 10 (1991): 11–21.

Keil, Charles, Angeliki V. Keil, and Dick Blau. *Polka Happiness.* Philadelphia: Temple University Press, 1992.

Lomax, Alan. "Brief Progress Report: Cantometrics-Choreometrics Projects." *Yearbook of the International Folk Music Council* 142 (1972): 142–44.

Loza, Steven. *Barrio Rhythm: Mexican American Music in Los Angeles.* Urbana, IL: University of Illinois Press, 1993.

McLane, Daisann. "In the Footsteps of the Conga and the Alley Cat." *The New York Times,* August 18, 1996, Section 2, 30.

Romani, G., and Ivor Beynon. "Accordion." In *The New Grove Dictionary of Musical Instruments,* ed. Stanley Sadie. New York: Macmillan, 1984. Vol. 1.

Russell, Melinda. "Give Your Body Joy, Macarena: Aspects of U.S. Participation in the Dance Craze of the 1990s." In *From Tejano to Tango: Essays on Latin American Popular Music,* ed. Walter Aaron Clark, 172–92. New York: Routledge, 2002.

Sharma, Ashwani. "Sounds Oriental: The (Im)Possibility of Theorizing Asian Musical Cultures." In *Dis-Orienting Rhythms: The Politics of the New Asian Dance Music,* edited by Sanjay Sharma, John Hutnyk, and Ashwani Sharma. London and Atlantic Highlands, NJ: Zed Books, 1996.

Thomas, Helen, ed. *Dance, Gender, and Culture.* Basingstoke, England: Macmillan, 1993.

Recordings

Secteto Mayro Orchestra. *A Passion for Tango.* Angel/Columbia Records CDC554857.

Squeeze Play: A World Accordion Anthology. Produced and edited by Richard Spottswood. Rounder CD 1090.

Web Sites

Bhangra:
www.bhangrablowout.com
sangeet group
www.bayoubhangra.com
www.generasianradio.com
www.zibamusic.com

Astor Piazzolla:
www.piazzolla.org
Includes "A Sad, Current, and Conscious Tango" (*Un Tango Triste, Actual, Consciente*), an interview of Astor Piazzolla, by Gonzola Saavedra, July 1989, Barcelona, Spain, shortly before Piazzolla's death, translated into English.

Morris dance:
www.cdss.org
www.mit.edu/people/ijs/blackjokers.html
www.sheldonbrown.com/banbury
www.angelfire.com/folk/polka/texas.html

Tango and *La Cumparsita*:
totango.net/cumpar.html

Chapter 8

For the Tibetan case study, I have depended on the work of Walter Kauffman and Ter Ellingson and the recordings by Lewiston and Hart. The discussion of *Santería* draws on María Teresa Vélez's article in *Diaspora* and her book; I am grateful to her also for help with the *Santería* chant text transcribed by David Lyczkowski. My own fieldwork with Ethiopian Christian musicians in Ethiopia and the United States is the source for the major case study, much of which was originally drafted for the 1999 Ethel V. Curry Distinguished Lecture in Musicology at the University of Michigan. Interviews with Hailegebriot Shewangizou and Tilahun Gebrehiwot were of great help in clarifying the sources of new directions in Ethiopian diaspora church music. Monica Devens and Thomas Kane were helpful with translations.

Notes

[1] Arnold Van Gennep, *The Rites of Passage*, trans. Monica B. Vizedom and Gabrielle L. Caffee (Chicago: University of Chicago Press, 1960).

[2] Victor Turner, *The Ritual Process* (Ithaca, NY: Cornell University Press, 1977).

[3] Judith Becker, *Deep Listeners: Music, Emotion, and Trancing* (Bloomington, IN: Indiana University Press, 2004), pp. 38–39.

[4] Diana Eck, "Neighboring Faiths," *Harvard Magazine* 99 (1996): 38–44.

[5] Ricardo Canzio et al., "Tibetan Music" (II), *New Grove*, 2nd ed., Vol. 25, p. 443.

[6] Canzio et al., p. 443.

[7] Huston Smith, Kenneth N. Stevens, and Raymond S. Tomlinson, "On an Unusual Mode of Chanting by Certain Tibetan Lamas," *Journal of the Acoustical Society of America* 41 (1967): 1262–64.

[8] Ter Ellingson, "The Mathematics of Tibetan *Rol Mo*," *Ethnomusicology* 23 (1979): 225–43; p. 236.

[9] Ellingson, pp. 148, 226–29.

[10] María Teresa Vélez, *Drumming for the Gods: The Life and Times of Felipe García Villamil, Santero, Palero, and Abakua* (Philadelphia: Temple University Press, 2000), p. 7. Unless otherwise indicated, information about *santería* is drawn from this work.

[11] John Amira and Steven Cornelius, *The Music of Santería: Traditional Rhythms of the Batá Drums* (Crown Point, IN, and New York: White Cliffs Media, 1992).

[12] Steven Gregory, *Santería in New York City: A Study in Cultural Resistance* (New York: Garland, 2000), p. 85.

[13] Gregory, p. xiii.

[14] María Teresa Vélez, "Eyá Aránla: Overlapping Perspectives," *Diaspora* 3 (1994): 289–304.

[15] Johann Wedel. *Santería Healing: A Journey into the Afro-Cuban World of Divinities, Spirits, and Sorcery* (Gainesville, FL: University of Florida Press, 2004), p. 31.

[16] As quoted in Vélez, "Eyá Aránla," p. 293.

[17] Unless otherwise indicated, all quotations are from ethnographic interviews held by the author with either Liga Berhanu Makonnen in Ethiopia during 1975 or with Hailegebriot Shewangizou and Tilahun Gebrehiwot in the United States during 1999.

[18] *Music, Dance and Drama*, Book IX of *Patterns of Progress* (Addis Ababa: Ministry of Information, 1968), pp. 43–44.

[19] The song *Lent* was released in the United States on the CD *Assiyo Belema* (Ethio-Grooves Record, 1994). Another of Mulatu Astatke's compositions from the 1970s titled *Dewel* after the resonant stones outside rural churches, has been reissued on *Ethiopiques. EthioJazz & Musique Instrumentale* 1969–74, Vol. 4, Paris: Buda Musique, 82964-2, no date.

Additional Sources
Books and Articles

Comaroff, Jean, and John Comaroff. "Introduction." In *Modernity and its Malcontents: Ritual and Power in Postcolonial Africa*. Chicago: University of Chicago Press, 1993.

Cox, Harvey Gallagher. *Fire from Heaven: The Rise of Pentecostal Spirituality and the Reshaping of Religion in the Twenty-First Century*. Reading, MA: Addison-Wesley, 1995.

Crossley-Holland, Peter. Review of *Tibetan Buddhism: Tantras of Gyuto: Mahakala*, ed. David Lewiston. *Ethnomusicology* 18 (1974): 339–41.

Dalai Lama. *Freedom in Exile: The Autobiography of the Dalai Lama*. New York: Harper Perennial, 1991.

Harrison, Frank Llewellyn. *Time, Place, and Music: An Anthology of Ethnomusicological Observation*. Amsterdam: Frits Knuf, 1973.

Helffer, Mireille. Review of *The Music of Tibet. The Tantric Rituals*. *Ethnomusicology* 16 (1972): 152–54.

Leach, Edmund Ronald. *Rethinking Anthropology*. London: Athlone Press, 1961.

Mercier, Jacques. *Ethiopian Magic Scrolls*. New York: George Braziller, 1979.

Nomachi, Kazuyoshi. *Bless Ethiopia*. Tokyo: Odyssey Publications, 1998.

Powers, John. *An Introduction to Tibetan Buddhism*. Ithaca, NY: Snow Lion Publications, 1995.

Rappaport, Roy A. "The Obvious Aspects of Ritual." In *Ecology, Meaning, and Religion*. Richmond, CA: North Atlantic Books, 1979.

Shelemay, Kay Kaufman. "The Musician and Transmission of Religious Tradition: The Multiple Roles of the Ethiopian Dabtara." *Journal of Religion in Africa* 22 (1992): 242–60.

———. "Zema: A Concept of Sacred Music in Ethiopia." *The World of Music* 24, no. 3 (1982): 52–67.

———, and Peter Jeffery. *Ethiopian Christian Liturgical Chant: An Anthology*. Madison, WI: A-R Editions, 1994–1998. Vols. 1–3.

———, Peter Jeffery, and Ingrid Monson. "Oral and Written Transmission in Ethiopian Chant." *Early Music History* 12 (1993): 55–117.

Tarocco, Francesca. "Buddhist Music," *The New Grove Dictionary of Music and Musicians*, 2nd ed. ed. Stanley Sadie. London: MacMillan, 2001. Vol. 4.

Tucci, Giuseppe. *Religions of Tibet*. Trans. Geoffrey Samuel. Berkeley: University of California Press, 1980.

Vélez, María Teresa. "The Trade of an Afro-Cuban Religious Drummer, Felipe García Villamil." 2 vols. Ph.D. dissertation, Wesleyan University, 1996.

Recordings

Jenkins, J., ed. "Ethiopia I. Copts." *An Anthology of African Music.* UNESCO Collection. Kassel: Bärenreiter Musicaphon BM 30 L 2304, 1965.

Lewiston, David, ed. *Tibetan Buddhism: Tantras of Gyuto: Mahakala.* Nonesuch, H-72055, 1973.

CD-ROM

Eck, Diana. *On Common Ground: World Religions in America (Pluralism Project).* New York: Columbia University Press, 1997.

Web Sites

The Pluralism Project Web site: www.fas.harvard.edu/ ~pluralism

Tibetan Music in North America: www.tibet.org/ chaksampa

Chapter 9

The case study on *Nkosi Sikelel' iAfrika* was compiled with the assistance of members of Kuumba, who provided details of their experience learning the new South African national anthem in September 1998. Veit Erlmann's discussion of *mbube* was an additional resource. The reggae case study was compiled from the secondary sources listed below and helpful suggestions by anonymous readers.

The Shoshone case study depends heavily on research published by Judith Vander, although the interpretations of the music's significance in Shoshone public life are my own. I gathered additional materials on the Shoshone powwow during a brief field trip to the Wind River Reservation during the summer of 1998, and am grateful for the generous assistance of Judith Vander. Tara Browner's recent study of the Northern plains powwow has provided a rich resource.

Notes

[1] James C. Scott, *Domination and the Arts of Resistance: Hidden Transcripts* (New Haven, CT: Yale University Press, 1990).

[2] Tricia Rose, *Black Noise: Rap Music and Black Culture in Contemporary America* (Hanover, NH: Wesleyan University Press, 1994), p. 101.

[3] Veit Erlmann, *Nightsong: Performance, Power, and Practice in South Africa* (Chicago: University of Chicago Press, 1996), pp. 54–57.

[4] Erlmann, pp. 46–47.

[5] www.safrica.info/ess_info/sa_glance/history/anthem.htm

[6] F. G. Brownell, *National Symbols of the Republic of South Africa* (Melville, South Africa: Chris Van Rensburg Publications, 1995), p. 2.

[7] Andrea Botha, "South Africa: Anthem Changes City Men's Lives," *Africa News,* December 15, 1998.

[8] Xolani Xundu, "Time to Dump *Die Stem,*" *Business Day (South Africa),* May 15, 2003, p. 12.

[9] Norman J. Singer, "Symbols of Ethiopian Culture in Jamaica Beyond Rastafarianism," *Proceedings of the Ninth International Congress of Ethiopian Studies, Moscow, August 26–29, 1986* (Moscow: USSR Academy of Sciences, Africa Institute, 1988), pp. 27–28.

[10] Dick Hebdige, *Subculture: The Meaning of Style* (New York: Routledge, 1988), p. 34.

[11] Eric Hobsbawm, "Inventing Traditions," in *The Invention of Traditions,* ed. Eric Hobsbawm and Terence Ranger (Cambridge: Cambridge University Press, 1983), pp. 1–14.

[12] Stephen Davis, "Reggae," *New Grove,* 2nd ed., Vol. 21.

[13] Kevin O'Brien Chang and Wayne Chen, *Reggae Rousters: The Story of Jamaican Music* (Philadelphia: Temple University Press, 1998), pp. 41, 95.

[14] Davis, p. 100.

[15] Kelefa Sanneh, "The Rhythm That Reggae's Clapping To," *The New York Times,* March 9, 2003, Section 2, p. 15.

[16] Chang and Chen, p. 54.

[17] Adrian Boot and Chris Salewicz, *Bob Marley: Songs of Freedom* (New York: Viking Studio Books, 1995).

[18] www.Bobmarley.com/songs/ram/zimbabwe.ram

[19] Davis, p. 101.

[20] Hugh Davies, "Synthesizer," *New Grove,* 2nd ed., Vol. 24, p. 851.

[21] Jeff Pressing, *Synthesizer Performing and Real-Time Techniques* (Madison, WI: A-R Editions, 1992), p. 12.

[22] Ian Peel, "Scratching," *New Grove,* 2nd ed., Vol. 23, p. 11.

[23] www.apple.com/pro/music/rothschild/index2.html

[24] Roger Steffens, "Ragga," *New Grove,* 2nd ed., Vol. 20.

[25] Raminder Kaur and Virinder S. Kalra, "New Paths for South Asian Identity and Musical Creativity," in *Dis-Orienting Rhythms: The Politics of the New Asian Dance Music,* ed. Sanjay Sharma, John Hutnyk, and Ashwani Sharma (London and Atlantic Highlands, NJ: Zed Books, 1996), p. 226.

[26] George Lipsitz, *Dangerous Crossroads: Popular Music, Postmodernism, and the Poetics of Place* (London and New York: Verso, 1994), p. 15.

[27] Jon Pareles, "Spicy Mix of Salsa, Hip-Hop and Reggae," *The New York Times,* August 7, 2003, Section E, p. 1.

28Hasse Huss, "The 'Xince-Fence Thing': When Will Reggae Album Covers be Allowed out of the Ghetto?" *Black Music Research Journal* 20 (2000): 181–94; p. 191.

29Mike Alleyne, "White Reggae: Cultural Dilution in the Record Industry," *Popular Music and Society* 24 (2000): 15–30, p. 15.

30The Rev. John Roberts (1883–1949), *Walk Softly, This Is God's Country: Sixty-Six Years on the Wind River Indian Reservation,* ed. Elinor R. Markley and Beatrice Crofts (Lander, WY: Mortimore Publishing, 1997), p. 121.

31Carey Goldberg, "Powwows Change, But Drummer Is the Same," *New York Times,* August 24, 1997, Week in Review, p. 4.

32Judith Vander, *Songprints: The Musical Experience of Five Shoshone Women* (Urbana, IL: University of Illinois Press, 1988).

33www.creative-native.com/biograp.htm

34www.cradleboard.org/2000/press.html

35Tara Browner, *Heartbeat of the People: Music and Dance of the Northern Pow-Wow* (Urbana, IL: University of Illinois Press, 2002), p. 48. Subsequent passages about powwow dance draw on this source unless otherwise indicated.

36For additional details, see Browner, Chapter 3, Dance Styles and Regalia.

37Vander, *Songprints,* p. 81.

38Goldberg, p. 4.

39Daniel J. Gelo, "Powwow Patter: Indian Emcee Discourse on Power and Identity," *The Journal of American Folklore* 112 (1999): 40–57.

40Tara Browner, "Making and Singing Pow-Wow Songs: Text, Form, and the Significance of Culture-Based Analysis," *Ethnomusicology* 44 (2000): 214–33.

41Vander, p. 194.

42Browner, p. 73.

43William K. Powers, "Ogala Song Terminology," in *Selected Reports in Ethnomusicology* 3, no. 2, ed. Charlotte Heth (Los Angeles: Program in Ethnomusicology, University of California, Los Angeles, 1980), p. 31.

44William K. Powers, "Plains Indian Music and Dance," in *Anthropology on the Great Plains,* ed. W. Raymond Wood and Margot Liberty (Lincoln, NE, and London: University of Nebraska Press, 1980), p. 219.

45Vander, p. 46.

46Vander, p. 143.

47Vander, p. 144.

48Anna Hoefnagels, "Powwow Songs: Traveling Songs and Changing Protocol," *The World of Music* 44 (2002): 127–36; p. 129.

49Vander, p. 156.

Additional Sources
Books and Articles

Bilby, Kenneth. "From 'Jamaica'." In *Reggae, Rasta, Revolution: Jamaican Music from Ska to Dub,* ed. Chris Potash. New York: Schirmer Books, 1997; pp. 29–36.

Burton, Bryan. *Moving Within the Circle.* Danbury, CT: World Music Press, 1993.

Campbell, Gregory R. "The Lemhi Shoshoni; Ethnogenesis, Sociological Transformations, and the Construction of a Tribal Nation." *American Indian Quarterly* 25 (2001): 539–78.

Dunning, Jennifer. "A Culture's Age-Old Rituals Made Fresh in a Journey Through Time." *New York Times,* August 10, 1998, E5.

Erlmann, Viet. *Music, Modernity, and the Global Imagination: South Africa and the West.* New York, Oxford University Press, 1999.

Foster, Roy. "What Is Political History?" In *What Is History Today?,* ed. Juliet Gardiner. Atlantic Highlands, NJ: Humanities Press International, 1988.

Harlan, Theresa. "Creating a Visual History: A Question of Ownership." *Aperture* 139 (Summer 1995): 20–33.

Haynes, George Edmund. "Negroes and the Ethiopian Crisis," *The Christian Century* 52, no. 27 (November 20, 1935): 1485.

Hutton, Ronald. "What is Political History?" In *What Is History Today?,* ed. Juliet Gardiner. Atlantic Highlands, NJ: Humanities Press International, 1988.

Jackson, Zig. "Social Identity: A View from Within." *Aperture* 139 (Summer 1995): 34–38.

Madsen, Brigham D. *The Northern Shoshoni.* Caldwell, ID: Caxton Printers, 1980.

———. *The Shoshoni Frontier and the Bear River Massacre.* Salt Lake City: University of Utah Press, 1985.

Morgan, Kenneth O. "What Is Political History Today?" In *What Is History Today?* ed. Juliet Garner. Atlantic Highlands, NJ: Humanities Press International, 1988.

Norton, Mary Beth. *A People and A Nation: A History of the United States,* 4th ed. Boston: Houghton Mifflin Company, 1994.

Pow Wow Time, a *Ranger* special edition. *Ranger,* Riverton, Wyoming, Thursday, May 21, 1998.

Reckford, Verena. "From *Burru* Drums to Reggae Riddims: The Evolution of Rasta Music." *Chanting Down Babylon: The Rastafari Reader,* ed. Nathaniel Samuel Murrell, William David Spencer, and Adrian Anthony McFarlane. Philadelphia: Temple University Press, 1998.

Rickard, Jolene. "Sovereignty: A Line in the Sand." *Aperture* 139 (Summer 1995): 51–60.

Scales, Christopher A. "The Politics and Aesthetics of Recording: A Comparative Canadian Case Study of Powwow and Contemporary Native American Music." *The World of Music* 44(1) 2002: 41–59.

Shabalala, Joseph Bekhizizwe. "Joseph Bekhizizwe Shabalala: A Unifying Force." In *Nightsong: Performance, Power and Practice in South Africa,* ed. Veit Erlmann. Chicago: University of Chicago Press, 1996.

Smith, Huston, and Reuben Snake, eds. *One Nation Under God: The Triumph of the Native American Church.* Santa Fe: Clear Light Publishers, 1996.

Smyth, Willie, ed. *Songs of Indian Territory: Native American Music Traditions of Oklahoma.* Oklahoma City: Center of the American Indian, 1989.

"South Africa's National Anthem." *The Times* (London). May 3, 2001.

Vander, Judith. "The Song Repertoire of Four Shoshone Women: A Reflection of Cultural Movements and Sex Roles." *Ethnomusicology* 26 (1983): 73–83.

———. *Ghost Dance Songs and Religion of a Wind River Shoshone Woman.* Los Angeles: Program in Ethnomusicology, UCLA, 1986.

———. *Shoshone Ghost Dance Religion: Poetry, Songs, and Great Basin Context.* Urbana, IL: University of Illinois Press, 1997.

Web Site

Biography of Enoch Mankayi Sontonga, by Genevieve Walker: www.polity.org.za/people/sontonga

Chapter 10

For this chapter I drew on the following sources as well as the help of a number of individuals. Gil Rose of the Boston Modern Orchestra Project and Reza Vali provided information, recordings, and scores for the Flute Concerto. I am especially grateful to Reza Vali for his willingness to share his thoughts and observations about his music and composition in general during telephone interviews.

For advice and translation of the *enka* example, I thank Takashi Koto and Tomie Hahn; Kazuko Mockett provided a transliteration of the Japanese text. Christine Yano's research on *karaoke* provided a wealth of historical and ethnographic detail. I thank Kerry Masteller and Andrew Wilson for assistance with the listening examples.

Ronald Emoff's work on Cajun poetics provided valuable insights. For help with the Creole repertories, I thank Asmara Tekle. The writings of Tisserand on zydeco have been a particularly valuable resource.

Barry Jean Ancelet kindly provided information concerning several photographs.

The note on the orchestra is based on the article "orchestra" in the *New Grove Dictionary of Musical Instruments.*

Notes

[1] Ronald M. Radano, "Interpreting Muzak: Speculations on Musical Experience in Everyday Life," *American Music* 7 (Winter 1989): 448–60.

[2] Gage Averill, *Four Parts, No Waiting. A Social History of American Barbershop Harmony* (Oxford: Oxford University Press, 2003), p. 91.

[3] This definition is based on Adelaida Reyes Schramm, "Ethnic Music, the Urban Area, and Ethnomusicology," *Sociologus* 29 (1979) new series: 1–18; p. 15.

[4] Hugh Trevor-Roper, "The Invention of Tradition: The Highland Tradition of Scotland," in *The Invention of Tradition,* ed. Eric Hobsbawm and Terence Ranger (Cambridge: Cambridge University Press, 1983), p. 15.

[5] Hormoz Farhat, "Iran, II," *New Grove,* 2nd ed., Vol. 12, pp. 536–37.

[6] Scheherazade Qassim Hassan and Jean During, "Ney," in *New Grove,* 2nd ed., Vol. 17, p. 853. Information about *ney* construction is from Hassan and During unless otherwise noted.

[7] Hossein 'Omoumi, Notes for *The Song of the Ney: Persian Classical Music* (London: Nimbus Records, 1992 and 1995). Information about *ney* playing techniques is from 'Omoumi unless otherwise noted.

[8] Quotations are drawn from telephone interviews between the author and Reza Vali.

[9] Farhat, p. 533.

[10] Georgina Born and David Hesmondhalgh, eds., *Western Music and Its Others: Difference, Representation, and Appropriation in Music* (Berkeley: University of California Press, 2000), p. 2.

[11] Christine R. Yano, "The Floating World of Karaoke in Japan," *Popular Music and Society* 20 (1996): 1–17.

[12] Tōru Mitsui and Shūhei Hosokawa, eds., *Karaoke Around the World: Global Technology, Local Singing* (London and New York: Routledge, 1998), p. 3.

[13] Hiroshi Ogawa, "The Effects of Karaoke on Music in Japan," in *Karaoke Around the World,* ed. Mitsui and Hosokawa, 45–54; pp. 45–46.

[14] Mitsui and Hosokawa, Introduction, p. 8.

[15] Ogawa, p. 46–47.

[16] Christine R. Yano, *Tears of Longing: Nostalgia and the Nation in Japanese Popular Song* (Cambridge, MA: Harvard Asia Center and Harvard University Press, 2002), p. 25.

[17]James R. Brandon, "Form in Kabuki Acting," *Studies in Kabuki: Its Acting, Music and Historical Context,* ed. James R. Brandon, William P. Malm, and Donald H. Shively (Honolulu: University of Hawaii Press, 1978), pp. 63–132, p. 65.

[18]This discussion of *kata* in the music of *kabuki* draws on William P. Malm, "Music in the Kabuki Theater," in *Studies in Kabuki,* ed. Brandon, Malm, and Shively, pp. 132–175.

[19]Marta E. Savigliano, "Exotic Encounters," in *Tango and the Political Economy of Passion* (Boulder, CO: Westview Press, 1995).

[20]Sarah Morelli, unpublished field notes on *no rae pang.*

[21]Casey Man Kong Lum, *In Search of a Voice: Karaoke and the Construction of Identity in Chinese America* (Mahwah, NJ: Lawrence Erlbaum Associates, 1996), pp. 29–31.

[22]Mike Toshi Kida, quoted in Damien Cave, "'Sweet Caroline' Never Seemed so Good: So Uncool It's Hip, Karaoke Enjoys a Comeback in New York," *The New York Times,* July 14, 2003, A 24.

[23]Lauren C. Post, *Cajun Sketches* (Baton Rouge, LA: Louisiana State University Press, 1977), p. 23.

[24]Ron Emoff, "A Cajun Poetics of Loss and Longing," *Ethnomusicology* 42 (1998): 283–301.

[25]Post, p. 31.

[26]Pekka Gronow, "Ethnic Recordings: An Introduction," in *Ethnic Recordings in America* (Washington DC: Library of Congress, 1982).

[27]Chris A. Strachwitz, "Cajun Country," *The American Folk Music Occasional,* No. 2, ed. Chris Strachwitz and Pete Welding (New York: Oak Publications, 1970), p. 15.

[28]Mark F. DeWitt, "Heritage, Tradition, and Travel: Louisiana French Culture Placed on a California Dance Floor," *The World of Music* 41 (1999): 57–83, pp. 63–64.

[29]Emoff, p. 292.

[30]Michael Tisserand, *The Kingdom of Zydeco* (New York: Arcade Publishing, 1998), p. 3.

[31]Tisserand, p. 3, quoting Wilbert Guillory, the founding director of the Southwest Louisiana Zydeco Festival.

[32]Tisserand, p. 222.

[33]Jennings, p. 38.

[34]Dana Jennings, "In Bayou Country, Music Is Never Second Fiddle," *The New York Times,* November 22, 1998.

Additional Sources
Books and Articles

Ancelet, Barry Jean, and Elemore Morgan, Jr. *Cajun and Creole Music Makers.* Jackson, MS: University Press of Mississippi, 1999.

Arceneaux, George. *Youth in Acadie: Reflections on Acadian Life and Culture in Southwest Louisiana.* Baton Rouge, LA: Claitor's Publishing Division, 1974.

Bendix, Regina. *In Search of Authenticity: The Formation of Folklore Studies.* Madison, WI: The University of Wisconsin Press, 1997.

Bernard, Shane K. *Swamp Pop: Cajun and Creole Rhythm and Blues.* Jackson, MS: University Press of Mississippi, 1996.

Borwick, John. "Sound Recording, Transmission, and Reproduction. 6. Recording." *The New Grove Dictionary of Music and Musicians,* ed. Stanley Sadie. London: Macmillan, 1980.

Brasseaux, Carl A. *Acadian to Cajun: Transformation of a People, 1803–1877.* Jackson, MS: University Press of Mississippi, 1992.

———. "Creoles of Color in Louisiana's Bayou Country 1766–1877." In *Creoles of Color of the Gulf South,* ed. James H. Dorman. Knoxville, TN: University of Tennessee Press, 1996.

Broven, John. *South to Louisiana: The Music of the Cajun Bayous.* Gretna, LA: Pelican Publishing Company, 1983.

Conrad, Glenn R. *The Cajuns: Essays on their History and Culture.* Lafayette, LA: Center for Louisiana Studies, University of Southwestern Louisiana, 1978.

Crowley, Larry. "Queen Ida Still Cookin' On, Offstage." *Arizona Republic,* May 15, 1997, C1.

Diagram Group. *Musical Instruments of the World: An Illustrated Encyclopedia.* New York: Facts on File, 1976.

Dorman, James H. *Creoles of Color of the Gulf South.* Knoxville, TN: University of Tennessee Press, 1996.

———. "Ethnicity and Identity: Creoles of Color in Twentieth-Century South Louisiana." *Creoles of Color of the Gulf South.* Knoxville, TN: University of Tennessee Press, 1996.

Evans, David. *Big Road Blues: Tradition and Creativity in the Folk Blues.* Berkeley: University of California Press, 1982.

Gleason, Philip. "Identifying Identity: A Semantic History." In *Theories of Ethnicity: A Classical Reader,* ed. Werner Sollors. New York: New York University Press, 1996.

Hanger, Kimberly S. "Origins of New Orleans Free Creoles of Color." In *Creoles of Color of the Gulf South,* ed. James H. Dorman. Knoxville, TN: University of Tennessee Press, 1996.

Hildebrand, Lee. "Queen Ida Cookin' in More Ways than One." *San Francisco Chronicle,* May 20, 1990, Sunday Datebook, 39.

Keil, Charles. "Music Mediated and Live in Japan." *Ethnomusicology* 28 (1984): 91–96.

Lawson, Kyle. "She's Still Ruling Zydeco's Roost: Queen Ida Plays a Mean Accordion But She's No Lawrence Welk." Minneapolis–St. Paul *Star Tribune*, July 9, 1995, 8F.

Koizumi, Fumio and David W. Hughes. "Japan" (VI, 3). *New Grove* 2nd ed., Vol 12.

Minton, John. "Houston Creoles and Zydeco: The Emergence of an African American Urban Popular Music." *American Music* 14 (1996): 480–526.

Monson, Ingrid. *Saying Something: Jazz Improvisation and Interaction.* Chicago: University of Chicago Press, 1996.

"More Good Stuff; Saturday." *The Phoenix Gazette.* May 19, 1994, Z2.

Nash, Manning. *The Cauldron of Ethnicity in the Modern World.* Chicago: University of Chicago Press, 1989.

Nettl, Bruno. "Streets." In *The Western Impact on World Music: Change, Adaptation, and Survival.* New York: Schirmer Books, 1985.

Proulx, E. Annie. *Accordion Crimes.* New York: Scribner, 1996.

Ratliff, Ben. "Frank Yankovic, Long-Reigning Polka King, Is Dead at 83." *New York Times,* October 15, 1998.

Rushton, William Faulkner. *The Cajuns: From Acadia to Louisiana.* New York: Farrar Straus Giroux, 1979.

Savigliano, Marta E. "Exotic Encounters." In *Tango and the Political Economy of Passion.* Boulder, CO: Westview Press, 1995.

Shane, Bernard K. *Swamp Pop: Cajun and Creole Rhythm and Blues.* Jackson, MS: University of Mississippi Press, 1996.

Spottswood, Richard Keith. *Ethnic Music on Records: A Discography of Ethnic Recordings Produced in the United States, 1893 to 1942,* 7 vols. Urbana, IL: University of Illinois Press, 1990.

Sollors, Werner. "Foreword: Theories of Ethnicity." In *Theories of Ethnicity: A Classical Reader.* New York: New York University Press, 1996.

Valdés, Alisa. "Fresh Squeezed." *Boston Globe,* January 3, 1998, D1.

Vali, Mahmood-Reza. "Breaking the Sound Barrier." Program notes for Concerto for Flute and Orchestra, Boston Modern Orchestra, February 13, 1998.

Vecoli, Rudolph J., et al., eds. *Gale Encyclopedia of Multicultural America,* vols. 1–2. New York: Gale Research, 1995.

Westrup, Jack, with Neal Zaslow and Eleanor Selfridge-Field. "Orchestra." *The New Grove Dictionary of Musical Instruments,* ed. Stanley Sadie. London: Macmillan, 1984.

Whitfield, Irene Thérese. *Louisiana French Folk Songs.* Baton Rouge, LA: Louisiana State University Press, 1939.

Yeh, Nora. Review of *In Search of a Voice: Karaoke and the Construction of Identity in Chinese America,* by Casey Man Kong Lum. *Ethnomusicology* 41 (1997): 565–67.

Web Site

Hawaii Star Bulletin:

http://www.starbulletin.com/96105/16/features/story2

Includes "Queen Ida Gets Down on the Bayou Sound," by Ann Marie Swan, May 16, 1996.

Epilogue

[1]Deborah Wong, "I Want the Microphone: Mass Mediation and Agency in Asian American Popular Music," *TDR: The Drama Review* 38 (no. 3) T143, Fall 1994: 152–67; pp. 161–62.

Additional Source

Takaki, Ronald. *From Different Shores: Perspectives on Race and Ethnicity in America,* 2nd ed. New York and Oxford: Oxford University Press, 1994.

Appendix

Notes

[1]Based on Curt Sachs, "Terminology," in *The History of Musical Instruments* (New York: W. W. Norton, 1940).

Glossary

Terms in *italics* refer to other definitions in the Glossary.

A 440 The *sound* produced when a string or air column vibrates at 440 cycles per second, assigned the *pitch* value A. Western *orchestras* tune to A 440.

accent Emphasis on a *pitch* by any of several means, such as increased *intensity*, altered *range*, or lengthened *duration*.

accompaniment *Instrumental* support for a foreground *melody* or *solo* instrument.

accordion A *free aerophone* with *reeds* that are hidden within two rectangular headboards that are connected by a folding bellows, with keys or buttons to play a *melody* and *chords*.

acoustics The science that deals with *sound*.

acrostic A word spelled by reading down the first letters of the lines of a poem.

aerophones Instruments that sound by means of vibrating air; one of the five main classes of instruments in the *Sachs-Hornbostel system*, subdivided into *trumpets* and horns, pipes (*flutes* and *reeds*), and *free aerophones*.

agbadza An Ewe dance performed at social gatherings and funerals.

air In Scottish *bagpipe* music, a long, slow, main theme, also known as a tune or ground. See also *allrd urlar*.

air and variations A musical form in which a main theme is repeated with a series of alterations to its *melody, harmony, rhythm,* and so on.

allrd urlar A *Gaelic* term for the *ground* or *melody* that is used as the *theme* in a *pibroch*.

antiphony A *performance practice* that features alternation between two or more groups of singers or players.

arbor The circular structure surrounding the courtyard where a *powwow* is held.

articulation The way a note is begun or finished. See also *slides*.

atumpan Large drums, the central instruments in ensembles used in Asante ceremonies and state occasions.

bagpipe An *aerophone* with one or more *drones* and a *chanter,* all attached to an air reservoir, or bag, allowing for uninterrupted sound production.

ballad A song *genre* commemorating important events and individuals, usually in *strophic form*.

ballroom dance Partnered, structured dances for recreation or competition.

bandoneón A button *accordion* associated with the *tango*.

banjo A plucked *lute* with a long neck, predominantly metal strings, and a shallow, single-headed *membranophone* as its body.

bar mitzvah The religious ceremony that marks the formal passage of Jewish boys to adulthood at age thirteen.

barrel organ A small, portable organ with a rotating barrel fitted with pins that trigger individual pipes to sound. The player is typically called an *organ grinder*.

barrio A Spanish term for an urban district or suburb.

batá Double-headed *membranophones* usually played in sets of three (the *iyá,* the *itótole,* and the *okónkolo*) in *Santería* ceremonies.

beat An individual *pulse*.

beating tones *Acoustical* phenomenon perceived as a shimmering *quality* when two slightly different *pitches* are played at the same time.

bellows shaking An *accordion* technique that results in an intensified *tremolo* or *vibrato*.

Bembé A traditional *Santería* religious feast.

bhangra A tightly choreographed men's group dance, originally from the Punjab region of North India and Pakistan, with pronounced leg and shoulder movements and occasional waving of arms high overhead; *bhangra* has become a popular competitive dance in the Asian diaspora.

bhangramuffin An amalgam of *bhangra, reggae, hip-hop,* and Anglo-American pop.

bimusicality Proficiency in two different musical traditions.

biphonic singing A singing technique of Inner Asian origin in which two tones, the *fundamental* and an *overtone,* are made audible simultaneously by a single singer; also known as harmonic singing.

birl A quick *ornamental* figure of two adjacent *pitches* in *bagpipe* music.

blowpipe The pipe through which a *bagpiper* blows to fill the air reservoir, or bag.

bolis A short solo phrase traditionally sung without *accompaniment* at the beginning of a Punjabi song.

bombo Peruvian *membranophone.*

bow An implement resembling an archer's bow used to sound string instruments; in some places, the bow itself is plucked to produce *sound.*

break dancing A dance form that emerged from the *hip-hop* movement.

broadside English or American narrative poem of the sixteenth to nineteenth centuries, printed on one side of a page, generally addressing contemporary events and personalities.

busker Public street performer who collects donations from passersby.

button accordion See *bandoneón.*

ca hue Vietnamese *chamber music.*

cadence A melodic or harmonic figure, typically at the end of a phrase or piece, that creates a sense of repose or resolution.

Cajun A corruption of the term "Acadian," a French-speaking people in Louisiana; their style of music; their cultural life.

call-and-response A *performance practice* in which a leader makes a musical statement and another performer (or group of performers) responds with a musical answer.

cancionero A Spanish term for a collection of lyric poems, sometimes including music.

canntaireachd See *mouth music.*

ceilidh A social or musical event dating back to the eighteenth century and associated with Celtic traditions.

chain migration A process of migration in which immigrants follow extended personal and familial networks to a particular community.

chamber music Music written for small ensembles, often played in more intimate performance venues than concert halls.

changgo A Korean double-headed hourglass *membranophone.*

chant A musical setting of a sacred text, or a repertoire of such works.

chanter A pipe with fingerholes on which a *bagpiper* plays the melody.

charro Mexican cowboy whose fancy dress, associated with the *mariachi* identity, consists of a *sombrero* (wide-brimmed hat), a short jacket, a large bow tie, and tight trousers with rows of *botonaduras* (shiny buttons).

chest voice Sound resonated from within the chest, with a low, powerful, throaty vocal *quality.*

chicken dance *Shoshone* war dance that imitates the behavior of the sage chicken.

chord A set of three or more pitches sounding simultaneously.

chordophones Instruments with strings that can be plucked or bowed, one of the five main classes of instruments in the *Sachs-Hornbostel system,* which subdivides them into *zithers, lutes, lyres,* and *harps.*

choreometrics Alan Lomax's system for comparing movement styles in dance.

chorus (1) A large *ensemble* of singers performing together, sometimes under the guidance of a conductor. (2) *Refrain.*

classical (1) A cultivated or esoteric musical tradition. (2) *Western art music.*

commodity A product that is bought and sold.

compadrito A type of urban *gaucho* reputed to be both Don Juan and pimp.

composition The process of creating *music.*

compound meter Groupings of six, nine, or twelve beats per *measure.*

concerto Music written for *orchestra* and a solo instrument.

concussion idiophones A subclass of *idiophones* consisting of instruments that are struck, often in pairs.

conjunct motion Stepwise melodic movement using small intervals, as opposed to *disjunct motion.*

conjunto A distinctive style of *accordion* music, popular among Mexican-Americans, whose ensemble includes an *accordion,* a *guitar,* bass, and percussion.

contour The shape of a *phrase* or section of music, generally understood as the way its *pitches* move; the pitches of an ascending contour go up, those of a descending contour go down.

contrafactum A song in which new text is set to a borrowed or preexisting melody.

conventional signs A category of Ethiopian *notational* signs that do not derive from the Ge'ez syllabary, consisting of dots, dashes, and curved lines.

copyright The legal protection of intellectual property.

corrido A type of *ballad,* usually *strophic,* that commemorates important events and memorable individuals in Mexican and Mexican-American history.

countermelody A *melody* that contrasts with a main *melody,* or tune, played at the same time.

cross-cultural Of more than one *culture.*

culture The collection of beliefs, concepts, arts, crafts, skills, ideas, customs, and practices held jointly by a group of people.

cutting The insertion of *grace notes* between two notes of the same *pitch* in *bagpipe melodies.*

dan bau A *Vietnamese zither* with a pitch-bending bar.

dan ken A *Vietnamese double-reed aerophone.*

dan nguyet A moon-shaped, long-necked *Vietnamese lute* with two strings.

dan nhi A Vietnamese two-stringed *lute.*

dan tranh A Vietnamese sixteen-stringed *zither.*

dabtara Ethiopian church musicians who are also scribes and healers.

darabukkah A Middle Eastern *membranophone* with a goblet shape.

dastgah Traditional Persian musical system consisting of a number of categories of melody that are distinguished by *pitch* content, melodic contours, and ornamentation.

dbyang A type of *biphonic* Tibetan chant characterized by sustained notes in a low *register* and audible *harmonics.*

dbyangs-yig A song book of Tibetan *dbyang,* literally "written account of the song."

development (1) The process of elaborating or varying a *theme.* (2) The middle, contrasting section of Western *sonata form.*

dhol A double-headed South Asian *membranophone* associated with *bhangra.*

diaspora People living outside their historic homeland who maintain memories of, and attachments to, their place of origin.

digital electronic instrument An *electrophone,* such as the digital *synthesizer,* in which a computer emulates acoustic patterns.

disjunct motion Melodic motion by leaps of large intervals, as opposed to *conjunct motion.*

dirge An instrumental lament played at a slow tempo.

dotted rhythm The pairing of a long and short rhythm, as in iambic meter, so named because a dot represents the rhythm in Western notation.

double reed A *reed* made of two thin strips of cane bound together so that they vibrate against each other.

drone A steady single tone or a pipe on a *bagpipe* that produces one.

duduk An Armenian wind instrument that symbolizes its native country.

duple meter A grouping, or *measure,* of two *beats.*

duration The way *music* organizes time; can be described in terms of *rhythm, pulse,* and *meter.*

dynamics The *intensity* of a musical event.

early music Music of the European past or its twentieth-century revival.

electromechanical instruments *Electrophones,* such as the *Hawaiian steel guitar,* whose vibrations are produced mechanically and transformed into electric oscillations that are amplified and reproduced by electric speakers.

electrophones Instruments that produce sound using electricity, one of the five main classes of instruments in the *Sachs-Hornbostel system,* subdivided into *electromechanical instruments, radioelectric instruments,* and *digital electronic instruments.*

engergari A group of celebratory *Ethiopian Christian chants.*

English ballad A *ballad* that commemorates important events and memorable individuals in British history; often based on the text of a *broadside.*

enka A *genre* of popular song with melodramatic themes of love, used in Japanese *karaoke.*

ensemble A group of instruments or musicians who perform together.

Ethiopian Christian chant The music of the Ethiopian Christian *liturgy.* See also *chant (zema).*

ethnic recordings 78-rpm discs issued from approximately 1900 to 1950, targeted for a particular subgroup united by a shared national, linguistic, racial, or religious background.

ethnomusicology A field of study that joins the concerns and methods of anthropology with the study of music.

ezengileer Literally "stirrup," a type of *khoomii* that features a *rhythmic* pulsing, said to imitate singing while riding a horse.

fado Literally "fate," a song *genre* closely associated with Lisbon and popular within Portuguese expatriate communities.

fais-dodo A *Cajun* term meaning dance music; the dance halls where such music is performed.

falsetto The process of singing by men in a high *register* above the normal male singing *range.*

fancy shawl dance A virtuosic *shawl dance* performed by Native American women.

fancy war dance A virtuosic *war dance* performed by Native American men.

fasola See *shape-note.*

fiddle (1) A name used for the *violin* in the context of a wide range of Euro-American *folk* and vernacular musics. (2) Any bowed instrument of the *lute* family.

fieldwork Research, including observation and participation, of living traditions, also called musical ethnography.

figure A stereotyped motion that is part of a given dance, such as the dos-a-dos in square dancing.

fixed form A musical *form* in which aspects of its content are predetermined.

fixed tuning The singing or playing of music at a pitch level determined in reference to a standard, fixed *frequency,* such as *A 440* for *Western orchestra* tuning. Contrasts with *relative tuning.*

flag song A Native American song performed during a *powwow* flag ceremony to honor the American flag.

flute An *aerophone,* such as the *ney,* that is generally tubular and whose air column is set into vibration by the player's blowing against a sharp edge.

folk music A category conventionally applied to styles of music transmitted by *oral tradition,* maintained in collective memory by a group of people, associated with nonprofessionals, and regarded as the cultural property of a group of people bounded by national, social, or ethnic identity, often called "traditional music" or *vernacular music.*

form The structure of a musical piece as established by its *qualities, pitches, durations,* and *intensities,* typically consisting of distinct sections that are either repeated or are used to provide contrast with other sections.

frame drum A *membranophone* with a skin stretched over a round frame, such as the tambourine or Tibetan *rnga.*

free aerophones *Aerophones* that act directly on the surrounding air, such as the Australian bullroarer.

free rhythm *Rhythm* that is not organized around a regular *pulse.*

frequency The number of vibrations per second of a vibrating string or column of air, usually measured either in cycles per second (cps) or in hertz (Hz) and kilohertz (kHz). Perception of frequency determines *pitch.*

friction idiophone An *idiophone* whose sound is produced by an object rubbing its surface.

fundamental tone The lowest tone in a *harmonic* series, also referred to as the "first harmonic" or "first partial," which determines the perceived pitch of a sound.

Gaelic The language associated with Celtic culture, including Irish Gaelic, Manx, and Scots Gaelic.

gamelan A large Indonesian ensemble consisting mainly of *metallophones*.

gaucho The Argentinian word for cowboy.

ge'ez The most important of three categories of *mode* in Ethiopian Christian ritual music.

Ge'ez The Ethiopian Christian liturgical language.

genre A type or kind (of music).

ghazal A strophic song sung in Urdu, traditionally performed for elite audiences in Northern India, that has exerted a strong influence on contemporary Indian film music.

Ghost Dance religion Indigenous Native American religion with associated ceremonial dances.

giddha A dance performed by Punjabi women that is equivalent to the male *bhangra*.

glide See *slide*.

glissando A musical gesture that entails sliding from one pitch to another.

gong kebyar A type of Balinese *gamelan*, known particularly for its shimmering sound and interlocking parts (*kotekan*).

grace notes The addition of one or more notes in slight anticipation of a *pitch*.

gracings The practice of inserting *grace notes* into *bagpipe melodies*.

grass dance A women's dance at a *powwow*, named after the fringed regalia worn in performance.

great Highland bagpipe The large Scottish outdoor *bagpipe* with a nine-note *chanter*, three *drones*, and a bag filled by mouth through a *blowpipe*.

grip A quick *ornamental* figure of two non-adjacent *pitches* that serves as a set of *grace notes* in *bagpipe* music.

ground An English term for the slow-moving *air* or *melody*, that is used as the *theme* for a set of variations in Scottish *bagpipe* music.

guitar A plucked *lute* that has a hollow resonating body with waisted sides, such as the *guitarrón*, *Hawaiian steel guitar*, *ukulele*, and *vihuela*.

guitarrón A large, plucked, four- or five-string bass *lute* with an expanded belly that serves as the bass instrument in a *mariachi ensemble*.

haflah A party held among Syrian Jews and other peoples of Middle Eastern descent, to celebrate a special occasion such as an anniversary, usually featuring a professional *vocalist* who sings popular Arabic songs with *accompaniment*.

harmonic series See *harmonics*.

harmonic singing See *biphonic singing*.

harmonic texture See *harmony*.

harmonics The series of simple vibrations that combine to create a complex pitched sound, also called the harmonic series. The lowest, or first, harmonic, called the *fundamental*, is perceived as the basic pitch of the sound. The remaining harmonics, called *overtones* or *partials*, influence the sound's *quality*. Harmonics are present in the sounding of any string or air column.

harmony The collective sound of a series of *chords*, serving as a support to a *melody*. The term also refers to a set of rules that govern the progression of *sound* in *Western classical music*.

harp *Chordophone* whose strings run at an angle away from the soundboard, subcategorized by shape, playing position, and *tunings*.

Hawaiian steel guitar An *electromechanical instrument* derived from the guitar, usually placed flat when played, whose characteristic sounds include a pronounced *vibrato*, *slides*, and "palm *harmonics*" or "chimes."

head voice A light, bright, high tone resonated in the head.

Hebrew The Semitic language used in Jewish prayers and spoken in modern Israel.

heterophony A musical *texture* in which two or more *parts* sound almost the same melody at almost the same time; often with the *parts ornamented* differently.

hip-hop The cultural movement associated with African American urban life in the 1970s that emerged at once in the graphic arts (graffiti), dance (break dancing), and music (rap).

ho A Vietnamese work song.

homophony A musical *texture*, as in the Western *hymn*, where the parts perform different *pitches* but move in the same *rhythm*.

hymn A sacred *vocal genre* sung during worship ceremonies.

Hymnary The most elaborate musical *ritual* of the Ethiopian church, performed before the *Mass* on Sundays and festivals.

idiophones Instruments that produce sound by being vibrated. One of the five main classes of instruments in the *Sachs-Hornbostel system*, idiophones are further classified by the way they are caused to vibrate: *concussion, struck, stamped, shaken, scraped, plucked,* or *rubbed.*

impresario A manager of performers or a director of a concert series.

improvisation The process of composing music as it is performed, drawing on conventions of preexisting patterns and styles. Examples include *cadenzas*, jazz riffs, and *layali*.

Indian Days Annual Native American gatherings that feature social and competitive events during the days and *powwow* ceremonies in the evenings.

instrumental Music produced on instruments, whether by one person or many.

intensity The perceived loudness or softness of a *sound.*

iterative Consisting of short, repeated melodic segments.

interculture The sphere of interaction between musical *subcultures.* Contrast with *subculture* and *superculture.*

interlocking parts *Instrumental* or *vocal* parts in which silences in one part occur simultaneously with sound in another, creating the sense of a single musical line.

intertribal Refers to an event or dance in Native American tradition that incorporates people of different tribal backgrounds.

interval The distance between two *pitches.*

Irish ballad A *ballad* that commemorates important events and memorable individuals from the Irish past while referring to contemporary political subjects.

irregular meter Asymmetrical groupings with different numbers of beats per *measure.*

itótole The middle-sized double-headed *membranophone* in the *batá* ensemble.

iyá The largest and deepest of the double-headed *membranophones* in the *batá* ensemble.

jazz funeral See *New Orleans jazz funeral.*

Jew's (jaw's) harp A *plucked idiophone* held in the mouth that consists of a metal tongue attached to a frame. The tongue of the instrument is plucked while the mouth provides a resonating chamber that can be shaped to emphasize particular *harmonics.*

jig A lively dance tune popular in Ireland and among Irish-Americans.

jingle dance Women's dance in present-day *powwows*, named after the metal jingles that cover festive dresses.

Judeo-Spanish songs Songs in a Judeo-Spanish dialect transmitted through *oral tradition* by descendants of late-sixteenth-century Jewish exiles from Spain (Sephardic Jews).

juke box A machine that plays recorded songs chosen from a list of current offerings.

karaoke Literally "empty orchestra"; live singing, usually into a microphone, with a recorded accompaniment, performed in restaurants, clubs, or private homes.

kargyraa A style of *khoomii* characterized by text sung in a low *register.*

kata A Japanese aesthetic principle, literally "patterned form."

katajjaq An Inuit form of throat music, literally "vocal game."

kebaro Ethiopian double-headed conical *membranophone.*

key The relationship between *pitches* in *Western classical music* as defined by a central *pitch* and related *harmonies.*

keyboard accordion An *accordion* with a keyboard on the melodic headboard.

khoomii *Biphonic* Tuvan throat singing, originally from rural *Inner Asia* and now heard in concert halls worldwide. Types of *khoomii* include *sygyt, kargyraa,* and *ezengileer.*

kotekan An Indonesian term for the *interlocking parts* heard in Balinese *gamelan* music.

Labanotation Rudolf Laban's system of dance notation, which uses ideograms to represent dance motion in great detail.

lahan (1) A tune, in Arab music theory; (2) the *melody* to which a *pizmon* is sung.

lament A song of mourning.

layali In Arab *vocal* music, an *improvisation* that introduces a song and establishes the *maqam* used in the rest of the piece.

liturgical order The order in which sacred *rites* are performed.

liturgy The content of a religious *ritual*.

lute *Chordophone* whose strings are stretched along a neck and body, such as the *'ud, ukulele,* and *guitar*.

lyre *Chordophone* whose strings are stretched over a soundboard and attached to a crossbar that spans the top of a yoke.

macarena A mid-1990s dance.

major mode A particular set of eight *notes* in *Western classical music*. See *major scale*.

major scale The series of *pitches* in the *major mode* possessing the following *interval* relationships, from lowest to highest: two *whole tones*, one *semitone*, three *whole tones* and one *semitone*.

maqam (*pl.* **maqamat**) The system governing *pitch* and *melody* in Arab music.

maqam ajam A *maqam* that resembles the Western *major mode*.

maqam nahawand A *maqam* that resembles the Western *minor mode*.

march A piece in *duple meter*, usually with a quick pace, suitable for accompanying and coordinating a group of people marching.

mariachi A Mexican *instrumental ensemble* that includes the *guitarrón, vihuela, violin,* and *trumpets*; the musicians in the group.

Mass A Christian *ritual* that includes the sacrament of Communion.

mbube A South African *vocal genre* popularized in recordings and spread internationally, featuring *falsetto* singing and Western-style *harmony*.

measure The unit of time in *Western music* and musical *notation* in which one cycle of the *meter* takes place.

melekket The *notational* symbols in *Ethiopian Christian chant*, derived from Ge'ez language characters, each representing a short melody.

melismatic text setting *Vocal* music in which each syllable of the text is sung to many *pitches*.

melody A sequence of *pitches*, also called a "tune," heard in the foreground of music.

membranophones Instruments whose sound is produced by a membrane stretched over an opening. One of the five main classes of instruments in the *Sachs-Hornbostel system*, membranophones are distinguished by their material, shape, number of skins (or heads), how the skins are fastened, playing position, and manner of playing.

metallophone *Struck idiophone* made of metal.

meter A term describing the regular *pulse* of much of *Western classical music* and its divisions into regular groupings of two, three, four, or six *beats*.

minor mode A *mode* of eight *notes* in *Western classical music*. See *minor scale*.

minor scale The series of *pitches* in the *minor mode* possessing the following *interval* relationships from lowest to highest: one *whole tone*, one *semitone*, two *whole tones*, one *semitone* and two *whole tones*.

mode A flexible term that can refer, depending on the context, to a musical system or a particular series of *pitches*. Examples of modes are *ge'ez, major mode, minor mode,* and *tizita*.

modulation The process by which music moves from one *key* or *scale* type to another.

monophony Literally a "single sound," the simplest musical *texture*.

Morris dancers English country dancers costumed in white, with bells strapped to their legs, who dance to the music of a *fiddle, bagpipe,* or pennywhistle.

motive A short melody or rhythm that recurs in a musical composition.

mouth music *Vocal* music ("*canntaireachd*") that imitates the sound of the *bagpipe*.

movement A large section of a musical composition typically separated from other such sections by a pause.

music The purposeful organization of the *quality, pitch, duration,* and *intensity* of *sound.*

musical ethnography The process of identifying a musical scene and studying the *soundscape* of which it is a part. See also *participant observation* and *fieldwork.*

muwashshah A *classical* Arab *vocal form* marked by a regular *rhythm* and rhyme scheme and a three-part *form.*

mu'yu A *genre* of traditional Chinese *vocal* music whose texts deal with the concerns of everyday life, performed by men or women in public or private. Also spelled as *muk'yu.*

Muzak Programmed, recorded music designed to create sonic background environments in public spaces such as elevators, shopping malls, and restaurants.

narco-corrido Drug *ballads* popular along the Mexican/US border. See *corrido.*

nasal A buzzing vocal *quality* produced by using the sinuses and mask of the face as sound resonators.

Native American Church A religion that blends indigenous Native American beliefs with Christian elements.

nduah Literally "tail," a Blackfoot Indian term that refers to a short section added to the end of a song.

New Orleans jazz funeral A ritual marking the death of a musician that includes a procession with a jazz band.

"new tango" A *tango* composed expressly for listening.

ney An end-blown Middle Eastern *flute* whose sound has a breathy *quality.*

no rae pang (1) Literally "song room," a Korean style of *karaoke* performed with a small group of friends in a private rented room; (2) the room where the *karaoke* takes place.

non-Western Outside the *Western classical music* arena; an increasingly problematic term in an increasingly transnational world.

notation The representation of musical sound in written form.

note A single *pitch,* or the representation of a single *pitch* in musical *notation.*

octave (1) The eight consecutive notes that make up a major or minor *scale*; (2) the interval spanning the first through the eighth notes of any such scale. The

pitch of the highest *note* of an octave has a *frequency* exactly twice that of the lowest *note.*

okónkolo The smallest of the double-headed *membranophones* in the *batá* ensemble.

oral tradition Tradition preserved in people's minds through singing or speech, in contrast to written tradition, which is recorded through writing or *notation.*

orchestra A large Western *instrumental ensemble.* See *Western orchestra.*

organ grinder Itinerant street musician who plays a small portable *barrel organ*; called *organito* in Spanish-speaking communities.

organito Spanish for *organ grinder.*

organology The study of musical instruments.

orisha Saint, in the *Santería* tradition.

ornaments Melodic, rhythmic, and timbral elaborations or decorations such as *gracings, rekrek,* and *grace notes.*

ostinato A short musical pattern that is continually repeated.

outdoor style A *vocal* or *instrumental style* with substantial *volume* or penetrating tone quality, originally meant to be performed out of doors.

overtones The *harmonics* above the *fundamental.*

panoptic mode View of an event or performance from a distance, from a detached vantage point. Contrast with *panoramic mode.*

panoramic mode View of an event or performance from within a setting into which the spectator enters. Contrast with *panoptic mode.*

parallel motion Occurs when different *parts* move in the same direction at the same time; a type of *homophony.*

part The *melodic* line of a particular voice or instrument.

partials Another term for *harmonics.*

participant observer What a researcher becomes when studying a living tradition during *fieldwork.*

pawwaw See *powwow.*

pentatonic scale A *scale* that contains five *pitches,* or the music that is based on such scales.

performance practice The manner in which music is interpreted and performed.

phrase A brief section of music, analogous to a phrase of spoken language, that sounds somewhat complete in itself, while not self-sufficient. One phrase may be separated from the next by a brief pause to allow the singer or player a moment to breathe.

pibroch, piobaireachd A *genre* of *solo bagpipe* music which consists of a set of elaborate *variations* on a theme, called the *allrd urlar*.

pìob mhór Literally "great pipes," the *Gaelic* name for the *great highland bagpipes*.

pipe band A military-style marching and performing *ensemble* consisting of *great Highland bagpipes* and drums.

pitch The highness or lowness of a *sound*.

pizmon (pl. pizmonim) Hymns sung by Middle Eastern Jews, featuring sacred Hebrew texts set to popular Arab melodies.

plainchant See *chant*.

plainsong See *chant*.

plectrum (*pl.* plectra) A small piece of hard material, such as horn, shell, or plastic, used to pluck a stringed instrument.

plucked idiophones *Idiophones* such as the *Jew's (jaw's) harp* that have plucked metal tongues.

polka A fast dance in *duple meter* that has become identified with Polish peoples, although it originated in Bohemia.

polka step The *polka* dance step, usually described as a heel-and-toe half step.

polyphony A musical *texture* in which the parts move in contrasting directions, as opposed to *homophony*.

polyrhythms Contrasting *rhythms* that are performed at the same time.

powwow Native American social gatherings that feature ceremonies, celebrations, and dance competitions; formerly "pawwaw" in the Algonquian language.

prayer staff A pole on which *dabtaras* lean when performing the *Ethiopian liturgy* and which is used as an *idiophone* that is pounded on the floor during dance.

pulse The short, regular element of time that underlies *beat* and *rhythm*.

push-button accordion See *bandoneón*.

push-ups Term used by the *Shoshone* and other Native Americans to indicate the number of times a song is repeated.

qanun A Middle Eastern trapezoidal *zither* with twenty-six sets of three strings, played polyphonically with *plectra* attached to the index fingers of both hands.

quadruple meter Rhythmic organization based on groupings, or *measures,* of four *beats*.

quality The color of a *sound,* arising from acoustical properties of the *harmonic* series. Also called *timbre*.

quinceañera A traditional Latino celebration marking the passage of fifteen-year-old girls into adulthood.

radioelectric instruments *Electrophones,* such as the analog *synthesizer,* in which the oscillations of electric circuits are amplified and transformed into audible vibrations by electric speakers.

rag-dung Tibetan *trumpet*.

raga The Indian system for organizing melodies according to their distinctive pitch content, ornaments, and range of associations.

range The distance between the highest and lowest *pitches* that can be sung or played by a voice or instrument.

rap The genre of musical expression that arose out of the *hip-hop* movement, featuring words recited rhythmically.

raspy A singing voice that is rough or gruff in *quality*.

Rastafarianism A religious movement from Jamaica whose adherents venerate the Ethiopian emperor Haile Selassie (Ras Tafari).

reed A thin strip of wood, metal, or plastic, that is fixed at one end and free at the other and that produces sound when set into vibration by moving air.

reel A *genre* of Scottish and Irish dance music, typically played on a *bagpipe*. See also *strathspey*.

refrain A fixed stanza of text and music that recurs between *verses* of a *strophic* song.

reggae A style of urban Jamaican popular music that originated among the *Rastafarians* of Jamaica in the 1960s.

register A subset of the *range* of a voice or instrument.

rekrek The *vocal slides* characteristic of the *ge'ez* mode in *Ethiopian Christian chant*.

relative tuning Singing or playing at a pitch level determined by what is comfortable for the performer, as opposed to *fixed tuning*.

revival The reintroduction or reinvention of an earlier tradition.

rhythm The temporal relationships within *music*.

rhythmic cycle A repeating *rhythmic* sequence that may be subdivided in complex and constantly changing ways.

riddim Insider term for the various marked rhythmic properties of reggae that convey, in coded form, the subversiveness of the *Rastafarian subculture* and its associated *soundscape*.

rite A religiously prescribed or customary act or observance.

ritual An established set of *rites*, or the observance of such a set of *rites*.

rnga Tibetan *frame drum*.

rol-mo Tibetan cymbals (*concussion idiophones.*)

ru A Vietnamese lullaby.

rub board A *scraped idiophone* made of metal, used in the *Zydeco* tradition.

Sachs-Hornbostel system A classification of musical instruments, named after the scholars who developed the system.

sacred service The performance of *liturgy*.

sadhana A Tibetan Buddhist *ritual* meditation text.

Santería An Afro-Cuban religious and musical practice.

saxophone A Western European *single-reed aerophone* made of metal.

scale A series of *pitches* set forth in ascending or descending order.

scraped idiophones *Idiophones*, such as the *rub board*, that vibrate by being scraped with a hand-held tool.

Sebet A Sabbath-afternoon songfest of unaccompanied *pizmonim* held among Syrian Jews in North America to celebrate a special occasion.

seconds Singing an octave or two above another singer in the *Shoshone* tradition.

semitone, half-step The smallest *interval* in *Western classical music*. There are twelve semitones (also called "half steps") in the Western *octave*.

Sephardim Descendants of Spanish Jews who were forced into exile in 1492.

setting The context of a musical performance, such as the place, the structure of the performing space, or behavior of those present.

shaken idiophones *Idiophones*, such as the Ethiopian *sistrum*, with sounding parts that strike together when the instrument is shaken.

shape-note Also called "fasola," a system of musical *notation* for American *hymns* in which the shape of the note indicates the *pitch*.

shawl dance A dignified, traditional dance performed by Native American women with shawls draped over their arms. See also *fancy shawl dance*.

Shoshone A Great Basin people who migrated to the Plains, some settling on the Wind River Reservation in Wyoming.

significance The range of meanings constructed by musicians and listeners in response to musical *sound* and its *setting*.

siku Andean panpipe.

silence The absence of *sound*.

simple meter Groupings of two, three, or four beats per *measure*.

single reed A *reed* constructed from a single thin, vibrating strip. Examples of single-reed instruments include *aerophones* such as the *accordion, saxophone,* and *clarinet*.

sistrum (senasel) *Ethiopian* Christian *shaken idiophone*.

slide Smooth linking of *pitches*, characteristic of the *Hawaiian steel guitar*.

smallpipes *Bagpipes*, such as the *Irish uilleann pipes*, with a low sound intensity, usually played indoors; the bag is generally filled by a bellows rather than by mouth.

sojourner A person who migrates with the intent to stay for a time and then return home.

solo Literally "alone," in Italian, refers to musical sound that is produced by only one singer or instrumentalist, either individually or with the *accompaniment* of a larger *ensemble*.

sonata form A *Western classical form* that generally consists of an exposition, in which one group of *themes* is presented in a "home" *key* and a second in a "foreign" *key*; a "development" section, in which the *themes* are elaborated on; and a recapitulation, in which both groups return, in the "home" *key*.

song cycle A group of songs that are composed as a set, sometimes because they have texts by the same poet or are connected in some other way.

sound Vibrations with *frequencies* in the audible spectrum (from 20 Hz to 20 kHz). Musical vibrations can be produced by voices, instruments, or electronic resources. A sound can be described in terms of its *quality, pitch, duration,* and *intensity.*

soundscape The distinctive *settings, sounds,* and *significances* of music.

sound sources The voices and instruments that produce musical *sound* and whose vibrations give rise to our perceptions of *quality.*

spiritual A genre of songs, usually with *verses* and a *refrain,* that emerged from the musical expression of slaves converted to New World Christianity.

stamped idiophones *Idiophones* that are stamped on, such as boards, pots, beams, mortars, or slit drums.

stamping idiophones *Idiophones* that are hit on the ground in a vertical motion, such as sticks, tubes, or gourds.

steel guitar See *Hawaiian steel guitar.*

straight tone A sound that lacks any *vibrato.*

strathspey A kind of *reel* with a slower *tempo* and more elaborate *melody* and *ornamentation* than a simple *reel.*

strophic form A form in which all *verses* of text are set to the same melody. Strophic form can include a *refrain* that is sung between *verses.*

struck idiophones *Idiophones,* such as the *triangle,* that are struck by a hand-held tool, such as a stick.

subculture A group of people who share a common identity and related practices, whether based on ethnicity, religion, language, or generation, that are perceived as distinct from others within a given society. Contrast with *interculture* and *superculture.*

Sunday School songs A repertory of Ethiopian Christian hymns that emerged in the early 1990s with texts primarily in Amharic instead of *Ge'ez.*

superculture The sphere of musical interaction that involves the power of the state and international industries, and the assumptions and expectations they generate. Contrast with *subculture* and *interculture.*

sygyt A type of *khoomii* that is sung in a high *register* with clear *overtones* that sound like whistling.

syllabic text setting *Vocal* music in which each syllable of text is sung to one pitch.

syncopation A *rhythmic* effect that provides an unexpected accent, often by temporarily unsettling the *meter* through a change in the established pattern of stressed and unstressed *beats.*

synthesizer Any *radioelectric instrument* or *digital electronic instrument;* a modern synthesizer is generally self-contained with a performance interface, sound-editing controls, and sound-generation circuitry.

tail See *nduah.*

tala An Indian rhythmic framework consisting of time cycles that contain a fixed number of counts.

tan nhac A *Vietnamese* popular song tradition of the French colonial period that used Western instruments and Vietnamese lyrics, and occasionally drew on Vietnamese *folk melodies.*

tango An Argentinian-derived style of song and dance.

tempo *Music's* rate of speed or pace.

Tet Vietnamese New Year.

text setting The way in which a text is sung or "set" to music. See *syllabic* and *melismatic.*

texture The perceived relationship of simultaneous musical sounds.

theme A short *melody* that is prominently stated and that recurs one or more times in a piece of music.

throat singing See *khoomii.*

Tibetan Buddhist chant See *dbyang.*

timbre The distinctiveness of a particular voice or instrument, arising from acoustical properties of the *harmonic* series. Also called *quality.*

tizita A category of *tuning* and *melody,* based on a *pentatonic scale,* widely used in secular music of the Ethiopian highlands.

tonal music Music in which a single *pitch* and its associated *harmonies* serve as the point of departure and return.

tone color See *quality.*

toque The *rhythmic* patterns played by the *batá* drum in *Santería* ceremonies.

traditional music See *folk* music.

transcription The writing down of music in *notation.*

tremolo A regular fluctuation or "trembling" of a sound, produced by varying the *intensity* of the sound.

triangle A small, triangular *struck idiophone* made of solid cylindrical metal and struck with a metal bar.

triple meter A rhythmic organization based on groupings, or *measures,* or three *beats.*

trumpet An *aerophone* in which the player's compressed lips cause the air in the instrument to vibrate.

tshig Tibetan term for sung syllables with actual meaning. Contrast with *vocables.*

tuning (1) The act of adjusting the frequencies produced by one or more instruments so that they sound at the same *pitch*; (2) any ordered collection of *intervals* that are organized around a system used in a particular cultural context.

'ud Plucked five-stringed Middle Eastern *lute* with a short neck and a large body with a rounded back.

uilleann **pipes** Irish *smallpipes* with three *drones,* a keyed *chanter,* and a bellows to fill the bag.

ukulele A small, four-stringed Hawaiian *chordophone* that became popular in the twentieth century.

ululation A vocal sound of joy or celebration commonly produced by women in Africa and the Middle East.

union pipes See *uilleann pipes.*

unison The playing or singing of exactly the same *pitch* at the same time by two or more performers.

universalism The belief that certain music traditions or practices are found in all *cultures.*

vernacular music Music linked to the commonplace aspects of life. See also *folk music.*

verse A variable strophe of text sung to a fixed, repeating melody in a *strophic* song.

vibrato A regular fluctuation of a sound, produced by varying the *pitch* of the sound.

vihuela A small, strummed *folk guitar,* a key instrument in the *mariachi ensemble.*

violin A small bowed *lute* with a hollow wooden body and a solid neck to which the fingerboard is attached. See also *fiddle.*

vocables An alternative word for nonsense syllables.

vocal Produced by the voice, whether by one person or many.

vocal style A particular, idiosyncratic manner of singing that features particular tone *qualities, articulations,* or uses of *vibrato.*

vocalise Untexted *vocal* music.

war dance A Native American dance performed by men. See *fancy war dance.*

washboard See *rub board.*

Western classical music The varied musical styles and practices derived from elite European and American musics of the eighteenth and nineteenth centuries. See also *classical.*

Western harmonic system See *harmony.*

Western music Most broadly, music found in the Western Hemisphere (and thus all of the musics discussed in this book); musics of Euro-American origins, especially *Western classical music.*

Western orchestra The major *instrumental ensemble* of *Western classical music* from the late eighteenth century to the present. Commonly consists of bowed *chordophones, aerophones, idiophones,* and *membranophones.*

whole tone The *interval* made of two *semitones* in *Western classical music.*

wind instruments *Aerophones* such as *trumpets, flutes,* and *reed instruments,* that rely on the vibration of an enclosed column of air for their *pitch* and *quality.*

world music A cover term for a variety of musical styles from around the globe, increasingly referring to "world pop."

yang-yig A songbook of Tibetan *dbyang.* See also *dbyangs-yig.*

zema Ethiopian Christian *chant*; the music of the *Ethiopian* Christian *liturgy.*

zither A *chordophone* without a neck or yoke whose strings are stretched parallel to the soundboard.

zydeco Dance music that emerged in the 1950s among the *Creoles* of the Gulf Coast. The name *zydeco* is said to derive from a French expression, *les haricots* (literally, "the beans"), alluding to a metaphor popular among *Creole* peoples of color that "the beans are not salty," that is, they are not flavored by expensive salted meat.

Credits

Every effort has been made to contact the copyright holder of each of these selections. If proper acknowledgment has not been made, please contact us.

Viswanathan; **p. 141:** Annie Wells/*The Press Democrat*, Santa Rosa, CA; **p. 142:** Joseph Sohm, ChromoSohm, Inc./CORBIS; **p. 146:** Reuters Pictures Archive; **p. 149 (left):** James Marshall/CORBIS; **p. 149 (right):** Yann Arthus-Bertrand/CORBIS; **p. 155:** Maíre Ní Ghráda; **p. 157:** Original held by the First Battalion, the Royal Scots, Edinburgh. Used with permission; **p. 158:** Kris Snibbe, the Harvard Gazette/Harvard University News Office; **p. 159:** School of Scottish Studies, University of Edinburgh; **p. 163:** The Royal Museum, Edinburgh. The Trustees of the National Museums of Scotland, 2000; **p. 164:** Alex Milne; **p. 165:** Joanne Reid; **p. 166:** David L. Ryan/*The Boston Globe*; **p. 168:** Courtesy Kay Kaufman Shelemay; **p. 171:** Sarah G. Partridge/Bettman/CORBIS; **p. 175:** Museum of the City of New York; **p. 176 (top):** "The Chinese in the World Today," from The Penguin Atlas of Diasporas by Gerard Chaliand and Jean-Pierre Rageau, translated by A.M. Berrett, copyright © 1995 by Gerard Chaliand and Jean-Pierre Rageau. Used by permission of Viking Penguin, a division of Penguin Group (USA) Inc.; **p. 176 (bottom):** Photo courtesy of Asian American Arts Centre, NY; **p. 182:** "The Lebanese in the Modern World," from The Penguin Atlas of Diasporas by Gerard Chaliand and Jean-Pierre Rageau, translated by A.M. Berrett, copyright © 1995 by Gerard Chaliand and Jean-Pierre Rageau. Used by permission of Viking Penguin, a division of Penguin Group (USA) Inc.; **p. 183:** Courtesy of Mrs. Russel Bunai; **p. 184 (top):** Courtesy of Virginia Solomon; **p. 184 (bottom):** MGM Grand Hotel and Casino Las Vegas, Nevada; **p. 185 (top):** © Jack Vartoogian/FrontRowPhotos; **p. 185 (bottom):** Courtesy Johnny Sarweh; **p. 190:** New York Public Library; **p. 191 (top):** Hulton-Deutsch Collection/CORBIS; **p. 191 (bottom):** Library of Congress; **p. 194 (top):** Philip Jones Griffiths/Magnum Photos; **p. 194 (bottom):** Inez Eskowitz; **p. 195:** AP/Wide World Photos; **p. 196:** Terry Miller; **p. 197 (top):** Adelaida Reyes; **p. 197 (bottom):** Courtesy Bui Huu Nhut; **p. 202:** Photo by Huynh Tam, Paris 1989; **p. 204:** Ngan Khoi Chorus; **p. 214:** Courtesy World Center for Alpetto Jews Traditional Culture, Tel Aviv; **p. 216:** Courtesy of Kay Kaufman Shelemay; **p. 221:** Courtesy Alan Paredes; **p. 224:** Getty Images; **p. 225:** Bettmann/Corbis; **p. 226:** Philip Gould/CORBIS; **p. 227:** Bettmann/Corbis; **p. 228:** Tim Wright/CORBIS; **p. 232:** Courtesy Kay Kaufman Shelemay; **p. 236:** Courtesy Sephardic Community Center, Brooklyn, NY; **p. 237:** Courtesy Sephardic Community Center, Brooklyn, NY; **p. 240:** Courtesy Tawil family; **p. 241:** Bettmann/CORBIS; **p. 244 (top):** Tawil family; **p. 244 (bottom):** Courtesy Maria Garcia; **p. 245:** Courtesy EMI, Arabia; **p. 249:** Tawil family; **p. 250:** Courtesy of Sephardic Community Center, Brooklyn, NY; **p. 256:** Courtesy Hohner; **p. 258 (top):** Corbis; **p. 258 (bottom):** Bettmann/CORBIS; **p. 259 (middle):** Courtesy Blix Street Records; **p. 260:** AP/Wide World Photos; **p. 263:** Wallis/Malm, Big Sounds from Small Peoples (Hillsdale, NY: Pendragon); **p. 265:** Courtesy Kay Kaufman Shelemay; **p. 266:** Haley S. Robertson; **p. 267, 270:** Courtesy of Ukulele Hall of Fame Museum; **p. 271:** Alicia Smith; **p. 272:** Jody Diamond; **p. 273:** Michael Tenzer; **p. 278:** Photo by Christine Southworth; **p. 279:** Michael Tenzer; **p. 282:** Courtesy Shreve, Crump, & Low, Boston; **p. 283:** Courtesy Kay Kaufman Shelemay; **p. 285:** Freer Gallery of Art and Arthur M. Sackler Gallery, Smithsonian Institution, Washington D.C.: Purchase, F1930.44; **p. 288:** Sam Sweezy; **p. 289 (top):** Andrea Bruce/The Washington Post Writers Group; **p. 289 (bottom):** AP/Wide World Photos; **p. 290:** Smithsonian Folkways and Theodore Levin; **p. 291:** Courtesy Gamelan Galak Tika; **p. 293:** Smithsonian Institution, Washington, D.C.; **p. 295:** Courtesy the Silk Road Ensemble; **p. 299 (second from right):** Courtesy Cairdin Accordions, Limerick, Ireland; **p. 300:** Christel Gerstenberg/CORBIS; **p. 302:** © Bonnie Kamin; **p. 303:** Wally McNamee/CORBIS; **p. 304:** Hanna 1979/1992, 321; **p. 305:** Michael S. Yamashita/CORBIS; **p. 308:** Alka Pande www.mapinpub.com; **p. 309 (top):** Folk Dances of Panjab by Iqbal Singh Dhillon, Delhi, India, National Book Shop, 1998. Reproduced with permission of the author; **p. 309 (bottom left and right):** Alka Pande www.mapinpub.com; **p. 311 (top):** Lindsay Hebberd/CORBIS; **p. 311 (bottom):** Jessie Singh Birring/Courtesy of 4x4 Dancers; **p. 312:** Photograph courtesy of Sujata Sundar; **p. 319:** Courtesy ISHQ Records; **p. 320:** Ben DeSoto photos/Chronicle, *Houston Chronicle,* Sunday November 16, 2000 p. 1E; **p. 321:** Courtesy Katherine Koperski; **p. 323:** Courtesy Hohner; **p. 324:** From *Histories de l'Accordeon* by Francois Billard and Didier Roussin, Climat, INA, 1991; **p. 325:** Pekka Gronow Collection; **p. 326:** Philip Gould/CORBIS; **p. 328 (top):** Dick Blau; **p. 328 (bottom):** Reuters Newsmedia Inc.; **p. 331:** Copyright 2005. *The Chronicle of Higher Education.* Reprinted with permission; **p. 338:** Courtesy Natalio Gorin; **p. 339 (top):** Adriana Groisman; **p. 339 (bottom):** Asahi Graph, June 1, 1987. Reproduced with persmission of Asahi Graph, Tokyo; **p. 342:** AP/Wide World Photos; **p. 344:** Courtesy Rossi and Rossi, London; **p. 346:** Courtesy Steve Dunn and Vanessa Drake-Johnson; **p. 348:** Diana L. Eck, The Pluralism Project, Harvard University; **p. 349:** © Bob Seidemann; **p. 352 (top):** Nik Wheeler/CORBIS; **p. 352 (bottom):** AP/Wide World Photos; **p. 353:** Getty Images; **p. 354:** Adriana Groisman; **p. 355 (top):** Terry Sanders; **p. 355 (bottom):** Courtesy Kay Kaufman Shelemay; **p. 360:** Courtesy of Harvard Map Collection, Harvard College Library; **p. 362 (top):** Kazuyoshi Nomachi/Pacific Press Service; **p. 362 (bottom):** Courtesy Kay Kaufman Shelemay; **p. 364:** Walter Kaufmann/Indiana University Press; **p. 365:** A-R Editions, Inc.; **p. 368:** Courtesy Braham; **p. 369:** Jacques Mercier, Ethiopian Magic

Index

NOTE: Page numbers in *italics* refer to illustrations; numbers in **boldface** refer to definitions. **Boldface** text indicates special features such as **Case Studies**.

Ethiopian, 93, 96–97, 362, 363, 375, 376–77
Ewe *agbadza*, 55
Flag Songs, 412, 414
Hawaiian song, 268–69
Hindu *aarati*, 68–69
Indian rap, 74–76
Irish American ballad, 89
Judeo-Spanish lullaby, 122–23
mariachi song, 268–69
Mexican *corridos*, 220–25
Mongolian long song, 9
Portuguese *fado*, 92, 94–95
Quebecois, 31
reggae, 392, 393
reggaeton, 397–98
rock steady, 389
Santería chant, 357–59
Shoshone war dance, 416–17
South African anthems, 386–87, 390–91
South African national anthems, 384
South Indian lullaby, 132–34
Syrian Jewish *pizmonim*, 232, 234–37
tango songs, 329, 332–33, 336–37
transplantation as theme in, 469
Tuvan, xxviii, xlv
Vietnamese *Ca Hue*, 196
Vietnamese-language, 197, 200–201, 202, 205, 206, 208–10, 470–71
zydeco, 458–59, 462–63
songman (Australian), 43
Songprints (Vander), 402
Sonic Meditations (Oliveros), 45
sonido ronco (accordion sound), 326
Sontonga, Enoch Mankayi, 384, *384,* 386–87
Soul of the Tango (album), 289
sound, **xxxvi–xxix,** 2–47, 468–69
  of accordion, 322
  of Arab music, 183–84
  of bagpipes, 147, 149–51, 153–55, 162, 166
  of *bandoneón*, 329
  of *bhangra*, 313–14, 319
  of Cajun music, 448–49, 454
  characteristics of, 6
  duration of, 27–30
  of Ethiopian chant, 363–67, 370–71
  of Ethiopian Sunday School songs, 376
  form of, 38–40
  of *gamelan* music, 102–4, 106–7, 275
  of Hawaiian music, 265–70
  intensity of, 22–23
  of jazz bands, 227

of *karaoke,* 438
mobility of, 298, 468–69
music compared with, 4–5
of Native American Flag Songs, 409–13
pitch of, 23–27
of *pizmon,* 232, 234–37, 241–51
quality of, 8–22
of reggae, 389–90, 392
of *Santería* ritual music, 356–57
Silk Road Project, 289–91, 295
of tango ensembles, 331–34
texture of, 30, 32–33, 35, 38
of Tibetan chant, 349–52, 353
of Tuvan throat singing, xxxvi, xxxviii–xxxix
of Vietnamese music, 196–97, 205–10
vocal, 8–10
of zydeco, 455–56
sound quality. *See* quality (sound)
sound recordings. *See also* cassette recordings; ethnic recordings
  of Arab music, 183–84, *214*
  of Balinese *gamelans,* 271–72
  of *bhangra,* 311
  of Ethiopian Christian chant, 373
  of Ganesh prayers, 67
  of Hawaiian music, 265, 269
  history of, 6–7
  of *pizmonim,* 234, 243
  of polka, 324–25, 328
  reggae, 396–97
  role in transmission, 170, 173, 218–19, 284, 325, 328, 466
  of spirituals, 190–91
  of tango, 339
  transmission and, 217
  of Vietnamese music, 200–201
  of zydeco, 457
Sound Sources, 8
  accordion, 322–24
  Balinese *gamelan,* 100–101
  instruments, 10–22
  mariachi ensemble, 143
  New Orleans jazz band, 227
  sacred drums, 355
  Scottish Highland bagpipe, 150–51
  steel guitar and ukulele, 266–67
  synthesized sounds and scratching, 396–97
  'ud and *qanun,* 185
  voice, 8–10
  voices and instruments, 16
  Western orchestra, 428–29

soundscapes, **xxxiv–xxxv.** *See also specific topics*
  changes in, xxxv, xlvi, 379
  locating, xxxv–xlv
  seascape analogy for, xxxiv–xxxv
  shared, 468–69
South Africa
  anti-apartheid movement in, 105, 303, 384, 419
  mbube, 108, 110–11
  national anthems of, 130, 382, 383–88, 390–91
  Simon in, 436
Southern Harmony (songbook), 229–31
Southwest Louisiana Zydeco Musical Festival, *420, 466*
Spain, *'ud* in, 185
speech-song, 114
Spies, Walter, 272, 274
spirituals, 189–93
sporran, **162**
sruti box, *135*
staccato, 332
Stahl, Ilene, 98
Starkman, Jane, 120–21
status, music and, 13, 15, 55–59, 131, 140, 302–3
steel drums, 11–12, 17, 26–27, 46, 263
steel guitar, 264–71, 454
Steiner, Jacqueline, 113, 114–15
Stem van Suid Afrika, Die (Afrikaans song), 385, 388, 390–91
step dancing, 153
Stevens, Peter, *461,* 464–65
Storm Over Asia: The Heir of Genghis Khan (film), xlii
straight tone, **9,** 119, 120, **122**
strathspey, **163–64**
Strathspey and Reel, The (Scottish dance number), 164
Strauss, Deborah, 98
Strauss, Richard, 428
Stravinsky, Igor, 339
street musicians, *xxx,* xl, *84, 85*
"stretching" a song, **411**
"stride" piano playing, 465
strophic form, **38,** 74, 90–91, 94–95, 114–15, 118, 120–21, 123, 144–45, 173, 192–93, 220–25, 230, 231, 242–43, 244, 246–49, 252–54, 268–69, 376, 384, 386–87, 390–91, 394–95, 452–53, 457, 462–63
Studying Music
  courtesy at powwows, 404–5